ESSAYS ON THE HISTORY OF EQUITY

The history of equity takes in questions of philosophy, theology, jurisprudence and legal history. When we speak of 'equity', do we mean Aristotelian *epieikeia*, civilian *aequitas*, a theological or juridical conscience, the common law concept of the 'equity of the statute', or merely the rules applied by the Court of Chancery before 1875? The purpose of this volume is to chart the evolution of equity in English legal history from the medieval period to the present day. Whether by investigating the historical foundations of the modern law, the jurisprudential underpinnings of the equitable jurisdiction, or the socio-political context of discrete legal developments, this collection exposes the strands of thought which 'equity' comprises and the mechanisms by which its rules evolved.

Essays on the History of Equity

Edited by
David Foster
and
Charles Mitchell

•HART•
OXFORD • LONDON • NEW YORK • NEW DELHI • SYDNEY

HART PUBLISHING

Bloomsbury Publishing Plc

Kemp House, Chawley Park, Cumnor Hill, Oxford, OX2 9PH, UK

1385 Broadway, New York, NY 10018, USA

Bloomsbury Publishing Ireland Limited, 29 Earlsfort Terrace, Dublin 2, D02 AY28, Ireland

HART PUBLISHING, the Hart/Stag logo, BLOOMSBURY and the Diana logo are trademarks of Bloomsbury Publishing Plc

First published in Great Britain 2026

A catalogue record for this book is available from the British Library.

A catalogue record for this book is available from the Library of Congress.

ISBN: HB: 978-1-50995-512-1
ePDF: 978-1-50995-514-5
ePub: 978-1-50995-513-8

Typeset by Compuscript Ltd, Shannon

For product safety related questions contact productsafety@bloomsbury.com

To find out more about our authors and books visit www.hartpublishing.co.uk. Here you will find extracts, author information, details of forthcoming events and the option to sign up for our newsletters.

This book is dedicated to the memories
of David Yale (1928–2021)
and Stephen Waddams (1942–2023)

CONTENTS

LIST OF CONTRIBUTORS

Sir John Baker KC (Hon) FBA is an Honorary Fellow of St Catharine's College, Cambridge and Emeritus Downing Professor of the Laws of England at the University of Cambridge.

MJ Cleaver is a Senior Associate at Allens and an Adjunct Lecturer at the University of New South Wales.

Laura Flannigan is Warner Woodring Chair and Assistant Professor in Early Modern History at Ohio State University.

David Foster is an Associate Professor of Law at University College London.

Joshua Getzler is a Fellow of St Hugh's College, Oxford, Professor of Law and Legal History at the University of Oxford, and Conjoint Professor of Law at the University of New South Wales, Sydney.

Julius AW Grower is the Ann Smart Fellow and Tutor in Law at St Hugh's College, Oxford and an Associate Professor of Law at the University of Oxford.

AJ Hannay is a Lecturer in Property Law at the University of Manchester.

David Ibbetson FBA is an Honorary Fellow of Clare Hall, Cambridge and Emeritus Regius Professor of Civil Law at the University of Cambridge.

Emily Ireland is a Lecturer in Law at the University of Liverpool.

NG Jones is a Fellow of Magdalene College, Cambridge and Professor of English Legal History at the University of Cambridge.

Michael Lobban FBA is a Senior Research Fellow at All Souls College, Oxford and Professor of Legal History at Oxford University.

Joanna McCunn is a Senior Lecturer in Law at the University of Bristol.

Catharine MacMillan is a Professor of Private Law at King's College London.

Mike Macnair is a Fellow by Resolution of St Hugh's College, Oxford.

Lorenzo Maniscalco is a Senior Assistant Professor in the History of Medieval and Modern Law at the University of Bologna.

Charles Mitchell KC (Hon) FBA is a Professor of Law at University College London.

Helen Saunders is an independent scholar who has held teaching posts at Keele University, the University of Sydney and the Australian National University.

Fleur Stolker is the Herchel Smith Teaching and Research Fellow at Emmanuel College, Cambridge.

Andreas Televantos is the Hanbury Fellow and Tutor in Law at Lincoln College, Oxford and an Associate Professor of Law at the University of Oxford.

Stephen Waddams was a Professor of Law at the University of Toronto at the time of his death in 2023.

DP Waddilove is an Associate Professor of Law at Delaware Law School, Widener University.

1

Historical Foundations of English Equity

DAVID FOSTER*

The history of equity is a tangled skein. How, why and to what extent the broad precepts of equity were instantiated in English law has been controverted since the medieval period. With its own terminology, doctrines and courts, equity is frequently considered in contradistinction to the common law. However, 'equity' is a capacious term; it contains multitudes. At times, 'equity' is used as a byword for 'fairness' or 'reason' – as a value inherent in the law itself.[1] In this vein, common law judges not infrequently dispensed equity in their own courts,[2] whilst the equity of the Chancery could be regarded as the 'fulfilment' of the common law.[3] Over the course of its long life, equity's meanings in English law have been modified depending on context, period and – all too often – the tastes and prejudices of the beholder.

The purpose of this volume is to chart the evolution of equity in English legal history from the medieval to the modern period. At base, the classical English notion of equity comprised a secondary set of principles which operated to assist, supplement, or even correct the primary rules and procedures of the common law. In its primitive form, it connoted a type of extraordinary justice – beyond the law – granting remedies not available in the common law courts and preventing abuse of legal process. Early English equity was not bound by precedent; its application was characterised by highly fact-sensitive inquiries and the exercise of an overarching judicial discretion. It is hornbook legal history that, over time, English equity lost much of its 'extraordinary' character and became a more-or-less regularised part of the law – at times, as ossified and inflexible as

* I would like to thank Benjamin Douglas, David Ibbetson, Michael Lobban, Lorenzo Maniscalco, Joanna McCunn, Charles Mitchell, Judith Skillen, and Ian Williams for their comments on earlier drafts. All errors are my own.

[1] N Doe, *Fundamental Authority in Late Medieval English Law* (Cambridge, Cambridge University Press, 1990) chs 4 and 5.

[2] P Brand, 'The Equity of the Common Law Courts' in E Koops and WJ Zwalve (eds), *Law and Equity: Approaches in Roman Law and Common Law* (Leiden, Martinus Nijhoff, 2014) 39–53. For early examples of equity in the common law courts, see *Clencham v Bale* (1278) in GO Sayles, *Select Cases in the Court of King's Bench, vol I* (1936) 55 *Selden Society* 41, and *Umfraville v Lonstede* (1309) in FW Maitland, *Year Books of Edward II, vol II* (1905) 20 *Selden Society* 58–9. See also Lord Ellesmere's observation in *Earl of Oxford's case* (1615) Chan Rep 1, 9, that *audita querela* writs were instances of common law equity.

[3] JW Brunyate (ed), FW Maitland, *Equity: A Course of Lectures* (Cambridge, Cambridge University Press, 1936) 17.

the rules it purported to gloss. This shift from extraordinary to regularised equity, from 'equity *beyond* the law' to 'equity *as* law', is the focus of this introductory chapter.

I. Origins of English Equity

The language of equity appears in English legal sources as early as *Glanvill* (c. 1189)[4] and *Bracton* (c. 1220s).[5] In its early usages, 'equity' might simply mean the abstract notion of justice which underpinned all law.[6] As a narrower aspect of justice, however, equity could also incorporate the need to treat like cases alike; most crucially, through the analogical extension of written rules to cases which were within the reason of the rule, but outside its strict wording.[7] In this form, equity became well known to English common lawyers through the doctrine of statutory interpretation known as the 'equity of a statute'.[8] How precisely this notion of equity was theorised in the medieval period is hard to pin down in the sources. JL Barton has noted a marked similarity with the civilian concept of *aequitas* as 'a device for filling gaps in the written law'.[9] Whereas Norman Doe regards such instances of 'equity' as merely a search for the 'reason' (or *ratio*) underlying the original written rule.[10] In that regard, however, this medieval notion of equity – restricted, as it was, to *written* law only – bore little resemblance to the classical English notion of equity as a discrete body of principles administered by a separate set of courts and most often associated with the Court of Chancery.[11]

The language of equity did not become associated with the work of the Chancery until the early modern period. However, the separation of the Chancery's jurisdiction from that of the common law courts was a medieval innovation – and one which has come to define the peculiar notion of equity administered under English law.[12] The origins of the separate equity jurisdiction lie in the medieval King's Council and the practice of petitioning the Crown in cases where the common law had failed to render justice. In such cases, the aggrieved party would directly petition the King – as the font of justice in the legal system – to grant an extraordinary remedy and prevent the injustice complained of at law. As the number of petitions grew, an administrative structure was required to transact this judicial business and, from the thirteenth century, the King's Council seems to have exercised a general jurisdiction to grant remedies where

[4] *Glanvill*, prologue; bk ii. 7; bk ii. 12; bk vii. 7.

[5] *Bracton*, bk ii. 25.

[6] JH Baker, *Oxford History of the Laws of England, Volume VI: 1483–1558* (Oxford, Oxford University Press, 2003) 40. For later usage in this sense, see W Blackstone, *Commentaries on the Laws of England, Book III* (Oxford, Clarendon Press, 1768) 429.

[7] Doe (n 1) 103–6 and 115–7.

[8] YB Hil 48 Edw III 1, pl 4 (Fyncheden CJCP); YB Mich. 48 Edw III 28, pl. 4 (Belknap CJCP).

[9] JL Barton, 'Equity in the Medieval Common Law' in RA Newman (ed), *Equity in the World's Legal Systems* (Brussels, Bruylant, 1973) 139–41. For detail on civilian conceptions of *aequitas*, see L Maniscalco, *Equity in Early Modern Legal Scholarship* (Leiden, Brill, 2020) 13–28.

[10] Doe (n 1) 115–7; DJ Ibbetson, 'A House Built on Sand: Equity in Early Modern English Law' in E Koops and WJ Zwalve (eds), *Law and Equity: Approaches in Roman Law and Common Law* (Leiden, Martinus Nijhoff, 2014) 56–7.

[11] Baker (2003) (n 6) 40–1.

[12] WS Holdsworth, *A History of English Law, vol III*, 3rd edn (London, Metheun, 1922) 446.

the common law had failed.[13] Over the course of the fourteenth century, significant elements of the Council's judicial work were delegated to high-ranking officers of state, of whom the Lord Chancellor was the most significant.[14] Already possessing a considerable administrative staff and oversight of judicial matters on the Latin (or common law) side of Chancery, the Chancellor's authority to grant remedies upon petition eventually matured into a discrete jurisdiction: the English side of the Chancery. The English side of the Chancery was only one of the so-called 'conciliar' or 'prerogative' jurisdictions which emerged in this way. By the early fifteenth century, the Court of Exchequer seems to have been developing an extraordinary jurisdiction to hear petitions relating to the royal revenue.[15] Whilst much of the Council's civil jurisdiction was delegated to the Chancery, the constitutional changes under Edward IV (r 1461–70 and 1471–83) and Henry VII (r 1485–1509) saw the birth of a 'Court' of Star Chamber to consider petitions on criminal matters and a 'Court' of Requests to hear petitions on 'poor men's causes'.[16]

The jurisdiction of the prerogative courts was broadly justified by reference to the King's role as the source of all justice in the legal system. Where the King's ordinary laws (embodying his *potestas ordinata*) had failed, it was the King's prerogative to use his absolute power (*potestas absoluta*) to provide ultimate justice to the grieved parties. This conception of extraordinary justice resting in the power of the Prince had its origin in Roman legal learning and was a commonplace of medieval legal and political thought in Europe.[17] This absolute power might be contrasted to the ordinary procedures of the law; it was an external influence affecting the law's normal operation, grounded in the extraordinary discretion of the monarch. We can detect a sense of this distinction in a proclamation of 1349 which publicly announced the availability of the Chancellor to deal with petitions touching the operation of the common law.[18] The wording of the proclamation specifically referred to such instances as matters of 'grace', as opposed to matters of common law.[19] Crucially, the delegation of this 'absolute power' from the King's Council to the prerogative courts ensured that the authority of these emergent jurisdictions would be closely tied to the Crown;[20]

[13] ME Avery, 'The History of the Equitable Jurisdiction of Chancery before 1460' (1969) 42 *Bulletin of the Institute of Historical Research* 129, 141–2; Barton (n 9) 145–6.

[14] On this process of delegation, see L Flannigan, *Royal Justice and the Making of the Tudor Commonwealth, 1485-1547* (Cambridge, Cambridge University Press, 2024) 43–9.

[15] TFT Plucknett, *A Concise History of the Common Law*, 5th edn (Indianapolis, Liberty Fund, 2010 reprint) 185. Although *cf* WH Bryson, *Cases Concerning Equity and the Courts of Equity, 1550–1660, vol I* (2000) 117 *Selden Society* xliii, noting that the Exchequer did not develop an *equity* jurisdiction until significantly later.

[16] See Flannigan (n 14) 59–61 and 68–71. The Council continued to exercise a broad jurisdiction over private law matters throughout the sixteenth and seventeenth centuries; for which, see JP Dawson, 'The Privy Council and Private Law in the Tudor and Stuart Periods' (1950) 48 *Michigan Law Review* 393 (Part I) and 627 (Part II).

[17] Barton (n 9) 141–7; K Pennington, *The Prince and the Law* (Berkeley, CA, University of California Press, 1993) 38–75 and 106–118.

[18] Close Roll, 22 Edw III, part 2, membrane 2d. See *Calendar of the Close Rolls, vol VIII* (London, HMSO, 1905) 615.

[19] WP Baildon, *Select Cases in Chancery, 1364–1471* (1893) 10 *Selden Society* xvii–xviii.

[20] For caution as to the association between Chancery and royal power in medieval legal theory, see IS Williams, 'Developing a Prerogative Theory for the Authority of the Chancery' in M Godfrey (ed), *Law and Authority in British Legal History, 1200–1900* (Cambridge, Cambridge University Press, 2016) 33, 35–7.

an association which would eventually come to define aspects of the equity they dispensed.[21]

Writing of the early jurisdiction of the Council and the Chancellor, SFC Milsom has emphasised that 'this was not the delegation of some sovereign power to override the law, and a petitioner did not see himself as asking the law to be overridden'.[22] Rather, the extraordinary jurisdiction of the Council was predicated on common law procedures having failed by reason of the parties' specific circumstances (typically, the plaintiff's poverty or because the claim was brought against an 'over-mighty' defendant).[23] Such cases formed the heart of the early medieval Chancery's jurisdiction c. 1400 and were particularly notable in their concern for the proper administration of the common law and preventing abuse of legal process. The distinguishing feature of the Council and the early Chancery was not in the law which they dispensed, therefore, but in their modes of proceeding. The prerogative courts were not bound by the common law's inflexible forms of action, its reliance on jury trial or its restrictive approach to the admission of evidence. Rather, they adopted the English bill procedure. With their open form of pleading by bill, proceedings in the prerogative courts lacked the technicality of the common law and were comparatively cheaper and speedier.[24] Similarly, the Chancery did not keep the usual legal terms; it was always open to receive bills and petitions.[25] Perhaps the most crucial of all the procedural advantages of the prerogative courts was the writ of *subpoena*.[26] By means of the *subpoena*, the Chancellor could compel a recalcitrant or over-mighty defendant to appear and answer the petitioner's complaint. Through these powerful procedural mechanisms, the prerogative courts distinguished themselves from the 'ordinary' course of the common law and laid the foundations for later medieval conceptualisations of their extraordinary jurisdiction.

The flexible procedures adopted in English bill courts were crucial to their conceptualisation in another regard: as courts of conscience. From the late fourteenth century, conscience had been regarded as a basis for the Chancellor's intervention.[27] In *Duram v Mell* (1433),[28] for instance, the petition insisted that the defendant's use of 'sorcerye' to draw water from the petitioner's pond was 'une mater de conscience' requiring relief from the Chancellor. The language of conscience operated to further distinguish the

[21] Writing c. 1470, Sir John Fortescue seems to have been the first English writer to connect the notion of equity (*epieikeia*) to the King's *potestas absoluta*: T Fortescue (ed), *The Works of Sir John Fortescue* (London, privately printed, 1896) 85–6, translation at 214–5. However, the connection to the work of the Chancery was not made until later.

[22] SFC Milsom, *Historical Foundations of the Common Law*, 2nd edn (Oxford, Oxford University Press, 1981) 83.

[23] JH Baker, *Introduction to English Legal History*, 5th edn (Oxford, Oxford University Press, 2019) 113.

[24] ME Avery, 'An Evaluation of the Effectiveness of the Court of Chancery under the Lancastrian Kings' (1970) 86 *Law Quarterly Review* 84, 85–6.

[25] N Pronay, 'The Chancellor, the Chancery, and the Council at the End of the Fifteenth Century' in H Hearder and HR Lyon (eds), *British Government and Administration* (Cardiff, University of Wales Press, 1974) 97.

[26] For the early history of the writ, see WM Ormrod, 'The Origins of the *Sub Pena* Writ' (1988) 61 *Historical Research* 11.

[27] M Beilby, 'The Profits of Expertise: The Rise of the Civil Lawyers and Chancery Equity' in MA Hicks (ed), *Profit, Piety and the Professions in Later Medieval England* (Gloucester, Alan Sutton, 1990) 82.

[28] Public Records Office (PRO) C1/12/168.

Chancery from the courts of common law.[29] By 1468, Stillington C could regard himself – in matters pertaining to conscience – as a 'judge de conscience', as opposed to a mere 'judge temporal'.[30] It has long been observed that this distinctive language of conscience may have had its source in the ecclesiastical training of the medieval chancellors and that the procedures adopted by the Chancery may themselves have been influenced by the canon law – most notably by the *aequitas canonica* of the *denunciatio evangelica*.[31] As early as 1415, a petition in the House of Commons had complained that pleas in Chancery were made by 'examination and oath of the parties, according to the form of the civil Law, and the Law of Holy Church, in subversion your [Majesty's] Common Law.'[32] The civilian *denunciatio evangelica* had a penitential origin, concerned with the reformation of the defendant's soul in accordance with the demands of Christian conscience. Factors such as the plaintiff's poverty and the defendant's might were as relevant to the *denunciatio* as to the medieval Chancery.[33] Similarly, if a remedy in the ordinary law were available, the *denunciatio* procedure could not be used,[34] and the same was equally true in Chancery.[35] Indeed, there is evidence that the Chancellors regarded the sanctity of the defendant's soul as relevant to their jurisdiction. In 1489, for example, Morton C asserted that an executor who failed to make restitution to the testator's estate would be 'damned to hell' and that the 'remedy for such a thing … is well done according to the conscience.'[36]

Despite the similarities, there are difficulties in identifying the *denunciatio* as the inspiration for Chancery practice – not the least of which is the absence of evidence for a direct transplantation of legal ideas.[37] If the Chancery's English bill procedure was not, in fact, influenced by the *denunciatio evangelica*, there was nevertheless scope for civilian influence by other means. MRT Macnair has drawn attention to usage of the civilian maxim '*iudex secundum allegata et probata non secundum conscientiam iudicat*'[38] in discussions of fifteenth-century Chancery procedure.[39] Whilst courts of common law were constrained to proceed *secundum allegata et probata*,[40] the English bill courts were privileged to proceed '*secundum conscientiam & non secundum allegata*'.[41] In this context, 'conscience' meant 'private knowledge' or 'facts which were not alleged and proved according to the

[29] See David Ibbetson's chapter in this volume (ch 2).

[30] YB Trin 8 Edw IV 5, pl 1.

[31] H Coing, 'English Equity and the Denunciatio Evangelica of the Canon Law' (1955) 71 *Law Quarterly Review* 223; Barton (n 9) 143–5; JL Barton, 'Introduction' in TFT Plucknett and JL Barton (eds), C St German, *Doctor and Student* (1974) 91 *Selden Society* xxxiv–xxxv and xxxix–xl. Although there is reason to believe that the language of conscience was a mainstay of English legal thought more generally in this period; for which see Doe (n 1) ch 6.

[32] Rot Parl iv, 84 (printed in J Parkes, *A History of the Court of Chancery* (London, Longman, 1828) 48–50).

[33] Coing (n 31) 232.

[34] ibid 233.

[35] YB Mich 39 Hen VI 26, pl 36.

[36] YB Hil 4 Hen VII 4, pl 8.

[37] MRT Macnair, 'Equity and Conscience' (2007) 27 *Oxford Journal of Legal Studies* 659, 669–672. The earlier historiography is conveniently covered in TS Haskett, 'The Medieval Court of Chancery' (1996) 14 *Law and History Review* 245, 256–266.

[38] 'The judge decides according to what is alleged and proved, not according to conscience.'

[39] MRT Macnair, *The Law of Proof in Early Modern Equity* (Berlin, Duncker & Humblot, 1999) 46–54; Macnair (2007) (n 37) 672–77.

[40] YB Hil 37 Hen VI 13, pl 3 (Prysot CJCP).

[41] YB Trin 9 Edw IV 14, pl 9 (Stillington C).

requirements of the common law'. What precisely proceeding '*secundum conscientiam*' entailed, however, remains debatable. In its original sense, the phrase suggested that the judge in conscience was entitled to proceed to a decree upon his own personal knowledge of the case (ie, upon knowledge which was neither alleged nor proved before the court).[42] By the later fifteenth century, however, the notion of proceeding according to conscience could also be associated with the flexibility of pleading in Chancery. Courts of common law were bound to exclude allegations not specifically pleaded or which could not be known by a jury, but these strict rules of pleading were not applicable in Chancery.[43] In a yearbook case of 1469, the defendant objected that the plaintiff's bill failed to assert particular facts, including the sum owing to the plaintiff and the agreed date of repayment. Rejecting the defendant's plea, Stillington C remarked:

> As to the uncertainty [in the bill], the plaintiff cannot know what sum has been paid or what day was given to … [pay], for this does not lie within his knowledge … But matters that lie within his knowledge he ought to set forth with certainty, but this will come upon the examination of conscience, and, sir, in this court, it is not required that the bill be entirely certain according to the solemnity of the common law, for here it is merely a petition, etc.[44]

According to Stillington, therefore, any imperfections in the plaintiff's pleadings could be ameliorated by examination of the defendant's conscience at the proofs stage (by compelling his answer under oath).[45] Proceeding according to conscience in this sense, Chancery might elicit the requisite knowledge from the defendant and proceed to a decree on that basis.[46] According to Macnair, 'this examination of the *conscientia* of the defendant was the absolute centre of the fact-finding procedure of the Chancery and other equity courts'.[47] Whether transplanted from civilian sources or not, the notion of conscience as a procedural concept may well have operated to distinguish the English bill courts from the courts of common law and give greater conceptual unity to the nascent equity jurisdiction of the fifteenth century.

The preceding discussion has highlighted three key characteristics which differentiated the English side of the Chancery from the ordinary course of the common law

[42] This meaning appears to lie behind the notion of jury verdicts rendered according to the conscience (or private knowledge) of the juror, rather than what had been alleged and proved before the court (see *Bracton*, bk iii. 74). See also the discussion of private judicial knowledge at YB Pasch 7 Hen IV 41, pl 5 (Tyrwhit sjt and Gascoigne CJKB).

[43] YB Pasch 4 Edw IV 8, pl 9: matters of intention, which could not be known to a jury, were regarded by Moyle J as 'good facts in the Chancery'. See also TFT Plucknett and JL Barton (eds), C St German, *Doctor and Student* (1974) 91 *Selden Society* 117.

[44] YB Mich 9 Edw IV 41, pl 26. Translation adapted from DJ Seipp, *Legal History: The Year Books* (Seipp Number: 1469.115): www.bu.edu/law/faculty-research/legal-history-the-year-books/. See also YB Trin 14 Edw IV 6, pl 8 (mispleading on the Latin side of the Chancery).

[45] In his *Forum Romanum* (written c. 1700), Jeffrey Gilbert regarded the advent of examination of the defendant under oath as the 'birth' of Chancery's equity jurisdiction (see *History and Practice of the High Court of Chancery, vol I* (Dublin, Watts, 1758) 33). On answers under oath, see Macnair (1999) (n 39) 54–60.

[46] It should be noted that, whilst the Chancery might proceed *non secundum allegata*, there was a continuing question as to the proofs necessary in proceedings *secundum conscientiam*. In YB Trin 9 Edw IV 14, pl 9, for example, it is not clear whether Stillington was discussing the private knowledge of the judge or private knowledge gained by examination of the defendant's conscience. This ambiguity is reflected in St German's 'Little Treatise Concerning Writs of *Subpoena*' (c. 1530), printed in J Guy (ed), *Christopher St German on Chancery and Statute* (1985) 6 *Selden Society Supplementary Series* 106 at 120–2 and 124 (discussing the personal liability of the Chancellor for issuing decrees on 'vehement conjectures' or inadequate proofs).

[47] Macnair (2007) (n 37) 676.

courts: the extraordinary jurisdiction delegated from the King (representing his *potestas absoluta*); the flexible mode of proceeding; and its conceptualisation in terms of conscience. These aspects of medieval Chancery jurisprudence were eventually woven together by the ecclesiastical Chancellor, Robert Stillington DCL. In 1469, Stillington C explicitly linked the Chancery's distinctive procedures with the 'absolute' power vested in that court:

> [In Chancery,] one will not be prejudiced by mispleading or by lack of form, but [will be adjudged] according to the truth of the matter, and we have to judge '*secundum conscientiam, & non secundum allegata*' because if one supposes by bill that another had done wrong to him, and the defendant says nothing, if we have knowledge that no wrong has been done to the plaintiff, he will recover nothing; and there are two kinds of powers and processes, that is, '*potentia ordinata et absoluta*'; '*ordinata*' is where a certain order is observed, as in positive law, but the law of nature '*non habet certum ordinem*', but by whatever means that the truth can be known, etc. and '*ideo dicitur processus absolutus*' …[48]

The union of absolute power, flexible procedure, and adjudication according to conscience had thus become the hallmark of the medieval Chancery. This concatenation of ideas was a sign of the court's extraordinary authority but also the central feature differentiating it from the ordinary procedures of the law.

Over the course of the fifteenth century, the substance of the Chancery's jurisdiction began to change, and its distinctive jurisdiction in conscience started to diverge from the work of the common law courts. Throughout the fourteenth century, the Chancellor had often been called to adjudicate on pure questions of common law, such as disseisin of land and trespass to goods or persons.[49] The rising significance of the Chancery, however, triggered protest from those concerned that the Chancellor was interfering in matters properly determinable at common law.[50] From the mid-fourteenth century, Parliament passed various due process statutes designed to protect the common law from external interference.[51] These statutes were informed by jurisprudence stemming from chapter 29 of *Magna Carta* but were put to significant use in restraining the extraordinary jurisdiction of the Council and Chancery in matters of life, limb and freehold property.[52] Over time, the view emerged that pure issues of common law were not to be stirred in Chancery, and it is to these developments that we owe the rule against Chancery determination of freehold title.[53] The due process statutes were not the end of the matter, however, and petitions against the Chancellor's jurisdiction were also lodged in the House of Commons in 1389,

[48] YB Trin 9 Edw IV 14, pl 9. Translation adapted from Seipp (n 44) (Seipp Number: 1469.049).

[49] For a charming example, see *Charles v Prior of Royston* (1432x1443) PRO C1/11/227-230 in which the petitioner had earned an income by charging the public to view 'the Kinges foul called an Estrich' but complained that the defendants had commandeered and exhibited the bird 'in the com[m]on street … and hym openly made to be seyn for nought of all man[ner] of people.'

[50] For early Parliamentary petitions regarding the Chancellor's jurisdiction, see Parkes (n 32) 37–42 and 48–50.

[51] 2 Edw III, c 8; 25 Edw III, stat 5, c 4; 28 Edw III, c 3; 42 Edw III, c 3.

[52] JH Baker, *The Reinvention of Magna Carta 1216-1616* (Cambridge, Cambridge University Press, 2017) 36 and 50–2. In 1393/4, an unsuccessful petition in the House of Commons demanded that 'no frank tenement or other Action whatsoever, which may be tried by the Common Law, shall be tried or brought into the Chancery': Rot Parl iii, 323 (printed in Parkes (n 32) 41–2).

[53] Plucknett (n 15) 176–77.

1393 and 1402.[54] In 1402, the statute 4 Hen IV, c 23 had prohibited interference with common law determinations after judgment. Whether this statute was intended to restrain Chancery's jurisdiction has been debated,[55] but it is undeniable that the statute was passed in an era where concern for the autonomy of the common law had been pricked.[56]

Parliamentary petitions against the Chancery continued into the 1420s, and by the 1450s, the Chancery's jurisdiction in cases of abuse of process, over-mighty defendants and poor men's causes had declined significantly.[57] By the end of the century, much of this work had been transferred to the Star Chamber and the Court of Requests.[58] Although the Chancery's extraordinary jurisdiction over the common law had been curtailed, the court retained its jurisdiction to *supplement* the procedures and remedies of the common law.[59] Mark Beilby has observed that, during the reign of Edward IV, 'petitions no longer simply alluded to the petitioner's inability to gain a common law remedy because of the power of his adversary. Rather they conceded that the petitioner had no claim at common law, but had a right in conscience which the Chancellor should recognise.'[60] This jurisdiction included relief against penalties and frauds, protection of sureties, and decrees to quiet the possession of land. Perhaps the most important aspect of this separate jurisdiction, however, was the enforcement of uses.[61] In recognising rights to land not cognisable at law, the Chancellor might be regarded as enforcing a body of rules entirely separate from those of the common law – and not merely as administering a distinct set of procedures for unearthing evidence not admissible at law. We can see a hint of this distinction in a yearbook case of 1464.[62] In that case, Serjeant Jenney had denied that a feoffment in confidence could be pleaded in an action for trespass at common law because 'a man's intention is uncertain; and one must plead facts which are or can be known to the jury'.[63] Moyle J agreed that '[t]hese would be good facts in the Chancery, for there the defendant shall aver the intention and purpose of such a feoffment; for in the Chancery, by conscience, one shall have a remedy according to the intention of such a feoffment.'[64] This discussion drew the familiar distinction

[54] P Tucker, 'The Early History of the Court of Chancery: A Comparative Study' (2000) 115 *English Historical Review* 791, 797.

[55] Baker (2017) (n 52) 213, n 412.

[56] See also 15 Hen VI, c 4. Designed to prevent abuse of process, the statute provided that writs of *subpoena* were not to be granted unless the petitioners found sureties to pay damages to the defendant in the event the matter in the bill proved untrue. See Avery (1970) (n 24) 96. For the position in the early sixteenth century, see J Guy, *The Cardinal's Court* (Sussex, Harvester Press, 1977) 81 and the discussion in St German (n 46) 119–120.

[57] Avery (1969) (n 13) 133.

[58] For developments in Requests, see Laura Flannigan's chapter in this volume (ch 5).

[59] EG Henderson, 'Legal Rights to Land in the Early Chancery' (1982) 26 *American Journal of Legal History* 97.

[60] Beilby (n 27) 78. See also YB Hil 4 Hen VII 4, pl 8 in which Morton C declared '*nullus recedat a Curia Cancellariae sine remedio*' but this was denied by Fyneux sjt on the grounds that '*si nullus recedat sine remedio, ergo nullus indiget esse confessus*'.

[61] See Ashley Hannay's chapter in this volume (ch 3).

[62] YB 4 Edw IV 8, pl 9.

[63] JH Baker, *Baker and Milsom: Sources of English Legal History: Private Law to 1750*, 2nd edn (Oxford, Oxford University Press, 2010) 106–7. For the general assertion that intention was not triable at common law, see also YB Pasch 17 Edw IV 1, pl 2 (Bryan CJCP).

[64] ibid 107.

between Chancery and common law proceedings according to their rules of evidence. However, Moyle J's intervention elicited the following exchange between bar and bench:

> *Serjeant Catesby*: The law of the Chancery is the common law of the land; and there the defendant shall have advantage of such facts and [may set out the] feoffment. Why, then, should it not be the same here?
>
> *Moyle J*: It cannot be, here in this court, as I have told you: for the common law of the land in this case differs from the law of the Chancery on this point.[65]

The reference here to variance between the common law and the 'law of the Chancery' was a significant indicator that the language of conscience was developing from a purely procedural notion and had gained greater substantive effect in the English legal system by the middle of the fifteenth century.[66]

As the Chancery's supplementary jurisdiction in conscience began to flower in the later fifteenth century, it became necessary to explain the status of the Chancellor's decrees at common law. Central to late medieval conceptions of the Chancery's supplementary jurisdiction was the notion that the Chancellor did not declare legal rights and obligations void; rather, the Chancery superintended their exercise by means of coercive decrees against the parties personally. By the *subpoena*, the Chancellor could compel parties to use their legal rights in accordance with the requirements of good conscience (under threat of imprisonment). In this respect, the Chancellor's decrees acted *in personam*, or on the person of the defendant, and thus did not involve adjudication of the underlying legal rights at stake.[67] The personal character of Chancery proceedings may also explain why records of the court's decrees were not kept or enrolled.[68] Chancery decrees were not judgments of record and, as such, could not be reversed on a writ of error to the King's Bench.[69] A Chancery determination of a right to land, for example, would bind only the parties to the dispute and did not operate to 'clear title' to the land as a common law judgment did.[70] These aspects of the Chancery's jurisdiction were blended together by Prysot CJCP in *Reynolde v Knott* (1459).[71] The question in that case touched on the legal effect of a Chancery decree to deliver up a bond for cancellation. In the Common Pleas, Prysot CJCP denied that the Chancellor's decree excluded the jurisdiction of the common law courts:

> It remains to be seen in what matters the Chancery is a court of record so that one can have a writ of error, and in what matters [it is] not. Sir … in the use of writs of *sub poena*, [the Chancery] is not … a court of record, for there conscience only has to be examined, because we here in this court proceed to judgment *secundum allegiatum et probatum*, and we cannot go beyond it; and it is their business to examine the conscience … And forasmuch as he cannot have remedy by our law, he sues there to have the obligation restored to him, and the effect of their power and their judgment is to restore the obligation to the party or cause the

[65] ibid.

[66] See also *Rede v Capell* (1492) YB Pasch 7 Hen VII 11, pl 2: 'by a feoffment on confidence, the feoffor has no remedy by common law, and yet by conscience he has' (Morton C).

[67] Milsom (n 22) 90 and 92.

[68] F Metzger, 'The Last Phase of the Medieval Chancery' in A Harding (ed), *Law-Making and Law-Makers in British History* (London, Royal Historical Society, 1980) 79, 87.

[69] JH Baker, *Reports of Sir John Spelman, vol II* (1977) 94 *Selden Society* 75.

[70] Bryson (n 15) xliv; Henderson (n 59) 116–7.

[71] YB Hil 37 Hen VI 13, pl 3.

> defendant to make acquittance or release. And to execute this [judgment] the court can do nothing except order him to prison to be there until he is ready to do this; and thus this is all that the said court can do. And if the party would rather lie in prison than hand over the obligation, the other party is without remedy, and thus the Chancellor has no power to make the obligation void.[72]

According to Prysot, therefore, the Chancellor's decree was not a matter of record such that it might prevent the common law courts proceeding to judgment. The distinction was drawn between proceedings *secundum allegata et probata* at common law and those according to conscience by writ of *subpoena*, but with the additional observation that proceedings in conscience bound only the person of the defendant and did not touch the validity of the underlying legal right.[73] The Chancery's supplementary jurisdiction was – at least in theory – designed to respect the autonomy of the common law and, for this reason, did not fall foul of the due process statutes of the previous century.

By the end of the fifteenth century, the Chancery had developed a body of rules and principles which were distinct from the common law. 'Conscience' in the late fifteenth century Chancery no longer merely denoted the procedures adopted by the court but the substance of its jurisdiction as well. In the first quarter of the sixteenth century indeed, More C could remark of Chancery's work that 'three things are to be helpt in conscience: fraud, accident, and things of confidence'.[74] At the close of the medieval period, therefore, the foundations of English equity had been set. The Chancery had developed a separate jurisdiction administering a discrete body of rules. Founded on conscience, the Chancery's jurisprudence was crafted to supplement – though, in theory, not override – the primary rules of the common law. The two jurisdictions were intimately connected, however, and the work of the Chancery necessarily brought it into intermittent conflict with courts of common law. There had been flashpoints of friction between the Chancery and the common law courts in the later fifteenth century,[75] but it was not until the chancellorship of Cardinal Wolsey (1515–29) that the issue reached fever pitch. Following Wolsey's fall from grace, a new theory of the Chancery was required to justify the jurisdiction and mediate relations between the courts. That theory was equity.

II. Crisis of Conscience

The period after 1480 had witnessed a significant expansion in the Chancery's business. Although exercising an 'extraordinary' jurisdiction, the Chancery had become a

[72] Translation adapted from M Hemmant, *Select Cases in the Exchequer Chamber* (1933) 51 *Selden Society* 147, 152.

[73] See also *Rede v Capel* (1492) YB Pasch 7 Hen VII 11, pl 2: 'the judgment in the court [of common law] … will not be impaired, but will stand: but the party will be restored according to conscience … [B]ecause the original feoffment will not come under examination, but only whether in conscience it ought to be restored' (Kebell sjt).

[74] 1 Rolle 374. Sir Edward Coke attributed the rhyme to Sir Thomas More. For discussion of this attribution, see Macnair (2007) (n 37) 677, fn 72.

[75] See, eg, *Russel's case* (1482) YB Mich 22 Edw IV 37, pl 21. In that case, the plaintiff had proceeded to judgment in King's Bench notwithstanding a Chancery injunction to the contrary. In awarding judgment, Huse CJKB threatened to release the plaintiff by *habeas corpus* in the event he was imprisoned for contempt of Chancery.

'court of constant resort'.[76] By the early sixteenth century, we once again find complaints that Chancery proceedings were undermining the common law, in contravention of the medieval due process statutes.[77] In a reading of 1514, John Hales observed:

> although *subpoenas* are sued in Chancery, yet it is not a court of record for this purpose, for it is only for conscience; and therefore judgment given there for this [conscience] shall not be reversed for error. [But] there is a statute which provides that no-one shall be vexed except by matter of record, and therefore if any man brings a *subpoena* where an action [lies at law, an action] on the statute lies and is maintainable against him.[78]

This argument was a step change from preceding complaints against the Chancery. The Parliamentary petitions of the late fourteenth and early fifteenth century had been concerned with the Chancery's overlapping jurisdiction with the common law courts (at least in matters of life, limb and freehold property). Hales' remarks were directed not at the Chancery's extraordinary common law jurisdiction, but at the jurisdiction in conscience itself. Not being a court of record, Hales was concerned that Chancery decrees were not subject to review by writ of error; after all, the statute of 4 Hen IV, c 23 had specifically provided that judgments at law were not to be disturbed other than by writ of error (or attaint), and no exception had been drawn for the Chancery.[79] This line of argument would later attract significant debate, but it was indicative of the objections that might be raised against Chancery's supplementary jurisdiction in conscience in the first decades of the sixteenth century.

It was, however, the appointment of Thomas Wolsey as Lord Chancellor in 1515 which marked a watershed in the history of the Chancery. Wolsey was an ecclesiastical chancellor – having been appointed Archbishop of York in 1514 and papal legate in 1518 – but lacking any formal legal training. In some respects, Wolsey's views on the Chancery were merely a continuation of previous practice; in other regards, he seemed to have pushed the Chancery beyond its medieval bounds. In his advice to Shelley J in 1529, for example, Wolsey observed:

> The kyng aught of his royal dignities and p[re]rogative mytigate the rigor of the lawe, where concyence hath the most force. Therefore in his royall place of equall justice, he hath constitute a chauncellor, an officer to execute justice w[ith] clemencie, where concyence is opposed by the rigor of the lawe. And therefore the court of chauncery hath been heretofore co[mm]only called the court of concyence, because it hath jurysdicion to command the highe mynysters of the co[mm]on lawe to spare execucion and judgm[en]t where concience had most effecte.[80]

Following his medieval predecessors, Wolsey considered that Chancery was instituted to wield the King's prerogative power in accordance with the requirements

[76] Baker (2019) (n 23) 114.
[77] Similar complaints were levied against the Court of Requests in this period. See Flannigan (n 14) 219–22.
[78] Baker (1977) (n 69) 75.
[79] See 2 *Statutes of the Realm* 142.
[80] British Library (BL) Egerton MS 2402, ff 59v–60r. George Cavendish's *Life of Cardinal Wolsey* circulated in manuscript from the mid-sixteenth century but was not published *in toto* for political reasons. This passage appeared in various garbled forms in J Stow, *Annales of England* (London, Newbery, 1592) 929 and G Cavendish, *Negotiations of Thomas Wolsey* (London, Sheeres, 1641) 85. A more accurate transcription was eventually published in SW Singer (ed), G Cavendish, *The Life of Cardinal Wolsey, vol I* (Chiswick, Whittingham, 1825) 216–7.

of conscience. In Wolsey's mind, conscience appeared to stand outside the law.[81] Associated with notions of justice and clemency, conscience was calculated to 'mitigate the rigour of the law'.[82] In these respects, Wolsey's understanding of conscience dimly reflected canonical conceptions of equity – in turn, deriving from the earlier notion of *misericordia* – as 'justice tempered by the sweetness of mercy'.[83] The phrase '*iustitia dulcore misericordiae temperata*' belonged to the thirteenth-century Italian canonist, Hostiensis, and was often associated with the notion of mitigating the strictness or rigour of the law. The phrase was picked up in the early fifteenth century in the moral theology of Jean Gerson, where it was associated with *epieikeia* and a concern to do justice in particular circumstances.[84] Around 1470, the English jurist, Sir John Fortescue, had connected the *potestas absoluta* of the king with equity ('*epikaia*'), which he explained as a 'super-laudable relaxation of the strictness of law'.[85] Whilst the juxtaposition between the conscience of the English Chancery and the rigour of the law ('*ex rigore iuris*') appeared in English sources in 1526,[86] it was the work of Christopher St German in 1528 which cemented the relationship between Chancery, conscience and continental equity discourses.[87] By similarly connecting the work of the Chancery to the language of the *aequitas canonica*, Wolsey's words indicate shifting notions in the conceptualisation of early modern Chancery and conscience.

In terms of Chancery practice, too, Wolsey's chancellorship appeared to break with the medieval past. It was alleged that, under Wolsey, the Chancery's jurisdiction expanded to encompass nearly any type of claim – including issues properly determinable at common law.[88] Wolsey's approach to adjudication gave fuel to the objection that Chancery undermined the operation of the common law, that its decrees were arbitrary and followed no fixed rule.[89] Without detailed reports or records of Chancery decrees for the period, it is difficult to come to an objective conclusion as to Wolsey's practices.[90] Nevertheless, it is tolerably clear that Wolsey's chancellorship elicited censure from many quarters – not least from the legal profession itself.[91] In his reading of 1526, for example, Thomas Audley complained that 'the good laws of the realm' had been rendered uncertain through their dependence 'on the whim (*arbitrement*) of

[81] G Behrens, 'An Early Tudor Debate on the Relation between Law and Equity' (1998) 19 *Journal of Legal History* 143, 154–5.

[82] For earlier use of this phrase, see Baker (2003) (n 6) 45 (quoting an address by the Chief Justice to new serjeants in 1521).

[83] On *misericordia*, *aequitas canonica* and *epieikeia*, see Maniscalco (n 9) 21–8 and 33–8.

[84] Z Rueger, 'Gerson's Concept of Equity and Christopher St German' (1982) 3 *History of Political Thought* 1, 9–11.

[85] Fortescue (n 21) 85–6, translation at 214–5.

[86] *Diversite de Courtz et lour Jurisdictions* (London, Pynson, 1526) sig A5 [recto of the following unnumbered leaf]. For the attribution and complex printing history of this work, see Baker (2003) (n 6) 894.

[87] St German (n 31) 94 ('*Equitas est* [*iustitia*] *pensatis omnibus circumstantiis particularibus dulcore misericordie temperata*') and 96 ('*obtemperare legis rigorem*').

[88] Metzger (n 68) 79; Macnair (2007) (n 37) 670–71.

[89] Baker (2003) (n 6) 175–77. See also Guy (n 56) 94–109 (discussing Wolsey's practice in Star Chamber); MRT Macnair, 'Arbitrary Chancellors and the Problem of Predictability' in E Koops and WJ Zwalve (eds), *Law and Equity: Approaches in Roman Law and Common Law* (Leiden, Martinus Nijhoff, 2014) 85–6.

[90] Although *cf Docwra's case* (1535) Trin 27 Hen VIII 15, pl 6 (reversing a former decree of Wolsey; this decision was specifically listed in Wolsey's articles of impeachment).

[91] Baker (1977) (n 69) 77–80.

the judge in conscience'.[92] In 1529, Wolsey's articles of impeachment likewise asserted that, in 'subversion' of the common law, Wolsey had granted injunctions after judgment at law (contrary to the statute 4 Hen IV, c 23).[93] Writing in the wake of Wolsey's fall, an anonymous serjeant lamented that:

> if the subjects of any realm shall be compelled to leave the law of the Realm, and to be ordered by the discretion of one man, what thing may be more unknown and more uncertain? … For most commonly the Chancellors of England have been spiritual men, that hath had but superficial knowledge of the laws of the realm … And [the Chancellor] regarding no law, but trusting to his own wit and wisdom, giveth judgment as it pleaseth himself, and thinketh that his judgment … is far better and more reasonable than the judgments that be given by the King's justices according to the common law of the realm.[94]

The perception of arbitrariness which pervaded Wolsey's chancellorship revealed the frailties of the office. If, as the sole judge in Chancery, the Chancellor followed no certain law and obeyed no clear jurisdictional boundary, then the law of the court simply collapsed into the personal conscience and discretion of the Chancellor himself.

III. Emergence of English Equity

Under Wolsey, conscience had become associated with notions of excessive subjectivity in adjudication and the exercise of autocratic power. As a juridical concept, conscience seemed to lose the structure with which it had been imbued in the medieval period. Writing towards the end of Wolsey's chancellorship, Christopher St German sought to place conscience and the work of the Chancery upon a non-arbitrary foundation by tying the Chancellor's discretion to the rules of the common law. St German's *Doctor and Student* (published between 1528 and 1530) has been credited with introducing the language of equity to conceptualisations of the Chancery's jurisdiction and uniting it with pre-existing notions of a jurisdiction based in conscience. Crucially – and unlike Wolsey – St German regarded equity and the work of the Chancery as *part of* the law, not as an extra-legal force which diverted the law from its ordinary course, but as the realisation of the law's underlying intent.[95]

St German's broad purpose in *Doctor and Student* is revealed in the original title of the work, *Dialogus de fundamentis legum Anglie et de conscientia* (published in Latin in 1528). After considering the various sources of English law, St German considered the role of conscience in the English legal system generally; namely, as a means for identifying the

[92] Baker (2010) (n 63) 118. *Cf* Flannigan (n 14) 211–3, suggesting that the Master of Requests (John Stokesley) was a likely target for these remarks. Stokesley – once accused of having baptised a cat – was removed from judicial office in 1523. For Stokesley's tenure in Requests, see L Flannigan, '"Allowable or Not"? John Stokesley, the Court of Requests, and Royal Justice in Sixteenth-Century England' (2020) 93 *Historical Research* 621.

[93] Baker (1977) (n 69) 79.

[94] 'Replication of a Serjeant at the Laws of England' in J Guy (ed), *Christopher St German on Chancery and Statute* (1985) 6 *Selden Society Supplementary Series* 101–2.

[95] For what follows, see especially: Barton (n 31) xx–lxvii; Rueger (n 84) 1–30; IS Williams, 'Christopher St German: Religion, Conscience and Law in Reformation England' in M Hill and RH Helmholz (eds), *Great Christian Jurists in English History* (Cambridge, Cambridge University Press, 2017) 69–92.

moral foundations of the law. To make this argument, St German followed the standard line of medieval theologians by dividing conscience into *synderesis* and *conscientia*.[96] *Synderesis* was the innate power to distinguish good from evil,[97] whilst *conscientia* was the application of *synderesis* to specific cases.[98] Through this intellectual structure, St German sought to demonstrate that conscience was not a purely subjective notion but a process of moral reasoning which was rational, predictable, and non-arbitrary. According to St German, conscience was implicit in all aspects of adjudication; he tells us at several points that 'conscience must always be grounded upon some law' (whether the law of God, the law of Nature, or the law of man).[99] For St German, conscience was the means by which, in cases of conflict between Divine, Natural, and human laws, the appropriate rule could be determined. Where human law conflicted with some precept of Divine or Natural law, the higher law was to be followed as a matter of conscience. If human law spoke to an issue on which the laws of God and Nature were silent, then conscience demanded that the human law be observed.[100]

Although providing for the invalidity of positive law in the event of conflict with higher legal norms, St German's general theory of law accorded a significant degree of autonomy for the substantive human law. In the state of nature, for example, we are told there can be no law of contract and no law of property.[101] As such, the entirety of the law of contract and property was to be determined by human law alone. This had significant implications for St German's notion of conscience. A conveyance rendered invalid by some defect at law was not to be aided in conscience; after all, on St German's account, there could be no conflict with Divine or Natural Law in this case, and so conscience was constrained to follow the human law.[102] Reflecting on this aspect of St German's theory, JL Barton observed that 'it must be confessed that it would seem possible to do some pretty odd things with a clear conscience'.[103] Such a narrow role for interventions based on conscience was clearly difficult to square with the practices of the Chancery – long reputed to be a 'court of conscience' by St German's day. On St German's theory, the law of property was to be determined by human law alone, but in practice the Chancellor regularly intervened to perfect imperfect conveyances where valuable consideration had passed or in cases of fraud.[104] Indeed, the very fact of Chancery intervention in such cases seemed to imply that the common law produced results which were themselves unconscionable. To account for the work of the English Chancery, therefore, St German's theory of conscience required an additional concept.

St German explained the conscience of Chancery through the principle of *epieikeia*,[105] which he drew from the *Nicomachean Ethics* (by way of Aquinas and Gerson).[106] Aristotle had observed that all general laws were liable to fail in specific cases. No human legislator

[96] Doe (n 1) 133–7.
[97] St German (n 43) 81–3.
[98] ibid 87–95.
[99] ibid 207 (see also 105, 133 and 163).
[100] ibid 75, 111–3, 129–31.
[101] ibid 133–5.
[102] ibid 121–5.
[103] Barton (n 31) xxvii.
[104] St German (n 43) 125, 208–13, 222–3 and 227.
[105] ibid 105: 'the law of England wills in many cases of conscience admitted by the law that there shall be such a remedy in Chancery upon diverse things grounded upon such equities'.
[106] Barton (n 31) xlvi–xlvii; Rueger (n 84) 16.

could account for the range of circumstances to which a rule might be applied, and its strict application could produce outcomes not intended by the legislator. *Epieikeia* was the means by which general rules could be modified in specific cases to reach results conformable with the intention of the legislator. Following Gerson, however, St German grounded the intention of the legislator in the Laws of God and Nature; after all (we are told), no legislator would intend an outcome which conflicted with Natural Law.[107] The courts were therefore justified in construing the general law according to *epieikeia* and granting an exception which would avoid conflict with the higher legal norms.[108] Crucially for St German, interpretation by *epieikeia* did not render the general rule void. Rather, the principle of *epieikeia* meant that all laws could be read as containing within themselves a 'secret' exception to their own terms, applicable in specific cases:

> in some cases it is good and even necessary to leave the words of the law, and to follow what reason and justice require, and to that intent equity is ordained, that is to say to temper and mitigate the rigour of the law. And it is also by some men called *epicaia*. The which is no other thing but an exception of the law of god, or of the law of reason, from the general rules of the law of man: when they by reason of their generality would in any particular case judge against the law of god, or the law of reason, the which exception is secretly understood in every general rule of every positive law … and so it appears that equity rather follows the intent of the law, than the words of the law.[109]

This was a crucial step in the argument. Applied to the Chancery, the principle of *epieikeia* suggested that the court was merely interpreting the law's underlying purpose and applying its 'secret exceptions' to unforeseen cases. Chancery intervention was not, therefore, grounded on the supposition that the common law rule was itself against good conscience but upon the realisation of the law's own intended effect. St German explained:

> equity takes not away the very right, but only that that seems to be right by the general words of the law … but equity follows the law [*equitas sequitur legem*] in all particular cases where right and justice require … [I]f any law were made by man without any such exception expressed or implied it were manifestly unreasonable, and were not to be suffered, for such cases might come that would observe that law should break both the law of God, and the law of reason.[110]

St German's approach was summed up in the pithy Latin tag, '*aequitas sequitur legem*'. This was an account of Chancery conscience, tied to the principle of *epieikeia*, which was grounded upon – and part of – the law.[111]

[107] St German (n 43) 77.

[108] ibid. St German specifies that such cases contravene the 'law of reason secondary', rather than the primary law of reason (or nature). Contravention of the primary law of reason would render the rule void, whereas contravention of the law of reason secondary merely justified an equitable construction of the general rule in specific cases. On which, see: Barton (n 31) xxiv; MJW Lobban, *A History of the Philosophy of Law in The Common Law World, 1600–1900* (Dordrecht, Springer, 2016) 16.

[109] St German (n 43) 97–99. This logic was equally applicable to the medieval notion of the equity of a statute; indeed in the English translation (but not the Latin), the Student follows the Doctor's comments on *epieikeia* with examples of statutory interpretation (see 99–100). This line of St German's thought would be adopted by Edmund Plowden in 1570s, albeit in conjunction with a markedly different conception of *epieikeia* (on which, see discussion below).

[110] ibid 97.

[111] See also St German (n 46) 122–3.

The stock example chosen by St German to illustrate his account of Chancery equity was that of double payment on a bond.[112] Where a bond debtor had repaid his debt but failed to procure a written acquittance, the debtor remained liable on the bond. In the common law courts, only written evidence was sufficient to discharge the debt, and the mere fact of repayment was no defence to the creditor's claim. The purpose of this general rule requiring writing was to ensure ready repayment of debts.[113] In cases where the debt had already been repaid, however, the failure to take a written acquittance produced an unintended outcome: the same debt might be repaid twice. Such an outcome was contrary to the Law of Nature and thus presumed contrary to the intentions of the lawgiver. Dispensing equity, the Chancellor would not declare the common law rule void; rather, he would intervene in this case to correct the operation of the common law rule and order cancellation of the bond. In so doing, St German's theory of *epieikeia* was able to explain and justify Chancery's existence as a separate jurisdiction,[114] allowing the common law to pursue general policies (such as efficient debt collection), whilst mitigating its effects in deserving cases.[115]

In certain respects, *Doctor and Student* was a remarkable break with the medieval past. For St German, the authority of the Chancery was not grounded in the king's absolute power, nor was its jurisdiction to be regarded as extraordinary. Rather, Chancery's jurisdiction flowed from *epieikeia* – a principle which inhered in the very nature of law and its application to specific facts – and was administered in accordance with the formal process of reasoning known as conscience. Through the principle of *epieikeia*, St German could explain how Chancery could respect the general validity of the common law whilst simultaneously mitigating its effect in specific cases. Nevertheless, the line between following and mitigating the law was undoubtedly a fine one.[116] The subtleties of St German's theory were apt to escape his successors and, ultimately, inadequate to convince his detractors. In 1531, for example, the 'Replication' of an anonymous serjeant at law sought to counter St German's theoretical arguments.[117] The serjeant rejected the notion that Chancery equity inhered in the law, complaining that:

> this good common law of the realm … should be made void or set at naught by the suit of any particular person made in the Chancery or any other place … For these two laws, one being contrary to the other, cannot stand together, but one of them must stand as void.[118]

The serjeant observed in the operation of the Chancery a direct conflict with the pretensions of the law. In conscience, he saw only 'a thing of great uncertainty' and regarded

[112] St German (n 43) 77–9 (and 98–100 for Latin version).

[113] ibid 77–9; St German (n 46) 112. See also *Waberley v Cockerel* (1541) Dyer 51a, 51a–b ('if a matter in writing may be so easily defeated, and avoided by such a surmise and naked breath, a matter in writing would be of no greater authority than a matter of fact').

[114] St German (n 43) 79: 'One can never be aided by equity of this sort in the same court [i.e. at common law] … But in some cases one can be aided by that sort of equity in the king's chancery by the writ of *subpoena*.'

[115] On this justification for the separate equity jurisdiction, see also: R Snagge, *The Antiquity & Original of the Court of Chancery and Authority of the Lord Chancellor of England* (written 1587, published London, Seile, 1654) 37–8; DEC Yale (ed), E Hake, *Epieikeia: A Dialogue in Three Parts* (New Haven, Yale University Press, 1953) 126.

[116] For critique of St German's explanation, see Barton (n 31) xlviii–li; Behrens (n 81) 151–2; Ibbetson (n 10) 60.

[117] On dating the 'Replication', see DEC Yale, 'St German's *Little Treatise Concerning Writs of Subpoena*' (1975) 10 *Irish Jurist* 324, 326, fn 13.

[118] 'Replication of a Serjeant at the Laws of England' (n 94) 100.

the Chancellors as 'spiritual men that hath had but superficial knowledge of the laws of the realm'.[119] In similar terms, the serjeant also attacked uses as an 'untrue and crafty invention', maintained in Chancery 'by the colour of conscience' and by which the common law was 'subverted and made void'.[120]

Notwithstanding the serjeant's complaints, analysis of English law in terms of *epieikeia* gained greater traction as the sixteenth century progressed. At the same time, the wellspring of new theories was causing the very concept to fragment – especially as it was stretched to encompass aspects of common law jurisprudence.[121] Around 1570, for example, Edmund Plowden made use of the language of '*epichaia*' in his reports of cases concerning the equity of a statute.[122] In Plowden's *Commentaries*, equity was the means by which the words of the statute were extended to or excepted from particular cases not foreseen by the legislator. In such cases, the equity (or purpose) of the statute was divined from the presumed intent of the lawgiver (rather than from Divine or Natural Law, as in St German).[123] However, grounding equitable interpretation in the extra-legal will of the legislator had consequences for Plowden's general conception of equity. In his report of *Eyston v Studd* (1574), Plowden wrote that equity 'is no part of the law, but a moral virtue which corrects the law'.[124] Herein lay the tension at the heart of early modern conceptions of equity; for Plowden equity could 'correct' the law because it lay *outside* the law, whereas St German was bound to regard equitable intervention as the realisation of the law's underlying intent.

The linking of *epieikeia* to both statutory interpretation and the work of the Chancery served to embed the language of equity and reinforce its respectability as a juristic concept in England. As David Ibbetson has remarked, however, this association of ideas 'served only to exacerbate the incoherence of the treatment of equity in the discursive works of the late 16th and early 17th centuries'.[125] This incoherence is perhaps most clearly seen in Edward Hake's treatise, *Epieikeia: A Dialogue in Three Parts* (written c. 1590s and updated in 1603).[126] Hake's concept of *epieikeia* was expansive; he saw *epieikeia* at work in all aspects of the common law, designed to draw out the 'secret exceptions' of the law and to fulfil its underlying intent (ie, to comply with the precepts of Divine and Natural Law). For Hake, the equity of the common law was the means by which the law was continuously reformed by the judiciary; it was the 'soul and spirit of the law', and its operation did 'not change the law, but is indeed to set the law in his right place'.[127] In his discussion of statutory interpretation, Hake tracked Plowden closely but denied Plowden's assertion that equity lay outside the law. Rather, Hake thought that equity was 'within the law, and that it being there found is to be applied by the judge of the law according as the particularity of the case that is before him, not aided by the

[119] ibid 101.
[120] ibid 104.
[121] *Cf* J Hales, *Oration in Commendation of the Laws* (c. 1540s) BL Harl MS 4990, ff 42–3, which was clear to distinguish the 'arithmetic equity' of all law, from the 'equity geometric' of the Chancery.
[122] *Stowel v Zouch* (1563) Plow 353, 375; *Eyston v Studd* (1574) Plow 459, 466. For details, see Lorenzo Maniscalco's chapter in this volume (ch 4).
[123] G Behrens, 'Equity in the *Commentaries* of Edmund Plowden' (1999) 20 *Journal of Legal History* 25, 35–7.
[124] *Eyston v Studd* (1574) Plow 459, 466.
[125] Ibbetson (n 10) 62.
[126] Hake (n 115). For detailed discussion, see Joanna McCunn's chapter in this volume (ch 8).
[127] Hake (n 115) 28.

latter of the law, shall require'.[128] Hake seemed to recognise, however, that the 'equity of the common law' could not explain cases such as double payment of a bond, where the law refused to dispense justice in specific cases.[129] Unfortunately, when he turned to the equity of the Chancery, Hake's theory collapsed into a list of commonplace descriptions of the medieval Chancery: the Chancery acts *in personam*, on particular circumstances, according to conscience, by means of a flexible form of procedure.[130] Ultimately, Hake's attempt to hitch the 'equity' of the common law to the 'equity' of the Chancery was unsuccessful; the two conceptions of equity possessed few commonalities, and the very attempt seemed to hint at an inherent instability of the concept of equity in English law itself.[131]

As the language of equity began to proliferate in late sixteenth-century legal theory, so too did it creep into Chancery practice.[132] By the 1590s, the Chancery had become a 'court of equity', rather than a 'court of conscience'.[133] Over the course of the century, however, criticisms of the equity jurisdiction continued to be voiced. Allegations of arbitrariness in adjudication and illegitimate interference with the common law were frequent. In 1547, Wriothesley C was removed from office for making decrees 'not grounded nor made upon any rule certain or law written' and for granting injunctions 'before verdicts, judgments and executions as after'.[134] The mid-century saw mounting challenges to the authority of the Chancery and conciliar courts by means of the prerogative writs.[135] Sir Robert Catlyn (Chief Justice 1559–74), for example, proclaimed the right of Queen's Bench to challenge imprisonment – even upon order of the Council – by *habeas corpus*, on the grounds that 'this is the most high court of the Queen (no matter what those of Chancery say)'.[136] Between the 1560s and 1590s, writs of *habeas corpus* were used to challenge imprisonments for contempt of Chancery[137] and Requests.[138] In 1587, serjeant Hele was even indicted for *praemunire* for seeking a Chancery injunction after judgment at common law.[139] The final decade of the century saw further attacks on the conciliar and other lesser equity courts, at times even challenging their very authority to decide cases according to equity.[140] In the face of rising

[128] ibid 46 (and see also 121).

[129] ibid 123 and 126.

[130] ibid 47–8, 122–7.

[131] *Cf* [Anonymous,] *On Equity* (dating from the late sixteenth century), Cambridge University Library MS Gg 2.31, f 12: 'There is nothing more usual than the name of equity and scarce any thing more obscure'.

[132] For the adoption of the language of the equity in Chancery records, see Neil Jones' chapter in this volume (ch 9).

[133] See, eg, Hake (n 115) 122.

[134] Baker (2003) (n 6) 179.

[135] Baker (2017) (n 52) 158–60 and 162.

[136] R Crompton, *L'authoritie et Jurisdiction des Courts* (London, Yetsweirt, 1594) 78v (trans). See also GW Sanders, *Orders of the High Court of Chancery, vol I* (London, Maxwell & Son, 1845) 20–4 (Bacon LK summoned Catlyn CJ to explain why the Queen's Bench had refused a *supersedeas* to discharge a Chancery litigant from arrest on a *latitat*).

[137] See *Glanville's case* (1614) Moore KB 836, 839, listing early Elizabethan precedents. See also C Monro, *Acta Cancellariae* (London, Benning & Co, 1847) 5–9.

[138] *Humfrey and Humfrey's case* (1577) 3 Leon 18 (it was observed by Bendloes sjt that the same remedy would lie on imprisonment for contempt of Chancery).

[139] *Heal's case* (1587) 2 Leon 115. Heal sjt had acted for the plaintiff in *More v Taylor* (1587) (reproduced from the records in Monro (n 137) 5–8).

[140] Baker (2017) (n 52) 206–14, 265–6, 277–84, 302–11, 376–90 and 398–406.

opposition from the common lawyers, defenders of equity were now required to look beyond *epieikeia* as a justification for the jurisdiction, to ideas which would renew and place beyond reproach equity's claims to legitimacy in the legal system.

IV. Prerogative Equity

The prerogative theory of equity arguably had its roots in medieval legal theory – perhaps most clearly visible in the writings of Stillington and Fortescue, c. 1470. Whilst Cardinal Wolsey had drawn a direct link between Chancery and the royal prerogative in 1529, the association appears to have gained strength from the 1570s onwards. In 1572, the House of Lords heard arguments in *Lord Cromwell's Case* on whether a peer could be arrested for contempt of a Chancery decree.[141] The jurisdiction against such 'overmighty' defendants had, of course, been a mainstay of the medieval Chancery, and the dispute seems to have encouraged a review of the origins of Chancery's authority.[142] In his remarks to Parliament, Sir Nicholas Bacon LK explicitly linked the court's extraordinary jurisdiction to the prerogative power of the prince 'to order causes otherwise than the law is',[143] explaining that 'the Chancery is warranted to hear and order causes by virtue of the Queen's Majesty's prerogative where otherwise by law the subject hath no help, and also to qualify the extremity of the law'.[144] For the Lord Keeper, contempt of a Chancery decree was equivalent to a contempt against the Queen's prerogative itself, and a peer's historical freedom from arrest in civil suits ought not to apply. Although ultimately unsuccessful in shaking the peers' immunity from arrest, Bacon LK's speech may have demonstrated the potential of appeals to the prerogative in defence of the equity jurisdiction. Implicit in Bacon's prerogatival theory of equity was the notion that equity was 'otherwise than what the law is'. The prospect of a justification for the jurisdiction which lay *outside* the common law was a tantalising prospect in an era of mounting dissatisfaction with equity's role within the legal system as a whole.

The prerogative theory of equity received its most elaborate airing in the writings of Robert Snagge, deriving from his reading in the Inner Temple on chapter 29 of *Magna Carta* in 1581. Aspects of the reading were written up in 1587 and presented to the Lord Chancellor, Sir Christopher Hatton.[145] As the first Chancellor to describe himself as the 'keeper of the king's conscience', Hatton's chancellorship (1587–91) was notable for the rising popularity of prerogative-based theories of equity.[146] The published version of Snagge's reading addressed a question of fundamental constitutional importance to the equity jurisdiction: whether the English side of the Chancery satisfied the *lex terrae*

[141] For detail, see MAR Graves, 'Freedom of Peers from Arrest: The Case of Henry Second Lord Cromwell, 1571-1572' (1977) 21 *American Journal of Legal History* 1; Williams (n 20) 39–40.

[142] The 'absolute' authority of Chancery over the nobility was discussed in these medieval terms by Snagge (n 115) 39 and 80–4.

[143] TE Hartley (ed), *Proceedings in the Parliaments of Elizabeth I, vol I: 1558-1581* (Leicester, Leicester University Press, 1981) 265.

[144] ibid 266.

[145] Subsequently published as *The Antiquity & Original of the Court of Chancery and Authority of the Lord Chancellor of England* (London, Seile, 1654). For details on the reading, see Baker (2017) (n 52) 251.

[146] Williams (n 20) 51.

requirement in chapter 29 of *Magna Carta*. Chapter 29 and the subsequent due process statutes provided that any interference with life, liberty or property must proceed *per legem terrae*. Yet, as Snagge observed:

> looking into the course of Practice, I found the Lord Chancellor sitting highest in Westminster Hall ... gave his judgment (as it seem'd to me) as it pleased himself, whatsoever the Law of the Land required in the case ... I was in a maze, not finding at first how it could stand with the *Great Charter*, that referred all judgment *ad legem terrae*.[147]

According to Snagge, the proceedings of the Chancery appeared to be:

> besides the Law, erected out of the absolute Authority that the Conquerors claimed; and that it hath been from time to time against the Law and the Provision of that *Charter* and Parliament, as it were a Prerogative above the Law.[148]

This conception of the Chancery grounded in the authority of the prerogative – 'beside', 'against' and 'above' the law – was a far cry from St German's conception of equity as a 'secret exception' contained *within* the law.[149] Snagge's account of equity owed much to the medieval conceptions of Chancery as an extraordinary jurisdiction, founded on the absolute power of the monarch, and distinct from the ordinary course of the common law. Drawing explicitly on Stillington C's remarks in 1469,[150] Snagge emphasised that Chancery was 'not tied to any Form of Trial'.[151] Rather, the Chancellor took evidence to 'inform his Conscience' and examined parties upon oath 'as it seemeth good to him in his private judgment'; he decreed cases according to equity and conscience 'howsoever the law is in the case' and imprisoned parties on grounds of 'unconscionable' conduct.[152] This divergence of Chancery process from the ordinary process of the common law courts thus appeared at odds with chapter 29 of *Magna Carta*. That the equity jurisdiction might not stand with the *lex terrae* requirement had been controverted in various readings since around 1500.[153] For his part, Snagge asserted that Chancery process – though distinct from that of the common law courts – was itself part of the *lex terrae* and did not fall foul of chapter 29.[154]

In the course of his reading, Snagge set out his broader view of the function and authority of the Chancery's equity jurisdiction. For Snagge, equity was the 'perfection' of the common law, where the law failed to give 'competent remedy'.[155] He defended the jurisdictional split between law and equity in Aristotelian terms but connected the Chancellor's jurisdiction to the authority of the Prince:

> For that the Common Law, Custom of the realm, or Law of the Land (term it as they list) standing of General grounds, Rules and Maxims, it was impossible but some particular Cases must fall out, that either the General Rule whereon it lighteth should be too hard for it, or too

[147] Snagge (n 115) 19–20.
[148] ibid 31.
[149] Indeed, Hake had expressly rejected the 'civilian' notion that equity was 'not drawn out of the law, but derived from ... the conscience of the Prince': Hake (n 115) 121.
[150] YB Trin 9 Edw IV 14, pl 9, discussed by Snagge (n 115) 59–64.
[151] Snagge (n 115) 31.
[152] ibid 32–3.
[153] Baker (2017) (n 52) 102–3 and 454–5.
[154] Snagge (n 115) 21 and 34–5.
[155] ibid 36.

> short to reach it; And therefore was it of necessity (to the end that all Cases might be judged according to Right and Equity) to have one under the Prince, above the rest, to have such an authority *secundum aequum, & bonum, & sanam conscientiam*, in these cases, and to mitigate where the Rule of Law would light too hard, and to supply where it came too short.[156]

Snagge explained that the common law stood on 'general grounds ... without respect of persons or other circumstances' and that the certainty of these general rules was required to avoid the 'confusion' and 'infinite inconvenience' of judicial discretion in common cases.[157] By contrast, the Chancery operated to protect those who were 'too simple, and [who] would trust untrusty persons'.[158] In such cases, the legal system was required to 'constitute one Supreme Judge further trusted than the rest, that might have an Authority absolute and extraordinary, to supply and reform those particular cases ... according to Equity and good conscience, and to bind the parties not to follow Law'.[159] Snagge's view of equity was instructive. Equity was to be administered by a separate tribunal in order to preserve the certainty of the general rules of the common law. In cases where the law proved deficient, equity could 'perfect' the law by going 'beyond' it in pursuit of ultimate justice, and its authority to do so was grounded in the power of the Prince.

Contending that equity lay outside the common law, Snagge nevertheless recognised the need to articulate certain boundaries for the jurisdiction and to counter the charge of arbitrariness in adjudication. Although the Chancellor's absolute and extraordinary authority was 'beside law', Snagge explained that the Chancellor's jurisdiction was 'allowed by the law ... and therefore he may not cancel or deface it ... but only bindeth the person not to follow the law in any unconscionable course'.[160] The Chancellor's office was thus constituted by and bound to respect the law. Moreover, Snagge was careful to explain that the conscience of the Chancellor was not purely subjective – rather, it was regulated and guided by previous practice:

> Conscience whereby his Lordship is to judge, is not to be understood *simpliciter*, and to be *simplex Conscientia*, but *Regulata Conscientia*, and therein to follow Order and Course accustomed; *viz.* to take order in such Cases as by the Course of the Court hath before-time, and in causes of like Equity ... wherefore oftentimes Presidents are sought for and required, and for lack of Presidents, it hath been sought how cases in the like reason ... have been used.[161]

In the subsequent discussion, Snagge outlined the meaning of this *regulata conscientia*. We are told that Chancery will not intervene without some unconscionable conduct on the part of the defendant,[162] that Chancery will never meddle with collateral warranties or common recoveries,[163] nor intervene against a statute (except in cases of fraud).[164] In spite of the attempt, Snagge struggled to set any clearer limits on the jurisdiction. He

[156] ibid 21–2.
[157] ibid 37–8.
[158] ibid 38.
[159] ibid 40.
[160] ibid 45–6.
[161] ibid 65–6.
[162] ibid 66–7.
[163] ibid 69–71.
[164] ibid 71–2.

ultimately concluded that 'in all that discourse none could find how far his Lordship's Absolute power went, nor within what limits certain it could be contained, nor by what means he might find out the truth'. Rather, Snagge asserted that, like the will of God, the authority of the Chancellor was 'infinite, and not limited in certainty'.[165] As such, Snagge thought there could be no appeal or review of a Chancery decree by the common law courts: 'if [the Chancellor] err in his judgment, which is given according to his Conscience, there is no Appeal to any but to God to reform it'.[166] Snagge's absolute conception of equity was, therefore, difficult to square with his assertion that Chancery proceeded by a form of 'regulated' conscience. Nevertheless, his notion that Chancery practices might be regularised – particularly by reliance on precedent – would gain greater traction in the following decades.

The prerogative theory of equity was also adopted by the influential jurist and legal antiquary, William Lambarde.[167] In the *Archeion* (written c. 1590, published 1635),[168] Lambarde regarded the Chancellor as the 'mouth … of the prince'.[169] According to Lambarde's version of history, the medieval kings had conferred on the Chancellor their 'own regal, absolute, and extraordinary pre-eminence of jurisdiction in civil causes, as well as for amendment as for supply of the common law'.[170] The Chancellor's authority was, therefore, 'extraordinary, and absolute even as the king's own'.[171] In turn, this royal imprimatur grounded the Chancery's authority to correct general rules in specific cases according to the principle of *epieikeia*.[172] Notwithstanding equity's pre-eminence, however, *both* law and equity were regarded as necessary to achieve justice in the legal system; the 'rigour of the law' and the 'pleasure of the Chancellor' were required to be 'well compounded together' so that 'a most sweet and harmonical justice will follow of them'.[173] For Lambarde, the juxtaposition and admixture of law to equity was productive of justice; the two were complementary, provided they were held in a proportionate harmony.

Like Snagge, Lambarde was aware of the need to place limits on the equity jurisdiction and warned that 'equity should not be appealed unto but only in rare and extraordinary matters, lest … the judge in equity should take jurisdiction over all'.[174] To prevent this calamity, Lambarde suggested that the Chancellor might 'publish to others

[165] ibid 74–6.
[166] ibid 86.
[167] On Lambarde, see WJ Jones, *The Elizabethan Court of Chancery* (London, Clarendon Press, 1967) 111–2.
[168] Lambarde had been writing in this vein from at least 1577. For detail on the development of Lambarde's thought, see Williams (n 20) 42–8.
[169] CH McIlwain and PL Ward (eds), W Lambarde, *Archeion or, a Discourse upon the High Courts of Justice in England* (Cambridge, MA, Harvard University Press, 1957) 39. Lambarde also referred to the Chancellor as the 'prolocutor or mouth' of Parliament (at 32); Lambarde's language is reminiscent of T Smith, *De Republica Anglorum* (written mid-1560s, published 1584) which described the Chancellor as the 'voice and orator of the prince' in Parliament (L Alston (ed), Sir T Smith, *De Republica Anglorum* (Cambridge, Cambridge University Press, 1906) 51). The same language also appeared in Edward Hake's treatise written around the same period: Hake (n 115) 138 and 140.
[170] ibid 39.
[171] ibid 41.
[172] ibid 42–3.
[173] ibid 44. This language appears to have been borrowed from the sixteenth century French jurist, Jean Bodin. On which, see Williams (n 20) 45.
[174] Lambarde (n 169) 44.

any certain *Rules & Limits of Equity*' – though he stopped short of advocating this innovation outright.[175] Lambarde seemed to recognise the difficulty of his proposed reform, having earlier observed that the equity side of the Chancery had 'no records; as well because extraordinary cases may not be limited to any times certain, as for that his judgments be in his own breast, not tied to any preceding records'.[176] For Lambarde, the extraordinary and absolute nature of the jurisdiction seemed to militate against an equity jurisprudence predicated on precedent.

By the 1590s, however, such a dim view of precedent in equity was falling increasingly out of step with Chancery practice. The mid-sixteenth century had seen major institutional reforms of the equity jurisdiction, not least of which was the advent of formal record-keeping in Chancery.[177] Whilst it might still be contended that Chancery was not a 'court of record' (in the sense that its determinations were not *res judicata* in courts of common law), the records kept by Chancery provided a guide to previous practice and permitted greater regularisation of its remedial practices.[178] Although far from a doctrine of precedent, the 'course' or common practice of the court provided an anchor for future development. Indeed, Lambarde himself – as a Master in Chancery from 1592 – became Sir Thomas Egerton's 'most enthusiastic and expert adviser pertaining to records' and has been credited with aiding Egerton's attempts to reform the Chancery in the mid-to-late 1590s.[179] By the end of the century, Chancery proceedings were becoming increasingly regularised,[180] eventually acting as a bulwark against allegations of arbitrariness in Chancery determinations – as the earlier jurisprudential work of Snagge and Lambarde had suggested. Armed with a potent theory of equity grounded in the prerogative and an increasingly regularised judicial practice based on precedent, the equity jurisdiction was ready to respond to the challenge posed by the common lawyers.

V. Chancery Equity and the Common Law

Perhaps the most significant development in the history of English equity lay in its confrontation with the common law itself. By the end of the sixteenth century, it was generally accepted that equity was part of the *lex terrae*, that its decisions were not merely the personal whim of the Chancellor, and that its jurisdiction had appreciable (if not precisely measurable) bounds. The extent to which equity threatened the autonomy of the common law, however, remained highly controversial. Whilst St German, Snagge and Lambarde saw equity as the perfection of the common law, there was a persistent concern that Chancery interference with the law was illegitimate and that its jurisdiction to intervene after judgment at common law would produce a system of 'endless

[175] ibid 46–7.

[176] ibid 40.

[177] Jones (n 167) 13, 143–5, 291–9, and especially 488–9; Baker (2003) (n 6) 186–7.

[178] On the rise of reporting in Chancery in this period, see MRT Macnair, 'The Nature and Function of the Early Chancery Reports' in C Stebbings (ed), *Law Reporting in Britain* (London, Hambledon Press, 1995) 123–32 (esp 125–6 and 128–30).

[179] Jones (n 167) 62.

[180] For regularisation of Chancery practice c. 1600, see David Waddilove's chapter in this volume (ch 7).

appeals', lacking finality of judgment. Much of the sixteenth-century debate centred on the statute of 4 Hen IV, c 23, which purported to prohibit review of common law judgments other than by writ of error or attaint. In *Doctor and Student*, the student had admitted that 'if judgments given in the King's courts should be examined in Chancery ... the law should never have end'.[181] However, the student continued:

> it appears from the said statute [4 Hen IV, c 23] that it does not prohibit equity, but it prohibits only the examination of the judgment, for the eschewing of the inconvenience before rehearsed. And so it seems that the said statute stands with good conscience.[182]

For the equity lawyer, therefore, the systems of law and equity – to use SFC Milsom's phrase – 'moved on two separate planes and could not collide'.[183] Decrees in Chancery did not review the common law judgment itself; they were merely directions to the parties to act in accordance with equity and good conscience. Although the anonymous serjeant in 1531 had warned that the two systems 'cannot stand together, but one of them must stand as void', the very question of legal validity only made sense in the context of the court in which it was raised. It was clear that the Chancellor could not decree common law rights void *simpliciter*; notwithstanding an adverse Chancery decree, an action at law could still be brought, and the Chancellor's decree could not be pleaded in bar.[184] In this sense, both courts were 'right by their own lights', and the question of validity was misconceived.[185] This learning was key to the conceptualisation of the Chancery's jurisdiction *in personam*, itself designed to demonstrate equity's limits.

These arguments never seemed to satisfy the common lawyers, and the point was agitated again at the end of the century in *Finch v Throckmorton* (1597).[186] In that case, Throckmorton sued Finch in Chancery, seeking relief against a common law judgment.[187] Finch demurred, but Egerton LK ordered Finch to answer, declaring that 'he would not meddle with the judgment, but punish the corrupt conscience of the defendant, in relieving the plaintiff in equity'.[188] Following Finch's petition to the Queen, the case was referred to the Exchequer Chamber where counsel for Throckmorton argued that 'the intention of the Lord Chancellor was not to impeach the said judgments, but ... to be relieved upon matter of equity'.[189] This equity lawyer's shibboleth notwithstanding, the judges of the Exchequer Chamber held unanimously that the Chancery could not interfere after judgment 'for though the Lord Chancellor ... would not examine the judgment, yet he would by his decree take away the effect of the judgment'.[190] Rather than serving to resolve the law-equity conflict, *Finch v Throckmorton* seemed merely to embed hostilities on either side. Egerton seems not to have abided by the decision, and

[181] St German (n 43) 107.
[182] ibid 109. See also the discussion in St German (n 46) 115–7.
[183] Milsom (n 22) 93.
[184] Baker (2017) (n 52) 103 (citing a reading in Gray's Inn, c. 1529).
[185] JH Baker, 'Why the History of English Law Has Not Been Finished' (2000) 59 *Cambridge Law Journal* 62, 68–9 (discussing the clash between Common Pleas and Requests in the late 1590s).
[186] 3 Co Inst 124, 4 Co Inst 86, Bulst 118, Cro Jac 344, 139 *Selden Society* 797–803.
[187] For detail on the case, see Sir John Baker's chapter in this volume (ch 6).
[188] 3 Co Inst 124.
[189] 4 Co Inst 86.
[190] ibid.

relations between the courts worsened considerably. The stage was set for the clash of jurisdictions in 1616.

The bitter rivalry between Sir Edward Coke and Sir Thomas Egerton (later Lord Ellesmere) leading up to the *Earl of Oxford's case* (1615–16) has been discussed in detail elsewhere.[191] For our purposes, however, the conflict sheds light on competing conceptions of Chancery equity in the early seventeenth century. Coke, for example, never denied a role for equity in the English legal system and accepted equity as part of the *lex terrae*, but argued forcefully that its ambit was to be strictly controlled by the common law and its judges.[192] In the fourth volume of his *Institutes*, Coke described the English side of the Chancery as an 'extraordinary' – rather than an 'absolute' – jurisdiction[193] and emphasised the medieval position which restrained the *subpoena* to cases of 'necessity', excluding matters properly determinable at common law.[194] For Coke, the equity jurisdiction was to be limited to the 'ancient rule' that 'three things are to be judged in court of conscience: covin, accident, and breach of confidence'.[195] Within these extraordinary and necessitous cases, Chancery's jurisdiction was further limited by the fact that it was not a court of record:

> This court of equity proceeding by English bill is no court of record, and therefore it can bind the person only, and neither the [e]state of the defendant's lands, nor property of his goods or chattels.[196]

As well as placing substantive limitations on the equity jurisdiction, Coke also emphasised the significance of the record when rejecting equity's jurisdiction to interfere with common law judgments. In his notebook entry for *Finch v Throckmorton*, Coke wrote that 'it is absurd that a court which (as to equity) is not a court of record should control judgments which are of record'.[197] Common law judgments, he later said, were

[191] JP Dawson, 'Coke and Ellesmere Disinterred: The Attack on Chancery in 1616' (1941) 36 *Illinois Law Review* 127; JH Baker, 'The Common Lawyers and the Chancery: 1616' (1968) 4 *Irish Jurist* 368; L Knafla, *Law and Politics in Jacobean England* (Cambridge, Cambridge University Press, 1977) 155–81; M Fortier, 'Equity and Ideas: Coke, Ellesmere and James I' (1998) 51 *Renaissance Quarterly* 1255; DC Smith, *Sir Edward Coke and the Reformation of the Laws* (Cambridge, Cambridge University Press, 2014) 176–212; DJ Ibbetson, '*The Earl of Oxford's case* (1615)' in C Mitchell and P Mitchell (eds), *Landmark Cases in Equity* (Oxford, Hart Publishing, 2012) 1–32; Baker (2017) (n 52) 410–22.

[192] Baker (2017) (n 52) 410–15 and 501–2.

[193] 4 Co Inst 79 and 82.

[194] ibid 83–4.

[195] ibid 84. Coke would repeat this mantra in remarks to the House of Commons in March 1621: W Notestein, *Commons Debates, vol V* (London, Oxford University Press, 1935) 297. Equity lawyers too made use of this classification; see *Earl of Oxford's Case* (1615) 1 Ch Rep 1, 7 (Ellesmere LC) and LM Hill (ed), Sir J Caesar, *The Ancient State, Authoritie and Proceedings of the Court of Requests* (Cambridge, Cambridge University Press, 1975) 9: 'causes triable by the common law are not to be determined in this Court [Requests], unless there be some matter of equity in them … *videt*, to remedy frauds, breach of trust, extremity of common law, or undue practices'.

[196] ibid 84. See also *Themilthorp's case* (1605) in JH Baker, *Sources of English Legal History: Public Law to 1750* (Oxford, Oxford University Press, 2024) 259 and SE Thorne, 'Courts of Record and Sir Edward Coke' (1937) 2 *Toronto Law Journal* 24, 47–9. This logic could conceivably be extended to deny equitable jurisdiction over *any* case touching freehold land, although this argument was never accepted by the equity courts *in toto*; see *Sir Moyle Finch's Case* (1600) 4 Co Inst 85, *AG v Abington* (1613) 118 *Selden Society* 408, 413 (Davenport *in arguendo*), and discussion in D Foster, 'Fraud, Trusts and Trusting: Enforcing Crown Forfeitures in Equity, c 1570-1620' (2023) 44 *Journal of Legal History* 256, 289–291.

[197] 139 *Selden Society* 797, 799 (citing *Reynolde v Knott* (1459) YB Hil 37 Hen VI 13, pl 3, discussed above).

'so sacred that there ought to be no meddling with them save only by error or attaint, as appears by the statute of 4 Hen IV [c 23]'.[198] Conjoined with Coke's concern for the sanctity of the record was a reciprocal issue: decrees in equity – not being matters of record – could not be reviewed by writs of error and so could not be appealed *at all*. In 1614, when Chief Justice, Coke complained that 'it was unreasonable for men's inheritances to be thus decided in the courts of equity, the sentence whereof is like the law of the Medes and Persians, which is inviolable and wherefrom no appeal lies'.[199] In *Vaudry v Pannel* (1615–16),[200] Coke went even further, remarking that the only form of appeal from the Chancellor was by petition to the King himself. According to Coke, the King in such cases would follow the procedure used in *Finch v Throckmorton* and refer the issue to the common law judges for final determination.[201] For Coke, therefore, it was the common law judges – not the Chancellor – who should have final say on points of equity.[202]

By contrast, Ellesmere rejected entirely the notion that a common law judgment could foreclose the equitable jurisdiction. Ellesmere had imbibed the writings of St German and Lambarde and it was upon the twin bases of *epieikeia* and the prerogative that Ellesmere defended the Chancery in the *Earl of Oxford's case* (1615).[203] Discussing the statute 4 Hen IV, c 23 in his breviate to King's counsel in 1615, Ellesmere wrote that:

> it cannot reasonably be conceived that the parliament meant to bind the Chancery (which is not named) or the King and his counsel and the parliament itself (which are expressly named) that they should not relieve parties which are grieved by the rigor of the Common Law against equity and Conscience in Cases wherein the Judges of the common law cannot relieve them, by attaint or error or otherwise. For *sententia Iudiciis non praeiudicat veritati*: And *Iudicatura naturalem obligationem non tollit*: *Ita conspurcatam laesam que conscientiam non purgat* [a judgement does not prejudice the truth; and judicial authority does not remove natural obligation; it does not cleanse a defiled and wounded conscience]. And some do truly and aptly define equity thus: *Equitas est publici Iuris moderatio a pectore regis velut ab oraculo pretenda* [equity is the moderation of public law, to be sought from the heart of the king as if from an oracle].[204]

For Ellesmere, equity channelled the will of the monarch to pursue truth and justice wherever the common law failed, and the legislature would not have intended to oust

[198] *Cottes and Suckerman v Warner* (1615) BL Hargrave MS 386, ff 80v–81 (see Baker (2017) (n 52) 388).
[199] *Downing v Hadlocke* (1614) BL Hargrave MS 385, f 225 (see Baker (2017) (n 52) 376).
[200] 3 Bulst 116.
[201] ibid 118. Notably, Coke also rejected the right of the monarch to determine such cases personally on the grounds that there could no appeal from the King; the only appropriate forum was the King's Bench. See Baker (2017) (n 52) 367 and 386–9; Smith (n 191) 263–69.
[202] Baker (2017) (n 52) 288–9.
[203] 1 Ch Rep 1, 6–7. See also DR Klinck, *Conscience, Equity and the Court of Chancery in Early Modern England* (Farnham, Ashgate, 2010) 157–65; M Fortier, *The Culture of Equity in Early Modern England* (Abingdon, Ashgate, 2005) 5–8.
[204] Lord Ellesmere, 'Breviate' in L Knafla, *Law and Politics in Jacobean England* (Cambridge, Cambridge University Press, 1977) 324–5. The breviate was published as *The Priviledges and Prerogatives of the High Court of Chancery* (London, Sheapheard, 1641). Similar ideas were canvassed in [Lord Ellesmere], *Certaine Observations Concerning the Office of the Lord Chancellor* (London, Walbanck et al, 1651) esp 41–2 and 46–50. For doubt as to the attribution to Ellesmere, see WS Holdsworth, *A History of English Law, vol V*, 3rd edn (London, Metheun, 1924) 272, fn 6.

this jurisdiction without express words to that effect.[205] Although the rigour of the law could clearly produce injustice, Ellesmere was nevertheless careful to emphasise that the separate jurisdictions of law and equity were bent toward the same arc:

> Law and Equity are distinct, both in their Courts, their Judges, and the Rules of Justice; and yet they both aim at one and the same End, which is, to do Right; as Justice and Mercy differ in their Effects and Operations, yet both join in the Manifestation of God's Glory.[206]

Echoing Lambarde, Ellesmere seemed to regard law and equity as held in productive opposition. Each characterised by their distinctive rules and procedures, their interaction was required to achieve perfect justice. For a common law judgment to oust the equitable jurisdiction, therefore, was for the legal system to sanction injustice.

Intermixed with this high theory were assertions that Chancery equity formed part of the *lex terrae* for the purposes of the due process statutes[207] and extensive references to Chancery practice grounded in the yearbook authorities.[208] Like Snagge and Lambarde, Ellesmere's dual focus on theory and practice was designed to justify the jurisdiction, whilst also demonstrating its boundaries. In the pseudo-Ellesmere tract *Certaine Observations*, the conscience of the Chancery was described as a '*lex conscientiae politicae*' which was ordered by the law, rather than a '*lex conscientiae Divinae*' which lay at the judgement of God alone and could not be compassed by the Chancellor.[209] The ordering of Chancery conscience according to law was reminiscent of St German and Snagge, but the discussion in *Certaine Observations* took the project further, with the entire second half devoted to laying out Chancery precedents relating to land disputes, uses and trusts, copyholds, leases, chattels, and aliens.[210] The conscience of Ellesmere's Chancery was no mere *arbitrement* therefore, but was grounded upon the law and regulated by precedents.

The Coke-Ellesmere debate eventually came to a head in 1616. The matter was ultimately resolved not by the judges, but by the King himself.[211] Following Coke's failed attempt to have senior Chancery officials indicted for *praemunire*, Ellesmere and Francis Bacon AG complained to James I, requesting his intervention in the matter. Persuaded that the equity jurisdiction was an extension of his own prerogative power, James I gave a speech in the Star Chamber in defence of his Chancery:

> [Chancery] is called the dispenser of the king's conscience, following always the intention of law and justice: not altering the law, not making that black which other courts made white, nor *e converso*. But in this it exceeds other courts, mixing mercy with justice, where other courts proceed only according to the strict rules of law. And where the rigour of the law in many cases will undo a subject, there the Chancery tempers the law with equity, and so mixeth mercy with justice, as it preserves men from destruction. And thus … is the king's throne established by

[205] See also [Lord Ellesmere], *Certaine Observations* (n 204) 41, describing the equity jurisdiction of the Chancery as 'being absolute without comptrollment, other than in Parliament'.

[206] 1 Ch Rep 1, 7.

[207] Lord Ellesmere, 'Breviate' (n 204) 319–20 and 322–3.

[208] [Lord Ellesmere], *Certaine Observations* (n 204) 46–50.

[209] ibid 48.

[210] ibid 79–113. See also Smith (n 191) 217.

[211] See Williams (n 20) 56–9. On James I's judicial work generally, see IS Williams, 'James VI and I, *rex et iudex*: One King as Judge in Two Kingdoms' in W Eves et al (eds), *Common Law, Civil Law, and Colonial Law: Essays in Comparative Legal History from the 12th to the 20th Centuries* (Cambridge, Cambridge University Press, 2021) 86–119.

> mercy and justice. The Chancery is independent of any other court, and is only under the king … From that court there is no appeal. And as I am bound in my conscience to maintain every court's jurisdiction, so especially this, and not suffer it to sustain wrong, yet so to maintain it as to keep it within its own limits and free from corruption. My chancellor that now is … I never gave him other warrant than to go on in his court according to precedents warranted by law in the time of the best governing kings and most learned chancellors. These were the limits I gave unto him; beyond the same limits he hath promised me he will never go.[212]

With this grand exercise of monarchical power, James affirmed the vital link between King and Chancery, confirming the absolute authority of equity's jurisdiction to mitigate the rigour of the law (albeit according to the precedents and never to the 'alteration' of the law itself). In James' speech, the medieval foundations of conscience, the early modern theory of *epieikeia* and the royal prerogative were each given voice in an effort to articulate the English notion of equity.

James I's theory of judicature marked a triumph for early modern equity but sowed the seeds of its ultimate destruction. The theory was put to the test sooner than the King might have imagined. By 1620, Chancery had developed a controversial jurisdiction to aid insolvent debtors by compelling creditors to accept a *pro rata* distribution of assets.[213] For some, this jurisdiction was tantamount to court-sanctioned robbery,[214] whilst others saw it as evidence of a dangerous 'swelling' of the Chancery's jurisdiction beyond its 'ancient course'.[215] Following an economic downturn and pressure from the King, the Lord Chancellor (Francis Bacon) reformed the jurisdiction by issuing new orders in Chancery and restraining its exercise.[216] The publication of new orders was insufficient to quell concerns in Parliament, where Sir Edward Coke declared the jurisdiction 'a detestable new project'[217] and Sir Thomas Roe demanded a resolution to 'pare the nails of the Chancery that scratcheth and taketh hold of every thing'.[218] Once again, James I was required to intercede – this time by a proclamation suppressing the Chancery's much-maligned insolvency jurisdiction. The proclamation was followed by Francis Bacon's removal from office for corruption in 1621[219] and statutory reform of the jurisdiction in 1624.[220] The incident

[212] Baker (2024) (n 196) 255–6.

[213] The jurisdiction had been developing since the 1540s; on which, see Fleur Stolker's chapter in this volume (ch 10). See also FC Stolker, 'The Forgotten History of Bankruptcy, 1543-1624' (2023) 44 *Journal of Legal History* 295; DA Smith, 'The Error of the Young Cyrus: The Bill of Conformity and Jacobean Kingship, 1603-1624' (2010) 28 *Law and History Review* 307.

[214] Notestein (n 195) 237 (Lionel Cranfield, Master of the Court of Wards).

[215] ibid 237 (Dudley Digs).

[216] Sanders (n 136) 129–30.

[217] Notestein (n 195) 297.

[218] ibid 298.

[219] For discussion of Bacon's poor reputation as a judge, see Macnair (1995) (n 178) 125–6; TG Barnes, 'Mr Hudson's Star Chamber' in DJ Guth and JW McKenna (eds), *Tudor Rules and Revolution: Essays for GR Elton* (Cambridge, Cambridge University Press, 1982) 285, 298–304. It is notable, however, that Bacon's aphorisms on the role of a judge and the importance of precedent were widely cited in subsequent juristic literature on equity – perhaps suggesting a more significant role in equity's history than has commonly been thought. For subsequent citation of Bacon's work, see, eg: John Lisle's *Abridgments of Chancery Causes* (c. 1659) Kansas University, MS D87, ff 163–164v and f 319; R Atkyns, *Enquiry into the Jurisdiction of the Chancery in Causes of Equity* (London, [s.n.], 1695) 5, 21, and 33–4; MJW Lobban (ed), Lord Kames, *Principles of Equity*, 3rd edn (Indianapolis, Liberty Fund, 2014) 20–1, 25, 28, and 31. For Bacon's concern to dispense equity according to certain rules, see Klinck (n 203) 165–72.

[220] 21 Jac I, c 19.

demonstrated that the heat was not gone from the debate over equity's proper scope in the English legal system.

The prerogatival basis of the jurisdiction drew increasing ire in the decades prior to the Civil War, leading directly to the abolition of the conciliar equity courts and attempted abolition of Chancery in the 1640s and 1650s. Ultimately, the Chancery was reformed rather than abolished outright, but the scope of the jurisdiction remained controversial throughout the mid-century.[221] Indeed, the issue of injunctions after judgment was revived once more with the publication of the third and fourth volumes of Coke's *Institutes* in 1644. An anonymous tract criticised the 'boldness' of the publisher for printing 'some old notes ... long after the author's death' and laid out *in extenso* the arguments in Ellesmere's breviate of 1615.[222] By the late 1640s, however, the tides were shifting. In Chancery, the House of Lords and the Exchequer, arguments from the statute 4 Hen IV, c 23 were successful in challenging James I's 1616 decree.[223] By the end of the century, Robert Atkyns could argue that the proper mechanism for policing the Chancellor's 'absolute, arbitrary and *Dictatorian* power' was by appeal to the House of Lords (rather than the King).[224] These developments notwithstanding, the prerogatival theory of equity had a more long-lasting effect in encouraging jurists to delimit the jurisdiction more clearly. If the jurisdiction was absolute and infinite, the charge of arbitrariness could be countered by tying equitable jurisprudence to the precedents. Over the course of the seventeenth and subsequent centuries, the substantive principles on which the equity jurisdiction was conducted were mapped out in greater detail in relation to contracts,[225] mortgages and trusts.[226] Over time, equity began to mature into a body of more or less regularised doctrine, and, once again, its essential nature was altered.

VI. Toward Modern Equity

The mid-seventeenth century resounded with continued complaints against the unpredictability of the equity jurisdiction. John Selden's famous quip that equity varied with the length of the Chancellor's foot found voice in many quarters.[227] When

[221] Klinck (n 203) 222–5; Fortier (n 203) 159–79; AJ Busch, 'Bulstrode Whitelocke and Early Interregnum Chancery Reform' (1979) 11 *Albion* 317; SE Prall, 'Chancery Reform and the Puritan Revolution' (1962) 6 *American Journal of Legal History* 28. For the position after the Restoration, see MRT Macnair, 'Common Law and Statutory Imitations of Equitable Relief under the Later Stuarts' in CW Brooks and MJW Lobban (eds), *Communities and Courts in Britain, 1150-1900* (London, Hambledon Press, 1997) 115, esp 116–8.

[222] [Anonymous], *Arguments Proving from Antiquity the Dignity Power and Jurisdiction of the Court of Chancery* (published 1693, bound with *Reports of Cases Taken and Adjudged in the Court of Chancery in the Reign of Charles I, Charles II, and James II* (London, Walthoe, 1693)) 2 and 43.

[223] *Cordell and Langham v Lambrey* (1647) 9 House of Lords Journal 53 and 407; *Morel v Duglas* (1655) Hardres 23; *Harris v Colliton* (1658) Hardres 120 (adjourned without resolution). For discussion of these cases, see Atkyns (n 219) 44–6. *Cf* the Restoration position in *King v Standish* (1667–71) 1 Lev 241, 1 Mod 59, Raym 227, 2 Keb 661 and 787, 3 Keb 221, and *Cole v Forth* (1672) 1 Mod 94.

[224] Atkyns (n 219) 22 and 30 (italics original). Atykns even sought to revive Coke's argument that common law judges might issue writs of prohibition and indictments for *praemunire* to restrain the equity jurisdiction (see 20–1 and 48).

[225] See the chapters by Helen Saunders, Mike Macnair and Julius Grower in this volume (chs 12, 13 and 15).

[226] See the chapters by David Foster, Emily Ireland, Michael Lobban, Charles Mitchell, Joshua Getzler, and Andreas Televantos and Mitchell Cleaver (chs 11, 14, 16, 17, 19 and 20).

[227] J Selden, *Table Talk* (London, Smith, 1689) 18.

invited to become a Lord Commissioner in Chancery in 1648, for example, Bulstrode Whitelocke initially sought to avoid the appointment, complaining that whilst the 'judges of the common law have certain rules to guide them, a keeper of the seals hath nothing but his own conscience to direct him, and this is oftentimes deceitful'.[228] By the Restoration, however, the tone of the discussion was starting to change.[229] In *Fry v Porter* (1670),[230] whilst sitting as an assistant in Chancery, Vaughan CJ 'wondered' at the citation of precedents in equity '[f]or if there be equity in a case, that equity is an universal truth, and there can be no precedent in it.'[231] Bridgman LK reassured the Chief Justice that this was common practice in Chancery:

> Certainly precedents are very necessary and useful to us, for in them we may find the reasons of the equity to guide us; and besides, the authority of those who made them is much to be regarded. We shall suppose they did it upon great consideration, and weighing of the matter; and it would be very strange, and very ill, if we should disturb and set aside what has been the course for a long series of time and ages.[232]

The regularisation of equity by tying the Chancellor's discretion to previously decided cases has been a theme much remarked upon in the scholarship[233] and linked most closely to the work of 'equity's architect', Lord Nottingham.[234] In his *Prolegomena*, Nottingham stated that 'if equity be tied to no rule ... everything becomes arbitrary'[235] and that the Chancellor should 'order his conscience after the rules and grounds of the laws of this realm'.[236] In *Coke v Fountain* (1676), Nottingham declared that 'with such a conscience which is only *naturalis et interna* this Court hath nothing to do; the conscience by which I am to proceed is merely *civilis et politica*, and tied to certain measures'.[237] In these statements, we hear echoes of St German, Snagge and Ellesmere, and these ideas informed the equity which Nottingham dispensed. Articulating key principles, developing foundational doctrines and adopting a more formal approach to precedent, Nottingham oversaw the emergence of a regularised equity jurisprudence which, whilst retaining its inherent flexibility, was increasingly capable of being mapped along doctrinal lines. It may be no coincidence, therefore, that the decades following Nottingham's chancellorship saw the first attempts to treat substantive equity in systematic form – most notably, in the treatises of Jeffrey Gilbert,

[228] B Whitelock, *Memorials of the English Affairs* (London, Ponder, 1682) 373.
[229] On the institutional factors affecting the regularisation of equity, see Macnair (2014) (n 89) 94–104.
[230] 1 Mod 86 and 330; Rep Ch 26; 1 Ch Cas 138.
[231] 1 Mod 300, 307. *Cf* Vaughan CJ's remarks in *Dixon v Harrison* (1670) Vaugh 36, 37–8: 'Where the law is known, and clear, though it be unequitable and inconvenient, the Judges must determine as the law is, without regarding the unequitableness or inconveniency.'
[232] ibid.
[233] See generally, WHD Winder, 'Precedent in Equity' (1941) 57 *Law Quarterly Review* 245, 246–53.
[234] The significance of DEC Yale's path-breaking work on Nottingham is hard to overestimate: *Nottingham's Chancery Cases, vol I* (1954) 73 *Selden Society*, *Nottingham's Chancery Cases, vol II* (1961) 79 *Selden Society*, and *Lord Nottingham's Manual of Chancery Practice and Prolegomena of Chancery and Equity* (Cambridge, Cambridge University Press, 1965). See also Klinck (n 203) 225–61.
[235] Lord Nottingham, '*Prolegomena*' in DEC Yale (ed), *Lord Nottingham's Manual of Chancery Practice and Prolegomena of Chancery and Equity* (Cambridge, Cambridge University Press, 1965) c 3, s 27.
[236] ibid c 4, s 17.
[237] 73 *Selden Society* 362, 371. For doubt as to the sincerity of these claims, however, see MRT Macnair, '*Coke v Fountaine* (1676)' in C Mitchell and P Mitchell (eds), *Landmark Cases in Equity* (Oxford, Hart Publishing, 2012) 33–61, esp 51–4.

Richard Francis, and the anonymously published *Treatise of Equity* (1737), often attributed to Henry Ballow.[238]

The degree to which equity had been regularised by the early-to-mid eighteenth century is captured in the classic judgment of Sir Joseph Jekyll MR in *Cowper v Cowper* (1734):

> The law is clear, and courts of equity ought to follow it in their judgments concerning titles to equitable estates; otherwise great uncertainty and confusion would ensue and though proceedings in equity are said to be *secundum discretionem boni viri* [according to the discretion of a good man] … that discretion is a science, not to act arbitrarily according to men's wills and private affections: so the discretion which is exercised here, is to be governed by the rules of law and equity, which are not to oppose, but each, in its turn, to be subservient to the other; this discretion, in some cases, follows the law implicitly, in others, assists it, and advances the remedy; in others again, it relieves against the abuse, or allays the rigour of it; but in no case does it contradict or over-turn the grounds or principles thereof, as has been sometimes ignorantly imputed to this Court. That is a discretionary power, which neither this nor any other Court, not even the highest, acting in a judicial capacity, is by the constitution entrusted with.[239]

In these remarks, Jekyll was careful to disavow the arbitrary and unpredictable aspects of equity.[240] Rather, for Jekyll, law and equity were administered according to a model of mutual subservience – neither superior to the other and each necessary to achieve justice. The means by which equity displayed its subservience to the law was through the 'scientific' exercise of judicial discretion according to the 'rules' of law and equity.

This process of regularisation continued throughout the eighteenth century.[241] By the 1780s, John Mitford (later Lord Redesdale) could observe that decisions in equity 'are considered by those courts as rules to be observed with as much strictness as positive law'.[242] In a similar vein, John Fonblanque wrote that 'even in cases of fraud … courts of equity constantly proceed upon some clear and established principle … and not upon a vague, arbitrary and indefinite power'.[243] In this context, Lord Eldon's oft-quoted remarks in *Gee v Pritchard* (1818) are readily understood:

> it is my duty to submit my judgment to the authority of those who have gone before me … The doctrines of this Court ought to be as well settled and made as uniform *almost* as those

[238] MRT Macnair, 'The Conceptual Basis of Trusts in the 17th and 18th Centuries' in RH Helmholz and R Zimmermann (eds), *Itinera Fiducia* (Berlin, Duncker & Humblot, 1998) 207, 208–13.

[239] *Cowper v Cowper* (1734) 2 P Wms 720, 753–4. On Jekyll's approach to precedent in equity, see WHD Winder, 'Sir Joseph Jekyll, Master of the Rolls' (1941) 57 *Law Quarterly Review* 512, 529–34. See also the views of Jekyll's contemporary, Richard Francis, in *Maxims of Equity* (London, Nutt and Gosling, 1727) 1–5.

[240] For similar sentiments, see *Wagstaff v Wagstaff* (1724) 2 P Wms 258, 259 (Macclesfield LC); *Heard v Stamford* (1735) 3 P Wms 409, 412 (Talbot LC); *Earl of Chesterfield v Janssen* (1750) 1 Atk 301, 353 (Hardwicke LC); *Gwynne v Heaton* (1778) 1 Bro CC 1, 9 (Thurlow LC); *Bond v Hopkins* (1802) 1 Sch & Lef 413, 428–9 (Lord Redesdale). I am grateful to Benjamin Douglas for these references.

[241] D Lieberman, *The Province of Legislation Determined* (Cambridge, Cambridge University Press, 1989) 71–87; CE Croft, 'Lord Hardwicke's Use of Precedent in Equity' in TG Watkin (ed), *Legal Records and Historical Reality* (London, Hambledon Press, 1989) 121–55.

[242] J Mitford, *A Treatise on the Pleadings in Suits in the Court of Chancery by English Bill*, 2nd edn (Dublin, Lynch, 1787) 4, n (b).

[243] J Fonblanque (ed), [H Ballow], *Treatise of Equity, vol I* (Dublin, Byrne et al, 1793) bk I, c 1, s 3, n (k). For discussion of the flexibility of fraud in equity, see B Douglas, '*Earl of Chesterfield v Janssen*: Equitable Foundations' in J Gardner and I Ramsay (eds), *Landmark Cases in Consumer Law* (Oxford, Hart Publishing, 2024) 23–38.

> of the common law, laying down fixed principles, but taking care that they are to be applied according to the circumstances of each case. I cannot agree that the doctrines of this Court are to be changed with every succeeding judge. Nothing would inflict on me greater pain, in quitting this place, than the recollection that I had done anything to justify the reproach that the equity of this Court varies like the Chancellor's foot.[244]

By the time of Lord Eldon, therefore, there was ample evidence to suggest that equity doctrine had become 'almost' as fixed as the common law.[245] Eldon's Chancellorship was also notable for renouncing equitable discretion in certain cases,[246] and it is perhaps justified that this period has been characterised as one of '*rigor aequitatis*'.[247] No longer founded on a broad discretionary principle of *epieikeia* designed to mitigate the rigours of the common law, the equitable jurisdiction had become nearly as rule-bound as the law itself.

It is one of the ironies of English legal history that, as equity became increasingly law-like, so the common law was being reformed along more equitable lines.[248] The rigid procedures of the law, which had long distinguished the legal and equitable realms, were subject to some significant reforms in the later seventeenth and eighteenth centuries.[249] Concerned with the costs occasioned by transferring cases from law to equity and back, reforms of common law procedure were implemented to avoid resort to equity (including reforms of pleading, discovery, and examination of witnesses by deposition). In this period, certain matters of equity were also brought within the purview of the common law courts, including aspects of relief against penalties[250] and the recognition of the right of the *cestui que trust* to sue in assumpsit for breach of trust.[251] In the middle of the eighteenth century, this convergence of law and equity was given greater impetus through the judicial work of Lord Mansfield CJKB (1756–88) and in the juristic literature of Sir William Blackstone.[252] Lord Mansfield

[244] 2 Swans 402, 414 (emphasis added). See also *Davis v Duke of Marlborough* (1819) 2 Swans 108, 163.

[245] For discussion of Eldon's equity jurisprudence, see DR Klinck, 'Lord Eldon on "Equity"' (1999) 20 *Journal of Legal History* 51; FR Burns, 'The Court of Chancery in the 19th Century: A Paradox of Decline and Expansion' (2001) 21 *University of Queensland Law Journal* 198.

[246] See, eg: *Kemp v Kemp* (1801) 5 Ves Jr 849 (judicial execution of trust powers) and *Hill v Barclay* (1811) 18 Ves Jr 56 (relief against forfeiture for breach of leasehold covenants). Lord Wilberforce would overrule both decisions in favour of wider judicial discretion in equity: *McPhail v Doulton* [1971] AC 424; *Shiloh Spinners v Harding* [1973] AC 691.

[247] CK Allen, *Law in the Making*, 7th edn (Oxford, Oxford University Press, 1964) 417.

[248] On equity reasoning in the common law in this period, see Stephen Waddams' chapter in this volume (ch 18).

[249] For what follows, see Macnair (1997) (n 221) 118–31.

[250] The practice had emerged by Nottingham's time (see Nottingham (n 235) c 5, s 11) and was placed on statutory footing in 8 & 9 Will III, c 11, s 8 and 4 Anne, c 16, ss 12 and 13.

[251] *Dutton v Poole* (1678–80) 3 Keb 786, 814, 830, 836; 1 Vent 318, 332; 2 Lev 210; Rep t Jones 102; Raym 302; 1 Freem 471. For detail on the case, see NG Jones, 'Aspects of Privity in England: Equity to 1680' and DJ Ibbetson and W Swain, 'Third Party Beneficiaries in English Law: From *Dutton v Poole* to *Tweddle v Atkinson*', both in EJH Schrage (ed), *Ius Quaesitum Tertio* (Berlin, Duncker & Humblot, 2008) at 135–74 and 191–213 respectively.

[252] In this regard, both Mansfield and Blackstone owed something of an intellectual debt to the Scottish jurist, Lord Kames, whose *Principles of Equity* was first published in 1760. Kames' work was cited by Blackstone (n 6) 430. For discussion, see MJW Lobban 'Editor's Introduction' in MJW Lobban (ed), Lord Kames, *Principles of Equity*, 3rd edn (Indianapolis, Liberty Fund, 2014) xxiii–xxv, and Lieberman (n 241) 166–75. Kames' pugnacious approach to equity jurisprudence was well summed up by the earthy couplet composed by Boswell in his *The Court of Session Garland*: '[Lord] Alemoor the judgment as illegal blames, / 'tis equity, you bitch, replies my Lord Kames' (printed in J Maidment (ed), *The Court of Session Garland* (Edinburgh, privately printed, 1839) 48).

regularly emphasised the 'equitable' aspects of the common law and tended to view the distinction between law and equity as purely procedural, rather than substantive in nature.[253] In *Moses v Macferlan* (1760),[254] for example, he famously described the action for money had and received as a 'kind of equitable action' which lies 'only for money which, *ex aequo et bono*, the defendant ought to refund'.[255] Similarly, in *Burgess v Wheate* (1759),[256] he declared that the 'only difference' between trusts and legal estates was 'the forum where it is adjudged'.[257] In both regards, Mansfield was followed by Blackstone; indeed, it has been suggested that the passages on equity in Blackstone's *Commentaries* did 'little more than reproduce, in a connected and literary form, the views held by Lord Mansfield'.[258] Nevertheless, Blackstone's formulation of the law-equity distinction in the *Commentaries* repays closer study.

In the third volume of his *Commentaries*, Blackstone emphasised that equity was part of the common law. He described equity as 'the soul and spirit of all law'[259] and regarded any attempt to distinguish law from equity as 'either totally erroneous, or erroneous to a certain degree'.[260] In Blackstone's treatment, however, the *principle* of equity was to be distinguished from the *courts* of equity. For Blackstone, the claim that courts of equity operated to mitigate the rigour of the law was exaggerated; there were many instances of hardship at law which went unremedied in the Chancery.[261] Moreover, in cases of statutory interpretation, courts of law too might pursue the spirit (or equity) of the rule, rather than its letter.[262] Even cases of fraud, accident, and trust were – according to Blackstone – cognisable in courts of common law.[263] Finally, given that courts of equity were now bound by precedent,[264] he argued that the jurisprudence of courts of law and equity were to be regarded as 'founded in the same principles of justice and positive law'.[265] In his view, the jurisprudence of the courts of law and equity were distinguishable only by their 'forms and mode of their proceedings';[266] namely, their modes of proof, modes of trial, and modes of relief.[267] Admittedly, Blackstone was careful not to

[253] W Swain, *The Law of Contract, 1670-1870* (Cambridge, Cambridge University Press, 2015) 107–26 and 133–5; Lieberman (n 241) 129–32.

[254] 2 Burr 1005, 1 Wm Bl 219.

[255] 2 Burr 1005, 1012. For the civilian learning which underlay Mansfield's conception of equity, see PBH Birks, 'English and Roman Learning in *Moses v Macferlan*' (1984) 37 *Current Legal Problems* 1, 20–2. Birks captures well Mansfield's technique, noting that 'Lord Mansfield's references to "equity" are to the Roman *aequitas*, not to the chancery jurisdiction … Nevertheless it is true that Lord Mansfield does exploit the chancery overtone in *aequitas*.' See also DJ Ibbetson, 'Unjust Enrichment and Lord Mansfield' in JH Dondorp, M Schermaier, and AJB Sirks (eds), *De Rebus Divinis et Humanis: Essays in Honour of Jan Hallebeek* (Göttingen, V&R Unipress, 2019) 193, 198–201.

[256] 1 Bl Wm 123; 1 Eden 177.

[257] 1 Bl Wm 123, 160. For discussion, see D Foster, *Legal Demands against the Beneficial Interest under a Trust, c 1590-1759* (2020) Queen Mary, University of London (unpublished PhD thesis) 182–8.

[258] WS Holdsworth, 'Blackstone's Treatment of Equity' (1929) 43 *Harvard Law Review* 1, 7.

[259] Blackstone (n 6) 429. This phrase is lifted almost verbatim from Edward Hake's *Epieikeia* (quoted above). Blackstone was not unfamiliar with the sixteenth-century literature, having also quoted Lambarde's *Archeion* at 440.

[260] ibid 430.

[261] ibid 430.

[262] ibid 430–1.

[263] ibid 431–2.

[264] ibid 432.

[265] ibid 433–4.

[266] ibid 434.

[267] ibid 436–9.

overstate the point, and he recognised the existence of 'two other *accidental* grounds of jurisdiction' in the equity courts – mortgages and trusts – which had been 'driven into those courts by narrow decisions of the courts of law'.[268]

Throughout this discussion, Blackstone was anxious to stress the degree to which courts of law and equity shared a 'concurrent jurisdiction' in respect of matters of account, debts, legacies, contract, and fraud.[269] By contrast, mortgages and trusts were hived off as 'an exclusive jurisdiction' of the equity courts.[270] Even within this exclusive jurisdiction, however, the courts of equity had 'by degrees' transitioned from courts of 'extraordinary' jurisdiction and had transformed 'the system of relief administered by a court of equity into a regular science'.[271] For this reason, Blackstone maintained:

> It were much to be wished, for the sake of certainty, peace, and justice, that each court would as far as possible follow the other, in the best and most effectual rules for attaining those desirable ends … And sure there cannot be greater solecism, than that two sovereign independent courts, established in the same country, exercising concurrent jurisdiction, and over the same subject-matter, there should exist in a single instance two different rules of property, clashing with or contradictory each other.[272]

For Blackstone, the categorisation of the jurisdiction according to 'concurrent' and 'exclusive' was designed to show that there was little unique about the substance of English equity and that that which was unique could be readily administered by courts of law. By the mid-to-late eighteenth century, therefore, the wheel had turned again: equity could be regarded as an aspect of the common law, and the separate 'equity jurisdiction' looked upon merely as a function of disparate procedures used in Chancery, rather than as anything qualitatively distinct from the law.[273]

Whilst revolutionary, Mansfield and Blackstone's views on the substantive fusion of law and equity found little favour with their contemporaries. In the period c. 1790–1820, Lords Kenyon and Eldon reasserted the strict law-equity divide.[274] In *Bauerman v Radenius* (1798),[275] for example, Kenyon CJ recognised that the common law courts were ill-equipped to dispense equity, remarking that:

> We all know, that if the courts of law were to take into their consideration all the jurisdiction belonging to courts of equity, many bad consequences would ensue … By these means [i.e. the separation of law and equity] the ends of justice are attained, without making any of the

[268] ibid 436–7 (emphasis added). *Cf* CC Langdell, *Summary of Equity Pleading* (Cambridge, MA, CW Sever & Co, 1877) xxvi, who attributed the growth of trusts and mortgages to equity's system of remedies. Blackstone's failure to link the emergence of substantive equity to its system of remedies was a clear weakness in his classification.

[269] ibid 436, 437, and 438. *Cf* J Gilbert, *Forum Roman*, discussing equity's 'assistant' jurisdiction in relation to specific performance of contracts: Gilbert (n 45) 81. The language of 'assistant jurisdiction' was subsequently deployed by John Fonblanque to describe bills for discovery and perpetuation of testimony: Fonblanque (n 243) bk I, c 1, s iii, n (f).

[270] ibid 439.

[271] ibid 440–1.

[272] ibid 441.

[273] MJW Lobban, 'Contractual Fraud in Law and Equity, c 1750-1850' (1997) 17 *Oxford Journal of Legal Studies* 441, 443–6.

[274] For discussion, see: Holdsworth (n 258) 13–24; Swain (n 253) 134.

[275] 7 Term Rep 663.

> stubborn rules of law stoop to what is supposed to be the substantial justice of each particular case; and it is wiser so to act, than to leave it to the judges of the law to relax from those certain and established rules by which they are sworn to decide.[276]

In Chancery, Lord Eldon similarly opposed the substantive fusion of law and equity. In *Prince of Wales v Earl of Liverpool* (1818),[277] Eldon said:

> Many doctrines have been introduced into courts of law on a supposed analogy to the practice in equity, but without the guards with which equity surrounds the case ... and it happens whimsically enough, that there are cases in which courts of law, proceeding on the principle of giving a remedy because one might be obtained in equity, have compelled the party to resort to equity for protection against that practice at law.[278]

For Kenyon and Eldon, therefore, the separate equity jurisdiction was conceived as permitting the creation of strict and certain rules at common law. In appropriate cases, equity could intervene and 'relax' the strictures of the law in pursuit of 'substantial justice'. Chancery was the appropriate forum for these interventions because its forms of relief were hedged with safeguards to protect defendants from unjust interference with their legal rights[279] – safeguards which were wholly absent in the courts of common law.[280]

Notwithstanding this reaffirmation of the jurisdictional split, Blackstone's categorisation of equity according to the 'concurrent' and 'exclusive' jurisdictions gained traction in the subsequent treatise literature. Blackstone's classification would be adopted and adapted by John Mitford in his treatise on pleading in equity in 1780 and elaborated upon by John Fonblanque in 1793 and Joseph Story in 1836.[281] In its classic form, the classification of equity according to the 'exclusive', 'concurrent' and 'auxiliary' jurisdictions became the orthodoxy for most of the nineteenth century.[282] Although not accepted by every treatise writer of the period,[283] the classification was important in emphasising the overlapping jurisdictions of law and equity and may have encouraged a widespread view that the essential difference between law and equity was one of procedure rather than substance.[284] In this sense, the classification

[276] ibid 667–8. See also Kenyon CJ's remarks in *Deeks v Strutt* (1794) 5 Term Rep 690, 629, and *Clayton v Adams* (1796) 6 Term Rep 604, 605.

[277] (1818) 1 Swans 114.

[278] ibid 120.

[279] See, eg, *Evans v Bicknell* (1801) 6 Ves Jr 173, 184 (defendant's answer admissible as evidence in Chancery, whereas the testimony of the defendant could not be heard in courts of common law).

[280] This reticence to administer equity in courts of common law survived the passage of the Common Law Procedure Act 1854 (17 & 18 Vict, c 125). Section 83 permitted the pleading of equitable defences at common law, but this provision was interpreted restrictively: *Wodehouse v Farebrother* (1855) 5 El & Bl 277, 288–90 (Campbell CJ); *Gee v Smart* (1857) 8 El & Bl 313, 319 (Coleridge J).

[281] For discussion, see DEC Yale, 'A Trichotomy of Equity' (1985) 6 *Journal of Legal History* 194, 195–6 (although Yale tends to denigrate Blackstone and Mitford's contribution, instead attributing the classification to Fonblanque).

[282] For criticism of the classification, see Macnair (2007) (n 37) 664–6.

[283] See, eg, G Spence, *Equitable Jurisdiction, vol I* (London, Stevens et al, 1846) 430–1.

[284] C Riley, 'Jeremy Bentham and Equity: The Court of Chancery, Lord Eldon, and the Dispatch Court Plan' (2018) 39 *Journal of Legal History* 29, 31–40; MJW Lobban, 'Preparing for Fusion: Reforming the Nineteenth-Century Court of Chancery (Part 2)' (2004) 22 *Law and History Review* 565, 594–8. For similar views circulating in the United States c. 1840–70, see KR Funk, *Law's Machinery: Reforming the Craft of Lawyering in America's Industrial Age* (Oxford, Oxford University Press, 2025) 251–4.

may be regarded as laying the seeds for reform of the judicature and the great 'fusion' of the jurisdictions in the later nineteenth century.[285]

With the passage of the Judicature Acts 1873–75,[286] English equity lost its separate jurisdiction.[287] Its formerly unique procedures were either abolished or diffused across the judicature. Equity's discretion was now so tied to precedent that any description of the jurisdiction as 'extraordinary' sounded outdated. There remained enough of the old jurisdiction – mainly concerning contractual frauds, trusts and fiduciaries – that it could continue to be regarded as a distinctive source of private law rights and duties, but even this distinction appeared vanishingly thin to many.[288] To these survivors of the old equity jurisdiction, the Judicature Act 1873 accorded statutory recognition in section 25(11):

> in all matters … in which there is any conflict or variance between the Rules of Equity and the Rules of the Common Law with reference to the same matter, the Rules of Equity shall prevail.[289]

By the provisions of the Judicature Acts, the 'conflict' which the entire edifice of equitable jurisprudence had been designed to bypass was brought into searing focus. Where once the separate jurisdictions had avoided the possibility of contradiction, fusion provoked the conflict and resolved the matter in equity's favour.[290] Unsurprisingly, this provision would engender heated debate over its intended effect.[291] Equally unsurprisingly – for it was not their intention – the Acts failed to settle the broader question of equity's proper place in the English legal system.[292]

The passage of the Judicature Acts did, however, mark a change in the tenor of the conversation. Having discarded its theoretical foundations in *epieikeia* and much of its extraordinary and discretionary nature, equity had lost many of the hallmarks that distinguished it from the law. By 1875, English equity could instead be regarded

[285] Although *cf* J Story, *Commentaries on Equity Jurisprudence, vol I* (Boston, Hilliard, Gray & Co, 1836) 34–7, coming down in (muted) favour of *retaining* the separate jurisdiction.

[286] 36 & 37 Vict, c 66, and 38 & 39 Vict, c 77. The literature on the Judicature Acts 1873–5 is vast, but see especially: MJW Lobban, 'Preparing for Fusion: Reforming the Nineteenth-Century Court of Chancery' (2004) 22 *Law and History Review* 389 (Part 1) and 565 (Part 2); P Polden, 'The Judicature Acts' in W Cornish et al (eds), *Oxford History of the Laws of England, vol XII* (Oxford, Oxford University Press, 2010) 757–84; RP Meagher, WMC Gummow and JRF Lehane, *Equity: Doctrines and Remedies*, 3rd edn (Sydney, Butterworths, 1992) 36–44.

[287] Although the name continued in the new 'Chancery Division' of the High Court. For which, see P Polden, 'The Chancery Division' in Cornish (n 286) 834–47.

[288] FW Maitland (n 3) 12–22. For discussion of Maitland's narrow conception of equity, see D Foster, 'Historical Conceptions of the Express Trust, c 1600-1900' in S Degeling, J Hudson and I Samet (eds), *Philosophical Foundations of the Law of Express Trusts* (Oxford, Oxford University Press, 2023) 129–37.

[289] 36 & 37 Vict, c 66, s 25(11).

[290] At least in theory. For the practical effect of s 25(11), see S Waddams, 'Equity in English Contract Law: The Impact of the Judicature Acts (1873-75)' (2012) 33 *Journal of Legal History* 185.

[291] See especially, the judgments of Sir George Jessel MR in *Redgrave v Hurd* (1881) 20 Ch D 1 and *Walsh v Lonsdale* (1882) 21 Ch D 9. The controversy would re-emerge in the mid-twentieth century in *United Scientific Holdings Ltd v Burnley BC* [1978] AC 904, 924–5 (Lord Diplock) and *Federal Commerce and Navigation Ltd v Molena Alpha Inc* [1978] QB 927, 974 (Lord Denning MR).

[292] MJW Lobban, 'What Did the Makers of the Judicature Acts Understand by 'Fusion'?' in JCP Goldberg, HE Smith and PG Turner (eds), *Equity and Law: Fusion and Fission* (Cambridge, Cambridge University Press, 2019) 70–96 (esp 87–94).

merely as a historical accident which had been multiplied over the centuries. In 1906, FW Maitland would say:

> Equity now is that body of rules administered by our English courts of justice which, were it not for the operation of the judicature Acts, would be administered only by those courts which would be known as Courts of Equity. This, you may well say, is but a poor thing to call a definition. Equity is a certain portion of our existing substantive law, and yet in order that we may describe this portion and mark it off from other portions we have to make reference to courts that are no longer in existence. Still I fear that nothing better than this is possible. The only alternative would be to make a list of the equitable rules and say that Equity consists of those rules. This, I say, would be the only alternative, for if we were to inquire what it is that all these rules have in common and what it is that marks them off from all other rules administered by our courts, we should by way of answer find nothing but this, that these rules were until lately administered, and administered only, by our courts of equity.[293]

At the dawn of the twentieth century, therefore, the answer to the question 'what is equity?' lay in a process of historical deduction. The systematisation and positivisation of English equity over the preceding two centuries had operated to remove much of what was qualitatively unique to the jurisdiction. In this context, the abolition of the separate equity courts lent credence to the view that the classical conception of equity had faded from English legal practice.

As the wider effects of the Judicature Acts came to be realised, equity appeared under threat, but its supporters seemed unable to explain in analytical terms what was distinctive about equity jurisprudence.[294] With the passage of the 1925 property legislation, however, equity in land law was placed on a new statutory footing, such that HG Hanbury could remark that 'equity is … at the present day almost all-pervading'.[295] Over the course of the twentieth century, scholars of equity have gravitated increasingly toward the notion of an equity *mentalité* to distinguish equity from law.[296] This equitable mindset is defined by certain characteristics not shared by common law doctrine, including: the language of fiduciaries, confidentiality and unconscionability;[297] reasoning from maxims;[298] certain judicial techniques;[299] and the availability of equitable remedies according to judicial discretion (rather than as a matter of right).[300] Claims

[293] Maitland (n 3) 1. See also 13–4. In these remarks, Maitland may have been drawing upon Joseph Story's description of equitable jurisprudence as 'that portion of remedial justice … exclusively determined by a Court of Equity': Story (n 285) 26. This view persisted well into the mid-twentieth century; see, eg, *Chapman v Chapman* [1954] AC 429, 444 (Lord Simonds).

[294] For equity after fusion, see Catharine Macmillan's chapter in this volume (ch 21). See also P Polden, 'Mingling the Waters: Personalities, Politics and the Making of the Supreme Court of Judicature' (2002) 61 *Cambridge Law Journal* 575; Meagher et al (n 286) 50–9.

[295] HG Hanbury, 'The Field of Modern Equity' (1929) 45 *Law Quarterly Review* 196. See also WS Holdsworth, 'Equity' (1935) 51 *Law Quarterly Review* 142, 158–61.

[296] Lord Millett, 'The Common Lawyer and the Equity Practitioner' (2014–15) 6 *UKSC Yearbook* 193: 'Equity is not a set of rules but a state of mind.'

[297] Sir Peter Millett, 'Equity's Place in the Law of Commerce' (1998) 114 *Law Quarterly Review* 214; J Martin, 'Fusion, Fallacy and Confusion: A Comparative Study' (1994) *Conveyancer and Property Lawyer* 13–30.

[298] Meagher et al (n 286) 71–100.

[299] PG Turner, 'Equity and Administration' in PG Turner (ed), *Equity and Administration* (Cambridge, Cambridge University Press, 2016) 1, 17–20.

[300] PG Turner, 'Fusion and Theories of Equity in Common Law Systems' in JCP Goldberg, HE Smith and PG Turner (eds), *Equity and Law: Fusion and Fission* (Cambridge, Cambridge University Press, 2019) 1, 19–21.

of a discrete equity *mentalité* have not been sufficient to quell equity's most vociferous critics,[301] but the recent scholarship has demonstrated that there is clearly more to modern equity than the historical hangover which Maitland had considered it in 1906.

VII. Conclusion

At the close of this survey of eight centuries of English legal history, we return to the notion of equity as a secondary set of rules designed to assist, supplement and correct the primary rules of the common law. Through its long life, equity has continually operated interdependently with the common law, permitting the law to develop strict and certain rules safe in the knowledge that equity would act as a valve in hard cases. Indeed, the complex interaction of law and equity has often been regarded as the key to dispensing a more perfect justice in individual cases. This impression is reinforced when considering equity's highly adaptable suite of remedies, which have imbued the jurisdiction with a flexible and discretionary character. However, equity's function has necessarily brought it into a recurrent conflict with the common law – or, more precisely, with the common *lawyers* who disliked the open-textured nature of equitable jurisprudence.[302] The successive ructions in relations between common lawyers and equity men ultimately necessitated the development of sophisticated theories to explain and justify equity's role in the English legal system.

The jurisdiction had emerged in the medieval period to grant extraordinary remedies outside the usual common law procedures and to prevent abuse of legal process. The legitimacy of the jurisdiction was tied to the authority of the monarch, but its proper scope was highly controversial. With separate courts, procedures and principles, the medieval jurisdiction in conscience was closely aligned with, and yet distinct from, the common law. Provided it respected the due process statutes and refused to intervene in pure matters of law, its separation from the common law might be tolerated. As the jurisdiction became one of constant resort, however, its reach expanded and impinged upon the common law once more – and did so most spectacularly under Cardinal Wolsey. As the common lawyers' dissatisfaction mounted, a rearguard action by Christopher St German placed the jurisdiction on a whole new theoretical footing. The principle of *epieikeia* conceived of English equity as part of the common law, inhering in the very nature of law's application to specific facts. Whilst highly influential, St German's theory could never hold sway in its entirety. The notion of equity as implicit in the common law itself was all too readily viewed as a threat to the common law's authority and could never become the orthodoxy.

[301] PBH Birks, 'Equity in the Modern Law: An Exercise in Taxonomy' (1996) 26 *University of Western Australia Law Review* 1–99 (esp 16–25); S Worthington, 'Integrating Equity and the Common Law' (2002) 55 *Current Legal Problems* 223 (esp 226–41).

[302] *Cf* J Getzler, 'Patterns of Fusion' in PBH Birks (ed), *The Classification of Obligations* (Oxford, Oxford University Press, 1997) 157–192, observing that, with the adoption of open-textured objective standards (such as 'reasonableness') in the nineteenth century, common lawyers have increasingly come to dispense 'a new type of equity in the common law'.

The idea that equity was in some way necessary to the operation of the common law nevertheless remained vibrant in the subsequent juristic literature. Conjoined with the prerogative theory of equity, the jurisdiction could claim an authority independent of the common law and which legitimised equitable interventions in the law. As equity's absolute authority was being affirmed, jurists simultaneously insisted that its ambit was to be rendered with greater certainty. Equity, they said, was to be balanced with the law to produce a 'most harmonical justice' and this could be achieved only through the regularisation of its remedial practices. Over time, equity became increasingly tied to precedents, and its field gained greater shape and depth. As this process unfolded, equity became positivised and it matured into a 'science'. At the same time, it was insisted that law and equity were mutually subservient, each with the pursuit of justice as their *telos*.

With the eventual loss of its separate jurisdiction, equity acquired its modern form, comprising largely of substantive doctrines touching (inter alia) relief of frauds and enforcement of confidences. Notwithstanding persistent attempts to fuse legal and equitable doctrine in the twentieth century, the jurisdiction has retained sufficient identity and coherence to resist complete absorption by the common law. In the early decades of the twenty-first century, equity continues to defy simple classification. As part of the English legal system, it nevertheless remains apart from the common law; rather, equity may be understood as a distinct source of legal rights and duties, albeit one which is critically dependent upon the common law for its existence. Modern equity is to be distinguished from the common law not by courts or procedures, but by its history, its language and – perhaps – a certain state of mind. Variously conceived as within, without, against, adjacent and complementary to the law, equity has throughout its history remained indispensable to the pursuit of justice through legal process. Whilst its underlying nature has never been easy to explain, its vitality has lain in the legal system's continual quest for a more perfect justice, and the familiar desire to maintain the certainty of general rules whilst preserving flexibility in deserving cases. In this endeavour, equity's significance in the grand arc of English legal history cannot be denied.

2

Semantics of Conscience in Medieval Law

DAVID IBBETSON*

There can be few more axiomatic commonplaces of English law than that the Chancery was (and according to some still is) a court of equity. Yet, as Neil Jones details in chapter nine of this volume, it was only in the sixteenth century that the terminology of equity came to dominate, grounded on Christopher St German's *Doctor and Student*. For St German, equity was just a subset of conscience: the last aspect of conscience discussed in chapter 13 (15) of the First Dialogue is 'that in euery generall rule of the lawe thou do obserue and kepe equytie', immediately after which he begins his discussion of equity.[1] Before his time – at least from the 1450s – it was conscience that was the dominant term to describe Chancery's work by contrast to the common law.[2] Michael Macnair touches on this in a wide-ranging article on the language of equity and conscience in the Chancery, though his principal focus is on the period after St German;[3] Dennis Klinck has sketched the various senses of conscience in both lay and legal sources, again as a preface to more detailed work on the sixteenth century;[4] Norman Doe dedicates a chapter to conscience in his work on the later Middle Ages, looking at the wider context of the common law;[5] and David Seipp has dedicated an article to the use of the word 'conscience' in the Year Books.[6] This chapter attempts to build on those works in order to trace the shifts in the usage of the language of conscience in legal sources up to the end of the reign of Edward V (1483). By this time the final piece of the medieval legal jigsaw puzzle, the conscience at the base of the Chancery's jurisdiction and the designation of the Chancery as a/the 'court of conscience', was firmly in place. This final step was taken just as the Chancery was coming to make greater use of civil and canon lawyers,

* I am grateful to Norman Doe for comments on an earlier draft of this chapter.

[1] TFT Plucknett and JL Barton (eds), *St German's Doctor and Student* (1974) 91 *Selden Society* 86–101: First Dialogue (English version), chapter 15 (conscience), chapter 16 (equity).

[2] Below, n 63.

[3] MRT Macnair, 'Equity and Conscience' (2007) 27 *Oxford Journal of Legal Studies* 659.

[4] D Klinck, *Conscience, Equity and the Court of Chancery in Early Modern England* (Farnham, Ashgate, 2010) 13–40, especially at 18–24, 36–37.

[5] N Doe, *Fundamental Authority in Late Medieval English Law* (Cambridge, Cambridge University Press, 1990).

[6] D Seipp, 'Trust and Conscience in the Early Common Law' in F Cranmer and others (eds), *The Confluence of Law and Religion* (Cambridge, Cambridge University Press, 2016).

and there is some reason to suspect that it involved the grafting onto earlier English usage of ideas which were current in the learned laws.[7] It is based substantially on the printed Year Books,[8] supplemented by parliament rolls[9] and other sources.

By the twelfth century, the Latin *conscientia* had two core meanings in English sources.[10] On the one hand, it was cognitive, a sense of knowledge or honest belief. From a wider European point of view, this may have been the dominant sense: in his massive *Glossarium*, based on medieval sources, Du Cange simply defines *conscientia* as *cognitio*. On the other hand, it was based on the sense of right and wrong, either identifying how one ought to behave or judging one's past behaviour. It is in this sense that it had been used by Saint Jerome in his Latin commentary on the Bible.[11] Although focusing on different aspects, both of these senses were internal to the individual.

For the theological authors of the later Middle Ages, it was the latter aspect which prevailed. Building on Saint Jerome, they explored the relationship between *conscientia* and its Greek equivalent, *synderesis*.[12] Although the two concepts were linguistically identical at root,[13] they had different functions. The early thirteenth-century Peter the Chancellor, for example, treated *synderesis* as a knowledge of general propositions of right and wrong which had been implanted into all humans, whereas conscience involved the application of this knowledge to specific situations. *Synderesis* could not be mistaken, whereas conscience could, as a consequence of humans having free will.[14] Others would take different lines, but common to all of them was that both *synderesis* and conscience focused on right and wrong actions rather than on purely theoretical knowledge. It is this that creates the link with later natural law thought: for Thomas Aquinas, the basic principles of behaviour apprehended by *synderesis* were the basic principles of natural law.[15]

For lawyers, it was different: the cognitive aspect was to the fore. So, in the twelfth-century *Dialogus de Scaccario*, it is provided that a person making an account at the Exchequer should swear that he has given a proper account according to his conscience (*secundum conscientiam suam*).[16] This is very much the sense of *conscientia* in the Latin of *Bracton* in the second quarter of the thirteenth century and *conscience* in the French of *Britton* towards the end of the century. Their focus was on the determinations of the jury in felony trials and civil jurors or recognitors in assizes concerning real property.

[7] I have suggested this in 'Comparative Legal History: Equity and Conscience' in H de Jong (ed), *Secundum Doctores: Essays in Medieval Learned Law in Honour of Harry Dondorp* (Amsterdam, VU University Press, 2023), a paper from which I borrow in part.

[8] It is a pleasure to acknowledge the use I have made of David Seipp's massive database, without which this chapter would never have been finished: www.bu.edu/law/faculty-research/legal-history-the-year-books/.

[9] C Given-Wilson and others (eds), *The Parliament Rolls of Medieval England, 1275–1504* (Woodbridge, Boydell & Brewer, 2005) (hereafter 'PROME').

[10] *Dictionary of Medieval Latin from British Sources*, sub verb.

[11] Commentary on Ezekiel 1.7 (translation in TC Potts, *Conscience in Medieval Philosophy* (Cambridge, Cambridge University Press, 1980) 79.

[12] TC Potts, 'Conscience' in N Kretzmann and others (eds), *The Cambridge History of Later Medieval Philosophy* (Cambridge, Cambridge University Press, 1982).

[13] ibid 690.

[14] ibid 690–5.

[15] ibid 700.

[16] E Amt (trans and ed), *Dialogus de Scaccario / The Dialogue of the Exchequer* (Oxford, Clarendon Press, 1983) 32.

So far as felony trials were concerned, the issue was whether a juror who reached an erroneous verdict (*vere-dictum*, truth-telling) committed perjury. The verdict itself could not be questioned; but perjury was a sin, and swearing falsely might lead to suit in the ecclesiastical courts.[17] *Bracton* is clear, though, that giving a false verdict was not in itself perjury. This was explained on the grounds that the juror swore to give a verdict according to his conscience, so that a false verdict given unwittingly was not perjurous: he did not act against his belief or understanding (*contra mentem*).[18]

The same was true for civil jurors: they swore only to give a verdict according to conscience and hence did not commit perjury if they acted under an honest misapprehension.[19] It was their conscientious belief that mattered. However, a verdict given in a civil matter was susceptible to the process of attaint by a jury of twenty-four, leading to the condign punishment of the original jurors if it was found that they had given a false verdict. However, the punishment might be reduced if they promptly admitted they had sworn falsely, not knowingly through malice aforethought and contrary to their conscience but through folly; if they had sworn through a foolish hastiness (*hastivesce*), or if they had sworn based on a false belief in some fact.[20] A *casus* in a glossed manuscript of *Britton* seems to analogise swearing contrary to conscience and swearing in accordance with a warped (*blesmie*) conscience.[21]

Recognitors' oaths were not quite the same, since they swore to tell the truth according to their knowledge.[22] It was recognised, though, that this might not always be possible. Bracton points to recognitors who had not viewed the land in question being able to swear according to their conscience, *salvo visu*, in the manner of jurors, in effect on the basis of imperfect evidence, so that then they would avoid the serious punishments unless they had been instructed to make the view and had negligently or contemptuously failed to do so: they would not have sworn contrary to their conscience.[23]

Other usages of *conscientia* in *Bracton*, away from this core, underpin the sense that conscience was something internal to the person, something close to intention. Hence a testator making a will or a sealed writing might do so '*ex conscientia et voluntate*',[24]

[17] W Lyndwood, *Provinciale seu constitutiones Angliae* (Oxford, R Davis, 1679) 316o.

[18] *Bracton* 3.337. *Cf Britton* IV.9.3 (Nichols 2.214) which is confused, saying that perjury is a lie affirmed by oath, defining a lie as a false expression of the voice with an intent to deceive; but in the same paragraph states that an untrue sworn statement believed to be true is perjury, reversing the sense of the passage in *Bracton* which is the work's exemplar. *Fleta* (V.21) is to the same effect as *Britton*, adding that the oath be sworn rashly: GO Sayles (trans and ed), *Fleta. Vol 4, Book 5 and Book 6* (1984) 99 *Selden Society* 66.

[19] *Bracton* 3.63, 3.74, 3.75.

[20] *Britton* 2.219.

[21] *Britton* 2.232n, from CUL MS Dd 7.6.

[22] See the *regula* in the Irish Register of 1227, contrasting the oath of the knights in the grand assize, who must tell the truth according to their own knowledge, with that of ordinary jurors, who only swear to the best of their knowledge: E de Haas and GDG Hall (eds), *Early Registers of Writs* (1970) 87 *Selden Society* 7 (Hib 17), on which see FW Maitland, 'The History of the Register of Original Writs' in HAL Fisher (ed), *Collected Papers of Frederic William Maitland* (Cambridge, Cambridge University Press, 1911) vol 2, 110, 132. See too WJ Whittaker and FW Maitland (eds), *The Mirror of Justices* (1893) 7 *Selden Society* 173 no 135.

[23] *Bracton* 3.63.

[24] *Bracton* 2.119, 2.299; *Britton* 2.174n. *Cf Lord Edward v Prior of Gisburn* (1268) in JM Rigg (ed), *Select Pleas, Starrs and Records of the Jewish Exchequer, 1220–1284* (1901) 15 *Selden Society* 39, 40 (= TNA E9/9 m.3d): '*carta non est bona, immo falsa, nec ex conciencia ipsorum numquam emanavit*'; but *conciencia* here is plausibly glossed by the editor of the volume as meaning 'community' (ie, the priory), and so may not be a reference to conscience.

or a fire might be started accidentally, negligently or intentionally, '*mala conscientia*'.[25] Here the sense has shifted away from pure cognition – justified honest belief – onto something volitional.

Yet further from the core, where paraphrasing ancient theological or juristic texts, *Bracton's* use of *conscientia* falls squarely into the theologians' sense of right and wrong, indicating critical judgement of one's behaviour.[26] It may be that *Britton's* usage (and that of the gloss cited above) owes more than *Bracton's* to the theologians, getting closer to the scholastic idea of *synderesis* that was always true and the recognition that conscience might be erroneous: conscience itself might be flawed, in the sense that there had been a failure properly to interpret a basic proposition apprehended through *synderesis*.

As we get into the fourteenth century, we see a wider range of usage of the concept of conscience. This range had two poles: on the one hand, there was the pole represented by the earlier texts, where conscience related purely to a state of mind of the individual; the other pole represented a purely external value, akin to the law of God.[27] Between these is an intermediate position, assessing the individual's conduct by reference to external standards. These shades of meaning are found in cases reported in the Year Books; in records of, and petitions in, Parliament; and, by the end of the century, in petitions to the Chancellor.

It is the external pole that predominates. In 1332, for example, a man had entered into a bond for £20 subject to a condition that it would be void should he have paid £8 by a certain day. An action was brought for the £20, and the debtor produced an acquittance for £7.10s and tendered the remaining 10s of the £8. It was suggested, unsuccessfully, by Cantebrigge J that although the bond had been made for £20, all that was due was the £8, of which £7.10s had been paid and the remainder tendered. 'It would be against the law of God and good conscience' to award more. Notwithstanding that, the court awarded the full £20 plus damages, less the £7.10s which the acquittance showed had already been paid.[28] In the same way, in 1339 Stonore J said that 'by conscience and the law of God' it would be against reason to disinherit a person by a void fine, though he was reluctant to accept an averment which might lead to the annulment of the fine, given that the Statute *De Finibus Levatis* had expressly striven to make fines conclusive.[29]

In both of these cases, it might be noted in passing, there was an implicit or explicit contrast between conscience and common law. This contrast is yet clearer in a case in the Eyre of London in 1321.[30] In a plea of detinue the defendant waged his law but failed to appear on the appointed day; the plaintiff was therefore entitled to judgment.

[25] *Bracton* 2.414.

[26] *Bracton* 2.22, 2.424; *cf* 2.136, quoting more or less verbatim from D.41.2.1.6 with the sense of belief or knowledge.

[27] See *Oxford English Dictionary*, sub verb Conscience, treating this external sense as a usage of the fourteenth century onwards.

[28] YB Pasch 6 Edw III f 18, pl 32.

[29] YB Mich 13 Edw III (RS) 83, pl 51, at 97. The translation inaccurately reads 'good' conscience. See Statute *De Finibus Levatis* (1299) SR 1.126, 128.

[30] *Note* in HM Cam (ed), *Year Book Series vol XXVI, Part II. The Eyre of London, 14 Edward II (1321), Vol II* (1969) 86 *Selden Society* 352.

The count had valued the detained chattels at twenty shillings, with damages claimed of 100 shillings. At first, Stanton J argued that the court had no alternative to an award of the damages counted upon, though Herle J thought this was against good conscience when the damages claimed were so outrageous. The plaintiff was given the choice of an adjournment or accepting half a mark; he chose the latter. The report ends, 'Note that by law he should have recovered according to his count.' Sometimes, however, conscience might have been a guide in situations where the law was highly uncertain.[31] In this external sense, conscience equates – sometimes explicitly – to the law of God, objectively knowable ethical rules.

Slightly separated from this, conscience may involve the judgement of an individual's conduct in terms of this external standard. Hence, it could be said that where a claimant to land had the older title, he or she might in good conscience use any means to obtain it;[32] or a judge might say that he believed the plaintiff to be of such good conscience that he would not wish to enforce his full legal entitlement.[33] Similarly, it might be argued that a dying man had, *per cause de conscience*, married a woman whom he had made pregnant.[34]

The purely internal sense of (justified) honest belief, central in the references in *Bracton* and *Britton*, is not wholly absent in the cases of the first half of the fourteenth century. In an action of *cessavit per biennium*, it was said, issue could not be taken on the value of services due from the tenant unless he had admitted the cesser: the jury should judge '*in leur conscience*' the services due and then go on to determine whether distraint to that value was feasible.[35]

The evidence is strong that by the middle of the fourteenth century the dominant sense of the concept of conscience in legal contexts was the external moral law. This could be used as a standard for evaluating personal conduct (as in the dominant usage of the theologians). Thirdly, and wholly separate from the moral law, it could have a purely cognitive sense of a (justified) belief.

This continues through the second half of the fourteenth century. The dominant sense is the external one,[36] though it is now tinged with an idea of fairness, as where the judges adjourned a case out of conscience: in 1369, for example, a woman who was within age was received to defend her own right on the default of her husband. The case was adjourned 'out of conscience and because of her nonage', after which she was

[31] YB Pasch 8 Edw III 33 pl 35.

[32] YB Pasch 6 Edw III 16 pl 18, per Shardlow J.

[33] YB Mich 7 Edw III 52 pl 30, per Shardlow J.

[34] YB Pasch 44 Edw III 12 pl 21 (= YB Trin 45 Edw III 28 pl 45). See further PROME 1.251 (1290); 1.459; (1290); 1.510 (1292); 1.638 (1293); 2.248 (1305); 2.249 (1305); PROME 2.95 (1315); 2.197 (1316); 4.11 (1330); 4.117 (1330); 4.395 (1346); 4.432 (1348); 5.18 (1351).

[35] YB Mich 22 Edw III f 21 pl 95.

[36] *Savage v Gisborne*, YB Trin 6 Ric II (AF) 5 pl 2: a certain result is consistent with 'law and good conscience' (at 7, per Belknap CJ). The result of the case conforms 'with the best conscience' (at 8). *Gamoigne v Ftizherbert*, YB Mich 7 Ric II (AF) 83 pl 17, at 86 (good conscience that writ be maintainable); YB Mich 1 Hen IV 1 pl 3, at 2b per Skrene (in conscience grantee of land who has received benefit is liable to perform services); YB Mich 1 Hen V 13 pl 28 (court granting writ *dedimus potestatem* 'pur conscience'); YB Hil 5 Hen V 6 pl 13 ('good faith and conscience').

able to reformulate her defence.[37] In the same way, in *Sutton's Case*,[38] a defendant in an action of replevin had avowed for payment of relief of 100 shillings but subsequently 'for conscience' changed his avowry to two marks according to the usage of Beverley, since otherwise the land would be perpetually subject to the payment of 100 shillings as relief.[39] Alongside this, the sense of self-judgement of right and wrong behaviour is found,[40] as is the purely cognitive sense of the verdict of jurors and the like.[41]

As well, in its cognitive aspect, conscience was beginning to take on the sense of knowledge. In the treason trial in the Parliament of 1388, the lords, 'by due examination, and by evidence and information with which they could in any way duly inform their conscience' found the defendants guilty.[42] This is, perhaps, not too far from the jury reaching a verdict according to their conscience as found in *Bracton* and *Britton*, though the conscience here is something that can be informed and not something reflecting the honest belief of the jurors. A few years later, though, the sense of 'knowledge' is clear, where the Year Book describes that the record of a previous case was in the conscience of a judge.[43]

Cases in the reigns of Henry VI and Edward IV continue to show these meanings of conscience.[44] The dominant sense refers to the assessment of right and wrong external to the actor, more or less equivalent to 'justice',[45] but very frequently it is slanted towards the individual's actions assessed by reference to this.[46] A very good example of this is a case of trespass in 1456, where the defendant in the action was only four years old. 'Can you find it in your conscience to declare against an infant of such a tender age?' Moile J asked the plaintiff's counsel. Occasionally, too, the moral judgement is tinged with an

[37] YB 43 Lib Ass 266 pl 5; see too YB 17 Lib Ass 54 pl 28 (= YB Mich 18 Edw III (RS) 57 pl 17, at 61).

[38] YB Hil 40 Edw III 9 pl 18, with the corrections in J Baker, *Baker and Milsom Sources of English Legal History: Private Law to 1750*, 2nd edn (Oxford, Oxford University Press, 2019) 76.

[39] See too YB Hil 12 Hen IV (CUL MS Gg5.8(4) f 84) in J H Baker, 'John Bryt's Reports' [1989] *Cambridge Law Journal* 98, 105. PROME 6.163 (1380); 6.367 (1384); 7.134 (1390); 7.253 (1394); 7.326 (1397); 7.366 (1397); 8.53, 77 (1399; 8.173 (1402); 8.406 (1406); 8.423 (1407); 8.487 (1410); 9.25 (1413); 9.101 (1414); 9.280 (1421); 10.59 (1422).

[40] YB Pasch 46 Edw III 10 pl 7, per Kirton J ('vous parles de bon conscience'); YB Trin 50 Edw III 13 pl 3 (matters lying in priest's conscience); YB Mich 7 Hen IV 31 pl 15 (judges' conscience in assessing damages). PROME 5.280 (1373); 5.375 (1376); 6.18 (1377); 6.18 (1377); 6.356 (1383); 7.42 (1386); 7.258, 263 (1394); 8.10, 22, 52 (1399); 8.335 (1406); 9.151 (1416); 10.109 (1423).

[41] YB Mich 1 Hen IV pl 1; YB Mich 1 Hen IV 5 pl 10; YB Hil 11 Hen IV 50 pl 27.

[42] PROME 7.102 (the translation blandly translates 'lour conscience deuement enfourmer' as 'inform themselves.'

[43] YB Mich 8 Hen IV 3 pl 6.

[44] Doe (n 5) 132–154.

[45] YB Pasch 11 Hen VI 42 pl 38; YB Pasch 38 Hen VI 29 pl 12; YB Pasch 4 Edw IV 19 pl 36; YB Pasch 5 Edw IV LQ 30 pl 26; T5 E4 4 pl 9; YB Pasch 8 Edw IV 1 pl 1; YB Trin 9 Edw IV 6 pl 3; YB Mich 9 Edw IV 41 pl 26; YB Pasch 16 Edw IV 1 pl 1; YB Mich 18 Edw IV 11 pl 4; YB Pasch 21 Edw IV 24 pl 10; YB Pasch 22 Edw IV 6 pl 18. Stat 31 Hen VI c 9; Stat 33 Hen VI c 3. *Calendar of the Proceedings in Chancery in the Reign of Queen Elizabeth* (London. Record Commission, 1827) vol 1, xxi, xxiii, xxiv, xxxv, xxxviii, xl, xli, xliv, xlvi, xlvii, xlviii, l, lvi, lvii, lix; W Paley Baildon (ed), *Select Cases in Chancery, 1364-1471* (1896) 10 *Selden Society* 132 (no 136), 144 (no 143).

[46] YB Mich 8 Hen VI 4 pl 11; YB Pasch 21 Hen VI 35 pl 2; YB Pasch 22 Hen VI 47 pl 2; YB Hil 33 Hen VI 2 pl 8; YB Pasch 34 Hen VI 38 pl 9; YB Pasch 8 Edw IV 1 pl 1; YB Pasch 10 Edw IV (47 SS) 80 pl 22; YB 36 Hen VI 17 pl 4; YB Pasch 4 Edw IV 19 pl 36; YB Pasch 10 Edw IV (47 SS) 80; YB Pasch 21 Edw IV 22 pl 3; YB Pasch 21 Edw IV 22 pl 3; YB Pasch 22 Edw IV 2 pl 8; YB Pasch 22 Edw IV 19 pl 45; YB Mich 22 Edw IV 45 pl 11.

idea of fairness.[47] And the old usage of the (justified) belief of a juror in giving a verdict is still found.[48]

By the reign of Henry VI the Court of Chancery, which emerged out of the King's Council in the middle of the fourteenth century,[49] had become well established, and the language of conscience found its peculiar place there. At first, we may have no doubt that the word, when used in Chancery petitions, had no technical sense, but simply adopted the already existing usages. From the 1420s, petitioners were seeking from the Chancellor that he should do what conscience demanded, and the repeated collocation with good faith and right (*bone foy* and *reson*) points clearly in the direction of reference to an external standard.[50]

We may freely dismiss these references to conscience as non-technical, but a Chancery petition which can be dated before 1426 cannot be so lightly set aside.[51] One John Pecham (or Pekham) had transferred land to feoffees on condition that when the land was sold £40 should be paid to his right heir. The land had been sold after John's death, and the action was brought against the feoffees by a distant cousin as heir. No claim, it was said, would lie by the law of the church or common law, and so the claim was raised in the King's Chancery, 'which is [a] court of Conscience',[52] where the Chancellor would do 'as reason and conscience demand'.[53] The description of a court as a court of conscience implicitly sets it up in contrast to a court of law, reflecting the contemporary *ius commune* discussed below.[54] This is parallelled by an instruction to the Chancellor in 1427 to act 'according to what is desired in the petition, according to his discretion and according to good faith and conscience'.[55]

From this time we begin to see in the Year Books traces of an antinomy between law and conscience, though at first without reference to the Chancery. In 1425, for example, a tangle arose in the Common Pleas in an application to reverse an outlawry by a man who had been sued in debt under two different names and had obtained a charter of pardon in one of those names. The debtor brought a writ of scire facias to reverse the outlawry. Serjeant Rolf, for the creditor, argued that at law he could not safely answer to the claim in the name in which the pardon had been granted since he would then be estopped from enforcing the obligation, which was in the other name. '*Conscience gist en le cas*', he said, seemingly drawing upon the opposition between law and conscience.[56]

[47] YB Hil 3 Hen VI 25 pl 6; YB Hil 33 Hen VI 2 pl 8.

[48] YB Pasch 34 Hen VI 36 pl 7; YB Mich 5 Edw IV LQ 58 pl 3; YB Mich 6 Edw IV 5 pl 14; YB Mich 21 Edw IV 37 pl 1; YB Hil 22 Edw IV 45 pl 11; YB Trin 1 Edw V 2 pl 3. Stat 2 Hen V, stat II, c 3.

[49] J Baker, *An Introduction to English Legal History*, 5th edn (Oxford, Oxford University Press, 2019) 109–112.

[50] Baildon (n 45) 119 no 121, 130 no 136, 135 no 139, 137 no 140, 138 no 141, 146 no 143, 151 no 144, 153 no 145, 155 no 146, 156 no 147. Similarly PROME 10.339 (1427) and *Manual of Chancery English*, nos 44, 62, 73, 78.

[51] 100, 120 no 123. The *terminus ante quem* is established by the date of death of Reynold Pympe, one of the respondents: JS Roskell and others, *The History of Parliament: The House of Commons 1386–1421* (Stroud, Alan Sutton, 1992) vol 3, 151.

[52] The translation has 'the court of Conscience', but there is no definite article in the French original.

[53] *Cf* too YB Trin 14 Edw IV 6 pl 8.

[54] Below, 50.

[55] PROME 10.339.

[56] YB Hil 3 Hen VI 25 pl 6.

The bifurcation between the common law and the conscience of the Chancery was clear by the 1450s. A case removed into the Exchequer Chamber from Chancery, dated 1452 in Statham's *Abridgment*, is very clear.[57] Land had been granted to feoffees on trust to perform the grantor's will. He made a declaration that he wished the land to go to a daughter after his death, but he subsequently revoked this in favour of another daughter on the grounds that the first daughter would not marry the man he had chosen for her and was not well governed. The issue before the court was which of the daughters should have the land after his death. On the one hand, it was said that the declaration in favour of the first daughter was effective to give her an immediate interest; on the other, it was argued that the first daughter had given no *quid pro quo*, so that this was a matter of 'mere will' which was freely revocable: it was not consistent with conscience that the ungovernable daughter should have the land. Prisot CJ favoured the former view, by analogy with a common-law grant on condition, but Fortescue CJ took the opposite line, rejecting the analogy: 'We are not to argue law in this case but the conscience.' His conception of conscience comes through in his later remarks: if, after the declaration in favour of a daughter had been made, the grantor had had a son, it would be conscience to revoke the nomination of the daughter in favour of the son, who was now heir. It is hardly far-fetched to see this as a reflection of the commonplace principle of natural law that males were to be favoured above females. This is strengthened by the etymology he gives for *conscientia*: from *con-scio, scis*, 'to know with God', 'to know the will of God as near as one reasonably can.'[58]

There is more than a whiff of the Schools here. Most clearly, Fortescue CJ's suggestion that it would have been consistent with conscience to have revoked the declaration in favour of the daughter if a son had subsequently been born, and his derivation of conscience from '*con-scio*' aligns with his treatment of justice in his *De Natura Legis Naturae*.[59] Here, basing himself on his understanding of Aristotelian *epieikeia* ('*epikaia*'), he says a law-giver resolving a dispute should not blindly follow the rule he had laid down but do what he would have done if he had had full knowledge of the circumstances. It may be significant, also, that Prisot CJ's use of 'mere will' echoes closely Bartolus' definition of *nuda voluntas*.[60]

Some four years later, a petition was brought in Chancery arising out of a promise to give money on the intermarriage of the petitioners. The respondent answered in standard form that nothing in their bill was sufficient to put him to reply to the claim (the rest of the answer is lost), and the petitioners in their replication reasserted that there was matter sufficient 'to putte hym to answer after the lawe of consciens, whiche ys

[57] Statham *Abridgment*, Conscience 1, discussed in Klinck (n 4) 15–18. At 15, Klinck erroneously attributes the case to the Exchequer, which probably had no 'equity' jurisdiction this early: WH Bryson, *The Equity Side of the Exchequer* (Cambridge, Cambridge University Press, 1975) 13–14. Statham is explicit that the case originated in Chancery.

[58] For the equation of natural law with the law of God in the fifteenth century, see Doe (n 5) 60–83.

[59] Thomas Fortescue, Lord Clermont, *The Works of Sir John Fortescue, Knight* (London, privately printed, 1869) vol 1, 85–86, 214–215. Fortescue was concerned with the law-giver himself not being bound by his own rules, whereas Aristotle, whom he cites, was concerned with the decision-maker having to interpret the rules laid down as the law-maker would have wished him to do had he had full knowledge of the facts. It is likely that he was following the gloss of Monachus on the *Extravagantes Communes* 2.3.1, which had been incorporated into the standard gloss on the *Corpus Iuris Canonici*, whose focus (and citation of Artistotle) is the same as Fortescue's. See L Maniscalco, *Equity in Early Modern Legal Scholarship* (Leiden, Brill Nijhoff, 2019) 39, fn 112. But cp ibid, 37, fn 102.

[60] Bartolus, ad D.3.5.10 no 6.

lawe executory in this courte for defaute of remedy by cours of the common law'.[61] The phrase is telling. The Chancery is doing law, but it is the 'law of conscience' in contrast to the common law. The terminology 'law of conscience' became fairly common in the next decade or so.[62]

An argument of Prisot CJ in 1459 reveals the hardening of the division between common law and Chancery and casts light on the developing conception of conscience in this context.[63] An action of debt on a bond was brought against a group of London merchants. They pleaded that there had earlier been an action in Chancery (in common form asking the court to do as good faith and conscience required), referred to the Exchequer Chamber, where it had been ordered that the bond be delivered up for cancellation. The creditor (who had been imprisoned for contempt for ignoring the order) demurred to the plea, arguing that the Chancery order itself revealed that the bond was still in force, and denying that the Chancery had any power to instruct the Common Pleas to stay the action. Serjeant Choke and Danvers J refer to the obligation in conscience, but it is the argument of Prisot CJ which is most revealing. Contrasting the Chancellor with the common-law judges, he says that the former acts according to conscience, whereas the latter are restricted to judging *secundum allegata et probata* (in Latin in the manuscripts).[64] This distinction is taken from the *ius commune* tradition, where it was a much-discussed question whether a judge who had private knowledge should make use of that knowledge in reaching a decision in a lawsuit, judging according to conscience, or should reach a judgment based solely on what had been alleged and proved before him.[65]

The same question had been discussed in England, including in a Year Book case of 1407 or 1408.[66] Tellingly, however, there is no reference to the language of conscience in that case. The *ius commune* may have been the source of Prisot's thinking, but the terminology of conscience has undergone a shift. In the continental tradition(s) the conscience referred to is that of the judge, his knowledge, whereas for Prisot – at least as the reports have it – the Chancellor is to seek out 'the' conscience (*le conscience*), so it is anchored to the external truth rather than the judge's perception of it.[67] This bifurcation was conceptual as much as jurisdictional, especially in cases involving uses or trusts. Thus, it was said, where a person bought land from a feoffee knowing it was held to the use of another, he was buying what was in conscience the land of the *cestui que* trust.[68]

[61] Baildon (n 45) 143 no 143, at 146 (1456).

[62] YB Hil 7 Edw IV 29 pl 15; YB Trin 8 Edw IV 5 pl 1; YB Mich18 Edw IV 11 pl4; *cf* YB Pasch 4 Edw IV 8 pl 9, YB Mich 18 Edw IV 20 pl 29, contrasting common law with 'law of Chancery'.

[63] YB Hil 37 Hen VI 13 pl 3. The record of the case shows that it was argued several times between 1459 and 1461: M Hemmant (ed), *Select Cases in the Exchequer Chamber* (1933) 51 *Selden Society* 147, 153–58; but the printed Year Book and the manuscripts attribute this report to 1459.

[64] The distinction in this form is found in the fifteenth-century manuscripts edited by Hemmant (n 63), though not in the printed Year Books.

[65] KW Nörr, *Zur Stellung des Richters in Gelehrten Prozess: Iudex Secundum Allegata non Secundum Conscientiam Iudicat* (Munich, CH Beck, 1967); A Padoa Schioppa, 'Sur la Conscience du Juge dans le ius commune Européen' in J-M Carbasse and L Depambour-Tarride (eds), *La Conscience du Juge dans la Tradition Juridique Européenne* (Paris, Presses Universitaires de France, 1999).

[66] YB Pasch 7 Hen IV 41 pl 5.

[67] YB Mich 9 Edw IV 41 pl 26.

[68] YB Trin 11 Edw IV 8 pl 13.

Prisot CJ's remarks suggest that by the 1450s the idea of conscience was taking on a hue from the *ius commune*. This may be associated with the greater use of civil lawyers in the Chancery, beginning with the appointment of Richard Wetton DCL, formerly head of the civil law school in Oxford, as a Chancery Master in 1448.[69] The appointment of Robert Stillington DCL as Chancellor in 1467 seems to have extended the influence of the *ius commune*. A Year Book case of 1469 reporting his opinion requires quoting in full (translating the Law French but not the Latin):[70]

> In the Chancery it was touched on by the Chancellor that a man will not be prejudiced by mispleading or defect of form, but according to the truth of his matter; and we have to judge *secundum conscientiam et non secundum allegata*. For should a man suppose by bill that someone has done wrong to him and the defendant says nothing, if we have knowledge that he has not done wrong to the plaintiff [the plaintiff] will recover nothing. And there are two sorts of powers and processes, *scilicet potentia ordinata et absoluta*. *Ordinata* is where a certain order is observed, as in positive law, but the law of nature *non habet certum ordinem*, but by whatever means the truth can be known etc *et ideo dicitur processus absolutus* &c. *In lege naturae requiritur* that the parties be present etc or that they be absent by contumacy, that is to say where they are summoned and make default, etc *et examinatio veritatis*.[71]

This is not easy to unpick. The first part of this quotation is straightforwardly an application of the orthodox distinction of the *ius commune*, as found in Prisot CJ's argument quoted above, that in law a judge must decide according to what has been alleged and proved, whereas in conscience private knowledge can be brought into account. The second part of the quotation leans in the same direction, this time as a distinction between positive law and the law of nature.[72] This is expressed in terms of the distinction between *potentia absoluta* and *potentia ordinata*, well known in later medieval theology and philosophy.[73] The normal focus of this distinction in theological discourse was on the question whether God might have chosen to organise the world, both physically and morally, otherwise than He did. In His *potentia absoluta* He might have done, but having exercised once this power He had only *potentia ordinata*, either having no further choice or retaining a power of choice but refraining from exercising it. Since it could be accepted that God had foreseen and foreordained all that would happen in the world, nothing in this prevented, for example, a wholly orthodox belief in miracles as an exercise of *potentia ordinata*.

The distinction, though, was used rather differently by the canon lawyers of the thirteenth century, who were concerned with whether the pope had a power to dispense from the law of the church. He had *potentia absoluta* to make law, but once he had made this law had he only *potentia ordinata* which bound him to act in accordance

[69] M Beilby, 'The Profits of Expertise: The Rise of the Civil Lawyers and Chancery Equity' in M Hicks (ed), *Profit, Piety and the Professions in Later Medieval England* (Gloucester, Sutton, 1990) 71, 82. See too AD Emden, *Biographical Dictionary of the University of Oxford to AD 1500* (Oxford, Clarendon Press, 1957) 2027.

[70] I borrow this section substantially from my 'Comparative Legal History' (n 7).

[71] YB Trin 9 Edw IV 14 pl 9.

[72] *Cf* YB Trin 8 Edw IV 5 pl 1, in which Stillington described himself as being both a temporal judge and a judge in conscience, mapping onto the distinction between his roles on the Latin side of Chancery and the English.

[73] WJ Courtenay, *Capacity and Volition: A History of the Distinction between Absolute and Ordained Power* (Bergamo, P Lubrina, 1990).

with the law which he had laid down?[74] This 'canonistic turn' was picked up by Duns Scotus and his followers.[75] For him *potentia ordinata* was an ability to act in conformity with a right law (*conformiter agere legi rectae*), *potestas absoluta* a power to act other than in conformity with a right law.[76] No longer was the distinction applicable purely to divine power, it applied equally to human agency. Moreover, it could be mapped onto the distinction between sovereign power (*potential absoluta*) and the more limited power to act in accordance with the law (*potentia ordinata*).[77]

We may be certain that Chancellor Stillington was well aware of this. His first appearance in the historical record was as Principal of Deep Hall in Oxford in 1442, a position which he still held in 1444.[78] In 1443 he took the degree of Doctor of Civil Law, and in the same year received a bequest of three canon law books from his godfather. As a regent master he would have been familiar with Duns Scotus, described as the 'guiding light' of the Oxford theology school in the middle of the fifteenth century,[79] and the evidence points to his not having been unfamiliar with canon law.

Interpreting his words in context, we have three related binary pairs: law and conscience; *potentia ordinata* and *potentia absoluta*; positive law and natural law. The first term of each pair is limited by the law, the second term unlimited. For Chancellor Stillington, the Chancery was associated with the second term, the common law with the first term. Moreover, within these pairings, conscience is related to natural law, equivalent to the ethical values laid down by God. This collocation links Stillington's remarks back to Thomas Aquinas and the thirteenth-century philosophical literature.[80]

On analysis, therefore, Stillington's remarks in 1469 can be seen to embody the two different ideas of conscience identified by Bartolus, traceable back to Jacques de Révigny in the late thirteenth century.[81] The core idea, found long before Révigny, was that a judge should decide a case on the basis of what had been alleged and proved, *secundum allegata et probata*, and not according to his own private knowledge, according to conscience. Révigny had qualified this: although in ordinary cases a judge was restricted by the *allegata et probata*, a sovereign acting as a judge was free to follow his conscience; since he was free to change the rules, he should not be bound by them. This was extended to situations where the court was acting as representative of the sovereign (which would include the Chancery – 'before the king in Chancery').

Coincidentally perhaps, at the same time as the role of the English court of Chancery was being articulated along Bartolan lines, in the Dauphiné in south-western France, Bartolus's text was expressly relied on by Guy Pape in settling that the *Parlement* could

[74] Hostiensis, *Lectura in Quinque Decretalium Gregorianarum Libros*, ad 3.35.6, quoted in Courtenay (n 73) 107–108 and discussed at 92–95.

[75] Courtenay (n 73) 100–103, 115–116; H Veldhuis, 'Ordained and Absolute Power in Scotus' *Ordinatio* I 44' (2000) 38 *Vivarium* 222–230.

[76] Ordinatio I dist 44, quoted by Courtenay (n 73) 112.

[77] Courtenay (n 73) 115, citing John de Bassolis.

[78] Emden (n 69) 1777–79.

[79] J Catto and TAR Evans (eds), *The History of the University of Oxford: Volume II: Late Medieval Oxford* (Oxford, Clarendon Press, 1992) 270.

[80] Compare Potts (n 12) 695.

[81] Above, n 60. For Révigny, see D Maffei, 'Il Giudice Testimonie e Una "Quaestio" di Jacques de Révigny (MS Bon. Coll. Hisp. 83)' (1967) 35 *Tijdschrift voor Rechtsgeshiedenis* 54.

judge according to conscience (and not be bound by what had been alleged and proved) since its decisions were equivalent to those of the sovereign himself.[82]

For Chancellor Stillington the court might have been reaching decisions on the basis of natural law,[83] but a qualification is visible in the charge from the King to Master of the Rolls Robert Kirkham when giving him custody of the great seal in 1467: 'that all matters in his court of chancery shall be directed and determined according to equity and conscience *and to the old course and custom*'.[84] The Chancery may not have been bound by the rules and procedures of the common law, but it was enjoined to act consistently with its own practices. It may have been underpinned by the more or less unbounded natural law, but it was none the less held in check by what it had done in the past, the *stylus curiae*.

By the 1470s the linguistic shift of conscience was complete. Already in the fourteenth century, alongside its cognitive sense associated with the conscience of the jury, there was an ethical sense associated with the law of God, and hence natural law, according to which right conduct could be assessed. By the beginning of the fifteenth century the Chancellor might be instructed to exercise his discretion according to conscience. On the face of it there was room for a misalignment between objective ethical standards and the individual's perceptions of those standards, but the subjectivism that this would lead to was avoided – at least in theory – by the assumption that *synderesis* could not be flawed. This accounts for the frequent association of conscience with the Law-French *reson*, translatable both as 'reason' and 'right'. The injection of Bartolism, if such it was, in the 1450s and 1460s provided a legal-theoretical justification for the Chancellor's wholly discretionary jurisdiction, but this was counterbalanced by the treatment of Chancery as to some extent rule-bound: there was now a 'law of conscience'. By the early sixteenth century, and especially under the chancellorship of Thomas Wolsey, the tensions which were implicit in this position, in particular the risk of uncontrolled subjectivism, were coming to the surface; and it was these tensions, perhaps, that lay behind Christopher St German's framework for the justification of Chancery jurisdiction in *Doctor and Student*.[85]

[82] Guy Pape, *Decisiones*, *quaestio* 29 (Geneva 1643, 33, first published 1490). The decision dates from Pape's time as a judge of the court and can be dated around 1450, perhaps just after the reorganisation of the court in 1453. See N Chorier, *La Jurisprudence du Célèbre Conseiller et Jurisconsulte Guy Pape dans ses Décisions* (Lyon, Jean Certe, 1692) 75.

[83] See also YB Pasch 13 Edw IV 9 pl 5 (alien sues not according to common law but according to natural law in the Chancery).

[84] *Calendar of Close Rolls* 1461–1468, 456 (original quoted by WS Holdsworth, *History of English Law, vol 1* (London, Methuen, 1922) 407). Emphasis added.

[85] Sir J Baker, *The Oxford History of the Laws of England, vol 6: 1483–1558* (Oxford, Oxford University Press, 2003) 39–48.

3

The Statute of Richard III (1484) and the Emergence of Beneficial Ownership in Freehold Land

AJ HANNAY*

I. Introduction

The first and only Parliament of King Richard III's reign met at Westminster on 23 January 1484.[1] Richard had usurped the throne the previous June by declaring his brother's heirs illegitimate and had conclusively seen off the somewhat anti-climactic rebellion of October 1483. The King's immediate concerns for this Parliament were thus the confirmation of his title and the passing of attainders against his political opponents. This highly volatile political background was the setting for the passage of one of the most important statutes in the history of English equity and the development of the trust – the Statute of Richard III.[2]

In the famous words of FW Maitland, the trust can be regarded as 'the greatest and most distinct achievement performed by Englishmen in the field of jurisprudence'.[3]

* I have been very fortunate in receiving helpful comments and feedback from the editors and my fellow contributors and attendees at the workshop at UCL in April 2022. I am particularly grateful to David Ibbetson, Neil Jones and Ian Williams for their comments on earlier drafts of this chapter.

[1] For general literature on Richard III see M Hicks, *Richard III* (New Haven, CT, Yale University Press, 2019); R Horrox, *Richard III: A Study in Service* (Cambridge, Cambridge University Press, 1989); C Ross, *Richard III* (Berkeley and Los Angeles, CA, University of California Press, 1981).

[2] Statute of Richard III 1484 (1 Ric III, c 1). Although other statutes were passed in the 1484 Parliament, reference to 1 Ric III, c 1 as 'the Statute of Richard III' is contemporary and perhaps suggests a recognition amongst common lawyers of the statute's importance. For examples, see YB Mich 7 Hen VII, f 6, pl 9 (1491): '*le Statute de Richard de feoffment sur confidence*'; YB Trin 15 Hen VII, f 12, pl 23 (1500): '*Et le Statute de R le 3*'. The importance of 1 Ric III, c 1 has long been recognised, and was, alongside the Statute of Uses 1536 (27 Hen VIII, c 10), central to seventeenth- and eighteenth-century understandings of uses and trusts. For Lord Nottingham C (died 1682), 1 Ric III, c 1 was of fundamental importance to the general understanding of equitable interests after 1536 because it was the source of exceptions to the Statute of Uses: DEC Yale, 'The Revival of Equitable Estates in the Seventeenth Century: An Explanation by Lord Nottingham' (1957) 15 *Cambridge Law Journal* 72.

[3] E Cam (ed), FW Maitland, *Selected Historical Essays of FW Maitland* (Cambridge, Cambridge University Press, 1957) 129.

The roots of this achievement are to be found in the trust's medieval precursor: the use. A use of freehold land was created where a landowner transferred legal title to his feoffees to uses for the benefit of cestui que use.[4] Following the creation of a use, the feoffees were seised of the land and thus, as far as the common law was concerned, owned the land, but they were bound in conscience to the feoffor's wishes. By the Statute of Richard III, cestui que use acquired a power to alienate land that was held for his use. This chapter seeks to consider the statute, particularly in light of its effect on the nature of the interest held by cestui que use.

II. Uses and the Origins of Beneficial Ownership in Freehold Land

A. The Use as an Interest in Land

In the early sixteenth century, title to freehold land was understood to consist of two distinct things.[5] This was set out by Christopher St German in the second dialogue of *Doctor and Student* in which the Student explained that

> every man that have lands has thereby two things in him, that is to say, the possession of the land … called freehold, and the other is the authority to take thereby the profits of the land.[6]

This understanding of the nature of title to freehold land is reflected in Audley's repeated references in his 1526 reading to landholders before they had enfeoffed feoffees as being seised to their own use.[7] This conceptual dualism is reflected in Neil Jones's description of the use before the Statute of Uses 1536 as being 'thinglike'.[8]

There is some indication from the late fourteenth century onwards that cestui que use was understood to have some form of interest in property held to his use. By the statute 50 Edw III, c 6 (1377), the practice of creating uses of tenements and/or chattels and then taking sanctuary to avoid creditors was prohibited.[9] The statute provided that for the purpose of recovering debts, if the transfer was found to be collusive, creditors

[4] The full phrase is '*Cestui a que use le feoffment fuit fait*.' A feoffment with livery of seisin was 'the classic medieval conveyance' made by a feoffor with seisin and usually accompanied by a charter or deed. For detail see AWB Simpson, *A History of the Land Law*, 2nd edn (Oxford, Oxford University Press, 1986) 119–121. Note that a use could also be created through other types of conveyance such as a fine or recovery. See generally JM Kaye, *Medieval English Conveyances* (Cambridge, Cambridge University Press, 2009).

[5] NG Jones, 'Uses, Trusts and a Path to Privity' (1997) 56 *Cambridge Law Journal* 175, 177–182.

[6] TFT Plucknett and JL Barton (eds), *St German's Doctor and Student* (1974) 91 *Selden Society* 222.

[7] BL MS Hargrave 87, ff 438v–439: '*home seisi a son proper use*'.

[8] Jones (1997) (n 5) 179. See too NG Jones, 'The Trust Beneficiary's Interest before *R v Holland* (1648)' in A Lewis et al (eds), *Law in the City: Proceedings of the Seventeenth British Legal History Conference, London, 2005* (Dublin, Four Courts Press, 2007) 95–118; NG Jones, 'Uses and "Automatic" Resulting Trusts of Freehold' (2013) 72 *Cambridge Law Journal* 91, 94–5.

[9] *The Statutes of the Realm: printed by command of His Majesty King George the Third, in pursuance of an address of the House of Commons of Great Britain: from original records and authentic manuscripts.* (1810–29) (hereafter '*SR*') vol 1, 398.

could have their actions 'as if no such [use] had been made'.[10] In the context of the creation of a use by this particular form of bad faith, that is to say, collusion, between the debtor and 'their friends',[11] the statute allowed creditors to have their action and enforce the debt against property held to the debtor's use. By the operation of the statute, creditors were permitted to proceed in their actions as if the debtor had an interest in property held to their use. This was analogous to the operation of the later statute 4 Hen VII, c 17 (1490), whereby cestui que use would be treated as if his ancestor had died seised.

Returning to the fourteenth century, we can see Parliament adopt a similar approach to the 1377 statute in the following year with regard to land held to the use of Edward III's mistress, Alice Perrers, who had been given significant landed wealth, much of which had been enfeoffed to her use. Following her trial, which has been described as a 'convenient piece of theatre'[12] and which symbolised the end of the old regime, Perrers was subjected to forfeiture which, in an extraordinary measure, because of her 'fraud and deceit', specifically included lands of which others were seised to her use.[13] Later in Richard II's reign, a broader application of the same principle was enacted: by 21 Ric II, c 3 (1398), lands held in use were to be included in any future forfeitures following attainder for treason.[14]

On one reading of 50 Edw III, c 6 and the forfeitures of Alice Perrers in the 1370s, they demonstrate that cestui que use was thought to have an interest in the property, but the statutes are perhaps better understood as providing for voiding of the transfers as a result, respectively, of the 'collusion' of the debtors and the 'fraud and deceit' of Perrers. In voiding the transfers, though, it can be seen that certain uses were viewed as being in bad faith, and there are clear echoes here of the 'fraud' and 'collusion' of the Statute of Marlborough.[15] Further fourteenth- and early fifteenth-century examples can be seen in the prohibition of the employment of uses to avoid the requirement to purchase a mortmain licence when alienating to the church,[16] and in the fact that a plaintiff in an action of formedon could have their writ against the pernor of profits, that is to say, against cestui que use.[17] The policy of these statutes was that the protection afforded to entails and remainders through writs of formedon was not to be frustrated by uses.

The final provision of the statute 21 Ric II, c 3 is, for our purpose, the most interesting because it specifically excluded from forfeiture the converse case, in which traitors

[10] The wording of the statute at this point is 'gift' but in context this is merely the method by which the use was created.

[11] *SR* (n 9) vol 1, 398.

[12] L Tompkins, *The Uncrowned Queen: Alice Perrers, Edward III and Political Crisis in Fourteenth-Century England, 1360–1377* (unpublished PhD thesis, University of St Andrews, 2013) 153.

[13] C Given-Wilson (gen ed), *Parliament Rolls of Medieval England, 1275–1504* (Woodbridge, Boydell & Brewerm 2005) vol 6, 30. For more detail on Alice Perrers's extensive employment of uses, her trial and forfeiture, see Tompkins (n 12) 90–94, 141–155. For her trial see also WM Ormrod, 'The Trials of Alice Perrers' (2008) 83 *Speculum* 366.

[14] *SR* (n 9) vol 2, 98–99.

[15] The Statute of Marlborough 1267 (52 Hen III, c 1), discussed in AJ Hannay, '"By Fraud and Collusion": Feudal Revenue and Enforcement of the Statute of Marlborough, 1267–1529' (2021) 42 *Journal of Legal History* 65, 67–69.

[16] 15 Ric II, c 5 (1391); *SR* (n 9) vol 2, 79–80.

[17] 1 Ric II, c 9 (1377); *SR* (n 9) vol 2, 3–4; 4 Hen IV, c 7 (1402); *SR* (n 9) vol 2, 134.

held to the use of another.[18] Beyond the potential implication that cestui que use had some interest in property held to his use by virtue of voided transfers, the statute 21 Ric II, c 3, and the later statute 5 Hen IV, c 1, which enacted the same policy, went further. They provided that land of which traitors were seised to the use of another was excluded from their forfeitures, indicating that Parliament effectively recognised that seisin was not the sole consideration and that by the late fourteenth and early fifteenth centuries cestui que use was understood to hold something in the land. The question for our present purpose is: what was that 'thing'?

B. The Nature of the Use

In seeking to understand the nature of the 'thing', it is imperative to consider the contemporary language used to describe it. The word 'use' in this context derives from the Latin *ad opus* and Norman-French *al oeps* meaning 'for the benefit of'.[19] Before our period, there are a number of examples of uses being described with the English words 'confidence' and 'trust'. In his limited treatment of uses, Littleton described them as 'feoffments upon confidence to perform the will of the feoffor'.[20] Further examples can be found in reported cases throughout the fifteenth century which demonstrate uses being understood as a 'trust' or 'confidence' placed in the feoffees by the feoffor.[21]

In examples from 1452 reported by Statham, 'trust' is used to describe uses, and in the later abridgement of Fitzherbert, the same case is referred to with the word 'confidence' being reported rather than 'trust'.[22] In 1462 references were made to 'feoffees on confidence' and persons 'enfeoffed on confidence',[23] and in 1464 the same description is used, with the defendant being described as having been enfeoffed 'on confidence' to the use of the feoffor, and in the same case, that the feoffment had been made 'by trust and confidence'.[24] In the remainder of Edward IV's reign, the phrases 'in trust' and 'of trust'

[18] The same provision was included in a statute of Henry IV following the battle of Shrewsbury: 5 Hen IV, c 1 (1405); *SR* (n 9) vol 2, 143.

[19] F Pollock and FW Maitland, *The History of English Law Before the Time of Edward I*, 2nd edn (Cambridge, Cambridge University Press, 1898, reprinted 1968) vol 2, 228–9; SFC Milsom, *Historical Foundations of the Common Law*, 2nd edn (London, Butterworths, 1981) 200. Adgore uses the French '*oeps*' in his reading that dates from c. 1490–91: Lincoln's Inn MS Maynard 3, ff 197–197v: '*Si diverse persons fait feoffment, ceo serra intend al use de touts ceux, mes si l'un deux* [sic] *le owner donquez serra a son oeps*'; '*ilz serront seisi a son oeps et a ses et a ses* [sic] *heirs*'.

[20] TE Tomlins (ed and trans), *Lyttleton, His Treatise of Tenures in French and English* (London, S Sweet, 1841) 463. (Sir Thomas Lyttleton's *Tenures Novelli* was originally published c. 1481 and appeared in numerous editions thereafter).

[21] DJ Seipp, 'Trust and Fiduciary Duty in the Early Common Law' (2011) 91 *Boston University Law Review* 1011, 1022–1023.

[22] Trin 30 Hen VI, *Stath Abr, Devise*, pl 8, per Fortescue CJKB: '*le dit devise fuit de trust &c.; il fuist de trust*'; Mich 31 Hen VI, *Stath Abr, Conscience*, pl 1: '*une feoffement de trust*'; *CF* Trin 30 Hen VI, *Fitz Abr, Devise*, pl 22: '*le devise fuit de confidence; il fuit de confidence*'; Mich 31 Hen VI, *Fitz Abr, Subpena*, pl 23: '*feffment de confidence*'.

[23] YB Pasch 2 Edw IV, f 2, pl 6 (1462), per Danvers JCP: '*mon feoffee sur confidence*'; YB Pasch 2 Edw IV, f 5, pl 11 (1462), per Littleton sjt: '*le plaintif enfeoffa certein persons sur confidence; le feoffees sur confidence*'.

[24] YB Pasch 4 Edw IV, f 8, pl 9 (1464), per Catesby sjt: '*al use le defendant &c. sur confidence; le defendant fist le feoffment al plaintif per trust & confidence*'.

were frequently used in reported cases to describe feoffments to uses.[25] David Seipp has suggested that there was a shift in Henry VII's reign, with 'confidence' being preferred to 'trust',[26] but this shift, if indeed there was one,[27] appears to have been merely linguistic, as uses continued to be characterised – apparently interchangeably – as a 'trust', 'confidence' or 'trust and confidence' placed in the feoffees.[28] However, the question of what a use was – that is to say, what, if anything, cestui que use had in property held to his use – appears to have been a more nuanced question than is suggested by a statement that it was universally understood as a mere 'trust' or 'confidence' which was upheld in conscience.

In the mid-fifteenth century, as far as the common law was concerned, cestui que use, even if he was in occupation, was considered to be at best a tenant by the sufferance of his feoffees.[29] However, as we have noted, in particular circumstances of bad faith, a number of late fourteenth- and early fifteenth-century statutes treated cestui que use as if he had something more than a mere trust and confidence in his feoffees – indeed, that he had something in the property itself. As we have seen, by the sixteenth century, title to freehold land was considered to consist of two things: possession and the right to take the profits, that is to say, the use.[30] By virtue of the statutes 1 Ric II, c 9 (1377) and 4 Hen IV, c 7 (1402), within the context of an action of formedon with regard to land that had been enfeoffed to his use, cestui que use was considered to be the pernor

[25] YB Mich 5 Edw IV, f 7, pl 16 (1465): '*si home fait feoffement de trust de terre; fait feoffement de trust sans declarer de son volunt*'; YB Pasch 8 Edw IV, f 4, pl 11 (1468), per Stillington C: '*si jeo enfeoffe un home en trust*'; YB Hil 8 Edw IV, f 29, pl 15 (1469): '*Nota que il fuit tenus per les Justices que un feoffe de trust est tenus de pleder touts plees*'; YB Mich 9 Edw IV, f 41, pl 26 (1469), per Catesby sjt: '*son pere luy enfeoff de trust*'; YB Trin 11 Edw IV, f 8, pl 13 (1471): '*si mon feoffee de trust*'; YB Mich 12 Edw IV, f 12, pl 5 (1472), per Catesby: '*lou home fait foffement de trust*'; YB Trin 16 Edw IV, f 4, pl 1 (1476): '*il est enfeoffe en trust*'; YB Mich 16 Edw IV, f 7, pl 2 (1476): '*plaintif ne fuist sinon que feoffee de trust*'; YB Pasch 21 Edw IV, f 24, pl 10 (1481) per Digas: '*feoffements de trust; si le pere fait feoffement de trust*'; per Littleton JCP: '*ces feffees de trust*'; YB Mich 21 Edw IV, f 37, pl 1 (1481): '*enfeoffa … auters de trust*'; YB Hil 21 Edw IV, f 20, pl 29 (1482), per Hussey CJKB '*issint est enfeoffement en trust*'; YB Pasch 22 Edw IV, f 6, pl 19, per Rotherham C: '*sur feoffement de trust*' and per Hussey CJKB: '*si home ust enfeoffe un auter de trust*'.

[26] Seipp (n 21) 1025–1026. See, eg, YB Mich 5 Hen VII, ff 5, 6, pl 11 (1489), per Fyneux sjt: '*Si un home qui ad feoffe sur confidence*', and per Tout le Court: '*les feoffees sur confidence*'; YB Mich 20 Hen VII, f 8, pl 18 (1504), per Kingsmill JCP: '*Et si feoffees sont sur confidence de un manor*'.

[27] There are examples of 'confidence' under Edward IV and 'trust' under Henry VII: Seipp (n 21) 1026, fn 102: YB Mich 18 Edw VI, f 20, pl 29 (1478), per Sulyard sjt: '*un soit enfeoffe sur confidence en ma terre*', and per Littleton JCP: '*en le case de feoffment sur confidence*'; YB Hil 15 Hen VII, f 2, pl 3 (1500): '*Issint est ou en feffee de trust*'.

[28] *Gervys v Cooke* (1522) YB Mich 14 Hen VIII, f 4, pl 5, per Fitzherbert: '*Et use nest forsque trust et confydens, que le feoffour mytte en le parson son feoffee*'; '*Quar si jeo enfeffe B, a aver a luy et a sez heirez et assugnez, ore mon tryst et confydens*'. A printed version of these statements appears in JH Baker (ed), *The Year Books of Henry VIII: 12-14 Henry VIII 1520-1523* (2002) 119 *Selden Society* 108 and 114–115. See also Adgore's Reading (c. 1490–91) Lincoln's Inn MS Maynard 3 ff 191–210, f 191: '*feoffment sur confidence*'; and f 199v: '*feoffee de trust*'; Pettit's Reading (1518) BL MS Harley 5013, f 18: '*per cest feffement de confidence est implie un confidence et trust inter le feffour et feffee*'; Knightley's Reading (1523) CUL MS Hh 3.9, f 91v: '*feffe de trust*'; St German (n 6) 222: '*feoffment of trust*'. For a number of further examples from Roger Yorke's notebook (c. 1520–30), see JH Baker, *Oxford History of the Laws of England, vol 6: 1483–1553* (Oxford, Oxford University Press, 2003) (hereafter Baker, *OHLE*) 654, fn 10.

[29] YB Pasch 4 Edw IV, f 8, pl 9 (1464), per Catesby sjt: '*enfeoffe le plaintiff en fee, etc al use le defendant etc. sur confidence, et puis le defendant per sufferance del plaintiff et a son volunt occupie cel terre*'; Littleton (n 20) 463: 'by the will of his feoffees'.

[30] BL MS Hargrave 87, ff 438v–439: '*home seisi a son proper use*'; St German (n 6) 222; Jones (1997) (n 5) 177–182.

of profits. Moreover, the idea that cestui que use was the pernor of profits continued into the late fifteenth century because the earlier statutes were reaffirmed by 1 Hen VII, c 1 (1485). This suggests that as a result of these statutes, cestui que use was considered to have something more tangible in the land than a mere 'trust' and 'confidence' with his feoffees.

By the late fifteenth century, in response to the common law rule prohibiting the devise of freehold land by last will, it had become commonplace for landholders to enfeoff feoffees to their own use and to perform their wills.[31] The increased popularity of uses in this form led to Serjeant Frowyk famously declaring in 1502 that by the 1480s: 'the greater part of the land of England was in feoffments upon trust'.[32] One of the effects of this practice was for landholders in visible possession of the land – perhaps even in possession of the title deeds – to be no more than unseised cestuis que use.[33] The uncertainty facing purchasers of land as a result of feoffments to uses was the mischief that Parliament sought to address in 1484.

III. Enacting the Statute of Richard III

The preamble to the Statute of Richard III declared that it had been enacted because of 'privy and unknown feoffments [causing] great uncertainty [...] and grievous vexations [...] among the king's subjects'.[34] Maitland and Holdsworth were both convinced by this statement of the motive for enacting the statute,[35] but Bean was somewhat more sceptical.[36] He argued that the uncertainty faced by purchasers as a result of feoffments to uses had existed for a number of years and was therefore insufficient to explain why legislating on the issue appeared to be so important in 1484. It is possible that the 'uncertainty' was more recent than Bean thought and was a result of an increased confidence in and employment of uses following developments in the Chancery protection afforded to cestuis que use in the 1460s,[37] or an increase in the proportion of military service land that was held in fee simple, as opposed to fee tail, as a result of an increase in the barring of entails by common recovery following the decision in *Taltarum's Case* (1472).[38]

[31] Milsom (n 19) 208.

[32] YB Mich 15 Hen VII, f 13, pl 1 (Baker states that the Year Book is misdated and this quote is from *Dod v Chyttynden* (1502): JH Baker (ed), *The Reports of John Caryll* (1999) 109–110 *Selden Society* (hereafter *Caryll Rep*) vol 2, 395–6.

[33] Baker, *OHLE* (n 28) 655. The point on possession of the title deeds was made in YB Trin 6 Hen VII, f 3, pl 2 (1491).

[34] *SR* (n 9) vol 2, 477.

[35] WS Holdsworth, *A History of English Law, vol 4* (London, Methuen, 1923) 444–445; AH Caytor and WJ Whittaker (eds), *Equity: A Course of Lectures by FW Maitland* (Cambridge, Cambridge University Press, 1936) 33–34.

[36] JMW Bean, *Decline of English Feudalism* (Manchester, Manchester University Press, 1968) 178.

[37] ibid 168–171. See too J Biancalana, 'Medieval Uses' in R Helmholz and R Zimmerman (eds), *Itinera Fiduciae: Trust and Treuhand in Historical Perspective* (Berlin, Duncker & Humblot, 1998) 111, 149–152.

[38] *Taltarum's Case* (*Hunt v Smyth*) (1472) YB 12 Edw IV 19–21. That the employment of uses grew following this decision was suggested by Joseph Biancalana in an unpublished lecture: JH Baker, *Introduction to English Legal History*, 5th edn (Oxford, Oxford University Press, 2019) 272, fn 32. Conversely, the fact that *Taltarum's Case* was reported has perhaps resulted in its importance being overstated; indeed, it was not until *Capel's Case* (1581–1593) 1 Co Rep 54a, 76 ER 121; 1 Co Rep 61b, 76 ER 134 that it was decided that remaindermen and reversioners, as well as issue in tail, could also be barred by common recovery. See also Simpson (n 4) 129–132.

It is often tempting for lawyer-legal historians to view legal change within its own doctrinal vacuum, but law reform and legal development are not devoid of broader context.[39] There is no reason to doubt that the uncertainty facing purchasers of land was genuine. However, notwithstanding the possibility that the uncertainty was more recent than Bean thought, questions remain as to why it was considered so pressing in 1484. These are best addressed by considering the other legislation enacted in the same Parliament.

The Statute of Richard III was one of sixteen public Acts passed in the 1484 Parliament which are, it is argued, best understood as part of a broad, populist legislative agenda promoted by the new regime. In addition to the Statute of Richard III, 1 Ric III, c 2 abolished benevolences, a forced loan which had been heavily utilised by Edward IV. 1 Ric III, c 3 allowed bail for those suspected of a felony and protected their goods from seizure. 1 Ric III, c 4 qualified the property requirements for men who could sit as jurors. 1 Ric III, c 5 removed Richard as a feoffee by transferring seisin to cestui que use, where the King was sole seised, or, to the other feoffees, where he was a co-feoffee. 1 Ric III, c 6 reinforced a statute of 1478 addressing courts of piepowder and introduced new penalties against rogue officials.[40] 1 Ric III, c 7 protected the rights of purchasers by condemning secret fines. 1 Ric III, c 8 was a detailed and technical statute addressing commercial dishonesty by legislating about the size and quality of cloth. The following six statutes were all protectionist trade measures,[41] and the final public statute, 1 Ric III, c 16, was highly political and concerned Elizabeth Woodville, the widow of Edward IV.

In considering the legislation passed by the 1484 Parliament, Hanbury described King Richard III as

> a singularly thoughtful and enlightened legislator, who brought to his task a profound knowledge of the nature of contemporary problems, and an enthusiastic determination to solve them in the best possible way.[42]

On first glance, Hanbury's conclusions do not appear to be unreasonable. However, more recent scholarship has taken a less favourable view of Richard III's legislation, dismissing Hanbury's characterisation as being implausibly pure and based upon a lack of understanding of Richard's immediate political situation.[43] Indeed, whilst Sir Francis Bacon, in his 1622 *History of Henry VII*, spoke of the 'politic and wholesome laws' passed by Richard III, he tempered this description by declaring them as being 'but the brocage of a usurper, thereby to woo and win the hearts of the people'.[44]

The politics of Richard's reign were dominated by the need for the King to find allies and bolster his position. Never before had a king usurped the throne with such a narrow base of supporters, and Richard's legislation should be viewed within that context. Previous usurpers, Henry IV and Edward IV, had been able to garner support

[39] DJ Ibbetson, 'Historical Research in Law' in M Tushnet and P Cane (eds), *Oxford Handbook of Legal Studies* (Oxford, Oxford University Press, 2005) 863.

[40] 17 Edw IV, c 2 (1478); *SR* (n 9) vol 2, 432.

[41] 1 Ric III, cc 9–15; *SR* (n 9) vol 2, 489–498.

[42] HG Hanbury, 'The Legislation of Richard III' (1962) 6 *American Journal of Legal History* 95.

[43] S Chrimes, *Henry VII* (London, Eyre Methuen, 1972) 82; Ross (n 1) 189.

[44] J Spedding et al (eds), *The Works of Francis Bacon, Baron of Verulam, Viscount of St Albans, and Lord High Chancellor of England* (Cambridge, Cambridge University Press, 2011; reprint of 1857 edn) vol 6, 26.

by appealing to those wanting change from the tyranny of Richard II and the incompetence of Henry VI. This was not the case for Richard III. While Richard's motivation for taking the throne lies far outside the scope of this chapter, it is important to note that there was clearly no general wish to see Edward V removed.[45] The legislation passed in 1484 can only be accurately viewed by acknowledging its context.

Following his usurpation, Richard initially pursued a policy of continuation from his brother's regime.[46] However, the 1483 rebellion, primarily led by Edward IV's former retainers, showed that this strategy had failed. There was an identifiable shift in policy at this point from appeasement and consolidation to more proactive attempts to bolster the regime; one manifestation of this change of tack was Richard's approach to law reform. As King, Richard was certainly active in his concern for the administration of justice.[47] This can be seen both in his legislation and in his taking the unusual step of summoning all the justices to appear before him in the Exchequer Chamber.[48] Whilst it can certainly be said that Richard took a genuine interest in the law, this is not to say that this concern for justice was not politicised.

Richard was particularly concerned to see that his consideration of justice was widely publicised.[49] The statute 1 Ric III, c 5 is a prime example of this practice. As we have noted, the statute concerned land that Richard had been enfeoffed of to the use of others and, by statute, transferred seisin from Richard to his co-feoffees or, if he were sole seised, to cestui que use. Through this, Richard sought to position himself as a neutral arbitrator in land disputes. He could simply have done this through conveying the land. However, by legislating, Richard was able to portray himself with the widest publicity as a fair and just king. The extent to which Richard was prioritising his public perception and reputation amongst the people can be further seen by considering his legislation in light of his financial situation.

By the statute 1 Ric II, c 2, Richard abolished benevolences, a form of forced loan which had become prominent and unpopular during Edward IV's reign.[50] That Richard was actively prioritising legislation which presented him favourably at the expense of his immediate financial interests can be seen in his repeal of Edward IV's statute from the previous year which had sought to limit the avoidance of feudal incidents by the employment of uses in the duchy of Lancaster.[51] In the preamble to the repeal, Richard declared that his concern for his people was of greater importance to him than personal profit.[52]

The political reality of 1484 was that Richard had an urgent need to appeal to a broader range of support and that this needed to be balanced against his financial

[45] Ross (n 1) 64–95, 47; Horrox (n 1) 89–137.

[46] Horrox (n 1) 138–149.

[47] Ross (n 1) 173–5.

[48] M Hemmant (ed), *Select Cases in the Exchequer Chamber before all the Justices* (1945) *Selden Society* xxxviii–xl, 86–94.

[49] Ross (n 1) 173–5.

[50] Benevolences were described by the Crowland Chronicler in 1486 as a 'new and unheard of imposition of a gift … whereby everyone was to give … what he wished, or more accurately, what he did not wish': N Pronay and J Cox (eds), *The Crowland Chronicle Continuations: 1459–1486* (London, Alan Sutton, 1986) 135–6.

[51] Hannay (2021) (n 15) 73–74.

[52] *Rot Parl* vol 6, 261b–262b: 'The king, notwithstanding that he conceives the said acts to be to his great profit and avail and to the great hurt and thraldom of his subjects having more affection to the common weal of this his realm and of his subjects than to his own singular profit' (I have modernised the text).

situation. The Italian spy, Dominic Mancini, who was in London during the spring and summer of 1483, noted that during the protectorate Edward Woodville took to sea with the majority of Edward IV's treasury and joined Henry Tudor in exile.[53] The Crowland Chronicler, who was unaware of this and thus considered Richard's financial situation to be far healthier than it was, tells us that by 1485 Richard was in serious fiscal difficulty and his financial situation was precarious.[54] When considering the administrative records, Steel suggested that Richard's financial crisis occurred much earlier in the reign than the Crowland Chronicler had thought.[55] In August 1483 Richard reduced the size of the Calais garrison, a decision which was largely driven by the reality of his financial situation.[56]

Given how precarious Richard's fiscal situation was, financial crisis was at the very least looming in early 1484, and we find further evidence of Richard's legislation being driven by his even more precarious political situation. Richard's finances were far from secure when he declared that 'affection to the common weal' was of greater, immediate importance than money.[57] And another illustration of this point can be found in 1 Ric III, c 2, a clearly populist statute, in which Richard abolished benevolences, a form of forced loan that had been used extensively by Edward IV. Although Richard was far from financially secure, his immediate need for popular support took priority, and by the early months of 1485 Richard had returned, in all but name, to utilising benevolences.[58]

In light of these considerations, Bean's concern that the 'uncertainty' facing purchasers alone was insufficient to explain the decision to legislate in 1484 can be addressed. It appears likely that Bean is correct in his assertion that the 'uncertainty' had existed long before 1484, since the practice of creating uses to perform a feoffor's last will had become commonplace by the late fifteenth century. The passage of the Statute of Richard III cannot be removed from its immediate political context, and it is through consideration of Richard's increasingly pressing need to bolster his regime that it is best understood.

As we have noted, in the first few months of his reign, Richard sought to pursue a policy of appeasement. The November 1483 rebellion, led by Edward IV's former household men, showed Richard that this had failed. It is probable that Richard's counsellors, in the short months between the Autumn rebellion and the opening of Parliament in January 1484, sought to promote legislation that presented the King in a favourable manner. In the Statute of Richard III, they likely saw the uncertainty faced by purchasers of land and sought to enact what they considered as a simple solution. However, a number of conceptual challenges arose, particularly around the nature of the interest, if indeed there was one at all, held by cestui que use, particularly as they

[53] CAJ Armstrong (ed), *The Usurpation of Richard III: Dominicus Mancinus ad Angelum Catonem de Occupatione Regni Anglie per Riccardum Tercium Libellus* (London, Alan Sutton, 1984) 80–81.

[54] *Crowland Chronicle* (n 50) 172–3. For more detail on Richard III's financial difficulties see A Brayson, 'The Fiscal Policy of Richard III of England' (2019) 40 *Quidditas: Journal of the Rocky Mountain Medieval and Renaissance Association* 139.

[55] A Steel, *The Receipt of the Exchequer, 1377–1485* (Cambridge, Cambridge University Press, 1954) 317–320.

[56] A Grant, 'Foreign Affairs Under Richard III' in J Gillingham (ed), *Richard III: A Medieval Kingship* (London, Palgrave Macmillan, 1993) 117.

[57] *Rot Parl*, vol 6, 261b.

[58] *Crowland Chronicle* (n 50) 172–175.

were now empowered to convey a legal title that would be good against his heirs and those holding only to his use. It is to the operation of the statute and these challenges that we now turn.

IV. Operation of the Statute of Richard III

The effect of the Statute of Richard III was to give cestui que use the power to convey a legal title, and that this title would be good against his heirs and those holding only to his use.[59] More specifically, it was enacted that every disposition of land or other hereditament,[60] which was made or had, or thereafter would be made or had,[61] by a person of full capacity,[62] would be 'good and effectual' against the disponor, his heirs, and those holding only to his use.[63] As Baker notes, the statute made no reference to feoffees but to those holding only to his use, and hence it applied to recoveries to uses and implied uses as well as express uses.[64] Whilst the statute was not enacted to give a power to cestui que use but to protect purchasers, its effect was to give cestui que use a power to convey the freehold estate that was held only to his use.[65]

On its face, the solution enacted by 1 Ric III, c 1 was a rather simple one. Purchasers faced uncertainty with regards to titles arising from 'secret and privy feoffments [to uses]', and the solution was to legislate for their titles to be 'good and effectual'. There was no need for anything further to affect the transfer. Indeed, in 1494 Bryan CJCP said that following a conveyance under the statute cestui que use could not instruct an attorney to enter and deliver seisin, for the statute only gave him the power to enter and make a feoffment.[66] The simplicity of the remedy could perhaps support the suggestion made previously that the statute was conceived in the short months between November 1483 and January 1484 as part of a broader, populist legislative programme. However, whilst the legislation was pragmatically designed to offer a simple solution to a clearly identified problem – that of uncertainty of title caused by the employment of uses – it raised a number of complex and intricate doctrinal questions.

[59] YB Pasch 4 Hen VII, f 8, pl 9 (1489) per Bryan CJCP: '*que chescun grant covien estre per custome, Common Ley, ou per Statut; et icy n'est ascun chose forsquez le Statut a faire le grant bon.*'

[60] For example, a rent: YB Pasch 4 Hen VII, f 8, pl 9 (1489); or an advowson: YB Pasch 6 Hen VII, f 3, pl 5 (1491); or an annuity: *Athowe v Waller* (1540) TNA PRO CP 40/969 m 309.

[61] That the statute acted retrospectively was confirmed in the Common Pleas in 1491: YB Mich 7 Hen VII, f 6, pl 9 (1501) per Kebell Sjt.

[62] There was no need for someone pleading a feoffment made under 1 Ric III, c 1 to allege that they were of full age: Yorke (n 28) 133, no 117 per Fitzherbert.

[63] The statute applied to 'every estate, enfeoffment, gift, release, grant, lease and confirmation': *SR* (n 9) vol 2, 477. Baker explains the statute in terms of a grant: Baker, *OHLE* (n 28) 655; however, 'disposition' is preferred here to reflect the wider range of terms in the statute.

[64] Baker, *OHLE* (n 28) 655, fn 22.

[65] Lincoln's Inn MS Maynard 3, ff 191–210 (Gregory Adgore's reading, c. 1490–91): '*C'est statute est fait tout pur l'advantage de vendees.*' YB Mich 5 Hen VII, f 3, pl 11 (1489): '*s'il entre et fait leas ou feoffment, pur ceo que le Statut don pouvoir a luy loyalment, et ceo tout pur avantage d'el lesse, et nemy pur avantage d'el feoffor.*' YB Hil 15 Hen VII, f 2, pl 4 (1490): '*[A]l Statut, ceo fuit fait en l'avantage de ceur que claim ascun interest pur le feoffor, et nemy per l'avantage le feoffor.*' YB Trin 15 Hen VII, f 12, pl 23 (1500): '*[L]e Statut de R. le 3 per feffment sur confidence ne fuit fait al feffor, mes al proft des auters qui purchase ve eur.*'

[66] YB Pasch 9 Hen VII, f 26, pl 13 (1494) per Bryan CJCP.

A particularly pertinent question arose with regard to what exactly it was that cestui que use was now empowered to convey. The statute depended on the disponor having the use, and following a disposition by cestui que use, the use would be in the purchaser. By operation of the statute, this alienation of the use gave the purchaser a legal title, and this title would be 'good and effectual' against cestui que use, his heirs and those holding only to his use. A title acquired under 1 Ric III, c 1 is perhaps best understood by considering relativity of title: such a title, by operation of the statute, would take priority over any other legal title.

Another question arises around the application of the statute where there were multiple cestuis que use. The statute provided for the plural,[67] but it is unclear whether cestuis que use had to sell together under the statute, as if they were joint tenants, or whether they could sell independently, as if they were tenants in common. Additionally, the statute had the effect of giving cestui que use what was essentially a legal power to devise land that was held to his use.[68] Although it was, technically speaking, the use that was devised, by the equity of the statute the devisee acquired the right to alienate the freehold.[69]

As well as questions concerning the interest of cestui que use, which will be considered in detail below, the statute also raised questions about the nature of the interest of those holding only to his use. Following the creation of an express feoffment to uses, this would be the feoffees. They were not themselves disseised by the statute, but their title was subject to a title acquired by conveyance under it. Therefore, if A conveyed the manor of Blackacre to B and C as feoffees to the use of A, and A then by operation of 1 Ric III, c 1 alienated to Z, the feoffees would retain a title in the fee simple, but this would be inferior to the title granted to Z. Further, if cestui que use granted a lease for a term of years under the statute, the feoffees would be liable to aid the lessee, as there was privity between them.[70]

Moreover, and in contrast to the effect of the later Statute of Uses (1536), the feoffees were not deprived of their power to alienate by the statute 1 Ric III, c 1. Thus, if the feoffees were to make a conveyance for valuable consideration and without notice of the use before a conveyance by cestui que use, then this would defeat cestui que use's power to convey under the statute. It has been suggested that this could have been used by a colluding cestui que use and his feoffees to deceive purchasers.[71]

The situation could be readily complicated if the estate that was held for the benefit of cestui que use was held for a term of years or was subject to remainders or, if entailed, to reversions. Perhaps even more complex were situations in which the use was conveyed for a term of years, or with remainders, or in tail.[72] The final clause of 1 Ric III, c 1 provided an exception from the operation of the law for anyone holding a 'right, title,

[67] *SR* (n 9) vol 2, 477: 'person or persons [...] seller, feoffor, giver or grantor [...] sellers, feoffors, givers or grants [...] his or their heirs.'

[68] Baker, *OHLE* (n 28) 657.

[69] YB Trin 19 Hen VIII, f 10, pl 4 (1527) per Shelley and Englefield JJ: '*[C]ar le dit Statut [1 Ric III, c 1] est, que feoffement, grant, release, ou confirmation, est fait per cestuy qui ad use est bon; et par l'equitie de mesme Statut chescun volunte de terre fait per cestuy que use est bon accordant.*'

[70] YB Mich 11 Hen VII, f 6, pl 26 (1496).

[71] F Sanders, *An Essay on Uses and Trusts and on the Nature and Operation of Conveyances at Common Law and of Those Which Derive Their Effect from The Statute of Uses* (London, E and R Brooke, 1791) vol 1, 23.

[72] A number of later Tudor cases that were difficult to reconcile on this point were explored by eighteenth century writers: J Gilbert, *The Law of Uses and Trusts* (London, R Gosling, 1734) 53–56; Sanders (n 71) vol 1, 23–30.

action and interest by reason of any gift in tail of the same'.[73] It appears that the provision in 1 Ric III, c 1 was intended to prevent the statute from being used by cestui que use in tail to bar entails, although this was subject to much subsequent debate.[74] However, notwithstanding these difficulties in the operation of the statute, its effect in strengthening the interest of cestui que use was clear.

V. Uses and the Beneficial Interest in Freehold Land after the Statute of Richard III

The issues raised by 1 Ric III, c 1 are both practical and deeply theoretical. That a conveyance made by cestui que use was now 'good and effectual' against him, his heirs and those holding only to his use raises a number of questions about what, if any, interest cestui que use had in the land. The importance of the statute, and the desire to understand its effects, was recognised almost immediately, with Gregory Adgore reading on the statute in the Inner Temple in around 1490–91.[75] Throughout his reading, Adgore was concerned with how uses – particularly in light of the statute – interacted with the broader common law of real property. It is likely that following the uncertainty about the effect of the statute, the lack of a secure doctrinal framework for the now widely employed use had become untenable.

As we have seen, upon the creation of a use, the feoffees would be seised of the land but were bound to the feoffor's wishes in conscience. Where a feoffor had enfeoffed feoffees to his own use, he was understood to retain the right to take the profits; however, the orthodox position, as outlined by Serjeant Frowyk in 1502, was that at common law he had 'no more to do with the land than the greatest stranger in the world'.[76] And as Audley noted in his 1526 reading,

> those to whom the use of such lands [...] belongs shall take the profits of such lands [...] through the confidence and sufferance of them in whom the possession exists at common law. And this is directly contrary to the learning of the common law ... for the common law adjudges the feoffee to be the true owner.[77]

Notwithstanding this common law orthodoxy, the position of cestui que use – particularly after the Statute of Richard III – was in fact more nuanced.

Adgore's reading is particularly noteworthy for the reader's repeated use of the English term 'owner' to describe cestui que use.[78] An important point which affects our

[73] *SR* (n 9) vol 2, 477.

[74] Baker, *OHLE* (n 28) 695.

[75] CUL MS Hh 3.10, ff 19–28; University of Kansas, MS D 127; Lincoln's Inn MS Maynard 3, ff 191–207; University College Oxford MS 162, ff 103–110. All subsequent references to Adgore's reading are to the Lincoln's Inn manuscript.

[76] *Dod v Chyttynden* (1502) YB Mich 15 Hen VII, f 13, pl 1; *Caryll Rep* (n 32) vol 2, 395–396, 396.

[77] BL MS Hargrave 87, f 437v. Printed in J Baker, *Baker and Milsom Sources of English Legal History: Private Law to 1750*, 2nd edn (Oxford, Oxford University Press, 2019) 118. Note that Baker cites the manuscript as f 438 but it is in fact 437v.

[78] Lincoln's Inn MS Maynard 3, ff 191–210, passim. See, eg, f 199v: '*Si un feoffee devie et son heir enter il est feoffee de trust et le owner poit enter sur luy*'. Note also YB Pasch 4 Hen VII, f 8, pl 9 per Wode sjt '*le Statut voile pouvoire a cestui que fuit owner a grant un rent*'.

understanding of both the Statute of Richard III and the nature of uses should be made here. Adgore used the term 'owner' in describing situations both before and after the statute. When describing situations before 1 Ric III, c 1, Adgore used the word 'owner' to describe a landholder before the creation of a use,[79] whereas after the statute he also uses 'owner' to describe cestui que use. This appears to suggest that in now having a power to convey legal title,[80] cestui que use was thought to have retained a degree of 'ownership' following the statute.[81]

Considering that feoffments to a feoffor's own use and to perform his will were common by the beginning of our period, it is not difficult to understand the description of a feoffor/cestui que use – particularly one who had now acquired a power to convey – as the 'owner'.[82] Soon after the statute was enacted, cestui que use had acquired a number of the hallmarks of ownership: he was now empowered to alienate the land by the statute, an action of formedon could lie against him,[83] and – as Serjeant Frowyk was forced to concede in *Dod v Chyttynden* (1502) – he could grant a lease for a term of years or to sell trees.[84]

The right of cestui que use to trees is particularly informative as to the effect of the Statute of Richard III on the developing nature of the interest held by cestui que use. That an effect of 1 Ric III, c 1 was the furtherance of the rights of cestui que use can be seen by contrasting Frowyk's 1502 concession with regards to trees with a number of earlier considerations of the issue. In a reported case from 1464, it was said by Moyle JCP that cestui que use could be sued for trespass if he felled timber.[85] Moreover, in his reading, Adgore stated that cestui que use could not licence another to fell trees.[86] Adgore did not consider the possibility of cestui que use felling timber himself, as in the 1464 case, presumably because he was concerned with the effect of the statute, which empowered cestui que use to alienate the land but, according to Adgore, did not empower him to licence another to fell trees.

The first positive indication that cestui que use was considered to have the right to trees on land held for his use came in 1492. In *Lady Hastings v Hungerford*, a case concerning the right to make the next presentation of an advowson, Serjeant Wode argued that, by the statute, cestui que use could grant the profits of the land, which included not only the presentation of the advowson but also trees; however, this point was contentious, and it was queried by the reporter.[87] The issue was also considered in

[79] Lincoln's Inn MS Maynard 3, f 191: '*Et avaunt le statute la ley voile a cel iour regard cestuy qui avoit estate en le terre [i.e. the feoffees] et done a luy power de faire estate et nemi l'owner et a cestui que use etc.*'

[80] YB Pasch 4 Hen VII, f 8, pl 9 per Bryan CJCP: '*que chescun grant covient estre per custome, Common Ley, ou per Statut; et icy n'est ascun chose forsquez le Statut a faire le grant bon.*'

[81] *Cf* Audley's later characterisation of the feoffees as the 'true owner': text to n 77 above.

[82] Another possibility is that the feoffor could also be amongst the feoffees, ie, a feoffment by A to A and B to the use of A. For a notable example of this see *Stonor's Case* (1497): YB Trin 12 Hen VII, f 19, pl 1; YB Mich 13 Hen VII, f 5, pl 3; *Caryll Rep* (n 32) vol 1, 363.

[83] 1 Hen VII, c 1 (1485).

[84] *Dod v Chyttynden* (1502) YB Mich 15 Hen VII, f 13, pl 1; *Caryll Rep* (n 32) vol 2, 395–396, 396: '*Et fuit touche que cesty a que use poit prender abres, auxibien come faire leas pur terme dans, per le equitie de novel estatut [1 Ric III, c 1], quaere: quod Frowike concessit.*'

[85] YB Pasch 4 Edw IV, f 8, pl 9 (1464). Printed in *Baker and Milsom* (n 77) 106, 107.

[86] Lincoln's Inn MS Maynard 3, f 202v.

[87] *Lady Hastings v Hungerford* (1492) *Caryll Rep* (n 32) vol 1, 75, 81, 102–104, 104 per Wode: '*Et par le statut il poit done une arber a une estrange et auter profits. Quere hoc, car semble que non. Et le presentment est*

two Year Book reports from Trinity term 1495.[88] The first case did not progress, as the pleading was adjudged jeofails. However, the report appears to suggest that if it had been pleaded correctly, it was not out of the question that cestui que use could licence another to fell trees on her behalf.[89] Although this initially appears to directly contrast with Adgore's point that cestui que use could not license another to fell trees, they may potentially be reconciled.[90] Whilst it is not clear from the report, it may be that cestui que use was able to fell trees himself, and it was at least arguable that he could permit a stranger to fell on his behalf.[91] Whereas, as was confirmed by the Common Pleas in the later Year Book report, he could not grant the right to fell trees to a stranger under the Statute of Richard III.[92]

Rather than one issue, it appears that these cases are in fact considering two distinct questions with regards to the rights of cestui que use to trees. Firstly, whether cestui que use could fell trees for himself (or perhaps licence another to fell for him, as in the mispleaded Year Book report); and, secondly, whether cestui que use could grant the right to the trees to a third party under the Statute of Richard III.

le profit del advowson'. Also reported in YB Trin 10 Hen VII, f 29, pl 24 (1495) and YB Hil 13 Hen VII, f 18, pl 24 (1498) where it is presumably misdated given that Caryll reports the case as being heard in Hilary and Michaelmas 1492. It was held in 1511 that cestui que use could not make the presentation himself: see n 102 below.

[88] YB Trin 10 Hen VII, f 26, pl 4 (1495); YB Trin 10 Hen VII, f 29, pl 24 (1495).

[89] YB Trin 10 Hen VII, f 26, pl 4. The case has been tentatively identified as also being a report of *Lady Hastings v Hungerford*. The unifying factor in the reports is the consideration of the question of whether cestui que use had the rights to take trees, but this is not enough to securely identify the Year Book report with *Hastings v Hungerford*. *Caryll's Reports* demonstrates that the primary issue in *Hastings v Hungerford* was the presentation of an advowson, and the case was sued with a writ of *quare impedit* with the taking of trees apparently as an illustrative example given by Wode. In contrast, in the Year Book, which reports a case begun by writ of trespass, the central issue was taking trees. Furthermore, there is biographical detail in the book report which appears to exclude *Hastings v Hungerford*, namely that the question centred on widow of cestui que use, which could not be Lady Hastings as Edward Hastings was her first husband, and he did not die until 1506. For the tentative identification of the Year Book report with *Hastings v Hungerford* see *Caryll Rep* (n 32) 75, no 81. Also identified as *Hastings v Hungerford* by Seipp in his year book database: www.bu.edu/phpbin/lawyearbooks/search.php (last accessed 22 August 2022), YB Trin 10 Hen VII, f 26, pl 4 (1495.054).

[90] Lincoln's Inn MS Maynard 3, f 202v.

[91] *Cf* it was mentioned in the *Damna Usuum* (c. 1533) that the feoffees could fine or imprison the third party if cestui que use licensed another to take timber, graze animals nor take them to slaughter on his behalf: SP 1/101, f 282 (JS Brewer et al (eds), *Letters and Papers of Henry VIII* (London, Longman, Green, Longman, & Roberts, 1862–1932) vol 10, no 246); Holdsworth (n 35) 579, nos 18, 19. For more detail on the *Damna Usuum* see AJ Hannay, 'Uses in the Later Fifteenth and Early Sixteenth Centuries' (unpublished PhD thesis, University of Cambridge 2022) 176–187.

[92] YB Trin 10 Hen VII, f 29, pl 24: '*Nota, que fuit tenur per les Justices de Comon Pleas, que cestuy que use ne poit done arbres, car Vavasour J. dit, que le Statut est encounter le Comon Ley, et ou ne poet borower de le Stat.*'. This case has also been tentatively identified as being a report of *Lady Hastings v Hungerford*, however, there is not enough to securely identify the report with *Hastings*. There is no mention of an advowson, the report solely concerns trees, and it is suggested by Bryan CJCP that although Kebell spoke he was not counsel in this case, whereas he was in *Hastings v Hungerford*: '*Si vraiment: Et vous avez un matiere pendant icy pur mesme la cause, de quel matiere vous ne parlez, nient obstant que il ad passe ove vous.*' It is perhaps more likely that two cases were being heard simultaneously, one concerning an advowson (*Hastings v Hungerford*), the second appearing in the two Year Book reports from Trinity Term 1495, concerning trees. The issues in the respective cases were clearly analogous, Wode made the comparison in *Hastings v Hungerford*, and Caryll reported both issues in his first report of *Hastings v Hungerford* (no 81), but it is more likely that they were separate cases. For the identification of the Year Book case with *Hastings v Hungerford* see: Baker *OHLE* (n 28) 657, fns 38, 42; *Caryll Rep* (n 32) 75, no 81. Also identified as *Hastings v Hungerford* by Seipp in his year book database: www.bu.edu/phpbin/lawyearbooks/search.php (last accessed 22 August 2022), YB Trin 10 Hen VII, f 26, pl 4 (1495.074).

As we have noted, it was held in 1464 that cestui que use could be sued for trespass if he felled trees,[93] but by the 1490s it appears to have been at least arguable that cestui que use could himself fell trees on land held for his use. The characterisation by Wode of the felling of trees with the taking of the profits of the land addressed the first question, that is, whether cestui que use had the rights to fell trees himself, and is interesting. When read alongside the mispleaded Year Book report, it suggests that there had been development in doctrinal thinking from the 1460s. This may be reflective of a more general, increasing understanding in the late fifteenth century of cestui que use as the pernor of profits, as also demonstrated by the statute 1 Hen VII, c 1, which allowed for writs of formedon to be brought against cestui que use.[94] Although Caryll queried Wode's characterisation, it was only his subsequent argument, that cestui que use could in turn grant the right to trees under the Statute of Richard III, that was expressly rejected by the Common Pleas.[95]

A decade after *Hastings v Hungerford*, questions around the rights of the cestui que use in land that was held for his use were once again revisited in *Dod v Chyttynden* (1502).[96] In the case, cestui que use was sued by a stranger for replevin after he had taken beasts for damage feasance. The case was first heard in Easter term 1502, and counsel for the defendant cestui que use, Kingsmill, argued that cestui que use was justified in his own right by his interest in the land. This was denied by the justices with the interesting exception of Wode, by now Chief Justice, who continued to argue for a more expansive view of the interest held by cestui que use.

The case was decided the following term when it was held that cestui que use could act but only on behalf of his feoffees.[97] However, the importance of *Dod v Chyttenden* for our purpose is an exchange in the first report.[98] In argument, Frowyk, relying on *Hastings v Hungerford*, made his famous remark that cestui que use 'by the course of the common law had no more to do with the land than the greatest stranger in the world'. However, he was forced to concede that cestui que use could, by the equity of the Statute of Richard III, lease the land for a term of years or sell timber.

The French verb in the report in relation to the trees is '*prender*', which directly translates as 'take'. However, Baker's preferred translation of 'sell' seems to be more appropriate in the context. As we have noted, the Statute of Richard III gave cestui que use a power to convey, and so, in interpreting the statute by its equity, it seems more appropriate that Frowyk was accepting that cestui que use could now grant the right to trees on land held for his use. This represents a significant doctrinal shift in the ten years since Wode first argued for cestui que use being able to grant the right to fell trees in *Hastings v Hungerford*, and Adgore had expressly rejected it in his reading, as the point

[93] YB Pasch 4 Edw IV, f 8, pl 9.

[94] Note also St German's subsequent characterisation of freehold land as consisting of two things: St German (n 6) 222: 'possession of the land … called freehold, and the other is the authority to take thereby the profits of the land'.

[95] YB Trin 10 Hen VII, f 29, pl 24.

[96] YB Hil 15 Hen VII, f 2, pl 4; YB Trin 15 Hen VII, f 12, pl 23; YB Mich 15 Hen VII, f 13, pl 1; *Caryll Rep* (n 32) vol 2, 395–396.

[97] *Caryll Rep* (n 32) vol 2, 407–409, 409. Note that this is reported as the first case that Frowyk argued as Chief Justice. He appeared as counsel in the first report, from Trinity term, but had been appointed Chief Justice following Wode's death before the case was decided the following term.

[98] ibid 395–396, 396.

was conceded without objection from Frowyk or even Vavasour, the judge who had initially rejected a wider interpretation of the statute in 1492.

Further developments saw confirmation that land held for the benefit of cestui que use could be sufficient qualification to serve on a jury,[99] although it was thought that this was at the discretion of the justices and, interestingly, would likely only be sufficient if the feoffees allowed cestui que use to take the profits.[100] It was also confirmed that, by virtue of 1 Ric III, c 1, cestui que use could grant the next presentation of an advowson to someone else[101] – though in 1511 it was acknowledged that he could not make the presentation himself[102] – and cestui que use could not distrain without his feoffees, nor could he support an action of trespass or forcible entry.[103] It was also debated in 1522 whether an action on the case at common law would lie against a disobedient feoffee.[104]

The Statute of Richard III was also important because it effected an increased familiarity with common law titles that were traced through uses, which caused common lawyers to consider the question of the devolution of the use.[105] That the right in use – *jus usus* or *jus in usu* – would automatically devolve to the heir of an intestate cestui que use was recognised by the late fifteenth century[106] and was central to the loophole addressed in 4 Hen VII, c 17 (1490). It is interesting to note in this context that Adgore appears to have considered a use to be a hereditament. Towards the end of his reading, Adgore discussed grants, and immediately following a short example of a use of land held for a term of years, he moved to discuss '*auter hereditaments*'.[107] The question of whether the beneficial interest under a trust was an hereditament was significant in the later seventeenth century, particularly following Lord Nottingham's work in

[99] *Lady Hastings v Hungerford* (1492) *Caryll Rep* (n 32) vol 1, 102, 104, fn 3; *Thorneden v Bewregard* (1507) TNA PRO KB 27/984, m 26; *Caryll Rep* (n 32) vol 2, 559; *Sandys v Bray* (1511) TNA PRO CP 40/993, m 541; JH Baker (ed), *The Reports of Sir John Spelman, vols 1 and 2* (1976–77) 93–94 *Selden Society* (hereafter *Spelman*) vol 1, 234, 236; JH Baker (ed), 'Anonymous Reports in the Time of Henry VIII' in *Reports of Cases from the time of King Henry VIII, vols 1 and 2* (2003–04) 120–121 *Selden Society* (hereafter *Anon Rep*) vol 1, 8–80, 24, 25–26; Littleton (n 20) 463.

[100] *Sandys v Bray* (1511) TNA PRO CP 40/993, m 541; *Spelman* (n 99) vol 1, 234, 236; *Anon Reps Henry VIII* (n 99) 24, 25–26. It is possible to speculate that this was limited to circumstances where a feoffor had enfeoffed feoffees for his own use and the feoffees held only to his use.

[101] *Litton v Harvey* (1502) TNA PRO CP 40/1070, m 103. See Baker, *OHLE* (n 28) 657, fn 37.

[102] *Sandys v Bray* (1511) TNA PRO CP 40/993, m 541; *Caryll Rep* (n 32) vol 2, 610; *Spelman* (n 99) vol 1, 234; *Anon Reps Henry VIII* (n 99) 24. Note that the question was left undecided in *Lady Hastings v Hungerford* (1492) YB Trin 10 Hen VII, f 29, pl 24; *Caryll Rep* (n 32) vol 1, 75, 81, 102.

[103] *Dokker v Slyngesby* (1488) TNA PRO KB 27/909, m 37; *Dod v Chyttynden* (1502) TNA PRO CP 40/960, m 437, *Caryll Rep* (n 32) vol 2, 391–393; YB Hil 15 Hen VII, f 2, pl 4; YB Trin 15 Hen VII, f 12, pl 23; YB Mich 15 Hen VII, f 13, pl 1; Baker, *OHLE* (n 28) 656, fns 27, 28.

[104] *Gresley v Saunders* (1522) TNA PRO CP 40/1046, m 415, CP Mich 1522. Reported: YB Pasch 14 Hen VIII, f 24, pl 2; *Spelman* (n 99) vol 1, 22–23; R Brooke, *La Graunde Abridgement* (1573), 'Feoffments al uses', pl 48. Printed in JH Baker (ed), *Year Books of 12-14 Henry VIII 1520–1523* (2002) 119 *Selden Society* 170–175.

[105] Baker, *OHLE* (n 28) 658, fn 45.

[106] For '*jus usus*' or '*jus in usu*' see: *Dod v Chyttynden* (1502) TNA PRO CP 40/960, m 437; *Glover v Lucas* (1502) CP 40/962, m 444; *Frebody v Baker* (1506) CP 40/978, m 454. For descent of '*usus*': *Atwode v Elice* (1498) CP 40/946, m 113; *Athowe v Waller* (1504) CP 40/969, m 309; *Carter v Grene* (1506) CP 40/974, m 594; YB Mich 21 Hen VII, f 33, pl 28 (1506); *Morton v Chippenham* (1507) KB 27/983, m 66. For descent to the customary heir in gavelkind land see *Parcywakk v Phylippe* (1502–4) CP 40/962, m 570. See also Baker, *OHLE* (n 28) 658, fns 46, 47.

[107] Lincoln's Inn MS Maynard 3, f 206v.

crystallising the beneficial interest under a trust as proprietary in nature,[108] yet its foundations appear to lie in the final decades of the fifteenth century.

VI. Conclusion

It is significant in the historical development of a tangible beneficial interest in freehold land that by the late fifteenth century – and particularly following the Statute of Richard III – cestui que use could alienate land that was held only for his use and that the use would descend in conscience to the heir of cestui que use.[109] It is clear that by the first decade of the sixteenth century, cestui que use had acquired a number of the hallmarks of ownership. However, this was far from absolute and created a number of difficult doctrinal questions.

It is important to note that the scope of the Statute of Richard III was limited. The statute sought to address a very specific problem, namely the uncertainty with regard to title facing purchasers of land caused by feoffments to uses. The statute did not apply to uses generally but only to those where the feoffees held freehold land only for the benefit of cestui que use.[110] That is to say, the statute was directed at the practice of landholders enfeoffing feoffees to their own use and did not apply more broadly. Notwithstanding this limitation, the situation was far from uncommon,[111] and the effect of the statute was significant.

In particular, the statute raised a number of questions about the interaction between the common law of real property and cestuis que use, whose rights were upheld in conscience and who had acquired a number of the key characteristics of ownership by the turn of the sixteenth century. Collectively these all went to the issue of whether the interest held by cestui que use was merely a personal right against the feoffees in conscience or had crystallised into a more tangible property right in land held for his use.

The issue was considered by the common law courts in *Gervys v Cooke* (1522) – a long and interesting case which concerned the question of whether a release by cestui que use would extinguish an annuity granted by his feoffees – in which it was acknowledged that uses were part of the common law.[112] Questions as to the personal or proprietary nature of the interest in cestui que use were also central to the arguments in *Dacre's Case* (1535).[113] Even Thomas Audley, in his highly critical 1526 reading, acknowledged that

[108] DEC Yale (ed), *Lord Nottingham's Chancery Cases* (1961) 79 *Selden Society* 90. For consideration of the question as to whether a use was a hereditament before the Statute of Uses see Jones (2007) (n 8).

[109] YB Mich 13 Hen VII, ff 5–6, pl 3 (1500), per Mordaunt sjt: '*le droit del terre en conscience discendist al heire le feoffour [...] le terre discend al heire en consciens*'.

[110] This distinction was central to Lord Nottingham's explanation of equitable estates after the Statute of Uses: Yale (n 2).

[111] YB Mich 15 Hen VII, f 13, pl 1; *Caryll Rep* (n 32) vol 2, 395–396, *per* Frowyk: 'the greater part of the land of England was in feoffments upon confidence'.

[112] *Gervys v Cooke* (1522) YB Mich 14 Hen VIII, f 4, pl 5, per Fitzherbert JCP: '*quar lez esez sount al comen ley*'; and per Broke JCP: '*Quar (come ad este dit) usez sount al common ley, et par comen reason, et solonque ceo serra pris et qualifie*'. Printed in 119 *Selden Society* (n 104) 108, 114–116.

[113] YB Pasch 27 Hen VIII, f 7, pl 22; *Spelman* (n 99) vol 1, 228–30. Printed in *Baker and Milsom* (n 77) 131–132. The second was whether cestui que use could make a will of land.

uses might be proprietary to an extent, but it must be noted that he argued that they were personal and based solely on the confidence and trust placed in the feoffees.[114] Detailed consideration of the answers given to these questions in the years building up to *Dacre's Case* lies outside the scope of this chapter, but it is likely that the interest in cestui que use by the 1520s was best understood as neither purely personal nor purely proprietary: it had elements of both. What is clearer, though, is that after the Statute of Richard III was enacted, cestui que use had a lot more to do with the land 'than the greatest stranger in the world'.[115]

[114] BL MS Hargrave 87, f 437v: 'Firstly, a use is a property or ownership of land or something else, real or personal, depending solely on the confidence and trust between those who are in actual possession and are accounted owners by the common law of such land and things whereon the use depends'. Printed in *Baker and Milsom* (n 77) 118.

[115] *Dod v Chyttynden* (1502) YB Mich 15 Hen VII, f 13, pl 1; *Caryll Rep* (n 32) vol 2, 395–396, 396, per Frowyk.

4

Epieikeia and the Common Law: The Rise and Fall of Equitable Interpretation of English Statutes

LORENZO MANISCALCO*

I. Introduction

It has been argued that the early modern association of the conscience-based jurisdiction of the Court of Chancery with Aristotelian equity, or *epieikeia* was a rather natural one, which found fertile ground among those lawyers learned in civil and canon law that occupied the Chancery in early modern times.[1] Indeed, medieval lawyers would probably have recognised the Chancery as a jurisdiction proceeding *ex aequo et bono* or *de aequitate*.[2] However, the concept of equity did not have anything to do with St German's *epieikeia* in this time. In fact, a more recent study by David Ibbetson has shown that anyone turning to civilian writings to explain the Chancery's jurisdictions in terms of *aequitas* or *epieikeia* would have found the landscape far from intuitive.[3]

Early modern civilians would also have shared Ibbetson's view that Aristotle's *epieikeia* was not particularly well suited for explaining the jurisdiction of the Chancery.[4] Alessandro Turamini (1554x8–1605), an auditor of the *Rota Fiorentina*, the highest court in the Grand Duchy of Tuscany,[5] wrote a commentary on the first book of the *Digest* of Justinian, published in 1590, which resembled that of his contemporaries in many respects, explaining that medieval lawyers had misunderstood the meaning of equity and that a proper understanding of it could only be had by looking to Aristotle,

* I am very grateful to Jacob Currie, Timothy Endicott, David Ibbetson, Joanna McCunn and Ian Williams for their helpful comments and suggestions. All translations are my own unless otherwise noted. English spelling has been modernised throughout.

[1] M Beilby, 'The Profits of Expertise: The Rise of the Civil Lawyers and Chancery Equity' in M Hicks (ed), *Profit, Piety and the Professions in Later Medieval England* (Gloucester, Sutton, 1990).

[2] See the discussion in C Donahue, 'Equity in the Courts of Merchants' (2004) 72 *Tijdschrift voor Rechtsgeschiedenis* 1.

[3] D Ibbetson, 'A House Built on Sand' in E Koops and WJ Zwalve (eds), *Law & Equity* (Leiden, Brill, 2014).

[4] ibid 60.

[5] L Martines, *Lawyers and Statecraft in Renaissance Florence* (Princeton, NJ, Princeton University Press, 1968) 126.

in the tenth chapter of the fifth books of the *Nichomachean Ethics*, where he dealt with *epieikeia*, in Latin *aequum et bonum* or more simply *aequitas*. For Turamini, the assimilation of equity to *epieikeia* distinguished 'civil equity' from the broader notion of 'natural equity'. Natural equity was that natural justice by reference to which a king or arbiter or other judge unbound by rules might decide:

> Aristotle [when discussing *epieikeia*] only talks about civil equity. [...] So those statutes that require a certain matter to be decided *ex bono et aequo*, should be intended to refer to natural equity only.

He gives an example, dealing with the civil law rule that a naked pact, an agreement not amounting to a recognised contract or 'clothed' by some other ground of recognition, gives no action. As Turamini explains,

> in courts of merchants, or before an arbiter, or whatever other judge deciding from what is *aequo et bono* [...] one's argument that a naked pact gives no action would be rejected. Because there *aequum et bonum* refers to natural equity. In respect of civil equity [i.e. *epieikeia*], however, such an addition would be superfluous be superfluous.[6]

The Chancellor's jurisdiction would have been, for Turamini, a fairly familiar example of jurisdiction deciding *ex aequo et bono* – by 'natural' equity – that is, as opposed to *epieikeia*, the 'civil' equity that pertains to the office of the judge.[7]

This chapter will focus on the extent to which common lawyers, following the diffusion of equity as *epieikeia* in the sixteenth century, developed equity in the sense that would have seemed more intuitive across the continent, that is, as a doctrine of interpretation of the law beyond the letter. I shall first briefly deal with the medieval development of equity, in particular with the case of the equity of the statute and the difference between these ideas and the more general doctrine of purposive interpretation with which equity became associated in early modern times. I shall then locate the diffusion of *epieikeia* thinking among English lawyers within the broader intellectual context of the Renaissance before moving on to the approaches of *epieikeia* in this sense that can be identified among legal writers in England throughout the period, showing that the time of greatest popularity for equity as a doctrine for equitable interpretation was that which ran from 1550 to c. 1630. Finally, I will sketch out its gradual decline and supplantation from the seventeenth century onwards with the familiar association of equity with the Court of Chancery.

II. Equity and Interpretation in the Medieval Period

It is well known that in the Middle Ages the meaning of equity among English lawyers resembled the meaning which it had among civil lawyers insofar as it was used as a broad synonym for justice. In that sense, 'equity'

[6] A Turamini, *Ad Rubricam Pandectarum de Legibus Libri Tres* (Florence, F Tosium, 1590) 162–3.

[7] The distinction between natural and civil equity can be traced back to Baldus: C Lefebvre, *Les Pouvoirs du Juge en Droit Canonique* (Paris, Sirey, 1938) 191, when it was associated with the distinction between natural justice and the justice derived from the application of civil law rules. It is perhaps in this sense that it was revived in the seventeenth century by Lord Nottingham when he distinguished between a natural (*naturalis et interna*) and a civil (*civilis et politica*) 'conscience' adopted by the Chancellor, distinguishing between one's sense of natural justice and the justice arrived at by applying the rules of Chancery. See DEC Yale (ed), *Lord Nottingham's Chancery Cases, vol I* (1954) 73 *Selden Society* 371.

> was known to English lawyers under the name of 'reason', or rightwiseness, the sense of right and wrong which inspired and explained all legal doctrine, preserved consistency, and prevented absurdities.[8]

It was in this sense that *Bracton* defined it, borrowing from Azo's well-known *Summa* of Justinian's *Institutes* as a 'harmony of things which requires like law in like cases'.[9] The association between equity and Aristotelian *epieikeia* was owed to theologians, and, apart from at least one passage in Sir John Fortescue, no particular attention was drawn to it by medieval English lawyers.[10] The association of equity with *epieikeia* was a matter for theologians, starting with Aquinas, but the theological understanding of *epieikeia* was not particularly influential among lawyers in the medieval period.[11]

There was a particular context, however, in which medieval English lawyers applied equity to interpretation, namely in the doctrine known as the 'equity of the statute'. Samuel Thorne, discussing the operation of the doctrine in the fourteenth and fifteenth centuries, explained that

> The strict, literal meaning of a statute may be extended, but only slightly extended, through use of the doctrine of the statute's equity.[12]

The examples provided by Thorne include the extension of an action given to 'tenants for years' to a tenant for merely half a year; the extension of a statute against a jailer letting out of prison a party in arrears for account to a case where the jailer lets out one condemned for debt; and the extension of an action granted to executors to administrators too.[13]

This use of equity has some parallel with uses of the concept found among medieval civil lawyers,[14] and indeed a few sources talk about the 'equity of the law' (*aequitas legis*) as the spirit or *ratio* of the law, but this was not developed by legists as a self-standing doctrine of interpretation.[15] In his comment to the *Libri Feudorum* of 1393, Baldus (1327–1400) had said that

> the [extension of the law] on grounds of similarity requires that equity which binds together similar cases, so that all extensive interpretations of statutes ought to be founded on equity.[16]

[8] JH Baker, *Oxford History of the Laws of England, Volume VI: 1483-1558* (Oxford, Oxford University Press, 2003) 40. See also N Doe, *Fundamental Authority in Late Medieval English Law* (Cambridge, Cambridge University Press, 1990) ch 5.

[9] SE Thorne (ed), *On the Laws and Customs of England* (Cambridge, MA, Harvard University Press, 1968) vol 2, 25; amesfoundation.law.harvard.edu/Bracton/Unframed/Latin/v2/25.htm (last accessed 20 November 2025). This definition of equity was originally based on Cicero, *Topica* 4.23, but *Bracton*'s source is Azo. For the relationship between *Bracton* and Azo see FW Maitland, *Select Passages from Bracton and Azo* (1894) 8 *Selden Society*. For Cicero's text see HM Hubbell (trans), Cicero, *On Invention. The Best Kind of Orators. Topics* (Cambridge, MA, Harvard University Press, 1949) 396.

[10] Sir John Fortescue, '*De Natura Legis Naturae* 1.24' in T Fortescue (ed), *The Works of Sir John Fortescue, Knight* (London, printed for private distribution, 1869) vol 2, 85–86. See also Doe (n 8) 102.

[11] L Maniscalco, *Equity in Early Modern Scholarship* (Leiden, Brill, 2020) 33–43.

[12] SE Thorne, 'The Equity of a Statute and Heydon's Case' (1936–7) 31 *Illinois Law Review* 202, 210.

[13] See the cases cited in Thorne (n 12) 210.

[14] See W Ullmann, *The Medieval Idea of Law as represented by Lucas de Penna* (London, Methuen, 1946) 41–4; A Gewirth (ed), *Marsilius of Padua, The Defender of Peace* (New York, NY, Columbia University Press, 1951–56) vol 2, 37–44, 58, 190.

[15] E Cortese, *La Norma Giuridica* (Milan, Giuffrè, 1964) vol 1, 268–271, 275–293, cited in L Maniscalco '*Interpretatio ex aequo et bono*: The Emergence of Equitable Interpretation in European Legal Scholarship' in M Lobban and I Williams (eds), *Networks and Connections in Legal History* (Cambridge, Cambridge University Press, 2020) 239, fn 18.

[16] Baldus, *Commentaria in Usus Feudorum* (Pidié, 1552) *ad LF* 2.53(54) f 77ra.

No evidence of direct borrowing from civilian sources has yet come to light, but the doctrine of the 'equity of the statute' had, by the fifteenth century, settled around a doctrine of *interpretatio extensiva* not too dissimilar from that advanced by Baldus. The first reference to such an interpretation of the law springing from the 'equity' of the law is from 1330, and the earliest reference to an 'equity of the statute' is from 1374, but before the fifteenth century many such extensions were also made without reference to either.[17] By the fifteenth century, references become very frequent. In 1410 alone we can count seven cases in the yearbooks decided under the equity of a statute, or where that doctrine is at least mentioned.[18]

The doctrine was a rather narrow one and did not have much in common with *epieikeia*. First, it only served to effect 'simple and reasonable' extensions of the words of the statute.[19] Of course, statutes could also be interpreted restrictively, but this operation was not described as having anything to do with the 'equity' of the statute; it was rather described as involving a '*construction reasonablement*'.[20] Second, the extension of statutes was limited by the judges' 'jealousy for the common law which was not to be modified by statute more than could be avoided'.[21] This meant that an extension by equity could not be had where the statute 'abridges' the common law, but only whenever it 'enlarges the common law'.[22]

Beyond that, in the words of TFT Plucknett,

> neither counsel nor judges enquired into the nature of statutes and legislation, the sovereignty of Parliament, the supremacy of the Common Law, the functions of the judicature, and all the other questions which the modern mind finds so absorbingly interesting.[23]

Equity in that period, on the continent as in England, had nothing in common with Aristotelian *epieikeia* or with a broader doctrine of purposive interpretation.[24]

III. *Epieikeia* and Equitable Interpretation

A. *Epieikeia* in European Legal Scholarship

Equity and *epieikeia* were only truly associated with one another to form a doctrine of equitable interpretation in the early modern period. I have traced this diffusion

[17] The earliest reference to the equity of the law (*equitie de ley*) I have found is in (1330) YB Hil 4 Edw III ff 4b–5b, pl 7; the earliest to an equity of the statute seems to be (1374) YB Hil 48 Edw III, ff 1b–2b, pl 4. But, for instance, in 1347 such a statutory extension was made without reference to either doctrine, see (1347) YB Trin 21 Edw III, ff 21a–21b, pl 1 and (1389) YB Trin 13 Ric II, ff 9–11, pl 4.

[18] (1410) YB Hil 11 Hen IV, ff 40a–40b, pl 4; (1410) YB Hil 11 Hen IV ff 45b–47a, pl 20; (1410) YB Hil 11 Hen IV, ff 54b–55a, pl 36; (1410) YB Pasch 11 Hen IV, ff 56a–56b, pl 2; (1410) YB Pasch 11 Hen IV, ff 65b–67b, pl 25; (1410) YB Trin 11 Hen IV, ff 76a–78b, pl [17, not 18]; (1410) YB Mich 12 Hen IV, ff 1b–3a, pl 3.

[19] See the cases cited in Thorne (n 12) 210–1.

[20] ibid 205–6.

[21] ibid 208.

[22] ibid 211–3. It may be interesting to compare this with the *ius commune* rules that a penal statute and one that went against the reason of the law (*ratio iuris*) should not be interpreted extensively, as to which see B Caepolla, *De interpretatione legis extensiva* (Venice, Montisferrati, 1557) ff 44, 59v–60.

[23] TFT Plucknett, *Statutes and Their Interpretation in the First Half of the Fourteenth Century* (Cambridge, Cambridge University Press, 1922) 70–1.

[24] P Vinogradoff, 'Reason and Conscience in Sixteenth-Century Jurisprudence' in id, *Collected Papers* (Oxford, Oxford University Press, 1928) vol 2, 191.

elsewhere and provided an outline of the reasons behind it. In brief, the association of equity and *epieikeia* was a product of legal humanism. It seems to have been linked to a resurgence of interest in the works of Aristotle and to their new translations. The first effect of these translations was to encourage humanist jurists commenting on the first book of the *Digest* and specifically on the passage describing law as the art of the good and the equitable (*boni et aequi*) (D.1.1.1.pr) to talk about this *bonum et aequum* as referring to Aristotle's *epieikeia*. Within 50 years from the first mention of this argument by Guillaume Budé (1467–1540), associations of both D.1.1.1.pr and of references to *aequitas* in general with Aristotle were ubiquitous around Europe.[25]

A number of legal writers went a step further and seized the chance to take Aristotle seriously and develop a theory of interpretation based on equity as *epieikeia*. For example, Mario Salomoni degli Alberteschi (c. 1460–1533) in his *Commentarioli* written in 1525 argued that equity understood as *epieikeia* is a

> perfect reason which interprets and amends laws as well as any writing or saying. [This happens when] we prefer the will over the letter, when we prefer what is benign, when we add what has been omitted and, generally, when we carry out whatever right reason requires, as opposed to an interpretation that treacherously points to the strict words under pretence of equity (*iniuriae calumnia et nimis callida iuris interpretatione*).[26]

Salamoni's ideas were rather successful among his contemporaries and found their way into most accounts of equity in legal works, including legal dictionaries[27] legal works of French Calvinists,[28] of Catholic scholastic theologians,[29] and generally among civil[30] and canon lawyers.[31] That said, the substantive role of *epieikeia* throughout this period was rather limited – the doctrines of interpretation departed little from the medieval ones of *interpretatio restrictiva* and *extensiva*, and *epieikeia* worked as little more than a theoretical justification for them.[32] It is perhaps for this reason that the role of *epieikeia* as the basis for theories of interpretation gradually lost its appeal over the following decades, and, aside from a role retained among canon law works, it had disappeared from most treatises on interpretation by the first half of the eighteenth century.[33]

[25] Maniscalco, *Equity* (n 11) ch 2.

[26] M Salamoni, *Commentarioli in librum I Pandectarum* (Rome, M Calvi, 1525) 7–8, 10–13. See Maniscalco, *Equity* (n 11) 54–63.

[27] Maniscalco, *Equity* (n 11) 107–109.

[28] See, eg, F Connan, *Commentariorum Iuris Civilis Libri X* (Paris, I Kerver, 1553) ff 44–47; F Douaren, *Omnia ... Opera* (Frankfurt, A Wecheli, 1592) 1057–74; Maniscalco, *Equity* (n 11) 85–91.

[29] See, eg, Martín de Azpilcueta (1491–1586), *Commentarius Utilis in Rubricam de Iudiciis* (Rome, I Tornerii, 1585) 48–54; Didacus de Covarrubias (1512–1577), *Opera Omnia* (Antwerp, G Lestenius, 1627) 425. See too Maniscalco, *Equity* (n 11) 139–49.

[30] See, eg, at either end of our period D Godefroy (1549–1622), *Corpus Iuris Civilis* (Lyon, B Honorati, 1583) *ad 'aequitatisque'*, col 192; N von Lyncker (1643–1726), *Commentaria Lynckeriana in Jus Civile Universum* (Jena, J Belckium, 1698) 69–70.

[31] EG Tellez (d 1649), *Commentaria Perpetua in ... Decretalium* (Lyon, A Posuel, 1673) 68; A Reiffenstuel (1642–1703), *Jus Canonicum Universum* (Venice, A Bortoli, 1700) 156; FX Schmalzgrueber (1663–1735), *Jus Ecclesiasticum Universitum* (Venice, Typographia Remodiniana, 1738) I 68.

[32] See Maniscalco, *Equity* (n 11) 153–64, 205–8.

[33] ibid 205–16.

B. *Epieikeia* in Christopher St German

Aside from a few references in earlier authors, the history of equity as *epieikeia* in English legal scholarship truly begins only with St German's publication of his *Dialogus de Fundamentis Legum Anglie et de Conscientia* in 1528.[34] St German's work came out exactly 20 years after Budé's *Annotationes* and three years after Salomoni's *Commentarioli.* The only other legal works to include a discussion of equity before St German's were Juan Luis Vives's *Aedes Legum*, published in 1519, and Claude Chansonnette's *Topica Legalia*, published in 1520.[35] However, it is easy to see that St German's work shared almost nothing with the approach to equity adopted in those works. Indeed, there is no evidence (apart from its timing) that St German's interest in equity and the analogy with *epieikeia* was connected in any way to the proliferation of discussions of equity on the continent.[36] As is well known, St German drew in part from the discussion of *epieikeia* found in medieval theology. In particular, many aspects of St German's analysis unmistakeably belong to the tradition of Jean Gerson (1363–1429).[37] But the most important ideas found in St German are entirely original. Both the idea that *epieikeia* can be performed by a judicial body separate from that of regular courts and that *epieikeia* should play a role in aligning human law with the requirements of conscience have no parallel in any other writings and are owed to the peculiar jurisdictional point of view from which St German was writing, one in which the body doing equity – the Chancery – was known as a court of conscience.[38] More generally, St German also provided an original definition of *epieikeia* as 'an exception of the law of God or of the law of reason from the general rules of the law of man', which, while consistent with the writings of Aquinas and Gerson, is put in these terms by neither author.[39]

The most important feature of *Doctor and Student* that substantively set apart its theory of equity from the contemporary learning on equity by humanist jurists was the fact that it separated *epieikeia* from equitable interpretation. The doctor asks the student (in relation to the equity achieved in Chancery) 'is there any mention made in the laws of England of any such equities?' And the student replies clearly that

> of this term equity to that intent that it is spoken of here there is no special mention made in the laws of England, but of an equity derived upon certain statutes mention is made many times and often in the law of England. But that equity is all of another effect than this is.[40]

[34] TFT Plucknett and JL Barton (eds), C St German, *Doctor and Student* (1974) 91 *Selden Society* xiv–xv. A 1523 edition is recorded in J Ames, *Typographical Antiquities* (Cambridge, Cambridge University Press, 2015) vol III, 86, but it may be a ghost created by its editor, William Herbert: EJ Devereux, *A Bibliography of John Rastell* (Montreal, McGill-Queen's University Press, 1999) 149.

[35] JL Vives, *Aedes Legum* (Louvain, T Martens, 1519); C Chansonnette, *Topica Legalia* (Basel, A Cartandrum, 1520) 115–7.

[36] Maniscalco, *Equity* (n 11) 53–97.

[37] P Vinogradoff, 'Reason and Conscience in Sixteenth Century Jurisprudence' (1908) 24 *Law Quarterly Review* 373; St German (n 34) xx–xxx; Z Rueger, 'Gerson's Concept of Equity and Christopher St German' (1982) 3 *History of Political Thought* 1.

[38] St German (n 34) 100–3.

[39] Compare St German (n 34) 96–7 with Gerson's '*De Non Esu Carnium*' in P Glorieux (ed), *Œuvres Completes* (Paris, Desclée & Cie, 1960–73) vol 3, 83. Aquinas only talks explicitly about equity addressing a violation of the law of nature in one passage of the *Summa*: *Summa Theologiae IIa IIae* q 60, art 5; online at www.corpusthomisticum.org/sth3057.html (last accessed 20 November 2025).

[40] St German (n 34) 104–5. More references to the doctrine of the equity of the statute are made in the second dialogue without further analysis at 178, 254 and 272.

The express separation of *epieikeia* from even the closest English analogy to equitable interpretation – the medieval doctrine of the equity of the statute – is striking and very clear: equity and interpretation belong to different spheres.

It is interesting to note, however, that in the later English edition of *Doctor and Student* from 1531, St German added a passage that sits oddly alongside the one mentioned above. The student later claimed that in some cases

> the parties shall be helped in the same court and by the common law. And thus it appears that sometime a man may be excepted from the rigour of a maxim of the law by another maxim of the law. And sometimes from the rigour of a statute by the law of reason and sometime by the intent of the makers of the statute, but yet it is to be understood that most commonly where any thing is excepted from the general customs or maxims of the law of the realm by the law of reason, the party must have his remedy by a writ that is called sub poena.[41]

It is unclear what this passage was meant to add to the discussion. One possibility is that it was meant to recognise the growing association of the equity of the statute with a broader doctrine of purposive interpretation associated with *epieikeia*. We shall return to this role for equity below. What is certain is that this passage, especially its reference to the rigour of a statute being mitigated 'by the law of reason and sometime by the intent of the makers of the statute', resonated much more strongly with the humanist concept of equitable interpretation.

Doctor and Student was as original in its approach to equity as it was successful among lawyers – whether or not it was meant for them.[42] This is significant, because it caused the work to operate as the most significant counterweight to the influence of the civilian approach to equity as interpretation, indeed eventually displacing it entirely.[43]

C. *Epieikeia* and Equitable Interpretation in English Law

(i) *Early Modern Statutory Interpretation*

It is well known that a number of legal works produced in early modern times showed an increasing interest in legal interpretation and specifically in the interpretation of statutes.[44] This seems to have been a response to the fact that late fifteenth- and sixteenth-century Parliaments achieved 'more or less unqualified sovereignty' and were producing an 'ever-increasing torrent of legislation'. Statutes were not only more numerous but were also longer and more complex, something that contemporary commentators did not necessarily associate with increasing substantive sophistication as much as with the many '*tautologia* and *cakaphonia* penned in barbarous English' that plagued their drafting.[45] The response of common lawyers was to

[41] St German (n 34) 103. See also the practical examples added to the 1531 edition to support this role for equity at pp 99–101. I am indebted to Timothy Endicott for pointing these out to me.

[42] Baker, *OHLE* (n 8) 501; I Williams, 'Christopher St German: Religion, Conscience and Law in Reformation England' in M Hill and RH Helmholz (eds), *Great Christian Jurists in English History* (Cambridge, Cambridge University Press, 2017).

[43] See Part V below, and generally NG Jones, ch 9 in this volume.

[44] SE Thorne, 'Introduction' in Anon (ed), *A Discourse upon the Exposicion and Understanding of Statutes* (San Marino, CA, Huntington Library, 1942) 1–13; Baker, *OHLE* (n 8) 76–82.

[45] JH Baker, *English Law under Two Elizabeths* (Cambridge, Cambridge University Press, 2021) 91–2.

develop techniques of interpretation that gave intentions a central role.[46] The intentions of the legislator appear with relative frequency from the 1460s onwards in the Year Books,[47] and around that time the latter also became associated with the equity of the statute.[48] This growing interest and association of the equity of the statute with the intentions of the legislator was fertile ground for the use of Aristotle's *epieikeia* in what was perhaps its most intuitive application, that is, the equitable interpretation of statutes.

Two examples from the first part of this period may be mentioned. One was *La Graunde Abridgement* by Sir Robert Broke (d 1558), published posthumously in 1573 but written at some time between 1555 and 1558.[49] Broke's was the first abridgement to devote a separate title to 'Parliament and Statutes', including 109 entries on statutory interpretation.[50] One of the first treatises making the link to equity explicit was the *Discourse upon the Exposition and Understanding of Statutes* by William Fleetwood (c. 1525–1594), which dates back to the 1560s.[51] In the seventh chapter of the *Discourse*, the author explains that the interpretation of statutes by equity 'concerns the sense and meaning of a statute'.[52] Fleetwood provides a series of rules concerning how one is to understand the meaning and purpose of a statute,[53] but does not break free from the medieval learning on construing statutes strictly whenever they abridge (ie, restrict, rather than extend the effect of) the common law or are 'penal'.[54] It is only once the relationship with the common law is established that one can move on to consider the intentions of the legislators (*mente legislatorum*), because the common law is based on common reason, and statutes should not be construed extensively against it.[55] Fleetwood reconciled the growing concern for the intentions of the legislator in statutory interpretation with the medieval doctrine of the equity of the statute without departing from the orthodox rules that allowed for the extensions of statutes by their equity depending on their relationship with the common law and on whether they were penal or otherwise.

[46] The 'intentions of those who made the statute' (*entendement de ceux qr firent lestatut*) can be found mentioned in argument as early as 1324, but only in few cases, and never associated with the statute's equity: (1324) YB Hil 17 Ed II, f 515, pl [7]; (1330) YB Trin 4 Edw III, f 30 pl 8; (1331) YB Pasch 5 Ed III, f 19, pl 23. More often in this period one finds the 'intention of the statute' (*lentendement de Statut*) referred to: (1325) YB 19 Edw II, ff 630–631, pl [26]; (1332) YB 6 Edw III, f 10, lib ass 3; (1333) YB Trin 7 Edw III, ff 24–25, pl 7; (1334) YB Pasch 8 Edw III, ff 35–6, pl 41; (1340) YB Mich 14 Edw III, ff RS 43–51, pl 16; (1344) YB Mich 18 Edw III, ff RS 27–29, pl 10; (1350) YB Mich (2) 24 Edw III, ff 67–69, pl 76.

[47] The 'intent of those who made the statute' (*entente del fesans/de ceux que fieront le statute*) appears in eg, (1463) YB Mich 3 Edw III, ff 19–20, pl 13; (1463) YB Mich 3 Edw IV, f 24, pl 18; (1464) YB Pasch 4 Edw IV, ff 3–5, pl 4; (1489) YB Trin 4 Hen VII, ff 10–12, pl 6; (1495) YB Hil 10 Hen VII, ff 15–16, pl 13; (1495) YB Hil 10 Hen VII, ff 17–18, pl 17. See also (1506) YB Hil 21 Hen VII, ff 16–17, pl 28, at 17.

[48] See, eg, (1463) YB Mich 3 Edw IV, ff 19–20, pl 13; (1499) YB Hil 14 Hen VII, ff 17–19, pl 7 at 18 and *Dod v Chyttynden* (1502) 2 Caryll 407 quoted in Baker, *OHLE* (n 8) 80, fn 185.

[49] JH Baker, 'Broke, Sir Robert (d. 1558)' Oxford Dictionary of National Biography (Oxford University Press, 2004) doi.org/10.1093/ref:odnb/3497 (last accessed 20 November 2025).

[50] R Broke, *La Graunde Abridgement* (London, R Tottelli, 1573), part 2, ff 119–123.

[51] JH Baker, *The Reinvention of Magna Carta 1216-1616* (Cambridge, Cambridge University Press, 2017) 232–237.

[52] See nn 22–23 above and Thorne (n 44) 140.

[53] ibid 142–3.

[54] ibid 143, 159–60.

[55] ibid 151.

(ii) Plowden and Equitable Interpretation by Epieikeia

The development outlined above had prepared the ground for Aristotelian *epieikeia* to become the basis for equitable interpretation, aligning it with its use among legal writers across Europe. The main evidence for this comes from the reports and commentaries of Edmund Plowden (1519/20–1585). Plowden himself had a peculiar interest in equity as *epieikeia*, and his approach to equitable interpretation has already been examined in some detail by legal historians.[56] It is important to bear this in mind because Plowden did not report the views of lawyers and judges word for word in his *Commentaries* and sometimes expressed them 'in other words added by [him], showing the matter more fully'; the interest in Aristotle's doctrine that may appear to have been shared by mid-sixteenth-century judges and lawyers throughout the *Commentaries* may therefore simply be a reflection of Plowden's own enthusiasms.[57] Aside from this, the publication of Plowden's *Commentaries*, in particular of the second volume in 1579, had a momentous impact on the diffusion of uses of *epieikeia* as the basis for equitable interpretation throughout English sources and was perhaps second only to *Doctor and Student* in terms of the influence it exerted on the English legal concept of equity.

If the reports are to be trusted, from the 1550s onwards a growing number of lawyers and judges were using *epieikeia* as a principle of statutory interpretation. The main features of the use of equity through Plowden's *Commentaries*, and those which distinguish it from the previous uses of the equity of the statute, are that: (i) references to the 'equity of the statute' depart from the medieval orthodoxy to describe the doctrine as a more general one related to interpretation beyond the letter, and (ii) such a general understanding of the equity of the statute is specifically linked to the meaning of equity as Aristotle's *epieikeia*.

As to the first point, it is important to bear in mind that most references to the equity of the statute in Plowden's *Commentaries* simply involve a use of it in line with medieval precedents.[58] However, a number of authorities display a tendency to take the doctrine of the statute in a different direction, either by using it for purposes other than the simple extension of statutes to cases not covered by their words or by departing from those medieval rules that confined the doctrine to cases where statutes enlarged the common law or were beneficial.

Fulmerston v Steward[59] was a case concerning the validity of a lease made by the Master and Fellows of Rushworth in Norfolk to one Simeon Steward. One of the arguments made was that the lease was rendered void by Henry VIII's Second Suppression Act.[60] One point turned on the interpretation of a section of the Act which held that

> if [any ecclesiastical governor] [...] hath made any demise, lease, or grant, to any person for years [...] then the same person, to whom any such demise, lease, or grant has been made, shall have and hold the same tenements for the term of 21 years only.

[56] G Behrens, 'Equity in the Commentaries of Edmund Plowden' (1999) 20 *Journal of Legal History* 25. It has been argued that the subject had 'a peculiar fascination for him': Thorne (n 44) 55–6. See too SE Prall, 'The Development of Equity in Tudor England' (1964) 8 *American Journal of Legal History* 1.

[57] E Plowden, 'Prologue' in *Les Comentaires ou les reportes de Edmunde Plowden* (London, R Tottelli, 1571) v.

[58] See, eg, *Wimbish v Tailbois* (1550) 1 Plow 38, 75 ER 63.

[59] *Fulmerston v Steward* (1554) 1 Plow 101, 75 ER 160.

[60] (1539) 31 Hen VIII, c 13.

The lease had been made for 50 years, and the question was whether the effect of the statute would be to shorten it to 21 years or make it void.[61] Bromley CJ (d 1555) argued that it would be against all equity and reason to interpret it in the second sense and that

> our predecessors, have sometimes expounded the words [of statutes] quite contrary to the text, and sometimes have taken things by equity contrary to the text, in order to make them agree with reason and equity.[62] [... If] the words of statutes shall be construed contrary to the text, and things shall be taken by the equity of statutes in other manner than the principal provision of the statute is, [...] then I say, that in our principal case the said words ('so that such lease or leases shall not exceed 21 years') [...] may not be conditional, nor defeat the whole estate, but shall be taken by reason to abridge the estate unto 21 years.[63]

Here the equitable interpretation of the statute does not involve its extension but rather a reading of its words in accordance with reason. Bromley CJ presents this as an orthodox meaning of the equity of the statute, citing a yearbook precedent which he argued was to a similar effect, but no such use of the doctrine can be found in it.[64]

The argument that emerges most frequently in the reported views of judges and lawyers is that a statute should be interpreted by its equity regardless of whether it is penal.[65] *Platt v Lock* is the first case where the argument appears explicitly. It was said for the defendant that a statute 'shall not be extended by equity to others, especially where the statute is penal',[66] and the argument made in response was that

> although it is penal against the warden, yet it is beneficial to all others, and therefore shall be extended by equity, for every statute is penal to somebody.[67]

In *Wimbish v Tailbois*, Mountague CJ (c. 1485–1557) posed an even more direct challenge to the doctrine, saying that 'it was no sure ground that a penal statute should not be taken by equity'.[68] Sir Edward Saunders (d 1576) also expressed this view on several occasions.[69] In 1555, the author of the *Graunde Abridgment*, sitting as Broke CJ, sought to tie this view to a number of previous authorities which had shown that a statute could be extended despite being penal as long as it was extended to a case within the same mischief the statute was meant to remedy. However, Broke's view was not unsupported by the authorities he cited.[70]

[61] *Fulmerston* (n 59) 1 Plow 106–7, 75 ER 168.
[62] ibid 1 Plow 109–10, 75 ER 172.
[63] ibid 1 Plow 110, 75 ER 172.
[64] Bromley CJ cites (1506) Hil 21 Hen VII, ff 9–11, pl 11, at 10.
[65] *Hill v Grange* (1555) 1 Plow 164, 178; 75 ER 253, 273 (Broke CJ). See also Behrens (n 56) 40, fn 29.
[66] *Platt v Lock* (1550) 1 Plow 36, 75 ER 57.
[67] ibid 1 Plow 36, 75 ER 59.
[68] *Wimbish* (n 58) 1 Plow 46, 75 ER 75.
[69] *Reniger v Fogossa* (1551) 1 Plow 1, 7; 75 ER 1, 10 (Saunders Sjt); *Partridge v Strange* (1552) 1 Plow 77, 82; 75 ER 123, 131 (Saunders J). See also *Buckley v Thomas* (1554) 1 Plow 118, 127; 75 ER 182, 196 (Saunders J).
[70] 'Broke, Robert III' in JH Baker (ed), *The Men of Court, 1440 to 1550: A Prosopography of the Inns of Court and Chancery and the Courts of Law, vol I* (2012) 18 *Selden Society Supplementary Series* 370–371. See *Hill v Grange* (1555) 1 Plow 164, 178; 75 ER 253, 274. Broke cited (1476) YB Hil 15 Edw IV, ff 18–22, pl 8, though the argument was not made in that case that the statute was penal. The closest one can find to an argument supporting the extension of penal statutes is that of Fyneux CJKB, cited in Broke's *Graunde Abridgement*: Broke (n 50) f 119, fn 20. The relevant judgment is (1499) YB Hil 14 Hen VII ff 13–14, pl 2, at 14. In this case, Fyneux seemed to imply that a statute would have been extended despite being penal if not extending it would have resulted in a mischief, but the case was not decided on this point. This was, to my knowledge, the closest any previous authority had gone to challenging the view that a penal statute should not be extended by equity.

Turning to the second point, that of relating equitable interpretations to *epieikeia*, a number of cases in Plowden, though not mentioning *epieikeia* directly, show evidence that judges and lawyers were growing familiar with arguments and lines of reasoning related to it.

One does not have to look far in the *Commentaries* to find an example. The first case to appear in the reports, *Reniger v Fogossa*,[71] features equitable interpretation being understood as capable of carving exceptions into statute other than just extending them and features arguments that appear to be drawn from St German's *epieikeia*. The case was argued in the Exchequer before Sir John Baker (c. 1489–1558) in 1550. A claim was brought by Reniger, a controller of customs, against Anthony Fogossa, a Spanish shipper, because he had not paid customs on 1,693 kintals of woad – this was a violation of an Act for the subsidy of tonnage and pondage of merchandise, which stated that if the subsidy should remain unpaid 'or the Collector of the same subsidy [...] not agreed with for the same [...] all the said [...] goods] [...] shall remain forfeit' and split between the Crown and the person who seized the goods.[72] Fogossa argued that he had complied with the statute by reaching an agreement with a customs officer. The controller argued that the agreement was unenforceable. One of the problems was that it was too uncertain, as Fogossa had agreed to pay customs on 2,000 kintals of woal, and for anything in excess of 2,000 should the amount of woal be more than that when weighed. The controller argued that this amounted to an uncertain and conditional agreement and was therefore not within the meaning of the statute, which tacitly assumed the agreement would be certain and unconditional. Among the arguments for Fogossa was that, even if that were the meaning of the words of the statute, Fogossa had entered into such an uncertain and conditional agreement by reason of necessity. That was because Fogossa had docked at Southampton after a great storm had forced him to throw some cargo overboard, so he was unsure what quantity of goods he had left on the ship when he dealt with the customs officer.[73]

Interestingly, each side argued for their own version of an equitable interpretation, neither of which was consistent with an orthodox understanding of the doctrine. We have briefly mentioned Saunders Sjt's argument above, challenging the rule about penal statutes. Saunders argued against Fogossa that the Statute should be construed for the benefit of the King, and that even though it was penal, nevertheless, where it was clearly the intention of the makers that it should be so extended, then even a penal statute should be construed by reference to its equity.[74] The argument seems to have been that even if the words of this statute were taken to only apply against someone who had entered into no agreement at all with the customs officer, they should be extended by their equity to cover one who had entered into an agreement that was uncertain and conditional. Arguing for Fogossa, we find again Broke CJ. However, on this occasion, he argued that interpreting by equity should mean something else:

> When laws or statutes are made, yet there are certain things which are exempted and excepted out of the provision of the same by the law of reason, although they are not expressly excepted. [...]

[71] *Reniger* (n 69).
[72] 1 Ed VI, c 13 (1547).
[73] *Reniger* (n 69) 1 Plow 5, 75 ER 7.
[74] ibid 1 Plow 10, 75 ER 15–6.

> [S]ome things are for necessity's sake exempted and excepted (by equity of reason) out of the prohibitory words of statutes, and other things which are not remedied by the words of statutes, are (by equity of reason) taken within the purview of the same statutes. And if any thing shall be in any case exempted out of the penalty of any statute, we shall here be aided by equity of reason, notwithstanding that the words of the statute had been against us.[75]

The idea of exempting a case out of a statute by the law of reason is strongly reminiscent of St German's own take on *epieikeia* as an exception of divine or natural law, or indeed of the law of reason, from human law. Another argument to that effect was put for Fogossa on a later day by Pollard Sjt:

> admitting that the words of the said statute had ordained that if an agreement certain was not made with the collector before the landing, the goods should be forfeited, yet here the agreement uncertain shall be adjudged good, and out of the penalty: for in every law there are some things which when they happen a man may break the words of the law, and yet not break the law itself; and such things are exempted out of the penalty of the law, and the words of the law is not breaking the law, so as the intent of the law is not broken. [...]And I have read in books that amongst the Romans there was a law that every one that scaled the walls in the night time should be condemned to death, and a certain person in the night scaled the walls in time of war to discover the approach of the enemy, and he was not only discharged by the senate from the penalty of death, but besides was well rewarded for the action and yet he had thereby broken the words of the law, but the wise senators expounded it to be no breach of the intent of the law, because that law was made to prevent hurt and danger that might come to the Romans by the scaling of the walls, and not to inhibit benefit and safety to the city; so that the said judgment may be given in order to avoid a great inconvenience which might come to the Romans by such an example; and this manner of expounding and construing laws is not a mistaking them or a wrong judgment of them, but it is a tempering the rigour of the law.[76]

Unlike Broke, Pollard did not make an explicit reference to equity. However, both the argument and the example used of a Roman scaling the walls are reminiscent of those found in medieval moral theology.[77] In *Reniger* we find a use of the equity of the statute taken beyond its medieval boundaries – in particular, using it to restrict rather than extend the meaning of a statute – but this time with a clear sign that this different approach to equity was prompted by a familiarity with Aristotle's *epieikeia* and writings connected with it.

One has to wait until *Stowel v Lord Zouch*,[78] decided a decade later, to find an explicit reference to *epieikeia*. This was a complex case which turned on the fact that Zouch's grandfather had disseised Stowel's grandfather and levied a fine to have title conveyed to him and his wife. The issue with which we are concerned is that a statute on fines held that, where a fine is levied, any party with an interest in the land 'shall pursue their title claim or interest by way of action or lawful entry within 5 years' from the time the fine is levied.[79] Stowel's grandfather had died after the fine was levied, and his heir

[75] ibid 1 Plow 13, 75 ER 21.

[76] ibid 1 Plow 18, 75 ER 30.

[77] The example of the citizen ascending the city walls seems to originally come from Albertus Magnus (c. 1200–1280); see '*Ethica* V.4.1.' in SCA Borgnet (ed), *Opera Omnia* (Paris, L Vives, 1890) vol 7, 383–387, the example is at 384 and 386. It was repeated in T Aquinas, *Sententia Libri Ethicorum*, 3.16 in *Summa Theologiae in Opera Omnia iussu impensaque Leonis XIII edita* (1888–1906), available at www.corpusthomisticum.org/ctc0314.html (last accessed 20 November 2025).

[78] *Stowel v Lord Zouch* (1563) 1 Plow 353, 75 ER 536.

[79] 4 Hen VII, c 24 (1489).

only became of full age after the five years had expired. The question was whether an exception should be carved in the statute in these circumstances. The judges decided that Stowel could 'not be aided at all by equity'.[80]

For present purposes, the most interesting statement comes from Sir Robert Catlyn CJ (c. 1510–1574). From Plowden's report it appears that Catlyn was among those common lawyers who were convinced by the connection between equity and *epieikeia*, and it is clear that he felt this required him to justify why an equitable interpretation would not be available in this case. He explained that 'Aristotle defines equity *correctio justae legis qua parte deficit quod generatim lata est*',[81] but this would not be available because

> this law here is special, and limits a certainty of time in every point, and it is defective in no part as to time, for which reason the time limited shall not be altered or enlarged by equity.[82]

This case combines the tendency to develop the equity of the statute as a general doctrine both restricting and extending statutes, with evidence of Aristotle's text being adopted to guide equitable interpretation substantively. Both Catlyn's argument that interpreting a statute by its equity could lead to a restriction and that the restriction ought to be justified by some defect were both statements that had no parallel in the medieval understanding of the doctrine.

That said, the most influential and developed discussion of *epieikeia* as a principle interpretation did not come from a judicial statement but from Plowden's own comment in *Eyston v Studd*, where he wrote something of a short treatise on the subject.[83] The text is well known and has already been analysed in detail elsewhere,[84] but its very significant impact on later writings on the point justifies considering it briefly. In his comment Plowden said that

> equity, which in Latin is called equitas, enlarges or diminishes the letter according to its discretion, which equity is in two ways: the one Aristotle defines thus (which is touched by Catline, Chief Justice in Stowel's case) equitas est correctio legis generatim latae qua parte deficit, or, as the passage is explained by Perionius, Equitas est correctio quaedam legi adhibita, quia ab ea abest aliquid propter generalem sine exceptione comprehensionem, both which definitions come to one and the same thing. And this correction of the general words is much used in the law of England [...]. So that in these cases the general words of the law are corrected and abridged by equity.[85]

Unsurprisingly, Plowden reiterated the view already expressed by many judges in the 1550s that a statute ought to be interpreted by equity regardless of whether it is penal:

> And if it be said that the law is penal in this case, to this it may be answered that so it is also in the other case, but equity known no difference between penal laws and others, for the intent [...] ought to be followed and taken for law, as well in penal laws as in others.[86]

[80] *Stowel* (n 78) 1 Plow 375, 75 ER 569.
[81] ie, 'as a correction of a good law which is in part defective in that it was laid down too generally'.
[82] *Stowel* (n 78) 1 Plow 375–6, 75 ER 569.
[83] *Eyston v Studd* (1573) Plow 459, 465–88; 75 ER 688, 695–700.
[84] See Behrens (n 56) 30–33; Ibbetson (n 3) 61–2.
[85] *Eyston* (n 83) Plow 465, 75 ER 688, 695–96.
[86] ibid Plow 468, 75 ER 700, citing *Stradling v Morgan* (1560) 1 Plow 199, 75 ER 30.

This statement contains all the elements of development we have observed through the *Commentaries*. The doctrine of the equity of the statute is construed broadly as covering both extensive and restrictive purposive interpretations. It is viewed as one of general application, that is, regardless of whether laws are penal or abridge the common law. Finally, and most importantly, its meaning is explicitly identified with that of Aristotle's *epieikeia*.

The judges and lawyers cited in Plowden's *Commentaries* show a tendency to associate a broad notion of *epieikeia* with the extension or restriction of statutes by reference to either natural law, the law of reason or the intentions of the legislator. Certainly, Plowden's own explanation of *epieikeia* has strong parallels with some of the civil law sources considered earlier. There is no evidence that Plowden or his contemporaries drew on civilian sources directly, but it can be observed that by the 1550s common lawyers and civil law jurists discussing equity were drawing on similar sources and making similar arguments, and the early modern reconceptualisation of equity as a principle of purposive interpretation grounded in *epieikeia* had taken ground, at least among some common lawyers.

IV. Equity as Interpretation after Plowden's *Commentaries*

Whatever the *Commentaries* mean for the thinking around equity of judges and lawyers during the mid-sixteenth century, there is little doubt that they had a momentous effect, once published, on the spread of the use of *epieikeia* as a ground for interpretation among legal writing more generally. Interestingly, that impact was much clearer in legal writings than in case law. No other reporter describes uses of equity by judges and lawyers which are as creative as those found in Plowden's own reports, and even after the publication of the *Commentaries*, only a handful of cases discuss equity in as much depth as that found in Plowden's reports.[87] Among the few examples available, Professor Baker has recently shown that William Fleetwood – the author of the *Discourse* on the interpretation of statutes discussed above – cited examples of equitable interpretation from Plowden on a number of occasions in argument describing the statutes as having been expounded 'epicarie' or 'to prove what exposition the justices have made of statutes according to *epieikeia* or equity, sometimes abridging them, sometimes enlarging their text'.[88] In 1609, Plowden's argument from *Eyston* was used in *The Duke of Lenox*'s case to explain that a statute should extend also 'to a thing which is not in *rerum natura* at the time of the making of the statute [...] for how can makers of statutes prevent all mischiefs [...]. Aristotle in [*Ethics*, book 5, chapter 10] says that *Aequitas est correctio*

[87] Cases discussing the equity of the statute for the period 1520–1579 simply involve the extension of a statute to a case not covered by its words in line with the medieval orthodoxy. See, eg, *Putbury v Trevilian* (1556) 2 Dyer 142, 73 ER 310; *Anon* (1559) Jenk 221, 145 ER 152; *Austen v Baker* (1560) 2 Dyer 201, 73 ER 444; *Anon* (1561) Jenk 226, 145 ER 157; *Dame Dennis' Case* (1565) 2 Dyer 248, 73 ER 549; *Anon* (1571) 3 Dyer 319, 73 ER 722; *Anon* (1576) 2 Leo 9, 74 ER 314; (1580) Broke's New Cases 97; *Borough and Holcroft's Case* (1578) 2 Leo 160, 74 ER 442.

[88] *Buttell v Wilford* (c 1580) BL MS Harley 4717, f 159; *Norris v Alsop* (1586) BL MS Harley 1331, f 14; MS Add 35944, f 2 cited in Baker, 'Reinvention' (n 51) 233, fn 113.

legis generatim late, qua parte deficit.'[89] Already by the end of the seventeenth century, the use of equity in the context of interpretation was almost completely extinguished. One of the last cases mentioning *Eyston v Studd* was *Malloon v Fitzgerald*, but *Eyston* was referred to as a case in which a statute was construed 'according to the intent of the makers, and not according to the letter of the law' – no reference to equity was made at all.[90]

A. Legal Dictionaries

Perhaps the sector of legal writing in which Plowden's influence was most remarkably long-lasting is that of legal lexicons and dictionaries. The first printed English dictionary of English law was John Rastell's *Exposiciones Terminorum*, published in 1527, and contained no entry for equity.[91] When in 1579 John and William Rastell's *Exposiciones Terminorum* was expanded with over 100 new lemmas by an unknown editor[92] as *An Exposition of Certaine [...] Terms of the Laws of this Realm*, an entry for 'equitie' was included, and Plowden's approach to equity in *Eyston* provided the entire content for it. Indeed, Plowden's text would long outlive its relevance within this work, providing the sole content for the entry until its last edition in 1742.[93]

This work's influence was extremely long-lasting. The next English dictionary to be published was *The Interpreter* by John Cowell (1554–1611); this contained no entry at all for equity.[94] Aside from a number of similar reprints of Cowell's work, the following two law dictionaries to be published were the *Philologicall commentary* by Edward Leigh (1603–1671) and *Nomolexicon* by Thomas Blount (1618–1679). Both works included an entry for 'equity', and although equity had almost entirely lost its association with the interpretation of statutes in both practice and theory by then, these works – almost certainly through Rastell's, which Blount edited between 1667 and 1685 – referred back to Plowden's definition of *epieikeia*.[95] When Cowell's *Interpreter* was substantially enlarged in a reprint of 1672 by Thomas Manley (c. 1628–1676), the editor, by his own admission, relied heavily on Blount's *Nomolexicon*.[96] Accordingly, an entry for equity was added which quoted the same passage from *Eyston v Studd* found in Rastell's, Leigh's and Blount's dictionaries – this work too remained unchanged until its last

[89] *The Duke of Lenox* (1609) 2 Brownlow and Goldesborough 301, 307; 123 ER 954, 957–8. See also *Le Residue del Case* (1620) 2 Rolle 174, 174; 81 ER 733, 734; *Ferrers v Fryer* (1621) Benloe 100, 73 ER 971.

[90] *Malloon v Fitzgerald* (1694) 3 Mod 28, 33; 87 ER 17, 20.

[91] JH Baker, 'John Rastell and the Terms of the Law' in id, *Collected Papers in Legal History* (Cambridge, Cambridge University Press, 2013) vol 2. A number of earlier manuscripts providing alphabetical lists of English legal words did exist, but none provided an entry for *aequitas* or equity. See JD Cowley, *A Bibliography of Abridgments, Digests, Dictionaries and Indexes of English Law to the Year 1800* (London, Selden Society, 1932) lxxix–lxxxi.

[92] Possibly Lawrence Twine (fl 1564–1588): Baker, *OHLE* (n 8) 718, fn 38.

[93] J Rastell, *An exposition of Certaine Difficult and Obscure Words and Terms of the Lawes of this Realme* (London, R Tottelli, 1579) ff 78v–80v. See Ibbetson (n 3) 63, fn 43.

[94] J Cowell, *The Interpreter* (London, J Legat, 1607).

[95] Cowley (n 91) lxxxix. E Leigh, *A Philologicall Commentary or an Illustration of the most Obvious and Useful Words in the Law* (London, T Mabb, 1652) 83–4. T Blount, *Nomolexicon, a law-dictionary* (London, T Newcomb, 1670) sv 'equity (*equitas*)'.

[96] Cowley (n 91) lxxxvii.

edition of 1727.[97] In 1729, when the *New law-dictionary* by Giles Jacob (1686–1744) was published, equity was still described almost entirely in words borrowed from Rastell, with a single sentence mentioning at the end that it 'seems to be the interposing of the law of reason exercised by the Lord Chancellor'.[98] As late as 1764, when the *New and Complete Law Dictionary by* Timothy Cunningham (d 1789) was published, Plowden was still the only source for the entry.[99] It was only in the edition of 1782 that the editor John Morgan (1757×8-?) added, after the text from Rastell, a discussion of courts of equity, aligning the dictionary definition of equity to the meaning it would have had by then for any English lawyer.[100]

B. Legal Treatises

The wave of interest which was taken in statutory interpretation and its theory in the sixteenth century has already been mentioned. One of the works sparked by that was, as considered earlier, Fleetwood's *Discourse upon the Exposition and Understanding of Statutes*. Thomas Egerton, later Lord Ellesmere (1540–1617) had his own copy of the *Discourse* on which he made his own notes. One of these is particularly telling of the impact that Plowden's *Commentaries* had on the contemporary debate about statutory interpretation. At the foot of Fleetwood's statement that 'sometimes statutes are taken by equity more than the words', Egerton added a reference to Aristotle's *epieikeia* quoting from *Stowel's Case*.[101] Egerton was not alone in finding parallels between the theory of the equity of the statute, purposive interpretation and *epieikeia* – Plowden's text found fertile ground among later treatise writers, and there is evidence that it encouraged them to think differently about equity's role within doctrines of interpretation.[102]

An example can be found in the *Treatise concerning Statutes*, a work composed around 1590 and presented as the work of Sir Christopher Hatton (1540–1591) though the authorship is uncertain.[103] The work's fifth chapter deals with the 'interpretation of statutes according to equity'. Interestingly, the text relies heavily on St German but redirects St German's text to a different purpose entirely:

> All statutes may be expounded by equity so far forth as *Epicaia* goes, that is, an exception of the law of God; and law of reason from the general words of the law of man.[104]

The *Treatise* collects a number of examples in which exceptions are carved from statutes and also how statutes may be extended, presenting both as exercises in *epieikeia*. It then lists other cases in which one moves beyond the words 'by equities', such as where one

[97] J Cowell, *Nomothetes, the Interpreter* (London, J Streater, 1672) sv 'equity (*aequitas*)'. See the same entry in J Cowell, *A Law Dictionary or The Interpreter* (London, E & R Nutt and R Gosling, 1727).

[98] G Jacob, *New Law-Dictionary* (London, E & R Nutt and R Gosling 1729) sv 'equity'.

[99] T Cunningham, *New and Complete Law Dictionary* (London, Law Printers [etc.], 1764) sv 'equity'.

[100] G Jacob, *New Law-Dictionary* (London, W Strahan and W Woodfall, 1782). See also the entries for the *New Law-Dictionary* editions of 1809, 1839, 1847 and 1850.

[101] *Stowel* (n 78). Thorne (n 44) 141, fn 114.

[102] Aside from the examples cited below see also A Fraunce, *The Lawyer's Logike* (London, W How, 1588) f 48, 73v.

[103] [? C Hatton], *A treatise concerning Statutes* [c. 1590] (London, R Tonson, 1677) 31–62. See Thorne (n 44) 10. The date is attributed by Baker, *Two Elizabeths* (n 45) 99.

[104] ibid 31.

needs to reach 'things of vicine nature' and where law and reason repugn to the open sense of the words.[105] It continues by attempting to deal systematically with the fact that many penal statutes have been taken by equity 'so far forth as the exposition applies to favour and benignity or to the propagation of a good law'.[106] In the *Treatise*, the role of equity in interpretation is stretched far beyond its medieval meaning and aligned with that which was prevalent in the reports and commentaries of Plowden – a broad theory of purposive interpretation as *epieikeia*.

Through the influence of Plowden, the late sixteenth and early seventeenth centuries became the time when interest in equitable interpretation seems to have reached its summit among treatise writers. The least surprising example is probably William Fulbecke's *Direction or Preparative to the Study of the Law*, a work heavily inspired by European works on civil law and rhetoric.[107] Fulbecke discussed equity and rigour in terms that perfectly mirrored its discussion by civilians all around Europe by that time. The eighth chapter of his book stated that 'the words and terms used in books of law ought to be understood and applied as the law does expound them and conceive them'.[108] To address this problem, Fulbecke distinguished between *ius merum*, which is 'that law that has no mixture nor regard of circumstances, but grounds a rigorous conclusion upon things done without further examination of how or why they were done' from that law which is *ius aequum et bonum*, explaining that

> The law which is termed aequum & bonum, is that which mildly interprets, amends and mollifies the hard and rigorous speeches, and censures of the other laws: and is sometime sharp and severe, where the other laws are remiss and connivant.[109]

Both the use of the binomial pair *aequum et bonum* and the discussion of it in terms of interpretation are clearly inspired directly by civil law writings, which is consistent with Fulbecke's well-documented interest in civil law.

Fulbecke's interest in *epieikeia* was, however, far from exceptional at the turn of the century. Between the 1590s and the 1610s no less than three works bearing the same title of *Epieikeia* were published by Edward Hake, William Perkins and Thomas Ashe, respectively.[110]

Hake's work circulated only in a limited way at the time and is dealt with in greater detail by Joanna McCunn elsewhere in this volume.[111] Hake adopts by far the broadest approach to equity. He sees equity as permeating the entirety of the law and as being

[105] ibid 41, 45.
[106] ibid 64ff.
[107] W Fulbecke, *Direction or Preparative to the Study of the Law* (London, T Wight, 1600). For the heavy reliance of Fulbecke on civilian and rhetorical sources see DJ Ibbetson, 'Authority and Precedent' in M Godfrey (ed), *Law and Authority in British Legal History, 1200-1900* (Cambridge, Cambridge University Press, 2016) 74, and J McCunn, '"An art obscured with difficult cases": Interpretation and Rhetoric in Fulbecke's *Direction*' paper presented at a workshop on 'Reasons and Context in Comparative Law' to mark the retirement of Professor John Bell, Murray Edwards College, University of Cambridge (September 2019), I thank the author for providing me with a copy of this paper.
[108] ibid 62.
[109] ibid 62. For the same use of *aequum et bonum* among civilians see, eg, F Duarenus, '*Disputationes Anniversariae*' in id, *Opera Omnia* (Lyon, G Rovilium, 1558) vol 2, 492–93 and Salomoni (n 26) 13.
[110] DEC Yale (ed), E Hake, *Epieikeia: A Dialogue on Equity in Three Parts* (New Haven, CT, Yale University Press, 1953); W Perkins, *[Epieikeia]: or a treatise of Christian equity and moderation* (Cambridge, J Legat, 1604); Thomas Ashe, *Epieikeia* (London, A Islip, 1608).
[111] J McCunn, ch 8 in this volume.

responsible for each and every change within it. Like Fulbecke, Hake's view was inspired by civilian writings – McCunn identifies links between this approach to equity and the early treatises on equity by Lutheran jurists, including Philip Melanchthon.[112] That said, there is little in Hake that would be capable of providing the basis for a doctrine of interpretation – indeed, despite the introductory sweeping statements about equity, Hake unproblematically states that 'a penal statute shall not be taken by equity' nor does that 'abridge the common law'.[113] In fact, despite relating equity to *epieikeia*, Hake seems to make no mention of the principal role of equity envisaged by Aristotle and theologians, that of interpreting statutes restrictively so as to carve exceptions into them.

The second work, by Perkins, is a theological one, which approaches equity very broadly from the point of view of moral theology.[114] After considering the 'private equity' which individuals have to exercise in their daily life, he moves on to consider the 'public equity [...] which is practised in publicke metings and assemblies of men, as in Courts of iustice, Assises, Sessions, Counsells, Parliments, and such like'.[115] Public equity is considered through a bird's-eye view which considers both the execution of laws and their creation as well as their administration by judges. The role of equity in courts of law is not discussed in particular detail, but it is clear that its scope is seen by the author as encompassing the duties of all judges in approaching the law. The equity judges' practice is described as the 'moderation and mitigation of the extremity of a law, upon honest and convenient reasons, and in such cases, as were not directly intended in the law'.[116] Perkins invites judges to strike a balance between severity and mercy but does not explore the nature of the equitable interpretation of law beyond reiterating the familiar point that a judge should not stick to the letter of the law at the expense of its meaning.[117]

The third book, Thomas Ashe's *Epieikeia*, is rather curious. It is dedicated to Edward Coke and, at first sight, appears to take equitable interpretation seriously. Unlike Hake's and Perkins's works, it promises to deal solely with the role of equity in interpreting statutes. Its preface is an erudite essay on equity jurisprudence, featuring a very great range of citations, including not only the usual reference to *Eyston v Studd*[118] but also spanning theology,[119] legal humanism,[120] and civil law more generally.[121] Ashe also reports the peculiarly humanist translation of *epieikeia* as *aequum et bonum*, which in English is rendered by him as 'equall and just', or 'good and equall',[122] and at least from the range of sources ostensibly employed, it is the treatise that comes closest to engaging

[112] ibid.
[113] Hake (n 110) 88–91 cited in McCunn (n 111), fn 129.
[114] For more on Perkins see PH Sedgwick, *The Origins of Anglican Moral Theology* (Leiden, Brill, 2018) 177–211; his views on equity are also discussed in DR Klinck, *Conscience, Equity and the Court of Chancery in Early Modern England* (London, Routledge, 2010) 142–144.
[115] Perkins (n 110) 6.
[116] ibid 14.
[117] ibid 14–17.
[118] Ashe (n 110) [x]–[xi]. The work is not thoroughly paginated and I follow the pagination of the first two folios which are marked at the bottom as §iii and §iiii respectively.
[119] Mostly through St German: ibid [viii], [ix], [xii].
[120] ibid [viii], [x].
[121] ibid [viii]–[ix], [xiii]. As pointed out by Ibbetson these references are mostly drawn from J Magirus, *Corona Virtutum Moralium* (Frankfurt, Collegio Musarum [etc], 1601) 548: Ibbetson (n 3) 64, n 52.
[122] Ashe (n 110) [vii].

with the early modern European learning on equitable interpretation. However, looking closer at Ashe's work, it is clear that his borrowing of civilian citations comes mainly from William West, who had discussed equity only in relation to the Chancery. The quotations are often taken outside of their context and seemingly with no regard to their relevance for Ashe's overall discussion. Beyond the preface, the remainder of the work contains no substantive doctrinal analysis relating to equitable interpretation. It features instead twenty headings ostensibly involving some aspect by which equity may extend a statute, ie, to other persons, things, actions etc, but without any particular link to *epieikeia*. Under each heading is listed an index of statutes and cases from Year Books and contemporary reports broadly raising points concerning the twenty headings but featuring no commentary by Ashe making any explicit links with the theory of equity or *epieikeia*. It has been said that the work 'can hardly have been of much practical value'.[123] This seems to be true of its theoretical value, too.

The publication of Ashe's treatise coincides with the end of this wave of interest in equitable interpretation, and from the later seventeenth century onwards, associations of equity with the role of the Chancery were becoming ubiquitous.[124] References to equitable interpretation can still be found in a handful of works. Henry Finch's *Nomotexnia* of 1613 mentions equity as *epieikeia* only very briefly but clearly identifies it with a principle of interpretation, juxtaposing Plowden's words in *Eyston v Studd* with Aristotle's. A second reference is found in Edward Coke's *Institutes*, where he described equity as

> a construction made by the judges, that cases out of the letter of a statute [...] shall be within the same remedy that the statute provided: And the reason hereof is, so that the lawmaker could not possibly set down all cases in express terms.

In support, Coke cites Salamoni describing equity as 'perfect reason that interprets and amends written law, not comprehended in any writing, but consisting solely in true reason'.[125]

Another reference is found in *The English Lawyer*, written by Sir John Doddridge (1555–1628) and published posthumously in 1631.[126] Doddridge deals with equity in familiar Aristotelian terms, saying that it is impossible for a lawmaker to make a rule that would not fail in some particular case, and he draws heavily on Plowden for the remainder of his description of the role of equity in interpretation.[127] And one of the last relatively lengthy treatments of equitable interpretation in this sense is found in Edmund Wingate's *Maxims* of 1658, where equity is described as

> a construction made by the judges, that cases out of the letter of a statute, yet being within the same mischief, or cause of making the same, shall be within the same remedy that the Statute provides: And the reason hereof is, for that the law-maker could not possibly set down all

[123] W Holdsworth, *A History of English Law, Vol 4* (London, Methuen & Co, 1924) 312.

[124] See Part V below.

[125] E Coke, *The First Part of the Institutes of the Lawes of England* (London, [A Islip], 1628) f 24. Compare with Salamoni (n 26) 7. The statement had been repeated in a number of civilian legal dictionaries: eg, P Duprat, *Lexicon Iuris Civilis* (Lyon, G Rovilium, 1567) f 11 sv '*aequitas*'.

[126] H Finch, *Nomote[ch]nia: Cestascavoir, un Description del Common Leys Dangleterre Solonque les Rules del Art* (London, Society of Stationers, 1613) 14–5.

[127] J Doddridge, *The English Lawyer* (London, Assignees of J More, 1631) 209–15.

> cases in express terms [...] *Aequitas est perfecta quaedam ratio, quae jus scriptum interpretatur & emendat, nulla scriptura comprehensa, sed solum in vera ratione consistens.*[128]

By that time, however, Wingate's understanding of equity could only have been shared by a small minority. Throughout the late sixteenth and seventeenth centuries, a wealth of very influential literature had been spreading the rival view of equity as the basis for the Chancery's jurisdiction, which had by then settled as the norm.

V. Increasing Competition with the Chancery and Decline of Equitable Interpretation

From the 1590s, the association of *epieikeia* with the Court of Chancery was gaining ground. Indeed, Hake's work already claimed in the 1580s and 1590s to be dealing with equity in a more general sense, primarily to clarify its role as a justification for the Chancery's jurisdiction.[129] The spread of this understanding of equity has been studied in detail elsewhere, and the publications that contributed most significantly to its spread, aside from *Doctor and Student*, were probably William West's *Symbolaeography* and *Archeion* by William Lambarde (1536–1601).[130] Though both works relied heavily on civilian sources, neither referred to equity as a principle of interpretation, confining its role to explaining the jurisdiction of the Chancery and – in the case of Lambarde – a political justification for it in terms of the royal prerogative.[131]

Some writings evidence the confusion around the turn of the century, when authors were writing about equity in such different terms. According to an anonymous author writing around that time, 'there is nothing most usual than the name of equity and scarce anything more obscure and difficult than the matter itself'. He was clearly aware of the interpretive function of equity, citing a number of civilians on the point and deducing that

> The whole power and strength of equity may be reduced to these three general properties or effects (i) To maintain the true intent and meaning of the law against the words and letter thereof; (ii) To regard and weigh particular circumstances of every action and not to rest in the general terms of the law (iii) To provide for such defects and inconveniences as may happen contrary to the purpose and expectation of the lawmaker[132]

However, he also seemed to understand such equitable judgments as falling within the remit of the Chancery, stating that

> the force and nature of equity better appears then by diligent consideration of the difference with the civil law, for in these, that is in *stricti iuris actionibus*, the judge was always fixed to

[128] E Wingate, *Maxims* (London, R & W L, 1658) 192.
[129] Hake (n 110) 7.
[130] W West, *Symboleography* (London, R Tottle, 1590–1594). See E Poole, 'West's Symboleography: An Elizabethan Formulary' in JA Guy and H Beale (eds), *Law and Social Change in British History* (London, Royal Historical Society 1984). W Lambarde, '*Archeion*' in CH McIlwain and PL Ward (eds), *Archeion* (Cambridge, Cambridge University Press 1957).
[131] Ibbetson (n 3) 66–8 (West) and 69–71 (Lambarde). See also I Williams, 'Developing a Prerogative Theory for the Authority of the Chancery: The French Connection' in Godfrey (n 107) 33–59.
[132] Anon, *On Equitie* (Cambridge University Library MS Gg 2.31).

> a strict and necessary form of proceeding from which it was not lawfull for him *nec latum quidem unguem discedere* whatever reason or conscience might move to the contrary. But in *bonae fidei iudiciis* [...] the praetor gave him *libera iudicandis facultatem iuxta id quod sibi bonum et aequum visum fuerit.*[133]

At the end of this paragraph the author wrote 'Chancery' on the margin, indicating perhaps the court that he thought was responsible for handing over those *bonae fidei iudiciis* and therefore doing equity in a way that seemed irreconcilable with his other statements about equitable interpretation.[134]

By the time of the *Earl of Oxford's Case* (1615), the association with the Court of Chancery was commonplace. The same Thomas Egerton who had annotated Fleetwood's treatise on statutory interpretation with references to *epieikeia* was by then describing the judge's role in interpreting the law by reference to the Chancery. He wrote that the judges

> play the Chancellor's part upon statutes, making construction of them according to equity, varying from the rules and grounds of law, and enlarging them *pro bono publico*, against the letter and intent of the makers.[135]

The treatises from this period cited above by Coke and Doddridge also mention equity only as an instrument of interpretation alongside its role in Chancery.

In 1656 William Shepherd published *An epitome of all the common and statute laws*, the first encyclopaedic abridgement and the first common law abridgement to be published in English.[136] In it, equity is only discussed in chapter 42, 'Of the Chancery', as the 'rule by which they go and proceed in their courts of equity to allay, qualify and temper the rigour of the common law in some special cases'.[137] Plowden's take on equity was briefly mentioned in chapter 90, 'of statutes', but, for Shepherd, this was clearly no longer anywhere near its central meaning.[138] The entry for 'equity' in William Hughes's *Grand Abridgment*, written as a supplement to Broke's around 1660, did include an entry for 'Statutes' under which he discussed 'where and what statutes shall by equity be construed to extend to other persons, other things, other places, other times, other estates and other actions or writs then are mentioned in the statute', but contained no discussion of equity in general terms and hardly mentions equity at all in its list of examples from the case law.[139] The *Abridgement* by Henry Rolle (1589/90–1656), written for his students and edited for publication in 1668 by Matthew Hale (1609–1676), almost exclusively referred to equity in relation to Courts of Equity, and most references to it are found under the heading 'Chancery'.[140] The next well known *Abridgement*, that in 23 volumes published by Charles Viner

[133] ibid ff 3v–4r.
[134] On this see Ibbetson (n 3) 68–9.
[135] (1615) 1 Chan Rep 1, 12; 21 ER 485, 488. See also *Calvin's Case* (1608) 7 Co Rep 1a, 77 ER 377.
[136] Cowley (n 91) lii–liii.
[137] W Shepherd, *An Epitome of all the Common & Statute Laws of this Nation Now in Force* (London, printed for W Lee [etc], 1656) 193.
[138] ibid 918, fn 4.
[139] W Hughes, *Grand Abridgment of the Law Continued* (London, JS, 1660) 1880–1886.
[140] H Rolle, *Un Abridgment des plusierurs cases et resolutions del common ley* (London, printed for A Crooke [etc], 1668). See, eg, part 1, 194, 373–81; part 2, 192, 299, 314, 780. One mention of the equity of the statute is found at part 2, 269.

(bap 1678–1756) published between 1742 and 1756, was known as *abridgment of law and equity*, and there was no hint that the latter could be related to anything other than Chancery practice.

The fate of *epieikeia* as a ground of equitable interpretation was bound up with the doctrine of the equity of the statute, and as the latter began to come under increasing criticism in the eighteenth century, so did the idea of equitable interpretation.[141] In his criticism of the association of Chancery with *epieikeia*, William Blackstone briefly revived it when he said that

> Both [the Chancery and common law courts] are equally bound, and equally profess, to interpret statutes according to the true intent of the legislature. In general laws all cases cannot be foreseen [...] some will arise that will fall within the meaning, though not within the words, of the legislator; and other which may fall within the letter, may be contrary to his meaning, though not expressly excepted. These cases, thus out of the letter, are often said to be within the equity, of an act of parliament; and so cases within the letter are frequently out of the equity. Here by *equity* we mean nothing but the sound interpretation of the law; though the words of the law itself may be too general, too special or otherwise inaccurate or defective. These then are the cases which, as Grotius says, *lex non exacte definit, sed arbitrio boni viri permittit*; in order to find out the true sense and meaning of the law giver.[142]

By that time, however, the association of *epieikeia* with equitable interpretation was, at best, an anachronism. The doctrine of equity of the statute, and with it the use of *epieikeia*, came under increasing criticism in the nineteenth and twentieth centuries as it came to be seen as an appropriation of the role of the legislature. On the rare occasions in which it is invoked by modern judges its history is usually summarised in very few words:

> That concept of the 'equity of a statute' fell into disfavour in the 18th century and was abandoned by the beginning of the 19th century, and the judges were no longer able in effect to exercise a direct legislative function.[143]

VI. Conclusion

The success of *epieikeia* was rather short-lived, both in relation to equitable interpretation and to the Chancery. At least in theory, legal interpretation would have provided a better home for the survival of *epieikeia* and, as we saw, a number of authors sought to understand it in this sense, providing a new justification for a more principled application of the medieval doctrine of the 'equity of the statute'. This tendency is well aligned with its fate around the sixteenth and seventeenth centuries all around Europe. Early modern equity may have been a contested concept, but it found a stable core as interpretation beyond the letter, and the match between Aristotle's doctrine and purposive interpretation was much closer than that with the Chancery's jurisdiction.

[141] JD Heydon, 'Equity and Statute' in PG Turner (ed), *Equity and Administration* (Cambridge, Cambridge University Press, 2016) 211–47, 238–39.

[142] W Blackstone, *Commentaries on the Laws of England* (Oxford, Clarendon Press, 1765–69) vol 2, 430–431.

[143] *Singularis Holdings Ltd v PricewaterhouseCoopers* [2014] UKPC 36, [2015] AC 1675 [82] (Lord Sumption).

All around Europe, this role for equity saw a steady decline from the mid-seventeenth century onwards. This phenomenon in the English jurisdiction cannot be attributed solely to the rival increase of its association with the Chancery, but it may have accelerated its process. The deeper reasons seem to have been mostly practical. As theories of interpretation grew in sophistication later in early modern times, Aristotelian *epieikeia* seemed to add little of value, except a lofty justification, for their consistent development. The decline of equitable interpretation did not have much to do with practical changes in doctrines of interpretation themselves – purposive interpretation is still invoked today in numerous contexts, but with no reference to the *Nichomachean Ethics*. Unlike the much contested development of the Chancery's equitable jurisdiction, doctrines of interpretation soon lost the need to be justified by an Aristotelian pedigree.

5

Conceptualising Conscience in the Early Tudor Conciliar Courts

LAURA FLANNIGAN

I. Introduction

In terms of the sheer number of tribunals and volume of business, the provision of equitable justice expanded and formalised in the reigns of the early Tudors. Not only was this the period in which Chancery transitioned from a supposedly 'medieval', in the sense of unsystematised, court for the 'undefinable absurdity of conscience' into something more codified.[1] It was also the age of a new set of even more nascent tribunals, emerging out of the main royal Council and offering similar civil justice in private cases. These included the court of Star Chamber at Westminster, the Court of Requests in the attendant household, and intermittent committees in the Marches of Wales and the North of England. Put simply, what united all these courts and commissions was that their determinations were not restricted to the precedents, maxims, and statutes of the common law. Consequently, they could make exceptions to the rigour of these rules without affecting the broader application of law; they themselves set no precedent, even for their own judges. As such, these conciliar tribunals can be said to have dispensed an early form of equity – or, to use the parlance of the time, justice shaped by conscience.

Conceptually speaking, 'conscience' provided the overarching ideals of reason and fairness that the developing doctrine of equity and its courts put into motion. This was essentially the delineation sketched out in the first dialogue of Christopher St German's *Doctor and Student*, first published in 1528.[2] Still, as Norman Doe's work reminds us, conscience was an ideal whose hold ranged far beyond the courtroom; it was central to the clerical training of many of the realm's judges and to the lives of ordinary English subjects, too.[3] When examining the meaning of 'conscience' from a juristic standpoint, we are really attuned to 'legal equity' and its central defining principle as part of a 'general

[1] F Metzger, 'The Last Phase of the Medieval Chancery' in A Harding (ed), *Law-Making and Law-Makers in British History* (London, Royal Historical Society, 1980) 89.

[2] TFT Plucknett and JL Barton (eds), *St German's Doctor and Student* (1974) 91 *Selden Society*.

[3] N Doe, *Fundamental Authority in Late Medieval English Law* (Cambridge, Cambridge University Press, 1990) 132, 153.

culture of conscience' in early modernity.[4] On the other hand, chronologically speaking, legal historians have tended to use 'conscience' and 'equity' respectively as shorthand terms for consecutive phases in the emergence of equitable remedies in late medieval and early modern England. Hence, we might talk only of conscience-based justice before the mid-sixteenth century and of an equity jurisdiction by Elizabeth I's reign. Even then, in exploring the application of 'conscience' in the aforementioned courts, there is a distinction to be made between its external and evidentiary element, subject to investigation by the Chancellor or judge, and the internal forum that lay outside the courts' purview. This chapter will explore these facets of 'conscience' as they pertained to the new and emerging conciliar tribunals of the early Tudor period, roughly 1485 to 1547.

For St German and for legal scholars in the centuries that have followed his work, conscience as well as equity have been taken as best represented by what the Court of Chancery did. This association between doctrine and court is understandable: it was, after all, in Chancery that the *Earl of Oxford's case* (1615)[5] enshrined the prevailing power of equity when judged against common law, and it was Chancery that outlived other like facets of the central justice system to become *the* principal equity court in Britain. Upon the dissolution of Star Chamber, Requests, the provincial councils, and High Commission in the early 1640s, it was almost certainly to Chancery that their prospective litigants turned for a remedy. But so far as the early history of the twinned concepts of conscience and equity is concerned, this monopoly of attention on one tribunal – albeit one that provides ample evidence for procedures and legal interpretations that might be defined as equitable – has left other, similar courts somewhat overlooked. It is socio-legal and constitutional historians who have perhaps shown the greatest interest in the controversial Court of Star Chamber, in both its civil and criminal dimensions.[6] But the other fifteenth- and sixteenth-century tribunals of this kind – Requests and the provincial councils – have generally received much less attention from lawyers and historians alike. This is not helped by the fact that, while historians have recognised the significance of litigation and legal developments to the development of state and society in early modernity, the first half of the sixteenth century is typically overlooked in favour of a starting point for analyses in around 1550. Meanwhile, though the criticisms levelled against the wider range of conciliar courts from the common law, particularly in the form of prohibitions and injunctions, have been explored by legal scholars, this has sometimes been with the sole aim of telling us more about Chancery's jurisdiction.[7]

Admittedly, in the late medieval period it is certainly 'difficult to distinguish "council" jurisdiction from "chancery" in judicial or quasi-judicial cases'.[8] Even once

[4] DR Klinck, *Conscience, Equity and the Court of Chancery in Early Modern England* (Farnham, Ashgate, 2010) 1–12.

[5] *Earl of Oxford's Case* (1615) 1 Ch Rep 1, 21 ER 485.

[6] For the most recent work, see KJ Kesselring and Natalie Mears (eds), *Star Chamber Matters: An Early Modern Court and Its Records* (London, University of London Press, 2021); RW Hoyle, 'Fountains of Justice: James I, Charles I and Equity' in M Lobban et al (eds), *Law, Lawyers and Litigants in Early Modern England: Essays in Memory of Christopher W Brooks* (Cambridge, Cambridge University Press, 2019).

[7] See, eg, C Gray, 'The Boundaries of the Equitable Function' (1976) 20 *American Journal of Legal History* 192.

[8] JB Post, 'Equitable Resorts before 1450' in EW Ives and AH Manchester (eds), *Law, Litigants and the Legal Profession: Papers presented to the Fourth British Legal History Conference* (London, Royal Historical Society, 1983) 69.

Chancery had become established as *the* 'court of conscience' in the fifteenth century, petitioners continued to present matters framed by conscience to the king or queen, the royal Council, Parliament, and provincial councils, requesting 'mercyfull petie ... att the rev[er]ens of god and [in] the wey of charite'.[9] By the early sixteenth century, new tribunals emerged out of the main Council with differing degrees and trajectories of institutionalisation. While the central courts of Star Chamber and Requests operated regularly, within the law terms and sometimes in the vacations too, they were more likely to dip and flow with the lifetime of the King than was Chancery. Requests, for instance, paused business altogether for a few months after Henry VII's death and for the duration of the French campaign of 1513. The provincial councils were even more intermittent, usually sitting under specific royal commissions for criminal and civil justice: the council at Ludlow in the Welsh Marches was active only in the middle years of Henry VII's reign and from the mid-1520s onwards, and the council of the North in brief phases under Henry VII and more regularly after the Pilgrimage of Grace in the later 1530s.[10]

It is fair to say, then, that the conciliar tribunals were characterised by greater institutional fluidity than Chancery was by this time. Yet, day to day, each adopted the bill procedure already in use in Chancery, with English petitions, summons under the privy seal writ *subpoena*, and pleadings taken under oath. In fact, St German himself gained some experience of early equity when working as an attorney in Requests near the beginning of his career.[11] Hence, if we are to account for all the strands that made up the broader patchwork of equitable doctrine in England, the threads represented by the conciliar courts must be examined more closely.

This chapter characterises the conceptualisation of conscience in the early Tudor conciliar courts through a survey of the rich archives they have left behind. It is based primarily on a study of all the surviving materials from the Court of Requests for the early Tudor years (1485 to 1547). This is the best recorded of the conciliar courts of this time, with 3,300 files of catalogued pleadings, around the same number of *un*catalogued case files, and eight complete books of orders and decrees still surviving. Whereas Chancery did not keep equivalent records until the 1530s, and its loose pleadings and other paperwork have become muddled somewhat by archival organisation, in the Requests archive we often find every document in a case, from petition to interlocutory orders and certificates, still bundled and tied together as they were returned to the Court from commissions. We might then also find their eventual ruling in the court's registers.[12] By comparison, Star Chamber also has in the region of 7,000 pleadings still surviving from the Henrician years. Its register books have not been seen since the early eighteenth century, though some decrees survive incidentally, in draft form or in copies in the other conciliar court archives, and in later transcriptions, which suggest that

[9] See examples in the National Archives (TNA) SC 8 and E 111 classes.

[10] CAJ Skeel, *The Council in the Marches: A Study in Local Government during the Sixteenth and Seventeenth Century* (London, Hugh Rees Ltd, 1904) 29, 31. See also REQ3/8 *Leighton v Leighton.*

[11] TNA REQ 1/3 f 215v. He was also named at the bottom of a list of 'Counsaillours as be appointed for the heryng of power mennes causes in the kynges Courte of Requests' in January 1529, though it cannot be proven that he ever worked there in the years that followed: REQ1/5 f 43v.

[12] The essential archival classes are TNA REQ 1 (books of orders and decrees), REQ 2 (catalogued pleadings), and REQ 3 (unsorted, uncatalogued pleadings, mostly early Tudor).

the court may have kept its own books from as early as 1493.[13] In contrast, provincial tribunals leave behind no centralised archives of their own today, although later copies tell us that the council in the North at least kept order books from about 1537 onwards, and snippets of paperwork from both survive in local archives and in unsorted central repositories.

To our early history of equity, these resources yield a socially diverse and, therefore, perhaps, conceptually grounded vision of that concept and the broader ideal of conscience – and of these principles in practice, too. The original documents of the conciliar courts of conscience offer a range of viewpoints: those of petitioners, informed by the common law counsellors whom they paid to draft their pleadings; but also, thanks to surviving decrees, the councillor-judges to whom royal justice-giving was delegated. This chapter will take up the general distinction made by other legal and historical scholars on the subject between the conceptualisation or appeal to 'conscience' and equity from the perspective of plaintiffs and their counsel on the one hand, and its application in the juridical, fact-finding procedures of the courts on the other. Part II will contribute to the picture already developed using Chancery pleadings about contemporary meanings of 'conscience' and the sort of matters for which this jurisdiction was deemed applicable. Part III does something that it is not always possible to do for Chancery, which is to read the interlocutory orders and final decrees of Requests (and, where they survive, the provincial tribunals) for a firmer statement on how conciliar judges applied conscience in individual cases. Part IV then reflects on the implications of these findings for the way in which the relationship between conscience and the common law was figured in this period.

II. Conceptualising Conscience

Existing studies of litigation in the late medieval Court of Chancery have made much of the lexicon of 'conscience' or 'equity' in the petitions that initiated suits there.[14] English bills remain popular and intriguing sources for socio-legal research: at once lucid and detailed about complainants' lives, while also overtly rhetorical in surprisingly 'conservative' ways; taken, in more positivist readings, to give us access to the 'voices' of litigants, their 'lived experiences', and their understandings of the world.[15] They are less useful in this particular jurisdictional context for legal theorising since they were largely functional and structured quite concisely to put forward a case in the clearest terms possible, with the added flourish of prayers for the King and evocations of general

[13] JA Guy, 'Wolsey's Star Chamber: a Study in Archival Reconstruction' (1975) 5 *Journal of the Society of Archivists* 169; D Gosling, 'The Records of the Court of Star Chamber' in Kesselring and Mears, *Star Chamber Matters* (n 6); KJ Kesselring (ed), *Star Chamber Reports: BL Harley MS 2143*, List and Index Society Special Series 57 (Kew, List & Index Society, 2018).

[14] N Pronay, 'The Chancellor, the Chancery and the Council at the End of the Fifteenth Century' in H Hearder and HR Lyon (eds), *British Government and Administration: Studies Presented to SB Chrimes* (Cardiff, University of Wales Press, 1974); Metzger (n 1).

[15] For some recent discussions, see J Bailey, 'Voices in Court: Lawyers' or Litigants'?' (2001) 74 *Historical Research* 392; C Beattie, 'Yor Oratrice: Women's Petitions to the Late Medieval Court of Chancery' in B Kane and F Williamson (eds), *Women, Agency and the Law, 1300–1700* (London, Routledge, 2013).

ideals of order that had been ridden over roughshod by the accused. In petitions to the early Tudor conciliar courts, as to Chancery, 'equity' appears only rarely as a metric for justice, but several different meanings of the much more common term 'conscience' begin to emerge. The most generalised was the abstract, though normative, principle of 'right and good conscience' in the community, the realm, the commonwealth – aligning essentially with a sense of right versus wrong that was treated as somewhat objective as much as individual. Below this was the appeal inherent in petitions for justice to the conscience of the receiving judge from whom plaintiffs begged mercy and charity. It was this forum of conscience that played on the minds of the common law commentators of the early sixteenth century, like St German, when he expressed concern for the impact of the 'discrecion and conscience of oon man', or at most of 'divers men, divers conscience', in extraordinary jurisdictions.[16] Perhaps most pressing was scrutiny of the defendant's conscience, where the internal forum and individual soul came into play. Extensive analysis of petitions to the King and his conciliar courts suggests a slightly different emphasis, however.

On searching through petitions to Requests and the other early Tudor conciliar courts for use of the word 'conscience', it is the degradation of that general principle of righteousness by the defendant that takes centre stage. The remit of these courts, as of Chancery, was capacious and bills of complaint could layer up numerous actions and even entirely separate allegations against multiple opponents. Within that framework, all manner of trespasses – everything from breaches of promises or duties, embezzlement and forging of deeds, forcible entries into houses and lands, and even the vague accusation of 'withholding' property – was figured as being, first and foremost, 'contrary to right and good conscience'. It is difficult to know in this lexicon whether there was any implied distinction between these cognate concepts. Occasionally 'good conscience' was instead paired with 'order', 'justice' or – more interestingly, perhaps – the 'laws' of the realm. We might speculate that in each combination the defendant's behaviour was characterised as equally wrongful (sometimes meaning illegal) *and* immoral. In any case, these coordinated notions each carried the implication of being inherent to society and somewhat objective.[17]

Only occasionally did plaintiffs and counsel write more literally of defendants' internal conduct beyond this general claim to unconscionability. A dispute over copyhold lands in the manor of Wick Episcopi in Worcestershire saw the tenant Richard Bachelor refer to Walter Born, who had 'labored out a convent seale of the same landes contrary to the aunsient custum ther' in order to put all the tenants out of their holdings, as 'a man without consciens'.[18] Elsewhere, a husbandman called Edward Lynner of Bedfordshire petitioned the King in 1517 to lament how as a 'very pore man having his pore wife & many childern at his gret charges' he simply could not challenge the

[16] JA Guy (ed), *Christopher St German on Chancery and Statute* (1981) 6 *Selden Society Supplementary Series* 101.

[17] These general comments, and those that follow, are based on examination of petitions in Requests, Star Chamber, and the Council in the Marches: TNA REQ 2 and REQ 3 *passim.*; IS Leadam (ed), *Select Cases before the King's Council in the Star Chamber, commonly called the Court of Star Chamber, vol I* (1902) 16 *Selden Society* and *vol II* (1910) 25 *Selden Society*; and Hereford Archives and Records Centre BG11/29 (I am grateful to Dr Tom Johnson for providing transcriptions of these documents).

[18] REQ2/7/51.

powerful Robert Butler for forgery of deeds and vexations at law, especially since Butler 'is a man of small conscience and yor said Orator not of power to withstand his malicious purpose by the course of yor [common] lawes'.[19] The short petition of the yeoman John Francis of Maidenhead in Berkshire similarly got straight to the point in describing his opponent, the testator of the man who had taken hold of his parents' tenements in Guildford, as a 'man of smale conscience & grete substaunce'.[20] Indeed, petitioners to these forums were typically more preoccupied with painting their adversaries as wealthy, powerful, and corrupt – the implication being that they were capable of manipulating processes in common law courts. More unusual was the plaintiff's concern for the cure of their *own* conscience, though this was very occasionally the effect of bills to conciliar courts. Hence, in c. 1520, the widow Ellen Brasier of Hereford petitioned the Council in the Marches about the execution of her mother's last will and testament, calling upon the judges to help her 'for preferment of Justice and discharging of yor bedwomans conscience'.[21] These examples demonstrate a marginally more *individualised* dimension to 'conscience' in the conciliar courts than Dennis Klinck once perceived in the late medieval Chancery (at least, based on the printed documents he surveyed).[22]

The especially individualised meaning and application of 'conscience' in this context was reflected in extensive emphasis on the malignant motivations of defendants here. Petitions to conciliar courts are full of references to opponents moved by 'evil will', 'malice', an ill or evil 'disposition', and/or of a 'devilish mind'. On these grounds, it seems, a matter that would normally be triable at the common law could become justiciable in conscience. A notable example in Requests is that brought in the later years of Henry VII's reign by Robert Reve, a husbandman and sub-collector of taxes in Kent, self-described as 'a man unlettered [who] can not reade'. Reve had been bound to a local 'high colectour' by obligation, the terms of which were read out to him 'upon trust' before its sealing. It had since transpired that the obligation contained further conditions which he claimed had not been relayed to him but which he had unwittingly broken, and for which he was now being sued in the Exchequer, 'contrarie to reason and conscience'. The instrument was technically legal, but the honesty of its creation and its execution was disputable – there had been a premeditated attempt to trick him.[23] It was on similar footing that, in 1489, Chancellor Morton made his response to Serjeant Fineux's objection that not everything could be remedied in Chancery, or else there would be no need for the confessional, in which he specified that Chancery could rule when the defendant (an executor, in that case) was found to have been moved by evil disposition to make release to the testator's debtor.[24] The same rhetoric also served to frame earlier suits between the parties in common law courts, often recounted within the narrative petitions to conciliar justice to have been moved not by 'right' or 'colour of title' but by malice, greed, and evil will.

[19] REQ2/12/155.
[20] REQ2/3/385.
[21] BG/11/29 (1520) f 11.
[22] Klinck (n 4) 17.
[23] REQ2/3/264.
[24] YB Hil 4 Hen VII, pl 8, ff 4b–5a.

There appears to have been some expectation that the conscience courts – and *only* these courts – could induce the full 'truth' of a matter. Petitions often alluded to the belief that summoning and compelling the defendant to make answer on oath would help the 'trouth be known'. In turn, warrants written and signed by Requests judges and sent to the clerks of the privy seal ordered the production of writs to bring defendants and third parties in to 'speak the truth' ('*dicendum veritatem*').[25] The oath itself had defendants swear that they would say and submit things they 'believe' and 'knowe to bee true'.[26] When petitions asked instead for the authorisation of a local commission in the first instance, this was also framed as an opportunity for indifferent parties to 'serche examine and knowe the trouth' or to elicit the 'very trouth and playnes' of the matter from both parties. It was insisted that proposed witnesses – friends and older neighbours – would be able to 'declare and justifie for trouth' the plaintiff's complaints. In this same vein, at least one commissioner rehearsed ahead of the depositions he took down for Requests that 'hit ys merytorius & a charytabell dede for every trew crystyn man to wytnys & testyfye all maters of trawthe'.[27] We find the same appeal to truthfulness in defendants' written answers, too; all such responses were framed as a 'declaration of trouth', and some as being 'upon his consciens and honestye'.[28] Such inferences suggest confidence in all quarters as to the fact-finding capability of pleadings and testimonies entered under oath in conscience courts, a process which made the internal forum of conscience justiciable. That this was deemed to be particularly within the special remit of this tribunal is implied in the plaintiff William Wright's replication to Requests in 1522, in which he begged 'to have the matier of trouthe to appere to this honorable courte of consciens ffor if he have not help in this courte he is uttrely doon in this world'.[29]

Yet something distinct to *conciliar* justice at this time was the evocation of the royal conscience. This derived from the extraordinary and flexible way in which these tribunals worked, in proximity to the King and more explicitly in his name (whereas Chancery had become firmly the domain of the Chancellor or Lord Keeper). It was still possible to gain a hearing in Requests and Star Chamber, elements of the main Council, by petitioning to the King in person: such was the route taken by William Clerk and his son, Thomas, who later described having 'knelyd byfore yor nobyll grace [Henry VIII] wythowt yor gatys of Grenwych', whereupon it behoved the King to advise that they 'move a byll unto yor noble grace of all maner of [their] busyness'. This took the form of a 'byll of supplycacyon unto my lorde Cardynalles grace' – to Thomas Wolsey – which he directed on to John Stokesley, who presided at that time over the Court of Requests.[30] And so in these courts conscience and its associated concepts were framed as characteristics embodied by the King himself. Above all, as a petition's narrative blended into a closing exhortation for the King's prosperity, he was presumed to be naturally possessed of 'abundant' mercy, pity, and charity, and willing to direct his prerogative in favour

[25] TNA PSO 2/4, items 98, 109, 112, 114, 11, as well as item 49 of the bundle labelled 'August 9 Hen. 8 to April 20 Hen. 8' in the same class.

[26] As per the text of the oaths used in Star Chamber, printed in JA Guy, *The Court of Star Chamber and Its Records to the Reign of Elizabeth I* (London, HMSO, 1985) 27–28.

[27] REQ3/22/2 *Evering v Drewe*.

[28] eg, REQ2/5/337.

[29] REQ3/5 *Wright v Parker*.

[30] REQ3/17 *Clerk v Clerk*.

of his subjects whenever required. The double meaning of 'conscience' in Requests is encapsulated by the petition of Richard Bigges, a clothmaker from Kent, who lamented that

> the said William Bowyer [the defendant] lytyll regarding his conscience good truth or equate hath delayed yor said orator in his payment … to [Bigges's] utter undoing except he be holpen here by conscience.[31]

Conscience was a standard to which both the adversary and the court's judges – and, by extension, the King – might be held.

It is in this royal element to conciliar justice, where the King's presence loomed larger, where we can most clearly perceive some blending with the concept of 'equity'. This was a term very rarely used in petitions, and it appears most often in conjunction again with 'right', 'conscience', and/or 'justice', either in the sense of virtues violated by the defendant or of ideals to which a potential determination should accord.[32] For example, in a bill to the 'Kings comiss[ioners] at Salop' – the Council in the Marches, sitting in Shrewsbury – a mercer from Ludlow complained of a default in a debt of £10 for the sale of woollen cloths under obligation as 'contrary to justice right equitie and good conscience'.[33] On occasion petitioners and their counsel appear to have construed equity in relation to law, and perhaps as a mode of interpretation. In this way, plaintiffs and counsel sometimes explicitly sought a remedy consonant with the 'equitie of yor [the king's] laws'.[34] Interestingly, a petition from Richard Strode to Star Chamber in 1546, part of a long-running dispute between the Strode and Halswell families over lands in Ermington, Yealmpton and Brixton in Devon that had been heard in Requests, Chancery, and Star Chamber since the 1510s, specifically requested a final remedy that could 'stonde wythe equyte & the dexteryte of [the] comen lawe of thys realm'.[35] This precise wording carries the classical connotations of equity as the mitigation of the rigour of law by acting on spirit instead of on word.

Otherwise, though, equity in this context cleaved closer to its 'normative' dimensions as perceptible in wider late medieval and early Tudor culture. There were several 'fitting means' by which a king might administer justice to his people, according to Chancellor Morton's speech before Parliament in 1489: overseeing laws and statutes, distributing offices, rewarding good, and punishing offenders, but also generally remaining 'calm in discussing and determining cases' and personally delivering 'equity in judgment'.[36] Justice was theoretically and practically in the gift of the sovereign, and the early Tudor conciliar courts worked on this principle. Similarly, in the mouths of more ordinary folk, equity was figured simply as a tempering force to government. A rhyme composed as an 'exhortation to the nobles and commons of the North' by the friar Dr John Pickering in the later 1530s, and said to be 'in every man's mouth' in Bridlington and Pontefract, prayed that God would preserve the King 'long time to reign with equity'.[37]

[31] REQ2/3/124.
[32] eg, REQ2/2/136, 2/4/55, 393, 2/7/6, 128.
[33] BG/11/29 (1520) f 6.
[34] REQ2/2/154, 2/3/290, 2/4/94, 123.
[35] TNA STAC2/28/1.
[36] *Parliament Rolls of Medieval England* xvi, 8–9 (1489 Parliament, item 1).
[37] TNA SP 1/118 ff 282–293v.

Hence, despite its classical origins, equity was not an unfamiliar concept among the wider populace and formed part of their lexicon about monarchy and governance, just as conscience did.

Such a literal reading of either term can only take us so far, of course. The use of this language was so formulaic across Chancery and all the central and provincial conciliar courts that we can only speculate about its meaning. It may in fact have been deployed simply to signpost an appeal to courts of conscience for the purposes of the internal direction of bills within the royal household and central administration. Along these lines, Nicholas Pronay supplied two identifiers for what we might class as 'specifically equitable cases': petitions in which suitors 'claimed failure at common law on a technicality' and those who sought 'essentially equitable remedy in the sense that their case was grounded on natural justice'.[38] Examples of the former include the classic case of the debtor who had satisfied their obligations but remained without an acquittance and so was at risk of being sued at common law by an immoral opponent. We might also include the innumerable suits in which arms of the council were asked to weigh an enfeoffment to use to which the petitioner was a beneficiary against a vague allegation of 'withholding' of the same estate by the defendant (who usually turned out to have a lease for their own part). These were matters in which the extraordinary capabilities of the conscience courts were called upon to defend subjects who could claim to have been made unfairly vulnerable by a common-law system seen as rigid or outmoded.

Yet much more often within conciliar court petitions do we see examples of the second of Pronay's categories, where social circumstances were perceived as granting suits in conscience whatever the subject of a dispute might be. Appeals to conscience and equity in petitions to the King were more usually framed on the basis of the defendant's unconscionable behaviour and – relatedly – barriers to accessible and fair justice in other courts rather than on a legal technicality. There is, then, good reason to perceive conscience and equity as being attached as much to the extraordinary, merciful capacity of monarchy as to any specific curial or jurisdictional remit. Indeed, what this amounted to in the early Tudor period was a perception from the perspective of litigants and their counsel that extraordinary conciliar justice offered a supplementary jurisdiction and not necessarily some supplementary body of law.[39] And this is most plain in the procedures of conciliar justice.

III. Applying Conscience

More straightforward than the obscure rhetoric of bills is the evidence for how 'conscience' was applied as a juristic, juridical principle – how the conscience of the defendant was tested, how the broader virtue was restored, and how the King's internal conscience was enacted, if at all. We would do well to keep in mind, as Mike Macnair has convincingly demonstrated, that neither 'conscience' nor 'equity' had their ordinary meanings when actually put into practice in legal contexts – though they did

[38] Pronay (n 14) 92.
[39] Post (n 8) 68–69.

manifest themselves in judicial procedures.[40] Key to the discussion of how conciliar justice worked is the acknowledgement that it was overseen largely by theologians, canonists, and civilians. Much has been made of the clerical and civilian backgrounds of the late medieval and early Tudor masters of the rolls and chancellors, including Robert Stillington, John Russell, and John Morton; and, later, of the work of Thomas Wolsey, as chancellor and cardinal, in Star Chamber as in Chancery.[41] Likewise, the earliest presidents of the attendant council of Requests were bishops educated in divinity – Richard Foxe (Durham), Thomas Savage (Rochester, then London), and Richard Fitzjames (Rochester). The provincial councils in the North and in the Welsh Marches were headed by prominent bishops of those regions, too: in Wales, a series of them from John Alcock (Rochester, then Worcester, then Ely) in the 1470s to John Veysey (Exeter), Rowland Lee and Richard Sampson (successive bishops of Coventry and Lichfield) towards the end of Henry VIII's reign; in Yorkshire, Thomas Savage (then Archbishop of York) in Henry VII's reign, then Cuthbert Tunstall (Durham) followed by Robert Holgate (Llandaff, then York) in the revived tribunal of the 1530s.[42] In this sphere, as in Chancery, we perceive a general trend away from theologians and towards doctors of canon or civil law, or both, across this period.

What expertise and insight could these judges offer to conscience-based justice? Since each of the men just mentioned was a practising ecclesiastic, educated in theology and canon and/or civil law, it is plausible that they were familiar with the *summae confessorum*, sometimes even called *summae de casibus conscientiae*, printed in this period. As a genre these manuals have been described as a 'hodge-podge of Roman Law, canon law, moral theology, and common sense'.[43] Yet recent research has shown them to have been treated as informative legal literature, perhaps equal to the *Corpus Iuris Canonici*, in late medieval church courts.[44] Meanwhile, elements of the well-circulated, Franciscan-authored *Summa Rosella* and *Summa Angelica* were cited by St German for some of his Doctor of Divinity's views about the strength of pacts and promises in conscience and in common law.[45] That petitioners and counsel so regularly put it to the conciliar judges that promises for sales and services had been made without writing but were nonetheless surely enforceable in conscience suggests some expectation that these courts *were* informed by commentary on the internal forum as a factor in decision-making. Certainly, on the grounds of their clerical practice, we might agree that these judges were 'exercising the temporal counterpart of the confessional' in their care for defendants' souls.[46] As to the royal element of conciliar justice, many of them had cared for the *King's* soul at one point or another, too, as royal almoners or deans of his

[40] M Macnair, 'Equity and Conscience' (2007) 27 *Oxford Journal of Legal Studies* 659.

[41] Pronay (n 14) 91–93; TS Haskett, 'The Medieval English Court of Chancery' (1996) 14 *Law and History Review* 245, 260; JA Guy, *The Cardinal's Court: The Impact of Thomas Wolsey in Star Chamber* (Hassocks, Harvester Press, 1977); AWB Simpson, *A History of the Common Law of Contract* (Oxford, Oxford University Press, 1975) 400–401.

[42] See the lists produced in existing studies of these courts: Skeel (n 10) 287; RR Reid, *The King's Council in the North* (London, Longmans, Green and Co, 1921) 487.

[43] Simpson (n 41) 378.

[44] J Kirkland, 'Confessors' Manuals and the Practice of Law in Medieval Ecclesiastical Courts' (2021) 42 *Journal of Legal History* 258.

[45] Simpson (n 41) 375–405; *St German's Doctor and Student* (n 2) xxviii, 276–79.

[46] JH Baker, *An Introduction to English Legal History*, 4th edn (Oxford, Oxford University Press, 2007) 106.

personal chapel. Hence we might take seriously Gwilym Dodd's point that the presence of 'bishop-councillors' and other clergymen in the administration of royal, discretionary justice was *integral*, not incidental.[47] Still, as Dennis Klinck aptly put it in his study of Chancery equity, it is simply not enough to advance the '"medieval Chancellor equals ecclesiastic equals canonist equals expositor of conscience in canonist terms" argument'.[48] We must instead seek instances of where such thinking was evidently applied.

In the first instance, it is widely acknowledged that 'conscience' in the context of equity had a 'substantive' or 'normative' element – denoting a generalised sense of right and justice – but also a procedural, fact-finding one. Where the common law operated on a system of proofs designed to prove a limited set of facts, and its judges were largely contented to allow circumstantial details to fall to the determination of juries, the bill procedure in use within Chancery and the conciliar courts brought a whole range of individual circumstances to the fore. This made the existence of a separate forum for conscience broadly acceptable to St German. Enough has been said about the evidentiary dimension of conscience – especially the way in which it echoed the *denunciatio evangelica* – built into English bill procedure to not bear repeating in too much detail here.[49] The salient point is that conciliar court judges could, like the Chancellor, order the production of writs to summon defendants *subpoena* and make answer under oath. This process was so essential to the ethos of these courts that if a defendant could not appear and instead sent some representative to declare before the court their infirmity and inability to ride to court, a commission would be established to take their answer at home and convey it back to the judges with haste.

As to what else the conciliar judges were privy to when they 'dylygently herde … groundely ryp[e]ly and with good delyberacion' each case, the surviving decrees are often vague. What does come through on comparison across the conscience courts is that whereas many Chancery decrees described considerations made 'by evidence and witnesses', the equivalent orders in Requests and in Star Chamber usually referred more generally to examination of all the 'circumstances of the case'.[50] In the first place, it seems that a much wider range of evidence could be considered in the conciliar courts; that is, the plaintiff was not obliged to state a fact and produce a particular piece of evidence to prove it. An especially creative and compelling use of evidence in Requests appears in the suit of the Pilbarowe family of London, after their adolescent son had died suddenly of the plague while away trading the family's tin in Cornwall and all of his ready cash and possessions had come into the hands of the local priest who conducted his funeral. Letters sent in earlier years from the son to his parents while studying abroad in Rouen were brought into court as evidence. Examination pertained not to their contents, which mostly consisted of complaints about the cost of living and the lack of 'Inglysh mens compeny', but to the sample of Edward's handwriting to compare to the signature

[47] G Dodd, 'Reason, Conscience and Equity: Bishops as the King's Judges in Later Medieval England' (2014) 99 *History* 213, 222.

[48] Klinck (n 4) 26.

[49] H Coing, 'English Equity and the *Denunciatio Evangelica* of the Canon Law' (1955) 71 *Law Quarterly Review* 223; and, more recently, Macnair (n 40).

[50] Metzger (n 1) 84. See, eg, W Brown and HB McCall (eds), *Yorkshire Star Chamber Proceedings* Yorkshire Archaeological Society vols XLI, XLV, LI (J Whitehead and Son, 1908–14) vol 2, 121.

on his hastily produced will – several witnesses swore that they recognised the hand in the letters, at least.[51] Elsewhere in the Requests archive we find family tree diagrams scrawled onto the back of pleadings, attempting to keep track of lines of inheritance that were so often central to plaintiffs' claims to title.[52] Decrees therefore sometimes rehearsed simply that the plaintiff had 'proved hym to be cousyn and next heyr … by reason wherof he ought to be preferred'.[53]

Otherwise, in determining land disputes, the conciliar judges were often expected to determine the validity of documentary evidence: the deeds, charters, and indentures that litigants described keeping in locked boxes and chests in their homes. One of the few decrees surviving from the Henrician Council of the North, recording the determination of a case between two Yorkshiremen in the early 1540s, saw the judges uphold the 'wryt of entre in the nature of assise' and 'wrytt of entre in the post' that the plaintiff was able to show for his recovery of various lands, which the defendant occupied without having paid rent. In this straightforward case the validity and propriety of the plaintiff's documentation was the default position, in the face of a defendant who had no justification except his poverty for his failure to pay up.[54] In instances like this, conciliar courts had to rely on their common law members, or else the King's justices, to interpret legal contracts. In the suit reportedly brought before Henry VII's Council by Robert Pilkington of Derbyshire in the early 1490s, his claims to lands in Mellor were pitted against deeds produced in the courtroom by his opponent, John Ainsworth. But Pilkington was vindicated when one of the Council's common lawyers and Chief Justice of King's Bench, William Hussey, 'lokyd on [them] but a lytyll whyle' and then 'cast thaym away from hym and said thay were enturlynyd, and alowyd thaym not'.[55] Similarly, in one Requests decree from 1526 it was said that the 'Counsaill havyng thadvice of diverse persons lerned in the kings lawes' had determined that a deed shown on the part of the Abbey of Dieulacres was made 'without consent of the convent & not sealed with theyr seal' and so was 'voyde & of no force ne effect in the lawe'.[56] This is all to say that the prevalence of ecclesiastical lead judges in conciliar justice, the centrality of confessing to the truth in its procedures, and the wide remit of its fact-finding mechanisms did not mean that these courts dropped normal legal standards in their assessment of evidence – particularly when they sought to prove matters raised within pleadings.

Another hitherto overlooked source of fact-finding in conscience at work in these tribunals was their reliance on the testimonies of witnesses and the commissions that gathered them. This was a consistent element of the provision that the attendant Council in Requests could offer petitioners; indeed, some requested a commission of 'indifferent' men in their region to bring the parties to peace in the first instance, rather than a central court hearing of their cause. In addition to the usual elderly members of a community brought in to speak to immemorial customs and land-holding arrangements in their

[51] REQ2/3/181.

[52] eg, REQ2/2/188, 2/7/68, 2/12/179, 2/13/67.

[53] eg, REQ1/4 f 76.

[54] These decrees survive in REQ3/9 *Fox v Vincent*; for transcriptions and commentary, see L Flannigan, 'New Evidence of Justice-giving by the Early Tudor Council of the North, 1540–43' (2022) 59 *Northern History* 281.

[55] *Report on Manuscripts in Various Collections* (HMSO, 1901–14) II 33.

[56] REQ1/5 f 28. See also REQ1/4 f 137; REQ1/5 f 112v; REQ2/3/165.

locality, commissioners might also question those present when ritualistic exchanges of land took place, when indentures were sealed, and when last wills were read or proved. It should be said that the commissioners themselves were not typically common lawyers; rather, they were drawn from the ranks of the local gentry and clergy. Consequently some of those tasked with balancing competing title claims were eventually forced to admit that their 'lernyng is not sufficient to determyn or fynyshe' the dispute and to return the case back to the central administration so that 'men learned therupon may have opon knowlegh and playne instruccion to diffyne … the same mater according to the law'.[57] Oftentimes, though, the questions they were asking were less legal and more personal and circumstantial – and additional to matters raised within the pleadings. Memorable examples from the Requests archive include the testimony of a local physician about the dying moments of one of his patients and whether he divulged to anyone that his round box was full of leases before it was stolen; the impression of the citizens of a London parish as to how far the defendants could expect 'justice with favor' in the city; and the question of whether one defendant, the allegedly unruly vicar of Tathwell in Lincolnshire, was 'a Scotte borne' or not.[58] In these cases we can observe commissioners working to expand the body of information and facts – some technical, others not – that might be relevant to a particular interpersonal dispute, all of which would be certified back to the conciliar courts to help inform a final decree.

Importantly, commissioners' enquiries often aided the central, conciliar judges in assessing litigants from a social and financial standpoint. They might not have always been cognisant of the finer legal details of a case before them, but they could use their certificates to highlight the plight of certain parties. In so doing they contributed to a specialised manifestation of conscience in the royal conciliar sphere that came closer to ensuring fairness, and even offering mercy, in the provision of litigation. An exemplary case is the investigation undertaken on behalf of the litigious Anthony Complay, a surgeon from Ipswich who sued to Requests several times in the late 1510s and early 1520s about the sale of his house and goods by his adulterous wife while he was on a voyage to Iceland. The commissioners, two gentlemen, reported that based on witness testimonies it appeared that Complay had licensed his wife to sell anything she needed in order to support their child, but that she had voided this agreement by giving all the proceeds to her lover. They also noted that 'the costys of the sewte of the said Antony amountyth to the summe of … C markes'.[59] This represents a straightforward accounting of legal fees that was no doubt offered in support of the petitioner's own standard claim to poverty and to help the judges determine the value of any recompense awarded.

Other commissioners were much more outspoken about the poverty of the people before them. Those appointed to hear the matter between brothers Thomas and Nicholas Jackson of Fincham, Norfolk, in 1527 beseeched the King and Council to 'be moved with pytee and to help this poor man Thomas Jakson in his right'; eventually the defendant's title was found to be 'of noo force ne effect' and he was moved to pay four marks for the petitioner's costs and charges.[60] Elsewhere, the commissioners in the

[57] REQ2/2/154; REQ3/3 *Carpenter v City of Coventry*.
[58] REQ2/8/317; REQ3/4 *Mone v Kyrton*; REQ3/11/1 *Dion v Story*.
[59] REQ2/8/84.
[60] REQ2/3/80; REQ1/5 f 35.

matter between the 'pore men' of Abbotsham against the Abbot of Tavistock, regarding their right to put up butts for longbow shooting in accordance with a parliamentary act of 1513, went further, pleading with the Dean of the Chapel Royal that he

> be gode maister on to the seide complaynauntes and of yor charyte to have pyte of them for without that you be gode & gracyous master on to them they ar[e] men undon in this worlde … for the seide pore men have borowyde of the score of ther church vj li … And those pore men ar most ungodeley handelyd that ever war pore men for doyng & executyng of the kinges comaundement.[61]

The same pity was extended to defendants too, with commissioners or witnesses occasionally writing into the courts asking them to 'be good master to [the accused] a poore man acordynge onto ryght and no other wyse'.[62] In cases like these, the commissioners measured not just specific economic worth and legal costs but the social disparity so often alleged within petitions.

This capacity for charity demonstrably fed into the conciliar judges' decision-making. In the end, and contrary to the commissioners' findings that Complay's wife had no right to sell all of his property, the Requests Council ruled that a prior who now had possession of the lands *did* have the right after all, owing to a previous lease made for a term of years by his predecessor. But, perhaps based on the pleas of the commissioners and Complay, they decreed that 'in consideracion only of the povertie and not for noo right nor title on his behalve proved' the prior would pay the plaintiff the sum of four pounds.[63] A similar decree passed under the remit of Bishop Richard Sampson in Requests in 1529 described the Council as 'having pety' on a defendant who had lost his suit and ensuring that he received fifty marks outstanding from an old debt owed by the petitioner even though this was beyond the remit of the case.[64] In Yorkshire in the 1540s, the Council of the North's consideration of a land dispute in which a poor tenant simply could not afford to pay his rent resulted in them overseeing the release of the lease to the plaintiff. Yet the final line of their last decree in this matter ordered that

> the seyd [plaintiff] of his good wyll is contented at the request of the court at the departyng of the seyd [defendant] if he do depart lovingly and quietly … to gyve unto the seyd [defendant] fourty shillynges sterlyng.

There was no legal justification for this; in a matter where the defendant plainly owed the plaintiff as much as £12 in arrears, it was purely an act of charity.[65] So, both or either of the parties could benefit from the Council's pity – though, since winners asked to pay up were said to have been requested and to have 'consented', it was the parties' consciences that were again put on the spot.

This disposition for charitable treatment of the poor was further regularised in other elements of the conciliar courts' activities in the early sixteenth century. In Doe's work on conscience as an element of common law judgments, he suggested that the judicial conscience might be identified 'in the assessment of damages', and this

[61] REQ3/1/1 *Lacy v Abbot of Tavistock*.
[62] REQ3/22/1 *King v Cely*.
[63] REQ1/4 ff 195v–196.
[64] REQ1/5 f 69.
[65] REQ3/9 *Fox v Vincent*.

holds true for the early Tudor conciliar courts.[66] In fact, there *was* some demonstrable canon law influence in conscience-based justice along these lines: in the admission of plaintiffs, and possibly defendants too, to litigate *in forma pauperis*. Fee waivers had recently been codified in the common law as well, with a statute at the 1495 Parliament ordering the King's courts of record to admit 'such persons as are poore' without costs for original writs and legal counsel.[67] Yet, to date, little evidence has emerged from the ample plea rolls of King's Bench and Common Pleas to suggest that they enacted this provision with much gusto (unless they chose to generally leave it off the record). In comparison, the conciliar courts administered it liberally. An initial wave of *in forma pauperis* admissions in Requests from the later 1510s onwards is well-documented through annotations on the reverse side of its petitions reading 'pauper'. The same notes appear on petitions in Star Chamber during Wolsey's tenure and on memoranda surviving from the Council in the Marches, while the Council in the North and a short-lived Council in the West, headed by Lord Russell in the year 1539–40, were ordered to 'appoint consalle and other requisites without paying of any money' for 'poure sueters havyng no money'.[68]

Importantly, much of the initial wave of *in forma pauperis* in the conciliar courts occurred under the auspices of their theologian and civilian clergymen-judges: under Wolsey in Star Chamber, the deans of the Chapel Royal and almoners in Requests, and the bishops heading the provincial councils. So we might plausibly suggest that the ideological foundation for such activities was the decretals of the canon law and the practice of church courts, as much as the common-law statute. John Veysey, the Dean of the Chapel Royal and leading judge in Requests in the late 1510s, is known to have been bequeathed a copy of William Lyndwood's *Provinciale*, the manual of the laws of the Province of Canterbury drawn from the decretals of Gregory IX.[69] In its pages he may have read Lyndwood's suggestions that a pauper at law could be defined in a number of ways – as being economically poor (having less than fifty 'gold coins'), reliant on labour, not of sound mind, and/or without dependents – and that it was the judge's duty to ensure all litigants were properly counselled by providing advocates for free where they could not be afforded.[70] These were principles that Veysey likely applied not only in Requests but also during his spell as the president of the Council in the Marches, when we also find 'pauper' annotations.[71] And this attempt to pre-empt the damages sustained by petitioners was increasingly followed up in Requests at the other end of a suit, with the formal regulation of costs and charges recompensed to the 'winning' party. Litigants submitted bills listing their costs, including for document production, termly counsel, travel and accommodation, and clerks' fees, which the judges signed off and awarded (though they might silently deduct costs claimed for lost husbandry while the party attended court). So, in the proposed distinction between 'solicitude for petitioners who

[66] Doe (n 3) 146–47.

[67] An Act to admit such as are poor to sue in forma pauperis, 11 Hen VII, c 12 (1495).

[68] Guy, *Star Chamber* (n 26) 62; REQ3/8 *Plommer v Ward*; *LP* xiii I, 1269 (SP 1/133 ff 211–221v).

[69] AB Emden, *A Biographical Register of the University of Oxford to AD 1500* (Oxford, Clarendon Press, 1957–59) vol III, 1948.

[70] W Lyndwood, *Provinciale seu constitutiones Angliae* (Oxford, R Davis, 1679) 68c.

[71] eg, REQ2/1/2, 2/2/54, 2/3/165, 2/4/52, 2/5/58, 2/6/34, 2/7/122, 2/8/339, 2/12/126, 155, 159; REQ3/8 *Plommer v Ward*.

lacked remedy' and the care for the soul of the wrongdoer, the conciliar courts leant more regularly towards the former.[72]

Commission certificates also echoed rhetoric about the poor and unconscionable conduct of the principal disputants, which also influenced court proceedings. Writs sometimes specifically asked examiners to relate the 'demeanure' of the accused party; that is, not as a part of the events that had already happened, but *during* the proceedings of the commission.[73] When the defendant Walter Born – the 'man without consciens', according to his accusers – was summoned to a commission, he 'little regarded the kinges writing' (the writ) and told the examiners that they had no authority over him. This was presumably very in character, since the curate of the parish reported that during a previous royal commission Born had stated that 'if the king sent his brode seale and my lord Cardynall his seale yet he wold do no lasse', among other 'diverse obstainte wordes & evill demeanor'. Along with the commissioners' other comments about Born's abuse of a convent seal and general terrorising of the residents of Wick Episcopi – it appears that 'all the pore tenauntes of that lordship' and further afield had turned up to complain to the commissioners about him – the Council was convinced to summon him for a hearing.[74] This principle of obedience and good conduct applied to petitioners as well. When two complainants in 1517 were 'not mynded to take eny other end or direccion' from the appointed arbiters, preferring to have 'ther title by [the Council] discussed', Veysey and his associate judges remitted the matter to the common law and dismissed the 'obbedyant' defendant from further appearance.[75]

The effect of this emphasis on obedience was that those who proved themselves contemptuous of the mechanisms of royal justice might receive a cold shoulder from the conciliar courts *regardless* of any evidence they might produce for their lawful title. An intriguing example from Requests is the suit between Richard and Mary Flint and Robert Hackett, concerning the right to a messuage in Turlington, Leicestershire. The plaintiffs claimed the property by inheritance from John Hackett, Mary's father, while the defendant argued for his part that the same John had bargained and sold it to his grandfather. A commission held in March 1542 heard testimonies confirming that John had been within age at the time of this sale, but the returned certificate also reported that the defendant had failed to turn up on five separate days given to him to show his own evidence.[76] When the matter was determined in Requests a couple of months later, the judges accepted that Robert Hackett possessed 'wytnes[es] and evidences whereby he clierly myght have had fynalle ende & direccion' – that is, that he had the right – but that he had so 'obstynatly disobeyde' the commissioners and vexed the plaintiff by delaying proceedings that although he was allowed to retain his possession he was ordered to pay the plaintiffs forty shillings 'in full satisfaccion for the costes afore assessed and specified'.[77] Here 'right' and 'conscience' proved to be separable concepts when put into action.

[72] Simpson (n 41) 398–99.
[73] eg, the commission writ in REQ3/5 *Slak v Colisen*.
[74] REQ2/7/51, REQ1/105 f 227v.
[75] REQ1/4 f 56.
[76] REQ3/13 *Flint v Hackett*.
[77] REQ1/7 f 114.

In all, litigants to conciliar justice and the judges in its courts appear to have shared an innate understanding of conscience as a universal, near-objective sense of right and wrong. Informed by pleadings and testimonies made under oath and by commissioners' interpretations of events, judges framed their recorded decisions with the same language as appeared in petitions. Their decrees similarly characterised the behaviour of the defendant as being contrary to 'right and conscience', where proven, and it was implied that they reviewed the evidence before them in the light of both 'law and conscience'. More specific formulations appear occasionally: one of the earliest usages of the word 'conscience' in a Requests decree of 1507 was in the statement that a previous legal ruling was found 'effectuall … by the holy lawes of co[m]men and good conscience'; and, a few decades later, the Council in the North felt that a rent 'ought to be approcyoned in consyence' between prospective owners of the lands in question.[78] But aside from such literal, ultimately abstract, evocations of conscience (and, occasionally, equity), the idea was defined most clearly within the procedures of conciliar justice. This included the testing of the individual conscience under oath, as in Chancery, but also mechanisms to ensure that everyone should have access to justice. Here we see not just the straightforward correction of consciences upon frauds and broken promises that Lord Ellesmere later identified as driving Chancery's jurisdiction.[79] Rather, in addition to procedural elements that trialled the internal forum of all parties, conciliar justice applied conscience and/or equity in its attempts to mitigate the unconscionable and unjust workings of the legal system and in its provision of mercy and charity to poorer suitors.

IV. Conciliar Conscience and the Common Law

It is worth reflecting briefly on what this seemingly capacious application of conscience in the conciliar courts meant for the broader course of English law. Of course, common lawyers played a key role in the workings of conciliar justice, as counsel, examiners, and (more so as time went on) as judges. In a couple of rare reports made to the Court of Requests by serjeants-at-law, apparently employed to examine the legal ramifications, we find appeals to conscience as much as to their training. John Rowe concluded in one dispute concerning the occupation and waste of lands in Exeter that 'I thinke this pore man [the plaintiff] ought not to be put from his land … as I cowde discerne [ei]ther be my lernytt or consciens.'[80] After examining a 'composicion' made by local 'smytheholders' limiting who could carry and sell iron in the Forest of Dean, the Chief Justice John Ernley wrote to the Dean of the Chapel Royal asking, 'pray you be good master unto this pore man [the plaintiff]', whose iron had been seized, since he had been 'gretly iniured and wronged as ffar as I can [discern by] my lernyng and in my conscyens'.[81] Still, notwithstanding this input, the right of the emergent 'conscience' jurisdiction to handle certain matters determinable at the common law was questionable both within and

[78] REQ1/3 ff 297–97v; REQ3/9 *Fox v Vincent*.

[79] *Earl of Oxford's Case* (1615) 1 Ch Rep 1, 21 ER 485.

[80] REQ3/22/1 *Tucker v Citizens of Exeter*.

[81] REQ3/22/2 *Waldorn v Cachemay*. The Requests council, including the Dean John Veysey, agreed that this composition was only to its authors' 'singuler advayles and proffettes': REQ1/4 f 112v.

outside these courts. I have written elsewhere about various moments across the early sixteenth century in which the main royal Council paused to consider and scrutinise the workings of its judicial branches and even to investigate the work of specific judges.[82] But there is also ample evidence of internal attempts to regulate what conscience could do.

The best evidence of the limits of conscience are in those instances where Requests declined to hear cases or specific elements of a dispute in the first instance. Many remittals and dismissals resulted from the social assessments just discussed: petitioners were found to have sufficient goods and lands to sue at the common law and to be ineligible to litigate in a jurisdiction increasingly characterised as being 'erect & established … in & for the relief of the kynges power subiecttes & for the spedy administracyon of Justyce'.[83] Yet there are other moments in which Requests dismissed cases on a technical basis, particularly where their remit over land disputes was concerned. In one interlocutory order entered into Requests' order books in January 1523, it was decided that a certain case ought to be sued at the common law if it not be resolved by local arbitrators, 'forasmoche as it concernythe the right and title of lande'.[84] This seems strange, given that more than half of that court's cases at this time revolved around title to land, which generally did not stop them from investigating and passing judgment; perhaps this instance was brought on by the Council's inquiry into the work of the leading judge and theologian John Stokesley, announced a week prior.[85]

Later on, in the 1540s and in response to a growing volume of business, the master of Requests and common lawyer Robert Dacres set out two limits on the sorts of land cases that his Court might hear. First, if neither 'the plaintif nor his auncestors have not bene possessed of such landes, as are in the complaint specified' for a long duration of time, then 'the same parties and the matter by them brought [was] to be remytted to the common law'. Unfortunately all surviving manuscript copies of Dacres's orders leave the specified duration blank, but at least one defendant quibbled a decree passed against him on the grounds that 'thorder of this court hath byn that where hath ben such possession by the space of xxx^{ti} yeres the seid Court hath dysmyssed the partie defendaunt'.[86]

Secondly, Dacres specified that 'all bills concerning Copie hold landes be alwayes remitted to the Lords officers of the mannour, wherof the landes are holden', though it might still examine other land-holding arrangements. This order put into words a principle that the judges in Requests already recognised, it seems, since more than a decade earlier they had determined the freehold elements of one case but stated that 'as to the copy hold of any suche be the p[ar]ties to trie ther title afor the lorde of whom the same landes are holden'.[87] That the Court provably made this shift contradicts IS

[82] L Flannigan, '"Allowable or Not"? John Stokesley, the Court of Requests, and Royal Justice in Sixteenth-Century England' (2020) 93 *Historical Research* 621.

[83] REQ1/5 f 189v, REQ2/3/34, 137, 2/8/84, REQ3/6 *Marmyon v Hasylwood*, REQ3/7 *Bracebridge v Swynerton*, REQ3/19 *Dakenfield v Sheffield*; REQ3/22/2 *Brooksbank v Allinson*.

[84] REQ1/5 f 11v.

[85] San Marino, Huntington Library, Ellesmere MS 2652 f 4v; London, British Library, Lansdowne MS 639 f 56v.

[86] REQ3/9 *Unknown v Abbot*. Another case remitted on this basis was REQ3/7 *Bracebridge v Swynerton*.

[87] REQ3/14 *Cobley v Denys and Kyrton*. See also an order from 1530 showing similar concern for the liberties of the lord of Uttoxeter in copyhold cases: REQ3/5 *Hogeson v Hogeson*.

Leadam's interpretation of Requests as the defender of the copyholder against voracious landlords; conversely, its judges were concerned about breaching manorial liberties.[88] Moreover, many of Dacres's orders for how the Court should act going forward restored the defendant's right to due process and protected against vexation: plaintiffs were to be examined under oath about their substance and remitted to the common law automatically if found to be rich; all parties were liable to a fine if they failed to bring in their pleadings in person by a set date; and petitioners were given one term in which to prosecute their cause before being summarily dismissed.[89]

Elsewhere, we glimpse some hesitancy on the part of the judges and masters surrounding specific cases that appears to come down simply to their ability to pass judgment on legal technicalities. One suit from early 1517 required the judges, then headed by the Dean of the Chapel Royal, John Veysey (a canonist), to determine who had the right between a plaintiff who had failed to fulfil the sale of quarts of wheat because they had been seized by the King's purveyors for the French campaign of 1513, and a defendant who had allegedly forged an obligation to regain his money. Although Requests sent the cause out to commission, they eventually ruled that 'fforasmoch as thys cause ys upon a specialte of obligacion which ys mat[er] det[er]minable at the comen lawe' it ought to be dismissed and remitted to trial elsewhere.[90] Later on, a suit submitted to Requests in 1533 between Roger Holt of London, goldsmith, and the upholsterer Philip Gunter was interpreted by the judges as 'an accion of discepte'. The bill detailed how two men of supposedly 'good credens & very good substans' had been sent by Gunter to purchase leather from Holt, but it had since transpired that the elaborate claims of their good credit supported by Gunter as surety were false, Holt had received no money other than £25 which Gunter was bound to pay (far less than the £60 owed), and the two abettors had fled the area.[91] Having heard contrary witness testimonies from both disputants, the judges – together representing canon, civil, and common law training – decided that they did not have enough firm evidence to proceed in 'ryght or consciens to adiuge'. So, even though this matter too was presumably suitable for a remedy in conscience, since it concerned bad faith on an unwritten agreement, it was dismissed from the Court with the recommendation that Holt seek remedy at the common law.[92] We have good reason to believe, then, that the judges' conscience and their theoretically unbounded remit over individual consciences and conduct in line with the universal idea of good behaviour was not, in fact, jurisdictionally limitless.

In any case, as in Chancery, the conciliar courts got around any insinuation that they were negatively affecting the law by not entirely formalising their decrees. It has been suggested that 'the personal character of the decrees was also the reason why they were not enrolled and codified' in Chancery until the 1530s.[93] But this explanation does not hold for the conscience-based conciliar courts, most of which *did* record decrees – and

[88] IS Leadam (ed), *Select Cases in the Court of Requests, AD 1496–156* (1898) 12 *Selden Society* liv–lxviii.
[89] For Dacres's orders, see British Library Additional MS 25248 ff 29–33; Leadam (n 88) lxxxv–lxxxvii.
[90] REQ3/22/1 *Wilson v Reynold.*
[91] REQ2/2/136.
[92] REQ1/5 f 219.
[93] Metzger (n 1) 87.

exemplified them too – in the early Tudor period, even as early as the 1490s. The rationale for doing so may lie not only in the fact that these rulings were *in personam*, touching only the titles of the relevant parties, but also in their conditional and indefinite nature. The decrees of Requests and Star Chamber explicitly left room for the 'losing' party to return if and when they had better evidence for their title, and there are some instances of parties taking up this invitation and successfully having a previous ruling overturned.[94] As one counter-petitioner had it,

> all decrees made in the kynges most honorabull councell be condicionell that if the partie defend can hereafter shewe better evidence then the plaintif to the same landes then to be restored agayn.[95]

Otherwise, many decrees in these tribunals appear not as firm verdicts awarding title in either direction but as formalised arbitrations, in which each party gained something – lands were divided, terms of occupation were agreed, and days were specified on which corn and wheat could be peacefully harvested. Indeed, as has been suggested of the emergence of Chancery in the fifteenth century, too, the conciliar courts likely developed as a kind of formalised arbitration of the kind available from local powerholders but with the added benefit of royally authorised leverage in interpersonal disputes.[96] To reiterate, then, this was demand-driven justice offered to mitigate practical limitations to litigation in other forums, not necessarily animated by some abstract sense of equitable law (at least, not at this point in time). But as this supplementary jurisdiction became increasingly institutionalised, more limits were placed on its conscionable remedies.

V. Conclusion: The Legacy of Conscience in Conciliar Justice

A letter from a man called John Lucas to Thomas Thirlby, Dean of the Chapel Royal and judge in Requests, is insightful for its summary of that Court's role in overseeing

> causes of pytie and the succour and helpe of poore men in ther causes of Justice, aienste suche wronge doers as wolde oppresse poor people.[97]

Certainly, to petitioners and the counsel who helped frame their pleas, 'conscience' was an ideal against which to measure their opponents' conduct and the broader (*in*)justice of a rigid common law system. The ideal manifested itself in several elements of the conciliar courts' proceedings thereafter: overtly in their emphasis on the internal forum as tried under oath, but also more subtly in the provision of justice for the poor and in the assessment of costs and damages, sometimes awarded to a party in spite of their losing the case for title. To put it simply, 'conscience' in the conciliar courts had a particular social meaning and application and was therefore especially ad-hoc and variable. There is something to be said for the old chronology of an 'informal' type of conscience-based justice in this period, compared to a more regulated and systematised

[94] REQ 1 passim; for Star Chamber examples see Guy, *Star Chamber* (n 26) 49.
[95] REQ3/21 *Coke v Child.*
[96] As is the argument of Post (n 8).
[97] REQ3/7 *Wylson v Garland.*

type later on; or, to put it another way, of tribunals initially animated simply by what litigants and judges *thought* justice could do, with jurisdictional certainty and clarity achieved further down the line, well into the later sixteenth century.[98] We can see that the judges in Requests at least were increasingly concerned with what they could *not* do, and many of their 'orders' as the years went on take the tone of common-law statutes and maxims, seeking to protect the defendant. A similar trajectory might be interpreted in clearer codification of the work of the provincial councils when they were revived in the later 1530s.

What does this mean for the broader development of equity? We are reminded that early equity, or its cognate and predecessor concept of conscience, was not limited to the high Court of Chancery. Nor did these concepts have exactly the same meaning within each distinct legal culture. In the later part of the sixteenth century the relationship between the central equity courts, eventually concentrated around Westminster, required further delineation; Star Chamber was taken to treat criminal and riot causes, and Requests as helping the pauper, thus setting them apart from Chancery. Yet overall, amid the gradual innovations of the early Tudor justice system, 'conscience' was conceptualised capaciously and applied variably – not as a juridical doctrine or even an entirely systemised set of processes, but as a governmental ideal in action.

[98] TS Haskett, 'Conscience, Justice and Authority in the Late-Medieval English Court of Chancery' in A Musson (ed), *Expectations of the Law in the Middle Ages* (Woodbridge, Boydell Press, 2001) 157.

6

The Ravenstone Litigation and the Jurisdiction of Chancery

SIR JOHN BAKER

The intriguing case of *Throckmorton v Finch* (1597) ought, on the face of it, to have been a landmark decision on the extent of the equitable jurisdiction of the Chancery, and in particular on its claim to interfere with common-law judgments by injunction. The case was once known in print only from Coke's summary in the *Institutes*,[1] and a nineteenth-century historian of the Chancery observed that, since this was published from Coke's notes after his death, 'it has been doubted whether the report of this case is in all respects accurate'.[2] In fact, the published *Institutes* were almost certainly copied verbatim from Coke's manuscripts. And the full report in Coke's contemporary notebook, now published for the first time,[3] dispels any doubt as to whether it represented Coke's contemporary understanding of the case. Whether it tells the whole story is another matter. The significance of the case in the history of the Chancery was blurred by the fact that no one seems to have attached as much weight to it as Coke did. It certainly is significant, if only as providing some background to the clash between Coke and Ellesmere in 1614–16,[4] though until now it has presented a major puzzle for the legal historian. According to Coke, the decision was made by all the judges on a reference requested by the Queen herself. How could a decision by all the judges of England on so important an issue be ignored by all the reporters and have no apparent effect? For this reason alone, the case is worth exploring in detail. Fortunately, a good deal of the detail is still discoverable. Even though the eventual outcome was hidden from sight at the time, the case is better documented – outside the law reports – than most cases of the period. Besides the usual record sources,

[1] 3 Co Inst 124; 4 Co Inst 86.

[2] G Spence, *Equitable Jurisdiction of the Court of Chancery* (London, V and R Stevens and GS Norton, 1846) 679, n (a).

[3] British Library [BL] MS Harley 6686B fos 226v–229 (in Coke's numbering). The text is published with a translation in *Reports from the Notebooks of Edward Coke, vol IV* (2023) 139 *Selden Society* 797–803.

[4] Coke himself cited it several times as chief justice in 1614–16: *Glanvill's Case* (1614) Calthorpe's reports, BL MS Hargrave 385 fo 313; 2 Bulst. 301; 118 *Selden Society* 441 (1615); Cambridge University Library [CUL] MS Dd.10.51 fo 200 (1615); CUL MS Gg.2.31, fo 202 (1616). There is a brief discussion in DC Smith, *Sir Edward Coke and the Reformation of the Laws* (Cambridge, Cambridge University Press, 2014) 235–7.

we have Throckmorton's own papers preserved in the Warwickshire County Record Office[5] and a few related letters among Lord Burghley's papers in the British Library.

Throckmorton's quest for equitable relief – which was not in the end forthcoming – arose from an obvious injustice which the common law (after prolonged argument) proved incapable of righting. In order to understand it, the proceedings at common law need first to be examined. The facts were undisputed.[6] The manors of Ravenstone and Stoke Goldington in Buckinghamshire had come to the Crown upon the dissolution of the Augustinian Priory of Ravenstone by Cardinal Wolsey in 1525. They were soon afterwards assigned to Wolsey's foundation at Oxford but then returned to the Crown when Cardinal College was dissolved in 1532. In 1557 Queen Mary I and King Philip leased them for 70 years to Sir Robert Throckmorton (d 1580), the Roman Catholic courtier, subject to a previous lease for lives granted by King Edward VI.[7] The Throckmorton lease of 1557 contained a 'proviso' that a rent of £63 13s was to be paid into the Exchequer at certain feast days and that if the rent was in arrears for more than 40 days after any of these feasts, the demise should be null and void ('*vacua sit et pro nullo habeatur*'). In 1565 the lease fell into possession, and on Sir Robert's death in 1580 it passed to his eldest son and executor, Thomas Throckmorton (d 1615).[8] Five or six years later, someone discovered that in 1567 Sir Robert had not paid one of the instalments of rent within the four weeks prescribed by the proviso, and it was supposed that the effect of this was to render the Throckmorton lease ipso facto void from the moment of default. An Exchequer inquisition of 5 July 1586 duly found the fact of the late payment, and on the strength of this finding, a new Crown lease was granted for 21 years to Henry Berkeley on 8 July.[9] Two years later, following a commission of inquiry on 25 May 1588,[10] the reversion was granted by letters patent of 30 May 1588 to Sir Moyle Finch and John Audley,[11] who the following day bargained and sold it to Sir Moyle's

[5] Throckmorton Muniments, Warwickshire County Record Office, CR 1998 [hereafter 'Throckmorton Muniments']. Box 53 includes several relevant papers, including Thomas Throckmorton's autograph draft account of the case [hereafter 'Throckmorton's Abstract'], scribbled in an atrocious and eccentric hand on the day before the matter was argued in the House of Commons. The Abstract is accompanied by a draft letter to 'your honor' dated 11 December 1597, and another of the same date entreating the recipient to deliver 'my letter with the abstracte of my casse' to 'Mr Secretarye'. It seems, therefore, that it was meant for Sir Robert Cecil.

[6] They are summarised here from the records and reports of the proceedings recounted below.

[7] This ended in 1565. The lessees were Sir Francis Bryan (d 1550) and his wife Joan (d 1565), countess of Ormond. An *inspeximus* (1592) of the inquisition *post mortem* after their deaths is in the Throckmorton Muniments, Large Carved Box [LCB] no 3.

[8] He was of Coughton in Warwickshire, Weston Underwood in Buckinghamshire, and the Middle Temple, and died on 13 March 1615 aged 81. His wife Margaret was the daughter and coheir of William Whorwood, bencher of the Middle Temple and Attorney-General to Henry VIII. He is not to be confused with Sir Thomas Throckmorton (d 1607) of Tortworth, Gloucestershire, who was the son of another Sir Thomas (d 1568). One of them reputedly wrote a tract on the title to the throne of Mary, queen of Scots: BL MS Add 35844 fo 225. The surname was sometimes spelt Throgmorton.

[9] Transcript in Throckmorton Muniments. This inquisition was later treated as invalid. It seems the difficulty was that it did not find the death of the countess of Ormond (see n 7); this was touched on in Manwood CB's report of 1591 to the Exchequer Chamber (BL MS Hargrave 5 fo 15v), which dismissed it as unnecessary 'surplusage' with respect to the non-payment in 1567.

[10] Docketed in E 221/1 fo 158v ('*Commissio sub magno sigillo Anglie ad inquirendum de solutione redditus scit[i] pro procinct[u]* [sic] *nuper monasterii sive prioratus de Ravenston alias Raunston ac quorundam maneriorum, terrarum et tenementorum ibidem, Ricardo Grafton armigero et aliis directa*').

[11] An exemplification of this patent, dated 12 June 1591, is in Throckmorton Muniments, Exhibition Boxes. It recited the lease to Henry Berkeley for 21 years at a rent of £63 13s, and included a covenant by the 1588 patentees to pay this rent over to the crown.

father-in-law, Thomas Heneage (d 1595), Vice-Chamberlain of the Queen's Household, and Anne, his then wife (d 1594), and the heirs of Anne.[12] A few days afterwards, in June, Heneage took the precaution of procuring yet another inquisition to be found and returned into the Exchequer, setting out all the relevant facts, including the 1567 late payment.[13]

Thomas Throckmorton was an easy target. His family were leading Roman Catholic recusants,[14] and (as with *Shelley's Case*) there was an undercurrent of religious prejudice in the affair. Thomas, a Member of Parliament in the 1550s, had himself been in confinement for recusancy since about 1580 and remained under restraint for most of his life, losing much of his substance in cumulative fines.[15] His friends credibly suspected that the Ravenstone dispute was a form of religious persecution, though it could just as well have been motivated principally by greed. Not surprisingly, Thomas did not acquiesce in this skulduggery. He and his father before him had remained in possession of the premises despite the late payment in 1567 and had ever since paid their rent promptly, the rent being accepted at the Exchequer without demur. He therefore took the view that the Berkeley lease was void[16] and that Heneage had acquired only the reversion on the 1557 lease. In June 1588, immediately after the Heneage purchase, 'one Mr Salworth[17] of the Temple was sent to enquire [of] Thomas Throckmorton whether he would stand to trial of the law for the validity of his lease or refer it to the opinion of Mr Vice-Chamberlain's counsel and his own'. Throckmorton tactfully replied that he would 'rather refer him to the opinion of counsel on both sides than to contend in law with so honourable a friend as he had found of Mr Vice-Chamberlain before that time'. But Heneage then had second thoughts about risking a reference to counsel. In August, he sent his servant John Audley to ask Throckmorton which of the judges he would have join with Manwood CB[18] to decide on the validity of the lease. Throckmorton replied that this was 'an unequal match for him, considering the judges were neither of their counsels, and he knew Mr Vice-Chamberlain might demand them to attend his cause'; he would therefore have preferred to refer the case to counsel chosen by both sides, as originally proposed. He said he would nevertheless consent if Heneage would be 'bound with others to

[12] Finch had married Elizabeth, their only daughter and heir apparent. In 1594 Heneage married as his second wife Mary, dowager countess of Southampton, but he died the following year and there were no issue of the second marriage. Mary will be encountered again below.

[13] E 178/1436.

[14] The Throckmorton Plot of 1583 took its name from Sir Francis Throckmorton of Warwickshire. Francis was Thomas's cousin, being the son of his uncle John (justice of Chester).

[15] The Latin life of Thomas Throckmorton in Throckmorton Muniments, LCB no 21, attributes the loss of much of his property to religious persecution; but this refers chiefly to the heavy recurrent fines imposed on him for recusancy and does not specifically refer to Ravenstone. This biography was written shortly after his death, probably by a Roman priest, and is accompanied by a contemporary translation.

[16] Throckmorton's Abstract (1597) includes 'Reasons to prove that the taking of Berkeley's lease in possession in June 28° of her majesty's reign [1586] for 21 years of the manor of Ravenstone could not enure through the former lease taken by Sir Robert Throckmorton 4 & 5 Phil. & Mar. [1557].' Throckmorton pointed out that the 1586 lease was granted 'without finding any office', and also that by procuring the 1588 inquisition Heneage had admitted the 1586 lease to be invalid.

[17] Unidentified; possibly Arthur Salwey of the Exchequer Office.

[18] There seems to have been some connection between Heneage and Manwood, who were both involved in a suit to the queen in 1578: Longleat House, Dudley Papers, vol II fo 176 (not seen). There was also a connection between Finch and Manwood, whose wife Elizabeth (née Coppinger) was godmother to Moyle Finch's son Heneage. Finch and Manwood were both seated in Kent.

abide the censure of Manwood, then Lord Chief Baron, Sir Thomas Gawdy, one of the judges, and Mr Peryam, now Lord Chief Baron'.[19] Heneage evidently deemed that too risky, and his response was that '[he] thought counsel on both sides might as well determine it as judges'. However, when the following Michaelmas term Throckmorton sent to ask Heneage to set a place and time, and also whether he should pay his rent to him at the Temple or at Heneage House, the reply was that he would neither receive any rent nor appoint any meeting of counsel, but that Throckmorton should look to the defence of his own as he would to his.[20]

Proceedings at common law commenced in Michaelmas term 1589 with an action of ejectment in the Court of Exchequer, brought by Sir Moyle Finch against Throckmorton and others for twenty messuages and various parcels of land in Ravenstone (or Raunston), Weston and Stoke Goldington.[21] No doubt the Exchequer was chosen because Manwood CB would preside, and he was evidently considered to be already on Heneage's side. The declaration alleged a lease on 24 August and an ejectment on 24 September 1589.[22] The action was brought by Finch as nominal lessee of the Heneages, and it is evident from the letters to be quoted below that the Vice-Chamberlain was the moving force behind Finch's suit and Throckmorton's principal adversary.[23] Although the relationship between Heneage and Finch thereafter soured, and Heneage complained in 1595 of being 'troubled greatly with an unkind and injurious son-in-law',[24] Finch nevertheless remained Throckmorton's formal opponent in the litigation until 1597.

The parties pleaded to a demurrer in Hilary term 1590, but the first argument in court was probably in May 1590, when Throckmorton was licensed by the Privy Council to go to London to attend to his cause, on giving a bond in £500 to return within four days of the argument on the demurrer.[25] Finch was represented initially by Coke, and later by the Attorney-General (John Popham), the Solicitor-General (Thomas Egerton) and Mr Serjeant Owen. The defendant was represented by Mr Serjeant Drew,[26]

[19] Gawdy died on 5 November 1588. Peryam CB voted for Throckmorton in the Exchequer Chamber.

[20] The preceding account is from Throckmorton's Abstract, written in 1597 to show that he had made every effort to reach a compromise. The chronology may be faulty: see n 21.

[21] *Finch v Throckmorton* (1590) E 13/375 mm 9–15; Cro Eliz 220; Moo 291 (Pas 1590); 2 Leo 134; 1 And 303; 2 Rolle Abr 184; BL MS Hargrave 5 fo 9; MS Lansdowne 1060 fo 129 (dated Mich 1589); MS Lansdowne 1062 fo 389; MS Lansdowne 1068 fo 49v (Trin, Mich 1590); MS Lansdowne 1101 fo 79; Lincoln's Inn [LI] MS Maynard 66 fo 23; Middle Temple MS 13 fo 69 (with marginal note: 'Vide cest case M. 32 et 33 El. [in] Sir John Walter's reportes, fo 43b'); CUL MS Ii.5.20 fo 11; Harvard Law School [HLS] MS 110 fo 35; HLS MS 200.1 (formerly 1180.1) fos 24v, 278v; HLS MS 206 (formerly 5066) fo 251v.

[22] Throckmorton's Abstract; corroborated by Cro Eliz 220. This leaves an unexplained interval of one year between Michaelmas term 1588 and Michaelmas term 1589.

[23] Throckmorton's Abstract consistently refers to his opponent as 'Mr Vyschamberlen' or 'Mr Vysc.'

[24] Historical MSS Commission, *Calendar of the Manuscripts … at Hatfield House* (London, HMSO, 1883–1976) vol V, 277 (11 July 1595). The principal reason for this dispute appears below.

[25] PC 2/17 fo 647 (on the petition of his wife Margaret, 4 May 1590). He was currently facing another recusancy prosecution: KB 29/226 m 88d; KB 27/1313, Rex, m 28 (indicted with others, Pas 1589; imparlance to Trin 1590). There are similar bonds of 1594 and 1598 in Throckmorton Muniments, box 62.

[26] The names of counsel, with their arguments, are given in 2 Leo 134; BL MS Hargrave 5 (omits Egerton); MS Lansdowne 1060 (similar); HLS MS 206 (Godfrey, Atkinson, Popham). An argument for Throckmorton is attributed to Serjeant Harris in CUL MS Ii.5.20 fo 11. Notes of 'mon argument' in the Exchequer, apparently written by Serjeant Owen, are in BL MS Harley 1059 fo 5. Godfrey's argument is reported in LI MS Misc 791 fo 138.

and by the recusant barristers Richard Godfrey and Robert Atkinson.[27] According to Throckmorton's account:[28]

> The suit continued until Midsummer Term next following, at the end of which term I demurred upon his office, and then his counsel, finding the imperfection of his office, surceased all that matter and in June or July next after he found another office after the inheritance was out of the Crown to make void Sir Robert's lease for non-payment in *nono* [9 Eliz], which office by my counsel was nothing worth for making void of Sir Robert's lease because it came after the inheritance was out of the Crown.

This is somewhat garbled, but the reports of the ejectment action make the position clearer. Coke's report of this stage of the case has been lost,[29] but there is no shortage of surviving reports by others.[30] The defendant's case was that the crucial proviso in the lease of 1557 was not a limitation of his estate but a condition, and therefore the late payment of the rent in 1567 did not result in an automatic nullification of the lease but required an inquisition of office to rescind it. The inquisition of June 1588 was ineffective for this purpose because it did not take place until after the grant to the Heneages, which had divested the Queen of whatever title she had. In any case, the slightly late payment in 1567 had in fact been accepted at the Exchequer, and a receipt given, and all subsequent payments of rent had been accepted by the queen's receivers.[31] Although it was a prerogative of the queen not to be estopped by legal fiction, these subsequent receipts – so it was argued – amounted in fact to a waiver of the breach.[32] Notwithstanding these persuasive arguments, Manwood CB and the two junior barons of the Exchequer decided in favour of the plaintiff in October 1590. They held the proviso to be a limitation, not a condition, so that the lease had become ipso facto void when the day of payment was missed in 1567. There was therefore no need for an inquisition, and the acceptance of rent between 1567 and 1589 was immaterial, since it could not revive a lease which was void rather than merely voidable.

Throckmorton at once brought a writ of error – in fact, he had taken the precaution of getting one sealed before judgment was given[33] – and in the meantime

[27] Atkinson had purportedly been disbarred by the High Commission for recusancy and expelled from the Inner Temple in 1572, while Godfrey had been conditionally expelled from Gray's Inn for recusancy 1582. They must have conformed sufficiently to be able to continue in practice, but neither became benchers of their inns. See JH Baker, *Readers and Readings in the Inns of Court and Chancery* (2000) 13 *Selden Society Supplementary Series* 6, fn 31.

[28] Throckmorton's Abstract (1597). All the English texts quoted in this chapter are rendered into modern spelling and punctuation.

[29] Regarding fo 34 of Coke's lost notebook for the years 1588–91, see J Baker, *Reports from the Notebooks of Edward Coke Vol II: 1579-1588* (2022) 137 *Selden Society* 406. For Coke's report of the final stage see n 59.

[30] See n 21.

[31] Throckmorton carefully preserved all the Exchequer receipts from 1565 to 1597, and some early ones: Throckmorton Muniments, LCB/24 and box 53. Some of the original tellers' bills are in the Centre for Buckinghamshire Studies, D-X38. These seem to have been collected by Sir Thomas Phillipps after the Exchequer fire.

[32] In making this argument, Serjeant Drew distinguished an estoppel ('conclusion') from a waiver: 2 Leo 134.

[33] 2 Leo 145: the defendant 'cast in a writ of error, and by his counsel prayed that the writ of error be not broken upon until the judgment be entered. Manwood: The judgment hath reference and relation unto the first day of this term, and therefore do not doubt of that.' The record is added to the proceedings at first instance in E 13/375 mm14–15.

remained in possession.[34] The court established by Parliament to redress errors in the Exchequer consisted of the Lord Chancellor (Sir Christopher Hatton) and the Lord Treasurer (Lord Burghley), with 'such justices and other wise men' as they should see fit to call.[35] In practice this meant the two chief justices. Throckmorton assigned three technical errors in the replication: (1) it was argumentative, since it pleaded the proviso without asserting that it was a condition; (2) it recited the lease incorrectly and had therefore not answered his plea; and (3) it was double, in relying both on the non-payment and on the finding of the inquisition. The record has a string of continuances for advisement from February 1591 to November 1594, noting the repeated absence of the Lord Chancellor and Lord Treasurer. But this lengthy period was not spent debating the alleged errors in pleading. To find out what was actually happening, recourse must again be had to the reports. In accordance with the statute, Manwood CB first stated in writing the reasons why judgment had been given for Finch.[36] On the first hearing, Godfrey argued for Throckmorton, and Coke for Finch. On a subsequent occasion, the plaintiff in error was represented by Mr Serjeant Harris and the defendant by Egerton.[37] The case was then referred to the judges in Serjeants' Inn by a means which will be considered below.[38] This worried Heneage, who had no qualms about using his position as Vice-Chamberlain of the Household, and his familiar acquaintance with the Lord Treasurer, to intercede privately with Burghley, somewhat offensively (it might seem) asking him not to prejudge the issue until he had heard both sides. He wrote on 8 February 1591:[39]

> My lord, finding your lordship possessed with an opinion of some great inconvenience in the justice of the judgment of the case betwixt me and Mr Throgmorton, I am drawn earnestly to beseech your lordship, according to your wisdom and love of justice, to look well into the inconveniences of both sides and not to settle your persuasion upon the conjectures and supposals of mine adversary till your lordship shall hear answer to them by my counsel, which I the rather crave because Mr Throgmorton hath delivered in writing to my Lord Chancellor a kind of clamorous complaint and arguments of supposition of (I wot not what) wondrous undoing of numbers of Her Majesty's subjects, which course it may be he will hold with your lordship, and then it is reason mine answers be received, which is now my desire. The which I humbly pray your lordship to give me leave to tell you, that this case will not be found so common as Mr Throgmorton would have it thought, but rather single or very rare, and not least without remedy to all other Her Majesty's subjects either by law or conscience if men condemn not the way to it. But admit there be inconvenience in it, who is the cause of it? I, that offered him mine interest for less than it was worth and another would have given for it; that told him before of the invalidity

[34] Note the entry and ejectment in 1591, below, 124–5. According to his brief of 1597 (n 63), 'the possession thereof was not by such suit recovered'. The reason is that the fictional lease alleged in the declaration was for four years from 24 June 1589 and had therefore expired before judgment was given.

[35] 31 Edw III stat 1 c 12. They were to call before them the barons of the Exchequer to hear their reasons, and so the barons were not themselves part of the court. Some of the reports say that they attended, but they are not reported as speaking.

[36] There is a text of these reasons, in English (dated Mich 1591), in BL MS Hargrave 5 fo 15v.

[37] BL MS Hargrave 5 fo 14; MS Lansdowne 1060 fo 136; MS Lansdowne 1068 fo 52; LI MS Misc 791 fo 142.

[38] Below, 126.

[39] Burghley Papers, BL MS Lansdowne 66 fo 105.

> of his estate; that offered to abide the judgment of two or four of the judges indifferently chosen: or he, that refused all this, before we entered into suit? No, my lord, he falsely conceiving (as he doth in greater things) that his dead lease (which he knew to be void by non-payment of his rent) should now be revived by the transferring of the inheritance from Her Majesty to me, did then refuse either to give me reasonable money for the land or to abide by the judgment of indifferent choice, and would needs to the law, whereto I assented. And now, having received judgment for me (without any manner of contradiction of any of the three of that bench), if Mr Throgmorton (that takes glory to disobey the law) by secret suggestions and clamours can be taken to debar me of the benefit of the law, I shall think my fortune worse than my cause. And he shall have reason to avaunt of a recusant's success against Her Majesty's servant, yea (by her gracious favour) one of her honourable Privy Council, howsoever I be accounted of. And that mine adversary hath not only hope but great confidence to obtain his will herein, some of his friends let not to give out that they be sure the judgment passed for me shall be reversed. But, your lordship shewing me your lawful favour, which it hath pleased you to promise, and I believe in, and may well be, he reckoneth without his host, which I leave to God's pleasure, who ever preserve your lordship.

It will be noted that his representation of the dealings with Throckmorton did not accord with Throckmorton's. Heneage was brazen enough to write again to Burghley on 13 May 1591, urging expedition:[40]

> My lord, it must needs [be]come me very ill to pass if your lordship cannot keep your appointed day for the ending of my cause, which hath been protracted in suit of law by Throckmorton these three years, and – I having had judgment in Michaelmas term last in public court (no one of the judges dissenting) – he still keeps the possession and hath since chiefly spoiled all the woods, myself being without all profit, and so must be except it please your lordship to give me expedition. I desire no whit of favour – only justice in my case, that I be not kept out of mine own, but that he which is the right owner of the land may possess it. The Queen going from your lordship's house upon Friday, it might please your lordship to be in the 'Chequer Chamber on Saturday as it was by yourself ordered, where I doubt not your lordship shall find small difficulty of the matter. I, my lord, have no little cause to desire this, for besides my great loss, if any one of divers persons should die before confirmation of the barons' judgment my cause were at the ground, or else greatly impeached, besides that it toucheth me not a little in my poor credit in the world that Throckmorton should boast of favours against me as he hath done. And therefore I beseech your lordship to pardon me that I importune you in this case, as also that I have used another hand than mine own, which for pain am not able to stir one limb.

The following day, however, Lord Chancellor Hatton wrote to Burghley that the two chief justices were not yet ready to deliver their opinions and that he would go alone to the Exchequer Chamber and adjourn the case until the following term.[41] Several of the judges had shown themselves sympathetic to Throckmorton's case, and indeed, Fenner J had interceded to suggest a composition.[42] Heneage, who rejected all such overtures,

[40] Burghley Papers, BL MS Lansdowne 68 fo 4. He added in a postscript that he had sent a brief of his case at Burghley's request. This is no longer present, unless it is the very brief statement of the case in MS Lansdowne 106 fo 196.

[41] Burghley Papers, BL MS Lansdowne 68 fo 7.

[42] Below, n 49.

evidently had cause to worry that the judgment was likely to go against him. On 3 June he wrote anxiously to Burghley:[43]

> My lord, my disease continuing and the term approaching, that [which] I purposed by myself I must perform by my letters. To discourse to your lordship my cause hanging before you in the Exchequer Chamber I little need: your lordship hath heard it openly and largely argued, and what the opinion of the chief judges was before I began I know, and what the judgment of the law is taken to be in this case the world knows, yet what courage mine adversary takes I hear. Notwithstanding, I have neither will nor reason to forsake myself, but rather to put your lordship in mind that Throgmorton, knowing there be in this land but eleven judges for the common law, by his writ of error hath taken away the voice of three of them, and hath obtained that all the other eight, whereof two of them having counselled and carried him to this course I cannot hold but as parties, shall have all voices in my cause, of whom now, though three be for me, the other five shall overrule them, and so five shall reverse a judgment against six.[44] Besides that my lord chief justice Wray[45] gives out (which I least looked for) that most of their voices will be for Throgmorton. Therefore my humble suit to your lordship is that, as the barons of the Exchequer have given and are to give the reasons of their judgments openly, so the rest of the judges that should reverse or affirm the same may deliver their reasons in open court as in other courts is accustomed and is most consonant with justice, whereby the world may take knowledge upon what reasons this judgment is reversed or affirmed. Thus shall I be in some part satisfied, that have deserved as well as Mr Throgmorton in the state of my calling. And so, humbly commending myself and my suit to your lordship, with desire that my lord chancellor may be acquainted therewith, I wish your lordship the health I lack, and what else you best like.

Heneage was doubtless correct in supposing that, prior to Wray CJ's death in 1592, there was a small majority of the entire judiciary in favour of reversing the judgment; but no judgment was entered at that time. Indeed, we are told that the justices 'differed much in opinion for a long time'.[46]

While the writ of error was pending, Heneage sought to take the law into his own hands by causing his men to attempt an entry into the manor by underhand means. The circumstances were set out by Throckmorton's servant Japhet Butler in a letter dated 25 May 1591:[47]

> These are to signify unto you that about three of the clock this present Tuesday in the afternoon, when people were at evensong, one of Sir Thomas Henage's men came to Ravenstone mill, and finding the miller standing at his door demanded the way to Tyringham, and therewithal commended the water, and the miller gave him a cup to drink of the water, whereupon immediately there came thither two other of his fellows, whereof Chuite was one, who did in like sort demand the way to Tyringham, and the miller directing them the way departed

[43] Burghley Papers, BL MS Lansdowne 68 fo 14.

[44] The excluded three were the barons of the Exchequer. One of the judges who had counselled Throckmorton was Fenner J (appointed JKB in May 1590): see n 49. The other must have been Walmsley J (appointed JCP in May 1589). Both of them were to vote for Throckmorton in the Exchequer Chamber.

[45] Wray CJ died on 8 May 1592 and was replaced by Popham CJ, who had acted as counsel for Finch and decided in his favour.

[46] Moo 296 ('*Sur quel judgement brefe d'error fuit port en l'Exchequer Chamber, et la le case argue, et auxi al Sergeants Inne devant touts les Justices d'Angliterre, queux differont mult en opinion long temps. Uncore en fine per le resolution del greinder part des Judges puis le mort de Manwood et Gent le judgment fuit affirme*'). For the practice of not giving full reasons in the Exchequer Chamber see J Baker, *English Law under Two Elizabeths* (Cambridge, Cambridge University Press, 2021) 14.

[47] Throckmorton Papers, box 60/3/6.

> from them, and they took the way to Tyringham so far as the floodgates. The miller being returned out of their sight, they presently came back again to the mill [and] broke open the door. The miller coming to make resistance before they were entered, two of them kept him back until they all were entered into the house, and being therein called unto one Sowthwicke of Ravenstone, who as it should seem was there ready at their appointment, bidding him bear witness that there they took possession in name of all the manor, and without putting such persons out as were in the house they called for drink, and so departed. Sir, I find a sort of simple men, and such as by their timorous simplicity may be drawn to that which may be hurtful to you and them. Wherefore I beseech you let me receive direction from you what we may do by law in assisting them, whereby nothing may pass prejudicial to your estate.

Throckmorton responded by writing from his lodgings in Holborn on 26 May to Thomas Buggins, one of his tenants (and perhaps his steward), advising everyone to stand firm in asserting their rights:[48]

> I understand what stir Mr Vice-Chamberlain's men keep with making entries, but I pray you pull your spirits to you and be not dismayed at every scarecrow, and likewise encourage the tenants that they be not made afraid to stand in their own rights so far as the law warranteth, and therefore be not from amongst them. And call all my servants that I have in that country to aid them, and in no case let them yield any possession, but with discretion do you so order it that if Mr Vice-Chamberlain's men or their adherents shall seem with force to make any further entries into any houses that they be withstood to the uttermost. And yet if you see any such matter likely to be attempted, call for the aid of some justices of peace and head constable and such substantial friends of your own acquaintance as may be witnesses that none of your side shall be breakers of the peace, unless the other side forcibly will enter, and then in your own defence give them that they shall deserve before they shall have any possession. And if they shall seem to take any more distresses, let them be withstood unless they say they distrain for the rent, and then let them distrain and let the parties go to the sheriff to replevy their cattle. For assure all the tenants from me that I will them do no more than law will justify, and so read my letters unto them. For if I by law with my great charge shall defend them, and they fairly yield their possessions, I shall think all I have bestowed lost. And, Thomas Buggins, conceive I write as well to yourself as to them, for I would have every man that is towards me carry a man's heart in an honest action and to see everything as well performed as if I were there myself, seeing it so standeth with me as it doth.

A month later, Throckmorton offered a composition with Heneage, which was declined.[49] But Heneage's claim to have gained possession by making entries provided the means whereby the case was removed from the statutory Exchequer Chamber before all the justices. In 1592 Finch brought two further actions, this time in the King's Bench. The first was an action of ejectment against Thomas Throckmorton's servant, William Nicholl,[50] in respect of a messuage in Ravenstone; the pleadings set out the patents and leases

[48] ibid, box 60/3/4.

[49] 'Offers made by Thomas Throckmorton for composition with Mr Vice-Chamberlain', document dated 12 June 1591 in Throckmorton Papers, box 53. This is a list of tenants and their rents, showing how they might be divided between the parties. *Cf* Throckmorton's Abstract: 'In Midsummer Term 33° [1591] Mr Justice Fenner, who had been of my counsel before in law, and [of] good will, moved me to send down officers for compounding with Mr Vice-Chamberlain, supposing as he told me he had a special friend that could do some good therein and persuade Mr Vice-Chamberlain to an end.' Enquiries were made, but this came to nothing.

[50] He justified as Throckmorton's servant, but he was tenant of a cottage and meadow, at a rent of 10s: ibid.

and asserted that Sir Robert Throckmorton in 1565 had granted his whole term in the messuage to one John Smythe should the countess of Ormond die before 25 March 1566, that she died on 24 March, and that on 26 March Smythe entered and granted his term to Heneage; the record ends with an undetermined demurrer.[51] The second action was against Throckmorton's tenant, John Risley,[52] in respect of a messuage and water-mill in Ravenstone, alleging a trespass on 30 September 1591. The pleadings this time raised exactly the same legal question, upon demurrer, as the Exchequer case, and it was this record, rather than that of the earlier case, which Coke chose to print in his *Book of Entries*.[53] The case was argued in the King's Bench by White and Godfrey for Throckmorton, and by the Solicitor-General (Coke) and Attorney-General (Egerton) for Finch, but no continuances were entered on the roll beyond Easter term 1593. By that time Popham – one of Finch's counsel – had become Chief Justice of the King's Bench, and according to his report the case was argued in Easter term 1594 before all the justices and barons in Serjeants' Inn, Fleet Street. Its purpose, evidently, was to meet the concerns in Heneage's petition to Burghley. In a hearing before all the justices of England, the barons recovered their voice and were able to carry the day by voting to uphold their own decision. It was the same ploy which Popham CJ was to use in *Slade's Case* to outvote the Common Pleas, and it is permissible to speculate whether it was not the result of some informal discussion between Popham and Coke (his successor as Attorney-General) in both cases.[54] In the King's Bench, Popham CJ had failed to persuade the two puisne justices to take Finch's side,[55] and this explains why judgment was never entered there. However, it was not necessary to pursue the matter to judgment in the King's Bench, for the reference to the judges had served its purpose. Another of Finch's counsel (Owen) was appointed to the Common Pleas in January 1594, and when the case was reargued that year, a decision was finally reached to affirm the judgment in Finch's favour by a majority of one, notwithstanding the strongly held opinions of the dissentients. But for the barons of the Exchequer (whose decision was in question), there was a majority of one the other way.[56] It follows that if the case had been left to the tribunal established by Parliament to correct errors in the Exchequer, Throckmorton would have succeeded at common law.

[51] *Fynche v Nicholl* (1592–93) KB 27/1323 m 159 (three skins) (cav to Pas 1593). The plaintiff alleged that the messuage had been leased to him by Heneage on 24 August 1589 for four years.

[52] He was tenant of the mill, at a rent of £5 17s 4d, six pike and four eels: 'Offers' (n 49).

[53] *Fynche v Risley* (1592–93) KB 27/1323 m 160 (four skins); printed in Co Ent 191v (ending with the first continuance for advisement); reported in Poph 25 (Pas 1593), 53 (Trin 1594); BL MS Hargrave 430 fo 125 (Popham CJ, Fenner and Clench JJ, summarised in English, followed by an argument for the plaintiff in Law French); Lansdowne 1060 fo 138; MS Lansdowne 1072 fo 186; LI MS Maynard 66 fo 18v; HLS MS 206 (formerly 5066) fo 251v. The argument for Finch in Christopher Yelverton's commonplace book, MS Hargrave 430 fo 126v, was attributed by John Anstis (transcript in BL MS Stowe 421 fo 113) to Serjeant Yelverton himself, though it is paraphrased in Law French rather than an English speech.

[54] The entry on the roll (previous note) was in Mich 1592, five months after Popham CJ's appointment, but it begins by reciting that the bill was preferred in Mich 1591 (the term when the Exchequer judgment was given).

[55] Gawdy and Fenner JJ both voted for Throckmorton in the Exchequer Chamber. There were only two puisnes at this date.

[56] The majority were: Popham and Anderson CJJ, Owen and Beaumont JJ, Ewens and Clarke BB. The dissentients (who dissented '*fortment*') were: Peryam CB, Gawdy, Clench, Walmsley and Fenner JJ. (Details from BL MS Lansdowne 1060 fo 141v.) Without the barons, therefore, the vote would have been five to four against Finch. Coke's report (138 *Selden Society* 598) says the dissentients were Peryam, Clench, Walmsley and Fenner; he does not mention Gawdy on either side.

But by convention all three common-law courts in Westminster Hall were expected to abide by any opinion given by the assembled judges, even though they had no formal status as a court and had no power to reverse judgments. The reporters accordingly treated the opinion of the assembled judiciary in the King's Bench case as having resulted in the Exchequer Chamber judgment in Michaelmas term following.[57] One reporter mused: '*Sic transit gloria mundi.* The law in these days will alter and change as the justices did alter and change.'[58] The final judgment was given by the Lord Keeper and Lord Treasurer in the Exchequer on 12 November 1594,[59] and the plea roll noted in the margin the reason for the judgment, namely that the proviso in the lease was a limitation and not a condition.[60] It is said that this unusual course was adopted at the insistence of Burghley.[61]

It is evident from these proceedings that at least half the judges who had considered the case since 1589 felt that Throckmorton had a good case even at common law, and it can hardly be doubted that the decision against him was harsh. Although it was not stated in the pleadings, the reason for the default in 1567 was allegedly the negligence of the servant who had been sent to pay the rent.[62] That could not affect the legal position as against the Crown, but Heneage and his son-in-law had on any view acted unconscionably in seeking to take advantage of a minor slippage over twenty years earlier, a slippage which had in fact been waived by the Crown in accepting the rent ever since. Throckmorton's case in conscience was that the Queen had not been deceived but had treated him (and his father before him) as lawful tenants by continuing to receive their

[57] Serjeant Owen wrote this note at the end of his argument in the Exchequer (BL MS Harley 1059 fo 7): '*Cest matter fuit depending in bank le roy et apres pur ceo que ilz ne poient agree le matter vient destre debat per toutz les justices et barons al Serjeants Inn et fuit resolve que le pleintife avera judgment, et judgment fuit done accordant.*' But his note of the pleadings (on fo 5) clearly refers to the case in the Exchequer, not the King's Bench. See also LI MS Maynard 66 fo 23: '*Al auter terme, sc. Trinitatis 36 Eliz. [1594], le case inter Finch et Riseley fuit in question devant touts les justices et barons pur ceo assemble a Serjeants Inne in Fleetsrteete ... Et sur cest resolution le greinder part des justices en termino Michaelis anno 31 & 32 regine nunc* [1589] *mesme le case fuit in question en le office des pleas en Leschequer enter le dit Moile Finch, plaintife, et Thomas Throgmorton et auters defendants, et la adjudge ... dun assent, puis long argument al barr et al bench ... sur quel judgment done un brefe de errour fuit port per les defendants devant le seignior garden del grand seale et seignior treasurer de Angleterre, ou il long depend, et apres argumentes fait loppinion avantdit pris des touts les justices et barons le judgment done en le Eschequer per ladvise de Popham et Anderson fuit affirme ...*'. The reports in MS Lansdowne 1072 and Moo. 296 (quoted in n 46) also conflate the two cases.

[58] BL MS Lansdowne 1060 fo 141v ('*Sic transit gloria mundi. Et le ley hiis diebus altera et chaungera come les justices did alter et chaunge*').

[59] *Throckmorton v Finch* (1590–94) E 13/375 mm 14–15; Coke's notebook, 138 *Selden Society* 598 (reported mostly on another point); BL MS Lansdowne 1060 fo 141v (12 November 1594) endnote; HLS MS 1042 (formerly 1058) fo 33. Pending the writ of error, on 1 December 1590, Finch obtained an interlocutory injunction in the Chancery to prevent waste: 117 *Selden Society* 136, fn 63. Throckmorton was released from custody for the Easter term 1593 to pursue the case: PC 2/20 fo 358.

[60] E 13/375 m 15d: '*Notandum est quod ratio affirmationis hujus judicii est pro eo quod le proviso contenta in dimissione supramentionata facta Roberto Throckmorton militi est limitatio et non conditio.*'

[61] A Collins, *The Life of ... Lord Burghley* (London, R Gosling, 1732) 54 ('He was so careful in the administration of justice, as many times he favoured the subject in the causes of the prince; as, when one Mr Thogmorton had a case in the Exchequer, which was hardly recovered for the queen upon a nice point, he would not suffer the judgment [to] be entered but with this condition, to enter the reasons, and [said] that it was a case of the queen's prerogative and not of law.') This account was printed 'from the original manuscript wrote soon after his lordship's death', then in the possession of the earl of Exeter.

[62] Throckmorton's brief of 1597 (n 63); 4 Co Inst 86. According to a recollection of 1615, the servant had absconded with the money: BL MS Lansdowne 1110 fo 15v (118 *Selden Society* 441). It was alleged in the Chancery pleadings that Throckmorton had been late with some subsequent payments as well; but this was irrelevant to the argument that the lease was avoided automatically on the first default.

rent; that Finch knew the 1557 lease was in being before he made his purchase; that it was unheard of for a patentee to seek to avoid a lease for a default committed before he purchased the reversion; and that to allow him to do so would frustrate all the underleases made by the Throckmortons and would beggar thirty families and five hundred persons maintained on the premises who were not guilty of any default.[63] Coke himself concurred with the judges who thought that Throckmorton had a strong case in equity.[64] But could these matters be raised in Chancery after judgment had been given at law?

Throckmorton was advised to prefer a bill in Chancery against Finch to prevent enforcement of the judgment. Unfortunately for him, he had not sought relief in equity until after the judgment had been given and affirmed upon the writ of error. Indeed, he seems not to have brought the suit until May 1597.[65] The explanation for the long delay may be that he had in the meantime been back in prison as a recusant,[66] and it was not until 1597 that he obtained a temporary release from custody in Banbury Castle in order to conduct the proceedings.[67] Finch pleaded the judgments of the Exchequer and the Exchequer Chamber in bar of the Chancery suit and thereby raised for formal decision the question of whether judgments at law were sacrosanct or whether they were liable to be bypassed or effectively annulled by recourse to equity, and in particular by parties who had slept on their equitable rights. He had the advantage that the new Lord Keeper (Egerton, appointed in 1596) had been his counsel both in the Exchequer and in the King's Bench. According to the later report in Coke's *Institutes*, Egerton LK was inclined to overrule the demurrer but agreed to refer the question to all the judges of England. He had done this, he said, 'because the case was of great consequence and likely to be a precedent for many others',[68] though in truth it was because the queen herself had told him to do it.[69]

[63] 'Reasons why Thomas Throckmorton is in equity to be relieved against Sir Moyle Finch for his lease of Raunston', in Throckmorton Muniments, box 53 (three contemporary copies).

[64] See his reminiscences in *Glanvill's Case* (1614) Cro Jac 343, 345, per Coke CJ ('the bill comprehended much matter of equity, and there was very good cause he should have been relieved, if he had complained before the judgment'); 3 Co Inst 124 ('it appeared to [the judges] that there was apparent matter in equity').

[65] The first entry in the decree and order books is on 28 May 1597: C 33/93 fo 6v; C 33/94 fo 6. There is a brief report in 117 *Selden Society* 216 no 281 (Trin 1597).

[66] In May 1596 he was under house arrest, and his petition to be allowed liberty so that he could pursue his litigation was referred to the archbishop of Canterbury, presumably with no success: PC 2/21 fo 248.

[67] *Calendar of the Manuscripts ... at Hatfield House* vol VII, 135 (letter to Sir Robert Cecil from Banbury Castle, 30 March 1597); *Acts of the Privy Council*, vol XXVII, 64; vol XXVIII, 14–15, 102; P W Hasler, *The House of Commons 1558-1603* (London, HMSO, 1981) vol III, 500. On 8 March he had obtained permission for his wife to visit him in custody to confer about the case: PC 2/22 fo 149. Later in the year he was also being pursued in the Exchequer by Coke for intrusion in the manor of Ladbroke, Warwickshire, formerly belonging to Combe Abbey: *Att-Gen v Throckmorton* (1597) E 159/413, Mich Recorda, m 464.

[68] *Throckmorton v Finch* (1597) BL MS Harley 6686B fo 223; 139 *Selden Society* 797. This is close to wording of the entry in C 33/93 fo 6 ('as the cause is of great weight and will be taken for a precedent hereafter in like cases').

[69] 3 Co Inst 124 ('Sir Thomas Egerton, then lord keeper, inclined to rule over the demurrer, saying that he would not meddle with the judgment but punish the corrupt conscience of the defendant in relieving the plaintiff in equity. Upon a petition to Queen Elizabeth, who ever favoured the due proceeding of her laws, she referred the consideration of the demurrer to all the judges of England'). *Cf* Coke's autograph report: 139 *Selden Society* 798 ('The lord keeper of the great seal, because the case was of great consequence and likely to be a precedent for many others, referred the consideration of this case, by order of the court and by the queen's command, to all the justices of England'). In 4 Co Inst 86 it is made clear that Egerton had expressed his view in court before the queen intervened.

The case was heard before the assembled judges after the Michaelmas term, on 6 December 1597.[70] Throckmorton's counsel argued that his intention was not to impeach the judgment itself but to be relieved from it on equitable grounds, relying on a recent decision by Egerton that such a suit should not be seen as reopening the point which had been adjudged, but rather as examining the 'collateral' matter in equity in order to 'conform the corrupt conscience of the party'.[71] The argument on the other side was presented by Coke, now Attorney-General, and Thomas Fleming, Solicitor-General.[72] It was not about the need for equity. The equitable jurisdiction of the Chancery was too well established to question,[73] and Coke conceded that equity was on Throckmorton's side. The point was that those who sought equity had to take the first step before losing their case at common law, for otherwise there would be no certainty in judgments.[74] Even if the Chancery suit was formally concerned with a collateral question not in issue at law, its real purpose was to deprive the judgment of any effect. In Coke's words:

> It would be perilous to permit men after judgment and trials in law to surmise matter in equity and thereby put the person who recovered to excessive charges. Suits by this means would be infinite, and no one could be in peace for anything which the law by judgment had given him, but a contentious and able person who has an unquiet spirit might continually surmise matter in equity and thus continually vex the person who recovered, which would be a great inconvenience. And it is absurd that a court which (as to equity) is not of record should control judgments which are of record.

Such proceedings, it was said, were contrary to the statute of 1402, which provided that after judgment given in the King's courts the parties and their heirs should be in peace until the judgment was reversed by error or attaint.[75] Moreover, the case of *Cobb v Nore* (1465)[76] showed that the Chancery would not at that time give relief in conscience against a judgment, even if it was obtained by fraud, unless it was authorised to do so by act of Parliament. The later precedents of injunctions granted after judgment were either distinguishable or simply against the law. There was a colourable argument that, since Finch's ejectment action

[70] In Throckmorton Papers, box 60/3/8, there is a copy letter written by Throckmorton from his lodgings in Fleet Street on 3 December begging a 'most honourable' recipient (probably Sir Robert Cecil) to be present 'upon Tuesday next at the commitment of the bill in the Exchequer Chamber at two of the clock in the afternoon'.

[71] *Warde v Fulwood* (1596) 117 *Selden Society* 215, 258; 139 *Selden Society* 798–9; C 33/91, fo 370 (demurrer overruled). *Cf Anon* (1596) IT MS Petyt 516.5 fo 58v ('*Nota que Egerton, segnior keper del grand seale, dist in Chancery que il ne voile la doner ascun reliefe in equitie contrary a ascun positive ley*').

[72] In his contemporary report, Coke originally attributed the argument to the Attorney-General, and several times used the first person, though he later crossed through 'Attorney' and wrote 'Solicitor': 139 *Selden Society* 799 (whence the next quotation in the text). The decree book records that the Attorney-General was counsel for Finch, and Coke later recollected that he had been counsel in the case (below at n 89).

[73] Coke had nevertheless reported the decision by all the judges in *Perrot v Mathew* (1588) that there was no prerogative power to establish a new equity jurisdiction without an act of Parliament because it would be against Magna Carta (1225) c 29: BL MS Harley 6687D fo 743v; 137 *Selden Society* 372.

[74] This principle was affirmed by the Chancery in *Lord Compton v Egerton* (1570s), reported in Coke's notebook, BL MS Harley 6687A fo 207v; 136 *Selden Society* 23 ('since he could have had a remedy by the common law but had let it slip past by his negligence, they would not relieve him').

[75] 4 Hen IV, c 23. St German had considered this binding on the Chancery, as did Richard Crompton in his treatise of 1594 on the Queen's courts: J Baker, *The Reinvention of Magna Carta 1216-1616* (Cambridge, Cambridge University Press, 2017) 213.

[76] KB 27/816 m 35 (unreported). Coke copied this record twice in his notebook: BL MS Harley 6686B fos 212v, 226v; 139 *Selden Society* 776, 801.

was a personal action founded on a term of years which had expired before judgment, no decree in Chancery could in any way affect the judgment; nevertheless, the basis of the Exchequer decision was that the lease of 1557 was void, and the suit in Chancery sought to undermine that.

Coke was even emboldened to drop hints of severe sanctions. 'It seemed to some', he suggested, 'that such proceedings might incur the danger of a *praemunire*'.[77] This was still a far cry from the fatal collision of 1616 between Coke and Ellesmere, when Coke (by then Lord Chief Justice) was overruled by King James I and soon afterwards dismissed from office. But in 1597 Coke, taking the same position in his capacity as the principal law officer of the Crown, seemed to have won. The result, as he noted at the time, was that 'upon great consideration it was resolved by all the judges of England that the said Thomas Throckmorton was not to be admitted to examine the matter in equity after the said judgment, for that is contrary to law and statutes'. There was in fact one dissenting voice, that of Walmsley J, who had been one of the strong dissentients in the Exchequer Chamber.[78] Sir Thomas Walmsley made something of a habit of dissenting in leading cases, and Coke was accustomed to edit him out of his reports. In the event, however, Coke decided not to publish this case in his *Reports*, and his account of it in the *Institutes* (written in the 1620s) was considerably abridged.

Given the potential importance of the decision, we must return to the puzzling fact that it does not occur in any other contemporary reports. The most probable reason is that few were aware of it. No doubt the judges did indeed reach the decision noted by Coke at a private meeting. But it was reported to the Chancery by Popham CJ verbally, rather than in a signed certificate, and probably not made public. An entry in the Chancery order books on Saturday, 12 November 1597, suggested some uncertainty on Egerton's part about what the judges had decided:

> Upon the opening of the matter this present day by Her Majesty's Attorney-General, being of the defendant's counsel, and praying the resolution of this court touching the defendant's demurrer, wherein this court meant to have the opinion of the judges: forasmuch as the counsel were not now present, and the Lord Chief Justice of England hath by word only and not by writing shewed the resolution of the judges touching this matter to the Lord Keeper, it is ordered that the counsel on both parts shall be present in court on Tuesday morning next, at which time his lordship mindeth to declare what opinion was signified to him from the judges, and will be pleased to shew his lordship's own opinion also and give such order in the cause as shall be thought meet.[79]

On the following Tuesday the judges' opinion was duly reported to the court by Egerton, though it seems still not to have been put into writing. One judge had been absent, and another had dissented, but it was otherwise unanimous:

> [T]he Lord Keeper, having understood by the Lord Chief Justice of England what the judges' resolution is touching this cause, did this day declare in open court that, where the defendant

[77] 139 *Selden Society* 800. This turned in part on the words 'autri court' in the *praemunire* statute of 1353 (27 Edw III stat 1 c 1). The French meant 'another's court' (ie, given the context, a court of the pope); but Coke, following the printed statute-books, read it as 'auter court' (ie, any another court).

[78] He had probably been of Throckmorton's counsel: see n 44. Coke mentioned the dissent in his manuscript report, though in 3 Co Inst 124 he made the decision unanimous.

[79] C 33/93 fo 361; C 33/94 fo 351v.

> hath by way of answer shewed that a judgment had passed at the common law against the title pretended by the plaintiff, which judgment was afterwards affirmed also by a writ of error, and therefore (and for other causes set forth in the same answer) the defendant demanded judgment whether this court will hold plea thereof or not, all the judges (saving one who was absent), having considered of this cause, are all – one of them who so considered thereof excepted[80] – of opinion that the particular case, as it standeth, is not meet to be retained and examined in this court. Wherefore his lordship mindeth to be advised thereof and to give such order therein hereafter as shall be fit.[81]

And there the matter seems to have ended as far as the Chancery was concerned. Egerton was not pleased to show his opinion afterwards, as promised, or to make any order for the time being. The entry in the order book conveys an impression that, although he was disinclined to accept the judges' opinion, he did not think it appropriate directly to reject it. At any rate, Throckmorton and his counsel now saw little hope of obtaining relief in Chancery and decided to press again for a reference to arbitrators. Given Finch's previous unwillingness to participate in arbitration, their thoughts turned to achieving it through parliamentary pressure.

The next Parliament met on 24 October 1597, and shortly thereafter Throckmorton asked Sir Walter Raleigh MP and other friends in the House of Commons to insert an *ad hominem* proviso concerning the case into a bill currently before the House. The 'special proviso for Mr Throckmorton' was read twice, and counsel for both parties were heard on 12 December. It was at this time that Throckmorton compiled his long memorandum showing how he had constantly since 1586 been requesting a reference or a settlement.[82] Sir Moyle Finch was no longer a Member of Parliament, though he sought re-election (unsuccessfully) when a vacancy occurred at the end of the year, having agreed with the other candidate that he would withdraw if his case went to arbitration as had been proposed. Simonds D'Ewes gave the following account of the outcome on 19 December:

> And one special proviso also for Mr Throgmorton being twice read, it was ordered after many arguments upon the said bill and last proviso *pro et contra*, that Mr Throgmorton and Mr Moyle Finch, being at the door of this House, should be severally called in and demanded by Mr Speaker whether they would assent to have the matter in controversy between them referred to be ended by such arbitrators as had been before nominated for that purpose unto them in the committee, viz. the Lord Keeper and the Lord Treasurer, and the two chief justices, and in what sum they would be bound each to other for their standing to and performing of such award therein so to be made. It was at last, after sundry such demands made, resolved by both their assents at the bar in this House, that each of them should enter into bond unto the other in the sum of £5,000 to stand to the order and arbitrament of the lord Archbishop of Canterbury, the Lord Keeper of the Great Seal of England, and the two chief justices, or any three of them, for and concerning the two leases in question; so as the same order or

[80] According to the report, above, this was Walmsley J.

[81] C 33/93, fo 386v. This entry was discovered by JP Dawson, 'Coke and Ellesmere Disinterred' (1941–42) 36 *Illinois Law Review* 127 at 134; but Dawson did not know of Coke's manuscript report. For the practice of giving written judicial opinions to the Chancery see below, n 97.

[82] Throckmorton's Abstract, probably sent to Sir Robert Cecil. The covering letter, dated 11 December 1597, is addressed 'Most honorable, with all duty' and signed 'Your honour's most bounden T. T.' It requested the recipient's presence to lend support ('where[as] … both Sir Moyle Finch and myself with one counsellor a piece towards the law are appointed to be there [on 12 December], my most humble suit to your honour is that you will vouchsafe your presence …').

> arbitrament be made before the first sitting of this court which shall happen to be held next after the feast of the Nativity of our Lord now next ensuing, and the condition of the bond to be drawn by the learned counsel of the parties, and to be perused and considered of further by Mr Speaker.[83]

The arbitration went ahead, and Throckmorton was awarded a fourteen-year lease at a somewhat higher rent.[84] Since the 1557 lease would have ended in 1626, this meant that he lost the final twelve years – and, in the event, he just outlived the term.

There is no indication that Egerton ever paid much heed to the opinion of the judges in Throckmorton's case. Early the following year it was apparently declared that a judgment at law was 'no let to examination [in] equity, so [as] the truth of the judgment [be] not examined, as where judgment against an acquittance without a seal or where the money paid after the day.'[85] There was another test case in 1599, though it was materially different. Magdalene Masters, an executrix, had recovered a debt in the King's Bench in *indebitatus assumpsit* against the executors of a debtor, following a jury trial. The judgment had then been reversed by the Exchequer Chamber, which at that time took the view – contrary to that of the King's Bench judges – that *assumpsit* did not lie against executors.[86] She had thereupon sued in Chancery, setting all this out, and seeking relief on the grounds that she had no remedy at law. There could be no denying that she had no remedy at law, because that had been settled conclusively by the judgment of the Exchequer Chamber. But the defendant demurred, on the ground that the judgment precluded proceedings in equity for the same debt. Egerton LK overruled the demurrer, saying that by the advice of all the judges he had allowed bills to recover debts without specialty against executors,[87] but nevertheless said he would confer with the judges. Nothing more is known about the case, which has not been found in the decree and order books and presumably was not allowed to proceed. Nor is anything as yet known about the opinion of the judges to which Egerton referred. Whatever distinction the judges had drawn between this case and Throckmorton's, Egerton LK's reaction was consistent with his doctrine that a judgment at law was irrelevant in Chancery proceedings because the Chancery interfered only with consciences and not with judgments. On the other hand, in another case not long afterwards, Egerton (by then Lord Ellesmere LC) is reported to have ruled that an injunction would only be granted after a common-law judgment if: (i) the party had commenced the suit in Chancery before the judgment; and (ii) the party 'examine not the judgment nor seek to reverse it but only pray relief against him that has such judgment for so much as he has obtained by his judgment'.[88] The first of these points was challenged by Coke in 1605

[83] P Bowes (ed), S D'Ewes, *The Journals of all the Parliaments during the Reign of Queen Elizabeth* (London, J Starkey, 1682) 575.

[84] Hasler, *House of Commons 1558-1603* (n 67) vol 2, 118 (Finch), 265 (Percival Hart, who was elected); see also vol 3, 500 (Throckmorton, MP under Mary I).

[85] *Hord v Dodington* (Hilary term 1598) BL MS Add. 48097 fo 54; 117 *Selden Society* 266 no 273 (slightly different); Toth. 115. This is not explicitly attributed to Egerton but is in a Chancery collection.

[86] The Exchequer Chamber had routinely reversed King's Bench judgments in *assumpsit* against executors since *Yolland v Yolland* (1593), affirmed in *Ross v Serle* (1596): 138 *Selden Society* 525; 139 *Selden Society* 671. This followed the death in 1592 of Manwood CB, who had sided with the King's Bench: 137 *Selden Society* 402.

[87] *Masters v Burde and Newton* (8 June 1599) Moo 556 (misdated 31 Eliz); correctly dated in BL MS Add. 36076 fo 59v; CUL MS Gg.2.5 fo 278v (*Maisters v Bucke*). Francis Moore was counsel for the defendants. This is evidently the case reported more briefly in 117 *Selden Society* 331 no 79 (misdated 44 Eliz in some MSS).

[88] *Anon* (c. 1601) CUL MS Gg.2.31 fo 470; 117 *Selden Society* 311 no 236.

when it was reiterated by Popham CJ in a case concerning the Court of Requests. Coke responded that 'if that were law, then the statute of 4 Hen. IV, c. 23, would serve for little or nothing … for it would be to the same effect as if they could undo the judgment by their decree … And he said it was adjudged accordingly by all the judges in a case in which he was of counsel.'[89] The reporter concluded, 'Quere de cest matter': as well he might, since the particular question had not arisen in Throckmorton's case. Throckmorton had not commenced his suit until after judgment, and Coke at the time had made much of that.

As for the Ravenstone business itself, the compromise in 1597 was still not the end of it. While Throckmorton's Chancery case was still pending, Finch and his wife Elizabeth were the subject of a second suit in Chancery in respect of the same property, commenced in or before 1596 by Edward, earl of Worcester; Mary, countess of Southampton (widow of Sir Thomas Heneage); and Sir John Fortescue, Chancellor of the Exchequer.[90] They claimed that the Crown grant of the manors of Ravenstone and Stoke Goldington in 1588 to Finch and Audley had been upon trust for Sir Thomas Heneage, and that Sir Thomas, who desired to advance his then wife Anne and to make provision for payment of his debts ('being then very great') and to make his last will, had requested them to bargain and sell the priory, advowson and manor of Ravenstone to Sir Thomas and Lady Heneage and her heirs, and the manor of Stoke Goldington to him, his wife and his own heirs, for the purpose of paying his debts, though this purpose was not recited in the deed. The plaintiffs alleged that Sir Thomas, believing that he had thereby acquired Stoke Goldington to dispose of at his pleasure, had in 1595 conveyed it to them by bargain and sale enrolled for the payment of his debts, whereby (they said) they ought in equity to be seised. Sir Thomas had soon afterwards died, leaving debts of over £16,000, and had appointed as his sole executrix his second wife, Mary, now Countess of Southampton.[91] The suit was brought against Lady Finch, as Heneage's heir at law, complaining that no conveyance had been made to the plaintiffs, and that they were thereby hindered from paying the debts and performing the will. The Finches sought to wriggle out of the arrangement by claiming that 'in extremity of law' there was no distinct manor of Stoke Goldington, that all the lands mentioned in the conveyance were in fact part of the manor of Ravenstone, and that they had therefore all descended to Lady Finch. They also pleaded by way of demurrer that Lady Finch, as a married woman, could not be charged with any trust.[92] The replication stressed what was said to be the true intention of Sir Thomas Heneage, who had been too busy about the Queen's

[89] *Cardinal v De la Broche* (1605) BL MS Lansdowne 1075, fo 167; MS Add 35954, fo 430v; CUL MS Gg.4.9, fo 188; Baker, *Reinvention of Magna Carta* (n 75) 284; *cf* 117 *Selden Society* 345. The report says that Williams J 'seemed to agree' with Popham CJ.

[90] It had been commenced before Trin 1596, when the earl of Worcester was fined 30s for not putting in a bill. The following term the bill of revivor was referred to Owen J, and on his advice it was abated: C 33/91, fos 266, 366. The filed bill was received on 18 April 1597: C 2/Eliz/W11/62/2 (with the other pleadings, damaged in the lower corners). The enrolled decree (below) shows that Theophilus Finch, the defendants' eldest son, was also joined as a defendant. John Hele's briefs in the case are in Egerton's papers, HE Huntington Library MS EL 5913, 5914.

[91] In November 1596, when Mary was settling his accounts in the Exchequer as executrix, there was still an outstanding balance of £7,809 12s: E 159/411, Mich 38 Eliz, Recorda, mm 447–448.

[92] This was one of three objections raised by way of demurrer (C 2/Eliz/W11/62/3), separately from the answer (C 2/Eliz/W11/62/3). The others were that the plaintiffs had not certainly alleged what trust the defendants were supposed to have failed to perform and had not certainly alleged that there was any such manor as Stoke Goldington.

business to take counsel on the wording of the indenture but had made clear by word of mouth at the time his purpose of paying his debts.

On 18 November 1598 the Lord Keeper (with the advice of Walmsley J) decreed that, after inspecting documents going back to the dissolution of Ravenstone Priory in 1525, they were satisfied that Stoke Goldington was a separate manor, at least in repute, and that the defendants should convey the manor and lands in accordance with Heneage's 'honourable intention' to pay his debts. The decree provided, however, that if the defendants could prove that any parcel of the lands mentioned in the conveyance were not part of Stoke Goldington, the decree would be amended accordingly.[93] That qualification provided a pretext for referring the case to the assembled judges, though the reference was widened into a review of the entire case as a result of a petition to the queen in person from Sir Moyle and Lady Finch.[94] From this point, we have the benefit of another report by Coke which tells us a great deal more than the Chancery record, and it is partly corroborated by Anderson CJ's report.[95] What Coke did not mention was that he was now retained as counsel against Sir Moyle Finch.[96]

The judges certified their resolution to the Chancery under their hands on 24 November 1600.[97] Whether or not the Chancery was correct in finding that Stoke Goldington was in fact a distinct manor, in reputation if not in right, they held that the decree could not stand, principally because the question whether the lands in question were part of the manor was a question of freehold property and therefore not determinable in Chancery. According to Popham CJ, the Chancery could not determine anything except in cases of fraud, breach of trust, or accident.[98] Even if a suit was brought for discovery of title-deeds, the chancellor could not proceed if the title came in issue. This resolution was sufficient for the purposes of the suit, and the final decree of 24 January 1601 merely recited that the judges had confirmed the decree concerning the status of Stoke Goldington but had advised that the issues ought to be tried at common law. The entry concludes:

> The Lord Keeper and this Court, upon consideration of the said certificate and upon the hearing of the counsel on both parts, do not see any cause that the said matter should be

[93] C 33/96 fo 429 (decree book 1598B). The decree book 1598A only refers to the final decree on fo 429 of 'the fellow of this book', ie, C 33/95 fo 440v. The decree was enrolled in C 78/106, m 28 no 12. *Cf Finch v Countess of Southampton*, concerning property in Essex and Yorkshire, C 3/269/41, 270/3 (pleadings).

[94] 4 Co Inst 85 ('upon a petition preferred by the defendants to Queen Elizabeth, she referred the consideration of the whole case to all the judges of England'); 2 And 163 ('*suit fuit fait a le roign que el voile commaund touts les juges a deliver lour opinions quel choce est convenient d'estre fait come ceo case est*').

[95] *Earl of Worcester v Finch* (1600) Coke's notebook, BL MS Harley 6686B fo 421; 140 *Selden Society* 1094; 4 Co Inst 85; 2 And 162; cited in *Vaudry v Pannel* (1615) 3 Buls 116, 118, per Coke CJ (apparently conflating the case with *Throckmorton v Finch*); 117 *Selden Society* 224 no 335; cited in Calthorpe's reports, BL MS Hargrave 386 fo 114v (n 97).

[96] C 33/99 fo 240 (which names the Attorney-General as counsel for the plaintiffs).

[97] Ellesmere kept the original: HE Huntington Library, San Marino, California, MS EL 5915. (MS EL 5916 is an undated opinion by Popham and Anderson CJJ in the same case); copied in 2 And 163–4; decree book, C33/99 fo 240. See also Coke's notebooks, 140 *Selden Society* 1085. The preceding relevant entry in the decree books, on 5 February 1599, indicated only that the extent of Stoke Goldington was contentious: C 33/95 fo 502v. On 26 August 1599 the Privy Council ordered that £600 per annum paid into the Exchequer by Sir Moyle Finch should be 'repaid' to the countess of Southampton: *Calendar of State Papers (Domestic) 1588-1601*, 310.

[98] Coke said this was an 'ancient rule': 4 Co Inst 84. See also D Foster, ch 11 in this volume, 229–32.

> any longer retained in this Court, but left to the trial of the common law, forasmuch as there is no inequality between the said parties but that they are well able to try their titles by the law. And the principal cause that moved this Court at the first to relieve the said suit was the supposed imperfection which the complainants alleged to be in the said assurance of Stoke Goldington made unto them by the said Sir Thomas Heneage, admitting the same to be a manor in deed or reputation as they affirm it to be, which doubt being now thus cleared by the opinion of the judges, there is no cause why the said suit should be any longer continued in this court. It is therefore ordered that the matter be referred to be tried by the common law upon some special issue to be joined upon the freehold, wherein all things material may aptly and properly be brought in question … And if upon such trial the right shall fall out for the complainants, then this court will consider what arrearages of the said lands shall be due or payable to the said complainants and will take order for the same according to justice and equity. And it is finally ordered that no former decree or proceeding in this court shall be prejudicial to either of the said parties, nor any advantage to be taken thereupon, but that the full and whole right and title of the premises shall be equally and indifferently tried in such suit at the common law as though the same had been originally commenced and prosecuted there and nothing had been before proceeded or done in this court touching or concerning the same.[99]

Thus was any major collision with the judges formally averted. But Coke, and perhaps the judges, saw things more broadly. Coke wrote an addendum to his contemporary report to the effect that if the Chancellor[100] made a decree contrary to right, the Queen (who had committed her conscience to the Chancellor) could refer it to the judges to decide whether to affirm or reverse it, implying that the present case was an example of this procedure. He later crossed this out in his notebook, though he continued to maintain that the decree had been 'reversed' upon the judges' certificate.[101] He was reported to have said in 1616 that the judges in such a case acted as delegates by letters patent to 'hear and determine the decree', and that this procedure had been used to reverse the decree in Sir Moyle Finch's case.[102] But no mention was made of such a patent or commission in 1600, and Coke may have been thinking of a subsequent reopening of the case in the time of James I.[103] The reference in 1600 was probably one of the many instances in which the Queen informally asked some or all of the judges to look into a case and give their advice to the appropriate court. According to Edmund Hadde,

[99] C 33/99, fos 422, 743v; C 33/100, fo 701.

[100] Coke meant this generically. Egerton remained Lord Keeper until 1603.

[101] *Vaudry v Pannel* (1615) 3 Buls 116, 118, per Coke CJ (*cf* the citation in n 102); 4 Co Inst 85.

[102] Calthorpe's reports, BL MS Hargrave 376 fo 114v (Hil 1616), per Coke CJ ('*Mich. 42 & 43 Eliz. en le cas dependant parenter le countee de Worcester et autres feoffees en trust a Sir Moyle Finche … il fuit resolve per touts les justices Dengliterre que si un decrea fuit fait en Chauncery ore sur un petition al roigne el puist per ses lettres patentes delegater ses judges pur oyer et determiner cest decrea, car sicome lordinary power de seignior chauncellor est subject al un brefe derror port devant les justices de bank le roy, issint son extraordinary power est subject al roy, que puist delegater ses judges pur le redres del decrea sil ne soit come il doit estre, et accordant il fuit fait en le cas de Sir Moyle Finche et le decrea fuit revers*'). This citation is in a report of *Vaudry v Pannel* (n 98).

[103] *Finch v Earl of Worcester*, 118 *Selden Society* 474 no 249. This report says that Finch obtained a commission of review under the privy seal in the time of James I and that the former decree was 'avoided'. Its precise date is uncertain. It refers to the 'late' Lord Chancellor Egerton (d 1617), though Finch predeceased him in 1614. The proceedings may have been brought by Sir Moyle's widow Elizabeth (née Heneage, created Viscountess Maidstone in 1623), though the report says the bill was Sir Moyle's. Perhaps Egerton (*recte* Lord Ellesmere, when Lord Chancellor) was 'late' only at the time of writing the report some years afterwards. There is another copy of the same report in Northamptonshire Record Office, Finch-Hatton MS 33 fo 1.

barrister of Lincoln's Inn, 'the two chief justices were, by the Queen's command, used as assistants in the matter; and they delivered their opinion to the Lord Keeper contrary to his decree'.[104] But Anderson CJ's report is probably more correct in saying that, in obedience to the Queen's command, all the judges and barons gave their opinion in writing subscribed with their names, and that no more was done by the Chancery thereafter.[105]

It seems from Coke's report of the 1600 decision that the judges incidentally ventured to decide several points of equity. For one thing, they held that since Lady Finch had acquired the freehold by inheritance from Anne Heneage, and was a married woman, she could not be bound by a trust. Secondly, Sir Thomas could not have assigned his beneficial interest under the trust to the plaintiffs. A trust, in their opinion, was like a chose in action, which could not be granted over, and 'not like a use, for that by general allowance was esteemed as a hereditament … of greater estimation than a bare confidence and trust'. They foresaw 'great inconvenience' if trusts could be assigned, because 'they might be assigned to great men and thereby justice would be subverted'. Thirdly, it was held by a majority (including the three chiefs) that if a feoffment was made expressly to the use of the feoffee and his heirs, the feoffor could not allege that this conveyance was upon trust unless this was supported by written or other independent evidence, 'for otherwise all the inheritances of England might by such bare averments be drawn in question'. None of this was in the judges' signed certificate, and so the Chancery was free to ignore it. But it seems to have been made public.[106] And it showed, to Coke's way of thinking, that the judges could reverse Chancery decrees on equitable as well as legal grounds. Egerton, no doubt, would have seen it more as a matter of consultation with the judges, something which happened on a regular basis with judges assistant to the court.

One other case concerning Chancery jurisdiction is revealed by Coke's autograph notebooks. In 1605 Coke ruled as Attorney-General that the Lord Chancellor had no power to impose a fine for not performing a decree, because if he had such a power 'the interest of the land would indirectly be bound, whereas he had power only upon the person'.[107] This was related to Coke's contention that the Chancery, in matters of equity, was not a court of record and only courts of record had the power to impose fines.[108] Like the other cases, however, it was not reported by others and therefore not well known.

These decisions all belonged to Coke's time as a law officer, and they were seen by him as qualifying the power of the Chancery by subjecting it to a higher prerogative. All courts and authorities, in Coke's view, were subject to the oversight of the King's Bench – a position he had taken long before he became a judge. Ellesmere had a more absolutist view of the Chancery as a court exercising an uncontrollable prerogative.[109]

[104] 'Notes de certaine Chauncery cases', BL MS Add. 25207 fo 1 ('*ut audivi ex relatione Mr Hadde*').

[105] 2 And 163 (*cf* n 94).

[106] The last point, about parol evidence, was reported (and attributed to the two chief justices) in 117 *Selden Society* 166 no 104. *Cf Killio v Taverner* (1595) Powle's reports, ibid 203 no 183. For another aspect of the case see D Foster, ch 11 in this volume.

[107] *Themilthorpe's Case* (1605) Coke's notebook, BL MS Harley 6686B fo 658v. Coke confessed the defendant's plea to this effect when the fine was estreated in the Exchequer. The land would have been bound with the execution to recover the fine. (*Pace* Baker, *Magna Carta* (n 75) 339, the decree itself did not concern title to land.)

[108] See SE Thorne, 'Courts of Record and Sir Edward Coke' in *Essays in English Legal History* (London, The Hambledon Press, 1985) 243, 259–68.

[109] *Earl of Oxford's Case* (1615) 1 Ch Rep 1. He cited a remark of Stillington C in 1469 (YB Trin 9 Edw IV fo 14 pl 9) as meaning that the Chancellor sat according to 'an absolute and uncontrollable power'.

The jurisdictional disagreement meant that the decisions reported privately by Coke did not bear the fruit that he wished. Throckmorton's case had in the end been settled by arbitration after a hearing in the House of Commons, and it is not clear how far (if at all) Egerton accepted the terms of the judges' informal resolution. In any case, the resolution was to be eclipsed by the Star Chamber decree of 1616. The Earl of Worcester's case did not inaugurate a settled practice of appealing from the Chancery to the judges, and it may even have been reversed.[110] Certainly the judges did not acquire an equitable jurisdiction to overrule the Chancery. As in the Throckmorton case, litigants often preferred to seek their remedy in Parliament.[111] As for punishments, the Chancery preferred to use imprisonment for contempt, though Ellesmere maintained that there was a power to fine as well.[112]

Sir Moyle Finch's contribution to the history of equity has an ironic aspect. Not himself a lawyer, his 'unkind' nature[113] may explain his embroilment in litigation not only with his brother Henry, the Gray's Inn barrister and future serjeant at law,[114] but also with his mother[115] and others.[116] Even his death, in 1614,[117] did not end the family's involvement with the Chancery. His eldest son, Sir Theophilus Finch, engaged in extensive (but unrelated) litigation in the 1620s.[118] Sir Moyle's second son, named Heneage after his mother's family, was a barrister of the Inner Temple and well known to Coke, becoming a serjeant at law and Recorder of London. And it was Heneage Finch's son of the same name who rose to become Lord Chancellor, with the title of Lord Nottingham, and has been reputed since the eighteenth century as the 'father of modern equity'. Ravenstone was to be Lord Chancellor Nottingham's country seat and his burial place.[119] He must have been aware, if only from Coke's *Institutes*,[120] that his possession of the estate there represented a major struggle over Chancery jurisdiction almost a century earlier.

[110] See n 101.

[111] WJ Jones, *The Elizabethan Court of Chancery* (Oxford, Clarendon Press, 1967) 290, fn 1.

[112] See 117 *Selden Society* 296 no 160, 379 no 539. Both these notes are attributed to Lord Ellesmere (ie, 1603 or later) but are undated.

[113] Mentioned by his father-in-law Sir Thomas Heneage (see n 24).

[114] In Chancery: *Sir Moyle Finch v Henry Finch* (1590) Moo 339; BL MS Add 35952 fo 82v; 117 *Selden Society* 154, 227, 260, 285; pleadings in C 2/Eliz/F1/1, F5/50, 62, F6/61. In the Common Pleas (1597): BL MS Harley 1631 fos 256v, 267; MS Hargrave 5 fo 69; Duck's reports, MS Hargrave 51 fos 138v, 155. And in the King's Bench (1600) BL MS Lansdowne 1061 fo 33v; (1606) MS Hargrave 5 fo 69. Note also *Finch* v *Sir Moyle Finch* (1597) BL MS Add. 48097 fo 51.

[115] *Sir Moyle Finch v Lady Finch* (1598) Coke's notebook, BL MS Harley 6686B fo 303; 139 *Selden Society* 923 (referred by the Star Chamber to Wray CJ and Manwood CB); cited in 4 Co Rep 62.

[116] *Dounton v Sir Moyle Finch* (1601) Coke's notebook, BL MS Harley 6686B fo 480v (action for not separating tithes).

[117] The full-length effigies of Sir Moyle and Lady Finch by Nicholas Stone, formerly in Eastwell church, Kent, are now in the Victoria & Albert Museum. Unlike her husband, Lady Finch is shown with her eyes wide open, presumably because she survived him. A formidable woman, she was created a viscountess in her own right in 1623, and Countess of Winchilsea in 1628. The bust of their son Sir Heneage Finch, in his serjeant's robes, is placed nearby.

[118] H Saunders, '*Lambe v Finch* (1626): An Early Seventeenth-Century Expectant Heir Chancery Suit in Context' (2019) 40 *Journal of Legal History* 257; Cro Car 294; W Jones 312.

[119] Another descendant, Heneage Finch (1849–85), seventh earl of Aylesford, was plaintiff in the celebrated Chancery case discussed by Helen Saunders, ch 12 in this volume.

[120] He might also have seen his father's abridgment of it from Coke's notebooks: Bodl Lib MS Rawlinson C 756 fos 50v-51. See 136 *Selden Society*, cix n 65; 143 *Selden Society* lxxvii.

7

Aspects of Equity in 1600: Wills, Forfeitures and Trusts

DP WADDILOVE

I. Introduction

Having emerged from the largely undocumented days of its early life, the Chancery in 1600 stood somewhere on the bridge between medieval dispenser of ad hoc justice and sclerotically rigid Regency court of punctilio. Equity was, it seems, in an uncertain state, not yet driven by demands of regularity to full, precedent-driven lawlikeness, but also not unpredictably free-form. Yet matters of the balance of theory and practice, doctrine and discretion, remain relatively unclear. That is partly down to the inherent nature of the development, but at least as much due to a lack of investigation in the relevant source, the court record. The Register, also known as the Entry Books of Decrees and Orders,[1] records the daily judicial activity of the equity side of the court. It amounts to the Chancery's plea rolls. Unlike the haphazard content of the printed sources upon which the received wisdom has been built, it is an essentially complete record of the Chancery's equitable activity.[2]

The period around 1600 holds special interest as a crucial point in Chancery's development. Sir Thomas Egerton held the seal from 1596 to 1617, beginning as Lord Keeper of the Great Seal and becoming, after James I's accession in 1603, Lord Chancellor and Lord Ellesmere.[3] Egerton was appreciated both in his own day and for some time subsequently as particularly important.[4] But his tenure has been little studied because the printed reports hardly represent it.

[1] TNA PRO C 33. All manuscript references herein are to TNA PRO unless otherwise noted. The year of grace is taken to begin on 1 January. For the name 'Register' see *Bradshawe v Bushell*, C 33/83 f 56: '… the same should have been entered into the Register where the plaintiff might have seen it upon record which it is not'. For use of the term 'entry books of decrees and orders' see discovery.nationalarchives.gov.uk/details/r/C3594.

[2] For more on the insufficiency of printed reports as a basis for the history of early equity, see DP Waddilove, '*Emmanuel College v Evans* (1625) and the History of Mortgages' (2014) 73 *Cambridge Law Journal* 142.

[3] DE Greenway et al (eds), *Handbook of British Chronology*, 3rd edn (Cambridge, Cambridge University Press, 1996) 89; Sir JH Baker, 'Egerton, Thomas, first Viscount Brackley (1540–1617)' Oxford Dictionary of National Biography (Oxford University Press, 2004) doi.org/10.1093/ref:odnb/8594.

[4] Cambridge University Library MS Gg 2.31 f 553ff, for instance, suggests that a superfluity of business flowing to Chancery could be due to Egerton's particular competence. Egerton's influence in Chancery's victory

This chapter therefore considers the Court of Chancery in the legal year beginning 1600[5] based on a comprehensive review of the Register for that year.[6] This is supplemented with the manuscript Chancery reports collected by Hamilton Bryson and first printed by the Selden Society in 2000–2001.[7] The topics considered are three of the major areas of equitable jurisdiction. Two are often regarded as the major jurisdictions of Chancery: trusts, and forfeitures of bonds and mortgages.[8] The third – disputes over testamentary matters and decedents' estates – is famously associated with Chancery through Dickens's *Bleak House*.

II. Testamentary Jurisdiction

Little work has been done to consider the Chancery's treatment of inheritance disputes.[9] That is surprising given not only *Bleak House* but Henry Horwitz's estimate that nearly 19 per cent of Chancery's business in 1627 was what he called 'estate' cases, a figure rising to as much as 40 per cent in later years.[10] He defined these as cases based on issues 'arising out of wills and intestacies – above all, claims for payment of legacies and for performance of other provisions of wills'.[11] Anecdotal observation from 1600 confirms the general accuracy of his calculations.

The proper court for suits about a decedent's estate at this time was complex. One might assume that wills meant church courts. But church courts actually had a relatively narrow jurisdiction, covering only chattels.[12] Both debts and the all-important topic of

over common law in 1616 is well known; see DJ Ibbetson, '*The Earl of Oxford's Case* (1615)' in C Mitchell and P Mitchell (eds), *Landmark Cases in Equity* (Oxford, Hart Publishing, 2012) 1; JH Baker, 'The Common Lawyers and the Chancery: 1616' (1969) 4 *Irish Jurist* 368; JP Dawson, 'Coke and Ellesmere Disinterred: The Attack on the Chancery in 1616' (1941) 36 *Illinois Law Review* 127; LA Knafla, *Law and Politics in Jacobean England: The Tracts of Lord Chancellor Ellesmere* (Cambridge, Cambridge University Press, 1977) 171–81.

[5] Running from the start of Michaelmas term on 9 October 1600 to the end of the long vacation after the following Trinity term (8 October 1601). For the dates of legal terms see CR Cheney (ed), *A Handbook of Dates*, revised edn by M Jones (Cambridge, Cambridge University Press, 2000) 98–105 and 141.

[6] C 33/99 begins on the first day of the legal year and runs until the beginning of the next. Virtually identical content appears in C 33/100. Certain orders appear in only one book with a cross reference directing the reader to 'the fellow of this book'.

[7] WH Bryson (ed), *Cases Concerning Equity and the Courts of Equity 1550-1660, vol I* (2000) 117 *Selden Society* and *vol II* (2001) 118 *Selden Society* (hereafter 117 SS and 118 SS).

[8] The forfeitures category has been described variously. David Yale called it 'mortgages' while citing to Blackstone who called it 'the true construction of securities for money lent': DEC Yale, 'Introduction: An Essay on Mortgages and Trust and Allied Topics in Equity' in DEC Yale (ed), *Lord Nottingham's Chancery Cases, vol II* (1961) 79 *Selden Society* 8 (citing Sir William Blackstone, *Commentaries Upon the Laws of England, vol III* (Oxford, Oxford University Press, 1768) 436–37). Mortgages are perhaps the core, while securities for money lent includes penal bonds. Forfeitures also includes leases and other conditions of land forfeiture, which, while distinct in certain particulars, shares much with the other areas.

[9] Some few works of relevance include J Biancalana, 'Testamentary Cases in Fifteenth-Century Chancery' (2008) 76 *Tijdschrift voor Rechtsgeschiedenis* 283; RJR Goffin, *The Testamentary Executor in England and Elsewhere* (London, CJ Clay & Sons, 1901); and selections from both F Pollock and FW Maitland, *The History of English Law Before the Time of Edward I, vol II*, 2nd edn (Cambridge, Cambridge University Press, 1898) and WS Holdsworth, *A History of English Law, vols 1-17* (London, Methuen, 1903–1966).

[10] H Horwitz, *Chancery Equity Records and Proceedings 1600-1800*, 2nd edn (London, HMSO, 1998) 35–6.

[11] ibid 36.

[12] RH Helmholz, *The Oxford History of the Laws of England, vol I: The Canon Law and Ecclesiastical Jurisdiction from 597 to the 1640s* (Oxford, Oxford University Press, 2004) 387.

land were reserved exclusively to common law.[13] The resulting difficulty in settling an estate involving land, debts, and goods – as very many did – is self-evident; hence criticism by Richard Helmholz, amongst others, of the jurisdictional framework.[14]

Perhaps for this reason, many testamentary suits wound up in Chancery, where the entire matter could be decreed through its personal jurisdiction. The power of the injunction enabled the Chancery to order litigation in one place. For instance, in *Cockshut v Parkes*, the plaintiff challenged the defendant's title to various property according to a will.[15] The defendant alleged that he had been subject to 'several suits in the Spiritual Court', another suit 'in the prerogative court', plus 'several actions at the common law', and now an action in Chancery.[16] The Chancery held that it would dismiss the cause 'because this Court doth not think meet to determine of nuncupative wills in this Court', but nevertheless ordered 'that one action at the common law shall be only brought' and 'all other actions at the common law to be stayed and further that all suits in the prerogative or spiritual court concerning this cause other than appeals shall stay …'.[17] Similarly, in *Oliver v Rigdon*, the defendant successfully moved the Court to order the plaintiffs 'to make choice in which of the Courts they will proceed since the suits in both the said Courts be for one cause'.[18]

As *Cockshut* shows, the Chancery would not hear certain testamentary questions itself. In addition to claims upon nuncupative wills, a particularly important question that the Chancery would not hear was the validity of any will. A report from roughly between 1598 and 1602 says:

> my lord keeper will never stand to examine a will or no will, or a true will or a forged will, by any proofs in Chancery, but will say: Go, make your proofs or disproofs in the spiritual court or at common law. Or if there be a forged will, he will send you into the Star Chamber.[19]

The report is confirmed and elaborated by the record. In *Payne v Cantrell* the Lord Keeper determined that 'the matter between the said parties will stand partly upon the validity of the will in question which is meet to be tried at the common law',[20] and so he dismissed the case to the common law while nevertheless providing detailed rules about a feigned trespass to try title to the land under dispute, and an order for the appearance of a particularly important witness. Likewise, in *Browne v Richards*, the court said that the

> matter being touching the validity of the will and Administration mentioned in the plaintiff's bill seemeth more meet to be decided in the Ecclesiastical Court than in this Court[.] It is therefore ordered that the matter be Referred to be there tried accordingly …[21]

The reason *Payne* was dismissed to common law while *Browne* went to canon law was freehold land. The Statute of Wills 1540 enabled the will of freehold for the first time,[22]

[13] ibid 388, 400–01.

[14] ibid. Helmholz attributes a similar sentiment to Maitland, but it is not entirely clear that the latter's indignation was directed at jurisdictional difficulties as opposed to substantive decisions of the church as to how to direct property. See Pollock and Maitland (n 9) 362–63.

[15] C 33/99 f 428 v.

[16] ibid.

[17] ibid.

[18] C 33/99 f 356.

[19] 117 SS 119.167, 297.

[20] C33/99 f 100 v.

[21] C33/99 f 335 v.

[22] 32 Hen VIII, c 1.

reserving issues arising thereabout to the common law. *Payne* involved land, while *Browne* apparently did not (though the record was not explicit).

One of the more difficult – and important – testamentary questions in this period was the extent to which the court would hear direct claims for legacies. On the one hand, the lack of available remedy elsewhere, normally necessary to maintain a bill in Chancery, was unlikely for legacy matters given the aforementioned profusion of potential *fora* for such suits. On the other hand, the need to control complex litigation and invoke the relatively effective procedures of the Chancery created good reasons to maintain such suits in equity. The theory in our period remained that a claim for a legacy should be heard in the spiritual court. A report of 1601 says:

> My lord now puts a difference in relieving men for legacies, for he says he will receive no bill exhibited by a legatory against an executor, because the matter is spiritual and the suit is properly in the spiritual court, but where the legacy is transmitted into a foreign hand out of the hand of the executor, there if a bill be exhibited, my lord will relieve it.[23]

Thus the basic premise was that these suits should be heard in the church courts. But as this report shows, there seem to have been exceptions. The case in question involved property that found its way into the hands of a third party; the record of the reported case is regrettably unhelpful in further illuminating this particular exception.[24]

But even if suits for legacies were properly heard in the spiritual court, many such cases appear in Chancery.[25] Indeed, Dr Matthew Carewe, a master in ordinary, stated most plainly in a report to the court in 1595: 'this court doth usually deal in matters of legacy although the same be of their own nature properly triable by the ecclesiastical laws'.[26] Such a situation may have evolved out of the ease with which ordinary bases of Chancery jurisdiction were implicated. In the case upon which Dr Carewe reported, he explained the equitable jurisdiction:

> this legacy in the bill mentioned, was given to an infant not *in rerum natura*, but in his mother's womb, whereby some difficulty in law may arise, [therefore] I think this Court may very well take the hearing thereof, notwithstanding the demurrer.[27]

Or the plaintiff might lack necessary evidences, a frequently asserted basis of Chancery jurisdiction.[28] Many cases seem to involve claims for an annuity or rent charge, which easily triggered a trust rationale insofar as one party manages property to generate revenue for another.[29] Indeed, all cases of testate inheritance potentially implicated the trust jurisdiction because an executor was trusted to perform the will of the testator, and

[23] 117 SS 119.251, 314.

[24] *Newton v Jackson* C 33/102 f 116 v.

[25] Horwitz (n 10) 36.

[26] *Curtys v Wye* C 38/1/IMG_0300, 12 February 1595; see also WJ Jones, *The Elizabethan Court of Chancery* (Oxford, Clarendon Press, 1967) 410.

[27] *Curtys* (n 26).

[28] See, eg, *Heath v Wilde* C 33/99 f 220 v; *Howe v Howe* C 33/99 f 54.

[29] See, eg, *Gente v Wormell* C 33/99 f 576 v: 'with such allowance as was devised unto her by the will of her Father which should have been vjli yearly and hath been unpaid by the space of ten years'. Of course, unlike a trust, the surplus above the required payment belonged to the trustee equivalent, which altered the dynamics considerably. The similarity lay in on-going activity of one for the benefit, although not exclusively, of another.

some Chancery cases refer to the failure to perform the functions of an executor as a 'breach of trust'.[30] But the exact status of an executor as a trustee was at the time confusing and complicated.[31] One of Cary's reports from 1602 says:

> *Nota que executor non poit estre a trust*, unless he have an especial gift in the will, and that may then be in trust, otherwise the general trust of an executor is to pay debts and legacies; and of the surplusage to account to the ordinary *in pios usus* ....[32]

Thus the executor was not per se a trustee on this rationale, but might be so by virtue of a specific bequest. References to an 'executor in trust' nevertheless occur in the record,[33] and it is not always clear whether the status derived from a specific bequest or simply from the general power over the decedent's estate.

In the face of the numerous ways to shoehorn a legacy claim into Chancery, opposition to the jurisdiction seems to have faded. Indeed, by 1612 at the latest, a rule developed effectively putting legacy jurisdiction at the discretion of the defendant, as indicated by four very similar reports.[34] Each says that while Chancery was not the appropriate forum for a legacy suit, such cases could go forward if the defendant did not demur to the Chancery's jurisdiction. This created a potentially expansive jurisdiction where defendants lacked incentive to object to suits in the Chancery. And one can easily imagine executors fearing re-litigation if the relatively inferior church courts settled the matter. No such fear was necessary in light of a decree from the High Court of Chancery.[35]

Regardless of how they arrived and stayed in Chancery, many testamentary suits were heard there, which leaves questions about how more particular testamentary issues were treated. To take one example: what was to happen to the surplus assets of an estate? In many circumstances the executor was entitled to keep a surplus.[36] But WJ Jones has described an evolving Chancery position that directed the surplus elsewhere:

> for a long time the Chancery went no further than to direct the surplus to be transferred to the ordinary for pious uses.[37] Charity so vague and dubious – as opposed to specific bequests – was hardly an adequate solution, and in the reign of James I this doctrine was modified to the point where the executor was being compelled to distribute the residue among relatives of the deceased.[38]

The record suggests that by 1600 the Chancery may have already abandoned pious uses. At least one case sees a surplus directed to the recipients of an estate. For example, in *Keate v Heron*, the Chancery ordered that

[30] See, eg, *Smith v Wood* C 33/100 f 228 v.

[31] NG Jones, 'Wills, Trusts and Trusting from the Statute of Uses to Lord Nottingham' (2010) 31 *Journal of Legal History* 273, 283ff.

[32] *Anon* (1602) Cary 21, 21 ER 11.

[33] See, eg, *Workington v Dosyns* C 33/99 f 24; *Stradlinge v Guylforde* C 33/99 f 692 v.

[34] 117 SS 167.266 377; 117 SS 167.275 377; 117 SS 198 401; 117 SS 167.435 379.

[35] Horwitz (n 10) 38: 'executors may well have become increasingly cautious about administering any sizeable estate without Chancery's involvement'. Enrolment of a final decree in Chancery was the best means of preventing further litigation.

[36] NG Jones (2010) (n 31) 287.

[37] Citing *Anon* (n 32).

[38] WJ Jones (n 26) 415; see also NG Jones (2010) (n 31) 286–87.

> the defendant shall pay and discharge the said debts and legacies … And if any overplus shall be remaining then the same shall be divided amongst the children of the said [Testator] according to equity and Justice …[39]

Both the context of the order and the language quoted here strongly imply that such 'overplus' would go to the children, not because of any residuary clause but by equitable direction.

The Chancery was thus part of a complicated contemporary jurisdictional arrangement for testamentary matters in 1600, and its role therein seems to have been changing. Both the church and the common-law courts had exclusive jurisdiction over what together comprehended all testamentary matters, and yet the Chancery heard many such cases. Indeed, it was probably difficulty with jurisdictional profusion that often predicated Chancery's jurisdiction for litigation management. Combined with various other reasons for an equitable hearing, the Chancery's jurisdiction expanded, eventually leading to the position that as long as the defendant did not demur, and they often had reason not to, it would hear the case. As to equitable doctrine in testamentary matters, we have seen some indication from the record that a principle may have developed sooner than previously thought that the surplus of an estate goes to the general recipients of the estate rather than to pious uses. Other matters await further investigation of the record.

III. Forfeitures and Penalties

Forfeitures and penalties were united categorically in 1600. Contemporaries spoke of the 'forfeiture' of a bond to mean incurring its penalty.[40] And it was self-evidently a penalty to incur forfeiture of property (or any other right) through other instruments. Their equivalence in equity appears in the very first report in the *English Reports* Chancery series:

> *Payment after the day upon bonds holpen.* – If a man be bound in a penalty to pay money at a day and place, by obligation, and intending to pay the same, is robbed by the way; or hath intreated[*sic*] by word some other respite at the hands of the obligee, or cometh short of the place by any misfortune; and so failing of the payment, doth nevertheless provide and tender the money in a short time after; in these, and many such like cases, the Chancery will compel the obligee to take his principal, with some reasonable consideration of his damages (*quantum expediat*), for if this was not, men would do that by covenant which they do now by bond.
>
> *Condition to undo estates in lands.* – The like favour is extendable against them that will take advantage upon any strict condition, for undoing the estate of another in lands, upon a small or trifling default.[41]

[39] C 33/99 f 448.
[40] See, eg, *Head v Head* C 33/99 f 87; *Hungerforde v Blunte* C 33/99 f 385 v; *Fytche v Wilcox* C 33/99 f 494.
[41] *Anon* (1602) Cary 1, 21 ER 1 (italics in English Reports).

A. Penal Bonds and Leases

As intimated in the above report, bonds were a ubiquitous contract form in 1600.[42] According to a bond, a party forfeited a penalty sum unless he or she performed a condition of defeasance representing the substance of the contract. The condition might be any proper subject of contract. Edith Henderson considered bond-forfeiture relief in Chancery from the beginning of the Register in 1544 up to 1568.[43] She noted that extenuating circumstances excusing the forfeiture appear in cases in which the court granted relief. She nevertheless believed that the trend was toward a later equitable principle, still present in modern law, that penalties are irrecoverable per se. She wrote: 'The highly impressional reports I have heard for the 1590s indicate that by that time Chancery's intervention was almost routine.'[44] While the record shows very many bond-forfeiture cases, it suggests a more complicated position on when relief was available under Egerton.

One extremely brief report, most likely from between 1599 and 1604, says:

> My lord will not help the frequent complaint in Chancery of wilful and negligent forfeiture of bonds, but only in cases of extremity when, by inevitable necessity, a bond is forfeited; then will he relieve the forfeiture.[45]

Two points are of particular interest from this report. First, it confirms that requests for relief from bond forfeitures were 'frequent', something also entirely evident from the record. Second, Egerton clearly appears not to have adopted a position that penalties are unconscionable per se. Another report, of a case called *Johnson v Cooke*, provides nuance to Egerton's treatment of bond forfeitures:

> if the conditions be of the nature of the bond, scil. to pay money, no penalty will be recovered, but the debt will be inquired into. But if the conditions be for a collateral thing, scil. to perform covenants, it is otherwise.[46]

In other words, the Chancery will relieve penalties upon money bonds, but not upon performance bonds.

Distinguishing relief of money and performance bonds is logical. Money bonds secure loans, for which the fundamental nature – finance – is patent, and for which appropriate damages, viz. interest for forbearing, are therefore equally patent. The Chancery could thus easily calculate and enforce actual damages in the money-bond context. Performance bonds are not so simple. The amount of damages depended upon the nature of the performance, and the difficult question of consequential damages was more clearly implicated. What if, for example, a bond secured a right to pasture sheep in a field that was denied? This implicates all the complexity of contestable matters of fact – what happened to the sheep and everything downstream – in addition to complicated

[42] AWB Simpson, 'The Penal Bond with Conditional Defeasance' (1966) 82 *Law Quarterly Review* 392.
[43] EG Henderson, 'Relief from Bonds in the English Chancery: Mid-Sixteenth Century' (1976) 18 *American Journal of Legal History* 298.
[44] ibid 299.
[45] 117 SS 120.74 330–31.
[46] 117 SS 116.[331] 24.

legal questions of how that all matters in rules about duties, causation, and remedies. How much simpler to resolve the whole issue back to the pre-determined sum named in the bond as the parties agreed. Judicial economy thus makes it logical to distinguish between relief from forfeiture of a money bond and a performance bond.

The record shows some distinction in the treatment of money and performance bonds. In *Jeffery v Carewe*, the Chancery refused to stay a suit on a performance bond. The plaintiff bound himself to the defendant for £100 to 'suffer the defendant and his assigns to have and quietly to take the possession of certain lands at all times at the pleasure of him the defendant'.[47] The plaintiff breached the covenant, and thus the bond, by initiating suits against the defendant and his tenants in respect of the land. With the bond in suit at common law, the plaintiff sued in Chancery for relief. The court was

> of opinion that if the said bond were made with such condition as aforesaid[,] And that the plaintiff hath so wilfully forfeited the said bond and hath vexed the defendant and his tenants by such suits as it is alleged[,] there is no cause to stay the said suit upon the said bond[.][48]

The question becomes whether the inherent difficulty of determining damages on a performance bond, or the conduct of the obligor was the reason to allow the penalty. Later evidence suggests that Egerton would relieve performance-bond forfeiture where there was another way of recompensing the bond-plaintiff. For instance, in a much later case called *East v Wogan*, Egerton (now Lord Ellesmere) enjoined proceedings on a bond for the performance of covenants of a lease that was put in suit over reparation of fences and suchlike on the allegation that the bond-plaintiff could be recompensed by actual damages in an action of covenant.[49] But in *Jeffery v Carewe*, how the obligor 'wilfully forfeited' and 'vexed' the defendant seems to do the work. More cases might illuminate the doctrine further.

In contrast, money bonds ordinarily founded relief. Many cases saw the penalty relieved, often without extensive engagement over why the bond was forfeit and why relief was justified.[50] This was the baseline even under Egerton. But the relief was not automatic, nor was it always granted.

In 1600, examples still appear of explicit permission for penalties upon money bonds in Chancery. In *Samwayes v Bonde*, the plaintiff sought, inter alia, to obtain relief from forfeiture of a bond he had given to the defendant for 20 marks defeasible for 20 nobles. But

> it clearly appeared unto his Lordship … that the same bond was forfeited and that the defendant was not paid or satisfied any part of the said xx nobles before the same was put in suit and therefore the defendant had just cause to put the same in suit And also to keep the money received thereupon[.][51]

[47] C 33/99 f 247 v.

[48] ibid.

[49] C 33/131 f 202 v, 2 December 1616.

[50] See, eg, *State v Vinion* C 33/99 f 120; *Brooke v Sprynt* C 33/99 f 197; *Cullacote v Chawner* C 33/99 f 166 v; *Young v Gilberte* C 33/99 f 203 v; *Franckton v Walker* C 33/99 f 244; *Prettiman v Woodwarde* C 33/99 f 293; *Wilmote v Beckenshawe* C 33/99 f 556; *Prettiman v Lowe* C 33/99 f 53; *Alder v Bullocke* C 33/99 f 629.

[51] C 33/99 f 104 v.

What seemingly accounts for this remarkable outcome was that

> his lordship is of opinion the defendant was vexed without just cause[,] and his lordship would also have given costs to the defendant if so be had he had not had judgment and execution for xviii^{li} upon the said bond of xx marks for the payment of xx nobles as aforesaid[.][52]

Thus, not only had the obligor-plaintiff 'vexed' the obligee-defendant sufficiently to justify a costs award against him in dismissing his Chancery suit, but the obligee-defendant already had judgment and execution upon the bond in question. And the penalty recovered, £11 13s 4d,[53] easily may have been less than costs, both because of the vexatious litigation, and because the sums at issue were actually much greater than the bond, which was only part of securities related to an underlying £50 annuity. The best course was thus to allow the completed common-law action to stand, avoiding any problems of 'common injunctions' that led to the famous Coke-Ellesmere controversy of 1616.[54] As the history of that controversy shows, Egerton was not opposed in theory to post-judgment injunctions. But he may nevertheless have forborne to grant such relief because the Chancery plaintiff was asking too much: he had both broken the condition of his freely agreed bond and failed to raise the matter in Chancery until after judgment.

Indeed, such delay in seeking equitable relief until after judgment at law may alone have been sufficient to deny relief. Another contemporary report says:

> Touching injunctions to stay judgments or executions, as either of them may well be prayed in Chancery, so let these two things be respected, first, that the party who prays the injunction have a suit depending in Chancery before such judgment general or execution awarded, then that he examine not that judgment nor seek to reverse it there but only pray relief against him that has such judgment for so much as he has obtained by his judgment[.][55]

Samwayes thus saw recovery of a penalty on a money bond permitted in Chancery, but in fairly extreme circumstances.

Other evidence nevertheless suggests that relief from forfeiture of a money bond may not have been forthcoming even in less extreme circumstances. George Norburie, a former cursitor in Chancery and harsh critic of the court, wrote in 1621 to Bishop John Williams on the latter's appointment as Lord Keeper, hoping to encourage Chancery reform. Norburie stressed that Egerton was reluctant to relieve forfeitures:

> For to what purpose are bonds made with penalties, leases with forfeitures *nomine poenae*, and clauses of re-entry, if the wilful violators shall be exempt from all punishments, and who will take care to pay either debt or rent? I have heard the late honourable and worthy Lord Ellesmere say, that he would not relieve any that forfeited a bond, unless it were in case of extremity, or that he could make it appear that by some accidental means he was occasioned thereunto; and if he did help any, the party here complaining should pay all the defendant's charges, both at the common law and in Chancery, (if he were able) if there was cause. Whereas of late much lenity has been used to all debtors, so that many, after four or five years,

[52] ibid. Another factor in the outcome may have been the relatively small sums involved.

[53] The due debt was 20 nobles. One noble is one third of a pound, viz. 6s 8d. 20 nobles is therefore £6 6s 8d. The sum recovered at common law was £18, which is £11 13s 4d in excess of the due debt.

[54] Regarding the controversy see, eg, Ibbetson (n 4), Baker (n 4); Dawson (n 4).

[55] 117 SS 119.236 311.

> suit and charges in this court, were glad to go away with their principal without either costs or damages.[56]

In part based on Norbury's claim, Professor WJ Jones was of the view that Egerton preferred to enforce agreements as stated and was consequently reluctant to relieve bond forfeitures.[57]

One case in the record from 1600 strongly supports Jones's view. *Riley v Flecton* was a remarkable case. To begin with, it saw Egerton quash, at least temporarily, a defendant's settlement offer on the grounds that it was too generous to the plaintiff.[58] In a suit at common law upon a bond of £150 for payment of £105, the obligor exhibited a bill in Chancery admitting that he failed to tender the £105 'until about vj days after' the due date in November 1600.[59] The defendant was generous the following August:

> the defendant doth by his answer deny the said tender[,] but doth offer and still is willing and ready to take his principal debt of Cv^{li} with his damages for the forbearance thereof sithence the said seventh of November last[,] with such costs as he hath expended in this court[,] and to deliver up the said obligation.[60]

Although, as discussed below, the Chancery sought dispute resolution in this period even to the point of sometimes holding parties to prior settlement offers,[61] the record continues unexpectedly: 'which offer his Lordship doth think unreasonable in respect the said obligation was[,] as is pretended[,] by the plaintiff's own bill showed to be either wilfully or negligently forfeited'.[62] Egerton thus disallowed the proposed settlement and referred the matter to a master to report on the facts from the pleadings and damages and costs proper for the defendant. While the original master's report appears to have been lost,[63] the record appears to contain its substance. It says that the plaintiff-obligor

> would put off from himself to his servants careless negligence or forgetfulness, which may seem to be but a colour of excuse[;] yet it appeareth the bond to have been forfeited either wilfully or negligently which in law is equalled *cum dolo malo*[;] and so the bond in very Justice and not in extremity of law only became forfeited[,] and ought rather by the Creditor's own conscience to be remitted than to be forced there to by Judgment[;] Seeing (as daily it is) how careless men do grow for satisfying of their debts in hope of relief by Chancery[,] the which should not *subvenire negligentibus sed necessitate rerum impeditis*.[64]

This is remarkable in at least two respects. First, the use of Latin maxims, here written in italics rather than the customary secretary hand, is essentially unheard of in the Chancery record at this time. Second, the general consideration of both principle and

[56] G Norburie, 'The Abuses and Remedies of the High Court of Chancery' in F Hargrave (ed), *A Collection of Tracts Relative to the Law of England Vol I* (Dublin, E Lynch, 1787) 431–32.

[57] WJ Jones (n 26) 425, 447–48.

[58] C 33/99 ff 750 v, 757 v.

[59] C 33/99 f 750 v. The pleadings appear to have been lost, but this quote from the record seems fairly to represent the substance of the complaint.

[60] ibid.

[61] See nn 104 and 111 below.

[62] C 33/99 f 750 v (italics original).

[63] The report does not appear in C 38/4, where it would be expected if extant. The early C 38s are, however, distinctly imperfectly arranged, meaning it may lurk somewhere unexpected. This nevertheless remains unlikely given that the vast majority of master's reports from the period have been lost.

[64] C 33/99 f 757 v.

broader effect is likewise uncharacteristic of a court whose orders usually hew closely to the case at hand. The substance nevertheless accords with Egerton's equity that refused to relieve plaintiffs from the avoidable consequences of their own actions. The result of the case was not, however, a triumph of individual responsibility. The record continued:

> although he [the defendant] hath been viperously stung by the plaintiff's bill with some Imputations[, he] is yet contented of his own offer not to take *plus justo etiam ex justa actione*[,] but to accept of x^{li} only beside his principal for all his charges and damages; and therefore the said Mr Dr Carewe thinks it meet the same be allowed unto him and presently paid unto him with his principal and the bond thereupon to be delivered up to the plaintiff to be cancelled.

It was ordered accordingly. The principle nevertheless appears starkly, if theoretically, that even upon money bonds, relief from forfeiture was not automatic. Not only was this Egerton's personal equity, but also the institutional sense as represented by Dr Matthew Carewe, one of the most active and longest-serving masters in ordinary, who had been in post since 1577.[65] *Riley v Flecton* thus illustrates clearly how far equity remained in 1600 from regarding penalties, even on money bonds, as unconscionable per se.

Bond penalties in equity in 1600 were not, it seems, as odious to equity as they would become. Some countenance of performance-bond penalties appears in the record; so too does approval of money-bond penalties. 'Vexatious' or 'wilful' conduct of the obligor justified penalty recovery in addition to other regular equitable ideas such as laches. The bond obligor of the period thus still had reason not to presume the Chancery's favour.

Forfeiture of leases or other rights to land also met less resistance in Chancery in 1600 than they would later. A report from between 1598 and 1602 goes remarkably far in approving them:

> If any man enter for condition broken or take the extremity of advantage by virtue of a condition, if there be no fraud or practice in the party so entering, but simply so that he enter for a condition broken and takes the extremity thereof, no relief in this case for the other party, for a condition is a man's hereditament, my lord says, and he will not take that away from any man.[66]

The presumption, according to this report, was in favour of the forfeiture rather than against it. Another report says that Egerton would not relieve someone who forfeited a lease, even for which he paid 'a great fine or income,' if 'the lessee do wilfully neglect and deny [the condition of] the scouring of [the ditches of the lessor] so that the lessor enter'.[67] Egerton's focus appears again to be more on the fault of the forfeiter than on the strength of the right to the condition, but the point is the same: he will not relieve the forfeiture of land here.

The unmistakably strong position favouring land forfeitures here may be due to a prevailing preference in equity for what can be called 'ancient inheritance'. Equity appears to have imputed deontic importance to freehold land rights of long-standing

[65] P Stein, 'Carew, Sir Matthew (c. 1531–1618)' Oxford Dictionary of National Biography (Oxford University Press, 2004) doi.org/10.1093/ref:odnb/4632.

[66] 117 SS 119.254 314.

[67] 117 SS 119.256 315.

links to families in primogeniture.[68] This found expression to some extent in the equity of redemption, although other views, such as socially proper conduct in financial transactions, ultimately mattered more for that doctrine.[69] It was in lower-profile issues like those addressed here that it appeared more clearly. Land forfeitures brought lands back to their 'rightful' owners, grantors who had pre-established terms of the lands' return triggered solely at the fault of the forfeiter. The condition is thus a hereditament because it returns the land – the quintessential hereditament – to the rightful line. The ease with which damages could be calculated for typical conditions of re-entry, such as non-payment of rent or covenants to repair, later drove toward greater disfavour of land forfeiture. The matter thus appears in 1600 to have scrambled typical relations of law and equity: conditions found inadequate remedy at (developed) equity, for which only specific performance of the condition – in this case the *legal* position – would do.

B. Mortgages

(i) Basic Relief

Not many cases of mortgage forfeiture appear in the Chancery record for the legal year beginning 1600. Indeed, only around 30 cases in the Register contain the word 'mortgage', and by no means is forfeiture, or even the mortgage in any sense, at issue in all of them. Few cases address the question of real interest – in what circumstances would the Chancery grant relief from mortgage forfeiture? But in those few cases, the Chancery granted forfeiture relief every time, provided, of course, that the mortgagor had sufficient funds to redeem. Whether this 100 per cent relief rate was because the Chancery was prepared to relieve mortgage forfeiture as a matter of course is not clear. But no cases suggest that the court would permit a mortgagee to retain property if a mortgagor could afford to repay the requisite sum.

Such extensive relief puts in question the accepted timing of the development of the equity of redemption.[70] The received wisdom dated such development to very shortly before 1625 and suggested that Sir Francis Bacon (1617–21) may have been responsible.[71] The key to distinguishing the equity of redemption from other sorts of mortgage forfeiture is the absence of circumstances excusing the forfeiture. Simply the ability to pay to redeem became enough. Good reasons to excuse the forfeiture appear in most mortgage cases in 1600.

One case has, as it happens, been known long enough to be the paradigm of the pre-equity-of-redemption approach. *Courtman v Convers* has been known to legal historians since it was printed in a nineteenth-century collection of excerpts from the

[68] DP Waddilove, 'Why the Equity of Redemption' in C Briggs and J Zuijderduijn (eds), *Land and Credit* (London, Palgrave Macmillan, 2018) 117, 128–31; see also *Ellyot v Nance* C 33/99 f 58 v, discussed in text to n 80 below.

[69] ibid 141.

[70] RW Turner, *The Equity of Redemption* (Cambridge, Cambridge University Press, 1931); C McNall, 'Mortgage; English Common Law' in SN Katz (ed), *Oxford International Encyclopedia of Legal History*, vol 4 (Oxford, Oxford University Press, 2009); Waddilove (2014) (n 2).

[71] Turner (n 70) 27; McNall (n 70) 189.

record.[72] Owing to the meagre extent of the sources from the period, it was given a prominent place in RW Turner's highly influential account of the doctrine.[73] The allegations of the plaintiff-mortgagor have an almost comic quality to them. He presents himself as a poor soul who knew not the redemption day 'by reason he was ignorant and could not read writing';[74] but because he was a diligent debtor, he 'repaired to the defendant's house where the money was to have been paid at the very day to the intent to have known the certain day'. Yet the nefarious defendant absconded to avoid seeing the plaintiff. '[W]hereupon the plaintiff on the morrow after thinking it to be the precise day went again to the defendant's house and tendered the money.' But (in a slightly confusing passage), the defendant again fled until returning home at 1 am, at which time he refused the tender as being late. The defendant-mortgagee then entered the plaintiff's lands. After recounting all this, the court said: 'which if it be true this court holdeth to be very unconscionable and hard dealing and ought in equity to be relieved'. The court referred the case to Tyndall, one of the masters in ordinary, to see if he could end the matter by mediation, and if not, to report back to the court. The case disappears from the record thereafter.

Metham v Phillips is similar in involving uncertainty of the redemption date.[75] The plaintiff was the administrator of a deceased mortgagor's estate. 'And finding no counterpane of the said mortgage whereby to know the day of the redemption of the said lease[,] he[,] the said plaintiff[,] did presently exhibit his bill into this court to compel the defendant to discover the same.'[76] But the defendant delayed answering until after the redemption day. With the answer in court, 'it manifestly appeared unto his lordship upon the reading thereof that the defendant hath thereby set forth that he was not bound to discover the day of redemption unto the plaintiff and that he was willing to get a forfeiture of the said lease'.[77] After the defendant showed what cause he could why the lease should not be redeemed for the mortgage price, the court ordered it assigned to trustees to raise that sum for the defendant; and, interestingly, the court punished the defendant by subordinating his debt for trying to cause forfeiture:

> the defendant shall not have the preferment of payment of his other debts which he supposeth are due to him by the said intestate before any other creditors are satisfied for that he craftily sought to get the said lease to himself to defeat the rest as it seemeth.[78]

Before the trust was established, the court granted, per the plaintiff's request, that a third party be allowed to buy the lease for the mortgage price, thus liquidating the asset and more quickly resolving the matter.[79] The court's strong dislike of the defendant's attempt to take the forfeiture, perhaps as much for its effect upon third-party creditors as the estate of the mortgagor, is manifest.

[72] C Monro, *Acta Cancellariae* (London, W Benoing & Co, 1847) 764.
[73] Turner (n 70) 26.
[74] C 33/99 f 628. All quotations refer to this order.
[75] C 33/99 ff 110 v, 208 v, 503 v, 700 v.
[76] C 33/99 f 208 v.
[77] ibid.
[78] C 33/99 f 503 v.
[79] C 33/99 f 700 v.

Ellyot v Nance presents the equity of ancient inheritance, discussed above, as a reason for forfeiture relief.[80] The lead plaintiff's father-in-law entered into complex financial transactions and mortgaged his manor and lands for far less than they were worth. He 'was altogether decayed by those usurious bargains and died in prison before or about the time that the said lands should have been redeemed'. The mortgagor's heirs as plaintiffs were 'contented to pay unto the defendant all such sums of money as he hath any way disbursed *bona fide* for or in respect of the said lands upon an account to be by him of the profits of the same lands made'. The court thought this reasonable and referred the matter to referees to

> take a true and perfect account of the defendant both what sums of money he hath aby ways disbursed for or in respect of the said lands[,] and what profits he hath any ways made or received of the same lands either by receipt of rents fines or otherwise … as that the plaintiffs may have the said manor and lands being the ancient Inheritance of their Ancestors[;] And the said defendant may have all such money as is due unto him to the uttermost[,] with such reasonable consideration for the forbearing thereof as they shall think meet[,] deduction being made of such rents fines and profits of the said lands to the plaintiffs as aforesaid.[81]

That the court apparently considered restoration to one's 'ancient inheritance' desirable is interesting. Approval of such restoration provides an underlying rationale for relief of forfeiting mortgagors independent of the circumstances of forfeiture. Indeed, it seems particularly powerful here, as the mortgagee had put an unusually strong case for his entitlement to the manor. Not only was the mortgagee not one of the usurers who had decayed the mortgagor (which the referees of the case confirmed), he was instead a surety for the mortgagor who had been 'enforced to sell a great part of his inheritance[,] better lands and more worth than the manor of Trewynard' for his debts, and taken the manor as previously agreed countersecurity for those debts. Despite the mortgagee having taken up personal residence in the manor, the court preferred the ancient inheritance of the mortgagor's heirs.

An extremely clear equitable justification for relief appears in two more cases where fraud on the part of the mortgagee caused the forfeiture. In *Day v Murrell*, the court relieved the mortgagor because, in the words of a report of two masters in ordinary adopted by the court in its entirety,[82] when the debt was due 'the defendant was content to forbear the same until about Christmas after the day of payment[;] at which time the plaintiff offered and tendered the same to the defendant[;] but the defendant then refused to accept of it and would needs take the forfeiture of the copyhold premises'.[83] The masters reported that,

> considering the hard and unconscionable dealing of the defendant towards the plaintiff in his case[,] we are of opinion and think it agreeable to equity to be ordered and agreed by this

[80] C 33/99 f 58 v; see n 68 above.

[81] C 78/132/6 m 15.

[82] C 33/99 f 229. The court ordered 'That the report of Mr Dr Legge and Mr Tyndall two of the Masters of this court who heard the cause in question shalbe ratified and confirmed by the decree and authority of this court and shalbe performed on all parts to all intents and purposes as well as if the matter thereof had been judicially pronounced upon a solemn hearing in open court according to the meaning of the said masters.'

[83] C 78/116/3.

> court that the defendant shall with all convenient speed sufficiently surrender up all the copy-hold premises formerly to him mortgaged[84]

with a condition requiring payment of £20, in two payments of £10 at the next ensuing Lady Day and Michaelmas.

Nearly identical is *Mason v Wilmote*, in which the plaintiff-mortgagor 'was drawn to forfeit his said land by the fair speeches and promises [of the mortgagee and the broker who arranged the mortgage] that the said money should be continued longer in the plaintiffs hands and that no advantage should be taken of any forfeiture of the said lands'.[85] In both cases the Chancery relieved the forfeiture. Given the normality of continuing debts upon payment of interest at the time,[86] cases of a similar nature might have been fairly common.

The foregoing cases all have some level of extenuating circumstances excusing the forfeiture. Other mortgage cases in the record have no clear extenuating circumstances, yet the Chancery granted relief. None, however, is a sufficient basis to infer that relief was available as a matter of course.

The closest case is *Wright v Wright*.[87] In this very brief, single record entry, the court states that the case was one 'touching certain lands heretofore mortgaged' by the plaintiff to one of the defendants. Without explaining any of the particular circumstances, it goes on:

> It is thought meet by this court that if the plaintiff will have the said land from the said [mortgagee,] he the said [mortgagee] should have all such money as he hath disbursed for or in respect of the said land.

And the case was referred to Dr Hussey, a master in ordinary, to determine that sum. Though on first glance such cursory treatment suggests relief as a matter of course, a deeper look shows that is not true. In addition to the fact that it is not clear that the mortgage was ever forfeit, one of the co-defendants was a co-mortgagor, and the pleadings indicate that this was a complex situation involving the establishment of a marriage settlement.[88] It is therefore not clear precisely for what *Wright* might stand.

What perhaps nevertheless shows how straightforward mortgage forfeiture relief was in Chancery are five cases in which mortgagees did not bother resisting relief. So little opposition appears in *Alkyn v Wilde* that it is not clear why it was litigated: the defendant-mortgagee 'confessed the payment and satisfaction of the said [mortgage] money and that he is willing to reconvey the said messuage and land to the plaintiff', which was ordered accordingly.[89] *Maytam v Whitfield* involved only a dispute about the sum to be paid to redeem. The plaintiff mortgaged lands for £100,[90] which the mortgagee offered to re-convey if the plaintiff repaid the £100 'and ten pounds more'

[84] ibid.

[85] C 33/99 f 238 v; C 78/111/11.

[86] Waddilove (2018) (n 68) 135–37.

[87] C 33/99 f 163 v.

[88] The pleadings appear at C 2/Eliz/W1/52. It has not yet been possible for the author to consult them. The catalogue entry indicates their subject: 'To establish a settlement on marriage. A messuage and lands in Primthorpe in the parish of Broughton Astley, Leicestershire which defendant Wright agreed to settle on the marriage of the plaintiff Wright his son with the plaintiff Elizabeth.'

[89] C 33/99 f 594 v.

[90] C 33/99 f 475 v; C 33/99 f 72.

(impliedly representing interest). 'And xx[li] more[,] which he supposeth he disbursed for the plaintiff[,] with consideration for the forbearing of the said money'.[91] The plaintiff was willing to pay the first £110 but wished a master in ordinary to consider the last £20 and related damages. After the defendant-mortgagee failed to attend a master as ordered, the court ordered that if the plaintiff-mortgagor paid £110, it would order reconveyance of the mortgaged property, adding that it would later deal with the further £20.

In *Mawchell v Deane* the defendant-mortgagee was 'content so he may have the money due to him by the same mortgages with damages for the forbearing thereof together with such costs as he hath been put unto by these suits and extent[92] he will relinquish both the benefit of the said lands and statute.'[93] The court ordered accordingly. In *Parsey v Bartholomewe* the defendant-mortgagee disputed only the terms of a sale of land requiring the mortgagee's participation that was necessary to raise funds for the plaintiff-mortgagor to redeem. That the mortgagor might redeem late was uncontested.[94]

The only other case clearly involving mortgage-forfeiture relief in the legal year beginning 1600 is similar. In *Wood v Effield*, the mortgagee had provided in his will that a third party, a certain Mr Denne, could redeem the property for the sum the mortgagor had received in loan from the mortgagee, £60.[95] The plaintiff alleged that neither he nor Denne knew about this provision in the will, and the plaintiff had always been ready to pay £60. Though the record is not clear, it appears that because the mortgagee was clearly willing for *someone* to redeem late in light of his will, and because Denne lost nothing through non-enforcement of a gratuitous legacy of which he was ignorant anyway, the court allowed the mortgagor to redeem.

In none of these cases did the mortgagee attempt to enforce his legal right to the property according to the condition of the mortgage. The disputes centred only on the particulars of the late redemption. Given that Egerton could, as discussed above, call a land-forfeiture condition (of which a mortgage condition was one) a man's hereditament with which he would not interfere, it is far from given that mortgagees would not insist upon these rights.[96] Of course the mortgagee in *Wood v Effield* attempted to dispose of the property by effectively redirecting the redemption condition to a third party, but the executor defendants offered little resistance to allowing the mortgagor to exercise it. More importantly, the mortgagee in *Metham v Phillips* seemingly did consider the condition his right, even to the extent that he admitted in his answer to attempting to procure the forfeiture. But these, especially *Metham*, are the exceptions. The instances of mortgagees making no attempt to defend the condition are far more numerous; indeed, they represent a significant proportion of the mortgage cases in the legal year beginning 1600. This suggests that the equity of redemption was well along in development, although not everyone yet realised it.

[91] C 33/99 f 72.

[92] For extents as execution upon a debt, see DP Waddilove, 'The "Mendacious" Common-Law Mortgage' (2019) 107 *Kentucky Law Journal* 425, 435–38.

[93] C 33/99 f 113; *cf* C 33/99 f 243; C 33/99 f 257 v.

[94] C 33/95 f 240; C 33/95 f 270; C 33/95 f 782; C 33/97 f 652v; C 33/99 f 3; C 33/99 f 202.

[95] C 33/100 f 230v; C 33/99 f 675v.

[96] See n 66 above.

No other cases directly presented the question of mortgage-forfeiture relief in the legal year beginning 1600. The record thus shows what appears to be forfeiture relief pretty routinely available in those few cases that touch upon the matter, though each shows extenuating circumstances to justify relief. But all such circumstances alleged were sufficient; in no cases did a mortgagor fail to obtain relief. It thus seems that the Chancery had a well-developed habit of relieving mortgage forfeitures in the legal year beginning 1600.

(ii) Post-Forfeiture Mortgage Redemption Terms

Once relief of mortgage forfeiture is forthcoming, the next question is upon what specific terms. As is already evident from the foregoing discussion, the court does not appear to have adhered exactly to any rigid formula.

Two cases nearly follow the developed doctrine in requiring payment of principal, interest, and costs, deducting any profits received by the mortgagee, in order to redeem. In *Ellyot v Nance*, the court ordered all those elements except costs, no mention of which ever appears, suggesting the parties were left to bear their own.[97] *Parsey v Bartholomewe* was similar but went further and with more complications. The mortgagee had provided redemption terms in his will, simply requesting repayment of the principal debt with standard, ten per cent interest damages.[98] The mortgagee's widow offered, along modern lines, to accept those terms, to count all profits received toward the redemption money; and, if she did obtain the property in order to sell it to fulfil dependent charitable legacies in her husband's will, she would disburse any resulting surplus above the debt to the mortgagor.[99] '[W]hich offer this Court taketh to be Reasonable',[100] and so ordered.[101] Again, no mention of costs appeared.[102]

In *Wood v Effield*, the underlying finances were extremely complex, the court failed to explain how it calculated a redemption price, and, interestingly, overrode its own calculation to force the mortgagor to abide by an offer he had previously made.[103] The mortgage was originally to have been for a loan of £100, but only 'threescore pounds of the same', ie, £60, was eventually given due to extremely complex (and contested) underlying financial matters. The mortgage was forfeit; the mortgagee died in possession and provided in his will that a third party could redeem for £60. The court ordered the plaintiff-mortgagor to pay £70 to redeem. How it calculated the additional £10 is entirely unclear, and one is left to infer that a round sum seemed best. In an unusual

[97] The court orders reimbursement of the mortgagee's improvements, which the plaintiffs offered to do *sua sponte* at the beginning. Such payments, as the converse of a mortgagee's accounting for profits, became part of standard accounting for late redemption.

[98] C 33/95 f 270.

[99] ibid.

[100] ibid.

[101] ibid; and also at C 33/99 f 202.

[102] Costs orders were not rare, but did not appear in every case. For cases including award of costs, see, eg, *Wenman v Stone* C 33/99 f 114 v; *State v Vinion* C 33/99 f 120; *Smaleman v Pollard* C 33/99 f 145; *Jermyn v Fylke* C 33/99 f 156 v; *Hutton v Wyf* C 33/99 f 154; *Heaton v Dighton* C 33/99 f 223 v; *Awbrey v George* C 33/99 f 266 v. In some cases the Chancery explicitly refused costs: *Copledike v Copledike* C 33/99 f 120 v; *Eastman v Dirdo* C 33/99 f 200. Wrongdoing most clearly justified an award of costs.

[103] C 78/101/3; C 33/100 f 230v.

move, the court did not leave the matter at that. Upon the allegation of the defendants who had succeeded to the mortgagee's interest

> that the plaintiff heretofore upon an agreement offered by others to pay unto them the said defendants lxxx^{li} if they might have had the said land[,] It is therefore thought meet by this court and so ordered and decreed that the said plaintiff shall pay unto the defendants the sum of lxx^{li} at or upon the feast day of St Michael the Archangel next coming[,] but if the defendants can prove by the affidavit of two sufficient persons that the plaintiff would heretofore have paid lxxx^{li} unto the defendants[,] then the plaintiff shall at the said day pay unto them the defendants the said sum of lxxx^{li} but if no such proof shall be made then he shall only pay the said sum of lxx^{li} as aforesaid.[104]

The defendants in fact made proof of the £80 offer.[105] This preference for a prior offer shows something of the court's focus on dispute resolution in the period.

Day v Murrell was, like the £70 in *Wood*, inexplicable in the calculation of the redemption price. The court ordered redemption upon payment of £20, the original debt amount, despite the fact that the mortgagee had admitted to having received £5 thereof. Why the court thus required an increase of 25 per cent above the original debt is unclear, and one is drawn to think it problematic carelessness in the use of a round figure.

Mason v Wilmote at first glance appears to contradict standard practice, in that it was 'thought meet by this court and ordered and decreed that for a final end of the cause the said Stookes shall go away with all the profits raised of or by the said lands and by him already taken'.[106] But Stookes was not the mortgagee. He was a purchaser from the mortgagee. While the record is unclear whether he had notice of the mortgage, it is not especially surprising to see such a party permitted to retain profits.

Metham v Phillips is as expected, but its unique posture distinguishes it from ordinary mortgage cases. The mortgagor's administrator exhibited a bill prior to forfeiture specifically to discover the redemption date in order to prevent forfeiting. Unsurprisingly, after the mortgagee delayed answering specifically to cause forfeiture, which he himself admitted, the court ordered redemption for the original price.[107]

Maytam v Whitfield provides little of interest, ordering payment of what appears to be principal and interest according to the offer and acceptance of the parties, and leaving a disputed £20 outstanding.[108] No other sums are ever mentioned.

Wright v Wright is also irrelevant for understanding mortgage-redemption terms because too little information about the case appears in the order discovered to make sense of the overall situation.[109]

The trend was therefore toward the modern position, but it was far from developed. Each case appears to result in its own order with little concern for anything like

[104] ibid (identical in both).

[105] C 33/99 f 675 v.

[106] C 33/99 f 238 v.

[107] The means of payment shifted, having initially been ordered as establishment of a trust of the property to raise the redemption money from profits, but then, at the request of the mortgagor's administrator, simply became sale to a third party apparently to liquidate the property and resolve the matter with the original redemption price remaining the mortgagee's entitlement.

[108] C 33/99 f 475 v.

[109] See n 87 above.

a standard practice. The specificity of relief tailored to individual cases gave equity an essential flexibility, one at odds with the uniformity necessary for principled doctrine on award of equitable relief. It is worth noting the absence of costs allocated against mortgagees, as this could be interpreted to suggest that the court did not deem resistance to redemption an obviously wrong position sufficient to justify imposing costs.[110] But then the court calculates the exact price of redemption ordered in each case inexplicably, perhaps including costs within awards that typically exceed the principal debt. So it is difficult to know. One of the more interesting points is the override of the court's own redemption price in *Wood v Effield*. The court's reinstatement of an offer previously made by the mortgagor demonstrates the court's highly case-specific, litigant-focussed approach in this period. It was more interested in settling particular disputes than applying principles.[111]

IV. Trusts

The field of trusts in this period has been better explored than any other topic in early-modern equity thanks to the work of Neil Jones. The cases in the record in the legal year beginning 1600 are consistent with Jones's work. Though relatively little novel appears regarding trusts, one or two points may be made.

First, it is perhaps surprising to discover a strong savour of case-by-case adjudication in at least one trust matter in the legal year beginning 1600. Trusts were, after all, at the forefront of the doctrinal development of substantive equity. One therefore expects to see relatively little of what looks like case-by-case ordering, and rather more of a reasoned application of rules. And perhaps the case discussed below does represent just such reasoned application, given the rather uncertain doctrine at the time. But it may also have been a relatively ad hoc decision, thus demonstrating equity's ongoing capacity for case-by-case adjudication even in a relatively well-developed area.

Higgins v Higgins displays two aspects that also seem ad hoc. William Higgins conveyed his inn to a trustee for his own benefit, subsequently leaving it in his will as property to fund his widow, to whom he granted an annuity of £20 per annum.[112] The widow Higgins, as beneficiary of the trust of the annuity, successfully sued her son as trustee for payments. After the Chancery ordered payment to the widow Higgins, the son's father-in-law sought relief from the annuity on the ground that he had taken the assurance of the inn in consideration of paying the son's debts when the latter had married his daughter.[113] The court held that since the assurance of the inn was taken 'hanging the suit in this court', the father-in-law would be subject to the annuity. In light of a report that 'those who have notice of the trust or take estate … without good

[110] See n 102 above for more on costs.

[111] *Cf* M Macnair, 'Development of Uses and Trusts: Contract or Property and European Influences' (2015) 66 *Studi Urbinati A – Scienze Giuridiche, Politiche et Economiche* 305, 314–15 (referring to the 'alternative dispute resolution' character of the Chancery from Wolsey to Egerton).

[112] C 33/99 f 47 v.

[113] C 33/99 f 241.

consideration, or come to it hanging the suit' will be bound by the trust, this comes as little surprise.[114] What is surprising, and has an ad hoc quality, was the court's provision at the end of the order:

> if any freehold lands can be found which by the last will and testament of the said William Higgins the testator may any way be charged with the payment of the said Annuity or arrearages thereof for the ease of the said [father-in-law] in the said payments of the said Annuity and arrearages thereof as shall be meet.[115]

This is confusingly worded, particularly at the end, but it seems plain enough that the court was willing to substitute the property to which the annuity was charged. Now in one sense this is just plain equitable charging insofar as the decedent established the annuity and his property ought to fund it. In another, this is tantamount to the court changing the trust property, not a typical move of established trust law. That gives the order an ad hoc feel of the case-specific sort previously mentioned in respect of relief of mortgage forfeiture.

The second, perhaps more radical, aspect of *Higgins v Higgins* was a threat to grant title both to the annuity and the inn to the widow Higgins if the trustees failed to pay. The court's own language explains the situation fairly clearly:

> if Default be made of or in the payment or satisfaction of the [Annuity and its arrearages] from henceforth … Then his Lordship will be pleased upon motion thereof made in open court to grant an injunction to the said Complainant for her having and holding of the possession of the said Inn and the goods during her life to the interest she shall and may thereby satisfy herself of the [Annuity and its arrearages] from henceforth And answer and pay the Residue of the Rents and profits thereof …[116]

In a sense the court would invert the trust: the widow beneficiary would be given title so that she could take her portion and pay the rest to the former trustees.

Neither of these remedies in *Higgins v Higgins* seems familiar to regular trust doctrine. Property put in trust was not fungible with other property even if the purpose of the trust could be preserved by substituting other property. And beneficiaries were not put in possession to satisfy themselves first and effectively act as trustees for others. But in both aspects of the order, the court displays an intuitive logic in preserving the basic interests implicated. The widow will get her annuity payments, though they may come from other property of the annuity's grantor. And if the trustees refuse to perform properly, the widow will take their position, subjecting them to her as she had been subjected to them; turnabout is fair play. Whether these moves represent unusual means to vindicate still-inchoate principles later recognised in trust doctrine, or basic ad hoc adjudication specific to this case, is a matter for debate.

Flexible trust adjudication might have stemmed in part from the extent to which the trust remained viewed as grounded in interpersonal confidence between individuals, rather than something more proprietary. The extent to which the trust had been reified

[114] See 117 SS 136, 348.

[115] C 33/99 f 241.

[116] C 33/99 f 47 v. The text does not say to whom the residue is to be paid, but from the context it is clearly the erstwhile trustees.

in this period remains difficult.[117] The idea of an interpersonal basis nevertheless had observable effects persisting in 1600.[118] One slightly difficult report from between 1598 and 1602 says

> If I convey a lease for years to A. to the use of B., though by the statute of 27 Hen. VIII [the Statute of Uses[119]] this use be not transferred but that the interest of the term do rest in A., yet upon a bill exhibited by B. or his executors etc., my lord will decree it for B. or for his executors as the case stands, for my lord says that an use at the common law was but a trust and was always to be excused or relieved by subpoena. So, says he, is in this cause where a use will not properly rise, yet for the trust's sake, I will relieve it. But this case must come before him as *res integra*; it must not be soiled with any trials, former decrees upon other points, or such like to discountenance the case.[120]

The Statute of Uses, sometimes referred to as the Statute for Extinguishing Uses,[121] was intended to eliminate certain forms of the use as a type of property right as distinct from possession.[122] But some uses, such as the use of a lease referred to above, were not executed by the statute; and, in any case, instances of genuine interpersonal trust and confidence, putting all technicalities to one side, presented a classic opportunity for equitable intervention. The Lord Keeper would relieve such trusts, it seems. The comment about the case being *res integra* points toward significance in interpersonal confidence: the pristine reliance of man upon his fellow man made a case for relief; the more that litigation and strife disfigured that relationship of reliance, the less it seems the Lord Keeper would willingly provide relief. At least aspects of these ideas appear operative in 1600.

Another question of interest regarding trusts was what happened to grants to superstitious uses. The Dissolution of Colleges Act[123] made popish and superstitious religious trusts, such as chantries, illegal. Bryson says: 'What to do with the endowments was a new problem to be solved by the courts of equity.'[124] Substantive doctrine changed significantly over time.[125] At first the property was forfeit to the crown. Later the grant was considered void ab initio, and the property descended to the heir. Later still it was put to the use *cy-près*, viz. the legal use as close as possible

[117] On the relationship of trusts, uses, and property rights, see NG Jones, 'The Trust Beneficiary's Interest before *R v Holland*' in A Lewis et al (eds) *Law in the City* (Dublin, Four Courts Press, 2007) 95; NG Jones, 'Aspects of Privity in England: Equity to 1680' in EJH Schrage (eds), *Ius Quaesitum Tertio* (Berlin, Duncker & Humblot, 2008) 135, 164–67; DA Foster, 'Historical Conceptions of the Express Trust, c 1600–1900' in S Degeling et al (eds), *Philosophical Foundations of the Law of Express Trusts* (Oxford, Oxford University Press, 2023); Macnair (n 111) 315–19.

[118] Consider, eg, the requirement that only natural persons could be trustees: *Chudleigh's Case* (1594) Poph 70, 71–72 ('an use at common law is no other than a confidence which one person puts in another, for a confirdence cannot be in land, or other dead thing … nor a corporation, because it is a dead body, although it consist of natural persons: and in this dead body a confidence cannot be put, but in bodies natural'); SC 1 Co Rep 120a, 127a.

[119] 27 Hen VIII, c 10.

[120] 117 SS 119.200 303.

[121] See NG Jones (2010) (n 31) 273.

[122] It was once thought to have been an unsuccessful attempt to eliminate all uses, but now appears less ambitious in its remit: NG Jones, 'Trusts Litigation in Chancery after the Statute of Uses: The First Fifty Years' in M Dyson and DJ Ibbetson (eds), *Law and Legal Process* (Cambridge, Cambridge University Press, 2013) 103.

[123] Stat 1 Edw VI, c 14. See WH Bryson, 'Introduction' in 117 SS, xxx, fn 103.

[124] 117 SS 'Introduction' xxx–xxxi.

[125] ibid.

to that intended. Bryson suggests that the period of Egerton and Bacon was one of fluxion amongst these doctrines and cites cases going all three ways in the general time.[126]

The evidence of 1600 bears out Bryson's belief. In 1597, both Egerton LK and Coke AG were reported to have said that grants to superstitious uses were merely void rather than causing forfeiture under the Dissolution of Colleges Act.[127] But these were only opinions expressed in a case that did not settle the matter; the reporter himself felt it necessary to note the question '*non terminabatur per judicium*'.[128] When the issue arose in *Throgmorton v Browne*, the record itself described the question as one 'of great consequence and may reach far into the state of this Realm'.[129] In *Throgmorton* the heir challenged a bequest in trust for recusants. A report of what seems to be the same case gives an answer. A Roman Catholic named 'Throckmorton' devised property to Catholics.[130] The report says that the Lord Keeper 'upheld the will for that and said that notwithstanding they were obstinate papists, yet they were men and ought to be pitied and relieved'. The outcome suggested by the report is that the devise was actually fully upheld: money was given to Catholics who, it appears, needed charity in fact because they were Catholics and consequently imprisoned.

Thus *Throgmorton* appears to stand for the proposition that Catholics may receive bequests occasioned by virtue of their papistry. Presumably they could not employ the bequest specifically in furtherance of their religion, but could use the money for their own needs as ordinary humans. This may have innovated from a prior position that recusants were not fit recipients of charitable bequests. By allowing the recusants money, the court moved toward the doctrine of *cy-près*.

In the comparatively well-explored field of trusts, little else noteworthy appears in the legal year beginning 1600. Only the flexibility and situationally responsive order of *Higgins v Higgins*, especially the willingness to require conveyance to the trustee, appears of interest regarding ordinary trusts. And in respect of charitable trusts, moves toward the doctrine of *cy près* appear. In *Throgmorton v Browne*, a trust to superstitious uses was neither declared forfeit nor awarded to the legal heir, but put to the use *cy-près*, which here even meant giving it to Roman Catholics.

V. Conclusion

The Court of Chancery and equity in the legal year beginning 1600 appear headed in familiar directions, but retaining a flexibility to respond to particular circumstances that it would later abandon. The court shows little sign of having progressed towards

[126] ibid.

[127] 117 SS 84, 153.

[128] ibid. By 1600 reports of non-judicial opinions were still made, but carried less force than they once had. The concept of judgment and holding as the locus of law was rapidly developing.

[129] C 33/99 f 17. A very similar, if not identical issue was raised in *Knighton v Fortescue* C 33/99 f 374, which was ordered a month after *Throgmorton*. But there the court did not describe the significance of the case, and sent the matter off to the common law for trial on the validity of the will in question, which had not been sufficiently proved to that point.

[130] 117 SS 119.150 294.

its moribund and dilatory final incarnation. Doctrines – to the extent that 'doctrines' is the right word – were still in development.

The testamentary jurisdiction of Chancery saw that theory had not necessarily caught up with practice. The church courts were still proclaimed the correct places for suits for legacies, yet functionally they were allowed in Chancery. Some questions, such as the validity of a will, were genuinely not allowed in Chancery. But even in the cases that the Chancery would not hear, it might have an important role by managing the litigation in other courts. Equitable jurisdiction in testamentary and estate matters was thus more real than the Chancery would have liked to admit.

Forfeitures found relief in Chancery along familiar lines, but the doctrine had not developed to its fullest form. Bearing in mind the baseline of many cases providing relief as expected, it is the exceptions that stand out. Bond penalties could still be recovered with Chancery blessing, sometimes even in money-bond cases, although this was highly unusual. Lease and other land forfeitures received theoretically positive backing from Egerton, but in practice were perhaps not so thoroughly approved. Mortgage forfeitures essentially always found relief in Chancery, but the terms were not yet regularised; a strong sense of individual remediation unconcerned with general rules pervades the cases.

Although trusts were at the forefront of doctrinal development in Chancery, the trust cases in the legal year beginning 1600 show some perhaps unexpected features. The nature of the trust appears to remain closer to an interpersonal confidence than a proprietary interest. And charitable trusts were marching toward the later-standard doctrine of *cy près*.

In preserving an observable flexibility while hewing closely to a recognisable doctrinal line, perhaps the Chancery and equity in 1600 was more true to itself than it would later become. If equity is the dispensatory jurisdiction of Aristotle's *epieikeia*, as St German suggested, it ought to pay attention to the particulars of its cases, and avoid binding itself with comprehensively predetermined rules. Only then can it fulfil its mission as the secondary corrective to a primary law that can never attain perfection. But in 1600, as it performed its true function, perhaps equity sowed the seeds of its own destruction. In its palpable success, it attracted litigants beyond its capacity to manage them according to his true nature. Only by adopting the form of its companion in governance for the mainstream law could equity manage the onslaught. In so doing, it arguably shed its nature and lost its way. The vision of equity in 1600 thus perhaps represents its noonday splendour. In the march of time, that sun would set. Might it rise again?

8

Concepts of Equity in Hake's *Epieikeia*

JOANNA McCUNN*

I. Introduction

In sixteenth-century England, theories of equity were ubiquitous, multifarious, and often incoherent. Mark Fortier identifies equity as an 'essentially contested concept', which drew on a complex network of ideas from law, religion, literature and politics, and which was continually adapted to new contexts.[1] David Ibbetson describes the legal meaning of equity as 'wholly unstable'.[2] Different concepts of equity were used in different legal contexts, leading to confusion. By the turn of the century, legal writers were struggling to make sense of equity in its many manifestations. Edward Hake's *Epieikeia: A Dialogue on Equity in Three Parts*[3] was the most comprehensive analysis of equity produced in this period.[4] As a lawyer, Puritan, poet and government official, Hake was connected to many of the communities that made use of the currency of equity. His treatise exemplifies the dynamism, as well as the disorder, of equity in his day.

Hake is a rather obscure figure, and his *Dialogue* has often been portrayed as a damp squib. It opens with a promise to explain the jurisdiction of the Court of Chancery, but it soon becomes clear that the Chancery was not Hake's main concern. In fact, he devoted almost three times more space to the 'Equity of the Common lawes' than to 'the Equity of the Chauncery'. The latter accounts for less than a fifth of the work. Reviews of the treatise have tended to focus on Hake's inability to explain the Chancery's jurisdiction[5] and have overlooked his real interest. In fact, Hake's idiosyncratic concept of equity extended far beyond the Chancery. He saw equity as the all-pervasive 'secreate

* Original spellings have been retained, though typography and punctuation has occasionally been modified to aid comprehension. Translations are my own unless otherwise noted. I am indebted to Lorenzo Maniscalco for his help with Latin sources, and I am grateful to Andrew Bell and Ian Williams for their comments.

[1] M Fortier, *The Culture of Equity in Early Modern England* (Aldershot, Ashgate, 2005) 21–2.

[2] D Ibbetson, 'A House Built on Sand: Equity in Early Modern English Law' in E Koops and WJ Zwalve (eds), *Law & Equity: Approaches in Roman Law and Common Law* (Leiden, Martinus Nijhoff, 2014) 55.

[3] DEC Yale (ed), E Hake, *Epieikeia: A Dialogue on Equity in Three Parts* (New Haven, CT, Yale University Press, 1953) (hereafter 'Hake, *Epieikeia*').

[4] L Knafla, 'Hake, Edward (fl. 1564–1604)' Oxford Dictionary of National Biography (Oxford University Press, 2004) doi.org/10.1093/ref:odnb/11881.

[5] See, eg, Ibbetson (n 2) 64; JP Dawson, '*Epieikeia*: A Dialogue on Equity in Three Parts' (1954) 64 *Yale Law Journal* 308, 310; MJ Prichard, '*Epieikeia*: A Discourse on Equity in Three Parts' [1956] *Cambridge Law Journal* 126, 126.

righteousnes of the lawe', and the common law, properly understood, as 'a lawe consisting for the most part of Equity'.[6] Other commentators have marvelled at 'the sheer scope' of Hake's equity;[7] it is astonishingly, and perhaps uniquely, expansive.

One reason for Hake's unusual approach is the range of sources that he drew upon. Many of his ideas about equity derived from the expected legal texts: Christopher St German's *Doctor and Student* and the *Commentaries* of Edmund Plowden, with some contributions from *Bracton* and John Fortescue.[8] However, Hake also injected ideas from theologians – and not established authorities, like Thomas Aquinas, whose theories had already been incorporated into English legal sources. Hake preferred more modern scholars, such as Peter Martyr Vermigli and Johann Ferus. He held the Lutheran reformer Philip Melanchthon in particularly high regard, and made use of his writings throughout the treatise.[9] The nature of equity was hotly contested amongst theologians as well as lawyers, and so the addition of these sources only added to the ferment of Hake's ideas. As a result, Hake juggled multiple concepts of equity, all of which he found at work in English law. He could not confine equity to any particular forum or doctrine. Instead, his repeated mantra throughout the *Dialogue* is that the working of equity is 'aboundan[t]', 'endlesse' and 'infynite'.[10]

Hake makes several attempts to pin equity down. He seeks to define equity by examining what it is, explaining what it does, and emphasising what it is not. This chapter will follow his approach. First, we will investigate Hake's general concept of equity. We will see that he takes the Aristotelian ideas of St German and Plowden and runs with them, producing an unusually wide-ranging account of the nature of equity. We will then examine the areas of English law where Hake sees equity playing a particularly important role: the interpretation of all kinds of legal documents, the provision of the action on the case, and the working of the Court of Chancery. We will observe Hake's struggle to match the law in practice with the concepts of equity he has laid out. Finally, we will consider the related concepts to which Hake compares equity: personal virtue and mercy. Again, we will see that Hake struggles to give equity any clearly defined boundaries. Ultimately, Hake's *Epieikeia* shows early modern equity 'on the loose'[11] and out of control.

II. Hake and his *Dialogue*

We have scant details of Hake's life. He spent three years studying at an Inn of Chancery, likely between 1564 and 1567.[12] In 1574, he explained that he had been appointed as an attorney of the Common Pleas, but had retired 'unto solytarinesse in the Countrey' with his wife[13] – though he could still be found in London, at Barnard's Inn, in 1575.[14]

[6] Hake, *Epieikeia* (n 3) 7, 55.
[7] A Cromartie, *The Constitutionalist Revolution: An Essay on the History of England, 1450-1642* (Cambridge, Cambridge University Press, 2006) 185.
[8] Hake, *Epieikeia* (n 3) xvi.
[9] DEC Yale, 'Introduction' in *Epieikeia* (n 3) xvii.
[10] Hake, *Epieikeia* (n 3) 51, 54, 57, 85, 122.
[11] Fortier (n 1) 2.
[12] Yale (n 9) xxv.
[13] E Hake, *A Touchestone for This Time Present* (London, T Hacket, 1574) (unpaginated).
[14] Yale (n 9) xxv.

From 1576 onwards, he served in local government offices in Windsor; he was mayor in 1586–87, and a member of Parliament for two months in 1589.[15] He had a room in Gray's Inn during the 1580s and 1590s,[16] and wrote from there to his patron, Julius Caesar, in 1603.[17] He served on a royal commission in 1595 but was unsuccessful in his other applications for advancement.[18] His letters complained about the 'many shrewde crosses' he had suffered,[19] and his poems about unreliable friends.[20] Nothing is known of him after 1604.

Hake published a number of literary works between 1567 and 1604. His collections of poetry had a strongly Puritan bent: he denounced Catholics ('wylie wincking wyzard Woolves'[21]), ineffectual Protestants ('luskish loytering Lubbers'[22]), and the sinfulness of commerce, fashion, dancing and the like. The *Dialogue* was his only legal work, and he lavished it with care. In 1597, he wrote to Caesar twice about his plan for the treatise. He had begun the work 'a good many yeres sythens' and had completed the section on equity in general 'longe sythens',[23] with 'a large provision of undigested matter' available for the rest.[24] In 1603, he informed Caesar that the work was complete. Two judges, Anderson CJ and Walmsley J, had read and praised it, as had the Lord Keeper, Thomas Egerton.[25] Hake had delivered copies to the King and to Edward Bruce, the new Master of the Rolls. He was confident that it would finally bring him preferment. To encourage his warm reception, he was also resolved to disburse 'convenient money where it is to be given'.[26]

As its title suggests, the treatise is written in dialogue form. The conceit is that Hake has met with his 'cosens', Eliott and Lovelace, before dinner. They prevail upon him to explain the nature of equity. The two men are 'amiable stooges',[27] who ask easy questions and greet Hake's answers with untrammelled enthusiasm. In one typical contribution, Eliott declares that he has 'received both pleasure and profitt' from Hake's discussion,

> pleasure in the variety of the matter, and profitt in the good end and purpose that hath byn of it … I have received very greate contentment as well by this your later as by your former discourse of *Epieikeia*.[28]

It has been suggested that Lovelace was based on Lancelot Lovelace, who was admitted to Gray's Inn in 1581 and may have encountered Hake there.[29] A better candidate might be Richard Lovelace, lieutenant of the castle and forest of Windsor, who

[15] ibid xxvi.
[16] Knafla (n 4).
[17] BL Add MS 12503, f 47.
[18] Knafla (n 4).
[19] BL Add MS 12503, f 47.
[20] For example, E Hake, *Of Golds Kingdome, and This Unhelping Age* (London, J Windet, 1604) 25–6.
[21] E Hake, *Newes out of Powles Churchyarde* (London, J Charlewood and R Jhones, 1579) (unpaginated).
[22] Hake, *Touchestone* (n 13) (unpaginated).
[23] BL Lansdowne MS 161, f 233.
[24] BL Lansdowne MS 161, f 43.
[25] Both Anderson and Walmsley were notoriously conservative, and neither was a friend to Puritans – perhaps suggesting that Hake did not know his early readers well.
[26] BL Add MS 12503, f 47; see Cromartie (n 7) 189.
[27] Dawson (n 5) 309.
[28] Hake, *Epieikeia* (n 3) 116–7.
[29] Yale (n 9) xxvi, n 28.

described Hake as his 'very loving friend'[30] and whom Hake praised in a poem.[31] Eliott could be Edward Eliott, the Queen's surveyor in Essex, whom Hake called his 'verie loving Cowsen'.[32]

It might be objected that neither of these men was a practising lawyer. However, Hake only identified his interlocutors as 'justices of peace of greate experyence' and as not 'unlearned in the lawe'.[33] The *Dialogue* was not written for an exclusively legal audience, but to secure political advancement. Hake intended to present it to the King on his visit to Windsor, with a speech praising James's commitment to 'true Religion and Justice'.[34] He was aware of equity's wider resonances in the world of politics, invoking, for example, the 'highe equitie' of the Queen in a 1587 oration.[35]

Yet the *Dialogue* is firmly focused on the role of equity in English law. Eliott's opening gambit is to ask why lawyers commonly tell their clients 'yowe have no remedy for this or that at the Common lawe but yowe must seeke your remedy in Equity'.[36] To answer, Hake explains, he must 'beginne with Equity in generall, shewing therein what Equity is and howe it is to be observed in every lawe of man'. The bulk of the work then examines 'Equity as it is to be used in the Common lawe', before Hake finally turns to 'the Equity of the Chauncery'.[37]

Within this tripartite structure, Hake's discussion is rambling. Different strands of his thought weave in and out of each other, tie themselves in knots, and sometimes disappear entirely. 'One has the sense,' writes Dennis Klinck, of being in a labyrinth, in which 'many suggestive threads' appear but ultimately lead nowhere.[38] Hake is easily distracted, including lengthy digressions on topics such as the 'cardinall vertues or properties' that a judge ought to have,[39] the royal prerogative,[40] a recent case on clerical misprision that involved a 'freend' of Eliott's,[41] and the history of the Chancery.[42] He even recites a poem, to the (predictable) delight of his companions.[43]

It seems likely that Hake assembled the *Dialogue* by extracting 'undigested matter' from his commonplace book.[44] Many early modern law treatises reflected the structure of commonplace books, consisting of rather disjointed lists of authorities

[30] PW Hasler, *The History of Parliament: The House of Commons 1558-1603, vol II: Members D-L* (London, HMSO, 1981) 491.

[31] Hake, *Of Golds Kingdome* (n 20) 37–40. See L Wilson, 'Edward Hake' in DA Richardson (ed), *Sixteenth-Century British Nondramatic Writers: Second Series (Dictionary of Literary Biography Vol 136)* (London, Gale, 1994).

[32] E Hake, *A Commemoration of the Most Prosperous and Peaceable Raigne of Our Gratious and Deere Soveraigne Lady Elizabeth* (London, W How, 1575) (unpaginated).

[33] Hake, *Epieikeia* (n 3) 6.

[34] Hake, *Of Golds Kingdome* (n 20) (unpaginated). Equity was an important part of James's political thought: M Fortier, 'Equity and Ideas: Coke, Ellesmere, and James I' (1998) 51 *Renaissance Quarterly* 1255.

[35] E Hake, *An Oration Conteyning an Expostulation* (London, E Aggas, 1587) (unpaginated); see Fortier (n 1) 87, 111.

[36] Hake, *Epieikeia* (n 3) 5.

[37] ibid 6.

[38] DR Klinck, *Conscience, Equity and the Court of Chancery in Early Modern England* (Farnham, Ashgate, 2010) 106.

[39] Hake, *Epieikeia* (n 3) 30–43.

[40] ibid 72–85.

[41] ibid 97–103.

[42] ibid 132–143.

[43] ibid 64–5.

[44] I am grateful to Ian Williams for this point.

arranged by topic.[45] Hake's work falls squarely within this category. He also seems to have relied heavily on a few key texts: for example, he appears only to have had access to one, perhaps commonplaced, excerpt from Melanchthon's work, which he quotes repeatedly throughout the treatise.[46] If Hake was indeed drawing from a commonplace book, he was unusual in mixing theological texts indiscriminately with lists of common law cases. As Ian Williams observes, it was rare for lawyers to use non-legal sources in their scholarship. Such material might appear at the back of commonplace books or on the flyleaves, but was not usually incorporated into the body of the text.[47]

Hake also failed to do as much 'digesting' as was perhaps necessary. Modern readers have generally found the *Dialogue* to be 'cumbersome',[48] 'diffuse' and overly reliant on 'filler'.[49] However, Hake entreated his readers to appreciate the 'coherence' in the treatise,[50] explaining that he had been 'loathe to omytte' anything that was 'profitable for our purpose'.[51] As we will see, even Hake's more outré meanderings can help to shed light on his understanding of equity.

III. Hake's Concept of Equity

A. St German, Plowden and Hake

The basic thrust of Hake's *Dialogue*, at least, is clear from the outset. In titling the work *Epieikeia*, he nailed Aristotelian colours to his mast. Aristotle had observed that laws framed in general terms are unable to provide the right answer to every possible case that might arise. *Epieikeia* is the correction of a general law to reach an appropriate answer in an individual case.[52] *Epieikeia* subsequently became entangled with equity, originally a separate concept.[53] Aquinas identified equity with Aristotelian *epieikeia*,[54] and later philosophers and theologians followed suit. Lawyers of the *ius commune*, influenced by new humanist scholarship, began to associate the two concepts in the sixteenth century.[55]

Neither equity nor *epieikeia* was unfamiliar to English lawyers.[56] For *Bracton*, equity was the principle that like cases should be treated alike.[57] This idea developed into the

[45] RJ Ross, 'The Memorial Culture of Early Modern English Lawyers: Memory as Keyword, Shelter, and Identity, 1560-1640' (1998) 10 *Yale Journal of Law and the Humanities* 229, 282, fn 184.

[46] Hake, *Epieikeia* (n 3) 14, 33, 48, 57. Hake identifies the passage as 'towardes the end of the booke', suggesting that he may have at least seen a copy of the full work.

[47] I Williams, 'Common Law Scholarship and the Written Word' in L Hutson (ed), *The Oxford Handbook of English Law and Literature, 1500-1700* (Oxford, Oxford University Press, 2017) 73–4. Compare Hake's use of legal maxims discussed in n 112 below.

[48] Knafla (n 4).

[49] Dawson (n 5) 309.

[50] Hake, *Epieikeia* (n 3) 120.

[51] ibid 7.

[52] Aristotle, *Nicomachean Ethics* V.10.

[53] L Maniscalco, *Equity in Early Modern Legal Scholarship* (Leiden, Brill, 2020) 13–4; Fortier (n 1) 3.

[54] Thomas Aquinas, *Summa Theologica* II-II.120.1.

[55] Maniscalco (n 53) 44–5.

[56] Ibbetson (n 2) 56–8.

[57] S Thorne (tr), *Bracton on the Laws and Customs of England* (Cambridge, MA, Harvard University Press, 1968) vol II, 25; see JL Barton, 'Equity in the Medieval Common Law' in RA Newman (ed), *Equity in the World's Legal Systems: A Comparative Study* (Brussels, Emile Bruylant, 1973) 139.

equity of the statute, a doctrine that enabled the extension of statutes to analogous cases.[58] St German brought *epieikeia* to the forefront of English legal thinking early in the sixteenth century.[59] His understanding of the concept was derived from both Aquinas and the theologian Jean Gerson.[60] Equity, he explained, is

> an excepcyon of the lawe of god or of the lawe of reason from the generall rewles of the lawe of man … the whiche excepcion is secretely understande in every generall rewle of every posytyve lawe.[61]

In England, equity could be seen at work through legal maxims, statutory interpretation, and, 'most commonly', the jurisdiction of the Chancellor.[62] A few decades later, Plowden melded Aristotelian *epieikeia* with English learning on the equity of the statute.[63] He argued that equity could both extend the scope of a statute and make exceptions to its words, in accordance with 'the intent and meaning of the makers of the law'.[64]

Hake's *Dialogue* was substantially based on the work of St German and Plowden. His analysis begins in relatively conventional style, with Aristotle's definition: equity is the correction of a defect in a general law. He quotes Plowden's gloss on this passage, derived from Joachim Perionius, before briefly citing St German and the theologian Ferus.[65] Aristotle and Perionius, he observes, agree that 'Equity is a correction of a generall lawe.' Plowden wrote that equity is 'no parte of the lawe, but a morall virtue which reformeth the lawe'.[66] However, Hake firmly rejects this idea:

> if the lawe we speake of be a good lawe and well grounded, then the Equity that must be used to the correction of the generalitye thereof cannot be said to be the Equitye of the judge, but of the lawe.[67]

Otherwise, the law would be 'a lawe without justice', and 'no lawe but a meare tyranicall constytution'. Equity, then, is not introduced by 'the righteousnes of the expositor',[68] but is 'a parte or vertue attributory to the lawe'.[69]

Equity, however, is 'not alwayes to be seene in the expresse letter of the lawe'. Here Hake returns to St German, who said that to follow the words of the law is sometimes to act against the law, and against reason and justice.[70] Equity, as St German put it, is 'an exception secreatlie understoode in every generall rule of every positive lawe'. Like St German, Hake recognises the theoretical possibility of a law without equity,

[58] SE Thorne, 'Introduction' in SE Thorne (ed), *A Discourse Upon the Exposicion & Understandinge of Statutes* (San Marino, CA, Huntington Library, 1942) 44.
[59] Barton (n 57) 152; G Behrens, 'Equity in the Commentaries of Edmund Plowden' (1999) 20 *Journal of Legal History* 25, 25.
[60] Ibbetson (n 2) 58; A Cromartie, 'Epieikeia and Conscience' in Hutson (n 47) 330–2.
[61] TFT Plucknett and JL Barton (eds), C St German, *Doctor and Student* (1974) 91 *Selden Society* 97.
[62] ibid 103.
[63] Ibbetson (n 2) 61.
[64] *Eyston v Studd* (1574) Plow 459, 465-88; 75 ER 688, 695-700. See generally Behrens (n 59).
[65] Hake, *Epieikeia* (n 3) 7–8.
[66] ibid 8–9; *Eyston* (n 64) Plow 466, 75 ER 696.
[67] Hake, *Epieikeia* (n 3) 11.
[68] ibid 9.
[69] ibid 16.
[70] ibid 12–3.

which contravenes divine and natural law and has no binding force.[71] A law without secret equitable exceptions, he says, would be 'manifestly unreasonable and not to be suffered'.[72] His argument is ultimately question-begging. We know that these secret exceptions are in the law because the law is reasonable and just, and the law is reasonable and just because of the secret exceptions.

The next turn in Hake's discussion draws on ideas found in Plowden. The letter of the law is 'the very huske or skyne of the lawe', while equity is its 'intent and hidden meaninge'.[73] *Summum ius*, an insistence on 'the very stricte and expresse words of the lawe', is '*summa injuria*', 'a meare contrariety unto the lawe'.[74] Eliott, who is a little slow on the uptake, objects that laws should not be expounded 'besides or contrary to the letter'.[75] Hake explains that, since *epieikeia* is 'the sowle and spyrit of the lawe', a judge who follows the 'hidden (but the righte and trewe) meaning of the lawe' does not really 'chaunge the lawe', but will 'sett the lawe in his right place', and 'give life to the lawe which otherwise in the letter thereof would be dead'.[76] The penny drops, and Eliott realises that a judge should never hold 'precisely or rather austerely to the letter of the lawe without regarding the Equity thereof'.[77]

Hake then gives three examples of equity at work. If, in contravention of the law, strangers climb the city walls to repel an attack, *epieikeia* will absolve them from punishment. To put them to death, Hake explains, would be 'againste the lawe of nature' and contrary to the legislator's intention.[78] If a man refuses to return a sword to its owner, who is 'starke staring madde', *epieikeia* says that he has acted in accordance with 'the lawe of God and the lawe of Nature'.[79] And if a 'poore inhabitant' steals food from a traveller in the Isle of Man, the thief is 'withoute the meaninge and intent' of a custom that would have him hanged, since this punishment is only imposed to safeguard the island's own supplies.[80]

All three examples are based on standard hypotheticals discussed by philosophers, theologians and rhetoricians. Hake credits the first to Plowden;[81] it was discussed by both Cicero and Aquinas.[82] The second can also be found in Cicero and Aquinas,[83] as well as in Melanchthon.[84] The third is an unusual twist on a case put by Aquinas and Melanchthon.[85] It is worth pausing briefly over Hake's discussion of these examples. He resolves the first by reference to both natural law and the intention of the legislator, the second by natural and divine law, and the third by 'the meaninge and intent' of the law.[86] Hake, then, identifies equity with both the true intent of the law and the precepts

[71] St German (n 61) 97.
[72] Hake, *Epieikeia* (n 3) 13.
[73] ibid 16; see *Eyston* (n 64) Plow 467, 75 ER 697.
[74] Hake, *Epieikeia* (n 3) 17; see *Throckmerton v Tracy* (1555) Plow 145, 161; 75 ER 222, 248.
[75] Hake, *Epieikeia* (n 3) 25.
[76] ibid 28.
[77] ibid 29.
[78] ibid 18.
[79] ibid.
[80] ibid 19–20.
[81] *Eyston* (n 64) Plow 466–7, 75 ER 696.
[82] Cicero, *De Oratore* 2.xxiv.100; Thomas Aquinas, *Commentary on the Nicomachean Ethics* 5.xvi.
[83] Cicero, *De Officiis* 3.xxv.95; Thomas Aquinas, *Summa Theologica*, II-II.62.5, arg 1.
[84] G Kisch, *Melanchthons Rechts- Und Soziallehre* (Berlin, De Gruyter, 1967) 171.
[85] Thomas Aquinas, *Summa Theologica*, II-II.66.7; ibid 170–1. See Part V.A. below.
[86] Hake, *Epieikeia* (n 3) 19.

of natural and divine law. Again, he assumes that the true nature of the law is to be just and reasonable. *Epieikeia*, he argues, is the force by which this is made known.

B. The Equity of the Common Law

Hake's opening salvo is largely based on St German and Plowden. It is only in the second part of the *Dialogue* that a more radical concept of equity emerges, as Hake begins to show equity at work within the common law. He has already warned his listeners that equity is rarely mentioned 'in any of our books of reports of yeeres and termes', and that he must draw his examples 'from suche cases as do appeare to have rule from the secreat righteousnes of the lawe'.[87] In fact, Hake sees equity almost everywhere in the common law; he describes it as 'an endlesse matter' and a 'banck-lesse sea'.[88]

Following St German, Hake begins his discussion with infants.[89] If a woman alienated her dower land, her son would ordinarily be barred from claiming it after her death. However, if the son was an infant when his mother died, he could claim the land.[90] Here, Hake explains, 'the righteousnes of the lawe doth secreatly minister an exception for infants'.[91] Thomas Smyth had credited the Chancery with giving relief in cases involving infancy, fraud and duress,[92] but 'in every of those cases of exception as in infynite others', the common law would also assist. Admittedly, these exceptions were not particularly 'secreate'. Hake explains that 'in the beginning' they were 'sylent exceptions from the generality of the lawe'. Only now, by 'length of tyme', had they

> become expressed even as the lawes themselves are, so as a man may saie of them that they are themselves become grounds or maximes aswell as the principall groundes whereof they are exceptions.[93]

Lovelace is suspicious: if Hake is right, 'the Common lawe of England woulde then seeme to be a lawe consisting for the most part of Equity'.[94] Hake explains further. The common law consists of 'generall growndes and maximes'. However, 'particuler cases have ever and anon happened which coulde not receyve rule by the generality of the same'. Instead, they must be 'expownded by the hidden righteousnes of those growndes and maximes'. Thus,

> no doubt as long as the Common lawe shall have any being the like cases will daylie and continually fall owt and yet nevertheless the maximes remayne still the same without alteration.[95]

[87] ibid 7, 49.
[88] ibid 50–1.
[89] St German (n 61) 103.
[90] Sir Edward Coke, *The First Part of the Institutes of the Laws of England, or, A Commentary upon Littleton* (London, The Societie of Stationers, 1628) 379a–381.
[91] Hake, *Epieikeia* (n 3) 50.
[92] Thomas Smyth, *De Republica Anglorum* (London, Henrie Midleton, 1584) 54.
[93] Hake, *Epieikeia* (n 3) 50.
[94] ibid 55.
[95] ibid 56.

The common law, then, consists of grounds and maxims, as well as equitable exceptions to those maxims. Equity not only makes these exceptions, but also generates new maxims:

> many of our expositions by *Epieikeia* through tract of tyme have obtained such approbation concerning the uprightnes and righteousnes thereof, as that they are nowe become and are to be reputed as maximes themselves.[96]

This theory of equity goes far beyond St German's or Plowden's. As Alan Cromartie puts it, Hake's *epieikeia* 'pervaded common law' and was 'the motor of its development'.[97] Hake saw equity at work whenever a general rule was applied to a particular case that did not fall precisely within its letter. There were a few unchanging 'growndes and maximes' that had been part of the law since 'the beginning'. However, all of the principles that had since unfurled from them were equitable ones, although perhaps now indistinguishable from maxims themselves. Through this continual process, the common law had become 'for the most part' equity. While other writers saw equity and law as implacably opposed,[98] Hake viewed equity as the 'very life, sowle and spirit' of the law.[99] Examples of equity at work in the law were 'infynite'.[100] Fortier describes Hake's equity as 'no longer an exception but a correction happening ubiquitously'.[101] Equity does not merely tweak the law in extreme cases, but is the whole of the law's creative force, the law's own desire for correction to itself.

Equity is also a process of historical development. 'In the beginning,' Hake tells us, the law consisted solely of maxims, their equitable exceptions immanent within them. These exceptions have been gradually drawn out as they are needed to address new cases. Over time, equity makes what is hidden in the law explicit.[102] Glenn Burgess argues that this understanding of history was a common feature of Renaissance humanist thought. History was viewed 'as a teleological process in which potentialities inherent in an entity were gradually made visible over time'. The historical development of a nation, constitution or law was a process by which it 'became more itself over time' and its potential 'gradually became actual'.[103] This teleological process is Hake's model of the equitable blossoming of the law. Equity is what the law is demanding to be; it is law in the process of becoming more truly itself. Hake borrowed Plowden's metaphor, describing the letter of the law as a husk and equity as the fruit within. A more accurate depiction of his thought would be the letter of the law as a husk and equity as the tree that has grown from it.

Hake pushed his concept of equity further than any other writer, and far beyond any English authority.[104] In fact, his view of the common law had more in common with contemporary theologians' views of the Bible than with other discussions of legal

[96] ibid 56–7.
[97] Cromartie (n 60) 335.
[98] eg, CH McIlwain and PL Ward (eds), William Lambarde, *Archeion, or, a Discourse upon the High Courts of Justice in England* (Cambridge, MA, Harvard University Press, 1957) 68–72; see Fortier (n 1) 69–71.
[99] Hake, *Epieikeia* (n 3) 121.
[100] ibid 51, 54, 85, 122.
[101] Fortier (n 1) 73.
[102] Cromartie (n 7) 185.
[103] G Burgess, *The Politics of the Ancient Constitution: An Introduction to English Political Thought, 1603-1642* (University Park, PA, Pennsylvania State University Press, 1993) 13–4.
[104] SE Thorne, 'Preface' in Hake, *Epieikeia* (n 3) ix.

equity. Biblical scholars, like the Puritan William Perkins, argued that God's law and human law worked in similar ways: as God moderates divine law because of his 'love and mercy towardes mankind', so man's law is moderated by equity.[105] Through these processes, the laws gradually unfurl themselves. John Donne, for example, preached, as Katrin Ettenhuber puts it, that 'Scripture caters for the exceptions to its own rules … although these exceptions are only actuated as history unfolds, certain deviations from the letter of Scripture are latent within it from the inception of time'.[106] For Hake, the equity of the common law functioned in just this way, offering a similar 'kind of perfect textual justice'.[107]

Indeed, the main source for Hake's identification of law with equity was a theologian: the Lutheran Melanchthon. Melanchthon had written that equity could be written or unwritten, and that there was no difference between written and unwritten equity. This confirmed, Hake believed, that equitable exceptions to legal maxims were still 'of the *Epieikeia* of the lawe', even though they were 'nowe become written, as were the auntient maximes themselves'.[108] As Lorenzo Maniscalco explains, Melanchthon's distinction between written and unwritten equity was derived from the medieval *ius commune*.[109] 'Written equity' consisted of legal rules that were deemed to be in some sense equitable.[110] This distinction had since been disavowed by legal humanists. However, Melanchthon, unusually, maintained it, arguing that written equity was simply the application of written laws in appropriate circumstances.[111] Hake does not seem to have been aware of the wider context of Melanchthon's remarks.[112] Instead, he took them to confirm that equity had a character all of its own, even when it seemed to be indistinguishable from law.

IV. Equity in English Law

A. Equity and Interpretation

We have seen that Hake found equity at work in all legal development. However, he struggled to maintain this account of equity consistently throughout the *Dialogue*,

[105] W Perkins, *Epieikeia: Or, A Treatise of Christian Equitie and Moderation* (Cambridge, J Legat, 1604) 4, 8–11; *cf* K Ettenhuber, *Donne's Augustine: Renaissance Cultures of Interpretation* (Oxford, Oxford University Press, 2011) 147, 164–6.

[106] Ettenhuber (n 105) 176, commenting on a 1629 sermon.

[107] ibid.

[108] Hake, *Epieikeia* (n 3) 57.

[109] Maniscalco (n 53) 15–17.

[110] ibid 19.

[111] ibid 69–70. Melanchthon was not totally consistent on the nature of written equity: see ibid 70.

[112] While Hake referred to theologians like Melanchthon, Ferus, Vermigli and Johannes Rivius, he was seemingly uninterested in legal writers of the *ius commune*. The breaks between his parts are ornamented with Latin maxims on equity and related topics, but these play no substantive role in his argument. They derive from a wide range of sources, including Ovid (Hake, *Epieikeia* (n 3) 44), the *Liber Sextus* (ibid 118), and the legal humanists Marius Salamonius and Claudius Cantiuncula (ibid 45). His quotations from the latter two can both be found in a reference book: J Spiegel, *Lexicon Iuris Civilis* (Strasbourg, Johannes Schott, 1539). They may be the 'dyvers apte sentences of Equity' that Hake had been given by Anderson CJ and which he had 'made use of disposedly in the booke'. If so, Hake was under the impression that they were of Anderson's 'own hatching': BL Add MS 12503, f 47.

quickly seeking to 'leave that bancklesse sea' and contain himself 'within bowndes more sensible'.[113] 'The Equity used in the Common lawe,' he explained, 'is either in exposition or in gyving of actions'.[114] He therefore focused his discussion of the common law on these two processes. Both had previously been associated with equity by English lawyers, but they were not necessarily a comfortable fit with Hake's idiosyncratic concept.

It is convenient to begin with statutory interpretation, since it was entirely orthodox to invoke equity in this context. As Samuel Thorne explains, medieval judges were prepared to depart from the words of a statute in two directions. A statute could be disregarded in a case where it caused injustice; the case was said to be outside 'the intent of the statute'.[115] It was more difficult to extend a statute to a similar case by analogy, and when this was done, it was justified by invoking 'the equity of the statute'.[116] As we have seen, this developed out of the equitable principle that like cases should be treated alike.[117] St German was the first writer to identify both kinds of departure as operations of equity.[118] When judges make exceptions out of statutes, he argued, they are making use of *epieikeia* – but 'that equity is all of another effecte' to the equity of the statute.[119] Plowden further amalgamated the two.[120] The equity that extended statutes was also *epieikeia*, which either 'enlarges or diminishes the letter according to its discretion'.[121] However, Plowden maintained that 'there is a great diversity between these two equities, for the one abridges the letter, the other enlarges it'.[122] In true Aristotelian fashion, Plowden linked equity to the intention of the legislator. In order to judge whether equity should restrain or enlarge a statute, he explained, one should imagine what the lawmaker would have done if he were present.[123]

When Hake lays out his concept of equity, he makes little use of the legislator and his intentions. Instead, he speaks of equity as the 'secreat sense and hidden (but the righte and trewe) meaning' of the law.[124] He does not ask what the lawmaker might have said if present, but what 'Equity … if it had breathe and life in the present case, wolde have determined'.[125] Hake was indifferent to the actual intentions of the legislator, focusing instead on the true meaning of the law itself – which, as we have seen, he identified closely with the precepts of divine and natural law.

Hake's approach changes significantly, however, when he comes to explain 'howe *Epieikeia* ruleth in the exposition of statutes'.[126] Again, he emphasises that he will not 'speake of all the statutes that have bin expounded by Equity', because 'those statutes are infynite'.[127] Instead, his main order of business is to set out six 'certayne generall

[113] Hake, *Epieikeia* (n 3) 51.
[114] ibid 49.
[115] Thorne, 'Introduction' (n 58) 69.
[116] ibid 44.
[117] ibid 46.
[118] ibid 78.
[119] St German (n 61) 105.
[120] Thorne, 'Introduction' (n 58) 54–5.
[121] *Eyston* (n 64) Plow 466, 75 ER 696.
[122] ibid Plow 467, 75 ER 697.
[123] ibid.
[124] Hake, *Epieikeia* (n 3) 23, 14, 16, 28.
[125] ibid 121.
[126] ibid 85.
[127] ibid.

rules' for the construction of statutes. First, doubtful words in statutes are 'to be taken and expownded according to the intent of those that were the makers of the same statute'.[128] Secondly, a penal statute shall not be taken by equity; thirdly, a statute that enlarges the common law shall be taken by equity; fourthly, general words may be restrained to avoid a penalty; fifthly, statutes that abridge the common law shall not be taken by equity; and sixthly, the common law must be considered when interpreting statutes.[129]

Hake makes no real effort to connect these six rules with his previous treatment of equity, although Lovelace and Eliott applaud them as 'altogither guided and dyrected by *Epieikeia*'.[130] His first rule mandates interpretation by the legislator's intention, but, unlike Plowden, he does not explicitly link this with equity. His other five rules are all to the effect that some statutes are to be taken '*ex stricto jure*', and others are to be 'amplifyed by Equity'.[131] Perhaps surprisingly, he only mentions equity in the context of extending statutes, and not abridging them. In this, he is more conservative than either St German or Plowden. Hake draws here on an older sense of equity, equity as the extension of like rules to like cases – not equity as *epieikeia*, or as the creative force of the law. There is nothing in his analysis of statutes that hints at the radical concept of equity set out earlier in the *Dialogue*.

Hake does not confine equity to statutory interpretation. 'In the exposition of deedes, contractes and willes,' he writes, 'it may be affirmed withowte absurdity that Equity in every of them beareth rule very greatly'.[132] First,

> at all tymes and in all ages the judges of the lawe have expownded both deedes and contractes not precisely or strictly accordingly to ye words, [but] by Equity, that is to saye, according to the intent of the parties.[133]

Secondly, 'the righteounes of our *Epieikeia* is aboundantly to be founde' in

> the exposition of willes & testaments, wherein the Common lawe seemeth so highly to respect the intent of a testator or devisor as that a man woulde thincke there were almost nothing else that the lawe therein hath regard unto.[134]

In both cases, he explains, it is 'of the Equity of the lawe' that the document is interpreted according to the intention of its writers.[135]

Hake was following Plowden in emphasising the intentions of the document's maker. He cites Plowden's reports of *Throckmerton v Tracy* (1555) and *Browning v Beston* (1555), cases in which it was stressed that 'the law always regards the intentions of the parties' to a deed,[136] and that judges should not 'cavil about the words in subversion of the plain

[128] ibid 85–8.
[129] ibid 88–91.
[130] ibid 104.
[131] ibid 88.
[132] ibid 51.
[133] ibid.
[134] ibid 57.
[135] ibid 54, 60.
[136] *Browning v Beston* (1555) Plow 131, 140; 75 ER 202, 215.

intent of the parties'.[137] He also refers to *Newis v Lark* (1571), in which Plowden reports that wills are to be interpreted 'according to the intent of the party'.[138] Hake was not the only lawyer to notice the similarity between these principles and rules of statutory interpretation. For example, Fitzherbert and Baldwin JJ observed that 'the intention of the makers and parties shall be expounded' in both 'deeds and statutes',[139] while Edward Coke wrote that both statutes and wills are 'always construed and expounded according to the intent and meaning of the parties thereto'.[140]

Hake was, however, the only lawyer of this period to identify the English courts' approach to deeds and wills as a product of *epieikeia*.[141] Plowden saw equity as a principle that applied only to the interpretation of statutes, while for St German, it was a means of understanding both statute and common law.[142] Neither identified equity at work in the interpretation of private documents, with the exception of a few occasional references. For example, St German used the example of a private vow to demonstrate the working of equity,[143] while Plowden invoked the equitable maxim '*summum jus, summa injuria*' to warn against the literal construction of a deed.[144] Both instances involved borrowing from sources outside the common law: the vow example is from Gerson,[145] and the maxim from Cicero.[146]

Some lawyers of the *ius commune* also identified equity as a principle for the interpretation of private documents. For medieval civil lawyers, equity guided every judicial activity, including all kinds of interpretation. The idea that equity lay behind all legal interpretation could be found in civilian treatises throughout the fifteenth and sixteenth centuries.[147] Even writers with a more focused concept of equity were prepared to extend it to contracts and wills. Marius Salamonius, for example, wrote that equity works 'by rightly interpreting writings, sayings and facts, not only in laws but also in testaments and other deeds of men'.[148] Unlike these jurists, however, Hake did not argue that private documents had their own equity in the same way as statutes. He simply thought that it was an equitable rule that the intentions of a writer should be respected.

[137] *Throckmerton* (n 74) Plow 161, 75 ER 248. See also *Colthirst v Bejushin* (1550) Plow 21, 23; 75 ER 33, 37; *Browning v Beston* (n 136) Plow 140, 75 ER 215; *Chapman v Dalton* (1565) Plow 284, 290; 75 ER 434, 443. See generally J McCunn, 'Revolutions in Contractual Interpretation: A Historical Perspective' in S Worthington et al (eds), *Revolution and Evolution in Private Law* (Oxford, Hart Publishing, 2018).

[138] *Newis et Ux v Lark and Hunt* (1571) Plow 403, 413; 75 ER 609, 623.

[139] *Bold v Molineux* (1536) Dyer 14b, 17a; 73 ER 31, 36.

[140] *Butler and Baker's Case* (1591) 3 Co Rep 25a, 27b; 76 ER 684.

[141] William Fulbecke wrote that conditions in contracts could be 'extended by equity' in English law. However, this was in the context of a comparative law discussion, and the terminology was that of the civil law: W Fulbecke, *The Second Part of the Parallele, or Conference of the Civill Law, the Canon Law, and the Common Law of This Realme of England* (London, T Wight, 1602) 68v–70.

[142] Behrens (n 59) 36.

[143] St German (n 61) 97.

[144] *Throckmerton* (n 74) Plow 161, 75 ER 248; see Fortier (n 1) 72.

[145] Z Rueger, 'Gerson's Concept of Equity and Christopher St German' (1982) 3 *History of Political Thought* 1, 14.

[146] Cicero, *De Officiis*, I.33.

[147] Maniscalco (n 53) 29.

[148] Marius Salamonius, *Commentarioli in Librum I Pandectarum* (Rome, M Calvi, 1525) 9 (Lorenzo Maniscalco's translation).

Hake's approach may also have been influenced by the theological writers of his day. We have seen that equity had been associated with attentiveness to intentions since Aristotle. This facet of equity was emphasised, not just by legal writers like Plowden, but also by theologians.[149] Perkins, for example, wrote about 'Equitie which is the intent of the law.'[150] Theologians also stressed that equity ought to govern contracts: Melanchthon thought that contracts should be 'equitable',[151] and Perkins argued that equity must guide 'all the publike actions of a mans life', including 'suing bondes', 'letting of leases', and 'all manner of mutuall bargains, betwixt man and man'.[152] If contracts were ruled by equity, and contracts were interpreted by intentions rather than words, it was a natural leap for Hake to argue that this interpretive approach was a product of equity.

B. Equity and the Action on the Case

The second common law process in which Hake saw equity at work was the 'gyving of actions'.[153] However, as soon as he turns to discuss this, he is obliged to issue a disclaimer: if the common law does not already provide a remedy, judges do not 'have power to supplie the defecte thereof by gyving of this or that action, which was never before knowne to the lawe'. This is because, he explains, 'that were indeed to sett the judge above the law'.[154] The parties must instead appeal to the Prince to 'supplie the defecte of the lawe'.[155] There are, then, limits to equity. If the law is 'defective as well in the letter as in the *Epieikeia* thereof', this can only be remedied 'by making of a newe lawe'.[156] Indeed, 'the multitude of statute lawes' were made for just such cases.[157]

Judges may not invent new actions – but they can make 'a generall wrytt or action' available where there is no 'expresse or specyall writt or action' that will fit the case.[158] 'Every action upon the case', Hake declares, is supplied 'by the only Equity of the Common lawe'.[159] His example is the action on the case for assumpsit. If you agree to sell lands to me and then sell them to another, I will have an action of covenant, and 'by the *Epieikeia* of the lawe I may have my action upon my case also by reason of the deceipte'.[160] The Chancery, he says, 'oughte to be alwaies so powerfull and helpfull as that a man mighte have from thense at all tymes an originall writte for every particuler wrong'.[161]

[149] Fortier (n 1) 36–7.
[150] Perkins (n 105) 31.
[151] HJ Berman and J Witte Jr, 'The Transformation of Western Legal Philosophy in Lutheran Germany' (1989) 62 *Southern California Law Review* 1573, 84.
[152] Perkins (n 105) 20.
[153] Hake, *Epieikeia* (n 3) 49.
[154] ibid 104.
[155] ibid 105.
[156] ibid 23.
[157] ibid 21.
[158] ibid 104.
[159] ibid 106.
[160] ibid 107. See *Dogge's Case* (1442) YB Trin 20 Hen VI pl 4, ff 34a–35b.
[161] ibid.

To explain why the action on the case is a creature of equity, Hake quotes a dictum of Yelverton J:

> In matters dowbtfull … wee must doe even as the sophonists and civilians doe, who, when a newe case cometh before them wherein they had no lawe before (meaning, no doubte, as in the verball sense of the lawe) they resorte thereuppon to the lawe of Nature which is reason and the grownde of all lawes, and therein owte of that that is moste for the Commonwealthe they make a lawe.[162]

Yelverton J was not speaking about the action on the case; he was arguing that natural law should be used to fill gaps in the common law.[163] Hake rejects this idea: his argument is that the action on the case is not in fact new law. Rather, it is provided by the equity of the existing law, which was only defective in its 'verball sense'. Again, Hake identifies equity with natural law and reason. He also links case to equity in its sense of analogical extension, comparing it to the process of 'equalling' actions under the Statute of Westminster II.[164] 'In every case of resemblance,' he explains, 'one action may be taken for another'. Thus, an action granted to executors will also be available to administrators, because they are 'in the same degree' and should 'have the same remedy'.[165]

Insofar as the action on the case was a flexible tool for doing justice in particular cases and was developed by analogical extension,[166] it had obvious links with the working of equity. Hake was not alone in connecting the two: William Lambarde, for example, described case as an action that was 'fitting to the Specialtie, Reason, and Equitie' of the plaintiff's case.[167] For Hake, case was further evidence that equity is done at common law as well as in the Chancery. Indeed, he complains that fewer cases would go to Chancery if only plaintiffs would fully exploit the action on the case.[168] He invokes the maxim '*nullus recedat e curia Cancellariae sine remedio*' (nobody should depart from the Court of Chancery without a remedy) to explain the availability of case.[169] This maxim had been used by Egerton to defend the Chancellor's equitable jurisdiction,[170] but Hake's usage accorded better with its original meaning.[171]

C. Equity and the Chancery

In the third part of the *Dialogue*, Hake finally turns to the question that originally prompted his discourse: why do lawyers say that their clients have no remedy at common

[162] ibid 108. See (1468) YB Mich 8 Edw IV pl 9, ff 9a–13a, f 12b.
[163] N Doe, *Fundamental Authority in Late Medieval English Law* (Cambridge, Cambridge University Press, 1990) 71.
[164] Statute of Westminster 1285 (13 Edw I, c 24) (In Consimili Casu). A number of Hake's contemporaries, including Lambarde and Coke, incorrectly believed that this statute was the origin of the action on the case: AK Kiralfy, *The Action on the Case* (London, Sweet & Maxwell, 1951) 24–5.
[165] Hake, *Epieikeia* (n 3) 108–9.
[166] Kiralfy (n 164) 14–5.
[167] Lambarde (n 98) 38–9.
[168] Hake, *Epieikeia* (n 3) 107, 117, 127–8. See (1481) YB Pas 21 Edw IV, pl 6, ff 22b–23b, f 23a. The development of assumpsit was influenced by Chancery practice: see (1505) YB Mich 21 Hen VII pl 66, f 41a.
[169] ibid 107.
[170] *The Earl of Oxford's Case* (1615) 1 Chan Rep 1, 6.
[171] Kiralfy (n 164) 26–9; see Lambarde (n 98) 72.

law, but must seek a remedy in equity? So far, Hake has laboured to show what this does not mean. Law and equity are not 'distincte things'. In fact, equity is profoundly at work within the common law – not just in the interpretation of documents and the giving of actions, but in all legal development, as new implications are continually drawn from old maxims. Hake, however, must confront the same problem as St German.[172] If equity is really part and parcel of the common law, why is there a separate equitable jurisdiction in the Chancery? Why do 'certayne civilians' argue that 'Equity is not drawne owte of the lawe', but derived from 'the conscience of the Prince' or his representative, the Chancellor?[173]

Hake argues that the distinction between common law and Chancery does not map onto the distinction between law and equity. These civilians are right, he says, that the Chancery has a 'greate regard unto circumstances', and that the equity of the Chancery 'is drawne owte and deryved allonly from the conscience of the Lord Chauncellor'.[174] However, neither of these features of the Chancery's equity makes it fundamentally different from the equity of the common law.

First, Hake explains, the common law will also 'admitte circumstances', and these circumstances are likewise 'of the very *Epieikeia* of the lawe'.[175] He had used the terminology of circumstances in connection with equity at the outset of the *Dialogue*, but it had slipped from his radar until now.[176] The difference between common law and Chancery is not that the Chancery respects the circumstances of the case, he argues, but that each court attends to a different kind of circumstances. The circumstances considered by the Chancery are 'merely collateral and from the case, and so owte of or beside the case',[177] while the only circumstances accepted by the common law are 'altogither within the facte, and so of the body of the case'.[178] Because the Chancery considers a wider range of circumstances, it 'helpeth where the Common lawe helpeth not'.[179]

Secondly, it is true that the Chancery is strongly associated with conscience. Hake writes that 'relief … sholde be at all tymes ready in the Chauncery for matters of Conscience'[180] and that Chancery will aid a party when 'in Conscience he oughte to be relieved'.[181] However, while the equity of the Chancery 'must be derived from the conscience of the judge of that highe courte',[182] it is at the same time 'drawne owte of the lawe'.[183] This is because the Chancellor 'must order his conscience after the growndes and rules of the lawes of the realme',[184] and he must be 'learned in the Common lawes'

[172] G Behrens, 'An Early Tudor Debate on the Relation between Law and Equity' (1998) 19 *Journal of Legal History* 143, 158.
[173] Hake, *Epieikeia* (n 3) 121–2.
[174] ibid 122.
[175] ibid.
[176] ibid 2, 8. Hake quoted St German; Melanchthon's concept of equity also focused on circumstances: see Maniscalco (n 53) 71–2; Kisch (n 84) 170–2.
[177] Hake, *Epieikeia* (n 3) 122.
[178] ibid 126.
[179] ibid.
[180] ibid 107.
[181] ibid 127.
[182] ibid 129.
[183] ibid 127.
[184] ibid 129.

in order to do so.[185] Like St German, Hake argues that conscience must be guided by 'the lawe of the realme' when it 'doth concurre with the lawe of God'.[186] To say that 'the Common lawe … is according to Conscience'[187] is therefore to say that it is in accordance with divine law – which, as we have seen, is guaranteed by the working of equity. Thus, Hake explains, equity ensures that the common law follows conscience, and the Chancellor's conscience follows the law.[188]

Equity, then, works slightly differently in the Chancery. It attends to collateral circumstances, and it is filtered through the conscience of the Chancellor. However, it is not fundamentally different from the equity of the common law, which also attends to circumstances and also accords with conscience. Hake adds a further distinction: the Chancery acts '*ad personam* and not *ad rem*', as the common law does: 'a decree in the Chauncery bindeth not the right but bindeth the person to obedyence'. This means that it is not 'contradictory' to the common law.[189] None of this explains, however, why England needs two jurisdictions to enact the requirements of equity. And Hake does not dispute that both jurisdictions are needed: he says that

> it hath always byne of necessity that there shold be a consistory of Equity for the releiving of such cases as are in Conscience to be relieved, and for the which there is no succor or redresse at the Common lawe.[190]

Why does the common law not always provide redress in accordance with conscience? Although Hake refers to theological understandings of conscience,[191] and insists that the common law is in accordance with divine law, he also speaks of conscience in another sense. Mike Macnair explains that conscience could refer to private knowledge, in contrast to facts that were '*allegata et probata*' (alleged and proved) at common law.[192] The Chancellor could make use of conscience in this sense, examining a defendant to establish facts that the common law could not take into account.[193] Like St German, Hake contrasts conscience with what is *allegata et probata*.[194] He compares 'the Common lawe, whose proceeding is wont to be *stricti juris* and (as it is said) *secundum allegata et probata*' with the 'absolute course of relieving which is in the Chauncery'.[195] He identifies the key characteristic of the Chancery as its more flexible system of proof, observing that 'in many cases where the Common lawe fayleth of gyving remedy … it is for that oftentimes the party who is to bring the action fayleth of his proofes'.[196] The Chancery's

[185] ibid 140.
[186] ibid 129. Compare St German (n 61) 111–3, 163.
[187] Hake, *Epieikeia* (n 3) 130.
[188] ibid.
[189] ibid 126–7.
[190] ibid 132–3; St German (n 61) 105.
[191] Hake mentions St German's discussion of conscience, and the work of the theologian Johannes Rivius: Hake, *Epieikeia* (n 3) 130–1. Rivius's *De Conscientia* had recently been translated into English: J Woolton, *Of the Conscience* (London, H Jackson, 1576); see A Stoll, *Conscience in Early Modern English Literature* (Cambridge, Cambridge University Press, 2017) 11, fn 10. Compare St German (n 61) 81–95.
[192] M Macnair, 'Equity and Conscience' (2007) 27 *Oxford Journal of Legal Studies* 659, 672–74.
[193] ibid 674–6.
[194] St German (n 61) 117.
[195] Hake, *Epieikeia* (n 3) 47–8.
[196] ibid 127.

more flexible rules of proof enabled it to provide remedies where the common law could not.

But did equity not demand that the common law relax its own rules, rather than sloughing off these cases to a separate jurisdiction? No, answers Hake: sometimes it can be beneficial to maintain strict rules and ignore the wider circumstances of the case.[197] If too many exceptions are made to help plaintiffs out of their 'mischief', 'in respecte of a generall inconvenience that wolde growe thereby unto many, that helping wolde proove very daungerous to the commonwelthe'.[198] Hake makes similar arguments elsewhere. For example, he quotes Plowden on statutory interpretation: a statute will be taken by equity if it is 'more beneficiall then preiudiciall to the greater number of people'.[199] Although this might be unfair to an individual, it is a 'maxime in the Common lawe that the lawe will suffer a mischief rather then an inconvenience'. Hake also cites Thirning CJ's dictum: it is better that an individual is 'undone then that the lawe should be chaunged for him'.[200]

A careful balance, though, must be struck. In other parts of the *Dialogue*, Hake argues that the interests of the commonwealth require departures from general rules. For example, usually 'it is not lawfull for any man to touche the person of another forcibly'. However, it is permissible to beat a person to prevent him from hurting another, 'by the *Epieikeia* of the lawe in such cases, and for the avoiding of greater hurte'. In 'sondry other cases of commonwelthe', it might be permissible to dig another man's land, enter his house, or pull down his buildings, 'by the exception and reasonable construction of the generalitie of the law' for 'the benefite of the commonwelthe'.[201] Hake sees, then, that the common good is sometimes served by maintaining strict rules, and sometimes by departing from them. In the same way, the common good sometimes requires that facts be *allegata et probata* at common law, and sometimes that a more flexible approach be taken in conscience. In either case, the interests of the commonwealth are paramount.[202]

Hake concludes that the Chancery is not 'the onely and proper consistory of Equity', which examines circumstances and is guided by conscience.[203] Equity is at work at common law no less than in the Chancery, albeit within the confines of its different procedures. Both kinds of court are necessary to pursue the common good. As has often been noted, however, Hake's explanation of the Chancery is not easy to square with the rest of his treatise.[204] Chancery did not work by drawing out the implicit exceptions within common law maxims, nor even by extending common law rules to like cases. Again, Hake is forced to add more and more to his theory of equity so that it fits the realities of English law.

[197] ibid 123.

[198] ibid 126.

[199] ibid 89; *Platt v The Sheriffs of London* (1550) Plow 35, 36; 75 ER 57, 58.

[200] Hake, *Epieikeia* (n 3) 92–3. Hake repeats the point at ibid 115–6. See (1401) YB Pas 2 Hen IV pl 6, ff 18a–18b, f 18b.

[201] Hake, *Epieikeia* (n 3) 69–71. It is even equity that allows fishermen to dry their nets on others' land, since 'fyshing is for the commonwealth and for the sustenance of the whole realme'.

[202] ibid 108, 128. In appealing to the common good to justify both law and equity, Hake was following Aquinas and others: Thomas Aquinas, *Summa Theologica*, I-II.96.6, co; St German (n 61) 87; Berman and Witte Jr (n 151) 1626.

[203] Hake, *Epieikeia* (n 3) 121.

[204] Macnair (n 192) 681; Ibbetson (n 2) 64; Dawson (n 5) 310.

V. The Quality of Equity

A. Equity and Virtue

Throughout the *Dialogue*, Hake associated equity with a wide variety of attributes. Equity makes exceptions to general principles; it functions as the creative spirit of the law; it extends rules by analogy; it attends to a writer's intentions; and it takes account of the circumstances of the case. Hake also sought to describe equity by comparing it with related concepts – a common strategy in the literature of the period.[205] However, Hake's concept of equity was so wide-ranging that he struggled to assign it any stable characteristics. Any distinguishing feature of equity could be turned on its head, as equity grew to encompass so many notions that it began to contradict itself. Two particularly important associations that run through the *Dialogue* are those of equity and personal virtue, and equity and mercy. Neither, however, is easy to pin down.

From the outset of the *Dialogue*, Hake is concerned to dissociate equity from the personal virtue of judges. The first substantial point he makes is a refutation of Plowden's claim that equity is 'a morall vertue which reformeth the lawe'.[206] He also criticises Lovelace for agreeing with Aristotle that 'a good judge weare farre better then the best lawe that coulde be devised'.[207] Instead, Hake insists that equity is not 'the uprightnes of a righteous judge', but 'an uprightnes or righteousnes conteyned or ymplyed' in the law.[208] He emphasises that he has 'a desire to be playne in this poynte', and Eliott describes it as 'a matter of very good consequence' and of 'the greatest difficultye'.[209]

Hake explains his argument by making use of *Bracton*. Properly speaking, said *Bracton*, a man is described as just, and his judgment is described as equitable.[210] Hake infers from this that, if a just man makes an equitable judgment, the equity in his judgment must be drawn from the law. This is so because 'no judgment can be said to be right and trewe but that which is framed according to the lawe', and a judge could not be said to be just if he did not follow 'the true patterne and direction of lawe'.[211] Hake rejects the idea that a just man will inject extra-legal virtues into a judgment: justice will only permit him to draw out the equity that is already within the law. Thus, equity does not allow judges to create new law, but only to uncover the exceptions that were hitherto implicit within it.

Hake's motivation for this argument seems to be his association of the law with security of person and property.[212] The common law, he writes, protects 'the person, goods and possessions of a man',[213] and grants 'every subiect of this realme' a remedy 'for iniuryes done unto him in his goodes, landes or person'.[214] He praises the kings of

[205] Fortier (n 1) 108–9; Cromartie (n 60) 322–3.
[206] Hake, *Epieikeia* (n 3) 8–9; *Eyston* (n 64) Plow 466, 75 ER 696.
[207] Hake, *Epieikeia* (n 3) 10.
[208] ibid 9.
[209] ibid 12.
[210] *Bracton* (n 57) 25.
[211] Hake, *Epieikeia* (n 3) 11.
[212] Thorne, 'Preface' (n 104) x.
[213] Hake, *Epieikeia* (n 3) 69.
[214] ibid 74.

England because they 'rule by their lawes' and do not 'raigne by their wills or absolute powers'.[215] They do not take 'anything awaie from the subiect whether it be life, landes or goodes', except by due process of law.[216] If judges follow the direction of the law, subjects can be assured that they and their property will be kept in safety.

In contrast, matters left to an individual's discretion are uncertain and unstable. 'Althoughe the law be never so good and iust', Hake observes, it may be 'suppressed or perhaps violated' by an unjust ruler. Similarly, 'good and iust lawes may suffer detryment' by 'want of dewe and upright execution' by a sheriff or bailiff, or they may be perverted 'by evill and sinister interpretations' through 'the faulte of the judge'.[217] Hake's poetry demonstrates a keen awareness of the influences that can pervert justice. Judges may be misled by lawyers' 'well sounding' and 'subtilly declarde' arguments.[218] Other judges are corrupt and hypocritical: they seem 'iuste and holy', but will 'smoother troth' for 'spyte or gayne, or private wreke'.[219] Lawyers are 'false and subtil', and litigants are assailed by 'troupes of bribing fists'.[220] The virtue of men is unreliable, but law flows 'from Justice, even as from a fowntayne', and cannot be perverted.[221] The king may impose tyranny, writes Hake, but the law would always be against it.[222]

Hake is determined to establish equity as an attribute of the law, distinct from the personal virtue of those who administer it. However, he is unable to fully separate the two. In fact, it turns out that the implementation of equity is entirely dependent on virtuous judges. Judges must be knowledgeable about the law, since equity can only be identified by those who are 'groundedly read and travelled in every parte and learning of the law'.[223] Citing Melanchthon again, Hake explains that a judge is a 'a skyllfull artizon' who draws equity out of the law. Without this knowledge, judges may be misled by lawyers' 'writhing and wreathing', 'quercks and quiddityes' and 'false or fayned suggetions'.[224] To knowledge, a judge must add 'innocency of handes and holynes of life … diligence, zeale, courage and constancy'.[225] Hake admiringly recounts incidents in which the courts have administered the law impartially and refused to make concessions to powerful parties.[226] A good Chancellor will have similar qualities: he will be 'learned in the Common lawes of the realme',[227] and have a 'good and sownde conscience'.[228]

[215] ibid 79.
[216] ibid 81.
[217] ibid 79.
[218] Hake, *Of Golds Kingdome* (n 20) 16–20.
[219] Hake, *Newes out of Powles Churchyarde* (n 21) unpaginated.
[220] ibid.
[221] Hake, *Epieikeia* (n 3) 37.
[222] ibid 84.
[223] ibid 33, 14.
[224] ibid 34.
[225] ibid 36–7.
[226] ibid 39–40. Perhaps remembering his intended audience, Hake hastens to add that a 'couragious and stowte' judge should not go so far as to 'oppose himselfe presumptuously to the prerogative of the Prince': ibid 42.
[227] ibid 140.
[228] ibid 130.

Equity, then, is part of the law, but it can only be recognised and implemented by virtuous judges. While they do not create equity, they are able to reveal and make use of it. Luckily for Hake,

> no nation under the heavens have more sincearly, more iustly, yea (and I mighte saye) more holily expownded the textes of their lawes then the judges of our Common and statute lawes from age to age have done.[229]

Lovelace enquires whether, since equity is 'owte of the expresse letter of the lawe', it is not difficult for judges to discern it? Hake brushes this aside: if a judge is 'qualifyed', and does not wish to act 'against the lawe of God or the lawe or rule of Reason', it will be 'easy' for him to follow equity.[230] The fact that he must add the caveat shows that he has not fully succeeded in distinguishing equity from personal virtue.[231] Equity may be part of the law, but it can provide no security to subjects without good judges to draw it out.

B. Equity and Mercy

This kind of ambiguity is also evident in Hake's treatment of equity and mercy. Mercy had an enduring association with equity, stretching back to Aristotle's connection of *epieikeia* with clemency and leniency.[232] Thirteenth-century canon lawyers identified Christian *misericordia* with equity; the canonist Hostiensis described equity as 'justice tempered with the sweetness of mercy'.[233] This definition was adapted by Gerson,[234] from whom St German borrowed it: 'equytye is a ryghtwysenes that consideryth all the pertyculer cyrcumstaunces of the dede, the whiche also is temperyd with the swetnes of mercye'.[235] Unsurprisingly, Hake was also keen to invoke mercy as a hallmark of equity. Even before he repeats St German's definition at the outset of his *Dialogue*,[236] his note to the reader describes the equity of the Chancery as 'adourned & beautified with the sweete ornaments of clemency and mercy'.[237] Lovelace later observes that *epieikeia* 'signifieth sweetnes, gentlenes, goodnes, myldnes, moderation, and such like'.[238]

However, there is another thread running through the *Dialogue*. Lovelace goes on to note that 'by the same *Epieikeia* the letter of the lawe is otherwhiles sharpned or quickened by exposition to the ponishing of some particular offences (which likewise is done by *Epieikeia*)'. There is, he explains, '*misericordia puniens*' (punishing mercy) as well as '*misericordia parcens*' (forgiving mercy).[239] Hake argues that in some cases, equity will

[229] ibid 104.
[230] ibid 21, 16.
[231] Fortier (n 1) 73.
[232] ibid 16.
[233] Maniscalco (n 53) 24.
[234] Rueger (n 145) 9.
[235] St German (n 61) 95; see Rueger (n 145) 16.
[236] Hake, *Epieikeia* (n 3) 8.
[237] ibid 3.
[238] ibid 103–4.
[239] ibid 104.

dispense with punishment, as when a felony is committed by an infant.[240] In other cases, however, equity will 'enlarge' the punishment.[241]

Hake gives the example of *R v Saunders & Archer* (1576), a case reported by Plowden.[242] Saunders, intending to murder his wife, gave her a poisoned apple; she fed the apple to their daughter, who died. By 'the verball or literall sense of the lawe', explains Hake, Saunders was not guilty of murdering his daughter, because he had not intended to harm her. However, 'the *Epieikeia* of the lawe sayeth otherwise', because he 'had an intente of death in that acte which caused the death'.[243] Meanwhile, it might seem that Archer, the apothecary who had provided the arsenic, was guilty as an accessory to murder. However, 'it well holdeth in the *Epieikeia* of the lawe that Archer was no accessary', because Saunders had done 'another distincte acte' from that which Archer had directed.[244] Thus, equity had 'most iustly enlarged the letter of the lawe for the punishing of this so horrible an offence in Sawnders', but it had also 'streightened that which wee would take to be the letter of the lawe' to ensure Archer's acquittal.[245] Whether punishment is extended or remitted, then, Hake saw equity at work – no matter that it was not mentioned at all in Plowden's report.

Hake is keen to emphasise that, while equity may be 'beautified' with mercy, the two are separate concepts. He distinguishes cases involving equity from cases in which a judge acts from his own 'discretion, favor or pity'.[246] Where an exception is provided for an infant, for example, it is 'the favour of the lawe' itself at work, and not 'the favour of the judge'.[247] Hake would doubtless have agreed with his contemporary William West, who argued that

> there is a difference between Equitie, and Clemencie: for Equitie is alwaies most firmely knit to the will of the Law, which way soever it bendes, whether to clemencie, or to severitie.[248]

Hake's equivocal position on equity and mercy reflected broader contradictions in contemporary theories of equity. Two further examples can be given. It had been established that statutes enacting penalties, or restraining the common law, could not be extended by equity.[249] However, this rule was not always observed in practice.[250] Plowden even argued that 'equity knows no difference between penal laws and others',[251] although the orthodox rule was frequently reiterated in his reports.[252] Hake recounts Plowden's view that even penal laws should be taken by equity.[253] As we have seen, however, he also mandates that penal statutes, and those in restraint of the common law,

[240] ibid 60.
[241] ibid 65.
[242] *R v Saunders & Archer* (1576) 2 Plow 473, 75 ER 706.
[243] Hake, *Epieikeia* (n 3) 66–7.
[244] ibid 68.
[245] ibid.
[246] ibid 109–10.
[247] ibid 115.
[248] W West, *Of Symboleography the Second Part* (London, T Wight and B Norton, 1597) (unpaginated); see Cromartie (n 60) 333.
[249] Thorne, 'Introduction' (n 58) 48–52.
[250] ibid 52–3.
[251] *Eyston* (n 64) Plow 468, 75 ER 698.
[252] Behrens (n 59) 40.
[253] Hake, *Epieikeia* (n 3) 50.

'shalbe expounded *stricti juris*, and not by Equity'.[254] Here, Hake's conflicting accounts reflect the ambivalence of the common law of his day.

Uncertainty about equity and mercy stretched far beyond the common law: theological concepts of equity could also be inconsistent. Equity was associated with Christ-like mercy,[255] a notion that Hake invokes when he describes equity as 'patterned by the lenitye of the mylde Savioure of mankynde, the Lorde Jhesus'.[256] However, equity was also equated with divine justice and punishment.[257] For Martin Luther, equity entailed submission to authority as well as meekness and forbearance,[258] while for Melanchthon, *epieikeia* worked both moderation of the law and intensification.[259]

Hake draws on theological ideas about equity in an unexpected part of the *Dialogue*. In the middle of his discussion of *epieikeia* and criminal law, he announces abruptly that his cases are becoming 'wearisom'. To refresh his listeners, he has a poem 'lately devised', which he recites to great acclaim.[260] The poem is about two kinds of thief: 'him that steales throughe Neede, and him that steales throughe Covetousnes'. The first thief only steals because of his 'distressed state' – his 'body pynes and entrayles gnawe' with hunger – and he has lost his 'dreede / Of lawe' as a result. The second thief, in contrast, is a 'greedy wretche' who steals 'to fill / His hungry, thirsting hart'. Hake observes that 'the punishment of thefte by lawe is death', but 'Justice wold' that the two thieves 'be deemed asunder'. His argument isn't, he emphasises, that 'the lawes intent shold make it free / To steale through want'.[261] Indeed, it would be 'very daungerous and absurd' not to punish the needy thief at all.[262] However, the 'foresighte' of judges is needed to make sure that each thief gets what he 'deserveth most in righte'.[263]

The case of the needy thief was often discussed by theologians. Aquinas, for example, argued that it is lawful to steal in a case of immediate need, when there is no other possible remedy.[264] Melanchthon used the case to illustrate the working of equity. A thief who stole from hunger should not be subjected to the same rule as a thief who stole from malice, he argued; *epieikeia* would alleviate the usual punishment because of the mitigating circumstances.[265] English theologians also adopted Melanchthon's approach. Perkins, for example, explained that equity would mitigate the law in the case of a needy thief. Instead of death, a punishment should be imposed 'as shall be sufficient, to reforme the partie from his sinne to punish the fault, to terrifie others, and to satisfie the law'.[266]

Hake returns to the issue of capital punishment several times in the *Dialogue*. He argues that the death penalty should be remitted where nobody 'could take example

[254] ibid 88, 91.
[255] Fortier (n 1) 29–30.
[256] Hake, *Epieikeia* (n 3) 3.
[257] Fortier (n 1) 36.
[258] ibid 38–9.
[259] Kisch (n 84) 171.
[260] Hake, *Epieikeia* (n 3) 63–5.
[261] ibid 64–5.
[262] ibid 63.
[263] ibid 64.
[264] Thomas Aquinas, *Summa Theologica*, II-II.66.7, co.
[265] Kisch (n 84) 170–1; see Fortier (n 1) 44.
[266] Perkins (n 105) 13–4.

by' the execution, as in the case of an infant or 'a madd man',[267] or where the crime falls outside the mischief of the law.[268] However, he gives no clear resolution in this case. He is reluctant to say that 'there sholde be scope to steale for neede',[269] but he also feels the injustice of executing the hungry thief.[270] Hake's concept of equity is so wide-ranging that it is unable to offer him the answer: it may either extend or remit punishment, depending on what is appropriate in the circumstances. Hake can only make the trite point that judges should do what is 'righte'. As we have seen, his theological sources were caught in a similar bind.

VI. Conclusions

Throughout the *Dialogue*, Hake is barely in control of equity. We have seen him associate it with a dizzying array of attributes. Equity is the hidden meaning of the law, its creative spirit and its secret exceptions. It treats like cases alike; it attends to intentions and circumstances; it acts in accordance with conscience, the law of nature and the law of God. Hake's equity is unstable, even paradoxical. It works for and against the common good; it is merciful and punishing; it is independent of and dependent on judges; it is derived from the common law and the Chancellor's conscience. It is associated with the interpretation of written documents, the action on the case, the working of the Chancery, and almost every other aspect of English law imaginable. Hake is unable to set any limits to equity: it is infinite, he says, a bankless sea.

Hake's treatise, too, is paradoxical. In some ways, it is very conventional. Much of Hake's material was recycled from St German and Plowden, and he hit the usual notes – *epieikeia*, the extension of statutes, and the Court of Chancery. However, there are also flashes of originality. Hake blended legal theories and precedents with theological ideas, and he pushed them far in unexpected directions. His treatise was 'at the apex of the systematic elaboration of equity in early modern England'.[271] The landscape was already shifting under Hake's feet, and his way of thinking about equity would soon be eclipsed in the early seventeenth-century conflict over the Chancery.[272] Hake's *Epieikeia* is a dazzling vision of the dynamic force of equity in the late sixteenth century; the last glimpse of a bankless equity before the walls closed in.

[267] Hake, *Epieikeia* (n 3) 60.
[268] ibid 19–20.
[269] ibid 65.
[270] This injustice was discussed by length by Thomas More: G Logan and R Adams (eds), T More, *Utopia* (Cambridge, Cambridge University Press, 2003) 15–25. Hake praises More as a man of 'good and sownde conscienc[e]', despite being a 'Catholicqu[e]': Hake, *Epieikeia* (n 3) 143.
[271] Fortier (n 1) 73.
[272] Thorne, 'Preface' (n 104) v–vi.

9

'*Equitatis Causa*': 'Equity' in the Practice of the Court of Chancery, 1515–1615

NG JONES*

I. Introduction

It is well known that in Tudor times there was a 'shift from "conscience" to "equity"'[1] in the Court of Chancery, reflected in Serjeant Barham's dictum in 1572 that in relation to uses upon uses, the 'course of the Chancery by reason of equity (*equitatis causa*) is used contrary to the common law'.[2] In this period lie the roots of the lasting association between the term 'equity' and the English-side jurisdiction of the Court of Chancery.

Much has been written on the meanings and uses of 'equity' in our period, in relation to the Chancery, but also in the context of religion, politics, poetry and drama.[3] Much was written on equity by contemporaries too: early-modern England was 'a

* Unless otherwise indicated, all manuscripts are in The National Archives (TNA). Where available, references to TNA manuscripts are accompanied by the relevant image number in the digital archive assembled by Robert C Palmer, Elspeth K Palmer, and Susanne Brand, 'The Anglo-American Legal Tradition', available at www.aalt.law.uh.edu/aalt.html, which has much assisted with the research for this chapter. In footnote lists of references to TNA manuscripts, series numbers are generally provided at the first reference but not thereafter in the same footnote for manuscripts in the same series. For reasons of space, in some instances complete lists of references in relation to quantitative statements have not been provided here, but are available, if required, from the author. Quotations from manuscripts have been rendered into modern spelling and orthography. The year is taken to begin on 1 January.

[1] J Baker, *An Introduction to English Legal History*, 5th edn (Oxford, Oxford University Press, 2019) 115.

[2] '*Nota quod cursus cancellarie equitatis causa contra communem legem utitur*' ('note that the course of the Chancery by reason of equity is used contrary to the common law'), British Library MS Lansdowne 1067, fo 27, translated in J Baker, *Baker and Milsom, Sources of English Legal History: Private Law to 1750*, 2nd edn (Oxford, Oxford University Press, 2010) 143, from Barham's report of *Bertie v Herenden* (1560), written in 1572.

[3] For equity and the Court of Chancery see, eg, TFT Plucknett and JL Barton (eds), *St German's Doctor and Student* (1974) 91 *Selden Society* xliv–li; DR Klinck, *Conscience, Equity and the Court of Chancery in Early Modern England* (Farnham, Ashgate, 2010); DJ Ibbetson, 'A House Built on Sand: Equity in Early Modern English Law' in E Koops and WJ Zwalve (eds), *Law and Equity: Approaches in Roman Law and Common Law* (Leiden, Brill, 2014), 55; M Macnair, 'Equity and Conscience' (2007) 20 *Oxford Journal of Legal Studies* 659. For equity in England more broadly see, eg, M Fortier, *The Culture of Equity in Early Modern England* (London, Routledge, 2005).

particularly dynamic time for thinking about equity',[4] but reflection on equity's meaning is sparse in the law reports and the Chancery record of the period. The reports contain 'no real exploration of equity as an idea, nor is there any extensive discussion of the relations between equity and the common law'.[5] Ibbetson is equally direct:

> [t]he case law of the [early-modern] Court of Chancery will be largely ignored, since nowhere in this is there anything even purporting to give a theoretical insight into the nature of the Chancellor's equity; the one exception is the *Earl of Oxford's Case* (1615), which, it is argued, is not really a report of a decision at all, but rather a justificatory essay on the nature of the Chancery's jurisdiction by the Lord Chancellor, Lord Ellesmere.[6]

But the rise of 'equity' in the Court of Chancery cannot be understood from contemporary theoretical writings alone, absent an assessment of the practice of the court – '[e]quity in [a]ction'[7] – both to establish the chronology and path of the term's adoption in Chancery's daily practice, and to shed such further light as is possible upon contemporary lawyers' understandings of the meaning and role of Chancery equity.[8]

The period of this study spans the century between Thomas Wolsey's appointment as chancellor in 1515 and Lord Ellesmere's 'justificatory essay'[9] in 1615, a period encompassing the shift from the fifteenth-century ecclesiastical chancellors to chancellors trained in the common law;[10] the publication of St German's influential treatise *Doctor and Student*;[11] the commencement of record-keeping in Chancery;[12] the first steps in the English-side jurisdiction's hardening into a body

[4] Fortier, *Culture of Equity* (n 3) 1. This was true also in Europe more widely. For discussion see L Maniscalco, '*Interpretatio Ex Aequo et Bono*: The Emergence of Equitable Interpretation in European Legal Scholarship' in M Lobban and I Williams (eds), *Networks and Connections in Legal History* (Cambridge, Cambridge University Press, 2020) 233.

[5] Fortier, *Culture of Equity* (n 3) 60.

[6] Ibbetson, 'A House Built on Sand' (n 3) 56. For the *Earl of Oxford's Case*, see D Ibbetson, '*The Earl of Oxford's Case* (1615)' in C Mitchell and P Mitchell (eds), *Landmark Cases in Equity* (Oxford, Hart Publishing, 2012) 1. WJ Jones likewise observed that 'The only authoritative sources for the Elizabethan Chancery, the records of the court, do not appear to provide the evidence to sustain notions of an elevated theory of equity': WJ Jones, *The Elizabethan Court of Chancery* (Oxford, Oxford University Press, 1967) 420.

[7] Fortier, *Culture of Equity* (n 3) 4.

[8] The Chancery was not the sole 'equity' jurisdiction in England in the period. A fuller study of the meaning of 'equity' for early-modern English lawyers would require consideration also of the equity side of the Court of Exchequer, the Court of Requests and other conciliar tribunals, and regional courts of equity. For the Court of Requests and regional conciliar and equity courts see Baker, *Introduction* (n 1) 128–31. See also Laura Flannigan, ch 5 in this volume.

[9] Ibbetson, 'A House Built on Sand' (n 3) 56.

[10] Wolsey was the last of a line of ecclesiastics holding the great seal stretching back to the appointment of Thomas Arundel, bishop of Ely, in 1386, broken only by the brief tenure of Richard Nevill, earl of Salisbury, in 1454–55. On the backgrounds of the fifteenth-century chancellors see AWB Simpson, *A History of the Common Law of Contract: The Rise of the Action of Assumpsit* (Oxford, Oxford University Press, 1975) 400–01. After Wolsey, the holders of the great seal in our period were all laymen, with the exception of 1552 to 1558, when the seal was successively in the hands of three bishops (Thomas Goodrich of Ely, Stephen Gardiner of Winchester, and Nicholas Heath of York): EB Fryde et al (eds), *Handbook of British Chronology*, 3rd edn (Cambridge, Cambridge University Press, 1986) 88.

[11] *Doctor and Student* (n 3). The work was printed in two parts, the first dialogue in 1528 and the second in 1530: NG Jones, 'Doctor and Student' in S Dauchy et al (eds), *The Formation and Transmission of Western Legal Culture: 150 Books that Made the Law in the Age of Printing* (Cham, Springer, 2016) 70.

[12] The entry books of decrees and orders, or Register's books (TNA series C 33), begin in 1544. The earliest decree in the decree rolls (series C 78) dates from July 1534.

of rules;[13] the beginnings of reference to precedent in Chancery;[14] and the intermittent jurisdictional tensions between the common law judges and the Chancery reflected in Ellesmere's 'justificatory essay'.[15] The analysis is based upon a sample of approximately 750 bills in Chancery[16] and of the court's record in the entry books of decrees and orders[17] and decree rolls,[18] together with a sample of Chancery masters' reports and certificates.[19] Reference is made also to reports of cases in Chancery,[20] and to a number of Court of Requests entry books of appearances, final orders and decrees in the earlier part of the period.[21]

II. The Pattern of the Emergence of 'Equity' in Chancery

There being no cases in the Chancery entry books and decree rolls before 1534, early use of the term 'equity' must be traced through the surviving pleadings. In Wolsey's

[13] Baker, *Introduction* (n 1) 118–19. What appear to be substantive rules in Chancery concerning uses may be seen by the second half of the fifteenth century: see the cases printed in Baker, *Sources* (n 2) 106–10.

[14] The earliest reference to precedent as yet encountered in Chancery is in 1566, in *Cooke v Wootton*, where Bacon LK deferred making an order, having had insufficient time to 'consider the precedents of this court and to confer with the judges concerning the cause and matter in question': C 33/33 fo 82v [IMG_1297a]. Reference to precedent to guide decision-making in Chancery gained pace by the late sixteenth century. See, eg, the observation in 1592 in *Raglande v Wilgosse* that 'the matter is of great weight and importance and may hereafter be vouched for a precedent in other like cases': C 33/85 fo 79v [IMG_0082a]; also Egerton LK's statement in *Throckmorton v Finch* (1597) that 'the cause is of great weight and will be taken for a precedent hereafter in like cases': C 33/93 fo 6 [IMG_6130], referred to by Sir John Baker, ch 6 in this volume; and Lord Ellesmere's reference to a 'leading case' in 1613 in *Goulding v Tiffin* C 33/123 fo 413 [IMG_0419].

[15] There is a large literature on the controversy in the 1610s over the scope and limits of the Chancery's jurisdiction. For recent discussion see JH Baker, *The Reinvention of Magna Carta 1216-1616* (Cambridge, Cambridge University Press, 2017) ch 10.

[16] This figure includes a number of bills which are only partly legible, or only partly complete. There are bills in the sample from every chancellorship or lord keepership from Wolsey to Ellesmere, other than the brief tenure of Paulet LK in 1547. These bills are those in files C 1/394, 547, 563, 616, 636, 702, 720, 877, 1073, 1317, 1320, 1397, 1400, 1520; C 2/Eliz/A1, A2, M1, M2; C 2/Jas I/B20. They have been supplemented by a sample of 122 bills largely from the time of Wolsey, but including a small number from the time of More, chosen as containing a reference to uses. While outside the period of the article, 238 bills in files C 1/276, 302, 339 and 370 from the chancellorship of Archbishop William Warham, 1504–15, have been examined for context. While it may well be possible that relevant material occurs in subsequent pleadings, the focus here is upon the bills, both because they introduce the essential basis of the suit, and for reasons of practicality.

[17] C 33/1 (complete), 2 (complete), 3 (complete), 19 (first 150 folios), 41 (first 150 folios), 61 (first 150 folios), 81 (first 150 folios), 99 (first 150 folios), 119 (first 150 folios), supplemented by reference to a substantial number of entries previously selected as concerned with trusts.

[18] From a substantial number of enrolled decrees previously selected as concerned with trusts, together with 108 enrolled decrees for the period 1534–43, representing the large majority of such decrees in the period before the entry books begin (these decrees were identified from the 'chronolists' of the Chancery decree rolls on the Anglo-American Legal Tradition website).

[19] Books C 38/1 (1562–95, but mostly from the early 1590s); C 38/3 pts 1 and 2 (1599–1600); C 38/5 (1603–04); C 38/9 (1607, A–I); C 38/17 (1611); and C 38/20 (1614).

[20] Comprising those printed from manuscript in WH Bryson (ed), *Cases Concerning Equity and the Courts of Equity 1550-1660, vol I* (2000) 117 *Selden Society* and *vol II* (2001) 118 *Selden Society*, and those identified by a word-search for 'equity' in the printed reports for the period available in the JustisOne online database at www.app.justis.com.

[21] The following books were read (completely, except where indicated): REQ 1/4, 1/5, 1/6, 1/7, 1/8, 1/9, 1/10 (first 400 folios), 1/11 (first 400 folios), 1/22, 1/26 (first 250 folios), 1/42, 1/47.

time[22] the term rarely appears in Chancery bills. Of the 212 bills in the sample addressed to Wolsey, 'equity' appears in nine (a little over four per cent).[23] Bills may be dated at this time only by reference to the name, style and title of the chancellor to whom they are addressed, allowing bills addressed to Wolsey to be assigned to either 1515–18 or 1518–29.[24] All nine bills in the sample containing the term 'equity' in Wolsey's time are from the latter period,[25] though this may be an artefact of the sample: the term is found, albeit very rarely, in the time of Wolsey's predecessor, Archbishop Warham,[26] a sample of 238 bills in that period revealing three (a little over one per cent) referring to 'equity'.[27]

It has been said that 'equity' 'was rarely associated with the English side of the Chancery before St German',[28] and it seems probable that St German's discussion of equity in the first dialogue of *Doctor and Student*,[29] printed in 1528, contributed substantially to the term's adoption in Chancery practice:[30] '[i]t is St. German, as much as any single individual, who is responsible for the fact that today we have courts of equity rather than of conscience'.[31] As appears from the sample of bills in Warham's time, the term 'equity' was present in Chancery pleadings more than a decade before the publication of *Doctor and Student*, but then – as in Wolsey's time – appeared very infrequently.

The term appears somewhat more frequently in bills addressed to Wolsey's successor, Thomas More:[32] a sample of 72 such bills includes 12 containing it (a little under

[22] Chancellor 1515–29.

[23] C 1/498/30, 'as shall stand with equity and justice'; 547/9, 'as shall stand with equity right and good conscience'; 547/16, 'according to right equity and good conscience'; 547/31, 'according to reason equity and good conscience'; 552/34, 'according to equity right and good conscience'; 563/18, 'as shall stand with equity right and good conscience'; 563/31, 'as shall seem agreeably with the equity of justice and good conscience'; 563/33, 'according to reason equity and good conscience'; 586/62, 'according to equity right and good conscience'. The sample comprised 90 bills chosen without regard to the subject-matter of the petition, and 122 chosen as being concerned with uses. It seems improbable that a concern with uses would affect the likelihood of the presence of the term 'equity' in the bill.

[24] Wolsey was appointed papal legate *a latere* in 1518, from which time he is addressed as such in Chancery bills.

[25] All nine address Wolsey as legate *a latere*.

[26] Chancellor 1504-15.

[27] The sample excluded bills from the period of Warham's lord keepership, 1502–04. C 1/276 unnumbered [IMG_0011] 'before your grace in the king's Chancery where right justice and equity may be ministered'; C 1/276/23 [IMG_0039] 'such order and direction as shall be consonant to equity and good conscience'; C 1/276/40 [IMG_0087] 'according to right equity and good conscience'. The sample comprised four files of bills (C 1/276, 320, 339 and 370). It appears to be chance that the examples of the term 'equity' appear in the same file, the files being no longer in their original arrangement.

[28] Baker, *Introduction* (n 1) 114 n 57.

[29] In particular in the chapter headed 'Quid Sit Equitas'/'What Is Equitye': *Doctor and Student* (n 3) 95–98.

[30] *Doctor and Student* was very widely read, indeed a 'bestseller': I Williams, 'Christopher St German: Religion, Conscience and Law in Reformation England' in M Hill and RH Helmholz (eds), *Great Christian Jurists in English History* (Cambridge, Cambridge University Press, 2017) 69, 75.

[31] *Doctor and Student* (n 3) xlvii. Barton suggested that St German, 'introduced English lawyers to the theological doctrine of equity, or *epikeia*': JL Barton, 'Equity in the Medieval Common Law' in RA Newman (ed), *Equity in the World's Legal Systems* (Brussels, Établissements Émile Bruylant, 1973) 139, 154 (quoted in Klinck, *Conscience* (n 3) 45). As Klinck observes however, after Aquinas the concept of *epieikeia*/*aequitas* was familiar to theologians and canonists, and one would expect 'at least the ecclesiastical chancellors to have been familiar with it': Klinck, *Conscience* (n 3) 45 (referring to JC Grayson (trans), GHM Posthumous Meyjes, *Jean Gerson, Apostle of Unity: His Church Politics and Ecclesiology*, (Leiden, Brill, 1999) 243). See also on equity in medieval scholastic theology, Maniscalco, '*Interpretatio Ex Aequo et Bono*' (n 4) 233, 239–41.

[32] Chancellor 1529–32.

17 per cent), invariably accompanied by at least one other term.[33] The same increase in frequency is repeated in the time of More's successor, Thomas Audley,[34] where in a sample of 81 bills, 23 contain the term (a little over 28 per cent),[35] once again always accompanied by at least one other term. By the end of our period, of 88 bills in the sample addressed to Thomas Egerton as such, or as Lord Ellesmere,[36] no more than a handful lack the term.[37] In bills in Chancery, 'equity' thus appeared very infrequently in the time of Warham and Wolsey, became gradually more common over the succeeding decades, and was almost universally present by the mid-1590s.

Turning to the Chancery record, the enrolled decrees for the period 1534–43 reveal no instances of the term 'equity', though it appears in the entry books shortly after their commencement in 1544; the earliest instances, in 1545–46, take the form of descriptions, in the Latin texts of injunctions, of conduct to be enjoined, in such phrases as '*contra omnem equitatem*' and '*contra omnem iustitiam et equitatem*'.[38] The entry of the texts of injunctions did not long persist, but the term 'equity', now in

[33] C 1/616/28, 'as may stand with right equity and good conscience'; 616/29, 'contrary to right equity and good conscience'; 616/39, 'as may stand with equity and good conscience'; 616/40, 'shall stand with the law equity and good conscience'; 619/1 'as to equity and justice shall appertain'; 623/8, 'contrary to right equity and good conscience'; 636/2, 'contrary to right equity and good conscience'; 636/16, 'shall stand with equity and justice'; 636/18, 'ordered and determined according to right justice and equity'; 636/19, 'as to equity and good conscience shall appertain'; 636/24, 'as shall stand with equity right and good conscience'; 636/55, 'according to reason equity and good conscience'. The sample comprised 60 bills chosen without regard to the subject-matter of the petition, and 12 chosen as being concerned with uses. As above, it seems improbable that a concern with uses would affect the likelihood of the presence of the term 'equity' in the bill.

[34] Lord keeper of the great seal 1532–33, chancellor 1533–44.

[35] C 1/702/7, 'according to right equity and justice', 'against truth and equity'; 702/21, 'according to equity and justice'; 702/35 'against all right equity and good conscience'; 702/38, 'shall be thought convenient to stand with equity and good conscience'; 702/40, 'to stand with reason equity and good conscience'; 702/48, 'according to reason equity and good conscience'; 720/2, 'contrary to all right equity and good conscience'; 720/15, 'contrary to right equity and good conscience', 'as to … equity and good conscience shall appertain'; 720/19, 'as shall be consonant with reason equity and good conscience'; 720/20, 'to stand with right equity and good conscience'; 720/29, 'contrary to all equity and justice'; 877/6, 'with right equity and good conscience', 'as good right conscience and equity wills them so do to'; 877/9, '… equity and good conscience'; 877/11, 'according to equity and good conscience'; 877/27, 'to stand with equity and good conscience'; 877/51, 'contrary to right equity and conscience'; 877/53, 'as shall stand with equity and good conscience'; 877/54, 'according to right equity and good conscience'; 877/68 'as may stand with right equity and good conscience'; 877/71, 'contrary to all equity and good conscience'; 1073/1, 'contrary to all right equity and conscience', 'according to equity and conscience'; 1073/23, 'to accord with equity and good conscience'; 1073/26, 'to stand with equity and good conscience', 'against all right equity and good conscience'; 1073/32, 'contrary to right equity and good conscience'; 1073/36, 'as may stand with equity and conscience', 'contrary to all right equity and conscience'; 1073/37, 'as shall stand with equity and good conscience'; 1073/47, 'contrary to all right equity and good conscience'; 1520/21, 'as shall stand with equity and good conscience'; 1520/23, 'according to all right and equity'; 1520/144, 'with good equity and conscience'.

[36] Egerton was lord keeper 1596 to 1603, and chancellor, as Lord Ellesmere, between 1603 and 1616, and, as Viscount Brackley, between 1616 and 1617.

[37] C 2/Eliz/M2/27/2, 'shall seem most meet and convenient'; Jas I/B20/17/2, 'shall seem meet and convenient'; Jas I/B20/56/1, 'shall seem most meet and convenient'. C 2/Eliz/M2/56/1 also contains no reference to equity, though the bill seeks an injunction, for which it asks without need to express the grounds upon which an order might be reached.

[38] C 33/2, fo 9 [IMG_3576], *Stradling v Long*, '*contra omnem equitatem*'; ibid, *Reve v Leye*, '*contra omnem equitatem*'; 2, fo 47v [IMG_3617], *Broke v Brikilbank*, '*contra omnem equitatem*'; 2, fo 77 [IMG_3645], *Collingborne v Leighe*, '*contra omnem iustitiam and equitatem*'; 2, fo 131v [IMG_3699], *Gurney v Smythe*, '*contra omnem equitatem*'; 2, fo 181 [IMG_3746], *Dean of St Paul's v Prebendaries of St Paul's*, '*contra equitatem et mandatum nostram*'; 2, fo 184v [IMG_3750], *Gyve v Kyrton*, '*contra omnem iustitiam et equitatem*'.

English, appears in the succeeding books, albeit infrequently.[39] It has been found once in C 33/3, in 1548, in a commission to determine a matter 'according as to equity and justice sha[ll] appertain'.[40] It has not been found in C 33/5 for Easter term 1549 to Easter term 1550. Some ten years later, it has been found three times in the first 150 folios of C 33/19, for Michaelmas term 1558 and Hilary and Easter terms 1559.[41] Similarly limited occurrences, six in total, have been found in the first 150 folios of C 33/41, for Michaelmas term 1570 and Hilary term 1571.[42] Numbers increase modestly to 10 in the first 150 folios of C 33/61,[43] for Michaelmas term 1580 and Hilary term 1581.[44] A decade later, in the first 150 folios of C 33/81, for Michaelmas term 1590 and Hilary term 1591, the number of occurrences shows a slight decrease,[45] to nine, while seven instances have been found in the first 150 folios of C 33/99, for Michaelmas term 1599,[46] and in the first 150 folios of C 33/119, for Michaelmas

[39] The term *equitas* has not been found in the samples of bills and masters' reports. There is one instance of the phrase *bono et aequo*, in *Woode v Nevell* (1594), Masters Matthew Carew and Legge thinking it 'most agreeable *bono et aequo*' that a certain sum be paid to the plaintiff, C 38/1 (the volume is not paginated or foliated), 28 June 1594.

[40] C 33/3, fos 294–95, 295 [IMG_7816-17] (also entered in 4, fos 313–14 [IMG_8152-53]).

[41] C 33/19, fo 78v [IMG_0851], *Bell v Mosier*, arbitrators 'do likewise think in equity and conscience the same meet to be paid'; 19, fo 139v [IMG_0922], *Watton v Praus*, if necessary a master to make a final order 'as to his wisdom and discretion shall be thought agreeable to justice and equity'; 19, fo 142 [IMG_0924], *Cuturwell v Broughey*, the parties to appear before the lord keeper and abide by such order as 'he shall think convenient therein according to equity and conscience'.

[42] C 33/41 fo 15v [IMG_8791a], *Polstead v Bruce*, 'as the equity of the cause shall require'; 41, fo 73, 73v [IMG_8851a], *Wythe v Harbotell*, 'as in justice and equity it shall be thought meet'; 33/41, fo 82v, 83 [IMG-8861], *Kenne v Beckwith*, 'according to the equity of the cause'; 33/41, fo 84 [IMG_8862], *Hyde v Chowne* [IMG_84], 'what in equity is due to the children', 'they ought in equity to have'; 33/41, fo 104 [IMG_8882], *Randall v Stukeley*, 'should think in justice and equity it ought to be'; 33/41, fo 131, 131v [IMG_8910a], *Exetor v Hamond*, 'why their interest in equity ought to be allowed'.

[43] Comparisons between the numbers of occurrences from entry book to entry book should be taken with caution, both because of the small number of occurrences, and because it is unlikely that the number of cases entered in a given book, or in a particular range of folios, is consistent from book to book.

[44] C 33/61, fo 14 [IMG_0017], *Wilson v Stubley*, 'as in equity and conscience seemed unto him most fit'; ibid, fo 22 [IMG_0025], *Moundford v Sheldon*, 'think right in equity or conscience'; ibid, fo 47 [IMG_0050], *Dymock v Birde*, 'may have remedy in her majesty's Exchequer for any matter in equity'; ibid, fo 57v [IMG_0060a], *Hyde v Lady Elizabeth Warham*, 'ought in equity and conscience to go to the relief of … More and his children'; ibid, fo 72v [IMG_0075a], *Cole v Finche*, 'in equity and conscience'; ibid, fo 87v [IMG_0090a], *Dalton v Hargyll*, 'to be relieved in equity'; ibid, fo 126 [IMG_0129], *Carye v Mathewe*, 'in equity and conscience'; ibid, fo 132 [IMG_0135], *Napper v Napper*, 'relieved … as in equity and conscience shall by this court be thought most meet and convenient'; ibid, fo 146v [IMG_0149a], *Dotson v Dotson*, 'neither in equity nor conscience to be relieved'; ibid, fo 148 [IMG_0151], *Lenthall v Dean and Canons of Windsor*, 'for no other cause in equity'.

[45] C 33/81, fo 13v [IMG_0015a], *Gylman v Rothermaker*, 'there is no cause in equity'; ibid, fos 25v–26, 26 [IMG_0028], *Androws v Allen*, 'such order and direction as in right and equity shall in [the archbishop of Canterbury's] opinion conscience and discretion be thought most meet and convenient', 'in all equity and conscience'; ibid, fo 37v [IMG_0039a], *Burye v Conisbye*, 'contrary to all equity'; ibid, fos 54v–55, 54v [IMG_0059a], *Godderd v Godderd*, 'any matter of equity'; ibid, fo 60v [IMG-0062a], *Tooleye v Northey*, 'heard in equity'; ibid, fo 65–65v, at fo 65v [IMG_0067a], *Browne v Dighton*, 'in all equity to discharge it'; ibid, fo 95v [IMG_0091a], *Crofte v Acton*, 'for good causes in equity'; ibid, fo 133–33v, 133v [IMG_0135a], *Wincole v Whyte*, 'to discharge him in equity'; C 33/81, fo 145v [IMG_0147a], *Story v Kercherver*, 'equity of the plaintiff's cause'.

[46] C 33/99, fo 2 [IMG_8974], *Stafforde v Thynne*, 'the matter of mortgage or any other equity', 'what matter of equity', 'agreeable to equity'; ibid, fos 13v–14, 14 [IMG_8986], *Coniston v Askewe*, 'the matter of equity'; ibid, fo 68–68v, 68v [IMG_9043a], *Shere v Glanville*, 'the matter in equity'; ibid, fo 90v [IMG_9065a], *Lee v Lord Morley*, 'matter of equity'; ibid, fo 98 [IMG_9073], *Bysse v Willes*, 'in all equity and conscience'; ibid, fo 102v [IMG_9077a], *Kinge v Abbot*, 'in all equity'; ibid, fo 116 [IMG_9091], *Hyde v Holland*, 'relieved in equity', 'such order in equity'.

term 1610.[47] In recording its daily business, the Chancery of the sixteenth and early seventeenth centuries found little need expressly to refer to 'equity'.[48]

III. A Shift from 'Conscience' to 'Equity'?

As has been seen, it is commonly understood that a shift from conscience to equity occurred in the Tudor Chancery. The evidence considered for this chapter suggests that the terminological aspect of the shift was gradual, gaining strength only in the final decade of the sixteenth century and the first decade of the seventeenth, as the Tudors gave way to the Stuarts.

In Wolsey's time, almost two-thirds of the bills in Chancery in a sample of 212 employed either the phrase 'right and good conscience'[49] or, less frequently, 'right and conscience', in describing the defendant's misconduct, the desired remedy, or both. This reflected long-established practice: the phrases 'right and good conscience' and 'right and conscience' are not uncommon in fifteenth-century Chancery bills.[50]

As has been seen, a small number of bills in the sample addressed to Wolsey contained the term 'equity', but none used it in isolation. Fortier has observed that in

[47] C 33/119, fo 49 [IMG_0030], *Rogers v Parker*, 'for cause of equity'; ibid, fo 57v [IMG_0038a], *Hall v Leicester*, 'sufficient in equity for discharge of the … bonds'; ibid, fo 64 [IMG_0045], *Walker v Coleman*, 'before any further hearing had of the cause in equity'; ibid, fo 64v [IMG_0045a], *Foster v Crompton*, 'the equity of the cause'; ibid, fo 129 [IMG_0110], *Drewry v Saunder*, 'no matter in equity to relieve the … plaintiff'; ibid, fo 130–30v, 130v [IMG_0112a], *Beare v Seymor*, 'the matter of equity'; ibid, fo 141 [IMG_0123], *Mays v Brooke*, 'no matter of equity'.

[48] By way of comparison, the Court of Requests entry books of appearances, final orders and decrees commence earlier than those of the Chancery. REQ 1/4 (1515–20), reveals no reference to equity. REQ 1/5 (1523–33), shows one reference, in 1529 (fo 68 [IMG_0623] *Gylby v Mulsho*, 'as may stand and be consonant to equity right and good conscience'). No references have been found in REQ 1/6 (1538–46), while three references have been found in each of the two following books, REQ 1/7 (1540–45) [versos IMG_0063], 'to stand with equity of the law right and good conscience', REQ 1/7 [versos IMG_0167], 'according to equity and conscience', REQ 1/7 [versos IMG_0173], 'to stand with equity and good conscience'; and REQ 1/8 (1547-55) [versos IMG_0142], 'as to equity and justice shall appertain', REQ 1/8 [versos IMG_0143], 'contrary to equity and good conscience', REQ 1/8 [versos IMG_0145], 'contrary to all right equity and good conscience'.

[49] Of 212 bills, 105 employed the phrase 'right and good conscience'; 25 the phrase 'right and conscience'; and five the phrase 'good right and conscience', giving a total of 135 among 212 bills (a little under 64 per cent). See, eg, C 1/394/3, defendant alleged to have acted 'contrary to right and good conscience'; 547/11, plaintiff sought such order as 'shall be thought to stand with right and good conscience'; 547/17, defendant alleged to have acted 'contrary to all right and conscience'; 547/7, defendant alleged to have acted 'contrary to good right and conscience'. In calculating these figures the phrase 'law right and good conscience', which occurs three times in the sample (C 1/394/9, 547/10, 547/38) has been omitted, as has the one instance of the phrase 'equity right and good conscience' (C 1/563/18). Other phrases employed in bills in the sample in Wolsey's time include: 'shall be thought reasonable' (C 1/394/3), 'contrary to all right or truth and good conscience' (C 1/394/4), 'as … shall be thought necessary' (C 1/394/22), 'as shall be thought … most reasonable in the premises' (C 1/547/6), 'as shall be thought according to justice and good conscience' (C 1/563/29), 'according to reason equity and good conscience' (C 1/563/33), and 'as shall be thought convenient' (C 1/563/51).

[50] See, eg, *Calendars of the Proceedings in Chancery, in the reign of Queen Elizabeth* (London, G Eyre and A Strahan, 1830) vol 2, vii, *Abbot of Tynterne v Zonge*, '*droit & bone conscience*' (1426x32, or 1450x52) (the bill is printed as in the time of Henry V, though the chancellor is addressed as 'Archbishop of York', which must refer to John Kemp, chancellor in the time of Henry VI); xix, *Roper v Rollyng*, 'right and gode conscience' (the bill does not address a particular chancellor, it is printed as from the time of Henry VI); xxvii, *Saundre v Gaynesford*, 'right and consciens' (1426x1432, or 1450x52); l, *Baker v Parson*, 'right and good conscience' (1426x32, or 1450x52); lxix-lxx, *Penteney v Lady Lovell*, 'right and good consciens' (the bill does not address a particular chancellor, it is printed as from the time of Edward IV).

poetic works in early-modern England, 'equity can be found grouped with a startling range of somehow related words', including both 'conscience' and 'right', but extending more broadly to such concepts as 'charity', 'faith', 'religion', 'manhood', 'piety' and 'the law of Nature'.[51] While bills in Chancery addressed to Wolsey employ a relatively narrow range of terms, just as in poetry, 'equity' in Chancery bills in Wolsey's time is grouped with other words, in the phrases 'equity right and good conscience',[52] 'right equity and good conscience',[53] 'reason equity and good conscience',[54] 'the equity of justice and good conscience',[55] and 'equity and justice',[56] the most frequent form being 'equity right and good conscience'.

As in those addressed to Wolsey, of the 72 bills in the sample addressed to More, a clear (though smaller) majority still employed either the phrase 'right and good conscience'[57] or, less frequently, the phrase 'right and conscience', in describing the defendant's misconduct, the desired remedy, or both.[58] Again, as in the bills addressed to Wolsey, in those in More's time the term 'equity' – occurring in twelve instances – continued to be accompanied by other words, in the phrases 'right equity and good conscience',[59] 'equity right and good conscience',[60] 'equity and good conscience',[61] 'law equity and good conscience',[62] 'equity and justice',[63] 'right justice and equity',[64] and 'reason equity and good conscience',[65] the most frequent form being 'right equity and good conscience'.

In the time of Audley, the old phrases 'right and good conscience' and 'right and conscience' appeared in bills markedly less frequently than in the time of his two immediate predecessors, with under half of a sample of 108 bills containing them.[66] This reduction in frequency set the future pattern. In the chancellorships of Wolsey, More, and Audley – a period of 29 years – 214 instances of the phrase 'right and good conscience' have been found in the sample of bills.[67] Thereafter, only 30 examples have

[51] Fortier, *Culture of Equity* (n 3) 109. Compare Swinburne's observation in relation to wills that 'the testator cannot commaunde any thing that is wicked, or against iustice, pietie, equitie, honestie, &c.': H Swinburne, *A Briefe Treatise of Testaments and Last Willes* (London, J Windet, 1590) fo 5v.

[52] C 1/547/9, 563/18, 552/34, 586/62.

[53] C 1/547/16, 623/8.

[54] C 1/547/31, 563/33.

[55] C 1/563/31.

[56] C 1/498/30.

[57] Or, in one instance, 'good right and conscience'.

[58] Of 72 bills, 31 employed the phrase 'right and good conscience'; 12 the phrase 'right and conscience'; and one the phrase 'good right and conscience', giving a total of 44 among 72 bills (a little over 60 per cent).

[59] C 1/616/28, 616/29, 636/2.

[60] C 1/636/24.

[61] C 1/616/39, 636/19.

[62] C 1/616/40.

[63] C 1/636/16, 619/1.

[64] C 1/636/18.

[65] C 1/636/55.

[66] Of 81 bills, 25 employed the phrase 'right and good conscience' at least once; 9 the phrase 'right and conscience', and one the phrase 'good right and conscience', giving a total of 35 among 81 bills (a little over 43 per cent).

[67] This total includes the phrase 'right and conscience', and a small number of instances of 'good right and conscience'.

been found in the 73-year period from the beginning of Wriothesley's chancellorship[68] to the end of Ellesmere's.[69]

Over the course of the period, the dominant phrase in Chancery bills thus shifted from a widespread 'right and good conscience' at its beginning, to a predominant use at its end of the phrase 'equity and good conscience', combined with the persistent appearance, in a gradually diminishing minority of instances, of a phrase which mixed the two: 'right equity and good conscience'. It thus appears that the broad pattern of evolution in the language of the bills in our period was from 'right and good conscience' to 'equity and good conscience', with 'right equity and good conscience' providing a transitional form.[70] In this context the 'shift' from conscience to equity took the form of the replacement by 'equity' of the term 'right' in the phrase 'right and good conscience', reference to 'conscience' being retained throughout.

Turning to the language of the record, the Chancery entry books, as has been seen, infrequently refer to 'equity' in our period. The standard phrase in the bills early in the period – 'right and good conscience' – has not been found in the sample of the entry books, perhaps because by the mid-1540s, when they begin, 'equity' was beginning to

[68] 1544–47.

[69] As the numbers of bills sampled for each chancellor are neither uniform, nor proportionate to the length of each chancellorship, these figures are not directly comparable, but nevertheless indicate the general trend. For example, two bills containing the phrase 'right and good conscience' have been found in the sample in the time of Egerton/Ellesmere, as compared with 52 bills in the same period containing the phrase 'equity and good conscience'. Considering the terms 'right' and 'conscience' separately, 'right' never appears in bills in the sample unaccompanied by either 'conscience', 'equity' or both; one instance has been found in the sample of the entry books: C 33/19, fo 110v [IMG_0892] *Eston v Carpynter*, the court to take such order as is 'meet and right' following perusal of evidences by the parties' counsel. The term 'conscience', in contrast, appears in a small number of bills in the sample unaccompanied by reference to 'right' or 'equity': C 1/394/10 (Wolsey, 1515x18), petition for such order and direction 'as shall stand with conscience'; 636/22 (More), alleged that the plaintiff has done nothing 'whereby he is or ought to be bound in conscience'; 1073/35 (probably Audley), 'order of this court in conscience'; 720/7 (Audley), petition for such order and direction as thought to 'stand with conscience'; 1320/18 (Goodrich), petition for such order and direction as thought 'to stand with conscience'; 1397/28 (Gardiner), petition that the matter be 'considered and reformed by your lordship in conscience for by the common law there is no remedy'; C 2/Eliz/M2/56/1 (Egerton), claim by the plaintiff that he has offered the defendant satisfaction for costs and damages recovered at law 'although in conscience he be not bound so to do'; Jas I/B20/3/1 (Ellesmere), offer by plaintiff to pay 'so much as in conscience the [defendant] can prove due'; Jas I/B20/12/2 (Ellesmere), alleged that the defendant sought to set counterbonds on foot 'unduly and against conscience', and that a party 'was no way damnified and therefore ought not in conscience to take any benefit'. 'Conscience' has been found similarly unaccompanied in a small number of instances in the sample of the entry books and of masters' reports and certificates, either as an abstract concept or in reference to the conscience of the court or of individuals. C 33/5, fo 342v [IMG_8480], *Cokerell v Milles* (1549), assertion that the defendant 'in conscience is to be charged' with certain chattels, and reference to the defendant being allowed certain payments as the lord chancellor and the court should think 'in their conscience meet'; C 33/81, fo 1v [IMG_0003a], *Ringwood v Bulkley* (1590), reference to a bill exhibited seeking 'to be relieved in conscience'; C 38/3 pt 1, fos 372–73, *Andrew v Brinkehurst* (1600), report of Master Matthew Carew that 'I think the defendant bound in conscience to satisfy for her husband's will in such sort as by his said will he disposed'; C 38/9 (the volume is not paginated or foliated, but is arranged alphabetically by the first letter of the plaintiff's surname) *Horton v Horton* (1607), report of Master Matthew Carew that the defendant said that 'in her conscience' a certain sum of money alleged to be owed to her remained unpaid.

[70] About mid-way between Audley and Egerton/Ellesmere, in a relatively small sample of 19 bills in the time of Nicholas Bacon LK, one referred simply to 'right and good conscience' (C 2/Eliz/M2/36/1), six to 'right equity and good conscience' (C 2/Eliz/A1/18, A1/19/2, A2/21, M1/16/3, M1/37/3), five to 'equity and good conscience' (C 2/Eliz/A1/17/1, A1/49/1, M1/17, A2/18/1, A2/19/2), and two both to 'right equity and good conscience' and 'equity and good conscience' (C 2/Eliz/M1/11/1, M1/14/1).

appear in the bills. 'Right equity and good conscience' and 'equity and good conscience' likewise do not appear in the sample from the entry books, though 'equity and conscience' appears in a number of entries in the sample between the 1550s and the 1590s.[71] A variety of other phrases are also encountered in the Chancery entry books, a number of which are considered below.[72]

IV. 'Equity' in Terminological Context

We have considered so far the three phrases which predominate in the sample of bills in Chancery in the period: 'right and good conscience', 'right equity and good conscience', and 'equity and good conscience'. But these do not exhaust the terminology encountered in the sample, either in bills or in the entry books.

Before considering 'equity' in terminological context, it should first be noted that throughout the period, in describing the defendant's misconduct and the remedy sought, bills might omit any reference to 'right', 'equity' or 'conscience', the term appearing most frequently unaccompanied by reference to any of these terms being 'convenient'. In describing the remedy sought, the phrases 'thought most convenient', 'thought convenient', 'thought meet and convenient', and 'thought fit and convenient' occur in a total of 30 bills in the sample, with instances in bills addressed to Wolsey, More, Audley, Nicholas Bacon,[73] Bromley, Hatton,[74] Puckering,[75] and Egerton/Ellesmere. Thus, for example, Thomas Cobwald sought from Wolsey 'such order and direction concerning the premises as then shall be thought by your grace most convenient',[76] and Richard Blacke sought from Ellesmere 'such further order and direction therein as to your lordship shall be thought fit and convenient'.[77] These petitions have a pragmatic ring to modern ears, though to contemporaries the term 'convenient' may have carried a stronger normative sense, as in avoiding

[71] C 33/19, fo 69v [IMG_0851], *Bell v Mosier* (1558), arbitrators 'do likewise think in equity and conscience the same meet to be paid'; ibid, fo 142 [IMG_0924], *Cuturwell v Broughey* (1558), parties to appear before the lord keeper and to abide by such order as 'he shall think convenient therein according to equity and conscience'; C 33/61, fo 57v [IMG_0060a], *Hyde v Lady Elizabeth Warham* (1580), 'ought in equity and conscience to go to the relief of … More and his children'; C 33/61, fo 72v [IMG_0075a], *Cole v Finche* (1580), 'in equity and conscience'; ibid, fo 126 [IMG_0129], *Carye v Mathewe* (1580), 'in equity and conscience'; ibid, fo 132 [IMG_0135], *Napper v Napper* (1580), 'relieved … as in equity and conscience shall by this court be thought most meet and convenient'; C 33/99, fo 98 [IMG_9073], *Bysse v Willes* (1599), 'in all equity and conscience'. The phrase occasionally appeared also in master's reports, eg, *Laurence v Sharp* (1604), 'as are in equity and conscience due to him' (Master Hunt), C 38/5 (the volume is not paginated or foliated, but is arranged alphabetically by the first letter of the plaintiff's surname).

[72] By way of comparison, the phrase 'right and good conscience' has been found once in the sample of the Court of Requests entry books of appearances, final orders and decrees, REQ 1/4, fos 116v–17, 117 [IMG_0465], *Camberlam v Tyrell*. 'Right equity and good conscience' has been found in four instances, REQ 1/8 [versos IMG_0145], 'contrary to all right equity and good conscience'; REQ 1/11 [versos IMG_0652], 'contrary to all right equity and good conscience'; REQ 1/11 [versos IMG-0846], 'contrary to all right equity and good conscience'; REQ 1/11 [versos IMG_0944], 'contrary to all right equity and good conscience'. And 'equity right and good conscience' has been found once, REQ 1/5, fo 68 [IMG_0623], *Gylby v Mulsho* (1529), 'consonant to equity right and good conscience'.

[73] Lord keeper 1558–79.

[74] Chancellor 1587–91.

[75] Lord keeper 1592–96.

[76] C 1/394/43 (1515x80).

[77] C 2/Jas I/B20/30/1 (1608).

inconsistency or being fitting.[78] Reference to 'convenience', without accompanying reference to 'right', 'equity' or 'conscience', is likewise encountered in the sample of the entry books in describing the remedy sought, occurring in a number of instances in 1580 of references to end and determine, provided that should the referees fail to do so, the court should take such order as should be thought 'most meet and convenient'.[79] The defendant's misconduct could likewise be described without reference to 'right', 'equity', or 'conscience'; it might be said, for example, to have been 'much against all charity and contrary to all true dealing and honesty',[80] or to have amounted to acting 'wrongfully and unjustly'.[81]

Turning to the use of 'equity' in combination with terms other than 'right' and 'conscience' or 'good conscience', the term 'reason' (or 'reasonable') occurs in a number of instances in the sample, most frequently in the phrase 'reason equity and good conscience'.[82] Thus Thomas Rushton and his wife petitioned Wolsey to have their right in the premises in question 'according to reason equity and good conscience',[83] and Peter Mariner complained to Puckering that the defendant had refused to deliver certain deeds and muniments 'against all reason equity and good conscience'.[84] Broke J's

[78] For discussion of use of 'inconvenience' by late-medieval common lawyers, see N Doe, *Fundamental Authority in Late Medieval English Law* (Cambridge, Cambridge University Press, 1990) 161–74, suggesting that the primary meaning of 'inconvenient' was 'divorced from conceptions of abstract right and wrong', merely emphasising 'legal symmetry, certainty and consistency', ibid 169. This suggests that Klinck's tendency to understand the term 'convenience' as referring to 'pragmatic/policy concerns' may be open to question: I Williams, book review of Klinck, *Conscience* (n 3) (2011) 15 *Edinburgh Law Review* 500, 502. References to convenience are also found accompanied by references to equity and conscience, which may strengthen the view that 'convenience' was not used in Chancery in the period simply to connote pragmatism or policy, eg, C 1/702/38, C 2/Eliz/A2/38. The term 'conveniently' could also be used to refer to the propriety of procedural steps to be taken by the court, as in *Napper v Napper* (1580) C 33/61, fo 132 [IMG_0135], where the question arose as to whether an allegation 'may conveniently be examined without any new bill to be exhibited in that behalf', or by litigants, as in *Markham v Molyneux* (1580), ibid, fo 109v [IMG_0112a], where in permitting the defendant to bring an action at law, it was provided that the plaintiffs 'shall and may plead in bar thereof what they shall think most meet and convenient for them'.

[79] C 33/61, fo 6 [IMG_0009], *Darrell v Brende*; ibid, fo 22 [IMG_0025] *Moundford v Sheldon*; ibid, fo 36 [IMG_0039], *Hille v Barty*; ibid, fo 42 [IMG_0045] *Sutton v Sutton*; ibid, fo 71v [MG_0074] *Nicholas v Ravenscroft*; ibid, fo 74–74v, 74v [IMG_0077a], *Hollingworthe v Verney*; ibid, fo 74v [IMG_0077a] *Hatche* v *Cawell*; ibid, fo 88 [IMG_0091], *Garnet v Newton*; ibid, fo 107v [IMG_0110], *Harbert v Herbert*. In one further instance of the same pattern, the commissioners to end and determine were to do so 'as to their wisdoms and discretions shall be thought most meet and convenient', while if they were unable to do so, such order was to be taken as 'shall be thought meet': C 33/61, fo 140v [IMG_0143a], *Beckingshawe v Kingesmill*. Provision for the court to make such order as 'shall be thought meet' (without reference to convenience) if commissioners were unable to end and determine the matter is found also, eg, in C 33/41 [IMG_8813a], *Shelley v Apseley* (1570), and in C 33/61, fos 39v–40, 40 [IMG_0042a], *Pickeringe v Asheby*.

[80] C 1/1397, the bill is unnumbered and lacks the names of the parties and the name of the chancellor to whom it was addressed.

[81] C 2/Eliz/A2/29/1 (1597).

[82] 'Reason' had long appeared in bills in Chancery, see, eg, *Calendars* (n 50) vol 1, ii, *Downham v ap Blethyn*, petition that the court do right 'solone ley & reson demande' (the chancellor is not named, the bill is calendared as in the time of Richard II); *Calendars* (n 50) vol 2, lxviii, *Cotys v Joly*, allegation that the defendant has acted 'contrary to all reason and good consciens' (1426x32, or 1450x52) (the bill is printed as in the time of Edward IV, but the chancellor addressed is described as 'Archbishop of York', which must refer to John Kemp, chancellor in the time of Henry VI), xl, *Furby v Martyn*, petition that the defendants 'do and resseive in that behalf as the court woll award, as reason and conscience requyren' (1460x61, or 1470x71). It appears also in the time of Warham, more frequently than the term 'equity', for example, C 1/339/34 [IMG_0052] 'such further order and direction as shall stand with reason and good conscience'.

[83] C 1/563/33 (1518x29).

[84] C 2/Eliz/M2/54/3. For other examples of the phrase 'reason equity and good conscience', see C 1/547/31 (Wolsey), 636/55 (More), 702/40 (Audley), 720/19 (Audley), 1520/82 (Wriothesley), C 2/Eliz/A2/19/1

observation in 1522 that 'conscience ne fait use, mes common reason, que est common ley'[85] notwithstanding, those who drafted these bills saw no necessary incompatibility between reason and equity or conscience.

Also encountered, in both bills and entry books, is the phrase 'equity and justice', and variants of it. Thus Nicolas Gade petitioned More that the defendant be required to appear and further steps be taken 'as shall stand with equity and justice',[86] and Edward Brooke likewise petitioned Ellesmere that the defendant abide by such order 'as shall seem to stand with equity and justice'.[87] It was said in *Hare v Blumfeld* (1544) that the defendant had acted in neglect of 'iustitia et equitatem',[88] and in *Sydney v Atye* it was said in 1592 that the defendants were willing to reconvey trust land to such 'as this court shall in equity and justice think they ought to do'.[89] Those responsible for these bills, at least, did not see themselves as operating within a 'legal system structured around the two poles of justice and equity'.[90]

A number of other terms are encountered alongside 'equity' in the sample of bills. There are a few instances of 'truth', in the phrases 'truth and equity',[91] 'truth right and equity',[92] and 'truth equity and good conscience';[93] one reference to 'charity', in the

(Nicholas Bacon), A1/39 (Hatton), M2/25/1 (Puckering). The phrase 'reason and conscience', or 'reason and good conscience' is also seen: C 1/394/48 (1515x18), complaint that the defendant had acted 'contrary to all reason and conscience', C 1/1073/10 (1532x44), prayer that the defendant abide by such order as is 'most agreeable to reason and good conscience', C 2/Eliz/A2/52 (1590), complaint that the defendant had failed to act 'as in reason and good conscience he ought to do'; as are references to what is 'reasonable', C 1/394/3 (Wolsey, 1515x18), petition that the defendant abide by such order 'as shall be thought reasonable', C 1/720/17 (Audley), petition that the defendant abide by such order 'as shall be thought … most reasonable in the premises'. As Baker has observed, medieval common lawyers knew the sense of 'equity' 'as the source and spirit of all law, an abstract concept of justice' 'under the name of reason, or rightwiseness': J Baker, *Oxford History of the Laws of England, vol VI: 1483-1558* (Oxford, Oxford University Press, 2003) 40. For discussion of the role of reason in the medieval common law see Doe, *Fundamental Authority* (n 78) ch 5, arguing that 'the theorists' concept of justice and the practitioners' reason' were 'not exactly the same'; though '[o]verlapping in substance, in many respects they are equivalent': ibid 120.

[85] *Gervys v Cooke*, YB Mich 14 Hen VIII, fo 4, pl 5: 'conscience does not make a use but common reason which is common law'.

[86] C 1/636/16.

[87] C 2/Jas I/B20/4/2. For other examples of 'equity and justice' in bills see: C 1/702/21 (Audley), 720/29 (Audley), 1317/55 (Rich), 1320/23 (Goodrich), 1320/27 (Goodrich), 1320/51 (probably Gardiner), 1320/57 (probably Gardiner), 1400/5 (Heath), 1400/53 (Heath), C 2/Eliz/M1/25/1 (Bromley), Jas I/B20/2/2 (Egerton), Jas I/B20/14/2 (Ellesmere), Jas I/B20/24/4 (Ellesmere), Jas I/B20/31/1 (Ellesmere), Jas I/B20/71/1B (Brackley).

[88] C 33/1, fo 109 [IMG_3430].

[89] C 33/83, fo 461v [IMG_0446a]. For other examples of 'equity and justice' in the entry books see, C 33/2, fo 74 [IMG_3645], *Colingborne v Leighe* (1545), 'contra omnem iustitiam et equitatem', ibid, fo 184v [IMG_3750], *Gyve v Kirton*, 'contra omnem iustitiam et equitatem', C 33/3, fos 294–95, at 295 [IMG_7817], *Ap Hugh ap Nicholas v Ap Hugh ap Nicholas* (1547), commission to adjudge the matter 'according as to equity and justice shall appertain', C 33/41, fos 73–4, 73v [IMG_8851a], *Wythe v Harbottle* (1570), reference to the court taking order 'as in justice and equity it shall be thought meet', ibid, fo 104–04v, 104 [IMG_8882], *Randall v Stukeley* (1570), reference to the mayor and aldermen of London inter alia to consider a bond and determine whether it should stand or be avoided as they 'should think in justice and equity it ought to be'.

[90] Fortier, *Culture of Equity* (n 3) 139: 'In travelling to North America, the English brought with them a legal system structured around the two poles of justice and equity.' See also, ibid 109: 'Equity also finds itself set against opposing terms. To some degree this is true of the phrases "justice and equity" and "law and equity"' (referring to usage in poetry). Compare Klinck, *Conscience* (n 3) 47: '"equity" could refer to the justice or reason which was regarded as essential to law', and, similarly, Baker, *OHLE, vol VI* (n 84) 40: 'In one sense [equity] was the source and spirit of all law, an abstract concept of justice.'

[91] C 1/702/7 (Audley), allegation that the plaintiff had been condemned in the sum of £5 by a common law jury 'against truth and equity'.

[92] C 1/1400/41 (Heath), allegation of conduct 'against all truth right and equity'.

[93] C 2/Eliz/A1/36/1 (Puckering), allegation of conduct 'contrary to all truth equity and good conscience'.

phrase 'against all right equity charity and good conscience';[94] and two references to 'honesty'.[95] Perhaps more unexpectedly, the term 'law' occurs a number of times in conjunction with 'equity', in the phrases 'law and equity',[96] 'law and good equity',[97] 'law equity and good conscience',[98] and 'law right equity and good conscience'.[99]

It thus appears that those drafting bills in the period did not regard the term 'equity' as essential, and that while reference simply to 'right and good conscience' rapidly withered after Audley's time, reliance, not upon 'equity', but upon 'convenience', and what would be 'convenient', appears in descriptions of the remedy sought in more than half of the chancellorships between Wolsey and Ellesmere,[100] even where the defendant's misconduct was said to have been contrary, inter alia, to 'equity'.[101] It was clearly thought possible throughout our period for the court to be guided by considerations not expressly including 'equity', and likewise of masters of Chancery and others required to end and determine, who might be asked to do so on the basis, not of 'equity', but of 'convenience'. In cases where 'equity' was absent from a description of the defendant's conduct, it was common for it nevertheless to be employed in descriptions of the remedy sought, but it was also possible to speak of misconduct as contrary to 'equity' where the description of the remedy sought was couched in other terms: to the drafters of the bills in our period, 'equity' could be employed in describing the remedy sought, the defendant's misconduct, or both. Other terms which (less frequently) accompanied

[94] C 78/165 no 2 [IMG_0040-0047], at [IMG_0043] (1611). This case concerned a charitable trust, which may explain use of the term 'charity', though it also appears in C 1/1397, concerned with private interests in land, in the phrase 'against all charity and contrary to all true dealing and honesty' (the bill is unnumbered and lacks the name of the chancellor to whom it was addressed).

[95] C 2/Jas I/B20/55/1 (Ellesmere), 'contrary to all honest dealing equity and good conscience', C 1/1397 (see n 80 above). See also *Castell v Baker* (1566), C 78/31 no 6, mm 6–11, 6, view of commissioners to determine, that 'Henry Brograve is bound in honesty to perform the said promise or at the least is bound in conscience to restore unto the said heir such sums of money as he has gained by the bargain and sale of the said lands'. No reference has been found to 'mercy'.

[96] 'Law and equity' has been found also outside the sample of bills, eg, C 78/105, no 15, mm 35–end, m 36 [IMG_0071], *Gostling v Kynge* (1600), allegation that the defendant had failed to keep an agreement or pay certain money 'contrary to all law and equity', in pleadings recited in the enrolled decree; C 33/107, fos 30v–31, 31 [IMG_5056], *Merrick v Mason* (1604), allegation that 'both by law and equity' certain land should have been assured in a particular way.

[97] C 2/Eliz/A2/12/3 (Bromley), allegation of defendants' failure to deliver up muniments 'as by law and good equity they ought to do'.

[98] C 2/Eliz/A2/21/1 (Nicholas Bacon), petition for such order as shall be thought to stand and agree 'to law equity and good conscience'; A1/16/1 (Hatton), allegation that the defendant had taken profits of a wood 'contrary to all law equity and good conscience'; M2/19/3 (Puckering), allegation that profits of land had been taken 'contrary to all law equity and good conscience'; M2/50/1 (Puckering), allegation of failure to pay certain money 'contrary to all law equity and good conscience'; A1/58 (Egerton), allegation of attempt to gain title to land 'contrary to law equity and good conscience'; C 2/Jas I/B20/59/1 (Ellesmere), allegation of action brought at law 'contrary to all law equity and good conscience'.

[99] C 1/1397/22 (Gardiner), allegation of detention of plate 'contrary to all law right equity and good conscience', C 1/1320/55 (probably Gardiner), allegation of refusal to deliver muniments 'contrary to all law right equity and good conscience'.

[100] Those of Wolsey, More, Audley, Nicholas Bacon (lord keeper), Bromley, Hatton, Puckering (lord keeper), and Egerton (lord keeper)/Ellesmere. See n 78 above.

[101] See, eg, C 2/Eliz/M2/46/1 (Egerton), defendant's conduct described as 'against all right equity and good conscience', and order sought as 'shall be thought meet and convenient', M2/24/1 (Puckering), defendant's conduct described as 'against all right equity and good conscience', and order sought 'as shall be thought most meet and convenient', A2/3 (Hatton), defendant's conduct described as 'contrary to all right equity and conscience', and order sought as 'shall be thought meet and convenient'.

equity, such as 'truth', 'charity', 'honesty', 'justice' and 'law', were, in contrast, normally employed only in descriptions of the defendant's misconduct, though it was possible at least for 'justice' and 'law' to appear in describing the remedy sought.

The frequency with which 'equity' was accompanied by other terms – a phenomenon seen more broadly in this period[102] – suggests a degree of flexibility, and perhaps imprecision in its meaning. A defendant might act contrary to 'equity', and an order might be made in accordance with it. Conduct which was contrary to 'equity' might simultaneously be contrary to 'right', 'conscience', 'law', 'justice', 'charity', 'truth' or 'honesty'. And while in describing the remedy sought a more limited range of terms was employed, orders in accordance with 'equity' would usually simultaneously be in accordance with 'conscience' and frequently also with 'right'. In this light we might well concur with Fortier that the 'complexity' of equity 'is a product of different ideas, each complex it itself'.[103] The terms accompanying 'equity' in the bills may give colour to its meaning as carrying a sense of rightwiseness, but the question remains why the chancellor's English-side jurisdiction came to be firmly understood as being simply in 'equity', such that as early as 1572 the Chancery's approach to uses upon uses could be described as being contrary to that of the common law, 'equitatis causa'.[104]

V. 'Equity' Alone

The term 'equity' used alone is not commonly encountered in bills in Chancery in the period, at least before the time of Egerton/Ellesmere. Before Egerton's time the sample provides only three clear instances of such unaccompanied use of 'equity' in Chancery bills, two in Bromley's time[105] and one in Hatton's,[106] with a further possible instance of uncertain date.[107] A somewhat larger number of instances of 'equity' used alone appears in the sample of bills in the time of Egerton/Ellesmere: four such instances have been found in bills addressed to Egerton,[108] and nine in bills addressed to Ellesmere,[109]

[102] See n 51, above.

[103] Fortier, *Culture of Equity* (n 3) 22.

[104] See n 2, above.

[105] C 2/Eliz/A2/57/1, complaint of inability at common law to recover a rent, 'although there be great cause in equity that your … orators should have the same', M2/52/1, assertion of lack of remedy 'except by the equity of this honourable court'.

[106] C 2/Eliz/A1/11, petition that defendant abide by 'such further order as to your lordship in equity shall be thought meet'. A further example Hatton's time may arguably be provided by A1/42/3, though here the term 'equity' is not far removed from a reference to 'conscience', the plaintiff seeking a remedy 'by the clemency and mercy of your good lordship as the equity of his cause in conscience shall deserve'.

[107] C 2/Eliz/M1/38, petition that defendant abide by 'such further order and direction therein as to your good lordship shall in all equity seem meet and convenient'. A substantial part of this bill is missing, rendering dating impossible; it is numbered between a bill addressed to Nicholas Bacon and one addressed to Egerton. The term 'equity' is not far removed here from a reference to what is 'meet and convenient'.

[108] C 2/Eliz/A1/44, petition for relief 'as shall stand with equity and the full intent and meaning of all the parties aforesaid', A1/45, allegation that a mortgage in question 'is not anything available in equity to bar your … orator', M1/10, argued that a conveyance 'ought in equity to be void', and that any conveyance was upon trust, and 'satisfied and discharged in equity and true meaning', M2/59/1, argument that certain writings obligatory were 'in equity and true meaning' intended to be held upon trust.

[109] C 2/Jas I/B20/5/1, reference to goods and chattels which 'in all equity did and do belong' to the plaintiff, assertion that the defendants seek to defraud the plaintiffs of certain debts, B20/10/4, 'which they will

though as a proportion of the 88 bills in the sample in the time of Egerton/Ellesmere, these numbers are small. Those who drafted bills in Chancery in the period rarely used the term 'equity' without accompaniment.

While 'equity' not infrequently appeared alongside another term or terms in describing the defendant's alleged misconduct, it was occasionally employed alone in that context. Thus, for example, Richard Bartlett and Thomas Wrenford complained to Ellesmere that the defendants would 'contrary to all equity', 'assuredly' defraud the plaintiffs of certain debts were remedy not provided in Chancery.[110] Again, while bills in the period not infrequently included 'equity' alongside another term or terms in describing the remedy sought, the term was also employed alone in that context. Thus, for example, in *Lord Stafford v Thynne* (1599), Egerton LK intended 'to have some of the judges with him' in the hearing of the matter, and 'then thereupon to take such order as is agreeable to equity'.[111]

The very large majority, however, of the instances in the sample of 'equity' used without accompaniment occur not in the bills but in reports of cases, in reports of Chancery masters, and in the entry books and decree rolls. The instances of such use in these contexts date predominantly from the last three decades of the period,[112] and broadly concern either 'equity' as a name for a jurisdiction or 'equity' as a body of rules, principles or standards. In some instances the use of 'equity' to denote a jurisdiction is clear. Thus in *Verney v Lee* (1535) it was reported that a decree had been made '[u]pon … hearing of the cause in equity',[113] phrasing which appears again in the report of *More v Taylor* (1587).[114] In *Kerrye v Shepparde* (1614), the Chancery plaintiff feared that tenants of the manor in question would 'exhibit their bill of complaint into some one of his majesty's courts of equity',[115] and in *Cleare v Lady Heydon*, Master Matthew Carew in 1595 regarded the defendant's demurrer as not 'sufficient in this court of equity to

assuredly do contrary to all equity', unless a remedy is provided in Chancery, B20/11/1, assertion that the plaintiff 'is the more to be pitied and his case in equity to be relieved', that certain land does 'in all equity belong' to the plaintiff, that certain conduct by the defendant would be 'fit and agreeable unto equity', and a petition for a remedy as 'in equity shall seem meet', B20/12/2, assertion that certain counterbonds 'ought in equity to be discharged', B20/14/2, petition for certain steps 'to the end that the [defendant] may in equity be compelled to deliver' an indenture to the plaintiff, C 2/Eliz/B20/15/2, assertion that the defendant had acted 'contrary to equity', and that the plaintiff had no other means of relief 'but only in course of equity … in this honourable court', C 2/Jas I/B20/20/1, assertion that the plaintiff had no means to recover 'but in equity', B20/21/1, assertion that the plaintiffs 'have no relief … but in this court in equity', B20/24/4, expression of hope by the plaintiffs that 'they shall be relieved in equity'.

[110] C 2/Jas I/B20/10/4. Outside the sample of bills, another example is provided by C 33/81, fo 37v [IMG_0039a] *Burye v Conisbye* (1590), where it was said that a verdict at law had been obtained 'upon a very strict and extreme point in law contrary to all equity'.

[111] C 33/99, fo 2 [IMG_8974].

[112] It should be remembered in considering the chronology that reports of Chancery cases appear in greater numbers in the final decade of the sixteenth century and later than earlier in the century, and that most of the surviving masters' reports are from the 1590s and later (the earliest volume of masters' reports and certificates, C 38/1, commences in 1562, though most of its contents are from the early 1590s).

[113] 117 *Selden Society* 366 no 165[1]. The case dates from Audley's time, though the manuscript contains reports of cases up to 1610 which concern judgments at common law examined in Chancery, suggesting a compilation made in the 1610s in the context of jurisdictional tension between the common law judges and the Chancery.

[114] 117 *Selden Society* 373 no 165[17]. The case appears in the entry books at C 33/73, fo 435 [IMG_0437] which, unlike the report, refers not to 'equity' alone, but to 'equity or conscience', and simply to 'conscience'.

[115] C 78/177 membrane unnumbered, no 1 (in the pleadings recited in the enrolled decree).

preclude the answering' of the bill.[116] A clear jurisdictional usage of 'equity' is likewise found in the period in reports of common law cases. In *Westwick v Wyer* (1591) it was said in the King's Bench that one to whose use copyhold land had been surrendered, 'had no remedy in a court of equity, to compel the lord to admit him';[117] in *Martin v Marshall* (1615) the Common Pleas considered whether 'a court of equity may be by prescription'; and in *Cotts and Suckerman v Warner* it was resolved in the King's Bench in 1615 that 'no court of equity ought to meddle after a judgment'.

In other instances, use of 'equity' to denote a body of rules, principles or standards is likewise clear. In *Solicitor-General v Lord Cromwell* (1593) Masters Matthew Carew and Legge reported that the plaintiff had exhibited a bill in Chancery against the defendant's father, who had died before the hearing. The plaintiff sought revival of the suit, the defendant demurring that he was not bound by the prior proceedings because the premises had descended to him in entail. While leaving the decision to the court, the masters observed that 'by the common and ordinary course of this court which has otherwise used it, and by the rules of equity, we think the same answerable in this court'.[118]

Master Matthew Carew again referred to the 'rules of equity' in *Coles v Thynne* (1595), where the defendant, executor of Sir John Thynne, had had certain land conveyed to him and others as trustees for payment of debts and a legacy. Having taken the profits, but failing to pay the legacy, the defendant demurred to a bill in Chancery, arguing that the covenant conveying the land was not 'good and effectual in law' to raise or make any use or to charge the land with legacies, as it was not supported by any 'matter or consideration valuable in law'. While not committing himself as to the law, Carew, referring to 'the rules of equity', held that 'the heir in conscience ought to perform his father's deed, whether it be profitable or burdening unto him', and that the defendant should answer to the bill, 'unless this court shall otherwise overrule it on point of law',[119] and it was in this sense that Coke CJCP reported in Chancery in *Kinge v Saunderson* (1612) that it stood well both with his order upon the defendant's submission at *nisi prius*, 'and with the equity of the cause', that the lease in question, or its value, be evenly divided between the parties.[120]

Turning from these relatively clear instances of 'equity' used to refer to a jurisdiction or to rules applied in Chancery, in a large number of instances in the sample where 'equity' appears alone, it is difficult to be certain whether it was understood as referring to a jurisdiction or to rules, principles or standards, or, perhaps, to both. This is true, for example, of some uses of the phrase 'the equity of the cause'. Thus in *Kenne v*

[116] C 38/1 (the volume is not paginated or foliated), the report is dated Trinity 1595. See also, eg, Master Thoresby's report in *Dysney* v *Thornhaughe* (1607) C 38/9 (the volume is not paginated or foliated, but is arranged alphabetically by the first letter of the plaintiff's surname) that 'the daughter of the plaintiff has good means to recover by the common law or in equity at her choice', and Master Bird's observation in *Marman v Reston* (1611) C 38/17 (the volume is not paginated or foliated, but is arranged alphabetically by the first letter of the plaintiff's surname) that the Oxford Vice-Chancellor's Court was 'as well a court of equity as of law'.

[117] 4 Co Rep 28a, at 28b. For other instances in this period see Sir John Baker, ch 6 in this volume.

[118] C 38/1 (the volume is not paginated or foliated), 18 May 1593. The plaintiff solicitor-general was Edward Coke. It was alleged that the copyhold had been surrendered to his use by 'one Franklyn' in consideration of marriage between Franklyn's son and Coke's sister, Dorothy.

[119] C 38/1 (the volume is not paginated or foliated), 15 July 1595.

[120] C 38/17 (the volume is not paginated or foliated, but is arranged alphabetically by the first letter of the plaintiff's surname), 15 February 1612.

Beckwith (1570), the court was minded 'to take further order according to the equity of the cause',[121] which might seem to suggest reference to rules, principles or standards, but might, alternatively, be understood as indicating the basis for jurisdiction, the latter sense appearing more strongly in *Carter v Smyth* (1614), where Master Tyndall 'thought reasonable' that a trial of title to certain land be held at common law, 'the equity of the cause being still reserved to this court'.[122] Both senses of 'equity' may appear in *Hyde v Holland* (1599), where the legal validity of a lease was referred from Chancery to Walmsley and Fenner JJKB, with direction that should they find the lease void at law, they were to certify 'how far forth in their opinions the plaintiff may be relieved in equity in this court', and that thereupon 'this court will be pleased to take such order in equity between the parties as shall be meet for the quieting of all further suits between them'.[123] Here the question of how far the plaintiff might be relieved 'in the equity of this court' seems closer to a question of how far equitable grounds existed for relief, while the making of an order 'in equity' appears to contrast the Chancery's jurisdiction with that of the common law courts. Further ambiguity in the term 'equity' used alone appears in Serjeant Puckering's opinion in Chancery in *Gylman v Rothermaker* (1590) that 'there is no cause in equity wherefore the plaintiffs' should pay past rents to the defendant.[124] It seems here close to impossible to be certain whether 'cause in equity' refers to jurisdiction or to the substance of the point, and the two are largely merged in Master Matthew Carew's view in *Ward v Langeman* (1594) that 'the equity of this court' might not permit a certain common practice of merchants in London: there was clearly a point of substance here, but it was the substance 'of this court'.[125] Instances could be multiplied,[126] but the ambiguity may ultimately be incapable of resolution: if a rule, principle or standard of equity were to be applied, its application might inherently be expected to occur in an equitable jurisdiction.[127]

VI. Conclusion

The evidence considered in this chapter suggests that the term 'equity', while present in Chancery bills no later than the end of Warham's chancellorship in 1515, was rarely employed before Wolsey's fall in 1529. Its rise thereafter surely owed much to St German's *Doctor and Student*, though there was no immediate 'shift' to equity in the bills following publication of the treatise; rather the term was initially combined with existing terms – particularly the long-established 'right and good conscience' – to

[121] C 33/41, fo 82v [IMG_8860a].
[122] C 38/20, fo 299.
[123] C 33/99, fo 116 [IMG_9091].
[124] C 33/81, fo 13v [IMG_0015a].
[125] C 38/1 (the volume is not paginated or foliated), 30 April 1594.
[126] Another instance of such difficulties of interpretation appears, eg, in the phrase 'great equity', as in Master Matthew Carew's view in *Hallowell v Tedcastle* (1593) that the matter set out by the plaintiff had 'show of great equity to be considered of by this court', C 38/1 (the volume is not paginated or foliated), 12 May 1593.
[127] As may be reflected in Master Tyndall's view in *Bird v Arblaster* (1607) that the matter was 'fittest for the common law no matter of equity appearing before me to retain the cause in this court', C 38/9 (the volume is not paginated or foliated, but is arranged alphabetically by the first letter of the plaintiff's surname), 24 June 1607.

produce 'right equity and good conscience' (and variants of it). Subsequently, 'right' began to fall into disuse, leaving by the end of the period 'equity and good conscience' as the predominant phrase in the bills, 'equity' being employed in bills both in descriptions of the defendant's misconduct and of the remedy sought. Certain phrases became common form, but variety remained possible. The term 'equity' might be accompanied in bills not only by 'right' or 'good conscience', but also by other terms, including 'truth', 'justice', 'law' and 'reason'; and while reference to 'equity' became standard in bills as the period progressed, at no stage was it thought to be essential in describing either the defendant's misconduct or the remedy sought.

References to 'equity' alone are infrequent in bills in the period, though they appear in some numbers in other sources, particularly in the period's closing decades. The meanings of 'equity' used in this way seem largely to connote either the jurisdiction of the court or the rules, standards or principles applied there, often in ways which overlap or coincide. As has been seen, discussion giving a more detailed or precise sense of the meanings of Chancery 'equity' in the period is not plentiful. There are, however, a few suggestions in the sample as to what Chancery equity was thought to be, and as to the grounds which might comprise 'matter in equity'.

While it has been observed that by Lord Nottingham's time 'it could even be said, without a hint of paradox, that a contract without consideration was binding in conscience but not in equity',[128] signs of a distinction between conscience and equity may be seen almost a century earlier. In *Fortescue v Forde* (1580) Bromley C, Wray CJKB and Cordell MR 'thought not meet either in equity or conscience' to agree to the defendant's petition that an interest in a lease be saved to him,[129] and in the same year it seemed to the court in *Dotson v Dotson* that the 'plaintiff is neither in equity nor conscience to be relieved by this court'.[130]

As to indications of what might comprise 'matter in equity', in 1582 commissioners of bankrupts reported their view that 'in equity and conscience … the said silks ought to pertain to [one of the parties] for that he bought the same upon his own credit'.[131] In *Earl of Cumberland v Bygate*, Master Matthew Carew reported in 1594 that the earl[132] had appointed the defendant captain of the privateer *Assuerance*, 'to do his best service to the earl in his voyage', but that having captured a vessel laden with goods of great value, the defendant had left the *Assuerance* and purloined some of the goods. This being so, Carew observed that 'the equity is that the service not being performed, the hire is not to be paid'.[133] In *Hayward v Trumble* (1596) Masters Cosin and Hunt found that the

[128] Baker, *Introduction* (n 1) 119, referring to a dictum of Lord Nottingham C in *Honywood v Bennett* (1675), in DEC Yale (ed), *Lord Nottingham's Chancery Cases, vol I* (1957) 73 *Selden Society* 214, no 307: 'if this note were voluntary and without consideration, though it did bind the son in honour and private conscience, with which I had nothing to do, it could not bind him in legal and regular equity'.

[129] C 78/80, no 5, mm 5–9, 8 [IMG_0017].

[130] C 33/61, fo 146v [IMG-0149a]. See also C 2/Jas I/B20/12/2 (1615), where it was alleged that certain counterbonds 'ought in equity to be discharged', but that the defendant sought to set them on foot 'unduly and against conscience'.

[131] C 38/1 (the volume is not paginated or foliated), 9 March 1582.

[132] Presumably the third earl, George Clifford (d 1605), a notable privateer, see P Holmes, 'Clifford, George, third earl of Cumberland (1558–1605)' Oxford Dictionary of National Biography (Oxford University Press, 2004) doi.org/10.1093/ref:odnb/5645.

[133] C 38/1 (the volume is not paginated or foliated), 25 January 1593/94.

plaintiff sought relief in Chancery from forfeiture of a bond at law, against which the defendant argued that as the defendant's father's executor, the plaintiff had deceived and diminished the defendant by more than the value of the bond, for which loss, action upon the bond was the defendant's only remedy. This being so, the masters observed that 'with good equity rigour of law may be extended against such as are only protected from payment by the like rigour'.[134] And in *Cranley v Foster* (1615), Master Bird reported that the 'substance of the matter in equity suggested in the bill, is a combination between' a father and a son 'to set on foot a deed of annuity' to defeat the plaintiff's extents upon certain land.[135]

There is little sophistication in most of these views,[136] which carry a similar sense of rightwiseness as is suggested by the terminology of the bills, bearing little, if any, connection with 'equity' either in the Aristotelian sense[137] or as it was understood in medieval scholastic theology.[138] It was at least possible during the period to enunciate aspects of substantive equity – even on occasion to speak of 'rules' of equity – and for chancellors to seek guidance in decision-making from the previous practice of the court, but the substantive development of 'equity' was as yet in its earliest stages. As a matter of terminology, however, 'equity' was becoming well settled during the period as a name both for the Chancery's jurisdiction and for the approach which it took in resolving disputes.

If a single term were to be adopted, the sample suggests two other possible candidates: 'right' and 'conscience'. While they should not be discounted in seeking to understand the nature of the Chancery's jurisdiction in the period, 'right', and indeed such other terms as 'justice', 'truth' or 'honesty', may well have seemed overly broad to be suitable. 'Conscience' was an ancient Chancery term, persistently present in bills throughout the period, and employed alone in both bills and the entry books and masters' reports.[139] The reasons why 'equity' prevailed over 'conscience' may be beyond certain recall, and perhaps no more than semi-apparent to contemporaries, though the movement after

[134] C 38/1 (the volume is not paginated or foliated), 27 January 1596.

[135] C 38/20, fo 307. And see also Serjeant Barham's dictum considered at p 187, above.

[136] Compare Ibbetson's characterisation of the treatment of equity in Lord Ellesmere's 'justificatory essay' in the *Earl of Oxford's Case* as 'theoretically unsophisticated', 'little more than a collection of standard points which could be said to justify equitable intervention': Ibbetson, 'A House Built on Sand' (n 3) 75. See also Master Matthew Carew's observation in *Danvers v Whyte* (1608) that 'it is agreeable to common sense that no man should be bound by a void agreement', C 38/9 (the volume is not foliated or paginated, but is arranged alphabetically by the first letter of the plaintiff's surname), the report is dated 9 February 1607/08.

[137] As Ibbetson has observed, in applying Aristotelian conceptions of equity to 'the situation which obtained in English law', St German was using tools which were 'simply not the right ones for the job': Ibbetson, 'A House Built on Sand' (n 3) 60.

[138] See Maniscalco, '*Interpretatio ex Aequo et Bono*' (n 4) 239–41.

[139] This was true even in the final decades of the period, eg, C 2/Jas I/B20/3/1 (1607), assertion by the plaintiff of willingness to pay 'so much as in conscience the said [defendant] can prove due', B20/12/2 (1615), assertion that a party 'was no way damnified and therefore ought not in conscience to take any benefit', C 33/81, fo 1v [IMG_0003a], *Ringwood v Bulkley* (1590), court informed by counsel that the plaintiff had 'exhibited a bill into this court against the defendant to be relieved in conscience' touching a lease made upon trust, C 38/99 (the volume is not paginated or foliated, but is arranged alphabetically by the first letter of the plaintiff's surname), *Dunscombe v Blake* (1607), Master Matthew Carew's opinion that the defendant 'in conscience' ought to ratify a lease, C 38/20, fos 49–50, *Baylye v Roper* (1614), at fo 50, opinion of Masters Hunt and Tyndall that 'in a good conscience' the defendants should accept an offered release of title to certain freehold, but 'we leave it to the conscience of the court'.

Wolsey to common law-trained chancellors and a desire to emphasise the jurisdiction's regularity – manifested, under the influence of *Doctor and Student*, by Lord Ellesmere himself, as he 'volubly insisted that equity was an aspect of law rather than a product of discretion'[140] – may have had a part to play. If the term 'equity', 'one of the key ideas in general currency' in early-modern England,[141] burgeoned in Chancery practice in consequence of *Doctor and Student*, the same influential treatise was to mould the jurisdiction itself, contributing to the formation, as Lord Nottingham put it, of 'legal and regular equity'.[142]

[140] JA Guy, *Christopher St German on Equity and Statute* (1985) 6 *Selden Society Supplementary Series* 94. Guy observes that notes from the first dialogue of *Doctor and Student* survive in Ellesmere's hand: ibid, 94, fn 184. Ellesmere referred to *Doctor and Student* in his 'justificatory essay' in the *Earl of Oxford's Case* (1615) 1 Chan Rep 1, 13; 21 ER 485, 488. In St German's view, as Plucknett and Barton put it, conscience 'must always be founded upon some law', and was thus by no means 'merely the subjective sense of right and wrong possessed by a particular individual': *Doctor and Student* (n 3) xxvi.

[141] Fortier, *Culture of Equity* (n 3) 2.

[142] *Honywood v Bennett* (1675) 73 *Selden Society* 214, no 307.

10

Insolvent Debtors in Law and Equity, 1543–1624

FLEUR STOLKER*

I. Introduction

On 10 October 1620, William Steward, a tradesman, was awarded a debt settlement by the Court of Chancery.[1] The order not only included his release from debtor's prison, but also consisted of the recovery of his estate and a reduction of his debts. Some of his creditors had put Steward in the prison of the King's Bench in May that year in the hope that he, or his wife, would pay his debts. In addition to his incarceration, some of his creditors had sued out a commission of bankrupts, accusing Steward of being a bankrupt, a fraudster who, despite owning a house the value of which seemed enough to pay his debts, was not willing to sell and pay his creditors.

However, the Commissioners of Bankrupts decided otherwise: Steward's house had been bought in jointure with his wife, and his wife was not prepared to sell it. This meant that Steward was unable to pay his debts. Steward had not defrauded his creditors and was cleared from the bankruptcy allegations. Therefore the creditors, who had seized the estate in the procedure, were not able to execute the bankruptcy and sell the house for their benefit.

Nevertheless, most of his creditors were eventually persuaded to give Steward a reduction of debts and, together with Steward, exhibited a petition for a debt settlement in the Court of Chancery. The Lord Chancellor, Francis Bacon, awarded the settlement and forced the remaining creditors to conform to the settlement. Steward was released from prison and had to pay his creditors a reduced rate within a year of his release.

The facts of *Steward v Mountford* (1620) show that even though William Steward was an insolvent tradesman and appeared to be fraudulent (because he appeared to have the sole ownership of the house), he was not certified as being a bankrupt, simply

* Unless otherwise indicated, all manuscripts are held in The National Archives in Kew, London. The image number of the manuscripts included is taken from the digital archive on 'The Anglo-American Legal Tradition' website, available at aalt.law.uh.edu/aalt.html. Quotations from manuscripts and printed sources have been rendered into modern spelling. The year is taken to begin on 1 January.

[1] *Stiaard (Steward) v Mountford*, 10 October 1620 C 33/139 f 75 [IMG_0080]. For the full case see the masters' report, *Steward v creditors* by Bowyer and Paule, 21 July 1620 C 38/40.

because he had not deceived his creditors.[2] Like bankruptcy law today, bankruptcy law in early modern England only applied to insolvent debtors who fell within the scope of the bankruptcy statutes and the accompanying legal process. From the enactment of the Statute of Bankrupts 1543, when bankruptcy law was first introduced in England, this meant that the insolvent debtor had defrauded their creditors by denying them financial satisfaction, and from the Bankrupts Act 1571 onwards, the insolvent debtor also had to be a trader.[3] The aim of these statutes was not to punish the insolvent debtor (although that was considered a welcome bonus for the creditors), but to give as much financial satisfaction to the bankrupt's creditors as possible. This objective was achieved by the pro rata distribution of the assets of the bankrupt.

The law that was not codified in the bankruptcy statutes was classed as insolvency law. In theory insolvency merely describes a state of financial distress, but the term was used for all insolvency matters that fell outside of the bankruptcy statutes. Today, fraudulent and blameless bankruptcy are separated into two distinct legal jurisdictions: criminal law and civil law.[4] In early modern England, law and legal practice made a similar distinction. The formal bankruptcy laws dealt with fraudulent insolvent debtors, who were effectively criminals, while the Privy Council, the Court of Requests and the Court of Chancery, all having a broadly equitable jurisdiction, dealt with the blameless insolvents.[5] These three bodies all dealt with insolvent debtors who did not fit the requirements of the statutes. They could award debt settlements to a debtor and their creditors, thereby simulating the aims of the bankruptcy statutes for creditors of honest insolvent debtors, whether those insolvents were traders or not.

Scholarship in relation to insolvent debtors in early modern England has mainly relied on the interpretation of the bankruptcy statutes, and therefore has primarily been focussed on the law relating to fraudulent insolvent debtors.[6] It has been argued that before the Bankruptcy Act 1705, English law did not make a distinction between fraudulent and honest debtors.[7] However, the law concerning blameless insolvent debtors was simply not codified, has hardly been reported, and has therefore largely been forgotten.[8] This chapter aims to fill this gap in the literature and shows how insolvent debtors were treated not only at law, but also in equity from the mid-sixteenth to the early seventeenth centuries.[9]

[2] *Steward v creditors* by Bowyer and Paule, 21 July 1620 C 38/40.

[3] Statute of Bankrupts 1543 (34 & 35 Hen VIII, c 4), preamble; Bankrupts Act 1571 (13 Eliz I, c 7), s 1.

[4] A Keah and P Walton, *Insolvency Law Corporate and Personal*, 4th edn (London, LexisNexis, 2017) 711–721. Some misconduct can be pursued by civil actions.

[5] WJ Jones, 'The Foundations of English Bankruptcy: Statutes and Commissions in the Early Modern Period' (1979) 69 *Transactions of the American Philosophical Society* 5.

[6] See, eg, IPH Duffy, 'English Bankrupts, 1571-1861' (1980) 24 *American Journal of Legal History* 283; E Kadens, 'The Last Bankrupt Hanged: Balancing Incentives in the Development of Bankruptcy Law' (2010) 59 *Duke Law Journal* 1229; J Cohen, 'The History of Imprisonment for Debt and its Relation to the Development of Discharge in Bankruptcy' (1982) 32 *Journal of Legal History* 155.

[7] See, eg, WS Holdsworth, *A History of English Law, vol 8* (London, Methuen, 1925, reprinted London, Sweet and Maxwell, 1992) 229–230; Kadens, 'The Last Bankrupt Hanged' (n 6) 1229–1319.

[8] But see Jones (n 5) 5; DA Smith, 'The Error of Young Cyrus: The Bill of Conformity and Jacobean Kingship, 1603-1624' (2010) 28 *Law and History Review* 307–341; FJJ Cadwaller, 'In Pursuit of the Merchant Debtor and Bankrupt: 1066-1732' (University of London doctoral thesis, 1965) vol 2.

[9] This study is primarily based on a sample of the Chancery entry books of decrees and orders (class C 33) and the Decree Rolls (class C 78). The following Michaelmas terms in the entry book have been examined C 33/1 (1543–44 and 1544–45); C 33/2 (1545–46, 1546–47 and 1547–48); C 33/3 (1548–49

First, it sets out the main idea of statutory bankruptcy and its accompanying procedure, referred to by the Court of Chancery as the 'common law procedure'.[10] It shows that the procedure was introduced as an alternative to debtor's prison, but while it was not introduced with the aim of punishing insolvent debtors, it effectively worked as a criminal procedure. This rationale behind the bankruptcy statutes is important because it explains why equitable insolvency was more flexible and allowed a discharge of debts.

Secondly, the chapter examines the practice of debt settlements of the Court of Chancery. It reveals that the Chancery showed consistent practice in favour of honest insolvent debtors. In theory, the Court of Chancery balanced the interests of the debtor and his creditors. However, in practice the Chancery almost always supported the vulnerable, such as widows, the elderly and orphans. In every instance, these debtors were the financially weaker party. Thirdly, this chapter examines the link between statutory bankruptcy and insolvency practice in the Chancery. It shows that interactions mainly took place at the level of the commissions of bankrupts, but some cases also show that the Court of Chancery explicitly distinguished bankruptcy from insolvency. Finally, it concludes that bankruptcy and insolvency, while based on similar principles and ideas and existing alongside each other since the first introduction of bankruptcy law in 1543, were two procedures that ultimately had very little to do with one another.

II. Insolvent Debtors at Law: Statutory Bankruptcy and the Bankruptcy Procedure at Common Law

Before the introduction of the first bankruptcy statute in 1543, England had relied on the common law writ system in order to deal with insolvency.[11] By the mid-sixteenth century, of these writs, *capias ad satisfaciendum* was the most used.[12] *Capias ad satisfaciendum* used the body of the debtor as a security for a debt.[13] It gave the sheriff the power to put the debtor in debtor's prison until the debt was satisfied, with the aim of trying to push

and 1549–50); C 33/37 (Michaelmas 1568–69); C 33/77 (Michaelmas 1588–89); C 33/97 (Michaelmas 1599–1600); C 33/111 (Michaelmas 1606–07); C 33/119 (Michaelmas 1610–11); C 33/127 (Michaelmas 1614–15); C 33/135 (Michaelmas 1618–19); C 33/139 (Michaelmas 1620–21); C 33/143 (Michaelmas 1622–23); C 33/157 (Michaelmas 1627–28). The Chancery decree rolls were surveyed by using and relying on the calendars between 1543 and 1628 provided on the AALT website. The search term used was 'bankrupt', which would include both 'bankrupt(s) and 'bankruptcy', as well as 'conformity' and 'settlement'. The search term 'settlement' resulted in many results, as this is not only limited to settlements after insolvency, but also, for example, land disputes. Only the summary of the cases given in the calendars were examined to decide whether to read a case in full or not. A total of over 50 debt settlement cases were found in this sample. All volumes of the Acts of the Privy Council dating between 1543 and 1628 have been read. The State Papers from that period have been consulted by search terms, bankr*, insolvent, bill of conformity and debt settlement. The terms trade, merchant, conformity, debt settlement, debtor and fugitive provided too many entries. Petitions to the Crown to issue commissions of bankrupts found in the State Papers have been deliberately excluded from the analysis, because it is not clear whether such petitions were dealt with by the Court of Chancery, the Privy Council or Parliament.

[10] *Howse v Lea*, 2 December 1591 C 33/83 f 255 [IMG_0247]. See below for details about the common law procedure.

[11] DP Waddilove, 'The Mendacious Common-law Mortgage' (2018) 107 *Kentucky Law Journal* 425.

[12] Holdsworth (n 7) 231.

[13] The Statute of Westminster 1352 (25 Edw 3 st 5 c 17).

the debtor or their family and friends to pay the debts.[14] This meant that the writ was only effective when the debtor or his associates were able to pay the debts, but unwilling to do so.[15] This meant that in practice, *capias ad satisfaciendum* was often not a very effective method for creditors to get their money back. The writ was particularly unhelpful in two scenarios, namely when the debtor was either fraudulent or destitute. If the debtor had conveyed his assets away to others, the writ gave no power to creditors to get hold of these hidden assets. When the debtor was destitute and unable to call on assistance from relatives or friends, the debtor simply had no prospect of ever being released. In that case, the debtor became reliant on charity donations in order to survive his time in prison, which was of no benefit to anyone, and certainly not to creditors.

Another shortcoming of *capias ad satisfaciendum* was that it could only be used by one creditor at a time. This mechanism could have a negative impact on the credit status of the debtor, because creditors could only get financial relief on a first-come, first-served basis, which in turn could incentivise a run on the debtor's assets. The Statute of Bankrupts 1543 was intended to address this problem and introduced an alternative to debtor's prison: a system of collective debt recovery.[16] In this new procedure all the creditors could pursue the insolvent debtor at the same time. In order to give every creditor as much financial relief as possible, all the creditors would accept a reduction in the debts owed to them, and the proceeds of the available estate of the insolvent debtor would be divided pro rata amongst the creditors.[17]

A. The Bankruptcy Statutes

The bankruptcy procedure could not be used in every state of insolvency. The Statute of Bankrupts 1543 was only designed to address the problem of debtors who were able to pay their debts but took fraudulent steps to avoid payment.[18] Bankrupts were fraudulent debtors, who had committed one of the acts set out in the statute with 'the intent or purpose to defraud or hinder any of his or her creditors'.[19] In the 1543 statute these fraudulent acts were limited to those who left their usual dwelling place ('flee to parts unknown') or stayed in their houses ('keep their houses') in order to avoid paying their creditors, but these 'acts of bankruptcy' expanded over the course of the century.[20]

At least three government officials at a time could be asked to form a committee to deal with the bankruptcy procedure, eventually ending up in the Privy Council.[21] One of these committee members was generally the Lord Chancellor, the other being other Privy Councillors, and in some cases including one of the common law Chief

[14] JH Baker, *An Introduction to English Legal History*, 5th edn (Oxford, Oxford University Press, 2019) 74.
[15] Holdsworth (n 7) 231.
[16] The Statute of Bankrupts 1543 (34 & 35 Hen VIII, c 4).
[17] The Statute of Bankrupts 1543 (34 & 35 Hen VIII, c 4), s 1.
[18] The Statute of Bankrupts 1543 (34 & 35 Hen VIII, c 4).
[19] The Statute Bankrupts Act 1543 (34 & 35 Hen VIII, c 4), preamble; Bankrupts Act 1571 (13 Eliz I, c 7), s 1; Bankrupts Act 1604 (1 Jac I, c 15), s 1; Bankrupts Act 1624 (21 Jac I, c 19), s 2.
[20] The Statute of Bankrupts 1543 (34 & 35 Hen VIII, c 4), s 1.
[21] ibid.

Justices.[22] The committee members were given special powers to get access to the property of the bankrupt. The most important provision was that the committee could get access to all landed property of the bankrupt and was able to sell it for the benefit of the creditors.[23] This was a significant improvement compared to the common law writs system, where the remedies for creditors were restricted to chattels and limited charges over land.

In the period covered by this study, Parliament supplemented the original bankruptcy statute three times, in 1571, 1604 and 1624.[24] This meant that all the statutes existed in parallel and had to be 'largely and beneficially construed and expounded for the aid, help and relief of the creditors'.[25] On rare occasions, the common law courts were petitioned to give clarifications over the interpretation of the bankruptcy statutes.[26] Three amendments made by the Bankrupts Act 1571 were especially important for the development of bankruptcy law.

First, it gave the Lord Chancellor the sole bankruptcy jurisdiction and the power to grant commissions of bankrupts.[27] The bankruptcy procedure was involuntary and a private procedure in the period. It seems that the Lord Chancellor would generally exercise his jurisdiction in the Court of Chancery, but the records of the Privy Council show that some cases ended up there as well.[28]

Secondly, the statute was confined to traders, who had to be English nationals, citizens of the overseas territories or denizens.[29] There was nothing in the statutes about the position of foreign creditors, and it was argued in 1580 that merchant strangers could not benefit from the existing bankruptcy statutes.[30] The rationale behind this was that merchant strangers in London had explicitly negotiated that they would not be liable as bankrupts within the 1571 statute, and why should they have the 'advantage to take the benefit and not be subject to the pain'?[31] Nevertheless, it seems that the Court of Chancery allowed merchant strangers to benefit from the bankruptcy statutes. This meant that foreign creditors of bankrupts could invoke the bankruptcy procedure but could not be classed as bankrupts themselves. This must have angered English creditors, especially as various countries on the continent had reciprocal arrangements for both

[22] ibid.

[23] ibid.

[24] Bankrupts Act 1571 (13 Eliz I, c 7); Bankrupts Act 1604 (1 Jac I, c 15); Bankrupts Act 1624 (21 Jac I, c 19).

[25] Bankrupts Act 1624 (21 Jac I, c 19), s 1.

[26] See, eg, *Smith v Mills* ('*The Case of Bankrupts*') (1584) 2 Co Rep 25a, 76 ER 441; *Smith v Mills* (1589) Moo 594, 805; 72 ER 780. The common law also dealt with a substantial number of defamation cases following the unjust suing out of commissions of bankrupts.

[27] Bankrupts Act 1571 (13 Eliz I, c 7), s 2.

[28] ibid. That cases could end up in the Privy Council as well could be concluded after reading the Acts of the Privy Council from 1540 until 1628.

[29] Bankrupts Act 1571 (13 Eliz I, c 7), s 1. Denizens were foreigners who were made subjects by royal prerogative under letters patent of denizenation. Sir John Baker, *Oxford History of the Laws of England, vol VI, 1483-1558* (Oxford, Oxford University Press, 2003) 615–616.

[30] 'Opinion on the right of strangers to partake of bankrupts goods rateably with English creditors' by an unknown source, 1580 SP 12/146 f 232. See also *Certain merchant strangers creditors v Pope*, 2 September 1597 C 33/93 f 182 [IMG_6310]; *Disley v Leman*, 30 August 1621 C 33/140 f 1275 [IMG_1302]; *Larmite v Somerman*, 21 October 1624 C 33/147 f 98v [IMG_0101a].

[31] 'Opinion on the right of strangers to partake of bankrupts goods rateably with English creditors' by an unknown source, 1580 SP 12/146 f 232.

foreign bankrupts and foreign creditors. That foreign creditors could benefit from the statutes was explicitly stated in the Bankrupts Act 1624.

Thirdly, the 1571 statute explicitly included women within its scope.[32] In practice, this meant that widows and *femmes sole* could also be classified as bankrupts.[33]

Throughout the entire period bankruptcy was classified as a crime, in the form of a misdemeanour, and a bankrupt was therefore classified as a criminal. A bankrupt had 'the intent or purpose to defraud or hinder any of his or her creditors'.[34] However, the preambles of the four statutes suggest that the English legislature had trouble defining exactly what a bankrupt was. In each statute the definition of a bankrupt was extended because insolvent debtors were 'avoiding and deluding' the existing laws.[35] The preamble of the Statute of Bankrupts 1543 states that

> where divers and sundry persons obtaining into their hands great substance of other men's goods … not minding to pay or restore to any of their creditors their debts and duties, but at their own will and pleasures consume the substance obtained by credit of other men, for their own pleasures and delicate living, against all reason, equity and good conscience.[36]

The definition used in the preamble of this early statute looks like a variation of theft, rather than fraud. In his *Treatise against Usury* from 1547, one of the first published English texts discussing bankruptcy, the clergyman Richard Porder explicitly made this connection: 'wicked men that spend other men's goods … with [the] mind to defraud the creditor: and such are worse than a thief, and ought to die as well as the thief'. He continued:

> the better sort, or rather such, as are not so ill (for there are no degrees in evil things) are those that borrow men's money or goods … and so make their creditors to bear the adventure … and then the bankrupts do pay all, or almost all that is left, to their creditors they think themselves discharged. And though these men be not so evil as the other: yet certainly they are greatly in fault, and worthy of sharp punishment, and to be bound men to their creditor.[37]

Porder thus made a distinction between two types of 'evil' bankrupts. The distinction between fraudulent and reckless or frivolous bankrupts was sometimes made in continental legal systems as well, for example in Germany, but England did not distinguish between those two types in its legislation:[38] the Acts were merely there 'to prevent the deceitful actions of bankrupts'.[39] Nevertheless, the language used in the preambles to

[32] However, the letter of the text in the 1543 statute does not necessarily exclude the possibility of female bankrupts.

[33] See, eg, E Allen, 'Bankruptcy, Law and the Economics of Gender: the Act against Bankrupts of 1571' (Utah State University doctoral thesis, 1999).

[34] Bankrupts Act 1571 (13 Eliz I, c 7), s 1. See also Bankrupts Act 1604 (1 Jac I, c 15), s 1; Bankrupts Act 1624 (21 Jac I, c 19), s 1.

[35] See, eg, Bankrupts Act 1624 (21 Jac I, c 19), preamble.

[36] Statute of Bankrupts 1543 (34 & 35 Hen VIII, c 4), preamble.

[37] R Porder, *A Sermon of gods fearefull threatnings for Idolatrye, mixing of religion, retayning of Idolatrous remnaunts, and other wickednesse: with a Treatise against Usurie. Preached in Paules Churche the xv. daye of Maye 1570. being Monday in Whitson weeke* (London, H Denham, 1570) www.proquest.com/books/sermon-gods-fearefull-threatnings-idolatrye/docview/2248518548/se- 2?accountid=13042 accessed 31 October 2022.

[38] M Lindemann, *The Merchant Republics. Amsterdam, Antwerp, and Hamburg, 1648-1790* (Cambridge, Cambridge University Press, 2017) 268. It is possible that Lindemann discusses the law at a later period in time, but this is not clear from her book.

[39] Bankrupts Act 1604 (21 Jac I, c 19), preamble.

define bankrupts became stronger over time. The 1604 bankruptcy statute refers to those who 'wickedly and wilfully become bankrupt', and the 1624 refers to bankrupts as 'evil minded persons'.[40] Each new statute expanded the definition of a bankrupt and increased the powers of the Commissioners. From the Bankrupts Act 1604 onwards, bankruptcy procedures no longer ended with the death of the alleged bankrupt, and in the Bankrupts Act 1624, the Commissioners of Bankrupts were even given the power to break open the doors of alleged bankrupts. This meant that the principle 'a man's house is his castle' as formalised by Lord Chief Justice Coke in *Semayne's Case* (1604), which is still a leading case in constitutional law today, did not apply in relation to bankruptcy.[41]

The punishment desired by Porder was not imposed by the early bankruptcy statutes, although there had been some fruitless discussion of making bankruptcy a felony with the suggestion that bankrupts should be whipped to death.[42] The punishment for bankruptcy in the four early statutes was largely monetary, but the Commissioners also had the power to imprison uncooperative bankrupts or outlaw them.[43] The Jacobean statutes introduced harsher punishments for bankrupts. The Bankrupts Act 1604 implemented corporal punishment for perjury, where false statements were made under oath by those accused of bankruptcy in an effort to avoid liability under the bankruptcy statutes.[44] In the Bankrupts Act 1624 the legislature extended this harsh punishment to all declared bankrupts who had wilfully defrauded or deceived their creditors for £20 or more.[45] The corporal punishment could be imposed after indictment and required the bankrupt to 'stand upon the pillory in some public placed by the space of two hours, and have one of his ears nailed to the pillory and cut off'.[46] The purpose of this shaming ritual seems to have been not only to destroy the reputation of the debtor, but also to deter other potential debtors from fraudulent practices. It is not surprising that all four bankruptcy statutes enacted in the period excluded the possibility for the bankrupt to be discharged of their debts.[47]

[40] Bankrupts Act 1604 (1 Jac I, c 15), preamble; Bankrupts Act 1624 (21 Jac I, c 19), preamble.

[41] Bankrupts Act 1624 (21 Jac I, c 19), s 7; *Semayne's Case* (1604) 5 Co Rep 91a, 77 ER 194. For a recent example, see *Fearn v Board of Trustees of the Tate Gallery* [2023] UKSC 4.

[42] Provision for this was part of the bill for the Statute of Artificers (1559) and the bill for the Bankrupts Act 1624. See for the bill for the Statute of Artificers (1559), *An industrial programme*, nr 17 Hist MSS Com MSS of the Marquis of Salisbury, vol I, 162–65 in RH Tawney and E Power (eds), *Tudor Economic Documents, being Select Documents Illustrating the Economic and Social History of Tudor History*, vol I (London, Longmans Green and Co, 1951) 328. See for the bill for the Bankrupts Act 1624, the 'brief of the bill exhibited against bankruptcy'. Mr Louther reports the Bankrupts Bill. Amendments twice read. A Proviso tendered from the Committee, to make it Felony, if the Bankrupt stand out Six Months, and come not in after Proclamation. The Proviso, upon Question, rejected. The Bill ordered to be 'ingrossed'. 'House of Commons Journal Volume 1: 29 April 1624' in *Journal of the House of Commons*: vol 1, 1547–1629 (1802), *British History Online* www.british-history.ac.uk/commons-jrnl/vol1/29-april-1624 accessed 23 February 2021; An Act for the further Description of a Bankrupt, and Relief of Creditors against such, as shall become Bankrupts; and for inflicting corporal Punishment upon the Bankrupts, in some special Cases: – Upon Question, passed. 'House of Commons Journal Volume 1: 03 May 1624', in *Journal of the House of Commons*: vol 1, 1547–1629 (1802), *British History Online* www.british-history.ac.uk/commons-jrnl/vol1/03-may-1624 accessed 23 February 2021.

[43] See, eg, The Statute of Bankrupts 1543 (34 & 35 Hen VIII, c 4), ss 1 and 5.

[44] Bankrupts Act 1604 (1 Jac I, c 15), s 4.

[45] Bankrupts Act 1624 (1 Jac I, c 15), s 6.

[46] Bankrupts Act 1604 (1 Jac I, c 15), s 4; Bankrupts Act 1624 (21 Jac I, c 19), s 6.

[47] Statute of Bankrupts 1543 (34 & 35 Hen VIII, c 4), s 6.

B. Bankruptcy Procedure at Common Law

As has been seen, the Bankrupts Act 1571 gave the Lord Chancellor (or Lord Keeper) the power to grant commissions of bankrupts.[48] These commissions dealt with bankruptcy matters at first instance, following a common law procedure.[49] When Commissioners of Bankrupts made a 'certificate' of a bankruptcy, they applied the law as set out in the various bankruptcy statutes. Commissions of bankrupts had to establish whether a debtor was bankrupt by considering three questions of fact: (1) whether the debtor was a trader within the statutes; (2) whether he or she had committed a fraudulent act of bankruptcy; and (3) what the amount of debt of the alleged bankrupt was.[50] The general procedure was that one or more of the creditors of the alleged bankrupt requested the Lord Chancellor to issue a commission of bankrupts. The creditors of the alleged bankrupt could nominate several Commissioners of Bankrupts, of whom the Lord Chancellor appointed about three to five to act as Commissioners.[51] These Commissioners were often local aldermen or fellow local traders. It seems that the bankrupt could approve or disagree with the choice of Commissioners, but it is unknown whether this took place before the appointment of the commission of bankrupts or after the Lord Chancellor had made the appointment of the commission.

The Commissioners were not acting as judges, but, under the Statute of Bankrupts 1571, the Lord Chancellor delegated an administrative power to imprison the bankrupt, and to seize and sell real and personal property in order to distribute the profits rateably to the creditors according to the quantity of their debts. After the bankruptcy proceeding, but before the execution of the bankruptcy, one of the creditors was generally appointed to act as an assignee in bankruptcy, effectively acting as a custodian of the bankrupt's property until the Commissioners of Bankrupts were able to sell the property. Once a commission of bankrupts was instructed, the Lord Chancellor lost the authority to deal with the matter. The Lord Chancellor could only review or rehear the case if the commission of bankrupts had finalised the process. The alleged bankrupt could petition the Lord Chancellor by petitioning the Court of Chancery or Privy Council. On very rare occasions, the Lord Chancellor exercised his discretion to review or rehear the case himself.[52]

It seems that, apart from the Standing Orders of the Court of Chancery of 29 January 1618–19, there were no formal rules in the period in relation to commissions of bankrupts.[53]

[48] Bankrupts Act 1571 (13 Eliz I, c 7), s 2.

[49] ibid.

[50] The standard formula of the dockets of the commissions was 'A commission of bankrupts against [bankrupt's name] of [place of residence] of the county of [county of place of residence], [trade], broken about [date] last past, for the sums of [amount of debt (or thereabouts/or upwards of)] [day of the granting of the commission]'. See the dockets of the commissions of bankrupts of Lord Keeper Puckering. The dockets of Puckering LK are held in the Huntington Library. They can be found in the Egerton family papers, Part I. Lord Chancellor Ellesmere, up to 1617, Domestic and Personal Papers, Official Papers. The relevant dockets used are EL 3076; 3241; 3258; 3397; 3414; 3421; 3481; 3522; 3523; 3543; 3558; 3566; 3583; 3853; 3854; 3991; 3998; 4036; 4072; 4092; 4093; 4098; 4270; 4271; 4279; 4395; 4640; 4732; 4799; 4871; 4973; 5313; 5370; 5392; 5521; 5525; 5579; 5608; 5610. It is possible that this list is not complete.

[51] The dockets of Puckering LK show that the Lord Keeper generally would choose the Commissioners of Bankrupts from a list of seven potential Commissioners. This can be derived from the dockets.

[52] See *Allen v Edwards* (*Allen's Case*), 20 October 1608 C 78/172/13 m unknown [IMG_0009]; *Allen v Hubberstye*, 3 February 1614 C 78/125/11 m 1 [IMG_0002]. *Allen v Hubberstye* is the final decree of *Allen's Case*.

[53] GW Sanders, *Orders of the High Court of Chancery and Statutes of the Realm Relating to Chancery. From the Earliest Period to the Present Time*. Vol I, part I (London, A Maxwell & Son, 1845) 122.

The main provisions in the Standing Orders set out that one Commissioner had to be learned in the law.[54] Care had to be taken 'that the same parties be not too often used in commissions', perhaps to safeguard the variety of people who acted as Commissioners and prevent corruption.[55] The petitioner also had to enter a bond with good security of at least £200 to prove the debtor a bankrupt.[56] This was to deter creditors from making false accusations of bankruptcy and unjustly suing our commissions of bankrupts. It was not uncommon that commissions of bankrupts were sued out without reason; generally this was done by rival traders.[57]

WJ Jones has suggested that the annual average number of bankruptcies in the late Elizabethan and Jacobean periods may not have been much over ten, allowing for the increase in the number of commissions of bankrupts granted in the depression years.[58] This small number seems to be an underestimate.[59] It seems unlikely that Parliament would have supplemented a statute three times if it was only applicable in a few cases a year. It seems probable that more bankruptcies were decided by commissions of bankrupts, which might also have resulted in mediation. It appears that evidence to that effect has not survived, though a list of bankruptcies in the Lansdowne Papers shows that in 1571 alone forty bankruptcies took place in various parts of England.[60] This number is significantly higher than that suggested by Jones.

III. Insolvent Debtors in Equity: Insolvency Procedure in the Court of Chancery

The Lord Chancellor (or Lord Keeper) had an equitable jurisdiction to supplement the bankruptcy statutes.[61] This meant that from the first introduction of the Statute of Bankrupts 1543, a parallel equitable insolvency jurisdiction emerged.[62] The Lord Chancellor could exercise this power in the Privy Council and in the Court of Chancery,[63] but it seems that in the period 1543–1624, insolvent debtors more often petitioned the

[54] ibid.

[55] ibid.

[56] ibid 141.

[57] See, eg, *Wood v Hayes*, 9 February 1606 C 33/111 f 436v [IMG_9003a] at f 438 [IMG_9005]; *Moseley v Alsopp*, 25 April 1627 C 78/426/2 m 1 [IMG_0258]; *Cornellius v Blackmore*, 15 October 1614 C 33/127 f. 25 [IMG_0026]; by Julius Caesar, 10 March 1614 C 38/20; by Julius Caesar, 19 July 1614 C 38/ 20; by Julius Caesar, 8 December 1614 C 38/20; May 1615 C 33/127 f 1048v [IMG_1041a].

[58] Jones (n 5) 5.

[59] Jones himself accepts that the number might be an underestimate.

[60] Lansdowne Vol/13 f 54. These bankruptcies mainly took place in London, but some occurred in other places, such as York and Devon.

[61] Baker (n 14) 116–118.

[62] It is unclear whether the equitable function in relation to insolvency matters existed before the introduction of the bankruptcy statutes. It seems likely that insolvent debtors could petition the Court of Requests, Privy Council and Court of Chancery for a debt settlement before the introduction of the Statute of Bankrupts 1543. See T Stretton, *Women Waging Law in Elizabethan England* (Cambridge, Cambridge University Press, 1998) 75; Smith (n 8) 316–324. However, more research needs to be done in relation to insolvent debtors in the Court of Requests. The records of the Privy Council before 1540 have sadly not survived. There were also other ways to deal with insolvency. It seems that commissions for relief of poor prisoners had decided in matters involving insolvent debtors according to equity and good conscience at least since 1539.

[63] The Court of Requests had also an equitable jurisdiction to deal with insolvency matters, however, it seems that the Privy Council did not have an equitable jurisdiction in relation to the bankruptcy statutes.

Privy Council than the Court of Chancery. The Privy Council mostly awarded moratoriums, which consisted of a delay of payment combined with a royal protection, which resulted in a temporary suspension of actions at common law.[64] This meant that it was not uncommon for some debtors to keep reappearing in the Privy Council. For example, Dame Mary Wroth (the famous poet) reappeared three times in the Privy Council to renew her royal protection.[65] It seems that the Court of Chancery was more drastic in its measures. It was not uncommon for the court to award debt settlements, which often included a discharge of debts for the insolvent debtor. It is therefore not surprising that some debtors and their creditors reappeared in the Chancery, after having already been to the Privy Council.[66]

A. Debt Settlements in the Court of Chancery

The Court of Chancery consistently awarded debt settlements to debtors and their creditors in order to achieve the same aim as the bankruptcy statutes: to give the creditors of bankrupts as much financial relief as possible.[67] This meant that if a debtor did not fall within the scope of the bankruptcy statutes, the debtor, together with their creditors, could petition the Court of Chancery for financial relief. If there was no support for a debt settlement from all the creditors, the majority of the creditors and the debtor could petition for a bill of conformity. Using this procedure brought the advantage that the Court of Chancery could then force refractory creditors to agree with the debt settlement. The Lord Chancellor would not only look at the interests of the creditors, but also balance these with the interests of insolvent debtors based on 'equity and conscience'. In this way, the Court of Chancery seems to have encouraged the release of insolvent debtors from debtors' prison and to have encouraged reasonable, and sometimes charitable, compromises between debtors and creditors throughout most of the period.

In a debt settlement the Court of Chancery simulated the bankruptcy statutes. The creditors generally took a deduction of their debts owed to them, in return for pro rata payment from the debtor's available assets. Creditors, especially those who had no higher security interest than a bond, generally accepted such a debt settlement, because a debt settlement gave most creditors pro rata relief, which meant that they would at least get some financial satisfaction, and would be better off than when only one of them sued at common law and obtained a *capias ad satisfaciendum*.[68] The Chancery had more flexibility to get financial relief for the creditors. It could award

[64] This is concluded after reading all the Acts of the Privy Council for the period 1540 to 1628. The Privy Council also awarded debt settlements, or alternative options to enhance the financial position of the debtor. The Acts of the Privy Council are not very detailed and the consideration sometimes why insolvent debtors would get a debt settlement is unclear.

[65] The name appeared 4 times in the Act of the Privy Council in the period 1540–1628. For information about Mary Wroth, see M Lamb, 'Wroth [*née* Sidney], Lady Mary (1587?–1651/1653)' Oxford Dictionary of National Biography (Oxford University Press, 2004) doi.org/10.1093/ref:odnb/30082 [Retrieved 30 Jan 2023].

[66] See, eg, *Leecheland v James*, 5 November 1596 C 33/91 f 444v. [IMG_477a]; *Shippe v Underhill*, 17 October 1620 C 33/139 f 47v [IMG_0052a].

[67] FC Stolker, 'Bankruptcy in Early Modern England: Bankruptcy and Insolvency in the Early Modern Court of Chancery, 1543-1628' (University of Oxford doctoral thesis, 2022). See also FC Stolker, 'The Forgotten History of Bankruptcy, 1543–1624' (2023) 44(3) *Journal of Legal History* 295–324.

[68] On the topic of secured lending in the period, see Waddilove (n 11) 425.

not only a reduction of debts, as authorised by the bankruptcy statutes, but also a delay of payment or alternative payment plan, under which the debtor would generally take a reduction of debts and pay those debts back over a period of several years.[69] Unlike the bankruptcy statutes, which expressly provided that a discharge of debts was not allowed because the debtor's conduct was fraudulent, the Court of Chancery could financially rehabilitate the debtor by awarding a part – or full – discharge of debts.[70] This was achieved by issuing injunctions against proceedings at common law.[71] The Court of Chancery did not have the power to extinguish the debts at common law but, by awarding an injunction, was able to prevent the creditors of the insolvent debtor from suing for their debts at common law. The Chancery sometimes only ordered a temporary injunction, which in effect was merely a moratorium, but it was much more common that an injunction would be awarded indefinitely, effectively leading to a discharge of debts.

Whether the Court of Chancery was willing to award a debt settlement was dependent on four factors: (1) the conduct of the debtor; (2) the debtor's cooperation in the settlement procedure and willingness to pay the debts; (3) the circumstances of the debtor; and (4) the circumstances of the creditors.[72] The main requirement for the Court of Chancery to award a settlement was that the debtor must have become insolvent in an 'honest' manner.[73] This meant that the debtor must have become insolvent through circumstances beyond their own control, either due to the insolvency or conduct of others, or by their own misfortune. In practice, this meant that the Court of Chancery awarded debt settlements if the insolvency of the debtor had occurred due to acts of God, such as flooding, 'casualties at sea', or simply 'great losses'.[74]

Widowhood and suretyship were two other common ways to acquire debts without any fault of the insolvent debtor.[75] For example, in *Palmer v Rudd* (1620), the Chancery awarded a debt settlement to Susan Palmer, a widow, who had become insolvent after she inherited her late husband's insolvent deceased estate.[76] Suretyship was slightly less

[69] Stolker (n 67) 94–97.

[70] See, eg, *Sandys v Gresham*, 28 November 1589 C 33/80 f 271 [IMG_0234]; *Finch v Hicks*, 19 January 1620 C 33/137 f 770v [IMG_0778a].

[71] See, eg, *Johnson v Wolmer*, 3 November 1551 C 78/6/28 m 13 [IMG_0028]; *Finch v Hicks* 19 January 1620 C 33/137 f 770v [IMG_0778a].

[72] Stolker (n 67) 134–145, 155–164.

[73] Indeed, when a merchant or trader had acted fraudulently and became insolvent, he or she would be considered a bankrupt.

[74] See, eg, *Pollard v Reeve*, 18 November 1620 C 33/139 f 224 [IMG_0218]; by Richard Moore, 28 November 1620 C 38/40; by Richard Moore, 5 December 1620 C 38/40; *Smith v Ashton*, 12 May 1620 C 33/137 f 1242 [IMG_0788]; 11 July 1620 C 33/137 f 1642 [IMG_1190]; 17 October 1620 C 33/139 [IMG_0353]. See also one of the reports by the commissioners, *Smith v Ashton* by Thomas Middleton and Thomas Bennett, 19 June 1620 C38/40; *Nicholls v Tryon*, 9 November 1620 C 33/139 f 525 [IMG_0519]; *Wright v Jennings*, 28 November 1614 C 33/127 f 141 [IMG_0138].

[75] For widowhood, see, eg, *Palmer v Rudd (Palmer v creditors)* 19 January 1619 C 33/135 f 422a [IMG_1592a]; 27 January 1619 f 465v [IMG_1636a]; 1 February 1619 f 480 [IMG_1650]; by Thomas Bernett and Edward Barkham, 27 November 1620 C 38/40.

[76] *Palmer v Rudd* (1620) was effectively a case concerning a deceased insolvent estate. Susan Palmer inherited the debts of her late husband, Robert Palmer. In *Palmer v Rudd* (1620) the deceased insolvent estate was part of a bill of conformity procedure. *Palmer v Rudd (Palmer v creditors)*, 19 January 1619 C 33/135 f 422a [IMG_1592a]; 27 January 1619 f 465v [IMG1636a]; 1 February 1619 f 480 [IMG_1650]. The certificate of the composition has survived. See *Palmer v Rudd* by Thomas Bernett and Edward Barkham, 27 November 1620 C 38/40. For suretyship see, eg, *Tyffin v Hart*, 22 April 1618 C 33/133 f 839 [IMG_0844];

straightforward, given that the surety had voluntarily taken a risk by entering into the suretyship arrangement.[77] An argument by a surety that they were a blameless insolvent debtor may only have carried weight where the surety could say not only that they had not acted fraudulently but also that the principal debtor had incurred the debts in an honest manner and had not tried to defraud the creditors. In other words, when considering the petition of a surety, the Court of Chancery would also take the conduct of the principal debtor into account.

For example, in *Tyffin v Hart* (1619), Bacon LC awarded a settlement to two brothers.[78] He explicitly mentioned in one of his orders that the debts of their father, the principal debtor, had been incurred bona fide.[79] The Court of Chancery also awarded debt settlements if the debts of the insolvent debtors were incurred as the result of the fraudulent conduct of others. For example, in *Sandys v Gresham* (1589), the debtor, an insolvent law student, was awarded a reduction of debts followed by a discharge of debts because he had acquired his excessive debts by entering usurious loan agreements.[80] Similarly, in *Brooke (or Little) v Goode* (1620), the Court of Chancery ordered a delay of payment of four years because the debtor had become insolvent due to unjust lawsuits brought against him, bad debts and 'evil' servants.[81]

In addition to the 'honesty' requirement, it seems that the Chancery was more willing to award a debt settlement if the debtor had been cooperative in the settlement proceedings and had made an attempt to pay their debts. In *Tyffin v Hart* (1619), Bacon LC explicitly complimented the Tyffin brothers for their cooperation in the debt settlement procedure. Furthermore, the debtor's circumstances could persuade the Court of Chancery towards a debt settlement, although these were generally not a stand-alone reason to award a settlement. Examples of persuasive mitigating circumstances were the debtor's age, their status in society and their family responsibilities. In *Sandys v Gresham* (1589), Hatton LC was

> moved with compassion as well towards the plaintiff's unfortunate estate thus driven either perpetually to lie in prison otherwise to fly the Realm, his native country, being a young gentleman who might have done good service therein.[82]

In contrast, in his master's report in *Middleton v Holt* (1620), Haywarde considered that 'partly also in consideration both of the complainant's age, and his decay by means of his imprisonment', Francis Middleton should be let out of prison for a year to settle his

16 May 1618 C 33/133 f 933 [IMG_0942]; 20 June 1618 C 33/133 f 1229 [IMG_1241a]; 26 October 1618 C 33/135 f 111 [IMG_1277]; 29 October 1618 C 33/135 f 115 [IMG_1281]; 12 November 1618 C 33/135 f 159v [IMG_1324a]; 5 December 1618 C 33/135 f 301v [IMG_1469a]; 16 January 1619 C 33/135 f 417 [IMG_1586]; 22 February 1619 C 33/135 [IMG_1869a]; 20 April 1619 C 33/135 f 997 [IMG_2169]; 15 May 1619 C 33/135 f 979 [IMG_2151]. The final decree shows that Robert Tyffin was in the 'trade of brewing': KC4/1/27 (held by the History Centre in Kingston-upon-Thames, Surrey).

[77] For sureties and debt settlements, see Stolker (n 67) 146–153.

[78] *Tyffin v Hart*, 12 November 1618 C 33/135 f 159v [IMG_1324a]. More details about the case are given in n 119 below.

[79] ibid.

[80] *Sandys v Gresham*, 28 November 1589 C 33/80 f 271 [IMG_0234].

[81] *Brooke (or Little) v Goode*, 23 November 1619 C 33/137 f 528 [IMG_0537].

[82] *Sandys v Gresham*, 28 November 1589 C 33/80 f 271 [IMG_0234] at 273 [IMG_0236].

affairs with his creditors.[83] Middleton was a seventy-year-old tradesman at the time of his imprisonment in the Fleet prison.[84] As has been seen already, the debtor in *Brooke (or Little) v Goode* (1619) was awarded a debt settlement.[85] Francis Brooke, the debtor, had been the mayor of Abingdon, Oxfordshire, four times at the time of his insolvency, where

> he had many ways well deserved and done good for the town and hath heretofore had an estate able to support the reputation and the said place, which is now decayed.[86]

The court was also motivated to support Brooke's petition because he was unable to maintain himself, his wife and seven children.[87] The Chancery records also show that petitions for a debt settlement were often supported when a father or widow could no longer support their families.[88]

The Court of Chancery did not only take the interest of the debtor into account, but aimed to strike a balance between the interests of the debtor and the creditors.[89] Most of the petitions for a debt settlement were supported by the majority of the creditors, and the Chancery was then easily persuaded to award the settlement. The Court of Chancery always decided in favour of the financially weaker party, which in practice was always the insolvent debtor. However, creditors with strong security interests, such as a mortgage, statute merchant or staple, or a recognisance, or 'those [creditors] that are trusted on the behalf of others being orphans', could be excluded from a debt settlement and had to be paid in full.[90]

B. The Equitable Insolvency Procedure

The procedure for obtaining a debt settlement in the Chancery took place in a slightly different way than the bankruptcy procedure at common law. It was generally the debtor, together with the creditors, who petitioned the Court of Chancery for a debt settlement. The bill could either be exhibited directly in the Chancery or could be referred to the court by either the monarch or the Privy Council.[91] A limited number of cases during

[83] *Middleton v Holt* by Haywarde, 15 August 1620 C 38/39. See for one of the entries of this case, *Middleton v Holt*, 28 October 1620 C 33/139 f 355 [IMG_0349].

[84] ibid.

[85] *Brooke (or Little) v Goode*, 23 November 1619 C 33/137 f 528 [IMG_0537].

[86] ibid.

[87] ibid.

[88] See, eg, *Dawley v West*, 11 January 1619 C 33/135 f 406a [IMG_1574a]; *Dawley v West* by Bowyer and Paule, 19 June 1619 C 38/30; *Petre v Waterhouse*, 16 May 1621 C 33/139 f 993 [IMG_0989]; 6 October 1621 C 33/140 f 1286v [IMG_2626]; 23 October 1621 C 33/141 f 53v [IMG_0055a]. *Petre v Waterhouse* by Hawarde, 29 July 1621 C 38/42; *Nicholls v Tryon* 9 November 1620 C 33/139 f 525 [IMG_0519]; *Brooke (or Little) v Goode* 23 November 1619 C 33/137 f 528 [IMG_0537]. It is possible that Bacon LC respected the jointure of the wife of Steward, and did not force a sale of the house, because if the wife were to become a widow, she would no longer have the property that her parents had set aside upon her marriage for her maintenance in later life: *Steward v creditors* by Bowyer and Paule, 21 July 1620 C 38/40.

[89] Stolker (n 67).

[90] *Tyffin v Hart*, 20 April 1619 C 33/135 f 997 [IMG_2169] at 998v [IMG_2170a].

[91] See, eg, *Leecheland v James*, 5 November 1596 C 33/91 f 444v. [IMG_477a]; *Shippe v Underhill*, 17 October 1620 C 33/139 f 47v [IMG_0052a].

the reigns of King Edward VI and Queen Elizabeth I suggests that bills in this period were directly exhibited into the Chancery.[92] During the reign of King James I, it was common for insolvent debtors to petition the King for debt relief. In fact, this was standard procedure in a bill of conformity case. Upon receiving the petition, James I would generally refer the case to the Lord Chancellor or Lord Keeper, who would deal with the petition in the Court of Chancery. Usually the case would then immediately be referred to a commission of bankrupts or committee to deal with factual evidence concerning insolvent debtors.[93] This meant that the case would (temporarily) be referred to an inferior tribunal.

The commission of bankrupts or another committee in charge of the settlement proceedings would often have to consider the same questions as in a bankruptcy procedure: (1) whether the debtor was a trader within the statutes; (2) whether he or she had committed a fraudulent act of bankruptcy; and (3) the amount of the insolvent debtor's debt. The Commissioners would use witness statements and affidavits to determine the answers to these factual questions.[94] Most witness statements were made by merchants and aldermen in the town of residence of the insolvent.[95] On some occasions the Chancery would also consider depositions of witnesses and documents.[96] Generally, most of the factual evidence was collected by the Commissioners of Bankrupts before the start of the Chancery procedure, although the Chancery was able to instruct Commissioners to provide the court with factual evidence throughout the entire process.[97]

Mediation played a major role in the equitable insolvency procedure.[98] It was mostly used to persuade creditors to agree to a debt settlement. Mediation seems usually to have been voluntary, but *Sir John Wentworth's Case* (1620) shows that mediation on occasion could be compulsory.[99] Mediation could take place before the commencement of the procedure, in which case it was mostly done by a committee or commission, usually consisting of aldermen.[100] During the insolvency procedure, mediation became the task

[92] This is based on the sample used to conduct this research. See above for the methodology of the sample. See, eg, *Johnson v Wolmer*, 3 November 1551 C 78/6/28 m 13 [IMG_0027]; *Sandys v Gresham*, 28 November 1589 C 33/80 f 271 [IMG_0234]; *Ashbye v Richardson*, 15 April 1597 C 33/91 f 770v [IMG_5094a]; *Warren v Eldrington*, 19 September 1600 C 33/97 f 681v [IMG_8265a]; 20 February 1601 C 33/99 f 380 [IMG_9355]; 15 July 1601 C 33/99 f 728 [IMG_9703]; *Peers v Ward*, 21 October 1614 C 33/127 f 49 [IMG_0051]; *Rudd v Gamsall*, 23 January 1602 C 33/103 f 288v [IMG_2501].

[93] *Ashenhurst v Bartlet*, 23 December 1622 C 33/143 f 335 [IMG_0337]; 12 February 1623 C 33/143 f 531 [IMG_0533]; 27 April 1623 C 33/143 f 724 [IMG_0726].

[94] See, eg, *Dacombe v Brocke* by Richard Riche, 31 May 1620 C 38/40; Appendix on 31 May 1620 C 38/38; *Middleton v Holt* by Haywarde, 15 August 1620 C 38/39.

[95] See, eg, *Sandys v Gresham*, 28 November 1589 C 33/80 f. 271.

[96] See for an example of a deposition and interrogatories, *Mildmay v Wentworth (Sir John Wentworth's Case)*, 15 July 1613 C 33/123 f 911v [IMG_0923a]; for a copy of articles to be read in court, see *Mildmay v Wentworth (Sir John Wentworth's Case)*, 15 July 1613 C 33/123 f 912 [IMG_0924].

[97] See, eg, *Warren v Eldrington*, 19 September 1600 C 33/97 f 681v [IMG_8265a]; 20 February 1601 C 33/99 f 380 [IMG_9355]; 15 July 1601 C 33/99 f 728 [IMG_9703].

[98] Eg, *Peers v Ward*, 21 October 1614 C 33/127 f 49 [IMG_0051]; *Kippax v Dacombe*, 4 February 1617 C 33/131 f 510v [IMG_0499a]; *Johnson v Endicott* by Richard Moore, 7 August 1618 C 38/32; *Walton v Creditors of Walton*, 16 November 1618 C 33/135 f 351a [IMG_1519a]; *Smith v Alston* by Thomas Middleton and Thomas Bennett, 19 June 1620 C 38/40; *Nicholls v Tryon*, 9 November 1620 C 33/139 f 525 [IMG_0519]; *Walton v Creditors of Walton*, 16 November 1618 C 33/135 f 351a [IMG_1519a].

[99] *Mildmay v Wentworth (Sir John Wentworth's Case)*, 19 February 1614 C 33/125 f 633v [IMG_0642a].

[100] See, eg, *Nicholls v Tryon*, 9 November 1620 C 33/139 f 525 [IMG_0519]; *Walton v Creditors of Walton*, 16 November 1618 C 33/135 f 351a [IMG_1519a]. The possible difference between a committee and a

of the masters of the Chancery.[101] Litigation often ended after mediation, followed by an order or decree in the Court of Chancery to bind the creditors of the debtor to the settlement.

IV. The Link between the Bankruptcy and Insolvency Procedures

Two cases decided by the Court of Chancery make it particularly clear that the bankruptcy and insolvency procedures were two different procedures. In the first of these cases, *Lavington v Maton* (1595), debtors tried to get a composition by pretending to be insolvent, thereby trying to abuse the Chancery practice of debt settlements.[102] The case dealt with a certain Leonard Maton from Chisenbury, Wiltshire. Maton was a yeoman, 'a farmer of good wealth and substance to common account and estimation in the said county'.[103] *Lavington v Maton* is different from most other settlement cases, because Maton's creditors petitioned the Court of Chancery, accusing Leonard Maton, Matthew Grove (Maton's son-in-law), John Maton (Maton's nephew) and Alexander Staples of defrauding and deceiving them.[104]

The creditors argued that Leonard Maton had, via Staples, conveyed his assets away in trust to Grove to put them out of reach of his creditors and to make him appear insolvent.[105] The same issue had already been dealt with in the Privy Council in 1586, but a decision had never been reached.[106] In the Chancery case, Leonard's creditors argued that

> the said Leonard was become in the quality of a bankrupt though not such as was within the compass of the statute made against such offenders for that he was no merchant nor lived only by buying and selling as the purpose of the said statute is expressed.[107]

As a yeoman, Maton did not fall within the scope of the bankruptcy statutes, which meant that the creditors had to recover their debts by bringing simple common law actions. Instead, the defendants tried to get the creditors to agree to a composition, assuming that the creditors would agree to a reduction of their debts rather than potentially ending up with no relief at all.[108] However, the creditors argued that Maton had sufficient assets to pay off his debts and petitioned the Court of Chancery seeking to recover the debts owed to them in full.[109]

commission of bankrupts is discussed in the text below. According to Jones it was not uncommon for the Chancery to award a commission to mediate between the parties (generally after examining witnesses): WJ Jones, *The Elizabethan Court of Chancery* (Oxford, Clarendon Press, 1967) 270.

[101] *Ashenhurst v Bartlet*, 27 April 1623 C 33/143 f 724 [IMG_0726].

[102] *Lavington v Maton*, 7 July 1595 C 78/115/6 m 18 [IMG_0036].

[103] ibid.

[104] *Lavington v Maton*, 7 July 1595 C 78/115/6 m 19 [IMG_0038]. The case was complicated, because it seems that Maton was himself defrauded by his co-defendants.

[105] *Lavington v Maton*, 7 July 1595 C 78/115/6 m 18 [IMG_0036], at m. 19 [IMG_0038].

[106] [Meeting at the Star Chamber], 22 April 1586 PC 2/14 ff 67–68.

[107] ibid.

[108] ibid.

[109] ibid mm 19–20 [IMG_0037]–[IMG_0038].

However, the defendants argued that Staples had given valuable consideration to Leonard Maton for the leases and stock transferred to Staples.[110] He had paid a part of the sum at the time of the conveyance, had become bound in a statute and, in addition, there was marriage consideration for the conveyance from the marriage between Grove and Johane, the only child of Leonard Maton.[111] Grove had the quiet enjoyment of the farm and even held sheep there.[112] Overall, the defendants argued that the conveyance had been made bona fide and not by fraud or the intent to defraud.[113]

Sir William Brouncker, a Wiltshire man local to the dispute, was instructed as a Commissioner and

> for that purpose had taken great care and pains as well for quieting of such suits as were or might be commenced for or abouts [*sic*] the premises as also for the relieving the said creditors.[114]

Brouncker found that the creditors were indeed being defrauded.[115] However, it was Grove and Staples who had deceived the creditors. Leonard Maton, the lead defendant, appeared to be unaware of their fraudulent conduct and had also been deceived by them. Brouncker did not award a standard composition with a reduction of payment but recommended an alternative payment plan for Grove, based on a schedule which set out days of payment and sums of payment for a number of years in the future.[116] Puckering LK confirmed the settlement 'as if the whole matter of the same final end, order or award had been judicially pronounced and set down upon a solemn hearing in open court'.[117] The case is a clear example of debtors trying to get a reduction of debts, and thereby defraud the creditors, by pretending to be insolvent. However, the Court of Chancery would intervene to protect creditors from fraudulent conduct, and it is not surprising that the court acted to relieve Maton's creditors on the terms that they wanted.

The other case that specifically refers to the bankruptcy statutes is *Tyffin v Hart* (1619).[118] This concerned the insolvent estate of Robert Tyffin, a brewer in Kingston-upon-Thames, Surrey.[119] His two sons had acted as his sureties, and in that capacity were sued for their father's debts at common law. The brothers petitioned the Court of Chancery for a bill of conformity procedure, because not all of their creditors wanted to conform. The case eventually led to a debt settlement between the Tyffin

[110] ibid m 20 [IMG_0039].
[111] ibid.
[112] ibid m 20 [IMG_0040].
[113] ibid.
[114] ibid m 22 [IMG_0044].
[115] ibid.
[116] ibid m 18 [IMG_0036] at [IMG_0051]. This included various sums for the creditors of Leonard Maton, but also a small sum to provide for the livelihood of Maton and his wife.
[117] ibid m 18 [IMG_0036] at [IMG_0052].
[118] *Tyffin v Hart*, 20 April 1619 C 33/135 f 998 [IMG_2169] at f 998v [IMG_2170a]. See also (n 78) above.
[119] *Tyffin v Hart*, 22 April 1618 C 33/133 f 839 [IMG_0844]; 16 May 1618 C 33/133 f 933 [IMG_0942]; 20 June 1618 C 33/133 f 1229 [IMG_1241a]; 26 October 1618 C 33/135 f 111 [IMG_1277]; 29 October 1618 C 33/135 f 115 [IMG_1281]; 12 November 1618 C 33/135 f 159v [IMG_1324a]; 5 December 1618 C 33/135 f 301v [IMG_1469a]; 16 January 1619 C 33/135 f 417 [IMG_1586]; 22 February 1619 C 33/135 [IMG_1869a]; 20 April 1619; C 33/135 f 997 [IMG_2169]; 15 May 1619 C 33/135 f 979 [IMG_2151]. The final decree shows that Robert Tyffin was in the 'trade of brewing': KC4/1/27 (held by the History Centre in Kingston-upon-Thames, Surrey).

brothers and their creditors. In this case, Bacon LC explicitly distinguished the situation of the brothers from ordinary bankruptcy for two reasons. First, 'the honest disposition of the said Tyffins and their filial respect and piety to their dead father',[120] and, second, 'the gracious recommendation of his Majesty and the power and authority of this court'.[121]

The first element of Bacon's decision is not surprising, because the early bankruptcy statutes were all restricted to fraudulent debtors. If the fraudulent aspect could not be proved, the bankruptcy statutes did not apply. That the Tyffin brothers had stood as sureties for their father, which was considered an act of neighbourliness, was obviously not considered to be a fraudulent act. The second element, that the case was recommended by the King to the Court of Chancery, is another distinguishing factor, because in a bankruptcy procedure the case would be put forward by one or more creditors when they sued out a commission of bankrupts.

Occasionally the Court of Chancery explicitly ordered that a case should be tried 'at the common law', which meant that the case had to be referred to and decided by a commission of bankrupts. For example, in *Howse v Lea* (1591), the creditors of John Edgcombe, the bankrupt, exhibited a bill for an equal distribution of all Edgcombe's goods and money. It was alleged that these goods and money had come to the hands of Lea, Glanvile and Stone by a gift from Edgcombe, not sufficiently warranted by law, and that the commission of bankrupts which was stayed by *supersedeas* ought to have been continued. However, the Court of Chancery (the great seal being in commission after the death of Hatton LC) decided that this request 'seemed more meet to be tried by the course of the common law than in this court'.[122] Therefore, the Court of Chancery referred the plaintiffs

> to take what remedy they can there [at common law] and sue out a new commission of bankrupts or proceed upon the old commission by *procedendo* if they may by law and proceed to trial thereof with effect.[123]

Sometimes, the process worked the other way around. As has been seen, in *Steward v Mountford* (1620), the Commissioners of Bankrupts had declared the insolvent debtor not to be a bankrupt.[124] From that point onwards, the debtor had the opportunity to apply for a debt settlement in the Court of Chancery. In this case, the majority of the creditors, thirty in number, were willing to give Steward a reduction of debts to five shillings in the pound, with only two of the creditors refusing to accept that reduction. The two refractory creditors were only willing to accept eight shillings in the pound. Eventually, Bacon LC decided that the proposal of the majority of creditors was reasonable and awarded the settlement with a reduction to five shillings in the pound to be paid within a year of Steward's release from debtor's prison.

It seems that Bacon LC tried to formally reconcile the Chancery practice with the bankruptcy statutes in his Standing Orders of the High Court of Chancery in 1620.[125]

[120] *Tyffin v Hart*, 20 April 1619 C 33/135 f 997 [IMG_2169].
[121] ibid.
[122] *Howse v Lea*, 2 December 1591 C 33/83 f 255 [IMG_0247].
[123] ibid. Lea, Glanvile and Stone were all to bring their moiety of their goods and money into the Court of Chancery until further order.
[124] *Stiaard (Steward) v Mountford*, 10 October 1620 C 33/139 f 75 [IMG_0080]; *Steward v creditors* by Bowyer and Paule, 21 July 1620 C 38/40.
[125] *Tyffin v Hart*, 20 April 1619 C 33/135 f 997 [IMG_2169].

The Standing Orders prescribed that an order in a bill of conformity procedure had to be 'according to the equity of the Statute of Bankrupts'.[126] The idea that a statute might be interpreted according to its 'equity' meant that the statute might be interpreted based on the underlying principle of the statute, its *ratio*.[127] This justified a slight analogical extension outside the express terms of the statute.[128] The main aim of the statutes of bankrupts was to relieve creditors, so the Chancery practice before the Standing Orders was already in line with what the Standing Orders required.

The equitable insolvency jurisdiction of the Court of Chancery was mentioned for the first time in a bankruptcy statute in the Bankrupts Act 1624. The Act was the result of an active lobby for the interest of creditors, who had argued that the rules for debt settlements and the discharge of debts were too lenient. This arguably had caused great losses for the city corporation of London and caused a decrease of trade and shipping.[129] The Act effectively abolished bills of conformity, with section 2 of the Act providing that a debtor would commit an act of bankruptcy if he:

> shall either by himself or others by his procurement obtain any protection or protections other than such person or persons as shall be lawfully protected by the privilege of Parliament, or shall proffer or exhibit unto his Majesty, his heirs or successors, or unto any of the king's courts any petition or petitions bill or bills against his or her creditor or creditors, or any of them, thereby desiring or endeavouring to compel or enforce them or any of them to accept less than their just and principal debts, or to procure time or longer days of payment, than was given at the time of their original contract, or being indebted to any person or persons in the sum of one hundred pounds or more, shall not pay or otherwise compound for the same within six months next after the same shall grow due.[130]

The abolition of bills of conformity did not end the distinction between fraudulent bankruptcy and the equitable insolvency jurisdiction. However, the Act set out that creditors could no longer be forced to take part in a debt settlement. *Rycroft v Hedd* (1627) shows that the Chancery would still award a debt settlement to the willing creditors, because it was in their interest to do so.[131] The refractory creditor had to be paid in full, but because the refractory creditor could still pursue the insolvent debtor at common law, it is unclear how useful this settlement really was. The number of insolvent debtors in debtor's prison increased from 1624 onwards, and there is a strong possibility that the Bankrupts Act 1624, by abolishing bills of conformity, had caused creditors to fall back on *capias ad satisfaciendum*.[132]

[126] 'Additional rules for the better governing of the Court of Chancery and the Great Seal. Published in open Court 31 October 1620'. See Sanders (n 53) 129–131.

[127] DJ Ibbetson, 'A House Built on Sand: Equity in Early Modern English Law' in E Koops and WJ Zwalve (eds), *Law & Equity: Approaches in Roman Law and Common Law* (Leiden, Brill, 2014) 55–57.

[128] ibid.

[129] SP 14/123 f 74 'Reasons concerning the decay of trade and shipping and the scarcity of money within the kingdom, collected out of the observations, and infallible rules of the merchants of best experience and judgment'; Speech of Mr Solicitor (Sir Robert Heath), *Commons Debates*, 24 March 1621 in W Notestein, FH Relf and H Simpson, *Commons Debates* 1621, vol 4 (New Haven, CT, Yale University Press, 1935) 67. For more political background, see Stolker (n 67) 108–127.

[130] Bankrupts Act 1624 (21 Jac I, c 19), s 2.

[131] *Rycroft v Hedd*, 20 November 1627 C 33/153 f 319 [IMG_2055].

[132] For the increase in numbers, see T Paul, *The Poverty of Disaster. Debt and Insecurity in Eighteenth-century Britain* (Cambridge, Cambridge University Press, 2019); RT Bell, 'Charity, Debt and Social Control in England's Early Modern Prisons' (2022) 47 *Social History* 1.

V. Conclusion

The traditional way to deal with insolvent debtors was to put them in debtor's prison. However, the Statute of Bankrupts 1543 provided England with two more effective ways to deal with insolvent debtors in a collective manner: the procedure set out in the bankruptcy statutes, and an equitable insolvency procedure. The bankruptcy statute dealt with insolvency matters relating to fraudulent insolvent debtors, whereas the equitable insolvency procedure dealt with matters involving honest insolvent debtors. Whereas England thus distinguished between two types of insolvent debtors, only the law relating to fraudulent insolvent debtors in the bankruptcy statutes was codified. The regulation of bankruptcy was a tricky business, because given individuals might be debtors in one transaction and creditors in another. In their role as creditors, they might prefer a stricter regime than they did in their role as insolvent debtors.

The question remains whether England should have distinguished between fraudulent, reckless, and blameless insolvent debtors in the period, as suggested by Porder,[133] and to what extent merchants and traders should have been able to qualify for a debt settlement. After all, merchants and traders would only be classified as 'bankrupt' if they had been fraudulent and met the other criteria set out in the bankruptcy statutes. However, the Court of Chancery, especially by accepting 'great losses' as a reason for a debt settlement, might have undermined the equitable insolvency jurisdiction for 'real' blameless debtors. It seems that especially those kinds of insolvent debtors that incurred 'great losses' in the course of risky business angered creditors, who thought that the Chancery was too lenient in its approach to financial rehabilitation of the debtor.[134]

It is also noteworthy that England in this period did not recognise an equivalent to the Roman *cessio bonorum*, a voluntary surrender of the insolvent's property in return for protection against infamy.[135] After all, the Romans did have a codified bankruptcy procedure dealing with fraudulent insolvents (*venditio bonorum*) and a debt settlement procedure dealing with honest creditors that could include a discharge of debts (*concordia*).[136] The *cessio bonorum* resettled the credit status of the debtor, so that they could participate again in economic life but did not discharge them from their debts. This might have been a good compromise between letting the debtor participate in economic life again, and responding to dissatisfied creditors, who thought the Court of Chancery was too lenient towards certain insolvent debtors.

[133] Porder (n 37).

[134] SP 14/123 f 74 'Reasons concerning the decay of trade and shipping and the scarcity of money within the kingdom, collected out of the observations, and infallible rules of the merchants of best experience and judgment'; Speech of Mr Solicitor (Sir Robert Heath), *Commons Debates*, 24 March 1621 in W Notestein, FH Relf and H Simpson, *Commons Debates 1621*, vol 4 (New Haven, CT, Yale University Press, 1935) 67.

[135] See, eg, W Pakter, 'The Origins of Bankruptcy in Medieval Canon and Roman Law' in P Linetan (ed), *Proceedings of the Seventh International Congress of Medieval Canon Law, Cambridge 23-27 July 1984* (Vatican City, Biblioteca Apostolica Vaticana, 1998); OO Vroom, 'Origin and History of the Bankruptcy Law' (1932) 37 *Commercial Law Journal* 127; P Stein (ed), WW Buckland, *A Textbook of Roman Law. From Augustus to Justinian*, 3rd edn by P Stein (Cambridge, Cambridge University Press, 2007) 402–403; R Obenchain, 'Roman Law of Bankruptcy' (1928) 3–4 *Notre Dame Law Review* 185; LE Levinthal, 'The Early History of English Bankruptcy' (1919) 67 *University of Pennsylvania Law Review* 235; MW Frederiksen, 'Caesar, Cicero and the Problem of Debt' (1966) 56 *Journal of Roman Studies* 135.

[136] Discussed in Pakter (n 135).

Both procedures ultimately aimed to get the most relief for creditors of insolvent debtors. The Court of Chancery seemed to release insolvent debtors from debtor's prison for all sorts of reasons. Interestingly, these reasons were not only financial: the Chancery also considered arguments of a more humane nature. It seems that the Court of Chancery at the end of the sixteenth century and in the early seventeenth century understood that there was nothing to be gained for creditors from continued imprisonment of certain debtors. Compositions were beneficial for the insolvent debtor, especially if the creditors approved of any kind of discharge of debts. However, this seems to have been a positive side effect of the Chancery practice, rather than its main aim. Indeed, when the Court of Chancery balanced the interests of the debtor and his or her creditors, the vulnerable creditors would receive full repayment, implying that the interests of the creditors prevailed.[137] However, the fast succession of the four early bankruptcy statutes shows that the legislature had trouble getting the bankruptcy legislation under control, causing creditors to mainly revert to *capias ad satisficiendum* to deal with insolvent debtors after the Act of 1624.

[137] Stolker (n 67) 207.

11

Enforcing Equitable Rights against Non-Privies, c. 1590–1680

DAVID FOSTER

I. Introduction

In the late sixteenth century, courts of equity would not grant relief to beneficiaries or mortgagors where the legal estate was claimed by the trustee or mortgagee's legal demandants (eg, a judgment creditor, dowress, disseisor or the lord by escheat). Such legal demandants were not 'privy' to the trust or mortgage and for this reason took free of any equitable rights attaching to the legal estate. The refusal to relieve against non-privies was, in part, grounded in a restrictive conception of the equitable jurisdiction as concerning only relief of fraud, accident, and breach of confidence. The legal demandant's title arose by operation of law – not by any fraud, accident, or confidence reposed in them – and equity was therefore powerless to assist. Over the course of the seventeenth century, however, the central equity courts began to slip the bounds of this tripartite conception of the jurisdiction and eventually came to grant relief against non-privies as a matter of course. The enforcement of equitable rights against non-privies marked a watershed in the evolution of equitable jurisprudence – ultimately leading to more 'proprietary' equities with significant third-party effect and with major consequences for how equitable rights were conceived by judges and jurists of the period.

II. Privity and the Enforceability of Equitable Rights

The doctrine of privity had governed the medieval use,[1] but was subsequently transposed into the trust in its formative period (c. 1536–1600).[2] In this way, privity provided some structure and coherence to the principles governing the nascent trust

[1] YB 8 Edw IV, f 5b, pl 1; YB Pas 22 Edw IV, f 6, pl 18; YB 5 Edw IV, f 7b, pl 16 and 18; *Anon* (1453) Fitz Abr tit *Subpoena*, pl 19; *Dod v Chyttynden* (1502) 116 *Selden Society* 395.

[2] DEC Yale, *Nottingham's Chancery Cases* (1961-2) 79 *Selden Society* 88; D Foster, 'Historical Conceptions of the Express Trust, c 1600-1900' in S Degeling, J Hudson and I Samet (eds), *Philosophical Foundations of Express Trust* (Oxford, Oxford University Press, 2023) 118–9.

concept – especially regarding enforceability against those who were not the original parties to the trust. Only those who claimed the legal estate by an act of the trustee (eg, by grant or assignment) were deemed privy to the trust; privies were said to claim *per* (or 'through') the trustee and to take an estate to which the beneficiary's right was annexed. The liability of privies was subject to the doctrine of notice; where transferees were purchasers, their liability was subject to a defence that they had taken without notice.[3] The interplay of privity and notice thus governed the enforceability of equitable rights against those deemed privy to the trust.

By contrast, those who claimed the estate by operation of law – rather than by act of the parties to the trust – were outside the privity of the trust. Such classes of legal demandant included the trustee's judgment creditor, surviving spouse (tenants by dower and curtesy), disseisors, and the lord by escheat. Where a legal demandant claimed the trust property by operation of law, they were said to take free of the beneficiary's pre-existing equitable rights. Crucially, the doctrine of notice had no application where trust property was claimed by a non-privy; legal demandants would take free of the beneficiary's right regardless of whether they had notice or not.[4] In the sixteenth century, therefore, there was no clear means by which beneficiaries could assert their equitable rights against legal demandants claiming the trust property by operation of law. In the landmark case of *Gervys v Cooke* (1522),[5] Broke J explained:

> Now, sir, although common reason dictates that if I enfeoff someone without consideration or *causa* it shall be to my use, still the land shall keep the same course in the feoffee's hands as any other land. Thus, if he has a wife and dies, his widow shall be endowed and shall hold the land to her use; for here is no act by the feoffee, and she does not claim to be in through the feoffee, but the law creates her estate. Likewise if he is bound in a statute-merchant. Likewise when a lord takes by escheat. In these cases no act was done by the feoffee to deceive or defraud the feoffor, but it is done by order of law.[6]

In a similar vein, Pollard J stated that:

> There is a distinction between the case where the feoffee defaults in order to defraud the feoffor and where he does not; for, if the feoffee dies, his wife shall be endowed and shall hold to her own use, and it is likewise in the cases of statute-merchant and lord by reason of escheat: for here there is no default in the feoffee, and he commits no act of fraud against the feoffor, but it is by operation of law, and the default is rather in the feoffor who allows it to happen.[7]

In these passages, Broke and Pollard JJ emphasised that the legal estate in the feoffee was bound by the rules of the common law; it was subject to the same rules of descent, escheat, forfeiture, and execution as any other legal estate vested in the feoffee. Moreover,

[3] *Gervys v Cooke* (1522) 119 *Selden Society* 108, 115 (Fitzherbert J); *Chudleigh's case* (1594) 1 Co Rep 120a, 122b and Pop 70, 71–2; *Cole v Moore* (1607) Moo KB 806; W Sheppard, *A Touchstone of Common Assurances* (London, Lee et al, 1648) 503.

[4] Foster (n 2) 119–21.

[5] 119 *Selden Society* 108. On its landmark status, see JH Baker, *Oxford History of the Laws of England, Volume VI: 1483-1558* (Oxford, Oxford University Press, 2003) 659–60, and DJ Seipp, 'Trust and Fiduciary Duty in the Early Common Law' (2011) 91 *Boston University Law Review* 1011, 1026–7.

[6] 119 *Selden Society* 108, 116–7.

[7] ibid 118–9.

where the legal demandant claimed by operation of law, the demandant did not claim 'through' the feoffee and would take the land discharged of the right of the *cestui que use*.[8] In the technical language of the time, the entry of the legal demandant onto the land 'changed the use', and the law deemed him to hold to his own use, rather than to the use of the beneficiary.[9]

In characteristically clear style, Charles Butler explained the effects of the doctrine of privity in the following terms:

> between the feoffee and *cestuy que use*, there was a confidence in the person and privity in estate … But this was only between the feoffee and *cestuy que use*. To all other persons the feoffee was as much the real owner of the fee, as if he did not hold it to the use of another. *He* performed the feudal duties; *his* wife was entitled to dower; *his* infant heir was in wardship to the lord; and, upon *his* attainder, the estate was forfeited.[10]

Under the sixteenth-century model of privity, therefore, equitable rights were rendered rather ephemeral; they were readily defeasible at common law by the trustee's legal demandants, and equity seemed unwilling or unable to assist. Over the course of the seventeenth century, however, the logic of privity was slowly eroded, and the legal estate was, by increments, made immune to the liabilities of the trustee and mortgagee. Although the rules on enforcing equitable rights against non-privies remain relatively untouched in the secondary literature, it was in this context that equitable rights were given greater substance and wider third-party effect. The cases discussed in this chapter thus played an important role in the proprietisation of equitable rights over the course of the seventeenth century.

III. Immunity of Non-Privies, c. 1590–1630

In the late sixteenth century, rights arising by operation of law 'changed the use' such that pre-existing equitable rights did not attach to the legal demandant's estate. By this logic, all classes of legal demandant – judgment creditors, disseisors, tenants by dower and curtesy, and the Crown by forfeiture and escheat – entered without privity and escaped liability to equitable rights. This logic was applied equally to trustees and mortgagees and may well have encouraged a greater assimilation of the rules governing trusts

[8] This learning was subsequently reflected in Coke's 1592 reading on the Statute of Uses (British Library (BL) Hargrave MS 33, f 135, 139r) and his report of *Chudleigh's case* (1594) 1 Co Rep 120, 121a–122a, albeit in such a truncated form that the reasons for the rule were not fully elaborated. *Cf* [Lord Ellesmere], *Certaine Observations Concerning the Office of Lord Chancellor* (London, Walbanck et al, 1651) 94 ('the said persons do come to the land by the operation of law, and not by their own act, nor by the act of the feoffees', citing *Gervys v Cooke*). On the disputed authorship of this latter work, see WS Holdsworth, *History of English Law, vol V*, 3rd edn (London, Methuen, 1924) 272, fn 6.

[9] 119 *Selden Society* 108, at 111 (Roo *in arguendo*), 115 (Fitzherbert J), 116 (Broke J), and 119 (Pollard J). See also D Fox, 'Purchase for Value Without Notice' in PS Davies, S Douglas and J Goudkamp (eds), *Defences in Equity* (Oxford, Hart Publishing, 2018) 57–62.

[10] C Butler (ed), *The First Part of the Institutes of the Laws of the Realm or, A Commentary upon Littleton, vol II*, 19th edn (London, J & WT Clarke, 1833) 271b, fn 1 (emphasis in original). See also JH Thomas' explanatory note to the 1826 edition of Coke's report of *Chudleigh's case*. The 1826 edition of JH Thomas and JF Fraser (eds), *The Reports of Sir Edward Coke* (London, J Butterworth, 1826), 13 parts in six volumes, was reproduced in the *English Reports*; Thomas' remarks can be found at 76 ER 270, 275, n S.

and mortgages in this period.[11] Whilst this learning had been stated by the common law judges in *Gervys v Cooke* (1522)[12] and repeated by Sir Edward Coke in his report of *Chudleigh's case* (1594),[13] it was subject to a further gloss by the judges in *Sir Moyle Finch's case* (1600).[14] In *Finch's case*, the judges explained equity's unwillingness to grant relief against legal demandants in terms of a general limitation on the equitable jurisdiction itself. For the judges, the 'ancient rule' that Chancery aids three things – fraud, accident, and confidence – set out a clear, if restrictive, conception of the jurisdiction.[15] Where legal demandants claimed by operation of law, their rights arose neither by fraud nor accident. Moreover, because they were not privies, their consciences remained untouched by any confidence reposed by the parties to the trust or mortgage. This tripartite conception of equity was, therefore, relied upon by the common law judges to delimit the jurisdiction and refuse equitable relief to non-privies.[16]

In *Finch's case*, the question put before all the judges of England was whether a disseisor could be bound by a trust of freehold land.[17] The common law judges held that a disseisor could not be so bound and gave three distinct reasons for the ruling. First, the plaintiff-beneficiary could not be relieved in respect of a trust 'to which the disseisor was not subject'.[18] According to the doctrine of privity, the disseisor's title, known as a 'tortious fee', arose 'in the *post*' by operation of law (rather than 'in the *per*' by an act of the trustees). The tortious fee was a new estate – not derived from the trustee's title – upon which the beneficiary's right was not engrafted. For this reason, the disseisor was not privy to the trust and thus took free of the beneficiary's equity.

The judges also observed that, as the trust concerned freehold land, the matter was not fit to be decided in Chancery:

> there is no reason … to try inheritances or freeholds in Chancery, for at common law it appears by our books that a disseisor shall not be seised to a use, and a *subpoena* does not lie against him, not only because he is in the *post* but because the right of inheritance or freehold shall not be tried in Chancery. Yet in the same case cestui que use had no remedy at common law.[19]

[11] Aspects of the mutual development of trusts and mortgages are discussed in DEC Yale's classic 'Essay on Mortgages and Trusts and Allied Topics in Equity' in Yale (n 2) 7-207. See also RW Turner, *Equity of Redemption* (Cambridge, Cambridge University Press, 1931) ch 3, discussing precedents on trusts and mortgages as mutual authorities.

[12] 119 *Selden Society* 108.

[13] 1 Co Rep 120a, 122a.

[14] 4 Co Inst 84; 2 And 162; 140 *Selden Society* 1094.

[15] 4 Co Inst 84.

[16] This discussion is not intended to suggest that the tripartite classification was used *solely* by common lawyers. The classification was attributed to More C (1 Rolle Abr 374) and had significant implications for the substance of equity in the early modern period: MRT Macnair, 'Equity and Conscience' (2007) 27 *Oxford Journal of Legal Studies* 659, 677–79. The classification was also relied upon by Ellesmere LC in the *Earl of Oxford's case* (1615) 1 Chan Rep 1, 7. Crucially, Ellesmere's use of the classification was conjoined with a rich and expansive theory of equity. Largely derived from Christopher St German, Ellesmere's conception of the equitable jurisdiction was most assuredly not shared by Coke and the majority of his common law brethren. For early modern theories of equity, see generally M Fortier, *The Culture of Equity in Early Modern England* (Abingdon, Ashgate, 2005) esp 4–8.

[17] For detailed discussion of this case, see Sir John Baker's chapter in this volume (ch 6).

[18] 140 *Selden Society* 1095.

[19] ibid 1096. On the non-justiciability of freehold title in Chancery and cognate prerogative courts, see JH Baker, *The Reinvention of Magna Carta, 1216-1616* (Cambridge, Cambridge University Press, 2017) 36,

Finally, it was explained that equity could relieve only in cases of fraud, accident, or confidence. By casting the equitable jurisdiction in such narrow terms, relief against non-privies could be refused on the basis of an inherent limitation on the jurisdiction itself. The refusal of the common law judges to countenance relief in Chancery was neatly summed up by Popham CJ:

> the Court of Chancery cannot determine anything except in three cases, namely, (1) when someone is circumvented by fraud or deceit; (2) for breach of trust; (3) for accident, without default of the party, as if someone is bound in a penalty for payment of a lesser sum and the obligor sends the money by his servant at the day of payment, and his servant is robbed on the way, now for this accident without default of the party there shall be a remedy in the Chancery.[20]

We have in *Finch's case* something of a guide to common law conceptions of the equitable jurisdiction at the turn of the seventeenth century. Equity was competent to grant remedies only in cases of fraud, mistake and confidence. As against non-privies (such as the disseisor), equity's jurisdiction was exhausted. To grant an equitable remedy against a non-privy would be tantamount to a Chancery determination of freehold title, which was the sole purview of the courts of common law.

The common lawyers' approach in *Finch's case* would prove influential in later decisions touching the enforceability of equitable rights against legal demandants. In *Nash v Preston* (1630),[21] a bill was preferred in Chancery by a mortgagor seeking relief against the mortgagee's dowress.[22] The widow's right of dower arose by operation of law,[23] taking the form of a tenancy for the life of the dowress over one third of the property of which her husband had been seised during the coverture. The dowress therefore claimed an estate to which the mortgagor's equity did not attach. The facts of *Nash v Preston* were hotly contested by the parties, but the case was eventually referred, on an agreed set of facts, to two common law judges to certify whether equity might relieve against the writ of dower. Jones and Croke JJ, upon conference with other judges at Serjeants-Inn,

60, 211, 265–6, 277–84, 288–9, 377–8, and 410–11. *Cf* BL Lansdowne MS 604, f 23 listing several authorities under the heading 'titles determined here [ie in Chancery]' (eg, *Wadham v Norris* (1585), 'a demurrer because the matter concerneth titles [was] overruled and [the defendant] ordered to answer'). EG Henderson, 'Legal Rights to Land in the Early Chancery' (1982) 26 *American Journal of Legal History* 97, fn 2, also noted that early objections to the Chancery jurisdiction regarded the *subpoena* as contrary to Magna Carta and other medieval due process statues (eg, 42 Edw III c 3 and 15 Hen VI c 4). According to Henderson, '[c]ommon lawyers have read these statutes as enacting that no *subpoena* could be granted concerning matters determinable at common law, and particularly not concerning freehold land unless held in use .... This limitation of the equitable jurisdiction, though based on rather one-sided legal history, has been for many years imbedded in the legal consciousness as an unchallengeable first principle.' On this point, see also TFT Plucknett, *A Concise History of the Common Law*, 5th edn (Indianapolis, Liberty Fund, 2010 reprint) 176–7, and D Foster, 'Fraud, Trusts and Trusting: Enforcing Crown Forfeitures in Equity, c 1570-1620' (2023) 44 *Journal of Legal History* 256, 290–291.

[20] 140 *Selden Society* 1096.

[21] Cro Car 190; The National Archives: Public Record Office (PRO) C78/298/3 (25 Nov 1630).

[22] PRO C33/160, f 193.

[23] *Cf* dower *ad ostium ecclesiae* – a form of nominated dower – which took effect as an assignment from the husband. The widow claiming dower *ad ostium ecclesiae* claimed 'through' the feoffee and would be subject to pre-existing equities. See *Gervys v Cooke* (1522) 119 *Selden Society* 108, 118–19 (Pollard J). For detail on medieval dower, see: J Biancalana, 'Widows at Common Law: The Development of Common Law Dower' (1988) 23 *Irish Jurist* 255; P Brand, 'Dower *Ex Assensu* and Trial by Jury and Trial by Witnesses in the English Medieval Common Law' (2021) 42 *Journal of Legal History* 147.

concluded in favour of the mortgagee's dowress and did so explicitly because she entered by operation of law without any supervening fraud:

> when she is dowable by act or rule in law, a Court of Equity shall not bar her to claim her dower; for it is against the rule of law, viz. "where no fraud or covin is, a Court of Equity will not relieve."[24]

Once again, the common law judges' narrow conception of the equitable jurisdiction was used as grounds for refusing relief against non-privies. The opinion of Jones and Croke JJ was subsequently certified into the Chancery, and, following the decision of plaintiff's counsel not to challenge the judges' opinion,[25] Coventry LK decreed 'that a third part of two parts of the premises shall be settled with the defendant in full satisfaction of her dower'.[26]

It must be recognised, however, that these cases merely represented the common lawyers' views of the proper ambit of equity's jurisdiction. Whilst reliance on common lawyers as judges assistant or requests for the judges' opinion to be certified into Chancery could lend an air of collegiality to the administration of equity, the common lawyers' views were not always reflective of equity practice in this period.[27] It is similarly salutary to remember that, in this period, equity was administered by several central courts – principally the Chancery, the Wards, and the Exchequer – and the issue of relief against non-privies could arise in any one of them. In providing relief against non-privies, we shall see that the central equity courts were generally able to coordinate their remedial practices, and that there was clearly room for departure from the principles espoused by the common law judges.

IV. Enforcement against Non-Privies, c. 1620–1680

Over the course of the seventeenth century – and particularly following the Restoration – the central courts of equity demonstrated a greater willingness to issue decrees against non-privies. The equity courts' remedial ambit thus began to expand beyond the sixteenth-century conception of equity as fraud, mistake and confidence. Tentative at first, equity issued decrees against non-privies only in limited and specific circumstances. As the century progressed, however, such relief became *de rigueur*.

[24] Cro Car 190, 191.

[25] PRO C78/298/3: 'to prevent the further expense of the plaintiff, the matter in question being not great, did not therefore oppose the said certificate but did humbly pray that this court would settle the same accordingly'.

[26] ibid. It is notable, however, that prior to the case being sent to the judges for determination, the plaintiffs had been ordered to give a bond to the value of the mesne profits of one third of the land since the time of the defendant's husband's death. At the hearing before Coventry LK, the defendants requested payment of the mesne profits, but Coventry refused and held that the 'the defendant ought not in equity to be relieved for her dower as this case is'.

[27] In ch 6 of this volume, Sir John Baker shows that the chancellor did not always consider himself bound by the opinions of the common law judges. See also NG Jones, 'The Trust Beneficiary's Interest before *R v Holland* (1648)' in ADE Lewis, P Brand and P Mitchell (eds), *Law in the City: Proceedings of the Seventeenth British Legal History Conference, London, 2005* (Dublin, Four Courts Press, 2007) 111–14, demonstrating that the common lawyers' view of the trust as an unassignable chose in action was not reflected in contemporary Chancery practice.

A. Court of Wards

It seems that it was the Court of Wards which led the way in granting relief against non-privies; this was unsurprising given the nature of the court's jurisdiction. Prior to 1646, where a tenant *in capite* died with an heir underage, the King was entitled to the feudal incidents of wardship and marriage (and relief when the heir assumed the inheritance).[28] Where there was some dispute concerning rights to the underage heir's lands, the Court of Wards had primary jurisdiction and could even enjoin proceedings taken in Chancery which touched lands in wardship.[29] As a result, the Court of Wards in the early seventeenth century was regularly required to adjudicate on matters touching trusts, mortgages and the rights of non-privies. Where the trustee or mortgagee of freehold land died leaving an underage heir, there was the possibility that wardship might attach to the legal estate and that the King might take the land unencumbered by any pre-existing equities. After all, according to the logic of privity, wardship was a right arising by operation of law to which pre-existing equities did not attach. By the 1620s, there is evidence to suggest that the Court of Wards was careful to protect equitable rights against claims of wardship of the legal estate. In *Butler v Manningham* (1623–24),[30] for example, wardship had attached upon the death of the mortgagee, but the court granted the mortgagor a lease of the mortgaged land below market rent until the mortgagee's heir came of age.[31] By decreeing a lease in the mortgagor's favour, the mortgagor was thereby permitted to retain possession of the land whilst it was subject to the King's right of wardship.

Perhaps a clearer indication of relief in the Wards against non-privies is found in the case of *Cholmeley v Cave* (1623).[32] The facts of *Cholmeley* concerned the rights of a trustee's judgment creditor who was seeking satisfaction from the trust property. The judgment creditor's title arose by operation of law and took the form of a statutory tenancy over the trustee's land until the debt was repaid.[33] According to the logic set

[28] Baker (n 5) ch 35.

[29] See, eg, *Tatton and Ballard* (1623) PRO WARD9/539, f 15 and *Dutton, Worral and Bache* (1623) PRO WARD9/539, f 16 (both cases concerned bills in Chancery to set afoot a lease of the inheritance which would prejudice the ward's estate; injunctions were granted against further proceedings in Chancery as this was an issue properly examinable in Wards); *Altham, Wyn and Sutton* (1623) PRO WARD9/539, ff 23 and 44 (creditors of the heir's father preferred a bill in Chancery against the heir's trustees for consent to sell land in which the heir was interested; injunction granted to stay suit in Chancery and creditors ordered to bring proceedings in the Wards).

[30] BL Lansdowne MS 608, f 36: 'The manor of Towingbury held *in capite* was mortgaged by Buckingham Butler esq to John Manningham esq to save the mortgagee harmless and the mortgagee died seised thereof inter alia with his son and heir being within age who was in ward to the King for his body and that land only, although the ward's father was saved harmless (though after the day) and therefore the mortgagor had a lease of the land at [£20] rent during the minority and the auditors (warranted by decree Mich 21 Jac) charged … the land at [£20] per annum and not by the office which was found at a higher yearly value'.

[31] *Cf Lloyd's case* (1625) BL Lansdowne MS 608, f 25: Allen Owen granted his daughter a portion upon her marriage to Thomas Lloyd. To secure payment of the portion, Owen mortgaged lands *in capite* to Lloyd. Before the mortgage was repaid, Lloyd died, leaving his underage brother as his heir. No outcome is reported, but it was remarked that 'if the money be not paid at the day, the father loseth his land (and his daughter her portion) and the brother is heir to it'.

[32] PRO WARD9/539, f 77.

[33] The writs of *elegit* (on a judgment debt) and *levari facias* (on a recognisance) entitled the judgment creditor to possession of the debtor's goods and a moiety of their land as security for the debt. See JH Baker, *An Introduction to English Legal History*, 5th edn (Oxford, Oxford University Press, 2019) 74.

out in *Gervys v Cooke*, the judgment creditor lacked the privity required to be bound by pre-existing equities. In *Cholmeley v Cave*, however, the records suggest that the Court of Wards was wary of giving the trustee's judgment creditors unfettered access to the trust property.

In that case, James Bury had made a gratuitous transfer of the manor of Easton to Sir Thomas Cave upon trust to raise portions for Bury's children. In order to raise the portions, Sir Thomas sold and conveyed the manor to Sir Henry Cholmeley and his heirs for £2140. Sir Thomas died, leaving a debt upon a recognisance unpaid, and the question was whether the legal title to the manor could be extended to repay Sir Thomas' debt.[34] Ultimately, the Master of the Wards decreed that the land ought not to be so extended:

> although this court doth conceive that the said manor … being estated upon the said Sir Thomas [Cave] is by law to be extended with the rest of the lands and estates of the said Sir Thomas Cave … yet for that it appeareth that the said conveyance from Bury to Sir Thomas Cave was not a true and clear purchase but only for the provision for children and no … consideration paid and that Sir Thomas received the [proceeds of sale] … to the end he might therewith be enabled to perform the conditions in the conveyance made unto him by Bury. And the said conveyance was but a preparation for the sale of the land which was effected within six months or thereabouts after the conveyance was made to Sir Thomas Cave, this court doth conceive that in equity the said manor being in a purchaser's hands for great and valuable consideration ought not to be charged with the recognisance.[35]

The court was clear that the general rule of the common law entitled the judgment creditor to an extent over the lands. Nevertheless, particular circumstances of the case justified equitable relief, namely: (i) the conveyance to Sir Thomas was not for value; (ii) the conveyance was merely upon trust to sell and raise portions; (iii) the conveyance to Sir Thomas was for short duration only; and (iv) a purchaser for valuable consideration ought not to be charged with the debts of the vendor in such circumstances.[36]

We cannot, of course, rely on this case as evidence of a clear doctrinal rule that trust property was not liable to the debts of the trustee; the existence of such firm doctrinal rules in equity is comparatively rare in this period, and, in any case, the involvement of the purchaser prevents us distilling a clear *ratio*. Nevertheless, taken together with the decision in *Butler v Manningham*, *Cholmeley v Cave* may well indicate a tenderness towards equitable rights in the face of claims to the legal estate by non-privies. Where the facts of the case were apt, there may have been a general practice or preference to relieve against non-privies in the Wards. Moreover, and contrary to the opinion of the common law judges in *Sir Moyle Finch's case* and *Nash v Preston*, here was a jurisdiction, exercised over freehold land, which was not based on fraud, breach of trust, or accident. By the early decades of the seventeenth century, therefore, the central equity courts seem to have pushed beyond sixteenth-century notions which militated against the granting of such relief.

[34] PRO WARD9/539, f 77: 'the question being whether in law or equity the plaintiff's manor of Easton … were to be charged with a recognisance of [£1500] being the debt of Sir Thomas Cave … or not'.

[35] ibid.

[36] Note the broad scope afforded to the defence of *bona fide* purchase which is here used as a defence to a legal demand (ie, to an extent claimed by the trustee's creditors on the recognisance).

B. Chancery

Early indications that the Chancery too might grant relief against non-privies can be seen in counsel's arguments in *Reynell v Peacock* (1619).[37] Although the case did not concern relief against a legal demandant, Sir John Walter asserted that:

> It is to be agreed that a trust is more strong and does more nearly fix and bind the land than a use at the common law … A tenant by curtesy shall not be seised to a use at common law but still he will be seised and subject to a trust, and thus all others if [there is] no valuable consideration.[38]

Walter's words suggested that the trust was developing more pronounced proprietary overtones which, in turn, were bringing the trust out of the shadow of the use and the restrictive doctrine of privity.[39] Over the course of the seventeenth century, the Chancery leant increasingly against the claims of legal demandants to trust and mortgage property. In the middle decades of the century, however, Chancery's forms of relief remained tied to the specific circumstances of the case and seem not to have been generalised in the way contemplated by Walter in 1619.

Between 1630 and 1660, disputes touching legal demands to trusts of copyhold lands appear regularly in the Chancery and illustrate well the particularistic form of relief available against non-privies. In *Petty v Styward* (1631)[40] – decided a year after *Nash v Preston* – the Chancery refused to aid a trustee's widow claiming her widow's estate in the trust property. In that case, Simeon Styward had held certain copyhold lands upon trust for his father, Nicholas Styward. Following Simeon's death,[41] his widow claimed her free bench over the copyhold lands, and Nicholas – the beneficiary – sought to resist her claim. Unlike *Nash v Preston*, the issue was not referred to the common law judges. Instead, it was decreed that:

> whereas the plaintiff claimed a widow's estate in certain copyhold lands forasmuch as it appeared that the defendant [Nicholas Styward] always received the profits thereof to his own use and as was conceived the defendant granted the same to his son [Simeon Styward] in trust[.] And it appeared not that his son paid anything for the same this court therefore could not give the plaintiff any relief therein.[42]

As with the Court of Wards' decree in *Cholmeley v Cave*, it seemed that, where the trustee had not given value for the legal estate, the Chancery would protect the beneficiary from the claims of the trustee's legal demandants. In the absence of valuable consideration moving from the trustee, therefore, the objection from privity might be overcome. If this was a jurisdiction based wholly on the trustee not having given value, it may also explain why relief was not forthcoming in *Nash v Preston*; unlike *Cholmeley v Cave*

[37] 118 *Selden Society* 479.

[38] ibid 480.

[39] For discussion of the proprietisation of the trust at this time, see Jones (n 27) 95–118 and Foster (n 2) 112–25.

[40] PRO C33/162, f 93; BL Lansdowne 640, f 41. See also Jones (n 27) 105.

[41] PRO PROB11/155/461 (will of Simeon Styward, date of probate was 1 May 1629); PRO PROB11/162/138 (sentence, 30 June 1632).

[42] PRO C33/162, f 93.

and *Petty v Styward*, which concerned voluntary trusts, *Nash v Preston* had involved a mortgage whereby the mortgagee had given valuable consideration for the mortgagor's legal estate. In that sense, the mortgagee might have been regarded as a purchaser of the estate and thus outside equity's remedial jurisdiction.[43]

Cases involving widows' rights to copyhold land continued to appear in the Chancery through the 1640s and 1650s. Whilst the absence of valuable consideration moving from the trustee had been a significant issue in *Petty v Steward*, the Chancery seems to have broadened the range of circumstances relevant to the grant of relief in the later cases. In his *Abridgment of Chancery Causes*, John Lisle (Lord Commissioner in Chancery, 1649–59) included several relevant cases under the heading 'Who shall and who shall not be said to stand seised to a Use or Trust'.[44] The impetus for including this heading in the abridgment was the case of *Thinne v Lewis*.[45] In that case, copyhold land was granted to a trustee. The trustee died and his wife claimed the copyhold as her widow's estate by the custom of the manor. The question was whether the widow should take the land subject to the trust, but the determination of the case appears to have been controversial. In Lisle's first entry for *Thinne v Lewis*, he wrote:

> Trustee of copyhold lands or any other lands in fee dies, and his wife by the law is entitled *al* dower, either by the custom or by the law, whether [the] *cestui que trust* shall set aside the dower; in which case [the] court did seem to be of opinion that he should not, [she] being in by the custom which was precedent *al* trust.[46]

On this reasoning, the widow was to be preferred to the beneficiary on the grounds that she entered by a precedent estate to which the trust was not annexed.[47] The case was subsequently re-argued before the court, and, on this occasion, Lisle recorded that:

> the question was whether a copyhold estate granted in trust, if the same falls out to be a trust where the custom admits widows' estates[,] whether the widow should not in equity hold her estate under the same trust as her husband did. The court did order to see precedents.[48]

Immediately following this entry, Lisle listed a number of precedents on point. The cases broadly seem to follow the *Nash v Preston* line that equity could not relieve against a dowress.[49] In *Miller v Coker*,[50] for example, the mortgagor of land in fee simple brought a bill to redeem against both the heir and dowress of the mortgagee. Lisle noted that 'if the wife [of the] mortgagee had been dowable at law, no decree could have been made against her'.[51] However, some of the precedents listed by Lisle appeared to permit an exception in cases involving trusts of copyhold lands where the legal demandant entered

[43] It was not until the later seventeenth century that the mortgagee was recognised as having primarily an interest in repayment, rather than in the land itself (see Yale (n 2) 40–44; Turner (n 11) 38–42 and 58–64).

[44] Kansas University, MS D87, f 426r–v.

[45] (c. 1650s) Kansas University, MS D87, ff 384 and 426. Pleadings at PRO C7/397/93 (1652) and PRO C7/348/101 (1653).

[46] Kansas University, MS D87, f 384.

[47] This logic echoed the explanation for the immunity of the lord by escheat to pre-existing equities. For discussion, see Foster (n 2) 119–120 and 123.

[48] Kansas University, MS D87, f 426.

[49] Lisle had included Croke's report of *Nash v Preston* in his *Abridgment* at f 388v.

[50] (1645x1650s) Kansas University, MS D87, f 426. Pleadings at PRO C6/149/35 (1645) and PRO C9/3/124 (1647).

[51] ibid f 426.

by the custom of the manor. In *Countess of Salop v Sayle*,[52] it was held that the heir of the trustee of copyhold land took subject to the trust 'for as he comes in by the custom [of the manor] so he comes in in privity of the trust thereof'.[53] In *Thinne v Bamfield*,[54] it was said that 'a trust may be annexed to a copyhold estate, for although custom doth … make good the estate, yet it is ruled by the act of the party, but he that is in merely by the act of the law as an occupant etc.,[[55]] a trust cannot be annexed to that estate'.[56] Following this discussion of the precedents, Lisle returned to *Thinne v Lewis*. In this entry, Lisle wrote:

> where a trust is annexed to an estate, whilst that estate can limit anyone who comes to have an estate or interest in that land … although he doth not come in in the *per*, but merely by act of law or custom, yet he shall be liable to the trust; and so many precedents cited to prove this.[57]

In *Thinne v Lewis*, therefore, it was resolved that, in trusts of copyhold land, the trustee's widow – like the trustee's heir in *Salop v Sayle* – was to be regarded as privy to the trust by virtue of the custom of the manor. *Thinne v Lewis* was clear that the widow did not enter in the *per*; nevertheless, the custom of the manor was sufficient to create a privity between the legal demandant and beneficiary.

By the late 1650s, therefore, the Chancery had developed specific reasons for granting relief against legal demandants in cases involving copyhold land. Following the Restoration, we can see a further expansion of Chancery's remedial jurisdiction against legal demandants with the advent of relief against special occupants. Initially denied in *Thinne v Bamfield*,[58] relief against a special occupant was ultimately granted in the case of *Stephens v Baily* (1665–67).[59] A special occupancy arose where a tenant *pur autre vie* died before the *cestui que vie*. An estate *pur autre vie* was neither descendible nor devisable and, where the tenant *pur autre vie* died, the land could be claimed by the first person to occupy it – known as a 'general occupancy'. Where the grant of the estate *pur autre vie* specified a person to take the estate in the event of the tenant's death, the specified person could enter as a 'special occupant'.[60] In *Stephens v Baily* (1665–67), the tenant *pur autre vie* had covenanted to mortgage the land to the plaintiff for £1,200, but died before the conveyance

[52] (1625x1632) Kansas University, MS D87, f 426. Pleadings at PRO C2/ChasI/S14/24 (1625–1660).

[53] ibid f 426.

[54] (1651x1658) Kansas University, MS D87, f 426. Pleadings at PRO C7/128/102 (1651); enrolled decree at PRO C79/193/2 (1658).

[55] For occupancy, see discussion of *Stephens v Baily* immediately below.

[56] Kansas University, MS D87, f 426. Immediately following the quoted passage, there is an interlineation in a different ink, which states 'nor to dower, either by custom or law'.

[57] ibid f 426v.

[58] ibid f 426.

[59] Nels 106. Records available at: PRO C6/173/33 and PRO C33/228, f 237. Prior to this date, there is evidence that relief might be available in Chancery against a special occupant where the tenant *pur autre vie* had attempted to devise the estate *pur autre vie* to another (such devises being ineffective at law); see *Hunt v Youngman* (1619) Toth 285, PRO C33/137, f 371r–v ('[the defendant had] of late set on foot a title of occupancy … which kind of title this court hath not heretofore favoured as doth appear by presidents of the same nature'). The availability of such relief was controverted and subsequently denied in *James & Draper's case* (1649) *Prolegomena*, c 20, s 6 (also cited in *Drake v Drake* (1673) 73 *Selden Society* 5 and *Venables v Bland* (1679/70) 79 *Selden Society* 795, 796). The rule against devises of estates *per autre vie* was reversed by the Statute of Frauds 1677 (29 Car II, c 29, s 12).

[60] For detail, see NG Jones, *Trusts: Practice and Doctrine, 1536-1660* (1994) University of Cambridge (unpublished PhD thesis) 244–7.

was effected. The defendant was the son of the tenant *pur autre vie* and entered the land as a special occupant. The plaintiff brought a bill in Chancery alleging that the defendant thus stood entrusted with the land for the plaintiff's benefit. Equity had long held that trusts were enforceable against the heir of the trustee,[61] but the special occupant was not in by descent. Rather, the special occupancy arose by operation of law, and the occupant (so it was argued) lacked the requisite privity to be bound by his ancestor's agreement. Indeed, the defendant demurred to the plaintiff's bill on the grounds that 'he was in possession as an occupant, and so was not privy to his father who made the contract'.[62]

For the plaintiff-purchaser, Maynard argued for an analogy with the heir of the trustee. He also drew particular attention to the fact that the plaintiff had given value for his equitable rights. Maynard argued:

> that an occupant was bound by this agreement in equity: that the plaintiff, who was out of his money, ought to have relief: that where a man contracts for the purchase of lands, and dies before the assurance is executed, the heir of the vendor stands trusted for the purchaser, and is compellable in this court to execute the estate to him, and that trusts here are of another nature than uses are at common law: that a covenant doth not bind an occupant at law, because the estate which he possesseth by the occupancy is not assets in law; but here it is a trust: that if a copyholder takes money, and covenants to convey, his heir is not bound at law, yet this court will compel him. So in this case, the lands are bound by the agreement in whose hands soever they fall.[63]

By contrast, Heneage Finch (later Nottingham LC), for the defendant-occupant, drew an analogy with the lord entering by escheat, against whom no equity lay. Where the trustee died intestate and without heirs, the trustee's legal estate came to an end, and the land went to the lord discharged of the trust.[64] Technically, the lord entered in the *post* by a 'title paramount' – an estate which preceded the trustee's and to which the trust was not annexed. For Finch, the special occupant entering by operation of law was to be treated as equivalent to the lord by escheat entering in the *post*:

> 'tis more like the case of one seised in fee, who contracts to sell, and dies before any assurance, and without heir, so that his lands escheat to the lord: this court will not compel that lord to convey to the vendee.[65]

The case was referred to Tyrrill J, who certified that the defendant ought to answer the plaintiff's bill and either make good the conveyance or repay the mortgage money.[66] No reason for the decision is reported, and the basis for the decree remains obscure. There

[61] YB Pas 22 Edw IV, f 6, pl 18 (Hussey CJ); *Dod v Chyttynden* (1502) 116 *Selden Society* 395, 396 (Vavasour J).

[62] Nels 106.

[63] ibid 106–7.

[64] See *Wickes' case* (1609) Lane 54.

[65] Nels 106, 107. See also Finch LK's decision in *Drake v Drake* (1673) 73 *Selden Society* 5, concerning the attempted devise of an estate *per autre vie*: 'the devise is void in law … and therefore the heir not claiming under his father nor by descent but by act in law as special occupant, I would not decree that from him which the law gave him'.

[66] PRO C33/228, f 237, dated 16 January 1667: 'the said judge having heard counsel on both sides and advised with the rest of the judges certified that the said defendant Bayly and his wife ought to answer and to make good the mortgage or pay the mortgage money.' See also Nottingham's remarks in *Elliot v Hele* (1680) 79 *Selden Society* 816.

is a hint in the records that stronger proprietary notions of the beneficiary's right under a trust may have been important to the court's disposal of the case. The bill of complaint in *Stephens v Bailey* is notable for its assertion that the plaintiff had 'an equitable interest and estate of all the said premises',[67] and this same language of 'equitable interest' is found in the Decree & Order book entries for the case.[68] There are, however, several other possible explanations for the decree. It may be that, following Maynard's argument for the plaintiff, the Chancery was unwilling to decree against a purchaser of equitable rights – even where the legal demandant entered by operation of law. Alternatively, the case may have followed the logic of *Thinne v Lewis*: the special occupant, claiming by the terms on which the estate *per autre vie* had been granted, might be regarded as equivalent to the widow claiming by the custom of the manor and hence privy to the estate to which the trust was annexed. In either event, the extant cases suggest that, by the time of the Restoration, the Chancery was willing to grant relief against certain classes of legal demandant in specific circumstances; in this sense, equitable relief remained constrained and particularistic. Relevant factors included the presence of valuable consideration moving either from the trustee or beneficiary, and whether the legal demandant entered by custom of the manor or by some other means. It was not until a significant decision on the equity side of the Exchequer, that the availability of relief against non-privies would become more generally available in the Chancery.

C. Equity Side of the Exchequer

The equity side of the Exchequer dealt most commonly with matters of equity pertaining to the Crown revenue. Where a trustee or mortgagee committed treason and forfeited the legal estate to the Crown, it was to the Exchequer that the dispossessed beneficiary or mortgagor would turn for a remedy. In the late sixteenth century, it seems that such claims were not heard sympathetically by the Barons of the Exchequer.[69] There were two major obstacles to equitable relief against the Crown: (i) the doctrine of the privity; and (ii) the absence of an equitable jurisdiction to make compulsory decrees against the Crown.[70] In the first place, the King by forfeiture or escheat entered by operation of law, taking free of prior equities. For as long as the logic of privity was respected, therefore, the Crown would be held immune to equitable claims. Even if the logic of privity were to be cast aside, the absence of a compulsory jurisdiction against the Crown remained a bar to equitable relief. In *Turberville v Swame* (1631),[71] for example, Coventry LK had explained that the proper means for bringing a claim against the Crown was by petition of grace:

> And though there is no compulsory equity in any court of equity to force the King to confirm his grant, yet there is a remedy by way of appeal to the person of the king by way of petition, and the King being informed of the truth, will have the patent amended in all conscience,

[67] PRO C6/173/33, dated 21 March 1664.

[68] PRO C33/226, f 106, dated 26 April 1666 (before Tyrrill J).

[69] *R v Boys* (1568) 3 Dyer 283b (forfeiture for trustee's alienage); *Pimb's case* (1585) Moo KB 196 (forfeiture for trustee's treason); *Wickes' case* (1609) Lane 54 (forfeiture for trustee's treason).

[70] *Prolegomena*, c 14, s 20.

[71] Lincoln's Inn (LI) MS Maynard 75, f 47v (printed in WH Bryson, *Reports of Cases in the Court of Chancery in the Time of Lord Coventry* (Indianapolis, IN, Dog Ear, 2018) 161–4).

> because it is the intention of the King that good conscience and right should be observed between him and his subjects as between subject and subject.[72]

Outside this procedure for petitioning the Crown, there seemed little scope for the legal system to provide a remedy to equitable right-holders whose expectations had been defeated by a forfeiture or escheat of the legal estate to the Crown.

Relief against the Crown for beneficiaries under a trust was further hampered by a general rule that the King could not be a trustee for a subject.[73] In *Wickes' case* (1609),[74] for example, Graunt made a lease to Somerfield and Wintour in trust for Graunt's wife and children. Graunt and Wintour were attainted of treason for their involvement in the Gunpowder Plot. The King seized the moiety of the lease which had been held by Wintour and became a tenant in common with Somerfield. Thereafter, Wickes married Graunt's widow (the beneficiary under the trust of the lease) and brought a bill in the Exchequer to enforce the trust against the King. It was decreed by Tanfield CB and the other barons that the King took the land discharged of the trust:

> the King … shall not be ordered in equity to perform the trust reposed in [the trustee] … for the King cannot be seised to another man's use, no more can his estate be subject to any trust at this day.[75]

By the early seventeenth century, therefore, a general view had emerged that the King could not be a trustee; where a trust estate came into the hands of the King, the beneficiary's right was unenforceable against him. The prospect of equitable relief against the Crown thus appeared bleak.

Following the Restoration, however, it seems that a new jurisdiction to make compulsory decrees against the Crown began to emerge on the equity side of the Exchequer. This new jurisdiction was coupled with a greater willingness to cast off the restrictive doctrine of privity when vindicating equitable rights to forfeited estates. It may be no coincidence that such equities did not emerge until after the Restoration.[76] The constitutional settlement of 1660 may well have encouraged the judiciary to show less deference to Crown rights than their Tudor and early Stuart forebears,[77] but it was the appointment of Sir Matthew Hale as Chief Baron of the Exchequer in particular which marked the turning point in

[72] ibid. In that case, the patentee had notice of the complainant's right and was, therefore, bound by the complainant's equity after the grant from the King.

[73] *Willion v Berkeley* (1562) 1 Plow 223, 238.

[74] Lane 54.

[75] ibid.

[76] On greater security of judicial tenure immediately after the Restoration and possibly greater judicial independence in this period, see AF Havighurst, 'The Judiciary and Politics in the Reign of Charles II, Part I, 1660-1676)' (1950) 66 *Law Quarterly Review* 62, esp 63–5 and 71–8. On greater royal interference with the judiciary after 1668, however, see D Lemmings, 'The Independence of the Judiciary in Eighteenth Century England' in PBH Birks (ed), *The Life of the Law* (London, Hambledon Press, 1993) 125, 128–9.

[77] *Cf* JL Barton, 'The Statute of Uses and the Trust of Freehold' (1966) 82 *Law Quarterly Review* 215, 225, remarking that the Tudor judges were 'by no means the submissive guardians of the royal financial interests they are sometimes represented to have been'. On this point, see also DJ Ibbetson, 'Elizabethan Revenue Law: The Practice of the Court of Wards' in J Tiley (ed), *Studies in the History of Tax Law, vol IV* (Oxford, Hart Publishing, 2010) 107–20.

equity's approach to Crown liability. In his judicial work, Hale was generally not unwilling to rule against Crown interests,[78] but the extent of the equities Hale contemplated against the Crown was revolutionary.[79] Hale's decisions on the enforceability of equitable rights against the Crown placed this area of law on a new – and greatly expanded – footing and laid the foundation for regularised relief against non-privies.

We can see an aspect of the emerging equity jurisdiction against the Crown in the case of *Hicks v AG* (1661).[80] The case is imperfectly reported by Hardres as holding that a beneficiary under a trust 'was [to be] relieved against the King upon this trust in equity'.[81] The case does not quite stand for the proposition attributed to it by Hardres, and recourse to the records is required to correct the report. In *Hicks*, Sir William Cooper and James Cooper borrowed £200 on a bond from William Toomes. Toomes held the bond on trust for Sir William Hicks. In 1655, Toomes became a *felo de se* and the bond was forfeited to the Crown. In a bill for payment, the Coopers refused to pay the money directly to Hicks on the grounds that, as a mere beneficiary under a trust, he could not give a lawful discharge for the debt. Following the Restoration of the monarchy and the passage of the Act of Oblivion 1660,[82] the Crown's interest in the debt was 'discharged'[83] and Toomes' forfeiture declared 'null and void'.[84] Granting relief on the plaintiff's bill, the Barons decreed:

> And for that by the Act of Oblivion the King's interest in the said debt if any is discharged, It is this day ordered, adjudged and decreed by the court That the said def[endan]t Sir William Cooper by his own consent shall forthwith pay unto the said pl[aintiff] or his assigns the sum of [£207] of lawful money of England in full discharge of the said debt and interest for the same, and that upon payment thereof the said pl[aintiff] shall deliver up the said bond to the said def[endan]t Sir William Cooper to be cancelled and made void; And that the said pl[aintiff], his heirs, executors and administrators shall save the said Sir William Cooper and James Cooper his son their and every of their heirs, executors and administrators harmless concerning the said debt against the administrators of the goods and chattels of the said William Toomes late deceased and against the King's majesty that now is, his heirs and successors and against all other person and persons whatsoever.[85]

The Barons thus ordered the defendant-debtors to pay the plaintiff-beneficiary and for the plaintiff to deliver up the bond to be cancelled. Contrary to Hardres' brief summation of the case, *Hicks v AG* (1661) does not provide clear evidence that the Exchequer would grant relief against the Crown. Rather, the peculiar operation of the Act of Oblivion seems to have been the basis for the plaintiff's successful enforcement of the trust in that case. The decision does, however, demonstrate that following the Restoration, the

[78] A Cromartie, *Sir Matthew Hale, 1609-1676: Law, Religion and Natural Philosophy* (Cambridge, Cambridge University Press, 1995) 118–35.
[79] Turner (n 11) 51–54.
[80] Reported as *Hix v AG* at Hardres 176 (which also misdates the case to 1671). What follows is drawn from the records of the case at: PRO E126/8/46.
[81] Hardres 176.
[82] 12 Car II, c 11, ss 1–2.
[83] PRO E126/8/46. This same language is used in section 2 of the Act of Oblivion.
[84] 12 Chas II, c 11, s 2.
[85] PRO E126/8/46.

Exchequer was increasingly required to adjudicate on competing claims to the legal estate between equitable right-holders and the Crown.

The key development came with the decision in *Pawlett v AG* (1667–69).[86] In this case we can see a clearer elaboration of equity's jurisdiction against the Crown. On the facts, the legal title to mortgaged lands had escheated to the Crown, and the question was whether the mortgagor's equity of redemption could be enforced against the Crown or its assignee. In the case, the plaintiff, Charles Pawlett (or Poulett or Powlett), mortgaged his lands in fee to Sir Henry Ludlow (upon a recognisance for £3,000). Sir Henry died in 1643, leaving Edmund Ludlow his heir. Edmund was ultimately attainted of treason by the Attainder of Regicides Act 1660[87] and barred from succeeding to his father's inheritance. As a result, upon Sir Henry's death, the legal title to the mortgaged premises had escheated to the Crown. Under the terms of the recognisance, Pawlett was still liable to pay the mortgage debt to the executors of Ludlow's estate, but owing to the escheat, the executors were unable to reconvey the mortgaged lands upon repayment.[88]

The facts of the case are further complicated by the Crown's subsequent grant of the escheated lands to the Countess of Falmouth. In late 1666, the Countess petitioned the King for a grant of the escheated lands.[89] The Countess' petition was referred to the Attorney-General (Sir Geoffrey Palmer) who found that the land had indeed escheated to the Crown. Palmer also observed that:

> if the mortgagor shall redeem, the money payable upon the redemption must be answered to your majesty's use, or as you shall please to dispose, and that the executor of the mortgagee … have no right to the lands or money either in law or equity.[90]

The Attorney-General's opinion clearly suggests that he conceived the mortgagor to have an equity of redemption which might be enforceable against the Crown (albeit that the Crown, rather than Ludlow's executors, would be entitled to the mortgage monies).[91] In January 1667, notwithstanding the Attorney-General's advice, the King granted some of the escheated lands to the Countess of Falmouth.[92]

By June 1667, Pawlett had brought a bill on the equity side of the Exchequer to redeem the mortgage against the King.[93] The Attorney-General demurred to the bill,[94] and, on 4 February 1668, the cause was listed to be heard but with a direction for

[86] Hardres 465; LI MS Misc 499, f 213, 394 (translation printed in WH Bryson, *Equity Cases in the Court of Exchequer, 1660-1714* (Arizona, ACMRS, 2007) 23); *Prolegomena*, c 12, s 12. Records found at: PRO E127/4/321v, 407v, 424v, 461v and 486v; PRO SP29/182/138; PRO SP44/18/243; PRO SP44/30/113.

[87] 12 Car II c 30.

[88] PRO SP29/190/61 (4 Feb 1667): 'the said mortgaged premises are escheated to your majesty and the petitioner Charles Powlett is thereby … compellable to pay the said moneys to the other petitioners; yet they cannot make, nor the said Charles Powlett have such reconveyance of his said mortgaged lands, as ought to have been made to him by the heirs of the said mortgagee.'

[89] PRO SP29/182/138 (4 December 1666).

[90] ibid.

[91] Palmer AG seems to have vacillated on this point; see PRO SP29/190/61 (4 Feb 1667) in which Palmer opined that 'the said mortgaged premises are escheated to your majesty and the petitioner Charles Powlett is thereby in strictness debarred of his benefit of redemption thereof'.

[92] PRO SP44/23/315.

[93] PRO E127/4/321v.

[94] PRO E127/4/407v.

Pawlett and Ludlow's executors to apply to the King on a petition of grace for regrant of the mortgaged lands.[95] On that same day (4 February 1668), Charles Pawlett and the executors petitioned the King to grant them the lands which had not been given to the Countess. The petition was again referred to the Attorney-General, who in March 1668 advised a grant in Pawlett's favour:

> I humbly conceive that Edmond Ludlow having lands only by way of mortgage from Charles Pawlett esq. and liable in his hands to an equity of redemption, It is a reasonable favour for your majesty to admit Mr Pawlet the mortgagor to a redemption which he must have by way of a grant from your majesty ... Upon the whole matter I conceive the executors are not entitled to the mortgage lands or money by law or any regular equity[.] But how far your majesty out of your goodness will consider them as to the mortgage moneys is humbly submitted.[96]

Upon the escheat of the mortgaged lands, therefore, the Attorney-General had considered that the mortgagor might attempt to redeem the mortgage. In this second opinion, the Attorney-General countenanced the regranting of the land to the mortgagor. Perhaps an obstinance in the Crown (having already granted some of the land to another) led to the Attorney-General's advice being ignored, but the reason is not clear from the records. In any case, no grant was made to the plaintiff, and the case in the Exchequer continued. The question which arose on the facts of the case was whether the Exchequer could order the Attorney-General to answer the plaintiff's bill of complaint.

In the Exchequer, counsel for the Crown argued that there could be no remedy against the King, and that the complainant's only course of action was to proceed by petition of grace:

> the question now upon a demurrer to the bill was, whether or no the plaintiff could have any remedy against the King, to have a redemption? And it was said for the King, that he could not. But that he must prefer his petition of grace and favour. For a mortgage is in the nature of a trust betwixt the mortgagor and mortgagee; and no more than the King can be seized to an use, or in trust for another, so as to have remedy against the King for it; Dyer, 8[[97]] ... no more is there any remedy against him to redeem a mortgaged estate. Also the King cannot be compelled to execute any conveyances ...[98]

Sawyer, for the King, argued on an analogy between trusts and mortgages:

> the case in question is only a trust and the King is not liable to the executor [for] a trust. And also insisted that the King is in by escheat of his title paramount, and [asked] whether relief should be [had] against him in such a case. In both cases, as well when a mortgagor as a mortgagee dying without heirs, the King would lose his escheat, if relief was allowed.[99]

On a similar line, the Attorney-General argued:

> that the King is not compellable in equity, because no *subpoena* lies against him. And if the King is not compellable to execute a use, he should not be compelled to execute a trust. And

[95] PRO E127/4/461v.
[96] PRO SP29/190/61, 62.
[97] *R v Boys* (1568) 3 Dyer 283b.
[98] Hardres 465, 465–6.
[99] Bryson (n 86) 23.

> he said that, though he is compellable to answer, yet the King is not compellable to convey … [T]hey said that a petition of grace was the plaintiff's sole remedy.[100]

At its core, the argument for the Crown was threefold: first, it was argued that mortgages were analogous to trusts and that, just as the King could not hold upon trust for a subject, so the King could not hold land encumbered by an equity of redemption; secondly, that the King by escheat entered in the *post* and was not privy to the plaintiff's equity; and, thirdly, that regardless of any equitable rights attaching to the legal estate, there was simply no mechanism in the Exchequer to enforce the plaintiff's right.

Following these submissions, Sir Matthew Hale CB inclined to the view that the Attorney-General should be compelled to answer the plaintiff's bill:

> because the King is in purely by escheat and not by prerogative, as a forfeiture. And though a wife of a mortgagee in fee will be endowed, yet there will be relief against her.[[101]] And also against a free bench of the wife of copyhold lands surrendered to her husband in trust.[102]

In this passage, the Chief Baron suggested that cases of escheat were analogous to cases concerning a widow's right to her husband's lands. Hale thus concluded that, as relief was available against the mortgagee or trustee's widow, so it ought to be available against the King by escheat. These remarks clearly indicate that privity was not the jurisdictional bar for Hale that it had been for his predecessors.

Following Hale's remarks, the case was adjourned and reargued at a later date. On this occasion, Montague, North and Sawyer appeared on behalf of the Crown. As authority for the lack of an equitable jurisdiction in such cases, Montague cited the *Earl of Cleveland's case*, which had involved identical facts but, not being resolved in the Exchequer, 'was constrained to go to Parliament'.[103] Montague further observed that 'there is not any relief in equity against a disseisor', with the clear implication that the same ought to be true of the Crown by escheat.[104] Thereafter, North relied on *Nash v Preston* (1630) to demonstrate (*contra* Hale) that no relief could be had against the dowress because 'where there is not any fraud or covin, a court of equity will not relieve'.[105] Finally, Sawyer presented an elaborate argument from the doctrine of privity:

> the King was in his original estate and by title paramount, and on account of that he is not liable to the collateral rights of a mortgagor and mortgagee, but inferior estate[s] as dower, curtesy, occupancy etc, which are carved out of the general estate, can be liable to encumbrances, and on account of that the courts of equity relieve against them. And all these cases hold in the case of a subject and then in the case of the King *a fortiori* for the reason of his pre-eminence and prerogative [citing *Wickes' case* (1609) among others] … But his great objection

[100] ibid 24.

[101] This appears to be a reference to the facts of *Nash v Preston* (1630) Cro Car 190. Contrary to Croke's report of that case, however, Hale suggested that relief *was* available in equity against the mortgagee's dowress.

[102] Bryson (n 86) 24.

[103] In *Pawlett v AG* (1667) Hardres 465, 467, Hale CB too spoke of the *Earl of Cleveland's case* (1666). The case is not otherwise reported but seems also to have concerned the forfeiture of mortgaged lands to the King. The case was pending before the Exchequer during the hearing of *Pawlett v AG* but was ultimately resolved by an Act of Parliament rather than by judicial intervention (for which, see *Statutes of the Realm, vol V*, 303, 320 and 622).

[104] Bryson (n 86) 24.

[105] ibid 25.

> was that if the mortgagor dies after forfeiture without heirs, the land will not escheat. And if the mortgagee dies after forfeiture without issue, if relief may be against him in equity, then in both cases the lord will lose his escheat, which is harsh, and in this question, the court cannot decree relief against the King.[106]

Sawyer seemed to recognise that the course of equitable jurisprudence had changed, and that relief *could* be had against certain 'inferior' estates arising by operation of law, including tenancies by dower, curtesy and occupancy. Sawyer's argument was, in effect, one concerning derivative title; the judgment creditor and the dowress all, in some way, derived their title from the act of the trustee/mortgagee and ought in principle to be bound by any pre-existing equities. This was clearly an advance on the more restrictive principles stated in *Gervys v Cooke* (1522), where Broke and Pollard JJ had observed that only heirs, grantees and assignees might be considered as claiming 'through' (or '*per*') the trustee.[107] According to Sawyer, certain classes of legal demandant claiming by operation of law were now to be regarded as bound by equitable rights. Provided the legal demandant claimed an 'inferior' estate, in some way derived (or 'carved out') from the mortgagee/trustee's estate, they would take subject to pre-existing equities.[108]

On Sawyer's logic, however, there were two classes of legal demandant against whom pre-existing equities remained unenforceable. Neither the lord by escheat nor the disseisor could be regarded as claiming 'through' the trustee/mortgagee. The lord by escheat had a title which was 'original' and 'paramount' – it was an estate precedent to that of the mortgagee and to which the mortgagor's equitable rights were not annexed. By contrast, the disseisor claimed a tortious fee by adverse possession; this was a new estate, not deriving from the disseised legal owner, and it was clear of any equities annexed to the disseisee's title. For these reasons, escheat and disseisin were treated as distinct from the 'inferior' titles arising by operation of law which Sawyer regarded as derivative of the trustee/mortgagee's estate.[109]

Ultimately, Sawyer failed to convince the Barons of the Exchequer as to the immunity of the Crown to the equity of redemption. Decreeing for the plaintiff, Hale CB and the *puisne* Barons ordered the Attorney-General to answer the plaintiff's bill:

> This court doth declare, That inasmuch as they are of opinion, That there is an equity of redemption in the plaintiff not taken away by the escheat of the mortgaged lands to his Majesty, It is therefore ordered by the court, That the demurrer do stand overruled, and Mr Attorney-General is to be attended to put in his answer to the plaintiff's bill, but without prejudice to any claim of the defendants as executors of the mortgagee.[110]

The terms of this decree are somewhat remarkable. Not only was the Attorney-General ordered to provide a full answer to the bill, but the Barons went so far as to declare the continuing existence of the plaintiff's equity of redemption in the land. The escheat to

[106] ibid 25.
[107] 119 *Selden Society* 108, 117 (Broke J) and 119 (Pollard J).
[108] It may be that it was Sawyer's remarks which inspired Thomas Lewin's account of derivative title in equity (T Lewin, *A Practical Treatise on the Law of Trusts and Trustees* (London, A Maxwell, 1837) 18–19). Note, however, the tension between the language of 'carving out' and the 'engrafting' principle when applied to equitable estates. On this point, see Foster (n 2) 125, fn 107.
[109] Foster (n 2) 122–3.
[110] PRO E127/4/486v.

the Crown had not had the effect of clearing title to the land of all pre-existing equities. This flew in the face of centuries of legal learning and marked a watershed moment in the history of equitable jurisprudence.

In a wide-ranging judgment, Sir Matthew Hale CB took the opportunity to consider the nature of the equitable rights of the mortgagor, the continuing significance of the doctrine of privity and the extent of equity's jurisdiction against the Crown. Rejecting the arguments from the Crown, Hale first observed that the analogy between mortgages and trusts was a false equivalence:

> There is a great diversity between trusts and rights of redemption. And he thought that there should be relief against all who come in in the *post*.[111]

This point is reported at greater length in Hardres:

> There is a diversity betwixt a trust and a power of redemption; for a trust is created by the contract of the party, and he may direct it as he pleaseth; and he may provide for the execution of it, and therefore one that comes in in the *post* shall not be liable to it without express mention made by the party; and the rules for executing a trust have often varied, and therefore they only are bound by it, who come in in privity of estate. A tenant in dower is bound by it, because she is in the *per*,[[112]] but not a tenant by the courtesy, who is in the *post*.[[113]] So all who come in in privity of estate, or with notice, or without a consideration. But a power of redemption is an equitable right inherent in the land, and binds all persons in the *post*, or otherwise. Because it is an ancient right, which the party is entitled to in equity.[114]

In this difficult passage, Hale distinguished the mortgagor's right of redemption from the beneficiary's right under a trust on the grounds that a trust bound only in privity, whilst the equity of redemption inhered in the land such that it might bind the possession.[115] Although the rights of the beneficiary remained generally unenforceable against legal demandants entering in the *post*, the rights of the mortgagor were now thought to bind any subsequent owner of the land, including the lord by escheat entering in the *post* by a title paramount.[116]

Having established that the mortgagor's equity bound all categories of non-privy, Hale turned to consider the equitable jurisdiction against the Crown. In his judgment, Hale stopped short of deciding the remedy but remarked that:

> although by the escheat the tenure is extinguished, that will be nothing to the purpose, because the party may be recompensed for that by the court, by a decree for rent, or part of the land itself, or some other satisfaction … But … the King is in actual possession, and cannot be removed in equity by an *amoveas manum*, as he may at law.[117]

[111] Bryson (n 86) 27.
[112] Hale may be referring to nominated dower here; on which, see n 23 above.
[113] Relief against tenants by curtesy was far from clear-cut in the sources. Cf *Reynell v Peacock* (1619) 118 *Selden Society* 479, 480 (Walter *in arguendo*) and Sheppard (n 3) 503.
[114] Hardres 465, 469. See also Nottingham's entry on *Pawlett v AG* at *Prolegomena*, c 12, s 12: 'But now an equity [of redemption] is an interest fixed on the land, and not lost on any pretence of coming in *en le post*, as a trust is.' As to Nottingham's views on the nature of the trust, however, *cf Prolegomena*, c 12, s 5: 'The … trust remains still as it was at Common law, *viz.* an equitable interest in the land, which enables no man to use or enjoy the possession or profits of the land without the help of a court of conscience by way of *subpoena*.'
[115] Rights annexed to the possession of land were contrasted to rights annexed in privity in *Chudleigh's case* (1594) 1 Co Rep 120a, 122a. See also, Foster (n 2) 120.
[116] See also *Roscarrick v Barton* (1672) 1 Ch Cas 17, *Prolegomena*, c 21, ss 22–3.
[117] Hardres 465, 469.

This point is made more explicitly in Ward's report of Hale's judgment:

> [T]he great question was in respect of the person of the King. And he said when the King is entitled by a single matter of record, it is not any entry upon him, but when it is granted over, that entry can be [made] upon the grantee, and thus he thought that if the King would grant over the lands in question that relief should be against the grantee.[118]

According to Hale, whilst it was true that the court could not order the King to reconvey the land to the mortgagor, the Exchequer could make such an order against the King's grantee.[119] By this stage, the King had already granted some of the escheated land to the Countess of Falmouth; had the litigation proceeded, the clear intimation of the judges was that compulsory decrees to reconvey and compensate might be made against the Countess. On this point, Atkyns was rather more strident than the Chief Baron. In Atkyns' opinion:

> The party ought in this case to be relieved against the King, because the King is the fountain and head of justice and equity; and it shall not be presumed, that he will be defective in either. And it would derogate from the King's honour to imagine, that what is equity against a common person, should not be equity against him.[120]

The clear view of the Barons of the Exchequer, therefore, was that the plaintiff ought to have an efficacious remedy in equity.

At this stage, the proceedings in the Exchequer came to an end; the Attorney-General was ordered to answer, and the plaintiff was declared to have an equitable right in the land. The facts of the case are completed by referring back to the records in the State Papers. In his petition on 4 February 1668, Pawlett had requested that the King grant the lands to Ludlow's executors;[121] no reason is given, but presumably, it was intended on the basis that this would discharge Pawlett's mortgage debt. In February 1669, after the order in the Exchequer, the Crown duly complied with Pawlett's request and granted the escheated lands to Ludlow's executors.[122] Having received the order to answer to the bill, the Crown had already provoked the creation of one unfavourable precedent in the Exchequer. To have pursued the litigation further would likely have incited the court to make another.

V. Conclusion

Following the decision in *Pawlett v AG*, privity ceased to be the jurisdictional bar to equitable relief that it had been in the late sixteenth and early seventeenth centuries. Whilst Francis North, as counsel for the Crown, had argued that 'where there is not any fraud

[118] Bryson (n 86) 27.
[119] On this point, see *Turberville v Swame* (1631) reported in Bryson (n 71) 161, 163–4.
[120] Hardres 465, 469. The language used here is reminiscent of that in the *Magdalene College Case* (1615) 11 Co Rep 72a, 77: '[the King] is the fountain of justice and common right and the King being God's Lieutenant cannot do a wrong'. For a discussion of the jurisprudence arising from the maxim that the King can do no wrong, see DC Smith, *Sir Edward Coke and the Reformation of the Laws: Religion, Politics and Jurisprudence, 1578-1616* (Cambridge, Cambridge University Press, 2014) 249–77.
[121] PRO SP29/190/63.
[122] PRO SP44/30/113.

or covin, a court of equity will not relieve',[123] little heed was paid to this old adage. Sir Matthew Hale's disregard for such restrictions on the equitable jurisdiction was shared by Lord Nottingham, and the 1670s saw increasingly regularised relief against legal demandants.[124] Indeed, in *Noel v Jevon* (1678),[125] Nottingham expressly overruled the decision in *Nash v Preston* (1630), declaring that relief against the trustee's dowress was 'the constant practice of the court now'.[126] The decisions of Hale and Nottingham were subsequently reaffirmed in the eighteenth century[127] and, taken together, rendered trust and mortgage property largely immune to the liabilities of the legal owner.[128] Where once equitable relief against non-privies had been denied and, latterly, granted only in limited circumstances, Hale and Nottingham had generalised the remedial jurisdiction and strengthened the protection afforded to equitable rights in the process.

Whilst the beneficiary's right under a trust never became enforceable against the lord by escheat or the disseisor as the mortgagor's equity of redemption had,[129] it was clear that both species of equitable right had gained greater substance over the course of the seventeenth century. Writing around 1670, both Hale and Nottingham would describe the right of the beneficiary as an 'equitable interest' in the subject matter of the trust – clearly a nod to strengthening proprietary notions in equity.[130] Equity now operated to vindicate equitable rights not only against the trustee, mortgagee, their heirs and assignees, but also against those claiming the legal estate by operation of law, including judgment creditors, surviving spouses and – in the case of the mortgagor – even the Crown by escheat. As the list of third parties against whom equitable rights could be enforced expanded, their proprietary character was enriched. The developments canvassed in this chapter thus capture a process by which – in FW Maitland's words – equitable rights came 'to look very like *jura in rem*'.[131] These cases demonstrate the mechanisms and the contexts by which equitable rights gained their proprietary hue, by which the right of the beneficiary became the 'beneficial interest' and the mortgagor's equity to redeem became the 'equity of redemption'. By the late seventeenth century, therefore, equity had produced two fully fledged 'equitable estates' with expansive third-party effect and a substantial proprietary aspect. The age of equitable property had begun.

[123] Bryson (n 86) 25.

[124] *Smith v Hanbury* (1673) Nels 70, 3 Ch Rep 82, *Prolegomena*, c 30, s 75 (mortgagee's dowress); *Medley v Martin* (1673) Rep t Finch 63 (trustee's judgment creditors); *Tassel v Hare* (1675) 73 *Selden Society* 230 (trustee's dowress). See also the discussion in D Fox, 'Bankruptcy Protection for Trusts before the Judicature Acts' in B McFarlane and S Elliott (eds), *Equity Today: 150 Years after the Judicature Reforms* (Oxford, Hart Publishing, 2023) 237–56.

[125] 2 Freem 43. See also: *Norman v Woodfall* (1680) 79 *Selden Society* 835; *Bevant v Pope* (1681) 2 Freem 71, 79 *Selden Society* 890.

[126] See also Nottingham's note on *Nash v Preston* in *Prolegomena*, c 30, s 28 (under the heading '*de anomalis*'): 'But I do not agree to this case.'

[127] *Finch v Winchelsea* (1715) 1 P Wms 277; *ex p Chion* (1721) LI MS Misc 384, f 243, and 3 P Wms 186, n 2; *Bennet v Davis* (1725) 2 P Wms 316.

[128] *Cf Morrice v Bank of England* (1736) Cas T Talb 217, 220, in which Talbot LC suggested that where the legal demandant had already taken possession of the land, equity would be powerless to assist.

[129] Foster (n 2) 120–1.

[130] Hale, *History of the Pleas of the Crown, vol I* (London, Nutt and Gosling, 1736) 247–248; Nottingham, *Prolegomena*, c 12, s 5.

[131] JW Brunyate (ed), FW Maitland, *Equity: A Course of Lectures by FW Maitland* (Cambridge, Cambridge University Press, 1936) 107.

12

A Re-examination of the Expectant Heir in Seventeenth-Century Chancery

HELEN SAUNDERS

I. Introduction

The archetypal expectant heir suit found in the printed reports, dating from the late seventeenth century to the end of the nineteenth century, involved a young man of an aristocratic or landed gentry family seeking relief in Chancery from disadvantageous bargains entered in order to obtain the money needed to maintain his place in society while he waited to inherit his family estate. These bargains commonly involved the heir entering a penal bond or other penal obligation to secure a loan of money or the provision of goods on credit, and were of a nature intended to circumvent the usury laws:[1] for example, a post-obit bond, in which no repayment was required from the obligor heir until a specified time after the death of his ancestor.[2] The contingent nature of the post-obit bond – the lender would not be repaid if the young heir died first – put the transaction outside the scope of the usury statutes, allowing unscrupulous lenders to double, or even treble, their money in a relatively short time. Another kind of bargain commonly found in these suits involved the provision of goods on credit, secured by a penal bond or other instrument. The goods were then sold on by the heir for the ready money needed; all too often he discovered that the goods were worth only a fraction of the amount secured.

Typically, the plaintiff obligor heir alleged that his entry into such bargains was the result of sharp practice, such as 'drawing in', either by the defendant lenders or, in a significant number of cases, at the hands of third parties. The young heir could run up large, and potentially ruinous, debts against his inheritance in this way, and it seems clear from previous examinations[3] of the expectant heir suits appearing in the printed

[1] By the beginning of the seventeenth century, the outright prohibition of the charging of interest had been lifted: the permissible rate of interest dropped to eight per cent in 1624 (21 Jac I, c 17), then six per cent in 1660 (12 Car II, c 13). This remained the legal rate until 1713, when it was lowered to five per cent (13 Ann, c 15). The majority of the bargains examined here afforded the lender a potential gain far beyond these legal rates.

[2] 'Inherit' here is used broadly, meaning both by testamentary disposition and succession.

[3] See, eg, LA Sheridan, *Fraud in Equity* (London, Pitman Publishing, 1957) 134.

reports that by the later years of the seventeenth century there was an established jurisdiction in Chancery to relieve these heirs from the consequences of their improvidence, though the basis for such relief is less clear.

Reported expectant heir suits – and modern courts' and writers' interpretation of them – have influenced the development of the modern doctrine of unconscientious dealing. Most of that influence has come from the leading eighteenth- and nineteenth-century cases of *Earl of Chesterfield v Janssen* (1751)[4] and *Earl of Aylesford v Morris* (1873),[5] but a number of reported expectant heir suits dating from the later part of the seventeenth century have also played a role. This chapter re-examines the leading modern interpretations of the basis of Chancery's jurisdiction to relieve expectant heirs in the context of new information derived from a far greater number of seventeenth-century suits than have previously been analysed. As well as the reported suits, mostly dating from after 1680, which have been frequently used both in the case law[6] and the academic literature,[7] the sources used for this re-examination of the jurisdiction comprise 35 previously unexamined suits gathered from a search of other printed reports,[8] the *English Legal Manuscripts* series,[9] the Chancery enrolled decrees, and the other great source of unreported Chancery suits, the entry books.[10]

The first result of this process was the conclusion that what is commonly described in the academic literature and the modern case law as a jurisdiction to relieve expectant heirs was, in practice and conception, a jurisdiction to relieve both expectant heirs and non-heir profligates. The type of relief granted to expectant heir and non-heir profligate obligors was the same, and there is demonstrably a great similarity between the two classes of obligors in relation to their shared characteristics of youth and necessity. Additionally, courts and reporters did not always appear to make a distinction: it is reported that in hearing the case of *Earl of Ardglass v Muschamp* (1684),[11] the court had reference to

[4] *Earl of Chesterfield v Janssen* (1751) 2 Ves Sen 125, 28 ER 82.

[5] *Earl of Aylesford v Morris* (1873) LR 8 Ch App 484.

[6] *Waller v Dale* (1677) Rep Temp Finch 295, 23 ER 162; *Nott v Hill* (1682) 2 Chan Cas 120, 22 ER 875; *Earl of Ardglass v Muschamp* (1684) 2 Chan Rep 266, 21 ER 675; *Wiseman v Beake* (1691) 2 Vern 122, 23 ER 688; and the four reported Berney cases, *Berry v Fairclough* (1681) (included in a note to *Davis v Duke of Marlborough* (1819) 2 Swans 108, 36 ER 555 and later published in DEC Yale (ed), *Lord Nottingham's Chancery Cases, vol II* (1961) 79 *Selden Society* 868, hereafter cited as 79 SS 868; note also that for the sake of consistency with the use of this suit in other sources, this chapter retains the incorrect plaintiff name of Berry); *Barny v Beak* (1683) 2 Chan Cas 136, 22 ER 883; *Barney v Tyson* (1684) 2 Vent 359, 86 ER 485; and *Berney v Pitt* (1687) 2 Chan Rep 396, 21 ER 697. In the analysis which follows, the numerous Berney suits are treated as one, on the basis that to treat them individually would distort the results.

[7] The suits listed in n 6 above, and *Fairfax v Trigg* (1677) Rep Temp Finch 314, 23 ER 172; *Pawlett v Pleydell* (1679) 79 SS 739; *Batty v Lloyd* (1683) 1 Vern 141, 23 ER 374; *Bill v Price* (1687) 1 Vern 467, 23 ER 592; and *Lamplugh v Smith* (1688) 2 Vern 77, 23 ER 660.

[8] eg, WH Bryson (ed), *Reports of Cases in the Court of Chancery from the Time of King James II* (Indianapolis, Dog Ear Publishing, 2015).

[9] JH Baker, *English Legal Manuscripts* (Zug, IDC, 1978).

[10] Given the large number of the entry books, three 'slices' of fifty folios each, from the beginning, middle and end of the entries for Michaelmas term in the B books of 1630, 1640, 1650, 1660, 1670 and 1680 were examined. However, the two suits included in the analysis which appear only in the entry books, *Earl of Lincoln v Fuller* (1618) C 33/135 f 90; C 33/131 f 1180 (28 June 1617), and *Symson v Murmay* C 33/184 f 53 (13 February 1644), were not discovered through this process but were brought to the author's attention by Neil Jones and David Foster respectively: each found these suits while looking for something else, illustrating both the serendipity required when dealing with C 33s, and the generosity of legal historians.

[11] *Earl of Ardglass v Muschamp* (n 6).

> precedents in this court, as well in the reigns of Queen Elizabeth, King James, King Charles the First, as in his now majesty's reign, where relief hath been given against over-reaching bargains and contracts made by young *heirs*.[12]

The obligor earl in this suit had succeeded to both title and estate at the time he entered the bargain, and was thus not an expectant heir in any sense.[13] Accordingly, this use of the term 'heirs' suggests the court considered previous suits involving expectant heirs to have been relevant to the non-heir profligate suit before them. Similarly, the report of *Bill v Price* (1687)[14] describes the defendant as an exchange-man[15] practising on young heirs, although the plaintiff in that particular suit, Charles Bill, was not an expectant heir, having already become 'seised of an estate of inheritance'.[16] This reference to heirs in a suit involving a non-heir profligate obligor appears to have been made by the reporter, rather than the court; however, and it is possible that the reporter was simply mistaken as to the facts.

The evidence of the suits analysed in terms of the characteristics of both expectant heir and non-heir profligate status suggests that if the court did make a distinction between the two types of obligors, it was arguably one without a difference. Expectant heir status almost always involved the characteristics of youth and financial necessity; the two key characteristics of a non-heir profligate obligor. Additionally, when it is considered that the type of relief granted by the court to expectant heir and non-heir profligate obligors was identical,[17] it is perhaps permissible to suggest that an expectant heir was just a particular sub-type of obligor whose youth and position of necessity justified the intervention of the court.

Perhaps not surprisingly, then, the analysis undertaken of this expanded number of suits, incorporating their historic, social and economic contexts, suggests a more nuanced understanding of the basis for the granting of relief than the various later explanations set out in the case law and academic literature.

II. Later Explanations of the Jurisdiction

There are two main interpretations of the expectant heir[18] suits found in the modern academic literature: the first, that they can be explained according to the modern

[12] ibid 2 Chan Rep 269, 21 ER 675; emphasis added.

[13] ibid 2 Chan Rep 266, 21 ER 675. Despite this fact, the reported cases involving the obligor earl are invariably treated in the case law and the academic literature as involving an expectant heir. This mis-categorisation may have initially arisen from the post-obit. nature of the bargain: repayment was to commence after the obligor earl's own death, providing he died without male issue (ibid 2 Chan Rep 268, 21 ER 675).

[14] *Bill v Price* (n 7).

[15] This term appears to have been used in the seventeenth century to describe a kind of broker: see Roger Whitley, '1 November 1685', Roger Whitley's Diary 1684–1697 Bodleian Library, Ms Eng Hist C 711, ed Michael Stevens and Honor Lewington ([s.l.], 2004), *British History Online* (www.british-history.ac.uk/no-series/roger-whitley-diary/1684-97/november-1685).

[16] *Bill v Price* C 6/277/15 (28 October 1685). This is also supported by biographical research.

[17] The most common form of relief granted to expectant heir and non-heir profligate obligors in the seventeenth century was an order that the bargain be set aside on payment by the obligor of the amount actually received – whether in ready money, or the true value of the goods provided – and interest. See H Saunders, '"Corrupt Bargains and Unconscionable Practices": The Expectant Heir in Seventeenth-Century Chancery' (University of Cambridge doctoral thesis, 2019).

[18] As the jurisdiction in the modern case law and academic literature refers only to expectant heirs, for the sake of clarity that approach will be adopted in this discussion.

doctrine of unconscionable dealing (that is, the unconscientious taking advantage of a weakness); the second, that they represent an attempt by the court to preserve the assets and prestige of the ruling classes. The latter case law overwhelmingly reflects the first of these interpretations, characterising the relief given by Chancery to expectant heirs as having been of the same nature as (and indeed one of the sources of) the court's concern with protecting the weak from exploitation.

A. Case Law

To set aside a contract on the grounds of unconscionable dealing in modern English law, three elements must be present: an oppressive bargain; a 'bargaining weakness' affecting the plaintiff; and an unconscionable taking of advantage of this weakness by the defendant.[19] While the exact nature and content of each requirement may vary,[20] there appears to be no dispute that the purpose of the doctrine is to protect a party to a contract who is suffering a 'special disability'[21] from exploitation by the other party. It is within that context, therefore, that references to the expectant heir suits are found in modern cases. For example, in *Alec Lobb (Garages) Ltd v Total Oil Ltd*,[22] Millett QC stated:

> In the development of the equitable jurisdiction to relieve against fraud and oppression, there was a natural tendency to categorise cases by reference to the relationship between the parties or *the special situation of the weaker party*. Thus equity frequently intervened to protect the expectant heir, the reversioner, and the mortgagor … It can now be seen that all those cases are merely particular examples of situations in which one party may be unfairly exploited by the other.[23]

Although no explicit consideration of seventeenth-century expectant heir suits in twentieth- and twenty-first-century reported cases on unconscionable dealing has been discovered, several significant modern cases cite the eighteenth-century leading case of *Earl of Chesterfield v Janssen*,[24] the nineteenth-century leading case of *Earl of Aylesford v Morris*,[25] or both.[26] Several seventeenth-century expectant heir suits were considered in *Chesterfield*, and, although *Aylesford* does not cite any seventeenth-century expectant heir suits, it does cite *Chesterfield*. Thanks to precedent, therefore, it is possible to trace the influence of *Nott v Hill* (1683),[27] *Earl of Ardglass v Muschamp* (1684),[28] *Wiseman*

[19] H Beale (gen ed), *Chitty on Contracts*, 33rd edn (London, Sweet and Maxwell, 2018) [8-135].
[20] eg, the sort of weakness for which relief may be granted: see *Boustany v Pigott* (1993) 69 P & CR 298.
[21] This is the terminology used in the leading Australian case of *Commercial Bank of Australia v Amadio* (1983) 151 CLR 447, a watershed moment in Australian law, a jurisdiction in which the development of the modern doctrine of unconscionable dealing has gone further than in England and Wales: Beale (n 19) [8-142].
[22] *Alec Lobb (Garages) Ltd v Total Oil Ltd* [1983] 1 WLR 87.
[23] ibid 99 (emphasis added).
[24] eg, *Amadio* (n 21).
[25] eg, *Alec Lobb* (n 22); *Hart v O'Connor* [1985] 1 AC 1000; *Boustany v Pigott* (n 20); *Credit Lyonnais v Burch* [1997] 1 All ER 144; *Portman Building Society v Dusangh* [2000] All ER (D) 582.
[26] *Kakavas v Crown Melbourne Ltd* (2013) 250 CLR 392.
[27] *Nott* (n 6).
[28] *Earl of Ardglass v Muschamp* (n 6).

v Beake (1690)[29] and the various reported Berney cases,[30] on the modern doctrine of unconscionable dealing through their use in the eighteenth and nineteenth centuries.

In *Chesterfield* and the other eighteenth-century cases in which the seventeenth-century suits appear,[31] the use made of the earlier authorities is largely confined to demonstrating the existence of the jurisdiction; in the nineteenth-century cases,[32] however, the use of suits such as *Wiseman v Beake* and *Barney v Tyson* has shifted more towards that of the basis of the jurisdiction: specifically, 'that expectant heirs dealing for their expectancy are entitled, for mere inadequacy of price, to have the contract rescinded, upon terms of redemption'.[33] The nineteenth-century view of the reported seventeenth-century suits as authority that mere status as an expectant heir, allied with inadequacy of price (termed 'outcome fraud' in the analysis below), is sufficient to attract relief is not supported by the examination of the larger number of suits drawn upon for this chapter. However, this nineteenth-century interpretation has greatly contributed to the 'special disability' analysis found in the modern cases and, arguably, the 'economic preservation' analysis found in some academic commentary.

B. Academic Literature

The special disability of the heir as the basis for relief is frequently encountered in the academic literature. Stephen Waddams, for example, rests his overall explanation of the underlying principle of unconscionability specifically on the concept of inequality of bargaining power, and it is apparent that he classes the expectant heirs as an example of weaker parties to a transaction.[34] Similarly, Rick Bigwood, discussing the role of the expectant heir cases in the development of modern unconscionability, asserts that '[e]arly unconscionability doctrine was concerned almost exclusively with protecting a person because of his or her own weaknesses'.[35] Joshua Getzler also identifies the protection of weakness as a key concern in these cases:

> Chancery's intrinsic jurisdiction to protect the vulnerable grew to embrace lunatics, children, women, sailors, expectant heirs, and other parties regarded as incapable of contracting rationally.[36]

The characteristics of the expectant heir which are perceived to constitute this weakness are most frequently identified in the literature as twofold: first, the youth

[29] *Wiseman v Beake* (n 6).

[30] The reported Berney cases of *Berry* (n 6); *Berney v Pitt* (n 6); *Barny v Beak* (n 6); and *Barney v Tyson* (n 6), make up 10 of the 25 references to seventeenth-century expectant heir suits in eighteenth- and nineteenth-century cases.

[31] *Twisleton v Griffiths* (1716) 1 P Wms 310, 24 ER 403; *Cole v Gibbons* (1734) 3 P Wms 290, 24 ER 1070; *Barnardiston v Lingood* (1740) 2 Atk 133, 26 ER 484; *Gwynne v Heaton* (1778) 1 Bro CC 1, 28 ER 949.

[32] *Bowes v Heaps* (1814) 3 V&B 117, 35 ER 423; *Davis v Duke of Marlborough* (n 6); *O'Rorke v Bolingbroke* (1877) 2 App Cas 814; *Fry v Lane* (1888) 40 Ch D 312.

[33] *Davis v Duke of Marlborough* (n 6).

[34] S Waddams, 'Unconscionability in Contract Law' (1976) 39 *Modern Law Review* 369, 385.

[35] R Bigwood, *Exploitative Contracts* (Oxford, Oxford University Press, 2003) 233.

[36] J Getzler, 'Chancery Reform and Law Reform' (2004) 22 *Law and History Review* 601, 607.

and/or inexperience of the heir;[37] and second, his financial necessity.[38] The necessary corollary to this is the advantage taken by the other party of that weakness,[39] which results in substantive unfairness.

Catharine MacMillan, in an examination of the leading case of *Aylesford* (1873)[40] – although still grounding her explanation of the basis of the jurisdiction in the concept of the protection of the weak[41] – places the expectant heir cases squarely within the economic and social context provided by the strict settlement.[42] In this analysis, the 'weakness' of the heir stemmed from necessity, arising both from the degree of monetary control exercised by the heir's parent, and also, in the nineteenth century at least, increased parental longevity.[43] However, MacMillan also posits that Chancery was at least as concerned with protecting the heir's family as it was with protecting the heir.[44] There were two aspects to this concern: certainly, 'the depredations of an expectant heir could destroy his family fortunes',[45] but also the non-parental money made available to the heir through these transactions was seen to encourage disobedience.[46]

This latter aspect of Macmillan's view of the jurisdiction – the protection of the family – is also reflected in a strand of the literature that this chapter refers to as the economic preservation analysis. Here, the court is concerned with the potentially disastrous effect improvident heirs' bargains could have on landed families. Robert Clark argues that they were

> not necessarily cases in which the courts were concerned with ensuring justice inter partes. Rather, they reflect a desire to uphold the unity and integrity of estates, that is, the need to ensure that a testator was not deceived into leaving landed estates to an heir who would promptly part with them in favour of a creditor.[47]

Others of this view include John Dawson, whose characterisation of the decisions of Chancery in the expectant heir cases as 'the protection of a landed aristocracy

[37] See, eg, Sheridan (n 3) 142; JL Barton, 'The Enforcement of Hard Bargains' (1987) 103 *Law Quarterly Review* 118, 133.

[38] See, eg, Barton (n 37) 133; AH Angelo and EP Ellinger, 'Unconscionable Contracts: A Comparative Study of the Approaches in England, France, Germany, and the United States' (1992) 14 *Loyola of Los Angeles International and Comparative Law Review* 455, 461; J Phillips, 'Protecting Those in a Disadvantageous Negotiating Position: Unconscionable Bargains as a Unifying Doctrine' (2010) 45 *Wake Forest Law Review* 837, 840.

[39] See, eg, Waddams (n 34) 386; Barton (n 37) 133; Angelo and Ellinger (n 38) 461.

[40] *Aylesford* (n 5).

[41] C MacMillan, '*Earl of Aylesford v Morris* (1873)' in P Mitchell and C Mitchell (eds), *Landmark Cases in Equity* (Oxford, Hart Publishing, 2014) 329, 329.

[42] ibid 329–30.

[43] ibid 330.

[44] ibid 332. Lobban also shares this view of the court's twofold concern: 'Chancery was seeking to protect the aristocratic family, as much as the individual in question': M Lobban, 'Contractual Fraud in Law and Equity, c 1750 – c 1850' (1997) 17 *Oxford Journal of Legal Studies* 441, 451.

[45] MacMillan (n 41) 332.

[46] ibid 333.

[47] RW Clark, *Inequality of Bargaining Power: Judicial Intervention in Improvident and Unconscionable Bargains* (Toronto, Carswell, 1987) 3.

against its own improvidence'[48] has proved influential with later writers.[49] Dawson is uncompromising in his analysis of these decisions: '[t]he motive was clear – to preserve for a dominant class the economic resources on which its prestige and power depended.'[50] Eric Posner, following Dawson, expands on the nature of the difficulty: '[w]hen heirs defaulted, important families lost their future wealth and power to common businessmen.'[51] The danger of this was that 'allowing heirs to take on debt and to default would undermine the social and political structure of the country'.[52] Additionally, Clark points out the courts' concerns on a more personal level: 'the possibility of relatives of the heir being ejected from an estate, as a result of the heir's improvidence, was a prospect too horrible for the courts to contemplate'.[53]

Some of the literature acknowledges that the basis of the jurisdiction to relieve expectant heirs shifted with economic developments over time. For example, Patrick Atiyah posits that because by the eighteenth century 'reversions and expectancies had acquired … a reasonably measurable and objective value'[54] and developments such as life insurance had taken the risk out of such dealings, the jurisdiction to relieve expectant heirs from that period onwards was more concerned with the protection of the weak:

> Like the common sailors, [the young expectant heirs of eighteenth-century England] had very little idea of the present value of a future right, and many of them did not even appreciate that they could apply for professional advice to discover what they did not know themselves. Inevitably, they fell a prey to those who understood how to value future rights, and frequently made dreadfully disadvantageous bargains.[55]

C. Problems with Existing Explanations

One of the methodological and conceptual constraints on these interpretations of the seventeenth-century jurisdiction to relieve expectant heirs is that only those suits which appear in the printed reports are considered. This means – given the nature of Chancery reporting during most of the seventeenth century[56] – that these discussions (and their conclusions) deal overwhelmingly with suits from the

[48] JP Dawson, 'Economic Duress – an Essay in Perspective' (1947) 45(3) *Michigan Law Review* 253, 267.

[49] See, eg, GS Alexander, 'The Dead Hand and the Law of Trusts in the Nineteenth Century' (1985) 37 *Stanford Law Review* 1189, 1247; KM Teeven, 'Decline of Freedom of Contract since the Emergence of the Modern Business Corporation' (1992) 37 *Saint Louis University Law Journal* 117, 137.

[50] Dawson (n 48) 268.

[51] EA Posner, 'Contract Law in the Welfare State: A Defense of the Unconscionability Doctrine, Usury Laws, and Related Limitations on the Freedom to Contract' (1995) 24 *Journal of Legal Studies* 283, 314. Posner, however, also asserts that as the jurisdiction developed throughout the nineteenth century, the focus of the court moved more towards the special disability analysis (ibid 315).

[52] ibid.

[53] Clark (n 47) 7.

[54] PS Atiyah, *The Rise and Fall of Freedom of Contract* (Oxford, Clarendon, 1985) 172.

[55] ibid 172–73.

[56] See M Macnair, 'The Nature and Function of the Early Chancery Reports' in C Stebbings (ed), *Law Reporting in Britain* (London, Hambledon Press, 1995) 123.

eighteenth and nineteenth centuries. Additionally, where reference is made to suits from the seventeenth century, often no distinction is made between the doctrinal, or historical, social and economic contexts operating during this period, and those of subsequent centuries.

Accordingly, it is possible to see a form of presentism[57] at work. Atiyah describes this in relation to later perceptions of Chancery's treatment of unconscionable, or unfair, bargains in the seventeenth and eighteenth centuries:

> [T]his body of equitable doctrine, on its way down to the twentieth century, had to pass through the nineteenth. And in the nineteenth century [seventeenth- and eighteenth-century equitable rules of fairness] came to seem increasingly anomalous, and many glosses were put on the older case law. It was always possible to find dicta here or there more in accordance with the views of nineteenth-century lawyers, and these dicta were given great prominence by those more concerned with the consistency of legal doctrine over the centuries than with authentic legal history.[58]

This 'glossing' process is arguably evident in the fact that very few modern courts, or academic writers, make any meaningful distinction between the approach of Chancery to expectant heirs in the seventeenth century, and the approach taken in later centuries. This is particularly problematic given the significantly different economic and social contexts which existed in the seventeenth and nineteenth centuries.[59] It is therefore possible that modern views of pre-nineteenth-century expectant heir suits have been skewed by the tendency of later courts and commentators to view these decisions through the lens of nineteenth-century contract law doctrines and theories. The following analysis of the suits found during this research attempts to overcome this by a more detailed examination of various aspects of this jurisdiction in the seventeenth century.

III. Analysis of the Suits

It is widely accepted by academic commentators that the jurisdiction was firmly established in Chancery by the later part of the seventeenth century;[60] it is much less clear

[57] This term is used here to mean an interpretation of the past through the lens of present, or more recent, normative frameworks. Milsom warns us that 'the largest difficulty in legal history is precisely that we look at past evidence in the light of later assumptions, including our own assumptions about the nature and working of law itself': SFC Milsom, *A Natural History of the Common Law* (New York, NY, Columbia University Press, 2003) xvi.

[58] Atiyah (n 54) 148.

[59] For a discussion of the economic and political contexts in which nineteenth century contract law cases were decided, see W Cornish et al, *The Oxford History of the Laws of England, vol XII: 1820–1914 Private Law* (Oxford, Oxford University Press, 2010) 297–300.

[60] See, eg, W Swain, 'Reshaping Contractual Unfairness in England 1670–1900' (2014) 35 *Journal of Legal History* 120, 125. Illustrations of the established nature of the jurisdiction at the end of the seventeenth century can also be found in suits such as *Lamplugh v Smith* C 5/70/83 (26 January 1688) (where the obligee accepted in his answer that, due to the operation of the jurisdiction, the expectant heir obligor would only be ordered to repay the true value received plus interest) and *Wiseman v Beake* (n 6) (in which the obligee, on the advice of counsel, exhibited a 'pre-emptive' bill against the obligor so that the obligor could affirm the validity of the bargain in his answer, in an attempt to avoid any future relief being granted on the basis of the obligor's status as an expectant heir).

whether that jurisdiction already existed in the first half of the century. Henry Ballow suggests that the jurisdiction originated in, and initially was exclusive to, the Star Chamber.[61] A comprehensive search of the records of that court to establish this point remains to be made; despite this, the analysis undertaken here does allow us to reach some conclusions as to the existence of the jurisdiction in the earlier part of the seventeenth century. In particular, an early reference by the court to the jurisdiction is found in *Earl of Lincoln v Fuller* (1618),[62] in which the court stated that it 'much mislike[d] that heirs of great families should be drawn by loans of small sums of money to pay a great deal more than was received'.[63] It is possible to infer from this statement that, at the very least, the court perceived that there was a practice of preying on heirs at this time, and disapproved – albeit not to the point of granting relief on that basis, at least in this instance.[64]

A similar inference can be drawn in relation to non-heir profligates from a suit heard a few years later, *Maddocks v Needham* (1621),[65] in which Sir Richard Moore and Sir Robert Rich, masters of Chancery, described the matter in their report – in a passage which can be interpreted as indicating familiarity with the practice – as

> being of this nature to draw young gentlemen at the Inns of Court into a statute for tufted fustians and wares and commodities which appear by the defendant's answer not to be worth the money defeasanced to be paid for them.[66]

While there are several examples from later in the century[67] of the court more explicitly identifying the jurisdiction, these two examples from the earlier part of the century suggest that, if the jurisdiction to relieve expectant heirs and non-heir profligates was not established at this time, it was at least emerging. This conclusion is further supported by two suits, *Beeve v Whitehead* (1622)[68] and *Thompson v Veysey* (1633),[69] in which the plaintiff obligors falsely characterised themselves as a non-heir profligate and expectant heir, respectively. This suggests that the jurisdiction was sufficiently established to prompt plaintiffs to claim such status in the hopes of attracting relief; but what were the characteristics required for an obligor to be identified as an expectant heir or a non-heir profligate?

[61] H Ballow, *Treatise of Equity with the Addition of Marginal References and Notes by J. Fonblanque* (London, Whieldon and Butterworth, 1793) 126.

[62] *Earl of Lincoln v Fuller* C 33/135 f 90v (24 October 1618).

[63] ibid.

[64] Although the report of *Williams v Smith* (1671) 3 Chan Rep 75, 21 ER 733, a suit heard by Bridgman LK, notes that precedents from the times of Coventry LK (Lord Keeper from 1625–1639) and Ellesmere LC (Lord Keeper, as Sir Thomas Egerton, from 1596–1603, then Lord Chancellor until early 1617) were cited in relation to these sorts of cases, in the absence of reference to specific suits this cannot be taken to be definitive.

[65] *Maddocks v Needham* (1621) C 78/204 no 4.

[66] ibid. In this instance, however, the plaintiff obligor was ordered to match a composition with the obligee made by one of his co-obligors.

[67] See, eg, Nottingham LC's statement '[t]hat this Court ought to discountenance and relieve against all corrupt traffic between the shopkeepers and young gentlemen who are usually drawn in and entangled with such kind of bargains' (*Fairfax v Trigg* (1676) 79 SS 448); and North LK's view that 'the practice of purchasing from heirs was grown too common, and therefore he would not in any sort countenance it' (*Johnson, executor of Hill v Nott* (1684) 1 Vern 271, 23 ER 464).

[68] *Beeve v Whitehead* (1622) C 78/328 no 8.

[69] *Thompson v Veysey* (1633) C 78/515 no 4.

A. Characteristics of Expectant Heirs

Expectant heir status comprised a number of characteristics. The most obvious is, of course, the obligor's expectancy. In identifying suits for this analysis, no distinction was made in terms of the type of expectancy: both obligors who stood to inherit real property by descent or through operation of a settlement, and those with expectations of personal property (and, in some cases, real property) by testamentary disposition were included. The court likewise seems to have made no distinction: such a conclusion is supported to an extent by the fact that in the handful of suits in which substantive relief[70] was not granted to plaintiff expectant heir obligors,[71] there is no reason to believe the nature of the obligor's expectancy was in any way relevant.

In addition to expectancy, two other characteristics are mentioned frequently enough to suggest their significance: youth and financial necessity. The age[72] of the obligor was mentioned in 19 of the 25 expectant heir suits, and this includes all 12 suits in which plaintiff expectant heirs were granted substantive relief.[73] In the vast majority of those suits the obligor was young; this description from the bill in *Hubberstie v Danser* (1614) is a typical example of the way in which this was expressed:

> the plaintiff being then young and altogether unexperienced in such affairs yet then the son and heir of George Hubberstie citizen and leatherseller of London and by that means likely to be owner and possessed of good estate after the death of his father being aged …[74]

In two suits, however, *Draper v Dean* (1679)[75] and *Wiseman v Beake* (1690),[76] relief was granted despite the plaintiffs in those suits being of full age. Sir Robert Jason, the obligor[77] in the former suit, was 33 years of age, and Samuel Wiseman somewhat older, at the time of entering the bargains from which relief was sought. The granting of relief in both these suits, at least in relation to youth as a factor, appears to have run counter to the previous approach of the court, with counsel for the defendant in *Wiseman v Beake* arguing that 'this was not *the ordinary case* of surprising a young heir into a hard bargain, but [the plaintiff] was above thirty, near forty years old when this bargain was made'.[78]

This despite Nottingham LC in the earlier case of *Draper v Dean* having 'declared that this kind of infamous traffic with sons in the lifetime of their fathers ought to be

[70] That is, relief against anything more than the penalty.

[71] There are five such suits: the failure to grant substantive relief appears to be based respectively on affirmation of the bargain (*Fines v Wheatley* (1616) C 78/311 no 23; and *Fairfax v Trigg* (n 67)), an absence of fraud (*Batty v Lloyd* (n 7)), and an apparent wish on the part of the court to hold the obligor liable for his own foolishness (*Earl of Lincoln v* C 33/135 f 90v *Fuller* (24 October 1618) and *Pawlett v Pleydell* (n 7)).

[72] The plaintiff obligors in the suits examined were all above the age of 21, and therefore were not protected by the rules regarding minors.

[73] Thirteen suits in which plaintiff expectant heir obligors were granted substantive relief were found, but in one of them, *Tirwhitt v Martyn* (1646) C 78/529 no 12, the plaintiff's status as an expectant heir was not mentioned by either party, or the court; the expectancy was discovered through biographical research.

[74] *Hubberstie v Danser* (1614) C 78/184 no 1.

[75] *Draper v Dean* (1679) 79 SS 602.

[76] *Wiseman v Beake* (n 6).

[77] Although Jason was not the plaintiff in this suit, the court found that the suit had been brought by Draper on Jason's behalf, the obligor having been outlawed (*Draper* (n 75)).

[78] *Wiseman v Beake* (n 6); emphasis added.

discouraged and destroyed, though the sons be of full age'.[79] Notwithstanding, it seems at least a plausible interpretation of the overall approach of the court to conclude that the youth of the obligor was an integral part of the jurisdiction to relieve; it could even be said that the stress laid on the grant of relief to the obligors in the two anomalous suits *despite* their relatively advanced years gives further support for this conclusion.

The characteristic of the financial hardship of the obligor expectant heir does not recur as frequently as that of youth, but is still significant: 14 of the 25 suits involving expectant heirs, including six[80] of the 12 suits in which plaintiff expectant heirs were granted substantive relief, mention necessity. The necessity of the expectant heir was in some instances expressed to be a result of the heir's own profligacy or extravagance,[81] and it was also often attributed to his father's lack of generosity; for example, in many of the bills brought by Richard Berney, he complained that his father had allowed him only 'a small sum of money'[82] on which to live, thus compelling him to borrow. Similarly, the plaintiff in *Neaste v Poole* (1608) alleged he was in financial difficulties due to the 'very small or little maintenance allowed him by his said father'.[83] This lack of generosity was linked, in some suits, to a difficult relationship between the expectant heir and the ancestor from whom their expectancy derived. In *Neaste v Poole*, for example, the small allowance complained of by the plaintiff was said to be a result of him being in disgrace with his father;[84] in other cases, expectant heir obligors sought to avoid such disgrace – with its concomitant risk of disinheritance – by seeking to keep their borrowings secret.[85]

B. Characteristics of Non-Heir Profligates

Unlike the expectant heir suits, in which suits selected by reference to a central attribute – expectancy – revealed other, associated, characteristics, the suits dealing with non-heir profligate obligors were selected for analysis on the basis of two key characteristics, so that by definition these characteristics are present and integral. These are the youth of the obligor, and an element of financial necessity.[86] Of the 14 profligate suits found, 12 suits contain a reference to the obligor's youth, 10 to necessity, and nine to both. In only one suit was neither mentioned; the obligor in this suit being identified as profligate

[79] *Draper* (n 75).

[80] *Neaste v Poole* (1608) C 78/176 no 12; *Symson v Murmay* (n 10); the Berney suits, for example, *Berney v Fairclough and Stystead* C 10/201/12 (14 February 1680); *Nott v Hill* (n 6); *Lamplugh v Smith* (n 7); and *Whitley v Price* C 9/420/225 (20 July 1686). It is possible that this is because only expectant heirs who were in financial difficulties would end up in court. However, the way in which necessity is treated by the court seems to suggest that it was viewed as a basis of relief, rather than simply a reason why relief was sought.

[81] See, eg, *Lamplugh v Smith* (n 60); and *Frevile v Atkins* (1628) C 78/473 no 13.

[82] *Berney v Pitt* C 10/208/7 (16 February 1680); see also *Berney v Passmore* C 10/495/27 (23 February 1679); *Berney v Mingay and Utting* C 20/495/26 (14 February 1680), amongst others.

[83] *Neaste* (n 80). Similar complaints were made by the plaintiffs in, eg, *Nott v Hill* (n 6); the Berney suits, for example *Barny v Beak* (n 6); *Whitley v Price* (n 80) and *Pawlett v Pleydell* (n 7).

[84] *Neaste* (n 80).

[85] See, eg, *Frevile v Atkins* (n 81); *Fairfax v Trigg* C 6/220/35 (20 April 1676); and *Earl of Lincoln v Fuller* C 33/131 f 1180 (28 June 1617).

[86] In this context, necessity is used to encompass extravagance as well as the state of financial hardship per se.

through biographical research.[87] Of the seven suits in which plaintiff profligate obligors were granted substantive relief, all[88] referred to the obligor's youth, five[89] to his necessity, and all but two[90] to both. That the court granted relief – at least partly – on the basis of an obligor having these characteristics can be determined, as well as by inference from the numbers of suits mentioned above, through explicit statements to that effect.[91]

C. Family Background

A final consideration when discussing expectant heir and non-heir profligate status is family background: one of the two main modern explanations of the jurisdiction to relieve such obligors was to preserve the assets of the ruling class. Accordingly, the social class of the obligors in the suits has been ascertained (where possible) and categorised according to the class divisions identified by Stone as operating in the seventeenth century.[92] Table 3.1 shows that the strata of society that Dawson might be expected to be referring to as a 'dominant class'[93] in the seventeenth century – the peers and the county elite – make up 64 per cent of expectant heir obligors in the suits examined for this essay, 50 per cent of non-heir profligate obligors, and 58.9 per cent of both groups combined. These two groups make up the largest number of obligors in all suits examined; the number of obligors from each of the merchant class and the lesser gentry are significantly lower, and only one suit was found in which the obligor came from any of the lowest three social classes.

Table 3.1 Family background, all suits

	Expectant Heirs (N = 25)		**Profligates (N = 14)**		**Both (N = 39)**	
	N	%	*N*	%	*N*	%
Groups 1–3[94]	1	4.0	0	0	1	2.6
Merchants	1	4.0	4	28.6	5	12.8
Lesser or parish gentry	4	16.0	0	0	4	10.3

(continued)

[87] *Ashley v Earl of Suffolk* (1656) C 78/560 no 7.

[88] *Bill v Price* (n 7); *Woodward v Alporte* C 33/121 f 1209 (28 July 1612); *Smythes v Weedon* (1623) C 78/224 no 3; *Godscall v Walker* (1663) 3 Chan Rep 10, 21 ER 713; *Earl of Ardglass v Muschamp* (n 6); *Smith v Burroughs* (1696) 2 Vern 346, 23 ER 820; *Prescott v Sotherton* (1632) C78/442 no 10.

[89] *Smythes v Weedon* (n 88); *Godshalke v Walker* (1665) C 78/746 no 5; *Earl of Ardglass v Muschamp* (n 6); *Bill v Price* (n 7); *Smith v Burroughs* (n 88).

[90] The exceptions being *Woodward v Alporte* (n 88) and *Prescott v Sotherton* (n 88).

[91] See, eg, the masters' statement in *Maddocks v Needham* (n 65).

[92] L Stone, 'Social Mobility in England, 1500–1700' (1966) 33 *Past & Present* 16, 18–19.

[93] Dawson (n 48) 268.

[94] This refers to the first three groups of Stone's model: Group 1 consisted of '[t]he dependents on charity, whether widows, aged, or unemployed; also the apprentices and living-in servants, domestic, agricultural, or industrial'; Group 2 was [t]he living-out labourers, both rural and urban, agricultural and industrial'; and Group 3 comprised '[t]he husbandmen, the lesser yeomen (both tenants and freeholders), and the more substantial yeomen; also the artisans, shopkeepers and small internal traders': Stone (n 92) 18.

Table 3.1 ***(Continued)***

	Expectant Heirs (N = 25)		**Profligates (N = 14)**		**Both (N = 39)**	
The county elite: squires, knights and barons	8	32.0	6	42.9	14	35.9
The peers: barons, viscounts, earls, marquises, and dukes.	8	32.0	1	7.1	9	23.0
Unknown	3	12.0	3	21.4	6	15.4

Narrowing this down to suits in which the obligor was the plaintiff, Table 3.2 shows that those percentages remain fairly stable: 63.1 per cent of expectant heir plaintiffs, 41.6 per cent of non-heir profligate plaintiffs, and 54.9 per cent of both groups combined, came from the peer and county elite classes.

Table 3.2 Family background, plaintiff obligors

	Expectant Heirs (N = 19)		**Profligates (N = 12)**		**Both (N = 31)**	
	N	%	*N*	%	*N*	%
Groups 1–3	1	5.3	0	0	1	3.2
Merchants	1	5.3	4	33.3	5	16.1
Lesser or parish gentry	3	15.8	0	0	3	9.7
The county elite: squires, knights and barons	7	36.8	4	33.3	11	35.5
The peers: barons, viscounts, earls, marquises, and dukes.	5	26.3	1	8.3	6	19.4
Unknown	2	10.5	3	25.0	5	16.1

Narrowing this down further to plaintiff obligors who were successful in obtaining substantive relief, Table 3.3 shows that the percentages of peer and county elite obligors again stay relatively stable: they made up 61.5 per cent of successful expectant heir plaintiff obligors, 42.9 per cent of successful non-heir profligate plaintiff obligors, and 55 per cent of both combined.

Table 3.3 Family background, plaintiff obligors granted substantive relief

	Expectant Heirs (N = 13)		**Profligates (N = 7)**		**Both (N = 20)**	
	N	%	*N*	%	*N*	%
Groups 1–3	0	0	0	0	0	0
Merchants	1	7.7	4	57.1	5	25.0
Lesser or parish gentry	2	15.4	0	0	2	10.0

(continued)

Table 3.3 ***(Continued)***

	Expectant Heirs (N = 13)		Profligates (N = 7)		Both (N = 20)	
The county elite: squires, knights and barons	7	53.8	2	28.6	9	45.0
The peers: barons, viscounts, earls, marquises, and dukes.	1	7.7	1	14.3	2	10.0
Unknown	2	15.4	0	0	2	10.0

Tables 3.4, 3.5 and 3.6 respectively show the percentage of peers and county elite, merchant, and lesser or parish gentry plaintiff obligors who were granted substantive relief.

Table 3.4 Peers and county elite plaintiff obligors granted substantive relief

	Expectant Heirs	Profligates	Both
	N	*N*	*N*
Total peers and county elite plaintiff obligors	12	5	17
Peers and county elite plaintiff obligors granted relief	8	3	11
Percentage of total peers and county elite plaintiff obligors who were granted relief	66.7	60.0	64.7

Table 3.5 Merchant plaintiff obligors granted substantive relief

	Expectant Heirs	Profligates	Both
	N	*N*	*N*
Total merchant plaintiff obligors	1	4	5
Merchant plaintiff obligors granted relief	1	4	5
Percentage of total merchant plaintiff obligors who were granted relief	100	100	100

Table 3.6 Lesser or parish gentry plaintiff obligors granted substantive relief

	Expectant Heirs	Profligates	Both
	N	*N*	*N*
Total lesser or parish gentry plaintiff obligors	3	0	3
Lesser or parish gentry plaintiff obligors granted relief	2	0	2
Percentage of total lesser or parish gentry plaintiff obligors who were granted relief	66.7	0	66.7

Thus, we see that 64.7 per cent of peers and county elite plaintiff obligors were granted substantive relief; 100 per cent of merchant plaintiff obligors were granted substantive relief; and 66.7 per cent of lesser or parish gentry plaintiff obligors were granted substantive relief.

While the numbers involved here are very small and, overall, insufficient to warrant the kind of definitive conclusions that a larger sample size would provide, it might be thought that if the economic preservation explanation was correct, the proportion of county elite and peer obligors gaining relief would be greater when compared to the lesser gentry and merchants. As can be seen in Table 3.7, however, this comparison shows that the percentage of the combined class of county elite and peers plaintiff obligors gaining relief remains stable, as does the percentage of lesser or parish gentry; while the percentage of the merchant class gaining relief rises, in terms of their representation as plaintiff obligors.

Table 3.7 Comparison (both expectant heir and non-heir profligates)

	Percentage of obligors	**Percentage of plaintiff obligors**	**Percentage of plaintiff obligors granted relief**
Merchants	13.2	16.7	26.3
Lesser or parish gentry	10.5	10.0	10.5
Peers and county elite	60.4	56.7	57.9

Despite the merchant class making up only 16.7 per cent of all plaintiff obligors, they make up 26.3 per cent of all plaintiff obligors who were successful; whereas for the combined peers and county elite groups, those two figures are 56.7 per cent and 57.9 per cent, a barely perceptible difference. From these figures, it appears plaintiff obligors of the merchant class were more successful in gaining relief than plaintiff obligors belonging to Dawson's dominant classes. It is possible, of course, that these figures are skewed by a difference in strength of claims between social groups: if plaintiffs of the lesser gentry and merchant class knew that the jurisdiction was more favourable to peer and county elite obligors, they may only have brought suit where their claim was particularly strong; this would be another potential explanation for the relative parity between the classes in terms of relief. The suits examined here, however, do not display any marked difference in the strengths of the cases according to social category: in fact, the only expectant heir plaintiff to belong to the social group below the merchants, the Group 3 artisan goldsmith in *Batty v Lloyd* (1683),[95] brought one of the weakest cases. There could be a number of explanations for the fact that there was only one suit found which was brought by an obligor belonging to any of the lowest three groups: the cost of litigation may have prevented such obligors from seeking relief; or it may be that people from these lower classes were less likely to have expectations, or the opportunity to be profligate. However, it is possible that it was generally known (or at least

[95] *Batty v Lloyd* (n 7).

believed) that the court was less likely to grant relief to obligors from lower social groups, and that possibility should be borne in mind.

Accordingly, while the sample size prevents any definitive conclusion, it can at least be said that plaintiff obligors of the merchant class – not the peers or county elites – appear to have enjoyed the most success when seeking relief from the sorts of improvident bargains dealt with in this chapter. This might suggest that, at least in practice, the court was not discernibly favouring the dominant peer and county elite groups, which seems to contradict the idea of economic preservation as a discrete basis of the jurisdiction. It must be noted, however, that if preservation of the assets of the ruling classes was the aim of the court, it may have manifested in a normative way. That is, the court may have granted relief to obligors of all social classes equally, on the basis that the types of bargains dealt with were of a nature which *could* damage the economic power of the ruling classes, rather than basing decisions in individual suits on the grounds that they *would*. If this were the case, then there would be no differentiation in treatment based on the social class of the obligor, or disparities in class between obligors and obligees, in individual suits.[96]

IV. Basis of the Jurisdiction

A. Fraud

It appears that merely possessing the characteristics, and thus status, of an expectant heir or non-heir profligate was not sufficient in the seventeenth century to secure an obligor Chancery relief from an improvident bargain. An element of fraud was also necessary, and the operation of fraud in the expectant heir and non-heir profligate suits examined here can be categorised as relating either to fraudulent features occurring at, or before, the formation of the contract, or to those occurring afterwards. It also appears that the only difference between expectant heir suits and non-heir profligate suits in relation to fraud is that there were certain circumstances attaching to a bargain with an expectant heir which afforded opportunities for fraud that were not available to those dealing with a non-heir profligate obligor: chief amongst these was keeping a bargain secret for fear the heir's ancestor would disinherit them,[97] and knowledge on the part of the obligee of the heir's ancestor's ill-health or great age, before entry into a post-obit bargain.[98] These aside, the types of fraud found in the suits do not differ between the two types of obligors, giving further support to the conclusion that only one jurisdiction to relieve – on the basis of youth and necessity – was operating in the seventeenth century, and that an expectant heir obligor was simply a sub-type covered by this jurisdiction.

[96] There is also an evidentiary difficulty here; as Swain puts it, '[b]y definition, if the law is being used covertly to further the interests of particularly powerful groups, then it is going to be difficult to find historical evidence that this is so': Swain (n 60) 6–7.

[97] See, eg, *Fairfax v Trigg* (n 7).

[98] See, eg, *Berry v Fairclough* (n 6).

The first category of fraud found – that at or before formation of the contract – is by far the most populous, with 17 of the 25 expectant heir suits, and 10 of the 14 non-heir profligate suits, containing allegations of this type of fraud; only two suits refer to fraud occurring after formation.

(i) Fraud at or before Formation

Fraud at or before the formation of the contract, for the purposes of this discussion, has been divided into that which relates to behaviour, and that relating to the outcome of the bargain.[99]

> [T]he said plaintiff being a young man was drawn in by the cunning and practice of the said [defendant] who was much given to deceit to enter into the said statute without any just consideration at all, there being some hope of benefit to come to the plaintiff after the decease of his father …[100]

'Drawing in' was the type of behavioural fraud most commonly referred to in both expectant heir and non-heir profligate suits.[101] This term appears to have encompassed behaviours such as befriending the young obligor who had recently arrived in London,[102] introducing him to helpful individuals with money to lend,[103] encouraging him to spend money,[104] and helping him to spend it.[105] It is no coincidence that all these behaviours appear to be motivated by kindness. It seems clear that pretended friendship and helpfulness were an integral part of the mechanism by which young and inexperienced obligors were brought to enter these bargains, and demonstrate the relationship between this key characteristic of the expectant heir/non-heir profligate status – youth – and the fraudulent behaviour in question.

Another common form of behavioural fraud was that, having entered bargains on the promise they would receive ready money, the obligors were instead given goods, alleged to be worth the equivalent of the promised sum.[106] As a form of fraud, this relied for its success on the other key characteristic of the expectant heir/non-heir profligate status, necessity: with an urgent need for funds, and the securities already sealed, the obligors were in no position to refuse to accept the goods in lieu of the promised cash, even had they been able to determine at that point the true value of the goods. Both 'drawing in'

[99] That is, the contract price. In modern terminology these two categories of 'behaviour' and 'outcome' would be referred to as procedural and substantive fairness.

[100] *Neaste v Poole* (n 80).

[101] Six of the 17 expectant heir suits, and six of the 10 non-heir profligate suits, in which fraud was alleged contained such allegations and/or findings. Of the expectant heir and non-heir profligate suits in which plaintiff obligors were granted substantive relief, five of 11 expectant heir suits, and three of seven non-heir profligate suits, contained such allegations and/or findings.

[102] See, eg, *Freeman v Lassalls* (1622) C 78/336 no 9.

[103] See, eg, *Berney v Mason and Stistead* C 10/197/19 (14 February 1680).

[104] See, eg, *Frevile v Atkins* (n 81); *Lamplugh v Smith* (n 60); see also *Beeve v Whitehead* (n 68), where such an allegation was made despite being patently false, presumably on the basis it was a recognised basis for relief at that time.

[105] See, eg, *Earl of Ardglass v Muschamp* (n 6).

[106] Seven of the 27 expectant heir and non-heir profligate suits in which fraud was present fall under this category: *Freeman v Lassalls* (n 102); *Symson v Murmay* (n 10); *Fairfax v Trigg* (n 7); *Waller v Dale* (n 6); *Lamplugh v Smith* (n 7); *Maddocks v Needham* (n 65); and *Smith v Burroughs* (n 88).

and 'goods instead of cash' frauds often involved the type of professional confidence men identified by Jones in relation to the Elizabethan period,[107] and clearly active in the seventeenth century in the form of individuals such as Edward Stistead, who, as well as providing this dubious form of assistance to Richard Berney,[108] figured in the suits of *Bill v Price* (1687),[109] *Witley v Price* (1688)[110] and *Lamplugh v Smith* (1688).[111]

Twenty-six[112] of the 27 suits involving expectant heirs and non-heir profligates in which allegations and/or findings of fraud were made contain reference to a fraudulent outcome; all of the suits in which plaintiff obligors were granted substantive relief contain such a reference. In one suit the plaintiff obligor was found to have received no consideration at all; in the others, the obligor either received goods worth significantly less than the amount promised to him, and secured by him,[113] or the obligor received the full amount promised to him, but the security was such that the obligee stood to make an excessive gain.[114]

It is also apparent that, while there were instances later in the century in which relief was granted purely on the basis of outcome fraud, it was far more likely that the court would grant relief in suits where both behavioural and outcome fraud were present. Of the six suits in which only outcome fraud was alleged, only two – both dating from the later years of the century – attracted substantive relief: *Nott v Hill* (1682)[115] and *Wiseman v Beake* (1690).[116] The decision in *Wiseman v Beake* appears to have been something of a surprise on a number of grounds, including with reference to the age of the obligor. In the case of *Nott v Hill*, however, there is explicit discussion of the outcome of the bargain, with Nottingham LC apparently granting relief on the basis that the obligee had received five times the amount advanced to the obligor.[117]

(ii) Fraud after Formation

Two suits involving expectant heir and non-heir profligate obligors contained references to fraud occurring after the formation of the contract. In *Frevile v Atkins* (1628)[118] the obligee had apparently refused to cancel the statute despite the sums secured by it having been fully repaid;[119] and in *Wiseman v Beake* (1691)[120] the obligee attempted to have the bargain confirmed by the obligor by means of a later 'sham' action in Chancery.[121]

[107] WJ Jones, *The Elizabethan Court of Chancery* (Oxford, Clarendon Press, 1967) 433–34.
[108] See, eg, *Barny v Beak* (n 6).
[109] *Bill v Price* (n 7).
[110] *Witley v Price* (1688) 2 Vern 78, 23 ER 660.
[111] *Lamplugh* (n 7).
[112] The one suit which does not, *Frevile v Atkins* (n 81), does contain an allegation of behavioural fraud; it also contains a reference to fraud after formation.
[113] See, eg, *Hubberstie v Danser* (n 74); *Waller v Dale* (n 6); *Lamplugh v Smith* (n 7); *Woodward v Alporte* C 33/127 f 765 v (31 January 1615); *Smythes v Weedon* (n 88); *Bill v Price* (n 7).
[114] See, eg, *Neaste v Poole* (n 80); *Fines v Wheatley* (n 71); *Nott v Hill* (n 6); *Wiseman v Beake* (n 6) and *Earl of Ardglass v Muschamp* (n 6).
[115] *Nott v Hill* (n 6).
[116] *Wiseman v Beake* (n 6).
[117] *Nott v Hill* (n 6) 2 Chan Cas 121, 22 ER 876. This decision was overturned by North LK in a rehearing of the matter the following year, who found no basis for relief.
[118] *Frevile v Atkins* (n 81).
[119] ibid.
[120] *Wiseman v Beake* (n 6).
[121] ibid.

In each case relief was granted; however, in addition to the post-formation fraud alleged in these cases, *Frevile v Atkins* also contained a reference to pre-formation behavioural fraud, and *Wiseman v Beake* contained a reference to pre-formation outcome fraud. It is difficult, therefore, to determine from this very small sample the significance of post-formation fraud to the granting of relief. Similarly, it is impossible to determine whether the presence of post-formation fraud in these suits removed the necessity, posited above, that *both* types of pre-formation fraud were required for a grant of relief: while in *Wiseman v Beake* the presence of pre-formation outcome fraud and post-formation fraud appears to have been sufficient, at least for Nottingham LC, in the earlier case of *Frevile v Atkins* relief was clearly based on the court's acceptance that the conditioned amounts had already been paid in full.

It is clear from the suits examined here that an element of fraud was required before Chancery would relieve an expectant heir or non-heir profligate obligor during the seventeenth century, and that mere status as an expectant, or a profligate, was not sufficient. Whereas modern explanations of the expectant heir suits have interpreted the granting of relief either as based on protection of the heir, necessitated by his special disability, or on the desire of the court to preserve the economic assets and thus influence of the ruling classes, there is a more nuanced way of understanding these explanations which takes into account the economic and social context in which these suits were brought, heard, and decided.

B. Explanations of the Jurisdiction in Context

One of the key aims of this analysis as a whole has been to examine the seventeenth-century expectant heir and non-heir profligate suits within their historical, social, and economic contexts. To this end, as much biographical and contextual detail as possible has been uncovered about the suits discussed. Of major significance to this analysis is the acknowledgement that the economic context of the seventeenth century was fundamentally different from that of the eighteenth and nineteenth centuries; recognising this difference is necessary to gaining an understanding of the history of the jurisdiction which is not skewed by later legal interpretations.

The nature of credit was understood very differently in the seventeenth century; this was a period before commercial banking was established, and largely before risk could be managed through the use of life insurance or other such mechanisms.[122] Accordingly, there was a strong social and ethical dimension to the extending of credit between individuals: Muldrew argues that 'credit' during this period meant 'a person's reputation, the estimate in which his or her character was held, their repute or trustworthiness',[123] rather than the modern understanding of a 'buy now, pay later' financial transaction. Thus, trust, in a personal sense, was crucial to the decision on the part of one individual to lend money, or provide goods without immediate payment, to another.[124]

[122] C Muldrew, *The Economy of Obligation* (Basingstoke, Macmillan, 1998) 17.
[123] ibid 3.
[124] ibid 7. For discussion of the importance of personal trust in the context of early modern mortgages, see D Waddilove, 'Mortgages in the Early-Modern Court of Chancery' (University of Cambridge doctoral thesis, 2014) 108–109.

From the middle of the sixteenth century, consumption increased; there was no corresponding increase in the amount of gold and silver in circulation, however, and so the expansion of commercial activity was largely based on credit.[125] There was also, over the next 100 years or so, an increase in the complexity of commercial activity, and as a result the interconnected chains of credit between individuals got longer and more complicated.[126] This meant that one debtor's inability to repay a debt to one creditor could start a domino effect of defaults: the first default could lead to that creditor being unable to repay his or her own debts, which could lead to their creditor's inability to pay theirs, and so on.[127] This was especially problematic, as Muldrew's research suggests that the majority of households owed more than they were owed, and indeed owed more than could be covered by their own credits and the sale of their moveable goods. If the household owned land, this could be sold to cover debt, but at the cost of reducing the patrimony.[128] In this context, the prodigality of the younger generation could have a highly detrimental impact on a family's credit, and consequently on its overall economic health.[129]

Perhaps because of the potential magnitude of the damage to households which could result from default, there was a moral aspect to the obligation to repay one's debts. Muldrew suggests that:

> Since the redistribution of wealth through defaults was random and unpredictable, it was considered to be unjust if it resulted from profitable households simply spending too much. It was only considered just when poor householders defaulted out of need.[130]

In this context, extravagance and a resulting default by an expectant heir had an impact not just on that heir's family but also, potentially, on the creditworthiness of everyone connected by a particular chain of credit. Therefore, in granting relief to expectant heirs and non-heir profligates in the seventeenth century, arguably the court of Chancery was to at least some extent concerned with preventing the disruption of the normal operation of this culture of credit by fraud.

This theory is not, of course, susceptible of incontrovertible proof: there are no express statements by the court to be found in the decrees and entries examined here on the subject of credit chains or overall household indebtedness. However, the absence of such statements cannot be taken to show that the theory is invalid: quite apart from the fact that judicial reasons (in the modern sense) are almost entirely lacking from the decrees, entries, and the printed reports examined, the pervasiveness of the culture of credit as described by Muldrew suggests that those individuals

[125] Muldrew (n 122) 3.

[126] ibid.

[127] As Yale points out, the ramifications of this in relation to conditioned bonds, which were involved in many of the bargains examined in this chapter, could be disastrous: 'Credit was very largely raised … by such bonds. Apart from there being no notion of limited trading liabilities the cumulative effect of a failure upon a series of these bonds was ordinarily complete financial collapse. Generally the risk was heavy and the incidence of casualties high' (Yale, 'Introduction: An Essay on Mortgages and Trusts and Allied Topics in Equity' (n 6) 13).

[128] Muldrew (n 122) 118.

[129] ibid 17.

[130] ibid 4. While many of the expectant heir and non-heir profligate suits examined for this chapter involve personal extravagance, only one suit was discovered in which a decision to not grant relief was – or appears to have been – made on the basis of disapproval of extravagance: see *Earl of Lincoln v Fuller* C 33/135 ff 90, 90v (24 October 1618). This suggests that extravagance per se was not sufficient to put a transaction outside the court's suggested concern with the normal operation of credit.

living in it – including judges, lawyers, and parties – would scarcely feel it necessary to explain it.[131] It must also be borne in mind, when assessing the existence or otherwise of evidence in support of the culture of credit explanation of the jurisdiction to relieve expectant heirs and non-heir profligates, that – as with the economic preservation analysis – the concern of the court in protecting the operation of credit may have been normative: that is, a concern with the presence and nature of conduct or circumstances of a type which would disrupt the normal operation of credit generally, not with the specific details of the chains of credit of individual obligors or their families, which might have been discoverable in the pleadings and depositions. Accordingly, the most claimed here for this explanation is that it is at least as plausible as the existing modern special disability and economic preservation explanations and, indeed, provides an elucidation of the elements of those explanations which takes account of the seventeenth-century context.

The types of fraud which occurred at or before the formation of the bargains examined for this chapter clearly disrupted the normal operation of credit. The first of these, behavioural fraud – for example, 'drawing in', or the substitution of less valuable goods for ready money – was disruptive in convincing individuals to incur debt (or, in some cases, extend credit[132]) on the basis of untrue representations, or carefully engineered circumstances. The numerous bargains entered by Richard Berney serve as an illustration of this, particularly in relation to the activities of Edward Stistead. Berney was not only assisted in finding sources of credit by Stistead, but also encouraged to adopt a more extravagant standard of living, thus necessitating higher levels of debt than he might otherwise have taken on;[133] this kind of 'drawing in' and encouragement in debauchery appears to have been particularly disliked by Chancery.[134]

The significance of outcome fraud in this explanation of the jurisdiction is that an individual (and by extension their family) ended up indebted, or extended, to an amount greater than they had either intended or could afford. It is difficult to draw any definitive conclusion as to the court's willingness – in the context of a concern with maintaining the normal operation of the culture of credit – to relieve on the basis of outcome fraud alone, based on the two suits involving outcome fraud in which relief was granted despite the absence of behavioural fraud. It is possible, however, given that outcome fraud was present in all of the suits in which substantive relief was granted, tentatively to conclude that some kind of outcome fraud was necessary to trigger the court's jurisdiction to relieve expectant heirs and non-heir profligates, and that it may have been enough on its own to warrant the court's intervention.

If this is so, it can perhaps be explained in these terms: rather than a focus on abstract ideas of what was 'fair' in individual bargains, in this analysis the seventeenth-century court of Chancery was concerned with the protection of an economic system underpinned by norms of trustworthiness. In this context, the nature of the relief

[131] As Milsom says, '[p]eople do not formulate their assumptions for themselves, let alone spell them out for the benefit of future historians, and in the case of the law there is never occasion to write down what everybody knows': Milsom (n 57) 76.

[132] See, eg, *Lambe v Finch* (1626) C 78/239 no 9; this suit is discussed in detail in H Saunders, '*Lambe v Finch* (1626): An Early Seventeenth-Century Expectant Heir Suit in Context' (2019) 40 *Journal of Legal History* 253.

[133] *Barny v Beak* (n 6) 2 Chan Cas 136, 22 ER 883.

[134] See, eg, *Earl of Ardglass v Muschamp* (n 6). This may also reflect the moral repugnance for debt through extravagance described above.

granted in these suits, the repayment of the principal plus reasonable interest, served to restore the normal operation of credit: the obligee was kept to what they should have had out of the deal, and the obligor was kept to what they had actually received out of the deal, thus removing an inflated gain on one hand, and inflated debt on the other.

In the culture of credit explanation of Chancery's jurisdiction to relieve expectant heirs and non-heir profligates, the modern 'special disability' and 'economic preservation' analyses become, rather than discrete explanations of the basis of the jurisdiction, accounts of different aspects of the disruptive effect fraud had on the culture of credit. In this context, the protection from exploitation described in the special disability analysis operates to prevent interference with the decisions of individuals in taking up or extending credit; correspondingly, the economic preservation analysis can be seen, rather, as a concern with the ability of households, or families, to maintain appropriate levels of creditworthiness, unaffected by the distorting effects of fraud. This is, of course, slightly different from the class-based analyses of Clark, Dawson and Posner discussed above, in which the social class of the families being protected is key, but these analyses draw largely on express statements from suits heard in the eighteenth and nineteenth centuries.[135] It is suggested, therefore, that twentieth-century theories of Chancery's intention to maintain the economic power of the dominant classes – while perhaps valid for the decisions of the later eighteenth and nineteenth centuries – are flawed by Atiyah's presentism when applied to the seventeenth century.

It is true that one of the seventeenth-century suits examined for this chapter includes an express statement by the court in regard to protection of the obligor's family. In his note of *Berry v Fairclough* (1681),[136] Nottingham LC said:

> At the hearing I relieved him … notwithstanding he were of full age at the time, for this infamous kind of trade and circumvention ought by all means to be suppressed. The Star Chamber used to punish it and this court did always relieve against it. No family can be safe if this be suffered.[137]

In the later rehearing of the same matter, but in relation only to the defendant Pitt, Jeffreys LC appears to concur with his predecessor's concern for the family, declaring that 'these bargains were corrupt and fraudulent, and tended to the destruction of heirs, sent [to London] for education, and to the utter ruin of families'.[138]

These statements, however, are at least equally consistent with a court motivated by the protection of the normal operation of the culture of credit as with modern commentators' theories of the preservation of the wealth of the ruling classes. This suggestion is further supported by the analysis of the incidence of the relief granted according to family background, which showed no evidence of any meaningful distinction in the granting of relief to obligors of different social classes. While the

[135] eg, Dawson quoted a passage from *Earl of Portmore v Taylor* (1831) 4 Sim 182, 58 ER 69, which reads, in part, 'this court will not allow the heir of a family of rank to be reduced to poverty and distress by dealing with his expectancies' as an indication of '[t]he snobbery with which these cases reek': Dawson (n 48) 268.

[136] *Berry v Fairclough* (n 6).

[137] ibid.

[138] *Berney v Pitt* (n 6) 2 Chan Rep 397, 21 ER 698.

small numbers involved in the family background analysis mean that no definitive conclusion on this point can be safely asserted, it is at least worthy of note that plaintiff obligors of the merchant class had a greater success rate in obtaining substantive relief than obligors belonging to the combined county elite and peer classes, suggesting – while bearing in mind the caveat in relation to a normative approach by the court in this regard – an explanation of the granting of relief to expectant heirs and non-heir profligates based on the court's concern with ensuring the normal operation of credit networks, rather than with preserving the assets of the dominant county elite and peer classes.

V. Conclusion

The analysis of these 45 expectant heir and non-heir profligate suits, 28 of which have never previously been discussed in published works, suggests several conclusions in relation to the jurisdiction in the seventeenth century. The first of these is that the jurisdiction, described in the academic literature and the case law as a jurisdiction to relieve expectant heirs, was in fact a jurisdiction to relieve both expectant heir and non-heir profligates.

Additionally, by considering the basis for relief in broader terms, including the social, economic and historical contexts in which these suits were brought, heard and adjudicated, problems with the two main modern interpretations of the basis of the expectant heir suits – the 'special disability' and 'economic preservation' analyses – have been revealed. The most significant of these is that modern understandings of the seventeenth-century expectant heir suits have been skewed by the influence of nineteenth-century contract law doctrines and theories, which developed in a significantly different economic, social and historical context.

In contrast, this chapter suggests an interpretation of these suits grounded in the 'culture of credit' view of the economy of the seventeenth century. Here, the concern of the court was to prevent the disruption of the normal operation of credit through fraud, and in this light, both modern interpretations, rather than providing discrete explanations of the basis of relief, become illustrations of different aspects of fraud. This view, at least in relation to the economic preservation analysis, is supported by the fact that – as far as can be concluded from the small sample size – there does not appear to have been any meaningful difference in either the incidence or type of relief granted to expectant heir and profligate obligors on the basis of social class. This is further bolstered by the restitutionary nature of the relief granted, which acted to restore the normal operation of credit by removing the over-indebtedness of the obligor – and the risk to the creditworthiness of the obligor's family – brought about by behavioural or outcome fraud.

It is hoped that this research has led to a more nuanced, and historically informed, interpretation of one equitable jurisdiction; in a small way it is also offered as evidence for the importance of examining the historical roots of modern legal doctrine.

13

Equity Agreement Doctrine in the Early Eighteenth Century

MIKE MACNAIR

I. Introduction

My original project for this chapter – to look at the evolution of equity contract doctrine between the revolution of 1689 and the deaths of Lord Talbot LC (February 1737) and Sir Joseph Jekyll MR (August 1738) – was too ambitious. On looking into the caselaw, it turned out that a very high proportion of arguments in equity between the 1690s and 1730s turn either on 'agreement' or on 'consideration', including a lot of trusts law, mortgage law, priorities in the administration of estates and in insolvency, and so on. This is an unmanageably broad subject for a chapter. What I offer here is, instead, some account of the *general conceptions* of the enforcement of (and refusal to enforce) agreements in equity in the period. I consider mainly the contemporary printed treatise and abridgment literature, which shows lawyers' efforts to try to make some sort of sense of the topic, and I focus in this mainly on the analytical structures the authors try to create, though I also discuss what they have to say about agreement in the sense of, in modern terms, the formation of contract, and consideration. The other issues which surface extensively in the treatises are equitable fraud and related matters, and the enforcement of 'unreasonable' agreements, examined in this volume by Julius Grower, Emily Ireland and Helen Saunders.

II. Agreement

The first point to be made is the dominance in equity of the expression 'agreement', as opposed to 'contract'. 'Agreement' is the relevant subject heading in William Tothill's *Transactions*, published in 1651,[1] and the relevant chapter title in Lord Nottingham's

[1] *The Transactions of the High Court of Chancery, both by Practice and Precedent. Collected by William Tothill, Esq. Late one of The Six Clerks* (London, printed by TW for R Best, 1649); as printed in the *English Reports* reprint vol 21, 3–5, 21 ER 106.

Prolegomena, written in the early 1670s.[2] Moving into our period, 'Agreements in general' is much of Book I of the *Treatise of Equity* traditionally attributed to Henry Ballow; 'Specific performances of agreements' forms the first part of Sir Jeffrey Gilbert's *Lex Praetoria*; the heading in the 1732 *General Abridgment of Cases in Equity* is 'Agreements, Articles and Covenants'; 'Agreements' is the relevant title in Matthew Bacon's 1736 volume 1 of the *New Abridgment*; and 'Agreements' is the relevant subheading under the heading 'Chancery' in Sir John Comyns's *Digest*, written sometime before 1740.

'Assumpsit' appears in equity in very few cases, only as common law proceedings against which equity gives relief, or references to the availability of remedies at law, or as common law analogies.[3] References to 'contract' in 1689–1718 equity cases are more commonly to contract *debts* than to contract as a general principle of liability, though in the period 1719–1737 this proportion is reversed.[4] 'Agreement' remains throughout the period substantially more common than 'contract' in the equity reports. Thus, to give a crude indication of proportions, the number of *hits* for 'agreement*' on search, as they appear in common law versus equity *reporters*, with the products of blank searches for comparison:[5]

	HL	Chancery	KB/CP	Ex	Adm	Tot	All hits	HL/Ch
1689–1698	11	77	168	0	1	257	3,584	542
1699–1708	50	98	151	0	0	299	3,328	741
1709–1718	38	79	36	3	0	156	1,511	578
1719–1728	64	91	91	9	0	255	2,982	764
1729–1737	34	90	113	3	0	240	4,140	725

To the extent that we may be concerned with the theory underlying the doctrine, this would be clearly enough 'contract as agreement' rather than 'contract as promise'

[2] DEC Yale (ed), *Lord Nottingham's 'Manual of Chancery Practice' and 'Prolegomena of Chancery and Equity'* (Cambridge, Cambridge University Press, 1965) 309–311.

[3] Relief against: *Graham v Stamper* (1690) 2 Vern 146, 23 ER 701; *Snowball v Vicaris* (1724) Bunbury 175, 145 ER 638. Remedy at law: *Dupleix v De Roven* (1706) 2 Vern 540, 23 ER 950; *Earl of Hindford v Decosta* (1724) Cas t King 4, 25 ER 191; *Lee v Rook* (1730) Mosely 318, 25 ER 415; *North v Earl of Strafford* (1732) 3 P Wms 148, 151; 24 ER 1007, 1008. Analogy: *Andrews v Brown* (1714) Prec Ch 385, 24 ER 173; Gilb Rep 41, 25 ER 30; *Marlow v Pitfeild* (1719) 1 P Wms 558, 24 ER 516; *Burrows v Jemineau* (1726) Cas t King 69, 25 ER 228 (as *Burroughs v Jamineau* (1726) Mosely 1, 25 ER 235); *Roberts v Roberts* (1730) 3 P Wms 66, 76; 24 ER 971, 975. In *Anonymous* (1728) Mosely 37, 25 ER 255, King C offered the petitioning creditors in bankruptcy a feigned issue on *non assumpsit infra sex annos* where it appeared that some of their debts were statute-barred, and superseded the commission when they refused it. This is the complete set of 'assumpsit' references in equity brought up by search in the *English Reports* CD-ROM between 1689 and 1737.

[4] In 1689–98 there are 10 instances of 'contract' referring to debt on contract, five to broader senses. In 1699–1708 there are 20 debt on contract, 19 broader senses, and in 1709–1718, 18 debt on contract, 9 broader senses. But in 1719–28 there are 18 debt on contract, 41 broader senses, and in 1729–1737, 26 debt on contract, 44 broader senses. These figures result from a search of the Juta-Hart *English Reports* CD-ROM for 'contract'; lists of cases available from the author on request.

[5] I have moved the 'Chancery' cases from 9 Modern and the 'common law' cases from W Kelynge into the relevant column, and counted equity Exchequer cases individually, but otherwise this table merely assumes that the reporters are reporting in the courts to which they are usually attributed. The cases in HL are predominantly equity; I have excluded post-1707 Scots appeals from the count, but not bothered to split equity and law in HL.

(the assumpsit form of action at common law might seem to suggest the latter).[6] Also suggestive of the dominance of 'contract as agreement' is the point which surfaces occasionally in the reports, and is also present in Comyns's account, that an agreement to be enforceable in equity must be 'mutual' – that is, that it must be enforceable on both sides, not merely a unilateral contract.[7] If what equity enforced was 'promises' as opposed to 'agreements', the requirement of mutual enforceability looks quite inappropriate. The table also indicates a considerable presence of 'agreement' in common law usage; but 'promise' is far more clearly predominantly a common law usage.[8]

III. Books

How do our authors structure their 'Agreements' material? I will discuss them in what I *think* is the order in which they were written, rather than the order of publication, since it is certain in some cases that there were considerable gaps between the original writing and the date of publication, and this also seems likely in other cases.

A. British Library MS Lansdowne 1125

The earliest dated text in the period is unpublished, an equity commonplace book which forms the first part of British Library MS Lansdowne 1125, 'finished the 31th of 8br 1702 att Foord in Surrey'. This is not a highly developed text. The title 'Agreements' contains nine cases, neither in logical nor in chronological order. We begin with *Parker v Plummer* (1662), cited for the points that a speculative or wagering contract is enforceable, and (made in argument, but not clearly accepted) that specific enforcement is discretionary

[6] As, also, might debt on an obligation or on a contract, given the unilateral character of the claims they make. Covenant is also unilateral *as an action*, and individual 'covenants' can relate to unilateral individual terms; but since 'covenant' is merely Law French for Latin *conventio*, which translates into English as *agreement*, in this case the issue is much less clear.

[7] Sir J Comyns, *A Digest of the Laws of England* (London, printed by H Woodfall and W Strahan, for J Knapton, T Longman, and R Horsfield, 1762) vol 1, ii, tit 'Chancery', sub-tit 'Agreement', 2 C 14 (p 98); the editors cite the dissenting opinion of Wyndham B in *Lord Cornbury v Middleton* (1671) 1 Ch Cas 208, 209; 22 ER 765, 765, and the irrelevant *Bagg v Foster* (1670) 1 Ch Cas 188, 22 ER 755 (penalty bond conditioned to make a settlement not to be construed as an agreement to do so – Bridgman LK). In the reports, *Bromley v Jefferies* (1701) 2 Vern 415, 23 ER 867, Wright LK (*v Fettiplace*) 2 Freeman 245, 22 ER 1187, (*v Jeffereys*) Prec Ch 138, 24 ER 66, SC but not SP; *Conway v Shripton* (1710) 5 Brown PC 187, 2 ER 617, HL, counsel arguing 'as to the agreement, they insisted that it ought not to be performed in a Court of Equity; because it was unreasonable, not mutual, and void by the statute of frauds and perjuries' (accepted); *Bryan v Woolley* (1721) 1 Bro PC 184, 1 ER 502, Raymond & Lutwyche in respondent's printed case (*semble* accepted) at 1 Bro PC 185–86, 1 ER 503, 'That it was the nature of all agreements to be mutual and reciprocal, so as that each party might be equally bound to a performance; but as this pretended agreement was defective in that circumstance, a Court of Equity ought not to carry it into execution'; *Lewis v Lord Lechmere* (1722) 10 Mod 503, 88 ER 828, counsel for plaintiff arguing for SP at 10 Mod 506, 88 ER 829 'upon mutual articles there ought to be mutual remedies: that if the vendee had a remedy both in law and equity, the vendor would not be upon a par with him, unless he had so too' (this point seemingly accepted by Lord Macclesfield, though plaintiff lost on another point); *Armiger v Clarke* (1722) Bunb 111, 145 ER 614 (Ex).

[8] Of 165 hits for 'promise' 1689–98, 156 at law and 9 in equity; 1699–1708, 130 hits, 117 at law, 13 in equity; 1709–1718, 52 hits, 41 at law, 11 in equity; 1719–1728, 100 hits, 62 at law, 37 in equity; 1729–1737, 96 hits, 76 at law, 20 in equity.

and hard bargains may be left to law.[9] *Casey v Phitton* (unprinted, undated, but probably after 1688)[10] is on enforcement against the promisor's successors of what would in more modern times be called a secret trust. *Pauly v Martin* (1690, unprinted) is a decision that the plaintiff's breach bars a bill for the price of an equity of redemption sold. *Hind v Phips* (1690, unprinted) is on 'equivalent performance' (satisfaction?) of marriage agreements. *Wheeler v Newton* (1690) is cited here for the point, not in either of the printed versions, that an agreement in writing, partly performed, though unsealed, is not defeated by a 'paroll disagreement'.[11] *King v Withers* (1690), which in the printed versions is on the objection that the agreement is voluntary, is here cited as a case on duress by threats.[12] *Burge v Parker* (1690, unprinted, in the Exchequer) decides that a marriage agreement to double a daughter's portion under the custom of London is good and has priority over general creditors. *Barnard's Case* (unprinted) is Bridgman LK in 1671, ruling that agreements by deed are specifically enforceable, parol agreements only in special cases, and catching bargains and wagers not enforceable. *Mosely v Maynard* (1674) is one episode in a long-running litigation; the point noted here (that the son's reference of the other party to the father's decision means that the son is treated as bound by the father's agreement) is only in print in Lord Nottingham's report.[13]

There is a separate title, 'Paroll Agreements', containing five cases (two in print) and a maxim out of 'Cary' (Lambarde), again neither in logical nor in chronological order (and not including reference to the Statute of Frauds).[14]

'Consideration' contains five cases (four in print) and a maxim out of Coke upon Littleton.[15] The emphasis is very heavily on marriage as a consideration. There is some interest in the text the author attributes to *Pitt v Pelham* (1670) in the House of Lords:[16]

> an heir shall be compelled to sell in 2 cases, tho' he ben't particularly named thereto. 1st in case of a moral consideration, as to pay debts, as wherever a man devises lands to be sold to pay debts, the heir shall be compelled to do it. The 2nd is in case of a naturall consideration, vizt. where the like devise appointment had been made for raising portions for children

[9] This title all at fo 7r *Parker v Plumer* = *Parker v Plummer* (1663) 2 Freem 167, 22 ER 1134; (*v Palmer*) 1 Ch Cas 42, 22 ER 685.

[10] Not in print; probably after 1688, since part of the objection to the heir's conduct is undue influence on him by 'priests and Jesuits'.

[11] Prec Ch 16, 24 ER 9; Gilbert, *Chancery* (below n 29 and text there; the London edition) 245.

[12] Prec Ch 19, 24 ER 10, Gilbert, *Chancery* 245.

[13] *Maynard v Moseley* (1674) 73 SS 38 at 41. Lord Nottingham's report is clearly same point but slightly differently formulated.

[14] fo 8r *Powel v Crompton* (undated; the text is said in sidenote to be a *regula*), no relief on a parol or written but unsealed agreement unless part executed; *Poll v Smith* = *Voll v Smith* (1669) 3 Ch Rep 28, 21 ER 719; 'Cary 7' = Cary 5, 21 ER 3, no relief on *nudum pactum* or against false wager of law; *Dr Barnard's Case* (1671) repeating the note in the previous heading; *Breamer v Thornton* (1661) Hardr 203, 145 ER 453, cited from the printed report.

[15] fo 12r *Goodsal v Walker & Wall* (1663) (*Godscall*) 3 Ch Rep 10, 21 ER 713; *Glanvill v Jennings* (1669) (*Glanville*) 3 Ch Rep 31, 21 ER 720; *Burge v Parker* (1690) (above text after n 12) Ward *arg* marriage is 'the most valuable consideration in the law'; a bare statement without attribution of Hale CB's line in *Jenkins v Kemishe* (1665) Hardr 396, 398; 145 ER 515, 517, that 'the consideration of marriage, and of the marriage portion, will run to all the estates raised by the settlement, although the marriage is not concerned in them, so as to make them good against purchasors and to avoid a voluntary conveyance;' Co Lit 9b.

[16] *Pit v Pelham* (1668, 1670) 1 Ch Rep 283, 21 ER 574; (*Pitt*) (1670) 1 Ch Cas 176, 22 ER 750; 2 Freem 134, 22 ER 1110; (*Pits*) 1 Lev 304, 83 ER 419; (*Pit*) T Jon 24, 84 ER 1130.

Overall, however, there is little substance here. In spite of the presence of cases from Hilary Term 1690, the discussion is mainly of 1660s–1670s material.

B. The Maxims of Equity

Of the early eighteenth-century published books about equity, the first written – as far as I can see – was the book *The Maxims of Equity*, printed anonymously in 1727, but from the 1739 second edition onwards attributed to Richard Francis. The main body of the text of this book is entirely built on cases decided before 1700. The sidenotes added cases down to 1727, and the book also added at the end a (separately paginated) report of the important case of *Dowager Countess of Coventry v Earl of Coventry* (1724).[17] It is reasonable to suppose that, rather than writing a text artificially on the basis of old caselaw and then updating it in sidenotes, Francis was actually the editor of a pre-existing text dating to around 1700.[18] However, the method of *Maxims of Equity* means that it has little to tell us about the 'agreement' concept, telling us merely under Maxim 12, 'Equity regards not the Circumstance, but the Substance of the Act', that '*Equity will enforce the performance of Agreements in specie*; as Equity looks upon Articles for a Purchase of Lands, equal to a Conveyance …'.[19] Notably *absent* from both the base text and Francis's notes is the maxim that 'Equity will not assist a volunteer': the issue appears in the form of 'Where Equity is equal, the Law must prevail' (Maxim 14).[20]

C. The Treatise of Equity

The same dating issue arises in a more complex form in the *Treatise of Equity* printed in 1737 and usually attributed to Henry Ballow or Bellewe (1704–82). The *Treatise* consists in its main body of a quite intricate analysis of caselaw down to 1716–17, heavily reliant for both structure and introductory wording, as David Ibbetson has pointed out, on Samuel Pufendorf's *Law of Nature and Nations* (translated into English in 1703).[21] Within the individual sections, cases in this period are organised in a logical or quasi-logical, rather than chronological or reporter-based, order. This

[17] London, J Stephens, 1727; reprint, Gale ECCO. *Coventry v Coventry* also reported (1722) 10 Mod 463, 88 ER 811; (1722, 1724) 9 Mod 12, 88 ER 284; (1724) 2 P Wms 222, 24 ER 707; '1721' Gilb Rep 160, 25 ER 112; 1 Stra 596, 93 ER 722.

[18] And as well as sidenotes, added references to Vernon's reports, then recently published. The significance of 'maxims of equity' around 1700 can also be seen in the MS Lansdowne equity commonplace: British Library MS Lansdowne 1125; this contained a title 'Maxims in equity' (fos 48r-v), but this text is *not* antecedent to Francis's text.

[19] At 53. Francis adds an extensive sidenote on agreements equity will *not* enforce – unreasonable, unfairly obtained; but not, it seems to Francis, merely for lack of consideration.

[20] This is again an area where Francis adds extensively to the base text (sidenotes at 67–71, and cross-reference to *Coventry v Coventry*).

[21] D Ibbetson, *Historical Introduction to the Law of Obligations* (Oxford, Oxford University Press, 1999) 218–219. Ibbetson compares the 1729 4th edition of the English translation by Basil Kennett. To the extent that differences between editions are material, the points in 'Ballow' are already in the 1717 3rd edition, which used Barbeyrac's notes to the 2nd edition of his French translation (Amsterdam, 1712); the 1710 edition was the first to include Barbeyrac's (1706) notes. It is more likely that the author used the 1717 edition than that he used Barbeyrac's French directly.

text has then been partially but erratically updated to 1737 by *in places* adding more recent caselaw (and in one place a statute) at the end of the relevant sections.[22] It seems likely that Ballow was, as I have argued Francis was, an editor working on a pre-existing text.

I would suggest, extremely tentatively, that the text *might* be part of the preparations made by Thomas Parker, Lord Parker and later Earl of Macclesfield, for his judicial responsibilities when he became Chancellor in 1718, thus analogous to texts produced by Lord Nottingham (*Practice* and *Prolegomena*) and Lord Guilford,[23] and to Jeffrey Gilbert's updating work on his Chancery texts in the early 1720s (below). In favour of this view, Parker is certainly known to have read Pufendorf on contract, since he cited the text in *Mitchell v Reynolds* on covenants in restraint of trade in 1713 (a case which is, in fact, cited in the *Treatise*);[24] his Enlightenment-Whig politics are more consistent with the *sort* of use made of Pufendorf in the first few pages of the *Treatise* than Ballow's known Toryism is;[25] and he died in 1732, a date consistent with some manuscript of his having found its way into the hands of a publisher in time to be edited up and then published in 1737. But, as I said, this suggestion is very tentative; the main point is that this is a book about equity doctrine circa 1716–17 with some later additions.

As Ibbetson pointed out, the *Treatise* author's use of Pufendorf was limited to the use of some conceptual-introductory verbiage, and of a classificatory structure, which the author substantially modified. But this usage nonetheless enabled a much more extensive and elaborate analysis of the caselaw than was achieved by any of the other equity authors of this period. The *Treatise* begins by stating the availability of specific performance much more generally than other authors (though, in this, consistently with the caselaw of the period) but then says that

> regularly, there are but four Cases, wherein an agreement will not be binding in Equity. 1st, for want of Assent. 2dly, for want of Testimony of the Assent. 3dly, where there is some Vice or Defect in the Subject Matter; or, 4thly, The want of a sufficient Consideration (ch 1 § 8)

[22] This is the product of following up the marginal citations added by the Dublin editor (Dublin, S Cotter, 1756) with some further cross-checking. A file of the relevant cases is available from the author on request. It is implausible to suppose that the result is the product of writing purely on the basis of Vernon and *Cases in Chancery* as in print, since the 'structured' part includes pre-1717 cases not printed in these sources but appearing in *Equity Cases Abridged* (1732), Gilbert's *Reports* (1733), or *Precedents in Chancery* (1734) – but, on the other hand, if the author is writing on the basis of those sources as printed, rather than from MSS that lie behind them, he has artificially limited his use of them to pre-1717 cases when constructing the structure, and added in later cases only erratically. It is a more economical explanation to suppose that the author was writing on the basis of printed and manuscript sources available in 1716–17, and the erratic insertion of later cases the work of an editor, probably Ballow.

[23] Lord Nottingham – Yale (ed) (n 2). Lord Guilford – some extracted material copied from North's commonplace book in BL Additional MSS 32518, 32519; more selective extracts in M Chan (ed), *The Life of the Lord Keeper North by Francis North* (Lampeter, Edwin Mellen Press, 1995) 323–54 (more on practice and procedure than on substantive equity).

[24] *Mitchell v Reynolds* (1711) 10 Mod 27, 88 ER 610; (1712) 10 Mod 85, 88 ER 637; (1713) 10 Mod 130, 88 ER 660; (*Mitchel*) 1 P Wms 181, 24 ER 347; (*Mitchell v Reynold*) Fort 296, 92 ER 859. The Pufendorf citation is in Peere Williams: 1 P Wms 191, 24 ER 350; also in 10 Modern (Lucas): 10 Mod 135 and 137, 88 ER 662 and 663. Lucas is the only one of these sets of reports printed before the publication of the *Treatise*, so that the *Treatise* author is most likely to have known the case in MS.

[25] On Parker, *cf* J Rudolph, *Common Law and Enlightenment in England, 1689-1750* (Woodbridge, Boydell Press, 2013) esp ch 6.

Chapter 2 then discusses under 'the Assent required in Agreements' issues of capacity; mistake; fraud, and in this context 'surprise' (bad faith non-disclosure); *laesio enormis*,[26] and in this connection 'catching bargains' with heirs; and the effect of these transactions as being capable of subsequent ratification. Chapter 3, 'Want of Testimony of the Assent', begins with intention versus forms issues and implied assent; the distinction between negotiations and completed agreement, and the need for certainty, before moving into parol agreements, the Statute of Frauds and the parol evidence rule, concluding with the requirement of *acceptance* in 'all conveyances and contracts', though the text is mainly addressed to conveyances (§ 12).[27]

Chapter 4 on 'the Subject Matter of Covenants' is extensive. It begins with antecedent impossibility, and in this context, dispositions of after-acquired property; and supervening illegality. It then moves to illegality and immorality more generally; and in this context gaming, usury, bottomry and marriage-brocage; agreements in fraud of marriage or of creditors, and fraudulent conveyances and devises; and fraud on the custom of London as to forced shares in inheritance. At § 19 it moves into legal restraints on alienation: entails; corporations; femes covert (partially duplicating the discussion of capacity earlier); time priority in voluntary conveyances, unreasonable agreements, and laches/length of time (§§ 25–27). Chapter 5, on consideration, is a great deal shorter, and moves from § 4 into discussing covenants which run with the land before ending with failure of consideration (§ 8) and, following from the latter, apportionment (§ 9).

Also short in page length, but complex, is Chapter 6, on 'the execution of the agreement'. It begins with conditions as distinct from mutual covenants; the requirement that the claimant in equity be ready, able and willing to perform; relief against conditions where compensation is available; and under this head the jurisdiction that Lord Nottingham called 'voluntary offer',[28] which is in modern law called 'promissory estoppel'; and then (very much in outline) the issue of conditions in restraint of marriage. This in turn leads back to the consideration issue, in the form of strict construction of voluntary dispositions, but intention-based construction of dispositions for value (including marriage) and the doctrine of conversion; then from §§ 11 on, to common law rules of construction (as applied in equity); ending at § 20 with implied intentions and terms. The author has here turned Pufendorf's category into something of a 'grab-bag' of miscellaneous issues.

As I said, the use of Pufendorf enabled the author to construct an elaborate analysis of a large body of authority. The author is still (in his own view) discussing contract in

[26] The point is not *purely* civilian, but relies on Lord Nottingham's *dictum*, that a *laesio* rule would be desirable, in *Nott v Hill* (1682) 2 Ch Cas 120, 22 ER 875.

[27] The Dublin editor failed to identify a source for the passage. Pufendorf 3.6.15 is, as Ibbetson pointed out, *approximately* and *structurally* relevant; but the emphasis in the content on acceptance in *conveyances* means that the passage is probably at least substantially influenced by the heavy emphasis on the need for acceptance in conveyances in the leading case *Thompson v Leach* (1690) 3 Lev 284, 83 ER 691; 2 Vent 198, 86 ER 391; 3 Mod 296, 301 87 ER 196, 199 (CP); *Leach v Thompson* (1691) 1 Show KB 296, 89 ER 584; (*Leech*) (1692) Carth 211, 90 ER 726; (1697–98) Comb 438, 498; 90 ER 577, 596; 1 Comyns 45, 92 ER 951; (1698) 12 Mod 173, 88 ER 1243; (*Leech's Case*) 1 Freem 502, 508; 89 ER 377, 383; Carth 435, 90 ER 852; 1 Ld Raym 313, 91 ER 1104 (KB); *Leach v Thomson* (1698) Show PC 150, 1 ER 102 (HL).

[28] 79 SS Index, sv. So also in *Harman v Vanhatton* (1716) 2 Vern 716, 23 ER 1071, where Lord Cowper equates it to *nudum pactum*.

Book II Part I (private trusts) and Book III (mortgages and pledges), but these can, for the purposes of this chapter, be set on one side as specialist. That said, other specialist forms of agreement/contract are absent: 'account' appears merely as a chapter in relation to executors, and conversely there is no discussion of the substantial equity business in partnership and agency matters, or, more broadly, in complex contractual relationships in which account served as a remedy for the absence (later, the limits) of set-off and cross-claims at law.

D. Gilbert's Lex Praetoria

Sir Jeffrey Gilbert's *Lex Praetoria* was published in 1758, both in London and Dublin, as the second part of *The History and Practice of the High Court of Chancery* (the first part, on Chancery history and procedure, being called *Forum Romanum*). The Dublin edition of the *Forum Romanum* is based on a very early state of the manuscript, coupled with some other texts, but the Dublin *Lex Praetoria* version is fairly full. The London edition has a fuller *Forum Romanum*, but a weaker *Lex Praetoria.* It is continuously paginated between the two parts, and removes Gilbert's citations to manuscript law reports (present in the Dublin edition) in favour of citations to printed reports (where available), eliminating all the citations in the Irish edition where citations to print are not available.[29] The *Forum Romanum* part had behind it a series of earlier draft versions in manuscript, being part of the 'Courts' section of Gilbert's larger project, originating before 1710; but the writing of the *Lex Praetoria* element dates, as far as can be seen from citations, to the early 1720s.[30] As I said above, it seems likely that Gilbert felt the need to update his work on equity procedure and substantive doctrine around the time of his appointment to be a Baron of the English Exchequer.

The *Lex Praetoria* begins with 'Specific performance of agreements'. The material used here contains relatively few cases, and though they include late seventeenth-century material, there is a prominent presence of cases which, where they are in print, date between 1710 and 1719 and form part of the corpus of Chancery reports in early eighteenth-century manuscript circulation which partially overlaps between the *General Abridgment of Cases in Equity (vol 1)* (1732), *Precedents in Chancery* (1733), and the reports later attributed to Gilbert himself (1734).

[29] J Gilbert, *Two Treatises on the Proceedings in Equity, and the Jurisdiction of that Court, in two Volumes…* Forum Romanum … Lex Praetoria (Dublin, Richard Watts, 1756, 1758); id, *The History and Practice of the High Court of Chancery …* (London, J Worrall and W Owen, 1758).

[30] *Forum Romanum:* Columbia University, Diamond Law School MS Singleton 26, ff 1–16 (first version of the courts in general) 37–40 (notes on Chancery); Singleton MS 34 (1), item (ii) (unfoliated) (early version with no material later than 1714); Harvard Law School MS 1064 ff 42–51, foliation restarts, ff 1–46, and Harvard Law School MS 5141, item 2, new foliation after f 95 (updated into 17-teens); Columbia University MS Singleton 28, and copy id 27, updated to 1722–23; Singleton 33, and Singleton 34(1) item (i), pp 1–111, updated to 1720s; closest to the printed text is Harvard Law School MS 1163. I have to say that these judgments of what is obviously a complex manuscript history are tentative and based only on the Columbia and Harvard manuscripts. *Lex Praetoria:* Columbia Law School MS Singleton 33 has references to 'MS Chancery cases' generally; Harvard Law School MS 1164, item (ii) is closer to the referencing to Gilbert's MS collections found in the Dublin edition. MS circulation before printing is shown by these and by Singleton MSS 34 (2) and 34 (3), containing imperfect copies with the addition of sidenotes to the printed Vernon and *Precedents in Chancery*, so later than 1733.

Within this heading, the analytical structure is at best rudimentary. Gilbert begins with the proposition that covenants or agreements are at common law *in personam*, but in equity have an effect *in rem* by way of specific enforceability. This is followed by the assertion that where a marriage is illegal by statute law, but legal by canon law, the wife's claim under the marriage settlement is enforceable, citing the undated *Dr Butler's Case*;[31] then that agreements before marriage can be taken to be waived by settlements executed before marriage, but not those executed after marriage, citing *Read v Read*.

Gilbert then moves on to a series of cases on points on the Statute of Frauds; then, at pp 14–18, to the point that equity will not enforce an agreement 'unreasonable, or obtained by fraud or circumvention' (p 14), which, however, continues to overlap with Statute of Frauds issues. From around p 18 the discussion moves into marriage agreements – not, however, limited to settlements on marriage, but also including issues related to the husband's disposal of the wife's assets – with a digression into *Frank v Frank* (1667) and *Ross v Ross* (1670) in relation to exchange agreements between brothers/half-brothers where there was a bad title (pp 24–5), and another on the parol evidence rule as applied to a shipping claim in *Foot v Salway* (1683) (pp 27–9) before coming back to marriage agreements and ending with the enforceability of a separation agreement in *Angier v Angier* (1718) (pp 42–3).[32]

Like quite a lot of Gilbert's work, this is very rough draft material not really worked up; all that can really be obtained from it is the prominence of the Statute of Frauds, and of marriage agreements among the class of agreements studied.

E. Equity Cases Abridged

The *General Abridgment of Cases in Equity* published in 1732, is of uncertain authorship, but very much most plausibly attributed to Matthew Bacon.[33] It seems likely that Bacon started as an editor of some pre-existing manuscript, but this possibility leads nowhere in relation to dating, since alphabetical indexes to Chancery precedents go back to the 1590s, with Tothill (already mentioned) an important printed example, two other 1650s versions, one in Lincoln's Inn and one (Lord Commissioner John Lisle's version) in Kansas, and the 1702 equity commonplace discussed above.[34] So the form is an old one, but it seems reasonable to treat Bacon as responsible for the analytical features of this printed version.

[31] This *may* be connected to *Butler v Gastrill* (HT 1723/24) Gilb Rep 156, 25 ER 110 (misdated to 1721 and misattributed to the Delegates), (*Gastrell*) Bunb 145, 145 ER 627, Ex (L), also on marriage within the prohibited degrees; but if so, this point is not in either report.

[32] *Frank v Frank* (1667) 1 Ch Cas 84, 22 ER 706; *Ross v Ross* (1670) 1 Ch Cas 171, 22 ER 747; *Foot v Salway* (1683) 2 Ch Cas 142, 22 ER 885; *Angier v Angier* (1718) Gilb Rep 152, 25 ER 107; Prec Ch 496, 24 ER 222.

[33] JD Cowley, *A Bibliography of Abridgments, Digests, Dictionaries and Indexes of English Law to the Year 1800* (London, B Quaritch for Selden Society, 1932) lxvi, cites an attribution by the contemporary judge Sir William Lee in his copy of the book.

[34] References to the precursors of Tothill, and the LI versions, in M Macnair, 'The Nature and Function of the Early Chancery Reports' in C Stebbings (ed), *Law Reporting in Britain* (London, Hambledon, 1995) 127; for Lisle's version, AJ Busch, 'The John Lisle Chancery Manuscripts: The 'Abridgements'' (1989) 10 *Journal of Legal History* 317.

These *superficially appear* to be significantly stronger than Gilbert's account. Bacon starts, as Gilbert does, with 'Agreements and covenants which ought to be performed in specie, and econt'. The first part of the subtitle is cases where specific performance was ordered, the second where it was refused. Head (B) on parol agreements and the Statute of Frauds puts in, early in the heading, cases used by Gilbert, but then goes on to include a significantly larger range of cases (and ones from earlier dates). Head (C) 'Voluntary Agreements, in what cases to be performed', adds a little more than Gilbert's casual reference to a couple of cases in point. (D) 'Agreements by whom to be performed' addresses mainly – as it suggests – questions of parties but includes *Cass v Rudele* where what would now be called a frustration argument seems to have been made unsuccessfully (the houses sold had been sunk in the sea by the 1692 Port Royal earthquake, but the risk had clearly passed to the purchaser before the event).[35]

(E) 'Concerning the manner and time of performing agreements' contains an odd mixture of cases from Vernon – *Gerrard v Vaux* (1683), read as a question of construction; *Scolefield v Whitehead* (1690) where 60 years' quiet possession was a bar to enforcement of a mining lease and anti-competition covenant; *Broom Whorewood v Simpson* (1690), a case of fraud and self-dealing by an agent; *Gardner v Pullen* (1700) where a sale of shares was specifically enforced; and *Wilcocks v Wilcocks* (1706) where buying land and allowing it to descend to the eldest son was taken to be a satisfaction of an agreement to purchase and settle which would have given the son an interest in tail after the widow's jointure.[36]

(F) 'Where the person or estate will be made liable to a covenant or agreement' is partly concerned, as the title suggests, with covenants running with the land, in the form of *Cook v Arundel* (1656) (covenant to exempt part of land sold from rent service is personal, not real) with a note that the opposite line was taken in *Lord Cornbury v Middleton* (1671), and the notorious case of *Holmes v Buckley* (1691) allowing a positive covenant (to keep a watercourse clear) to bind purchasers.[37] But the two intervening cases concern a vendor who sells a bad title and later buys a good title being decreed to convey and covenants to purchase and settle, or to grant an annuity out of lands of a warranted value, affecting after-acquired land.[38] (G) 'Where there may be Relief when the Agreement is not strictly performed' would, to modern eyes, look like the question of 'substantial performance'. But it actually consists of three cases of relief against common law contractual claims where the purchaser was evicted by title paramount;[39]

[35] *Cass v Rudele* (1692) 2 Vern 280, 23 ER 781 (the note corrects the report); *cf* also *White v Nutts* (1702) 1 P Wms 61, 24 ER 294.

[36] *Gerrard v Vaux* (1683) 1 Vern 121, 23 ER 357 (from the editor's note from the record, the reported point seemingly merely misunderstood by the young Thomas Vernon); *Scolefield v Whitehead* (1690) 2 Vern 127, 23 ER 690; *Broom Whorewood v Simpson* (1690) 2 Vern 186, 23 ER 722; *Gardener v Pullen* (1700) 2 Vern 394, 23 ER 853 (the editor's note from the record shows a more complicated transaction and decree); *Wilcocks v Wilcocks* (1706) 2 Vern 558, 23 ER 961.

[37] *Cooke v Earl of Arundel* (1656) Hardres 87, 145 ER 394; *Lord Cornbury v Middleton* (1671) 1 Ch Cas 208, 212; 22 ER 765, 767; *Holmes v Buckley* (1692) Prec Ch 39, 24 ER 20; 1 Eq Ca Ab 27, 21 ER 848.

[38] *Taylor v Debar* (1676) 1 Ch Cas 274, 22 ER 798; 2 Ch Cas 212, 22 ER 915; Lord Nottingham's report, *Taylor v Daborah* 73 SS 260, shows these to be wildly inaccurate; *Tooke v Hastings* (1689) 2 Vern 97, 23 ER 671.

[39] *Coldcot v Hill* (1662) 1 Ch Cas 15, 22 ER 671; (*Collicott*) 2 Freem 173, 22 ER 1139; *Anon* (1680) 2 Ch Cas 19, 22 ER 826, probably *Skip v Sir William Rich* 79 SS 805 in the same term and on the same point, though less helpful to purchaser than the *Cases in Chancery* (hearsay) report is; *Awbry v Keen* (1687) 1 Vern 472, 23 ER 597.

two of what moderns call promissory estoppel; one on a penalty increase in interest rate on default; one refusal to relieve against excessive jury damages; and one refusal to relieve a bankrupt agent on bankruptcy preference grounds where the agent's defrauded principal had insisted on a preference grounded on the agent's fraudulent breach of fiduciary duty.[40]

In substance, though the structure on its face as a set of subheads looks not implausible, the content attributed to each of the subheads is a lot less coherent.

F. Bacon's New Abridgment

Bacon's second effort was the title 'Agreements' in volume 1 of *The New Abridgment* (1736). This begins with a definition of 'Agreement':

> An Agreement is the Consent of two or more persons concurring, the one in parting with, and the other in receiving some property, right or benefit; the Notion of contracting or entring into Agreements arose from the Increase of Commerce, and the Necessity Men were under of Bartering their Superfluities for Things of real Use, and which lay out of the Way of their acquiring; that Men should execute their Agreements and perform their Promises, though made without Writing or Consideration, is enjoined by the Law of Nature; but in Civil Societies, and in ours in particular, Circumstances are required which protect the Weak, and those who are under the Power of others; also Provision is made against Fraud and Circumvention, and that no man should be injured in his Property by the Turn of an unwary Expression.

As Michael Lobban has pointed out, this is fairly obviously immediately derived (as a summary) from Gilbert's *Personal Property*, in the part of that text which is a general introduction to contractual obligations.[41] Bacon has, in fact, here slightly 'spun' his summary of Gilbert in the direction of narrowing it to applicability to equity jurisdiction.

The definition allows one substantial addition to the analytical structure relative to the *Lex Praetoria* and to *Equity Cases Abridged*: subhead (A) is concerned with capacity. This begins with persons *non compos*, infants and *femes coverts*, in each case merely cross-referring to the relevant general heading. The discussion then proceeds to the power of tenant in fee simple to bind the heir, and from there to the effect of dispositions by tenant in tail not completed by fine or recovery.

The following subheads do not exactly duplicate *Equity Cases Abridged*, but there is relatively little additional content. (B) 'Of Agreements which are good in Law, and will be decreed in *specie* in Equity' has as sub-subheads 1. 'Of unreasonable agreements, and such as may be said to be obtained by Fraud or Circumvention, 2. Of voluntary Agreements, 3. Of the Manner in which they are to be performed'.

The first sub-subhead begins with the general proposition that claims sounding in damages are remediable only at law, the ground offered being that 'the Damages cannot

[40] *Sewell v Musson* (1683) 1 Vern 210, 23 ER 420; and *Delamere v Smith* (1668) 1 Ch Cas 110, 22 ER 718; *Marquis of Hallifax v Higgens* (1691) 2 Vern 134, 23 ER 694; *Barker v Holder* (1685) 1 Vern 316, 23 ER 493; *Small v Brackley* (1708) 2 Vern 602, 23 ER 993.

[41] 135 SS 205–207. The opening sentence is, of course, ultimately derived under Ulpian D. 2.14.1.2.

be ascertained by the Conscience of the Chancellor, and therefore must be settled by a Jury'. But if the claim involves matters of fraud, or specific performance, it can be retained in equity. This is taken from the Gilbert manuscript from which chapter 12 of the London edition of the *Forum Romanum* was derived.[42] (It probably inverts the story: the underlying doctrine at law as well as in equity being that unliquidated damages are in the exclusive province of the jury.)[43] The bulk of what follows is merely taken from *Equity Cases Abridged*; but the subsection concludes with the point that all the cases depend upon circumstances, so that 'I shall only observe that a Court of Equity will much easier be prevailed upon to dismiss a bill which prays a specifick Execution of an unreasonable agreement, that to set aside an Agreement, though not strictly fair, on a bill for that purpose …'.

The pattern of adding a degree of increased generality is also to be seen in the second sub-subsection, 'Of voluntary Agreements'. But the third merely cuts down and amalgamates (E) 'Concerning the manner and time of performing agreements' and (G) 'Where there may be Relief when the Agreement is not strictly performed' from *Equity Cases Abridged*. The third subhead, (C) on parol agreements and the Statute of Frauds, again begins with increased generality in the form of a brief notice of formalities at common law and a recital of the statute. This is then followed by material from *Equity Cases Abridged*, which is in turn followed by a report at length of *Sansum v Butter* (25 Jan 1724 – presumably 1724–25) on part performance; a few more cases not in *Equity Cases Abridged*; and a collection of points on the Statute ruled at common law.

Thus, although *The New Abridgment* adds some increased generalisation of arguments, the converse is some cutting of material from *Equity Cases Abridged* (presumably for space reasons). The resulting text is not significantly more coherent.

G. Comyns's *Digest*

Sir John Comyns's *Digest* was published in 1762–67, in translation from the original Law French. The anonymous translators tell us in the preface to the first volume that they made significant editorial alterations by correcting Comyns's text by the printed books, by adding authorities where Comyns did not cite any, and additional reports, by moving the general titles into strict alphabetical order, and by adding letters and numbers to the divisions and subdivisions in the style of Rolle or Viner.[44] It is also clear that Comyns continued to commonplace on the text down to the 1730s (assuming the editors were not responsible for the later cases).[45] The editing work and the commonplacing make it practically impossible to date the text, or at least the

[42] Gilbert, *History & Practice*, London edition (n 29) *Forum Romanum* ch 12, 219–221.

[43] At 69. Unliquidated damages a jury issue: M Bacon, *A New Abridgment of the Law* (London, H Lintot, 1736) vol 2, 4, tit 'Damages', subhead (D) 'Of assessing the Damages', 1. 'Of the *quantum* of the Damages the Jury may give', and p. 10 (E) 'Where the Court may increase or mitigate the Damages'.

[44] J Comyns, *A Digest of the Laws of England, vol 1* (London, J Knapton, T Longman, and R Horsfield, 1762) iv–viii (Preface).

[45] eg, title 2 C 8 *Parry v Hughs* Hil 5 Geo II (*Parry v Hughes* (1728) 2 Eq Ca Ab 54, 22 ER 47 (Ex(E)).

Chancery material, at any level beyond the proposition that it must have been written before Comyns's death in 1740.

Comyns's subhead 'Agreement' in his heading 'Chancery' has seventeen sub-subheads, four of which are printed as subheads ('When decreed' 'But an Agreement shall not be decreed', 'Specific Performance in the Discretion of the Court' and 'In what Manner an Agreement shall be decreed to be executed'), and the remainder as sidenotes. They are 1. Agreements to convey land are enforceable. 2. They are enforceable against certain successors in title. 3. Parol agreements are enforceable if partly performed. 4. This is limited since the Statute of Frauds 1677 but still possible. 5. Inequality of consideration is not a bar to enforcement. 6. Nor is mistake. 7. Agreements for a remote consideration, as eg, to settle a contingent remainder, are enforceable.

On the other hand, 8. Agreements are not to be decreed if there is no consideration, or if the plaintiff is a remainderman outside the consideration. 9. They are also not to be decreed if *ex facie* unreasonable. 10. Or if void in law (as in the case of an agreement by husband and wife not binding the wife after the husband's death). 11. Or if discharged by agreement or prohibited by law between agreement and performance. 12. Or if obtained by 'practice', meaning fraud, but also including breach of fiduciary duty by an agent, and fraud on the marriage agreement by collateral pay-back agreements. 13. Or if the parties to the contract did not include essential parties. 14. Or where the agreement is not mutual, ie, is only enforceable on one side.

Subhead 15 is titled 'Failure of one party excuses the other'. The first two heads concern 'voluntary offer'/'promissory estoppel'; the third is straightforward discharge by breach; the fourth also involves non-payment of anything more than earnest, but was interpreted by the editor of *Cases in Chancery* and subsequent writers as a claim by *particeps criminis* in a transaction intended to defraud creditors.[46] 16. Specific performance is at the discretion of the court (the cases listed are rather various).[47] 17. 'In what manner an agreement shall be decreed to be executed' is headed by the statement that 'An agreement shall be decreed according to equitable construction, in pursuance of the intent of the parties, and not according to the words' – but none of the following cases listed actually support the point.[48]

Notwithstanding Comyns's reputation among early nineteenth-century judges as a strong author (which may perhaps fall to be explained by the congeniality of his early Toryism to the politics of the early nineteenth-century judiciary), this is not particularly strong work. This is relatively unsurprising, since Comyns's reports show him in King's Bench until 1705, in Common Pleas from then until 1726, when he was appointed Baron of the Exchequer, and he appears as counsel in other reports pretty much exclusively at

[46] 1. *Delamere v Smith* (1668) 1 Ch Cas 110, 22 ER 718; *Sewell v Musson* (1683) 1 Vern 210, 23 ER 420; *Ewes v Blackwall* (1673) Rep t Finch 22, 23 ER 12 (not in 73 SS, though there are two cases in same term on same point 73 SS 21–22). 2. *Glover v Portington* (1664) 1 Ch Cas 51, 22 ER 690 (*Partington* Nels 96, 21 ER 799 looks like a weaker copy of same report). 3. *Legate v Hockwood* (1679) 2 Ch Cas 5, 22 ER 819 (not in 79 SS). 4. *Barebone v Barnes* (1682) 2 Ch Cas 121, 22 ER 876.

[47] Discussed below nn 51–2 and text there.

[48] *West v Lord Delaware* (1683) 1 Vern 198, 23 ER 411 (North LK sent the parties to compulsory arbitration); *Burrel v Harrison* (1691) 2 Vern 231, 23 ER 749 (implied term that tenant to repair inferred from low rent); *Vane v Lord Barnard* (1708) Gilb Rep 6, 25 ER 5 (covenant to covenant, approached on a strict-construction basis; mainly argued on notice).

common law, so that he is unlikely to have had much equity expertise before becoming a judge.[49]

IV. Topics

What can be learned from these various efforts? The first point is that category structure was clearly a problem. The *Treatise* author is relatively successful, but by virtue of using Pufendorf as a crutch. Neither Gilbert, nor Bacon, nor Comyns really succeeds in creating a category structure workable on their own terms.

The background to this is that at common law at this period the forms of action remained dominant in the construction of category structures. And an 'agreement' in equity was neither a 'covenant' at law, nor a 'contract' (so as to produce liability in the action of debt on a contract)[50] nor a bond, nor a liability to account, nor an assumpsit. It made a certain sort of sense to think of 'agreement' as the pure underlying natural obligation underlying particular contracts, as in Ulpian's discussion of pacts in D.2.14.1, and that is in effect what the *Treatise* author is doing in his use of Pufendorf, and what Bacon in the *New Abridgment* is doing by starting with a summary out of Gilbert on contracts. But that does little to resolve the issue of the details of the category structure.

Secondly, the starting point for all our authors is specific performance. Here there is a fundamental difference between the *Treatise* author and Gilbert on the one hand, and Bacon and Comyns on the other. For the *Treatise* author and Gilbert, there is in principle no substantive limit on specific performance. There is no equity jurisdiction if only damages are *sought*, or for a claim merely for payment of a liquidated sum,[51] but if specific performance is sought, it is *generally* available, though there may be various objections to it. In contrast, Bacon and Comyns begin with a list of cases in which specific performance is positively available, before going on to cases in which it is not available. In Comyns this method of approach is absolutely dominant.

In this respect these two authors are closer to the modern view. In the caselaw, however, there is a serious shortage of supporting evidence. Comyns's subtitle 'Specific Performance in the Discretion of the Court', relies on a rejected argument in a case of 1663 and on *Cud v Rutter* (1719), which rejected specific performance of a sale of shares and which is also the only case in the period to be found on a search for specific performance where that remedy is rejected on the ground of the subject matter of the contract, as opposed to on grounds of lack of consideration, fraud or sharp practice, laches/length of time, illegality or immorality, or other such objections.[52]

[49] M Macnair, 'Comyns, Sir John (c. 1667–1740)' Oxford Dictionary of National Biography (Oxford University Press, 2004) doi.org/10.1093/ref:odnb/6050; the only equity case in which he appears in the printed reports is the Irish HL appeal of *Earl of Clanrickard v Bourke* (1717) 6 Bro PC 4, 2 ER 895.

[50] Viner, adopting the title 'Contract or Agreement', produces a startling confusion of late medieval debt on a contract cases with 16th–18th century cases in equity.

[51] *Cf* discussion of the treatment in Bacon, from Gilbert, above nn 33–4.

[52] *Parker v Palmer* (1663) 1 Ch Cas 42, 22 ER 685; *Cud v Rutter* (1719) 1 P Wms 570, 24 ER 521; more fully (*Cuddee*) 5 Viner 538. Comyns' other cases in this subhead are *Colt v Nettervill* (1725) 2 P Wms 304, 24 ER 741, where King C rejected a demurrer to a bill for specific performance of a sale of shares, on the ground that circumstances might support specific performance; and two cases of relief against purchaser's laches,

Third, for all our authors the Statute of Frauds is the most fundamental issue posed in the field of what moderns could call the formation of contracts. This does not mean that the courts of equity had nothing to say about formation beyond this. In *Turton v Benson* (1718), Jekyll MR said that

> Mr. Turton's offers made and not accepted signified nothing; that Lord Cowper had often said a man should not be bound by an offer made during a treaty which afterwards broke off, or upon terms that were not accepted.[53]

A good deal of literature dates 'offer and acceptance' doctrine in the caselaw to the nineteenth or at most the late eighteenth century; Sir John Baker has drawn our attention to Lord Nottingham's use of the mode of analysis in 1675 in *Parker v Serjeant*.[54] Jekyll MR here reports a general dogmatic assertion of the point by Lord Cowper, which can also be found from Cowper himself in *Ackworth v Mew* (1709).[55] There are a few other casual references in the cases.[56] But these, and analogous references to 'assent', are rare.[57] The background is that the sort of cases the court is dealing with – those worth spending Chancery costs on – are ones in which contracts were *normally* made formally: marriage articles, contracts for the sale of land, leases, and less frequently charterparties and other such instruments. So the questions of parol contracts, the effect of the Statute of Frauds and the parol evidence rule, are naturally more pertinent than the rules for the

Awbry v Keen (1687) 1 Vern 472, 23 ER 597 where specific performance was impossible because the death of the vendor vested the property sold in a person not bound, and repayment of the price was ordered, and *Vernon v Stephens* (1722) 2 P Wms 66, 24 ER 642, where purchaser's delay was partly affected by the shortage of money in 1720 and the death of vendor and time taken obtaining administration, and specific performance was ordered. Neither is really in point in support of a general discretion or of a limited subject scope of specific performance. Though *Colt v Nettervill* is only in a limited way an argument against *Cud v Rutter*, it should be noted that in *Gardener v Pullen* (1700) 2 Vern 394, 23 ER 853, specific performance *was* ordered of a sale of shares. I have searched the English reports database for 'specific', 'specifick' and 'specie' for the period to produce this negative result; the range of cases where specific performance is decreed is wide, and at the other extreme, in *Ball v Coggs* (1710) 1 Bro PC 140, 1 ER 471 (HL) a contract of employment seems to be specifically enforced at the instance of the employee.

[53] (1718) 1 P Wms 496, 497; 24 ER 488, 489; Lord Macclesfield C on appeal says 'no more than nudum pactum'. 2 Vern 764, 765, 23 ER 1099, 1099 has the statement as 'as to any promise made by Turton that he would pay it, that was but *nudum pactum*, and not binding'; (1719) Prec Ch 522, 24 ER 234, is only Lord Macclesfield C on appeal and does not have this point.

[54] 19th century: eg, J Gordley *Philosophical Origins of Modern Contract Doctrine* (Oxford, Clarendon Press, 1991) 135–36, 139–40; later 18th century: P Hamburger, 'The Development of the Nineteenth-Century Consensus Theory of Contract' (1989) 7 *Law & History Review* 241, 283–84; Sir John Baker, *Introduction to English Legal History*, 5th edn (Oxford, Oxford University Press, 2019) 373, fn 30; 73 SS 241.

[55] WH Bryson (ed), *Reports of Cases in Chancery in the Time of Queen Anne* (Tempe, AZ, ACMS, 2021) 200–01.

[56] eg, *Mansel v Mansel* (1732) 2 Barn KB 186, 188; 94 ER 438, 439, Dudley Ryder *arg*, citing *Keech v Sandford*, 'The lord of the market refused to make them such lease in the right of the infant, but offered to make them such lease in their own right, if they would accept of it. The trustees accepted the offer, and had a future term in the market made to them accordingly'; *Hall v Digby* (1735) 4 Bro PC 577, 577; 2 ER 393, 394 (Irish appeal), narrative of the facts: 'they thought proper, in the mean time, for the improvement of the testator's assets, and for the benefit of all parties interested therein, to let her out to freight; and accordingly accepted of an offer made to them for that purpose by Mr. Lynch, a merchant'. References to 'offer' are fairly frequent in the reports, but mainly to offers in judicial proceedings; references to 'acceptance' are mainly to acceptances in satisfaction of debts, and similar matters.

[57] 'Agreement or assent' of promise: eg, *Parish of Wansworth v Parish of Putney* (1740) Sess Cas 219, 93 ER 221 (as to existence of a contract of service for Poor Law settlement purposes). 'Assent' in the reports is much more commonly concerned with assent in the making of bylaws, and executors' assents to legacies. 'Consent' is predominantly concerned with parental, guardian's or trustee consent to marriage.

formation of contracts made orally or even by correspondence.[58] I have written about the reception of the Statute of Frauds in equity before now, stopping in 1714.[59] Although there are some interesting details in the 1715–1737 cases, I don't think they are worth pursuing here.

The fourth general feature of all the authors' accounts is the role of consideration – which is, however, ambiguous. The *Treatise*, Bacon and Comyns all give the issue a prominent place; in the *Maxims* and Gilbert, the requirement is less prominent but still present.[60] However, they are by no means consistent. As I already indicated, the *Treatise* has the issue of consideration in two places and is less developed than one might expect in the first (Ch 5 §§ 1–3). Bacon, in a sense, inverts the point: in *Equity Cases Abridged*, his subtitle is 'Voluntary Agreements, in what cases to be performed', and in the *New Abridgment* 'Voluntary Agreements', and both titles, though asserting the requirement of consideration, are mainly concerned (as the name suggests) with cases where dispositions not for value *are* effective. Comyns also has a sub-subtitle, denying that the agreement should be decreed 'if made without a Consideration' – but only two cases in it, *Parry v Hughes* (1732) and *Vernon v Vernon* (1731), the second of which decides that specific performance *is* available for the volunteer remainderman where the overall covenant to settle was originally for consideration. And the immediately prior subtitle, 'tho' the Consideration was remote', includes the statement that 'so, if an agreement for a Jointure, Provision for Children, &c., is voluntary, it shall be decreed'.[61]

There is startlingly little of this material in these books relative to the quantity of discussion of the issue in the caselaw. Just minimally for numbers, 'voluntary' produces 116 hits in Chancery reports 1660–1688, 25 in HL and 71 in Chancery 1689–1708, 32 in HL and 74 in Chancery 1709–1728, and 11 in HL and 59 in Chancery in 1729–1737.

There is some sense in the *Treatise* that 'consideration' and 'voluntary' are employed in more than one context: thus references in connection with frauds on marriage or on creditors (Ch 3 §§ 11–14) and in connection with construction and relief against 'inartificial words' (Ch 6 §§ 6–8). But this is still incomplete, and for the other authors, there is a fairly radical flattening of the doctrine.

Thus, in the cases, a disposition may in some circumstances be characterised as for consideration if it is by way of a settlement for an equitable wrong previously committed by the promisor (in this context, notably the *pretium pudicitiae* or *pudoris* in relation to a man who seduces a previously virtuous young woman and then

[58] In *Backhouse v Mohun* 3 Swans 403n, 36 ER 938, the Lord Chancellor ruled that an exchange of letters could satisfy the Statute of Frauds, where 'the last letter from Mohun was in 1731, who said therein that the Plaintiff had offered a certain sum which Mohun accepted' and the defendants failed to produce their side of the correspondence. (There is a clear error in the printed report; either the date given, Easter Term 1736, is right and the Chancellor should be Lord Talbot (which seems more likely, given the note citation to the D&O book), or the attribution to Lord Hardwicke is right and the date is wrong.

[59] M Macnair, *Law of Proof in Early Modern Equity* (Berlin, Duncker & Humblot, 1999) 157–164.

[60] *Maxims* (n 17); Gilbert, *Lex Praetoria*, Dublin edn (n 29) 14 (probably *Fursaker v Robinson* (1717) 1 Eq Cas Ab 123, 21 ER 929; Pre Ch 475, 24 ER 213; Gilb Rep 139, 25 ER 97. The sidenote to *Seagood v Neale (Meale)* (1721) Pre Ch 560, 24 ER 251, refers to the requirement of certainty immediately following) and 38–9, citing *Fursaker* above and *Fairebeard v Bowers* (1690) 2 Vern 202, 23 ER 731; *(Fairbeard)* Prec Ch 17, 24 ER 9.

[61] At 96. *Parry v Hughes* (n 45); *Vernon v Vernon* (1731) W Kel 9, 25 ER 468; 2 P Wms 595, 24 ER 875 (King C); 1 Bro PC 267, 1 ER 559 (HL).

promises to make provision for her);[62] or, in pursuit of the father's duty to provide for and advance his children, or the husband's to make provision for his widow.[63] All these cases could be variously characterised either as voluntary, but nonetheless enforceable;[64] or, alternatively, as dispositions done for a 'natural', 'moral', 'meritorious' or 'good', though not valuable, consideration.[65] I have not explored how far this distinction between 'valuable' consideration and other forms of consideration may also be present at law in the period.

This brings us back to the beginning. 'Agreements' was clearly the fundamental category of analysis for equitable remedies in this field. But *how to analyse* the 'agreements' category was a problem which at this period very much remained unsolved.

[62] *King v Withers* (1690) Prec Ch 348, 24 ER 10 illustrates the general point (defendant argued agreement was voluntary, but it was enforced: it was by way of compensation for defendant's self-serving negligence as plaintiff's agent); *Randal v Randal* (1728) 2 P Wms 464, 24 ER 816 (to correct a mistake in a previous settlement.) *Pretium pudicitiae* etc: *Cary v Stafford* (1725) Ambler 520, 831; 27 ER 336, 522; (*Carey*) 3 Swans 427n, 36 ER 935, Ex(E); *Marchioness of Annandale v Harris* (1728) 2 P Wms 432, 24 ER 801; (1729) 1 Bro PC 250, 1 ER 547 (HL); *Lady Cox's Case* (1734) 3 P Wms 339, 24 ER 1091 (would have been 'meritorious consideration' if bigamous husband had paid second wife for separation; not where they continued to cohabit); *Cray v Rooke* (1735) Cas t Talbot 153, 25 ER 713, where Lord Talbot treats the bond as voluntary, and to be paid after creditors, but before legatees.

[63] The principle of equitable relief against defective provisions in such contexts appears to go back to *Wilmer v Kendrick and Vylett* (1670) 1 Ch Cas 159, 22 ER 741; (*Miller*) Nelson 113, 21 ER 803 (which relies on *Prince*, or *Price v Green* (1598)). Stated generally in the widely reported decision in *The Duke of Albemarle's Case* (1693): *Bath and Mountague's Case* (1693) 3 Ch Cas 55, 89; 22 ER 963, 984 (Treby CJ); *Montague v Bathoniensem* (1693) 3 Ch Cas 96, 106; 22 ER 988, 99 (Holt CJ); *Duchess of Albermarle v Earl of Bath* (1693) 2 Freem 193, 195; 22 ER 1155, 1156. Children: eg, *Watts v Bullas* (1702) 1 P Wms 60, 24 ER 293 (Wright LK and Trevor MR); *King v Cotton* (1730) Mosely 259, 261; 25 ER 383, 385 (King C); *Carter v Carter* (1730) Mosely 365, 25 ER 442 (Jekyll MR); *Cook v Arnham* (1734) 3 P Wms 283, 24 ER 1066; Cas t Talbot 35, 25 ER 646 (Lord Talbot C). Widow: eg, *Fothergill v Fothergill* (1702) 2 Freem 256, 22 ER 1194; *Lord Dudley v Lady Dudley* Prec Ch 241, 244; 24 ER 118, 119 (Trevor MR) (reasoning later rejected); *Tollet v Tollet* (1728) 2 P Wms 489, 24 ER 828; (*Tollet's Case*) Mosely 46, 25 ER 262; *Sutton v Sutton* (1732) 2 P Wms 700, 705; 24 ER 922, 924 (Jekyll MR) (reasoning later rejected); *Smith v Baker* (1737) 1 Atkyns 385, 26 ER 246.

[64] Already present in before 1688; see, eg, *Thompson v Attfield* (1682) 1 Vern 40, 23 ER 294. In our period see, eg, *Barlow v Heneage* (1702) Prec Ch 210, 24 ER 103; *Kirk v Clark* (1706) Prec Ch 275, 24 ER 133 (voluntary but made good by subsequent detrimental reliance); *Harvey v Harvey* (1710) 1 P Wms 125, 24 ER 322 (voluntary but 'founded on natural Justice, though not on contract'); *King v Cotton* (1732) 2 P Wms 674, 24 ER 912 (mother's provision for children of first marriage); *Newstead v Searle* (1737) West t Hardw 287, 25 ER 942; (*Searles*) 1 Atk 265, 26 ER 169.

[65] Citations for these tags follow. 'Natural' consideration: BL Lansdowne MS 1125 (to force heir to sell); *Lord Grey v Lady Grey* (1677) Rep t Finch 338, 340; 23 ER 185, 187; 2 Swans 594, 597; 36 ER 742, 743 (to rebut presumption of resulting trust). 'Moral' consideration, BL Lansdowne MS 1125; Freeman's report of *The Duke of Albemarle's Case, Duchess of Albermarle v Earl of Bath* (1693) 2 Freem 193, 195–96; 22 ER 1155, 1156; Treby CJ in the elaborate report of SC in 3 Cases in Chancery is reported as referring to a 'foreign' consideration, which looks like the reporter's mishearing for 'moral': 3 Ch Cas 55, 89; 22 ER 963, 984. 'Meritorious' consideration: this goes back to Dyer's definition of consideration, in his notes on *Calthorpe's Case* (1574) 3 Dy 334 b, 336 b; 73 ER 756, 759, as 'a cause or meritorious occasion, requiring a mutual recompense, in fact or in law', thence being used for a variety of purposes; 'meritorious consideration' appears as a requirement of a prescriptive claim to toll in *Prideaux v Warne* (1673) T Raym 232, 83 ER 121; (*Warn v Prideux*) (1674) 3 Keb 275, 84 ER 718; (*Warren v Prideaux*) (1674) 1 Mod 104, 86 ER 766. In *The Duke of Albemarle's Case* (1693) 2 Ch Rep 417, 426; 21 ER 704, 706 counsel for the defendants argue that there should be no relief against the failed execution of the power because the original settlement was made 'upon such meritorious Consideration of Blood, Merit, &c'. In *Martin v Nutkin* (1725) 2 P Wms 266, 24 ER 724 the existence of 'meritorious consideration executed' was given as a reason for churchwardens to be bound by their predecessors' agreement. 'Good' consideration: *Fothergill v Fothergill* (n 63); *Stephenson v Hayward* (1710) Prec Ch 310, 24 ER 147 (trust for payment of existing debts); *Osgood v Strode* (1724) 2 P Wms 245, 253–54; 24 ER 716, 719 (counsel for plaintiff) *Thomas v Williams* (1729) Mosely 177, 179; 25 ER 335, 336 (Talbot S-G arg): 'good cause'.

14

Women, Infants and 'Lunatics' before the Court of Chancery in the Wake of the South Sea Bubble

EMILY IRELAND

I. Introduction

Equity originally emerged to mitigate the harshness of the common law. Such mitigation is often discussed in the context of the development of a more free-form style of pleading in Chancery than the common law writ system, and an inquisitorial method of adducing evidence. It also involved giving certain rights, benefits, or an alternative forum to people whose access to the common law courts was, for whatever reason, limited or entirely restricted.[1] In the eighteenth century (as in other periods), legal status, and consequently the ease with which an individual could access the common law courts, was defined by age, gender, marital status, and mental capacity. It was also affected by the question of whether a person was the outright owner of property or the beneficiary of a trust. Thus, married women, infants, and 'lunatics' were prohibited from suing independently at common law, as were trust beneficiaries.[2] Furthermore, because married women, infants, and the mentally incapable possessed limited property rights, it often happened that individuals who could not bring common law proceedings concerning property due to their diminished legal status also faced restrictions because they were trust beneficiaries.[3] Chancery had an 'intrinsic jurisdiction to protect the

[1] This was delegation of the monarch's obligation to protect the 'poor and weak': J Seymour, '*Parens Patriae* and Wardship Powers: Their Nature and Origins' (1994) 14 *Oxford Journal of Legal Studies* 159. See too *Falkland v Bertie* (1696) 2 Vern 333, 23 ER 814.

[2] Women, children and lunatics were distinct subclasses of legal persons, but they all lacked the legal status afforded to an adult male. The jurisdictions exercised by Chancery over infants and lunatics have been described as 'intimately connected': G Spence, *The Equitable Jurisdiction of the Court of Chancery* (London, V and R Steven and GS Norton, 1846) vol 1, 618. 'Lunatics' is a contemporary description for individuals who lacked the mental capacity to manage themselves and/or their property and so the term will, with some discomfort, be used throughout this chapter.

[3] Spence (n 2) 605 described Chancery's jurisdiction over infants' property as 'intimately connected with its jurisdiction for enforcing the performance of trusts'.

vulnerable'.[4] 'Vulnerable', in practice, meant either one or both of a marginalised status in society (for example, widows, who held the same legal rights as men but perhaps turned to Chancery due to the subordination they faced under patriarchy) or marginalised legal status (such as children, who had no legal rights to own property or bring legal proceedings until they attained the age of maturity).[5] The Court mitigated constraints on access to justice and property-holding for subordinate members of society through the development of trusts law, for example, by the creation of married women's separate estate, and procedural systems that gave married women, lunatics and infants under the age of twenty-one access to justice, for instance, through litigation by a next friend.[6]

This chapter examines how litigants and lawyers utilised Chancery's dedication to protecting the vulnerable in different contexts in the period 1720–1730, the decade that encompassed the South Sea Bubble and collapse. While historians have written thorough economic studies of this episode, there 'has been no extensive description of the legal environment or aftermath of the South Sea Bubble'.[7] The economic crash of late 1720 negatively, and in many cases catastrophically, affected the finances of countless people from various parts of society. Equity, and the court of Chancery, were both the conduit for litigation by vulnerable people during and following the South Sea Bubble and, in some cases, the cause of their distress.

South Sea stocks were commonly held as trust property. The South Sea scheme was considered low risk because the shares were backed by the national debt and thus easy to trade.[8] Investing in stocks and shares, therefore, became a common means of generating income within family settlements, for which Chancery was 'a key arbiter'.[9] In addition, the National Debt Act 1719, which authorised the swap of public debt for South Sea stock, empowered 'executors, administrators, guardians and trustees' to subscribe 'for and on behalf of their respective testators, intestates, infants, femes covert, cestui que trusts or others' with whose property they were entrusted. And by the same section the legislation also provided that such people 'are or shall be, by virtue of

[4] J Getzler, 'Chancery Reform and Law Reform' (2004) 22 *Law and History Review* 601, 607. See also in relation to married women: ML Cioni, *Women and Law in Elizabethan England With Particular Reference to the Court of Chancery* (New York, NY, Garland, 1985); in relation to infants: Seymour (n 1); H Ballow, *A Treatise of Equity, With the Addition of Marginal References and Notes by John Fonblanque*, 5th edn (London, J & WT Clarke, 1820) vol 2; and in relation to lunatics: *Ex parte Whitfield* (1742) 2 Atk 315, 26 ER 592.

[5] *The Infants Lawyer: Or, The Law (Ancient And Modern) Relating To Infants*, 3rd edn (London, J Crocket, 1726).

[6] S Staves, *Married Women's Separate Property In England, 1660-1833* (Cambridge, MA, Harvard University Press, 1990); Cioni (n 4).

[7] GS Shea, 'Sir George Caswall v the Duke of Portland: Financial Contracts and Litigation in the Wake of the South Sea Bubble' in J Atack and L Neal (eds), *The Origin and Development of Financial Markets and Institutions: From the Seventeenth Century to Present* (Cambridge, Cambridge University Press, 2009) 121, 123; S Bogle, 'Inequality, Just Price and Bad Bargains: Contracting Attitudes after the South Sea Crash, 1720' (2019) 40 *Journal of Legal History* 298; PGM Dickson, *The Financial Revolution in England* (London, Routledge, 1993); HJ Paul, *The South Sea Bubble: An Economic History of its Origins and Consequences* (London, Routledge, 2010); J Carswell, *The South Sea Bubble* (London, Cresset Press, 1960). Uncovering information about any investment in the South Sea Company is difficult because important documentation has not survived, including most notably all of the Company share registers and some of the subscription books.

[8] BP Levack, *Distrust of Institutions in Early Modern Britain and America* (Oxford, Oxford University Press, 2022).

[9] A Hofri-Winogradow, 'Children and Property in Late 18th-Century Chancery' (2012) 32 *Oxford Journal of Legal Studies* 741.

this Act, indemnified in and for doing the same', here using the word 'indemnified' to mean 'exonerated' from any possible legal liability for their actions.[10] Furthermore, Lord Macclesfield's ruling in *Bromfield v Wytherley* (1718), that solvent trustees who invested trust money and gained 'considerably' could keep the 'whole benefit' for themselves, surely attracted trustees to invest money they held on trust.[11] Indeed, Strange, in argument for the plaintiff in *Wilkinson v Meyer* (1724), noted that a clause in the National Debt Act 1721 was made 'on account of so many persons being made trustees' of South Sea stock.[12]

More nefariously, Lord Chancellor Macclesfield and the Chancery masters were personally involved in a scandal that broke in the wake of the crash. The masters had played the stock market with money paid into the Court by litigants. Great financial losses resulted for suitors, many of whom were women and children, denting the reputation of the Court. Lord Chancellor Macclesfield left office in disgrace and was replaced by Lord Chancellor King in 1725. King is not a renowned equity judge, but a series of decisions that supported 'fiduciary honesty', culminating in *Keech v Sandford* (1726),[13] secured him a place in legal history. It is generally agreed that the conduct of the Chancery masters under Lord Macclesfield played a role in inducing this judgment and that the South Sea catastrophe prompted a further tightening up of trustee duties during the rest of the eighteenth century.[14]

This chapter discusses forty-three items in Chancery's C11 series held at the National Archives.[15] The selected items contain pleadings brought between 1720 and 1730 in which the complainants included at least one woman, and the defendants included the South Sea Company.[16] These have been matched with relevant entries in the order and decree books.[17] The sample includes a number of suits concerning South Sea stock held on trust by or for widows, husbands and wives, children, and one lunatic. Pleadings may not represent the 'truth' or the 'voice' of the litigant, but they do show us the approaches and narratives lawyers and litigants favoured

[10] 6 Geo I, c 4, s 23. *The Oxford English Dictionary*, sv 'indemnify', gives several meanings, including '1. To preserve, protect, or keep free from, secure against (any hurt, harm, or loss); to secure against legal responsibility for past or future actions or events …' and '2.a. To compensate (a person, etc) for loss suffered, expenses incurred, etc.' In the eighteenth century, as now, the word was often used in its second sense to denote the provision of compensation for a trustee who sustained personal loss while managing the trust affairs; but the word was used in the first sense in the 1719 Act: see, eg, *Newland v Sheppard* (1723) 9 Mod 57, 88 ER 313; *Trenchard and Ippsley v Wanley* (1723) 2 P Wms 166, 24 ER 685; *Chambers v Chambers* (1730) 2 Eq Cas Abr 224; *Borrett v Goodere* (1769) 4 Brown 679, 691; 2 ER 462, 469–470; *A General Abridgment of Cases in Equity Argued and Adjudged in the High Court of Chancery, &c.* (Dublin, J Rice, 1793) vol 2, 601; and the MS sources discussed below.

[11] *Bromfield v Wytherley* (1718) Prec Ch 506, 24 ER 227; 1 Eq Ca Abr 239, 21 ER 1017.

[12] 7 Geo 1, st 2, c 1, s 8; *Wilkinson v Meyer* (1724) 8 Mod 232, 88 ER 166.

[13] *Keech v Sandford* (1726) 2 Eq Cas Ab 741, 25 ER 223; Sel Cas T King 61, 25 ER 223.

[14] J Campbell (Lord Campbell), *Lives of the Lord Chancellors and Keepers of the Great Seal of England, from the Earliest Times till the Reign of Queen Victoria* (London, J Murray, 1845); AD Hicks, 'The Remedial Principle of *Keech v Sandford* Reconsidered' [2002] *Cambridge Law Journal* 287; J Getzler, 'Rumford Market and the Genesis of Fiduciary Obligations' in A Burrows and Lord Rodger of Earlsferry (eds), *Mapping the Law: Essays in Memory of Peter* Birks (Oxford, Oxford University Press, 2006) 577, 585; J Getzler, 'Fiduciary Investment in the Shadow of Financial Crisis: Was Lord Eldon Right?' (2009) 3 *Journal of Equity* 219.

[15] The C11 series contains pleadings for the period 1711–1758.

[16] There are 532 items in the C11 index dated between 1720 and 1730 that list the South Sea Company as a defendant.

[17] *The National Archives* (TNA) C33.

as tactics that would bring redress at any point in time.[18] The submission of non-combative pleadings concerning the administration of South Sea stocks and shares demonstrates routine utilisation of Chancery's jurisdiction to aid the vulnerable and the power the court wielded when authorising transactions involving trustees, beneficiaries and the South Sea Company. Suits that take an accusatory tone and report losses after the crash directly appealed to Chancery to assist vulnerable litigants by recovering stocks or the value of stocks that had been lost due to reported unconscionable behaviour by trustees or the South Sea Company.

Similarly, documents pertaining to Lord Macclesfield's trial and impeachment show contemporary criticism of Chancery for failing to protect the property of vulnerable litigants. Chancery litigants and the prosecutors of Lord Macclesfield harnessed the same narrative of the misuse of arbitrary power, wielded at the expense of weak, marginalised subjects who sought protection. The paternalistic duty to protect the vulnerable (which influenced a variety of decisions in Chancery) implicitly or explicitly influenced the development of Chancery and Chancery procedure following the South Sea Bubble in relation to Macclesfield's impeachment, King's tightening up of Chancery rules, and the development of fiduciary duties.

II. Administrative Suits

Throughout the 1720s Chancery acted as a forum to legitimate and administer transfers of South Sea stocks held as trust property. The Court's administrative arm allowed individuals whose legal status was encumbered by common law, or the representatives of such individuals, access to asset management. Chancery's willingness to undertake administrative suits for the property of married women, children and lunatics, is a routine example of the court's aim of aiding the vulnerable. Litigants who were beneficiaries, or who represented beneficiaries (such as guardians of infants), sought orders from Chancery which authorised sales and exonerated trustees and the South Sea Company from any legal liability when undertaking transactions involving stocks and shares held as trust property. Chancery's paternalist approach to these suits is evident in the powers the masters were given in managing these transfers, such as the power to assess whether sales would be for the benefit of beneficiaries and to manage money paid into the court by suitors.

Before the South Sea Bubble burst, Chancery bills that concerned the property of women, infants and lunatics and named the South Sea Company as a defendant were largely administrative and described South Sea stocks as lucrative.[19] For example, in a bill dated 24 May 1720, Mary Ellord, a widow, and four of her infant nieces and nephews, by their next friend, stated that they 'were willing & desirous' that stock held by

[18] J Bailey, 'Voices in Court: Lawyers' or Litigants'?' (2001) 74 *Historical Research* 392; FE Dolan, *True Relations: Reading, Literature And Evidence In Seventeenth-Century England* (Philadelphia, PA, University of Pennsylvania Press, 2013); N Zemon Davis, *Fiction In The Archives: Pardon Tales and Their Tellers in Sixteenth Century France* (Stanford, CA, Stanford University Press, 1987).

[19] *Walton v Clarke* (1720) TNA, C11/1236/44; *Ellord v Hamilton* (1720) TNA, C11/2369/74; *Young v Carter* (1720) TNA, C11/2723/72; *Barlow v South Sea Company* (1720) TNA, C11/363/62.

trustees for their benefit be sold 'to the best advantage' and 'for the most that can be gott for' it because South Sea stock had 'considerably risen & advanced in … price & value'.[20] The 1720 bill of three infant complainants, brought by a next friend, in *Walton v Clarke* stated that as South Sea Stock had 'lately risen in value very considerably', it was 'most manifest that the selling' of stock held in trust for the infant beneficiaries would 'be very much for' their 'benefit'.[21] The trustees' Answer, submitted in April 1720, concurred. The Court ordered that a Chancery Master 'examine whether' selling the stocks would 'be for the benefit of the partyes concerned' or whether lottery orders and annuities, also held in trust for the infant beneficiaries, should be 'subscribed into the South Sea Company' instead.[22] The defendant trustees were then to act according to what was decided with the Masters 'approbation', and to 'bring the moneys ariseing thereby … before the … master and the … subscription is to be subject to the further order of this Court'.

Both trustees and the South Sea Company sought indemnification from Chancery when selling shares held on trust. Pleadings reported particular difficulties when the beneficiaries of South Sea stock were infants. Mary Ellord and her nieces and nephews reported that 'by reason of some of' the plaintiffs' 'Infancy', the executors and the South Sea Governor and Company refused a sale of stock held in trust for their benefit, fearing they could not 'safetly' sell or transfer it without a Chancery decree confirming that they would incur no legal liability.[23] Four days later, an answer was submitted to the court in which the defendants expressed their willingness to sell the stock and requested authorisation and indemnification.[24] Chancery, again, ordered that a master assess whether it would 'be for the benefit of the' plaintiffs 'to have the … South Sea Stock sold' and if the master thought it would be beneficial, the defendants were ordered to sell the stock.[25] They were then to 'bring the money arising by such sale before the … master to be put out at Interest on Government or other security to be allowed of by the … Master' for the plaintiffs' benefit. The defendants were to be excused from any legal liability that they might otherwise have incurred for their actions performed in pursuance of the decree.

William and Emblyn Young's bill dated 30 May 1720 similarly stated that the defendants, the trustees of their marriage settlement and the South Sea Company, sought an indemnity from Chancery so that they could safely sell South Sea stock which was 'in Trust for Infants'.[26] Some fear and uncertainty regarding the price of South Sea stocks, demonstrating awareness of the precarity of the market in 1720, is evident. William and Emblyn noted that two annuities held in trust for their benefit, having been 'subscribed into the South Sea Company' had 'become double the value that they were at the time they were purchased' but that there 'may be some Danger of their sinking againe'.

A July 1720 bill submitted by Mary Barlow, her husband Thomas, and Samuel Dubois, a trustee, similarly noted how South Sea stock had 'risen considerably in Value

[20] *Ellord v Hamilton* (1720) TNA, C11/2369/74.
[21] *Walton v Clarke* (1720) TNA, C11/1236/44.
[22] *Walton v Barry* (1719) TNA, C33/334/464-5.
[23] *Ellord v Hamilton* (1720) TNA, C11/2369/74.
[24] This short space of time suggests an administrative suit.
[25] *Ellord v Hamilton* (1719) TNA, C33/333/284.
[26] *Young v Carter* (1720) TNA, C11 2723 72.

but … the Continuance thereof at such value' was 'uncertain'.[27] The bill requested that Thomas, as the Committee of Sarah Belbin's estate, be authorised to sell stock Sarah had bought with her deceased husband's estate, which she had inherited a life interest in. The bill argued this would be for both Sarah's 'interest' and the benefit of Mary Barlow, who was to receive the remainder of the estate on Sarah's death as a separate estate. However, a 'Comition of Lunacy' had been issued against Sarah; thus the Lord Chancellor had granted 'the Custody of her person' to Edward Jasper, and 'the Custody of her Estate' to Thomas Barlow. On 21 May 1720 the Lord Chancellor 'was pleased to order' that Thomas Barlow, as Sarah Belbin's Committee, 'should be at Liberty to sell the … Stock as the … Master should Direct'.[28] The money raised was 'to be brought before' a 'Master to be by him placed out at Interest on good Government or other … Security subject to the terms' of the will. However, in a similar narrative to cases concerning stock held in trust for infant beneficiaries, demonstrating Chancery's 'intimately connected' jurisdiction over infants and lunatics,[29] it was reported that the 'Governor and Company or their agents', despite Chancery's order, 'struggle[ed] To permit' Thomas to make the transfer because, on the one hand, the stock was 'placed in their Bookes' in Sarah's name, so 'no person but her selfe ought to Transferr' them, but on the other, Sarah could not transfer the stock 'by reason of … her Lunacy & Incapacity'.[30] '[B]y such objections', the bill continued, 'Thomas Barlow and mary his wife as well as … Sarah Belbin are in Danger to loose the benefit and advantage of the present great Rise and Value of such Capitall stock'.

Mary and Thomas Barlow's bill requesting the sale of South Sea stock was submitted on the 26 July 1720. From September the price would plummet. It is impossible to know if Thomas did sell the stock, and if he did, when he did so. Chancery's administrative function provided a protective measure for transactions involving trust property, and aided the vulnerable by providing married women, children and lunatics, or their agents, the power to manage their trustees and the trust property they benefitted from. Such decision-making and administration was perhaps prudent to protect trust assets, but it also elongated the time it took to complete transactions, putting trust beneficiaries and their trustees at a potential disadvantage when it came to selling stocks at the right time. Because of the fluctuating price of South Sea stock in 1720, this could be fatal to the beneficiary's estate. The plaintiffs in *Young v Carter* (1720), for example, believed the 'delaye' caused by the trustees and South Sea Company refusing to transfer stocks without first obtaining an indemnity from Chancery meant they were 'in danger of being Deprived of the benefit of the said present Rise of the said securities'.[31]

Chancery fostered a form of paternalist protection that bestowed limited power upon beneficiaries and their representatives to manage the trust estate. However, as the suits above demonstrate, due to the impediments placed upon the legal personhood of married women, infants, and lunatics, seemingly simple transactions became convoluted, perhaps involving repeated petitions to Chancery to safely administer trust

[27] *Barlow v South Sea Company* (1720) TNA, C11/363/62.
[28] *Belbin v Belbin* (1719) TNA, C33/333/288.
[29] Spence (n 2) 618.
[30] *Barlow v South Sea Company* (1720) TNA, C11/363/62.
[31] *Young v Carter* (1720) TNA, C11/2723/72.

property and indemnify all relevant parties. Chancery wielded the power to authorise such transactions, to indemnify the parties involved and, as is shown in Mary Ellord's case, to manage the money raised. Masters were given the authority to decide whether selling stock would be for the benefit of *feme covert*, infant, and lunatic beneficiaries, and even to decide if other forms of investments should be converted into South Sea Company stock.[32] Once stock was sold, it was sometimes ordered that the funds raised be paid into the court. This directly brought the business of South Sea investments into the Court of Chancery, establishing it as a key institution involved in the scheme in relation to trusts.

III. The Crash

By December 1720, South Sea stocks were worth 80 per cent less than they had been at the height of the Bubble. After the crash, litigants appealed to Chancery's paternalistic aim through the use of heightened emotive language and accusations of wrongdoing and corruption against trustees and the South Sea Company itself. This reflected wider public discontent aimed at the South Sea Company and its directors. Increasingly, bills contained descriptions of litigants' losses with heightened emotive language. Anne Colemore, a married woman, in a 1722 bill reported that due to the 'unhappy tyme' of the South Sea crash, she had 'sustained a very great loss' on South Sea Stocks she had 'negotiated' using her separate estate.[33] The trustee defendant in *Edwards v South Sea Company* (1730) reported how part of the £3,000 trust money he subscribed into the South Sea Company had, following the crash, 'been there by greatly Diminished'.[34]

The directors of the South Sea Company were widely condemned and held directly responsible for the crash. This narrative appeared in the courtroom. For example, Fazakerley, for the defendant in *Wilkinson v Meyer* (1724), noted that the directors had 'cheated the people' and 'by fraud … raised the value of the South-Sea stock'.[35] Complaints in Chancery continued to be made against trustees and the South Sea Company, but narratives in pleadings were more likely to involve accusations of corruption that stretched back to before the Bubble burst, reflecting wider public outrage with the disgraced directors of the South Sea Company, who were sometimes listed as defendants, or South Sea Company employees, who were accused of mishandling trust property.[36] Some accused the South Sea Company of deliberately impeding transfers of shares in 1720.[37] For example, on 18 May 1724, Lucy Thomson, her husband Henry, their infant son George, via a next friend, and George Moult, Lucy's father, petitioned Chancery over property included in Henry and Lucy's marriage settlement that had

[32] *Walton v Barry* (1719) TNA, C33/334/464-5; *Webster v Guy* (1730) TNA, C33/356/55-56.

[33] *Colemore v Colemore* (1728) TNA, C78/1689, no 1.

[34] *Edwards v South Sea Company* (1730) TNA, C11/82/10.

[35] *Wilkinson* (n 12).

[36] This was often in relation to the South Sea Sufferers Act 1721 (7 Geo I, st 2 c 1). See, eg, *Richardson v Benson* (1727) TNA, C11/70/29; *Webster v Guy* (1728) TNA, C 11/2420/59.

[37] *Hildegard v South Sea Company* (1721) TNA, C11/1424/17; *Thomson v South Sea Company* (1724) TNA, C11/2007/50; *Short v South Sea Company* (1721) TNA, C11/749/5.

been subscribed, in George's name, as trustee, into the 'Capitall stock' and annuities of the South Sea Company.[38] Henry had been 'desirous to have the said stock sold' in 1720 'to lay hold of that Opportunity when the price of such stock was high'. George had consented to the sale, and the pair 'well hoped such sale might have been minded when the price of ... stock was at nine hundred pounds per Cent or upwards'. If this had happened, the bill continued, Henry and Lucy might 'have stood the hazard of the sinking of the price of the stock allowed for the said subscribed annuitys'.

However, the bill claimed that despite the plaintiffs' attempts to obtain permission to transfer the stock through 'all the very frequent tedious and chargeable applications' available, the South Sea Company refused to permit George to sell the stock in 1720, and had ordered an injunction to stop any transfer being made because the stock in George's name was held on trust. This was to the 'very great Loss and prejudice' of Henry and Lucy who were 'thereby deprived of the benefitt of a Sale of the ... stock when the price ... was high', and were 'still forced to continue the risk of the' price of South Sea stock 'falling ... lower'.

The narrative reflects the surrounding political and economic climate and loss of favour of the South Sea Company and its directors. According to the bill, the South Sea Company had claimed an 'Illegal and arbitrary' power to refuse transfers if they found proprietors had no right to sell it. The accusation that the South Sea Company used 'many indirect and unlawfull practices to Obstruct ... all sales of South Sea stock by other persons besides themselves and their accomplices ... so they ... might have the better opportunity of selling their own stock at the Extravagant Prices which it was then risen up to' reflects contemporary public resentment for the disgraced directors, who were widely thought to have caused the crash through corruption and greed-driven financial mismanagement.[39]

According to an order dated 9 July 1723, the South Sea Company failed to answer. It was decreed that 'all further process of contempt' be awarded against the defendants.[40] When the South Sea Company did answer, they denied their refusal to permit the sale or procurement of an injunction on the sale of the stock in 1720. The 1719 National Debt Act, which regulated the public debt swap for stock, provided that 'the stock ... given for' such debts 'subscribed for or on the behalf of Infant[s] feme Coverts or others by their Guardians or Trustees', 'should be lyable to the same uses ... as such Debts ... would have been had not the same been subscribed'.[41] Therefore, the South Sea Company, 'not knowing how farr they might be answerable in Case any stock should be transferred ... by any Guardian or Trustee ... to the Damage and Loss of ... Infants ... or Feme Coverts', on 29th of March 1721, 'tend[ed] to the ... resolution ... that no Transferr be made of any stock which stands in the Books of this Companey in Trust till the opinion of the Company Councill be first had ... that such Transferr can be safely permitted'.[42] The resolution was put in place

[38] *Thomson v South Sea Company* (1724) TNA, C11/2007/50.

[39] Dickson (n 7); RA Kleer 'Riding a Wave: The Company's Role in the South Sea Bubble' (2015) 68 *Economic History Review* 264.

[40] *Thompson v South Sea Company* (1723) TNA, C33/342/469.

[41] 6 Geo 1, c 4, s 23.

[42] *Thomson v South Sea Company* (1724) TNA, C11/2007/50.

'with safety' in mind, 'in Cases … where Infants and persons unable to act for themselves were concerned'. It was not made 'with any view to obstruct' legitimate sales of stock 'or for their own advantage'. It was stated that any refusal to sell the complainants' stock must have been after the resolution of 29 March 1721 'when stock did not bear so great a price as nine hundred pounds per Cent or any thing near that'. The resolution specifically applied to the property held on trust for *feme coverts* and infants, and restricted their ability, alongside their trustees and representatives, to manage stocks and shares.

In contrast, it appears to have been very difficult to claim the benefit of stock that was not recorded as trust property unless some form of 'title' or 'authority' could be shown by the beneficiaries.[43] In 1722 the bill of Mary and Sarah Welch, two infant beneficiaries, brought by their mother and guardian Hannah Welch, accused John and Mary Webb, executors of Richard Welch, the executor of Mary and Sarah's father's will, of 'confederating and combining' with the South Sea Company in pretending stock the plaintiffs claimed was held in trust by Richard Welch for their benefit was not listed as such in the company's books.[44] The South Sea Company, in their answer, reported that the stock remained in Richard's name 'without any Trust or condition whatsoever Declared' in their books and denied any knowledge of 'whether the … stock … was purchased with the mony ariseing from the Estate of Henry Wlsh … or what Right the complt[s] … have thereto.'

Chancery litigants thus adopted the narrative of corruption that ran through the story of the South Sea Company and the economic crash, contrasting this with trust beneficiaries' vulnerability. Self-portrayal as vulnerable or distressed was a common trope of women's Chancery pleadings. Lawyers and litigants harnessed vulnerability in order to appeal to the Lord Chancellor and the Court's stated aim of protecting the weak.[45] Yet, the South Sea Company itself was also able to utilise the narrative of corruption. Elizabeth Webster asserted several claims upon her deceased husband's estate in a bill submitted to the Court. The South Sea Company answered in 1728 that Elizabeth's husband, John, had, during his service as a South Sea Company clerk under Robert Knight, grown 'very rich', keeping 'a House in Town and sevrall Lodgings well furnished and also a country House furnished wth a variety of Household Goods plate and Linnen'.[46] The defendants apprehended this 'could not be done from his bare salary'. Thus, they had 'great Reason to believe … John webster did not behave himself so fairly … As the Duty of his office require'. They argued that John 'never brought to' their 'account Severall large sumes of money' he received, which, because of 'the Great Confusion' the company was 'thrown into' in 1721, 'he had the greater Opportunity to Effect'. The South Sea Company stated they hoped they would 'not be compelled to deliver up the said Bond but be at Liberty to take such proper method for obtaining a satisfaction … as they shall be advised'. This was one of a number of

[43] *Clergyman's Widows v South Sea Company* (1729) TNA, C11/1477/16; *Welch v East India Company* (1722) TNA, C11/1999/43.

[44] *Welch v East India Company* (1722) TNA, C11/1999/43.

[45] A Capern, 'Maternity and Justice in the Early Modern English Court of Chancery' (2019) 58 *Journal of British Studies* 701.

[46] *Webster v Guy* (1728) TNA, C11/2420/59.

answers 'By order of the Court of Directors', who were the new directors of the South Sea Company put in place to replace the corrupt directors and handle the claims of debtors under the South Sea Company Act 1720. This group were not directly connected to the events of 1720, but were responsible for raising money to pay off the South Sea Company's debts, which perhaps explains their willingness to condemn a former employee in an attempt to avoid paying a claimant.

On 22 December 1730 an order reported that the parties had reached an agreement in regard to John Webster's estate. The case was referred to a master to discover and state to the Court 'whether the … agreemt is … advantageous … for the Infants or not … whereupon such further Directions shall be given as shall be just'.[47] Two days later the master reported that the agreement would be for the infants' benefit, and the Lord Chancellor ordered 'that the sd agreemt be made an order of this Court'. Thus, Chancery continued to facilitate litigants' demands through the paternalist practice of assessing the benefit to the vulnerable parties beyond the Bubble. The circumstances reported, however, were often quite different, reflecting wider political developments and public discourse regarding the corruption of the directors of the South Sea Company and their misuse of arbitrary power at the expense of the general public.

IV. Trustee Duties

While some pleadings targeted the South Sea Company, others accused trustees holding South Sea stock of committing breaches of duty.[48] Most of these cases ended in failure because trustees were not judged to a particularly stringent duty standard in the later seventeenth and early eighteenth centuries.[49] While a trustee was held liable for failing to make a profit on a trust in *Palmer v Jones* (1678), this decision was reversed when the case was reheard five years later. Lord Keeper North declared that 'he would never charge a trustee with imaginary values … He thought it was a great hardship, that a trustee was allowed nothing for his own labour and pains'.[50] Only very strong proof of 'very supine negligence might … in some cases charge a trustee with more than he had received'.

A year later, in *Grosvenor v Cartwright* (1679), it was held that an executrix was not liable to account for profits made by lending out the principal money of the testator's estate.[51] The plaintiffs attempted to argue that the executrix should answer for profits made by calling in and lending out money unnecessarily, as the money had been 'lent by the Testator on good Security, and such Security continued good'. It was argued this was 'her voluntary Act', intended 'to deprive the Children', who were beneficiaries of the testator's estate, 'of the Benefit of the Money, till the Infants come of Age', and instead 'turn it to her self'. Forwarding a narrative of trustee power used at the expense of

[47] *Webster v Guy* (1730) TNA, C33/356/55-56.

[48] *White v Seamer* (1721) TNA, C11/378/31; *Soley v Taylor* (1721) TNA, C11/376/74; *Webster v Guy* (1728) TNA, C11/2420/59; *Edwards v South Sea Company* (1730) TNA, C11/82/10.

[49] DEC Yale (ed), *Lord Nottingham's Chancery Cases, vol II* (1961) 79 *Selden Society* 140–144; Getzler 'Fiduciary Investment' (n 14).

[50] *Palmer v Jones* (1678) 1 Vern 144, 23 ER 376.

[51] *Grosvenor v Cartwright* (1679) 2 Chan Cas 21, 22 ER 827.

vulnerable beneficiaries, it was argued that it would 'be great Gain to the Executrix, and Loss to the Children, for whom in Effect she is trusted'. The Lord Chancellor, however, stated that he would not change a 'fixed Rule of the Court'. It was reasoned that the executrix lent the money 'at her hazard, so that if it miscarry she shall make it good to the Estate'. This case thus cemented the rule that

> If an Executor or Administrator receives in Money which was secured to the Testator, and he lends it out again, and receives Interest for it, yet he shall not be accountable for the Interest; for he lends it out at his own Peril[52]

The concept of risk, 'hazard', or 'peril' repeatedly arose in justifications for a low standard of trustee duties.[53] *Linch v Cappy* (1680) confirmed that an executor who received 'great Sums of Money of the Testator's Estate, and put out the Money again at Interest, and received Interest for the same' should not 'answer the Interest so made and received by him'.[54] In *Haslewood v Baldwin* (1680), however, it was ruled that an executor should pay interest upon money placed out on good securities he had 'unnecessarily called in', but not interest upon 'the Rents and Profits of the real Estate'.[55] In *Ratcliffe v Graves* (1683), the Lord Keeper 'thought it reasonable' that an administratrix, having had the plaintiff's father's estate 'long in her hands, and employed the same in trade, and received interest for some part thereof' should 'answer' the 'interest … and not turn the same to' her 'own private advantage', although 'it was urged, that the constant practice of the court had been otherwise for twenty years past, … and that there were above forty precedents in the case'. Yet it was reasoned that

> the Objection of the Executors being answerable for the Money, if it should miscarry or be lost, was of little Force now, because a Man may insure his Money for one per Cent., and therefore decreed the Executor liable[56]

Yet, it seems there was some tightening of rules regarding trustees at the turn of the eighteenth century. In *Keylinge's Case* (1702) an executor, who had been directed, via the testator's will, 'to turn his Estate', which consisted in 'great Part' of East India Stock, into Money, as soon as conveniently might be', was provided with no relief against legatees he had given bonds to when East India Stock 'bore … a good Price'. The executor had 'kept the Stock so long' that 'it fell so low, that he had not Assets to pay the Legacies'. The Lord Keeper held 'he was to answer for the Stock at the Value it was … at the End of the Year, after the Testator's Death'.[57] In *Lee v Lee* (1706) it was held that even in cases where 'an Executor or Trustee is not impowered or directed to place out Money at Interest; yet if he makes Interest, he shall be accountable for it'.[58]

However, in *Bromfield v Wytherly* (1718), Lord Macclesfield ruled that an executor or trustee who, without authorisation, placed trust money 'in the Funds, or on

[52] *Grosvenor v Cartwright* (1679) 1 Eq Ca Abr 238, 21 ER 1017.

[53] *Soley v Taylor* (1721) TNA, C11/376/74; *Bromfield* (n 11); *Thomson v South Sea Company* (1724) TNA, C11/2007/50.

[54] *Linch v Cappy* (1680) 2 Chan Cas 35, 22 ER 834.

[55] *Haslewood v Baldwin* (1680) Rep Temp Finch 457, 23 ER 248.

[56] *Haslewood v Baldwin* (1680) 1 Eq Ca Abr 238, 21 ER 1017.

[57] *Keylinge's Case* (1702) 1 Eq Ca Abr 239, 21 ER 1017.

[58] *Lee v Lee* (1706) 1 Eq Ca Abr 398, 21 ER 1130.

other Security', and made considerable gains 'shall have the whole Benefit thereof to himself, in respect of the Hazard he run of being a considerable Loser thereby'.[59] The concept of running a 'hazard' was key to this ruling, as the rule was different if an executor or trustee was insolvent. Then, the beneficiary was to have the whole benefit, 'as he only would have borne the Loss thereof, if any had happened; the Trustee or Executor, by reason of his Insolvency, being incapable thereof, and consequently running no Hazard at all'.

Then came the South Sea Bubble and crash. The argument that trustees refused to sell South Sea stocks when the price was high appeared in *Crookshanks v Turner* (1723), where the appellant 'pretended (though untruly)' that the respondent trustees, who were money scriveners, had 'refused to sell' his stocks in August 1720, 'when such subscription receipts were at a much more advanced price'.[60] This case ruled that a trustee was not to be held liable for a mistake from which he derived no benefit.

Beneficiary consent was also a contested issue in Chancery pleadings. Despite the fact trustees were indemnified for investing in the debt for stock swap under the 1719 Act, the trustee defendant in *Edwards v South Sea Company* (1730) stated how he had subscribed part of £3,000 trust money 'into the South Sea Company' specifically 'with the privity and Consent both of the Complainant and her said late Husband'.[61] In contrast, the bill brought by two widowed daughters, Frances White and Beata Hall, dated 27 November 1721, claimed they did not know that the estate they inherited from their mother, Lady Wyndham, had been invested into the South Sea Company until after the latter part of 1720 when the 'subscription to the South Sea were fallen greatly in … value'.[62] The bill claimed that James Seamer, one of the defendants, had subscribed bank annuities he held on trust for Lady Wyndham, who had died in early 1720, into the South Sea Company on 14 July 1720, presumably as part of the second debt subscription. The bill stated that James Seamer possessed no 'power authority order or direction' to do this and that the complainants had never requested he do so.

Utilising the narrative of an arbitrary use of power to take advantage of a vulnerable beneficiary, it was argued that James Seamer and the South Sea Company 'act[ed] fully contrary' to their required management of the property in order 'To make use of the same' and, if 'Advantageous', to 'Claime the benefit for themselves'. The plaintiffs requested relief from Chancery, the court where 'matters of plain breachs of Trust' were resolved. Yet, it is questionable whether James Seamer's investments would have been considered a breach of trust, as *Bromfield v Wytherley* stated a trustee was not only allowed to invest trust funds, but keep the profit accrued.[63] There were no immediate legal barriers preventing trustees from using women's separate property as capital in pursuit of their own economic interests.[64] Perhaps because of this, after filing a replication on the 26 November 1721, the order and decree books reported that the plaintiffs

[59] *Bromfield* (n 11).
[60] *Crookshanks v Turner* (1723) 7 Bro PC 255, 3 ER 166.
[61] *Edwards v South Sea Company* (1730) TNA, C11/82/10.
[62] *White v Seamer* (1721) TNA, C11/378/31.
[63] *Bromfield* (n 11).
[64] M Berg, 'Women's Property and the Industrial Revolution' (1993) 24 *Journal of Interdisciplinary History* 233.

had 'not since proceeded any further in the cause' and 'It was therefore prayed that the … Bill may stand dismissed out of this Court' with costs to the defendant.[65]

According to *Bromfield v Wytherley*, a trustee was also accountable for any loss sustained through investment.[66] Yet the bill of legatees Anne Soley and her husband William, submitted on 20 November 1721, reported that the defendants, the executors and a trustee of the complainants' deceased mother, had subscribed a 'Great part of the … Testators Orders or annuityes in the Exchequer' into the South Sea Company, 'whereby the same are much lessened in value'.[67] The bill reported that when Anne and William married, William requested Robert Taylor transfer a £1,200 legacy left to Anne. Robert Taylor refused, reporting, amongst other things, that there were not enough assets left to fulfil the testator's legacies because 'there hath been since the … Testators Death a considerable Loss happened to the said Testators estate by the fall of the credit of the South Sea Company'. Robert threatened that if he did pay the couple, 'they shall bear what loss he has sustained by subscribing the said orders or annuities into the South sea company'.

William and Anne's bill argued that 'there was not at the Testators death any part of the Testators Estate subscribed into the … South Sea Company and … if any hath been since subscribed thereto the same hath been done by the said Robert Taylor (without either your orator or oratrixes privity or knowledge) at his own hazard'. Use of the word 'hazard' here, as was also used in the bill of *Thomson v South Sea Company*, discussed above, was perhaps a direct reference to the report of *Bromfield v Wytherley*, and that a trustee who invested trust property ran the 'hazard' of personally being a 'considerable loser'.[68] Indeed, the bill requested that 'if any Loss happen thereby so as to sink the said Testators estate', Robert Taylor 'shall be obliged to make good' any loss 'or at least … satisfy' William and Anne's 'Just Demands'.[69] The complainants offered the further suggestion that it would be 'most Equitable' for any loss to 'be born equally by the several Legatees in the … will in p[rop]portion to their several Legacies thereby given', unless 'there be sufficient left to pay the particular Legacyes', in which case the loss might 'fall upon the residue of the estate'. The bill perhaps shows a greater awareness of the extent of trustee duties but still demonstrates uncertainty, or perhaps a challenge, to the question of who would ultimately bear the loss sustained through the trustee's investment of trust property in South Sea stocks without the beneficiaries' consent.

A decree from 1723 stated that Robert Taylor had not yet answered the bill of complaint, but, as the plaintiffs were 'apprehensive that there may be danger' of the testator's estate 'being misappliyed', an injunction was awarded to prevent Robert from transferring any of the stock.[70] The South Sea Company was also enjoined 'from paying any further Dividends or annuityes for the … stock to … Robt Taylor until' he answered the plaintiffs' bill. Robert then submitted an answer that 'Denyed the whole Equity thereof'.[71] On 28 January, an earlier order that the injunctions be dissolved unless

[65] *White v Seamer* (1724) TNA, C33/344/458.
[66] *Bromfield* (n 11).
[67] *Soley v Taylor* (1721) TNA, C11/376/74.
[68] *Bromfield* (n 11); *Thomson v South Sea Company* (1724) TNA, C11/2007/50.
[69] *Soley v Taylor* (1721) TNA, C11/376/74.
[70] *Soley v Taylor* (1723) TNA, C33/342/36.
[71] *Soley v Taylor* (1724) TNA, C33/344/81.

the plaintiffs provided 'notice or proof' to justify the contrary, was 'made absolute', suggesting that Robert had not breached his duties as a trustee.

Emilie v Emilie (1724) might reflect a slight shift in thinking regarding trustee liability. The case concerned £4,315 trust money raised from the sale of £2,000 bank stock, which had been Frances Emilie's fortune prior to her marriage to Francis Emilie, and placed in trust to the use of Francis for life, as per their marriage agreement. John Emilie and Martha Emilie, the mother of Francis Emilie, borrowed the money to purchase South Sea stocks, agreeing to pay the money back with interest. Following the South Sea Bubble, Martha and John Emilie, to the 'prejudice of the respondent Frances', claimed that the South Sea stocks were, in fact, the trust property itself, and that they did not have to account for the loss.[72] Before a decree, Martha died. John Emelie brought a bill of revivor to Chancery. The question to be decided by the Court was the amount to be returned to Francis and Frances's trust out of Martha's estate. The initial decision by the Master of the Rolls was appealed twice to the Lord Chancellor. On the second appeal, Francis, touching upon the question of trustee duties and liability, argued that as a beneficiary, 'in case any profit had arisen from this South-Sea stock, the respondent Francis and his wife had not any right or claim whatsoever thereunto; and consequently, in case of any loss, they ought not to make good the same'.[73] The vulnerability of Frances Emelie, the married female beneficiary's position in relation to keeping hold of her separate estate, is evident in the fact that she and John Elwill, another trustee, 'were no way consenting, or even privy to such proceedings'.[74] It was therefore argued that 'she, and those who might hereafter be interested in the trust, ought not to be prejudiced, or their estate affected therewith'.[75] In light of this, the Lord Chancellor affirmed the decree ordering the £4,315 be returned to the trust, recognising Frances's lack of involvement in the buying of the South Sea stock, and the bond made between Martha and the trustees to pay the money back.

This case highlights a juxtaposition between two women. Francis's mother Martha, the female investor, and wife Frances, the female beneficiary. Historians have demonstrated the financial acumen and decision-making of single women investors during the eighteenth century.[76] There was apprehension and disdain regarding female investors, as they wielded a form of power that stretched beyond gender norms.[77] Indeed, Julia Rudolf believes that 'the attack on Macclesfield's Chancery masters as investors was also part of a pointed critique of women in particular as investors'.[78] Women beneficiaries, who were often married, under 21 years old, or both, were somewhat separated from this discourse by trust mechanisms. They did not invest themselves, but were

[72] *Emilie v Emilie* (1724) 7 Bro PC 259, 3 ER 168.

[73] ibid 7 Bro PC 265, 3 ER 172.

[74] ibid.

[75] ibid.

[76] A Laurence et al (eds), *Women and their Money 1700-1950: Essays on Women and Finance* (London, Routledge, 2009); L Newton and PL Cottrell, 'Female Investors in the First English and Welsh Commercial Joint-Stock Banks' (2006) 16 *Accounting History Review* 315; M Freeman et al, '"A Doe In The City": Women Shareholders in Eighteenth- and Early Nineteenth-Century Britain' (2006) 16 *Accounting History Review* 265.

[77] J Rudolf, 'Jurisdictional Controversy and the Credibility of Common law' in D Coffman et al (eds), *Questioning Credible Commitment Perspectives on the Rise of Financial Capitalism* (Cambridge, Cambridge University Press, 2013) 104.

[78] ibid 120.

to benefit from investments made by trustees on their behalf. They possessed limited property rights and held only equitable title to the investments they decided upon.[79] While Amy Froide argues that we should not presume that such women were 'passive' or 'dependent' investors, it was perhaps easier for decision-makers in Chancery to justify a protectionist stance, such as that exemplified in *Emilie v Emilie*, for married female beneficiaries because they were perceived as posing less of a threat to traditional gender expectations.[80]

V. Lord Macclesfield

The 'old corruption and the South Sea mania' that influenced the lowering of the standard of care trustees owed may have inspired the Chancery officials who invested Chancery suitors' money in the South Sea Company.[81] As demonstrated above, litigants were ordered to pay money into Chancery for investment or because the assets were under dispute. During the South Sea Bubble, the masters used this money for personal gain, only to make heavy losses when the crash occurred.[82] An enquiry revealed that Lord Macclesfield and the Chancery masters had abused their positions at the expense of Chancery litigants, many of whom were the vulnerable parties whom the Court was supposed to protect. Macclesfield was accused of illegally extending 'the Power and Authority of Lord Chancellor, and of the Court of Chancery, beyond their Lawful and just Bounds', giving himself 'an unjust and unlimited Power … to the great Oppression of the Suitors of the … Court'.[83] Macclesfield had 'Illegally, Corruptly, and Extorsively take(n) and receive(d) to his own Private Use … great Sums of Money' by selling off Chancery masterships, amongst other practices.[84] Advertisements in newspapers and in Chancery itself invited suitors who had sustained losses to make claims against individual masters, alerting the general public of the corruption.[85] The subsequent published articles against Macclesfield and accounts of his trial demonstrate the narratives the prosecution used during his impeachment.[86] Similar to Chancery pleadings, the prosecution forwarded a narrative that contrasted the vulnerability and weakness of women, infant and lunatic litigants with the arbitrary power of those employed to protect them.

[79] A Froide, *Silent Partners: Women as Public Investors during Britain's Financial Revolution, 1690-1750* (Oxford, Oxford University Press, 2016).

[80] ibid 99–100. M Freeman et al, 'Between Madam Bubble and Kitty Lorimer: Women Investors in British and Irish Stock Companies' in A Laurence et al (eds), *Women and Their Money 1700-1950: Essays on Women and Finance* (London, Routledge, 2009) 105; K Barclay and E Ireland, 'The Household as a Space of the Law in Eighteenth-Century England' (2020) 7(2) *Law & History* 98.

[81] Getzler 'Fiduciary Investment' (n 14).

[82] ibid.

[83] *Articles exhibited by the Knights, Citizens, and Burgesses in Parliament assembled, In the Name of Themselves, and of all the Commons of Great Britain, against Thomas Earl of Macclesfield, In Maintenance of their impeachment Against Him for High Crimes and Misdemeanors* (London, J Basket, 1725) 29.

[84] G Wilson, *The Trial of the Earl of Macclesfield, faithfully abridg'd* (London, A Moore, 1727) 4.

[85] N Paxton, *The Report of the State of the Offices of the Deficient Masters of the High Court of Chancery* (London, S Buckley, 1725).

[86] *Articles exhibited* (n 83); Wilson, *The Trial* (n 84); T Parker, *The Tryal of Thomas Earl of Macclesfield* (London, S Buckley, 1725); G Wilson, *Bribes no Perquisites: or, the Case of the Earl of Macclesfield* (London, A Moore, 1726).

Many of the accusations involved specific complaints regarding the mismanagement of estates of women, infants and lunatic suitors. For example, one article stated that Lord Macclesfield, in a series of orders, had removed Francis Tyssen's wife, Rachel, 'from the Management and Receivership of' the estate held in trust for their infant son.[87] Robert Doyley, Macclesfield's confidant and 'a Person altogether Unfit and Unqualified for so great a Trust', was appointed 'to be Receiver of the Rents and Profits of the … Infant's Estate, and to have a Salary for the same'.[88] Robert, over several years, embezzled the estate for his own use. He died insolvent and greatly 'Indebted to the … Infant'.[89] It was argued that Macclesfield's actions were 'a Dangerous Exercise of Illegal and Arbitrary Power' that resulted in 'the great Damage and Loss of the Infant … and a Notorious Violation of Property'.[90] Here we see the deliberate juxtaposition of Macclesfield's position of power and the infant beneficiary's loss – a loss that Macclesfield was supposed to protect infants from suffering.

A further article alleged that Macclesfield had refused the resignation of a master from a Chancery office concerning the administration of the estates and custody of 'Ideots and Lunaticks', until the officer paid him £105, 'contrary to the Duty of his Office'.[91] Other articles concerned women, such as the widow Elizabeth Chitty.[92] As Rudolf notes, 'large numbers' of the suitors who were 'undone' by Macclesfield's corruption were female.[93] Thus,

> prosecutors launched a powerful and sustained complaint against the Lord Chancellor's refusal to protect the property of female suitors in Chancery. Those women who rightly looked to him for protection and support of settlements, they said, were now left penniless and powerless. Counsel made the case for impeachment, in part, by providing evidence of women whose fortunes were lost in the Chancery masters' risky investment scheme.[94]

It was repeatedly stated, in the courtroom and in broader public discourse surrounding the trial, that Macclesfield had taken the property of widows and orphans for his own gain.[95] By mishandling the property of women and infants, Lord Macclesfield had acted directly against his obligation to protect them.

At the heart of this critique was the trust mechanism. The masters acted as trustees for funds paid into the Court. It was argued that by selling the offices of Chancery masters, Lord Macclesfield was 'Selling a Licence to abuse and defraud the Suitors of the Court'.[96] The 'fatal Consequence' of this was 'the Loss which the Suitors are likely to sustain by it'.[97] This was directly linked to investments in the South Sea Company. One master, Dormer, was singled out, 'his Misfortune being wholly brought upon him by

[87] *Articles exhibited* (n 83) 30.
[88] ibid 31.
[89] ibid 32.
[90] ibid.
[91] Wilson, *Bribes* (n 86) 33.
[92] ibid 24; Parker (n 86) 5.
[93] Rudolf (n 77) 118.
[94] ibid 119.
[95] For example, Wilson stated how Masters were charged 1,500 Guineas as admission, and 'all Comers were to pay alike for this Stamp of Authority, whereby they were impower'd to strip the Widow and the Orphan': Wilson, *The Trial* (n 84) 14. See also Rudolf (n 77) 119.
[96] Wilson, *The Trial* (n 84) 8.
[97] ibid.

Trafficking the Suitors Money, and lending it to Goldsmiths, in the Reign of South Sea.'[98] It was noted of the suitors that 'The Hazard was all theirs, but the Profit belonged to the Masters.'[99] The injustice, then, concerned the fact that trustees, in this case the Chancery masters, were able to make a personal profit through investment of trust property, seemingly without liability for any losses sustained. Key to this, as already shown, was who bore the 'hazard' of the loss. This was a high-profile iteration of the same issue that arose in the pleadings of suits involving trusts of South Sea stock held for women, infant and lunatic beneficiaries. As Julia Rudolf states,

> trusteeship was seen as the essential factor that allowed corruption. And if trusts were prone to abuse even by those in Chancery who upheld them, it could be argued, then this kind of equitable remedy was inherently unstable and ultimately unjust.[100]

VI. Conclusion

Lord Macclesfield's 'impeachment operated as a gesture to appease public anger'.[101] Yet, it directly led to a number of reforms in Chancery, perhaps aimed at restoring public confidence in the court and wider economic policies.[102] Reforms included the streamlining of the 'administration of Chancery funds', increased oversight 'to support new financial and judicial practices' and the halting of the sale of Chancery masterships, despite this being a 'traditional perquisite of the office'.[103]

The actions of the masters and Lord Macclesfield also influenced the tightening up of trustee duties during the eighteenth century.[104] Lord Chancellor King, who assumed office in 1725, tackled the corruption of those that came before him. He 'disciplined his own officials and prohibited them from using other people's money'.[105] A 'run of stringently moralistic decisions disciplining trustees, guardians, co-owners, mortgagees and so on' followed, which suggests King was implementing a policy of 'commercial and fiduciary honesty'.[106] Some law reports demonstrate how the crash directly influenced certain decisions in Chancery.[107] After the events of 1720, legal practice 'turned against the trustee', and riskier investments were discouraged.[108] As John Langbein puts it, 'The Chancellors took fright and developed a restricted list of presumptively proper trust investments.'[109] '[T]raditional trusts were more or less barred from bearing stock

[98] ibid.
[99] ibid.
[100] Rudolf (n 77) 119.
[101] ibid 120.
[102] ibid 117.
[103] ibid 120.
[104] Yale (n 49); Getzler, 'Fiduciary Investment' (n 14).
[105] Getzler, 'Fiduciary Investment' (n 14) 231.
[106] Getzler, 'Rumford Market' (n 14).
[107] *Scould v Butter* (1720) 2 Eq Ca Abr 19, 22 ER 15. Other reports list this case as *Cud v Rutter* 1 P Wms 570, (1719) 24 ER 521; 2 Eq Ca Abr 50, 22 ER 43.
[108] Yale (n 49) 147.
[109] J Langbein, 'The Uniform Prudent Investor Act and the Future of Trust Investing' (1996) 81 *Iowa Law Review* 641, 643.

market risk' without clear authorisation from the settlor or beneficiaries.[110] By the late eighteenth century, only 'a narrow list of court approved investments' protected trustees from action at equity for lost trust capital.[111]

Then came *Keech v Sandford* (1726), or the 'Rumford market case', as it is colloquially known.[112] The case adopted a stringent approach towards trustee conduct in a specific context and is regarded as the oldest precedent for the concept of fiduciary loyalty.[113] It involved an infant beneficiary and a trustee's 'fraudulent' purchase of a lease previously held on trust for the benefit of the infant. In a direct sense, it had nothing to do with the South Sea Company, the Bubble, or the subsequent crash, yet it is widely regarded as a deliberate move to effect a sea-change in trusts law, prompted by Lord Chancellor King's efforts to distance himself from the actions of his predecessor. King's 'uncompromising stance' perhaps reflected an attempt to 'prevent all fiduciary powers being exploited for personal gain'.[114]

Case law that followed continued to flesh out the obligation of fiduciary loyalty with the aim of protecting the vulnerable,[115] one aspect of the greater role played by Chancery than by the common law courts in providing certain groups of vulnerable people with access to justice.[116] This was particularly important during periods of socio-economic upheaval. Chancery litigation from the 1720s demonstrates how the narratives of pleadings could change, almost instantaneously, when society suffered an extrinsic shock such as the bursting of the South Sea Bubble, how such narratives were shaped by wider public and political discontent with figures and institutions of authority, and how pleadings connect to legal change. Chancery lawyers and litigants, and those involved in Macclesfield's prosecution, embedded the corruption of the powerful at the expense of the vulnerable within their legal discourse. Dynamics of power were inherent in the relationships between vulnerable litigants, trustees, the South Sea Company, and the court of Chancery. Such powers were, theoretically, wielded in a non-despotic manner because of the duties that came with such positions. Such duties were called into question in the wake of the South Sea Bubble, with the trust instrument playing a leading role in the fallout and subsequent reformation of the court of Chancery and rules regarding trusteeship.

[110] Getzler, 'Fiduciary Investment' (n 14).
[111] ibid 231.
[112] *Keech* (n 13); Hicks (n 14).
[113] Hicks (n 14).
[114] J Getzler, '*Keech v Sandford*' in P Cane and J Conaghan (eds), *The New Oxford Companion to Law* (Oxford, Oxford University Press, 2008).
[115] Getzler, 'Fiduciary Investment' (n 14).
[116] Getzler, 'Chancery Reform' (n 4).

15

Constructive Fraud in the Time of Hardwicke and Thurlow

JULIUS AW GROWER*

I. Introduction

The purpose of this chapter is to establish the meaning of the phrase 'constructive fraud' during the period running from the start of Lord Hardwicke's Chancellorship (1737) to the end of Lord Thurlow's second term in that office (1792). The way in which lawyers have used this term has changed over time. As a matter of modern law, it is tolerably clear that 'constructive fraud' is a catch-all – albeit not a commonly used catch-all – which takes in 'breach of fiduciary duty, undue influence, abuse of confidence, unconscionable bargains and fraud on a power'.[1] As Dunn LJ put it in *O'Sullivan v Management Agency and Music Ltd*:

> In equity the term 'fraud' embraces not only actual fraud but certain other conduct which falls below the standards demanded by equity, and is known as constructive fraud, one of the examples of which is a transaction which has been procured by undue influence, or where one party is in breach of a fiduciary duty to another.[2]

Sometimes judges use the term '*equitable* fraud'[3] to describe their jurisdiction to protect against such behaviour. However, nothing turns on this alternative labelling, which merely reflects a natural variation in lawyers' preferences as to names. As Mummery LJ said in *Swindle v Harrison*, 'equitable fraud [is] sometimes called constructive fraud'.[4] Likewise, in *Armitage v Nurse*, Millett LJ was content to use the two terms as synonyms.[5]

* This chapter is a condensed version of the first third of my PhD thesis. Thanks are therefore due to my supervisors Charles Mitchell and Ben McFarlane. Additional thanks are due to Mike Macnair, Neil Jones, and David Foster for their comments at the April 2022 symposium. Any errors are solely my own.

[1] *Barnsley v Noble* [2016] EWCA Civ 799, [2017] Ch 191 [62].

[2] *O'Sullivan v Management Agency and Music Ltd* [1985] QB 428, 455.

[3] *Pitt v Holt* [2011] EWCA Civ 197, [2012] Ch 132 [165] (emphasis added).

[4] *Swindle v Harrison* [1997] PNLR 641, 663.

[5] *Armitage v Nurse* [1998] Ch 241, 250–252.

The modern definition of constructive fraud originates in the House of Lords' decision in *Nocton v Lord Ashburton*.[6] There, in order to restrict what was then thought to be the scope of *Derry v Peek*,[7] each of the judges emphasised that various equitable claims traditionally said to involve 'fraud' – not least those brought 'to keep persons in a fiduciary capacity up to their duty'[8] – were not based on 'such a *mens rea* as would found an action for deceit'.[9] This allowed a majority of their Lordships, including the Lord Chancellor, to make an award of equitable compensation for breach of fiduciary duty in favour of a lender whose solicitor had, though acting in conflict of interest, only *carelessly* misrepresented that the chances of the debt being repaid would be unaffected by a restructuring of the lender's security. Here is one relevant part of Viscount Haldane LC's speech:

> It is ... settled that nothing short of proof of a fraudulent intention in the strict sense will suffice for an action of deceit. This is so whether a Court of Law or a Court of Equity ... is dealing with the claim. ... But when fraud is referred to in the wider sense in which the books are full of the expression ... it is a mistake to suppose that an actual intention to cheat must always be proved.
>
> A man may misconceive the extent of the obligation which a Court of Equity imposes on him. His fault is that he has violated, however innocently, ... an obligation which he must be taken by the Court to have known, and his conduct has in that sense always been called fraudulent. ... It was thus that the expression 'constructive fraud' came into existence. ... What it really means in this connection is, not moral fraud in the ordinary sense, but breach of the sort of obligation which is enforced by a Court that from the beginning regarded itself as a Court of conscience.[10]

As later judges recognised,[11] the Lord Chancellor was not the first propagator of this idea. That was Joseph Story, writing in a section of his *Commentaries*, first published in 1834.[12] That is one reason why the focus of discussion in this chapter is on a period well before then, during the Chancellorships of Lord Hardwicke and Lord Thurlow (and the years between them). Another reason is that this period takes in Hardwicke's decision in *Earl of Chesterfield v Janssen*,[13] the case which has long been identified as the seminal authority on 'constructive fraud' in the eighteenth century. In the 1780s, for example, counsel in *Heathcote v Paignon* cited it 'in point of principle' as the leading statement of what 'courts of equity ... will treat as fraud'.[14] In the mid-nineteenth century, the first editors of *White and Tudor* described it as:

> A case of very frequent reference, celebrated ... above all for the learned judgment of Lord Hardwicke ... in which he ... so admirably classified the different species of fraud against which equity will give relief.[15]

[6] *Nocton v Lord Ashburton* [1914] AC 932.
[7] *Derry v Peek* (1889) 14 App Cas 337.
[8] *Nocton* (n 6) 963.
[9] ibid 963–964. For an example of the prevailing view of *Derry* at the time, see *Low v Bouverie* [1891] 3 Ch 82, 100–101.
[10] *Nocton* (n 6) 953–954.
[11] See, eg, *R Griggs Group Ltd v Evans (No 2)* [2004] EWHC 1088 (Ch), [2005] Ch 153 [45]–[47].
[12] J Story, *Commentaries on Equity Jurisprudence: As Administered in England and America* (Boston, MA, Hilliard, Gray & Co, 1836) §258–§259.
[13] *Earl of Chesterfield v Janssen* (1751) 2 Ves Sen 125, 28 ER 82.
[14] *Heathcote v Paignon* (1787) 2 Bro CC 167, 174; 29 ER 96, 99.
[15] F White and O Tudor, *A Selection of Leading Cases in Equity*, vol 1 (London, W Maxwell, 1849) 410.

In 1906, Upjohn KC referred to *Chesterfield* in argument before the House of Lords as the 'leading authority [on] the doctrine of "constructive fraud"',[16] and in *Nocton v Lord Ashburton*, Haldane LC endorsed the same proposition.[17] Again, in 1957, Lionel Sheridan used the case as the starting point of his own treatment of the subject.[18]

The main argument in this chapter will be that, although the term 'constructive fraud' means something different today, the term initially referred to a single doctrine which concerned the abuse of interpersonal power – a conception which is discussed in detail below. If this is correct, then while there may be a material degree of overlap between the abuse of interpersonal power and the substance of at least some of the doctrines that are nowadays covered by the label 'constructive fraud', it must be accepted that, when the same term was used in the eighteenth century, the judges did *not* make the categorical distinctions between different *types* of constructive fraud as judges do nowadays. Moreover, unlike today, there were no substantive differences between the rules which governed different types of 'constructive fraud' – including conduct that is now described as breach of fiduciary duty or undue influence.[19] One must therefore be careful when seeking to invoke seemingly similar older cases in support of modern propositions of law.[20] Furthermore, one might also expect to see some degree of inconsistency within the overall body of older cases that are now generally supposed to underpin certain discrete modern doctrines.[21]

Discussion in this chapter will be divided as follows. Part II will begin by positing several wider propositions of eighteenth-century equity. Establishing these points before considering the nature of 'constructive fraud' as it existed in the same period is important because they provide a context without which it is impossible to properly understand the relevant authorities. Part III will advance a theory of what 'constructive fraud' involved in the second half of the eighteenth century, arguing that it concerned only what is referred to in this chapter as 'the abuse of interpersonal power'. Part IV will analyse Lord Hardwicke's judgment in *Chesterfield v Janssen* in detail. Although it will take time to unpack what is undoubtedly a complex decision, it will be concluded that, properly understood, his Lordship's words provide strong support for the abuse of interpersonal power analysis advanced here. In other words, it will be demonstrated that at the time it was introduced, the term 'constructive fraud' referred to just one substantive ground of judicial intervention. Part V will look at a letter sent by Lord Hardwicke to Lord Kames shortly after the former's retirement. This has been invoked as evidence to support the proposition that, contrary to the view expressed here, the

[16] *Samuel v Newbold* [1906] AC 461, 462.

[17] *Nocton* (n 6) 952.

[18] LA Sheridan, *Fraud in Equity: A Study in English and Irish Law* (London, Pitman Publishers, 1957) 7.

[19] For a modern account of the differences between fiduciary law and the law of undue influence, see M Conaglen, *Fiduciary Loyalty: Protecting the Due Performance of Non-Fiduciary Duties* (Oxford, Hart Publishing, 2011) 236–241.

[20] Consider the anachronistic invocation of *Keech v Sandford* (1726) Sel Cas Ch 61, 25 ER 223 for the proposition that a fiduciary holds unauthorised profits on constructive trust in *FHR European Ventures LLP v Cedar Capital Partners LLC* [2014] UKSC 45, [2015] AC 250.

[21] Consider the difficulties faced by Lord Neuberger, first as Master of the Rolls and subsequently as President of the Supreme Court, in making sense of the authorities on the question of bribes and constructive trusts in *Sinclair Investments (UK) Ltd v Versailles Trade Finance Ltd* [2011] EWCA Civ 347, [2012] Ch 453 and in *FHR* (n 20).

term 'constructive fraud' had no fixed and determinable meaning in Lord Hardwicke's time. It will be argued that this understanding of the letter depends on a misreading of Lord Hardwicke's words. Part VI will finally bring the discussion to an end by describing later developments in the law governing the abuse of interpersonal power which led to the phrase 'constructive fraud' undergoing a change in meaning.

II. Setting the Scene

The cases which show what constructive fraud originally meant must be construed in their own context. Equity has developed too greatly since these cases were decided for their substantive content to be understood without noting several wider propositions of eighteenth-century equity.

A. Fraud in its Jurisdictional Sense

The first point to make is that, as a matter of mid-eighteenth-century equity, the word 'fraud' had a jurisdictional sense. Amongst other things, it could relate to the bringing of justiciable proceedings. A suit seeking relief from the Court of Chancery, for example, had to be commenced by preferring a bill to the Lord Chancellor (or, as appropriate, the Lord Keeper or the Lords Commissioners).[22] That bill would have to complain of some injury which the person exhibiting it had suffered, and it needed to show that it was 'the peculiar office of a court of equity to relieve [them from it]'.[23] In modern terms, that meant jurisdiction.

In the eighteenth century, lawyers understood that fraud – or, as it was sometimes labelled, 'fraud and imposition'[24] – was one of the three great heads of equity's jurisdiction. Indeed, it was by then trite law that for equity to intervene in any matter, a plaintiff would have to show that his case involved at least one of 'fraud, … a trust, or some accident'.[25] Establishing fraud in its jurisdictional sense was therefore a sufficient, though not a necessary, precondition for obtaining equity's aid.

Two sets of cases underline these points. The first concerned proceedings in which bills grounded solely on fraud, complaining about a wide variety of (sometimes

[22] J Mitford, *A Treatise on the Pleadings in Suits in the Court of Chancery by English Bill*, vol 1 (London, W Owen, 1780) 1.

[23] ibid 2.

[24] See, eg, *Law v Law* (1735) Cas t Talb 140, 25 ER 705; *Langley v Brown* (1741) 2 Atk 195, 26 ER 521; *Baldwin and Alder v Rochford* (1748) 1 Wils KB 229, 95 ER 589; *Brown v Pring* (1750) 1 Ves Sen 407, 27 ER 1109; *Searle v Lord Carpenter* (1754) Amb 242, 27 ER 162; *Williams v Duke of Bolton* (1768) Dick 405, 21 ER 327; *Barrow v Barrow* (1774) Dick 504, 21 ER 365.

[25] *Lord Bath v Sherwin* (1706) Prec Ch 261, 261; 24 ER 126, 126. See, alternatively, *Earl of Bath v Sherwin* (1710) 10 Mod 1, 1; 88 ER 596, 596–7; *R v Hare and Mann* (1718) 1 Str 146, 151; 93 ER 439, 442; Anon, *A General Abridgment of Cases in Equity* (London, H Lintot, 1756) vol 2, 242. For earlier statements to the same effect, see DEC Yale, *Lord Nottingham's 'Manual of Chancery Practice' and 'Prolegomena of Chancery and Equity'* (Cambridge, Cambridge University Press, 1965) 191; H Rolle, *Un Abridgement Des Plusieurs Cases et Resolutions Del Common Ley* (London, A Crooke and others, 1669) vol 1, 374; (and possibly) *Earl of Oxford's Case* (1615) Rep Ch 1, 6–7; 21 ER 485, 486. Whether this was true of Elizabethan law is contested: M Macnair, 'Equity and Conscience' (2007) 27 *Oxford Journal of Legal Studies* 659, 677, fn 72.

admittedly) sharp practices, were rejected on the basis that the actions complained of did not amount to that conduct.[26] The second covered litigation in which the defendant successfully raised a defence by way of a demurrer grounded on a want of equity, this having been a defence based on a contention that, whatever else had happened,[27] in the absence of any fraud by the defendant, the court had no jurisdiction.[28]

B. Two Types of Fraud

The next point to make is that, in the same period, the concept of fraud in its jurisdictional sense was wide enough to cover more than one ground of intervention, and in fact, it concerned *two* distinct types of legally operative events.

The first of these propositions is borne out by cases including *Bosanquett v Dashwood*[29] and *Baldwin and Alder v Rochford*.[30] In *Bosanquett*, Talbot LC distinguished between 'fraud as is properly [labelled] deceit' and 'such proceedings as lay a particular burden or hardship upon any man'.[31] Nevertheless, he was clear in stating that '[both] those cases [carried] somewhat of fraud with them'.[32] In *Baldwin*, Hardwicke LC identified that 'the general head of equity' upon which the bill before him rested was 'fraud and imposition', and then he also said that he was able to grant the plaintiffs relief on two separate but equally potent bases:

> '1st, here is a presumption of fraud arising from the circumstances appearing in the cause, and the great value of the thing sold in proportion to the small price paid for it; and although it is generally laid down … that fraud shall never be presumed, yet an evidence of fraud may arise from the circumstances and nature of the contract.[33]
>
> 2dly, here is actual fraud proved, and appearing upon the face of the bargain'.[34]

Authority for the proposition that fraud in its jurisdictional sense covered *two* distinct legally operative events may be found in the judgement of Hardwicke LC in *Langley v Brown*.[35] In her capacity as her brother's heir, the plaintiff brought a bill seeking to be relieved against several deeds which he had executed a little before his death. The plaintiff alleged that the deeds had been procured by fraud on the part of a woman with whom her brother had been infatuated. It also appears that her brother had previously been indebted to that woman for the sum of £1,050.

[26] See, eg, *Langley* (n 24); *Willis v Jernegan* (1741) 2 Atk 251, 26 ER 555; *Cory v Cory* (1747) 1 Ves Sen 19, 27 ER 864; *Cory v Cory* (1747) 1 Ves Sen 20, 28 ER 444; *Cray v Mansfield* (1750) 1 Ves Sen 379, 27 ER 1093.

[27] And assuming there was no other reason for the court to intervene.

[28] See, eg, *Robertson v St John* (1786) 2 Bro CC 140, 29 ER 81.

[29] *Bosanquett v Dashwood* (1734) Cas t Talb 38, 25 ER 648.

[30] *Baldwin* (n 24). See too *Smith v Downing* (1737) West t Hard 90, 25 ER 836; *Woodhouse v Shepley* (1742) 2 Atk 535, 26 ER 721; *Griffin v De Veulle* 3 Wooddeston's Lect App 334.

[31] *Bosanquett* (n 29) Cas t Talb 40, 25 ER 649.

[32] ibid.

[33] *Baldwin* (n 24) 1 Wils KB 229, 95 ER 589.

[34] Baldwin (n 24) 1 Wils KB 229–230, 95 ER 589. For more examples of cases in which relief was available on the basis that more than one different type of fraud was present on the facts, see *Taylour v Rochfort* (1751) 2 Ves Sen 281, 28 ER 182; *How v Weldon and Edwards* (1754) 2 Ves Sen 516, 28 ER 330; *Alden v Gregory* (1764) 2 Eden 280, 28 ER 905; *Griffin* (n 30).

[35] *Langley* (n 24). See also *Cray* (n 26).

In rejecting the bill – and so in holding that, on the facts, there was no ground upon which a court of equity could come to the plaintiff's aid – the Lord Chancellor first noted that she 'founded [her claim for] relief [on] fraud and imposition'.[36] He thus began by identifying the alleged jurisdictional basis of the claim. His Lordship then said that this was because there was neither '[any] proof of actual fraud',[37] nor proof of the other type of fraud: that which was – in the case before him – capable of being inferred 'from the internal evidence in the deeds themselves'.[38] Crucially, no further option was given. Indeed, in the absence of either of those two grounds of intervention, he said he was bound to conclude that whatever had happened between the plaintiff's brother and the woman he loved '[was] not a foundation in a court of equity to set aside [any] deed'.[39]

These cases establish that the jurisdiction exercised by the eighteenth-century courts of equity over cases of fraud covered just two grounds of intervention. There was actual fraud, and there was a second legally operative occurrence that could be inferred from the transaction which had been entered in any particular case. As shall be explained in Parts III and IV, below, this second ground of intervention was 'constructive fraud'.

C. Actual Fraud

What, then, did actual fraud entail? In *How v Weldon and Edwards*,[40] after breaking down the court's jurisdiction over 'fraud and imposition' into two parts: 'actual … fraud', and that 'head of equity arising partly from the person with whom the transaction was, and [partly from] the value of the thing purchased',[41] Clarke MR stated that actual fraud was '[charged] in the bill [before him as both] *suggestio falsi* [and] *suppressio veri*', and that it had been 'made out by evidence'.[42] These comments are instructive because at the start of the eighteenth century, Harcourt LC had described both *suggestio falsi* and *suppressio veri* in *Broderick v Broderick*.[43] In that case, he had set aside the release in issue before him which had been signed by an heir in response to various acts of actual fraud on the part of a putative legatee. The legatee had informed the heir that the testator's will, under which the legatee had just taken property, had been duly executed. In fact, the legatee knew it had not been. Consequently, it was the heir who was entitled to everything. 'Either *suppressio veri* or *suggestio falsi* is a good reason to set aside any release or conveyance', the Lord Chancellor noted, '[and] both circumstances concur [in this case]':

> To recite … that [a] will was duly executed, when it was not, is *suggestio falsi*, and to conceal from [an] heir … that [a] will was not duly executed is *suppressio veri*.[44]

[36] *Langley* (n 24) 2 Atk 201, 26 ER 524.
[37] *Langley* (n 24) 2 Atk 202, 26 ER 524.
[38] ibid.
[39] ibid.
[40] *How* (n 34).
[41] *How* (n 34) 2 Ves Sen 517–518, 28 ER 331.
[42] *How* (n 34) 2 Ves Sen 518, 28 ER 331.
[43] *Broderick v Broderick* (1713) 1 P Wms 239, 24 ER 369.
[44] *Broderick* (n 43) 1 P Wms 240, 24 ER 370.

Two important points about actual fraud emerge from this. One is that both misrepresentations and concealments were potentially covered by the label.[45] The other is that the occurrence of either was sufficient, and neither was necessary to justify the court's intervention in any case.[46]

A full study of all eighteenth-century actual fraud cases, or at least all those considered by the courts of equity, is beyond the scope of this chapter. However, it is still possible to say that together they indicate that, at that time, the term 'actual fraud' referred to all knowingly made[47] and reckless[48] misrepresentations and all failures to disclose information in breach of a duty to do so.[49] All other things being equal, then, neither wholly innocent,[50] nor merely careless misrepresentations[51] were actionable as actual fraud. Nor were intentional non-disclosures, provided they were not wrongful.[52]

D. Concurrent and Exclusive Jurisdictions

The last background point to make is that, in the period under consideration, both judges and commentators distinguished between equity's so-called concurrent and exclusive jurisdictions over fraud. Equity's jurisdiction over cases involving actual fraud was 'concurrent'[53] in the sense that, subject to the rule that they had no jurisdiction over disputes concerning the creation of wills,[54] the eighteenth-century courts of equity could intervene in any proceedings which involved actual fraud, even though that conduct *might* also have been actionable at common law.[55] It was therefore open to the victims of actual fraud to choose the court in which they would initiate litigation, and defendants could not raise demurrers against equitable proceedings on the basis that their victims had yet to exhaust all their potential legal remedies.[56]

One consequence of this was that there was a high degree of substantive harmonisation between the legal and equitable regulation of actual fraud. The equitable definition of such behaviour, for instance, was essentially the same as it was at common law.[57]

[45] See also *Young v Peachy* (1741) 2 Atk 254, 26 ER 557 (on misrepresentations); *De Costa v Scandret* (1723) 2 P Wms 170, 24 ER 686 (on concealments).

[46] See also *Baugh v Price* (1752) 1 Wils KB 320, 95 ER 640; *Merry v Ryves* (1757) 1 Eden 1, 28 ER 584; *Salkeld v Vernon* (1758) 1 Eden 64, 28 ER 608.

[47] See, eg, *Broderick* (n 43).

[48] See, eg, *Griffin* (n 30).

[49] See, eg, *Fox v Mackreth* (1788) 2 Bro CC 400, 420; 29 ER 224, 234.

[50] See, eg, *Whitton v Russell* (1739) 1 Atk 448, 26 ER 285; *Merewether v Shaw* (1789) 2 Cox Eq Cas 124, 30 ER 58.

[51] See, eg, *Plumb v Fluitt* (1791) 2 Anst 432, 440; 145 ER 926, 929.

[52] See, eg, *Ibbottson v Rhodes* (1706) 2 Vern 554, 23 ER 958.

[53] See, eg, *Colt v Woollaston* (1723) 2 P Wms 154, 156; 24 ER 679, 680; *Stent v Bailis* (1724) 2 P Wms 217, 220; 24 ER 705, 706; *Bright v Eynon* (1757) 1 Burr 390, 396; 97 ER 365, 368; J Fonblanque, *A Treatise of Equity* (Dublin, P Byrne, 1793) 61.

[54] See *Andrews v Powys* (1723) 2 Bro PC 504, 1 ER 1094.

[55] C Barton, *An Historical Treatise of a Suit in Equity* (London, W Clarke and Son, 1796) 21.

[56] See, eg, *Colt* (n 53) 2 P Wms 156, 24 ER 680; *Sowerby v Warder* (1791) 2 Cox Eq Cas 268, 270; 30 ER 124, 125–126.

[57] See, eg, *Scott v Lara* (1794) Peake 296, 170 ER 162 (on misrepresentations); *Carter v Boehm* (1766) 3 Burr 1905, 97 ER 1162 (on concealments). See, generally, CM Reed, '*Derry v Peek* and Negligence' (1987) 8 *Journal of Legal History* 64, 65–71.

Likewise, many of the rules of proof were the same on both sides of the institutional divide. As Jekyll MR noted in *Trenchard and Ippsley v Wanley*:[58]

> The rule of law as to fraud is also a good rule in equity, *viz.* that fraud is never to be presumed.[59]

Yet when it came to constructive fraud, things were different. That conduct had no analogue at common law, and so equity's jurisdiction over it was 'exclusive'.[60] As the judge in *Trenchard* went on to say: 'but it is true, that [something] may be a fraud in equity, which is not so at law'.[61] Indeed, it was for this reason that, in relation to this type of fraud, the courts of equity did *not* see themselves as required to maintain any particular consistency between their rules and practices and those of any other court. In Michael Lobban's words:

> Treating things as fraud which would not be regarded in that light at common law, … Chancery lawyers were willing to look far to root it out.[62]

A good example of this mindset in action can be found in the relevant rules of proof. As Hardwicke LC stated in *Chesterfield*: equity went 'farther than the … law' and provided that those acts of fraud over which it alone had jurisdiction 'may be presumed from the circumstances and condition of the parties contracting [rather than specifically proved]'.[63] As will be explained in Part IV, this was a reference to the fact that, unlike actual fraud, one element of constructive fraud could be established by the provision of circumstantial rather than direct evidence, namely evidence which *itself* demonstrates the existence of a certain fact.

III. What Constituted Constructive Fraud?

Perhaps unsurprisingly, there are examples of eighteenth-century equity judges using the phrase 'constructive fraud' in a different way from most other judges,[64] but a generally common usage of the term can be identified.[65] It was employed in combination with the label 'actual fraud' (which was also referred to as 'deceit')[66] to describe the entirety of fraud in its jurisdictional sense. In his judgment in *Forbes v Ross*, for example, Thurlow LC spoke of 'fraud … constructive, or otherwise'[67] when considering (so as to rule out) the possibility that the court had jurisdiction over the proceedings before him on the

[58] *Trenchard and Ippsley v Wanley* (1723) 2 P Wms 166, 24 ER 685.

[59] *Trenchard* (n 58) 2 P Wms 167, 24 ER 685.

[60] Fonblanque (n 53) 10.

[61] *Trenchard* (n 58) 2 P Wms 167, 24 ER 685.

[62] M Lobban, 'Contractual Fraud in Law and Equity, c 1750 – c 1850' (1997) 17 *Oxford Journal of Legal Studies* 441, 448.

[63] *Chesterfield* (n 13) 2 Ves Sen 155, 28 ER 99.

[64] See, eg, *Pearson v Morgan* (1788) 2 Bro CC 388, 29 ER 214, where Buller J used it to refer to an intentional concealment.

[65] Indeed, *mutatis mutandis* the same is true today. Contrast the standard definition set out in Part I with that put forward in *Manifest Shipping Co Ltd v Uni-Polaris Insurance Co Ltd (The Star Sea)* [2003] 1 AC 469 [40].

[66] See, eg, *Bosanquett* (n 29) Cas t Talb 40, 25 ER 649; *Chesterfield* (n 13) 2 Ves Sen 155, 28 ER 99.

[67] *Forbes v Ross* (1788) 2 Cox Eq Cas 113, 117; 30 ER 54.

basis of fraud. Likewise, in his *Treatise* of 1793, John Fonblanque advanced the following proposition about 'fraud or imposition' as a head of equitable intervention:

> If there be any fraud, either direct or constructive, ... courts of equity will interpose, and give relief.[68]

Having said that, it is harder to pin down exactly what types of behaviour amounted to 'constructive fraud'. The brevity of many judgments, the obvious incompleteness (perhaps even outright unreliability) of many law reports,[69] and the liberality with which judges sometimes expressed themselves,[70] all contribute to this uncertainty. Nevertheless, by taking samples from across a range of courts, and by focusing in on some of the longer, ostensibly more complete reports of their decisions, it is possible to ascertain several key facts:

1) In the second half of the 18th century, the label 'constructive fraud' covered just one substantive ground of judicial intervention.
2) That substantive ground of intervention can be adequately termed the abuse of interpersonal power.
3) An abuse of interpersonal power occurred when:
    i. One party (D) had a power – either legal or factual – over another (C),
    ii. C entered into (what this chapter shall call) a one-sided transaction with either D or a third party, and
    iii. There was a causal link between an *exercise* of D's power and C's entry into that transaction.[71]

Consider *Ward v Hartpole*,[72] *Heathcote v Paignon*,[73] and *Griffith v Spratley*.[74] In each case, all three of the elements of an abuse of interpersonal power just identified were more or less specifically set out and put into action.

In *Ward v Hartpole*, an appeal to the House of Lords from the Court of Chancery in Ireland, Lord Mansfield identified three requirements for relief in any case of 'fraud', absent 'evidence of [a] misrepresentation'.[75] On the facts of the case itself, he noted, the first was satisfied by the fact that the alleged victim's '[legal] affairs were exceedingly embarrassed'.[76] This meant that he was under his then attorney's power. 'In this situation', his Lordship said, 'one [is] very apt to give, and the other [is] too ready to take, a good bargain'.[77] He then linked the existence of that power with the transaction in issue before him by asking whether that transaction had been procured by its exercise. The

[68] Fonblanque (n 53) 238.

[69] See, eg, JW Wallace, *The Reporters*, 3rd revised edn (Philadelphia, PA, T & JW Johnson, 1855) 319–321.

[70] See, eg, C Croft, 'Lord Hardwicke's Use of Precedent in Equity' in TG Watkin (ed), *Legal Record and Historical Reality: Proceedings of the Eighth British Legal History Conference* (London, Hambledon Press, 1989).

[71] In other words, if C entered a one-sided transaction because of D's exercise of his power, an 18th century court of equity *would* have jurisdiction to intervene on the basis of fraud.

[72] *Ward v Hartpole* (1776) 3 Bli 470, 4 ER 671.

[73] *Heathcote* (n 14).

[74] *Griffith v Spratley* (1787) 1 Cox Eq Cas 383, 29 ER 1213.

[75] *Ward* (n 72) 3 Bli 487, 4 ER 680.

[76] ibid 3 Bli 488, 4 ER 680.

[77] ibid 3 Bli 488, 4 ER 680.

fact of the transaction, and the fact of the causal link, were the second and third requirements Lord Mansfield stated. Here is the operative part of his speech:

> The [transaction] in question was [entered into] for a consideration grossly inadequate; [the victim] knew it, but his distress compelled him to give way. [The defendant] availed himself of the advantage of his situation, and thus obtained it at an undervalue. [It is] upon the ground of undervalue, coupled with the other circumstances which I have stated, [that] the [transaction] is void as to the [defendant], and … should be set aside.[78]

In *Heathcote v Paignon*, Thurlow LC, sitting in the English Court of Chancery, was asked as to when (what he referred to as) inadequate bargains could be set aside for fraud. His Lordship stated:

> If [such a] transaction [involves] over-reaching on one side and imbecility on the other it puts [a burden on the defendant] to shew that it could not have taken place without [his use of] superior powers … over the other.[79]

These words also touch on all three of the elements of the abuse of interpersonal power listed above. The inadequate bargain obliquely referred to is what has been described as a one-sided transaction. The over-reaching on one side and 'imbecility' on the other point to the existence of a power on the part of the transferee and a vulnerability on the part of the transferor. As the Lord Chancellor noted, what was required was that '[a] person did not understand the bargain he made, or was so oppressed that he was glad to make it, knowing its inadequacy'.[80] Lastly, putting aside any doubts over the alleged location of the burden of proof, the idea that the defendant would have to *disprove* the fact that the bargain in issue could not have taken place *without* his use of power is manifestly a causal one.

Lastly comes *Griffith v Spratley*, a decision from what was commonly called the 'English side' of the Court of Exchequer.[81] The plaintiff brought a bill seeking the rescission of a deed. While short of money, he had conveyed his interests in several properties to the defendant. The transfer had been made at something of an undervalue and so constituted a bad bargain from his perspective. The plaintiff alleged that he had been the victim of fraud. Yet by the time of trial, the parties were agreed that there was no actual fraud in issue. Consequently, as Cox's report notes, this meant that, to win, the plaintiff would have to 'rest his case on [either] the … ground of inadequacy of consideration, or the fraud [that was] to be presumed from [it]',[82] ie, constructive fraud.

The court unanimously dismissed the action. It rejected out of hand the idea that the mere 'inadequacy of consideration [was] of itself a distinct principle of relief in equity'.[83] As Eyre CB put it: 'I know of no such principle: the common law knows no such [principle either].'[84] On the issue of constructive fraud, the court made clear that, although the plaintiff *had* been somewhat necessitous at the time he entered the impugned transaction, 'the

[78] ibid 3 Bli 489, 4 ER 681.

[79] *Heathcote* (n 14) 2 Bro CC 174; 29 ER 99.

[80] ibid 2 Bro CC 175; 29 ER 99.

[81] In the 18th century, the Court of Chancery was not the only court with an original equity jurisdiction. See, generally, W Bryson, *The Equity Side of the Exchequer* (Cambridge, Cambridge University Press, 1975).

[82] *Griffith* (n 74) 1 Cox Eq Cas 386, 29 ER 1214.

[83] ibid 1 Cox Eq Cas 388, 29 ER 1215.

[84] ibid 1 Cox Eq Cas 388, 29 ER 1215.

consideration [he received] more or less [supported] the contract'.[85] As a result, he could not be said to have been a victim of *that* behaviour either. The Chief Baron stated:

> When you see distress on … one side and money on the other and a wish on … one side to press that distress into a submission [on certain] terms, inadequacy of price goes a great way in warranting the court to infer … that some sort of fraud was used to draw the other party into the bargain; [but it is only in such cases that] the Court [can] presume more than is in actual proof.[86]

These comments nicely encapsulate the tripartite nature of 'constructive fraud' and the fact that, at its heart, it involved the abuse of interpersonal power. They also explain why, as a matter of principle, the proceedings in *Griffith* failed. The plaintiff might well have been subject to a (factual) power on the part of the defendant. Indeed, generally speaking, the eighteenth-century courts of equity were prepared to assume that '[where a] borrower [was] under some necessities, [he was] therefore in the power of [a] lender'.[87] However, he could not establish that such a power had been *abused*.

Of course, as indicated above, it is not this chapter's argument that the term 'abuse of interpersonal power' itself appears in any of the relevant eighteenth-century authorities. Having said that, it is worth noting that some judges from that period *did* speak in highly similar terms.[88] In *Kinchant v Kinchant*,[89] for example, Gould J dismissed a son's bill, grounded on his father's alleged fraud, seeking to have a family settlement he had entered into set aside. His Lordship observed:

> Suppose the father *had* exercised some paternal authority, it would not have been sufficient to set the transaction aside. If the father *had* exercised his authority in this case, it would seem to have been very happily applied. There is no reason to suppose he abused his power [and so] there is no ground to set the deed aside.[90]

Like the plaintiff in *Griffith*, the son in *Kinchant* could not prove that he had entered a one-sided transaction.[91] However, it is still, on its face, a case which supports the tripartite abuse of interpersonal power analysis set out above.[92]

It is also true that the phrase 'one-sided transaction' is not a label which was used in the cases. As the Chief Baron's words in *Griffith* demonstrate, 'inadequacy of price'[93] *was* a phrase used to describe the transactional disparity involved in 'constructive fraud' cases, but so too were 'inadequacy of consideration',[94] 'inadequacy of … value',[95] and 'some unfair

[85] ibid 1 Cox Eq Cas 388, 29 ER 1215.

[86] ibid 1 Cox Eq Cas 389, 29 ER 1215.

[87] *Ord v Smith* (1725) Sel Cas Ch 9, 10; 25 ER 193, 193. Of course, the plaintiff in *Griffith* was not seeking a loan per se, but instead hoped to realise the value an asset by transacting with someone solvent.

[88] See, eg, *Gartside v Isherwood* (1783) 1 Bro CC 558, 560; 28 ER 1297, 1298, where Thurlow LC said: 'The only principle upon which [the fraud case of *Filmer v Gott* (1774) 4 Bro PC 230, 2 ER 156 can] be supported [is] that if a confidence is reposed, and that confidence is abused, a court of equity shall give relief.' Throughout the Lord Chancellor's decision, the words 'confidence' and 'power' are used interchangeably.

[89] *Kinchant v Kinchant* (1784) 1 Bro CC 369, 28 ER 1183.

[90] *Kinchant* (n 89) 1 Bro CC 374, 28 ER 1186 (emphasis added).

[91] For further examples of such cases, see *Oldin v Samborn* (1737) 2 Atk 15, 26 ER 406; *Cory v Cory* (1747) 1 Ves Sen 19, 27 ER 864; *Fox* (n 49).

[92] For examples of cases which failed as the plaintiff could not establish that they were the subject of a power held by the defendant, see *Osmond v Fitzroy* (1731) 3 P Wms 129, 24 ER 997; *Tendril v Smith* (1740) 2 Atk 85, 26 ER 452; *Smith* (n 30).

[93] *Griffith* (n 74) 1 Cox Eq Cas 389, 29 ER 1215.

[94] *Gartside* (n 88) 1 Bro CC 563, 28 ER 1299.

[95] *Heathcote* (n 14) 2 Bro CC 175, 29 ER 99.

advantage.'[96] Indeed, it is tolerably clear that equity's jurisdiction over constructive fraud was also wide enough to cover cases involving gifts.[97] Thus, provided one distinguishes between what was said in any particular case from the substantive idea consistently invoked across them, it should be convenient to use a broad term like one-sided to describe any transaction capable of satisfying the second limb of the tripartite definition.

IV. *Earl of Chesterfield v Janssen*

A. Lord Hardwicke's Judgment

There is good reason to think that the account of 'constructive fraud' which has been posited here should stand or fall by reference to its consistency with Lord Hardwicke LC's judgment in *Earl of Chesterfield v Janssen*.[98] At base, that case concerned the validity of a *post-obit* bond used to facilitate a substantial loan. The circumstances in which it was granted were suspicious. However, the litigation itself – which was also heard by Strange MR, Lee CJ, Willes CJCP, and Burnet J – turned on the fact that, at some point after the impugned bond's issue, the borrower had voluntarily affirmed it. This meant that any fraud exercised by the lender during the parties' initial dealings was rendered otiose, and it was unnecessary for the court or any member of it to express a 'direct and conclusive opinion'[99] on whether any such behaviour had really occurred. Nonetheless, Hardwicke LC felt it was appropriate 'to say something'[100] on the issue:

> This court has an undoubted jurisdiction to relieve against every species of fraud.
>
> 1. Then fraud, which is *dolus malus*, may be actual, arising from facts and circumstances of imposition; which is the plainest case.
>
> 2. It may be apparent from the intrinsic nature and subject of the bargain itself; such as no man in his senses and not under delusion would make on the one hand, and as no honest and fair man would accept on the other; which are unequitable and unconscientious bargains; and of such even the Common Law has taken notice; for which, if it would not look a little ludicrous, might be cited … *James v Morgan.*
>
> A 3rd kind of fraud is, which may be presumed from the circumstances and condition of the parties contracting: and this goes farther than the rule of law; which is, that it must be proved, not presumed; but it is wisely established in this court to prevent taking surreptitious advantage of the weakness or necessity of another: which knowingly to do is equally against the conscience as to take advantage of his ignorance: a person is equally unable to judge for himself in one as the other.
>
> A 4th kind of fraud may be collected or inferred in the consideration of this court from the nature and circumstances of the transaction, as being an imposition and deceit on the other persons not parties to the fraudulent agreement. … Of this kind have been marriage-brocage contracts; neither of the parties herein being deceived: but they tend necessarily to the deceit on one party to the marriage, or of the parent, or of the friend. …

[96] *Cory* (n 91) 1 Ves Sen 19, 27 ER 864.
[97] See, eg, *Ward* (n 72) 3 Bli 488, 4 ER 680; *Bridgeman v Green* (1757) Wilm 58, 61; 97 ER 22, 24.
[98] *Chesterfield* (n 13).
[99] ibid 2 Ves Sen 155, 28 ER 99.
[100] ibid 2 Ves Sen 155, 28 ER 99.

> The last head of fraud, on which there has been relief, is that, which infects catching bargains with heirs, reversioners, or expectants, in the life of the father, etc., against which relief always extended.[101] These have been generally mixed cases, compounded of all or several species of fraud; there being sometimes proof of actual fraud, which is always decisive. There is always fraud presumed or inferred from the circumstances or conditions of the parties contracting: weakness on one side, usury on the other, or extortion or advantage taken of that weakness. There has been always an appearance of fraud from the nature of the bargain; …
>
> In most of these cases have concurred deceit and illusion on other persons not privy to the fraudulent agreement: the father, ancestor, or relation, from whom was the expectation of the estate, has been kept in the dark: the heir or expectant has been kept from disclosing his circumstances … which might have tended to his relief and also reformation. This misleads the ancestor; who has been seduced to leave his estate not to his heir or family, but to a set of artful persons, who have divided the spoil beforehand.[102]

B. Preliminary Observations

Before fully unpacking these remarks, five preliminary points should be made. The first is that prima facie his Lordship's description of the eighteenth-century law of fraud can be visually represented as follows:

Table 15.1

Fraud (in its jurisdictional sense)			
1. The fraud constituted by '*dolus malus*'.	2. The fraud 'apparent from the intrinsic nature and subject of [an unfair] bargain itself'.	3. The fraud involved in 'taking surreptitious advantage of the weakness or necessity [or ignorance] of another'.	4. The fraud constituted by an act of 'deceit' on a third party.
5. The fraud 'which infects catching bargains with heirs, reversioners, or expectants, in the life of the father, etc.'			

The second point is that, by beginning his statement of law with the words: 'this court', Hardwicke LC was emphasising that, in general, he was speaking only of equity. Thus, aside from when he specifically says otherwise, none of his observations should be taken to apply to the common law of the same time.

The third point is that the Lord Chancellor's words demonstrably concern more than just the law of constructive fraud. By referring to different 'kinds' or 'species' of fraud, his

[101] 'Catching bargain' was not a term of art, but a label commonly used to refer to the sort of extortionate *post-obit* bond that was in issue in *Chesterfield*. See, eg, *Matthews v Lewis* (1792) 1 Anst 7, 145 ER 783.

[102] *Chesterfield* (n 13) 2 Ves Sen 155–157, 28 ER 99–101.

Lordship *must* have intended that the fraud mentioned in the very first sentence quoted above was the whole of his court's jurisdiction over such conduct. Indeed, as previously stated in Part II, fraud in its jurisdictional sense *was* wide enough to cover more than one different ground of intervention in the eighteenth century. Thus, to determine exactly what was meant by the term 'constructive fraud' (as opposed to 'fraud' more generally), a process of selection vis-à-vis the entirety of the judge's remarks will be necessary.

The first step in this process is to weed out Hardwicke LC's first type of fraud ('type one fraud'). This is 'actual fraud' in the sense discussed in Part II. Omitting its subordinate clause, the main sentence of the first passage quoted above reads as follows: 'fraud … may be actual, arising from [the] facts and circumstances of imposition'.[103] What it was about those facts and circumstances which made the fraud actual is not specified, but those terms are wide enough to cover the making of knowingly made or reckless misrepresentations, and failures to disclose information made in breach of a duty to do so. What is more, even if it is a little opaque, his Lordship's reference to '*dolus malus*' in the subordinate clause suggests that this is the correct analysis. As a matter of mid-eighteenth-century equity, *dolus malus* was a synonym for actual fraud.[104]

Turning to the Lord Chancellor's fourth type of fraud ('type four fraud') – that which 'may be collected or inferred … from the nature and circumstances of the transaction, as being [a] deceit on [third] parties'[105] – it seems clear that it involved no more than certain fact-specific instances of actual fraud: actual fraud against third parties. The legally operative occurrence in issue in each case was therefore the same as that in type one fraud authorities. One clue comes from his Lordship's repeated use of the term 'deceit'. As has been said already, at the time, deceit was an alternative label for actual fraud. Furthermore, Hardwicke LC's own *draft* judgment confirms this point. In it, he wrote that this category of cases covered '*dolus malus* in respect of other persons who stand in such a relation to either of the parties as that they may be affected by the contract or the direct consequences of it'.[106]

In the end, then, when it comes to testing whether this chapter's analysis of constructive fraud is consistent with the decision in *Chesterfield*, it only needs to be asked if the concept of the abuse of interpersonal power provides the best way of understanding the second, third, and fifth types of fraud the Lord Chancellor set out.

The fourth preliminary point to make is that, even though no judge may have posited such an account before,[107] in delineating the various different types of fraud that he did, Hardwicke LC was *not* attempting to introduce any hard and fast taxonomy of that behaviour. Consequently, his judgment should not be read as doing so. Its terms were meant to be descriptive, rather than definitive. He was providing guidance on how to view the subsisting cases, not drafting parts of a statute. Indeed, why else would his Lordship have specifically caveated his remarks by saying that he was not 'giving any direct and conclusive opinion'[108] on the law? Why else would some of the categories he set out be self-confessedly mixed ones?

Furthermore, think back to what the Lord Chancellor said about the type of fraud which infected 'catching bargains [made] with heirs, reversioners, or expectants, in the life of the

[103] ibid 2 Ves Sen 155, 28 ER 99.
[104] See, eg, *Le Neve v Le Neve* (1747) Amb 436, 446; (1747) 3 Atk 646, 654–655; 26 ER 1172, 1176.
[105] *Chesterfield* (n 13) 2 Ves Sen 156, 28 ER 99.
[106] See G Harris, *The Life of Lord Chancellor Hardwicke* (London, E Moxon, 1847) vol 2, 429.
[107] See W Holdsworth, *A History of English Law, vol 12* (London, Methuen & Co, 1938) 262.
[108] *Chesterfield* (n 13) 2 Ves Sen 155, 28 ER 99.

father, etc.'[109] ('type five fraud'). Disputes involving such transactions, he stated, '[were] generally mixed cases, compounded of all or several species of fraud'.[110] This indicates an understanding on his part that type five fraud cases did *not* constitute a substantively separate head of the wider jurisdiction then under his contemplation. In every case there was always some other already-classified type of fraud in operation. Sometimes this was type one and/or type four fraud (ie, actual fraud), but, even if that was not present, there was always *both* type two *and* type three fraud. His Lordship's words also make clear how to treat those decisions which might otherwise be thought to fall into a distinct category of fraud. Bearing in mind that, as a matter of mid-eighteenth-century equity, actual fraud and constructive fraud were concurrent causes of action, then unless their facts *also* disclose instances of deceit, they should always be treated *only* as cases involving *both* type two *and* type three fraud. In other words, type five fraud cases are *always* best understood as a sub-category of at least one other type of fraudulent behaviour.

As shall be explained below, Hardwicke LC *did* sometimes acquiesce in the grouping together of factually similar authorities. However, this was usually only to provide analogies as to what was occurring in the particular case before him. As Croft's general examination of his Lordship's use of precedent demonstrates, in cases of fraud, what mattered to him more than anything were broad principles of equity.[111] Thus, insofar as this part of the judgment involves such behaviour, his sequestration of cases involving so-called catching bargains should be seen as no more than an instance of his habit in operation. Further, it may not be a coincidence that *Chesterfield* itself involved just such a transaction.

The final preliminary point to make is that, considering what has just been said, and – for clarity's sake – omitting type five fraud cases which *also* involved actual fraud, the contents of eighteenth-century equity's jurisdiction over fraud can be more accurately visually represented as follows:

Table 15.2

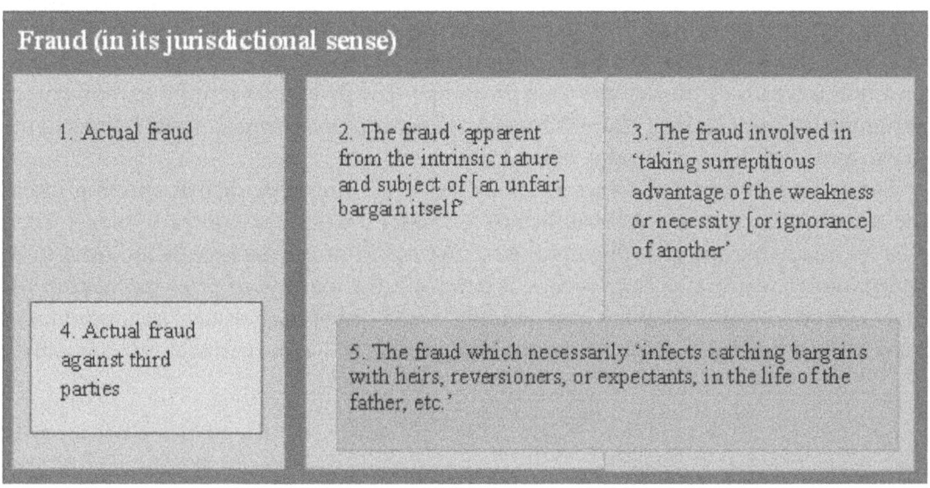

[109] *Chesterfield* (n 13) 2 Ves Sen 157, 28 ER 100.
[110] ibid.
[111] Croft (n 70) 145–149.

C. Unpacking Type Two Fraud

Consistently with the above, and assuming Hardwicke LC's judgment in *Chesterfield* entailed an exhaustive account of the scope of mid-eighteenth-century equity's jurisdiction over fraud, constructive fraud as it subsisted at that time could only have been constituted by cases falling within three of the five categories he set out. Actual fraud authorities – whether they involved two or three parties – must, by definition, have been outside of its scope. Moreover, as type five fraud cases formed no substantively separate category from both type two and type three fraud cases, to test this chapter's argument that constructive fraud was focused solely on the abuse of interpersonal power, it is to those two groups of decisions that the discussion must turn. The key question to be asked in relation to each of them is: what particular legally operative occurrence did they concern?

I start with the second type of fraud Hardwicke LC identified: that which may have been 'apparent from the intrinsic nature and subject of [a] bargain itself'.[112] Exactly what that involved has been the subject of some debate.

(i) *The Irrelevance of* James v Morgan

One way of interpreting Hardwicke LC's words is that the act of entering into a one-sided transaction was, in and of itself, fraud by the party getting the better of it. This, for example, is how Sheridan read them.[113] The problem is that this is neither the best construction of the words used, nor – as he recognised[114] – is it consistent with most eighteenth-century authorities.

The only decision which the Lord Chancellor referred to when substantiating his description of type two fraud was the late seventeenth-century common law case of *James v Morgan*.[115] There the defendant agreed to exchange a horse for 'a barley-corn a nail, doubling it every nail'.[116] A barley-corn was a unit of grain, and the horse had 32 nails in its shoes. In total, then, the defendant owed the plaintiff 500 quarters of barley (an amount worth 12 times more than the horse). The defendant refused to perform his side of the bargain, and the plaintiff brought an action for *assumpsit*. Hyde J directed the jury to award him only the value of the horse.

Some have interpreted *James* as a case in which the mere fact of entering into a one-sided transaction was held sufficient to render a would-be contract void.[117] Yet it is by no means certain that this is correct. The report of the decision is too brief to be determinative. All that is clear is that, if enforced, the method of price calculation the buyer agreed to would have left him handing over a disproportionately large amount of grain to the seller. Indeed, for this reason, Warren Swain has argued that *James* is merely

[112] *Chesterfield* (n 13) 2 Ves Sen 155, 28 ER 99.
[113] Sheridan (n 18) 125.
[114] ibid 127–128, 167.
[115] *James v Morgan* (1662) 1 Lev 111, 83 ER 323.
[116] ibid.
[117] See, eg, S Harrison, *A Treatise on the Law of Vendors and Purchasers of Personal Property*, 2nd edn (London, H Butterworth, 1826) 214.

a decision which reflected a judge's ability to pick which measure of damages to instruct a jury to adopt in an action for *indebitatus assumpsit* based on a contract.[118]

However, even if *James* is authority for the proposition that, in some cases, the early-modern common law held that the act of entering into a one-sided transaction was sufficient to invalidate an otherwise-binding agreement, it could simply have been wrongly decided. Sheridan, for example, describes the case as 'isolated'[119] as a matter of authority, and otherwise unsupportable on what was then subsisting legal principle. It seems inconsistent with the House of Lords' decision in *Keen v Stuckely*.[120] That case involved an appeal from a decision to order the specific performance of a contract which entailed a substantial inequality of consideration. While their Lordships were split over whether such relief should be granted, they were agreed that the contract between the two sides was valid. The idea that it may have been so one-sided as to render it void was not entertained. Crucially, if *James* was indicative of general legal principle at the time, one would have expected the opposite to have been true.

Indeed, even if *James* was rightly decided, and so even if it was true that, at common law, one-sidedness was *sometimes* sufficient to prevent a contract from being formed, that was not the position in equity. There are many cases – including ones decided by Hardwicke LC himself – in which that point was made explicitly.[121] Furthermore, writing in 1793, Fonblanque stated that he '[had] not been able to find a single case'[122] which suggested otherwise.

(ii) The Best Construction of the Lord Chancellor's Words

The best interpretation of Hardwicke LC's description of type two fraud is that the legally operative event in issue was that which could, in some cases, be inferred from, amongst other things, the fact of a one-sided transaction. It therefore covered what has been referred to as the abuse of interpersonal power. Unlike the view just analysed, this construction has the advantage of being more consistent with the words that the Lord Chancellor actually used, as well as fitting with several other leading authorities.

Starting with the judge's words themselves, consider the fact that Hardwicke LC described the type of fraud in issue as that which 'may be apparent from the intrinsic nature and subject of [a] bargain'.[123] The word 'apparent' is significant. Fraud which is apparent from something else is fraud which can be inferred from it. It is *not* constituted by the thing under consideration in and of itself. One who takes the view that entering into a one-sided transaction was, in and of itself, an act of fraud thus leaves no room for the idea that that conduct requires some interpretation. In contrast, this chapter's understanding of this part of the judgment takes that into account. It therefore involves a more complete reading of his words.

[118] W Swain, *The Law of Contract 1670–1870* (Cambridge, Cambridge University Press, 2015) 101–104.
[119] Sheridan (n 18) 168.
[120] *Keen v Stuckely* (1718) Gilb Ch 155, 25 ER 109.
[121] See, eg, *Wood v Fenwick* (1702) Prec Ch 206, 24 ER 100; *Willis* (n 26); *Nichols v Gould* (1752) 2 Ves Sen 422, 28 ER 270; *Heathcote* (n 14); *Griffith* (n 74).
[122] Fonblanque (n 53) 116.
[123] *Chesterfield* (n 13) 2 Ves Sen 155, 28 ER 99.

The second point to keep in mind is the welter of cases decided both before and after *Chesterfield* which are consistent with this view. Think back, for instance, to *Griffith v Spratley*, an authority referred to in Part III.[124] There it was recognised that, as there had been no actual fraud, if the plaintiff was to succeed in getting the deed in issue set aside, he would have to rest his case on 'the … ground of inadequacy of consideration, *or the fraud to be presumed from [it]*'.[125] Ultimately, the Court of Exchequer dismissed his claim. The plaintiff's necessity may well have meant that the wealthy defendant had a (factual) power over him, but 'the consideration [he received] more or less [supported] the contract'.[126] As the Lord Chief Baron stated:

> [While an] inadequacy of price goes a great way in warranting the court to infer … that some sort of fraud was used to draw the other party into the bargain; it [is only when it is combined with other circumstances that] the Court [can] presume more than is in actual proof.[127]

A similar point was made by Thurlow LC in *Fox v Mackreth*, where he said:

> It will be in vain to argue that there was any … fraud committed by [the defendant] if no loss accrued to [the plaintiff]. [However], that does not make an end of the matter, unless the [plaintiff's loss] was procured by [one] of those frauds which the Court has taken notice of.[128]

Ultimately, both these cases support the proposition that, in the absence of deceit, a bill grounded on fraud could still succeed if some other form of fraud could be inferred from, amongst other things, the fact of a one-sided transaction.

(iii) Unpacking Type Three Fraud

(a) Surreptitious Taking of Advantage

When it comes to ascertaining what amounted to type three fraud, the first problem is that Hardwicke LC's words are not just often misreported by the secondary sources, but they are misreported to such an extent that they become incoherent. Consider, for example, Hovenden's proposition that the third category of fraud mentioned in *Chesterfield* was that fraud which may be 'presumed from the circumstances and condition of the parties contracting'.[129]

The issue here is that, aside from raising as many questions as it answers – what circumstances? what conditions? – this interpretation elides the contents of the start of a main clause and the entirety of a subordinate clause so as to produce a corrupt statement of what was actually said. It omits the end of the main clause, which in fact provides substance to the description of the particular type of fraud then under the Lord Chancellor's consideration, and replaces it with words which make a purely procedural

[124] See also *Arglas v Muschampe* (1684) Rep Ch 266, 21 ER 675; *Gartside* (n 88); *Heathcote* (n 14); *Speed v Philips* (1795) 3 Anst 732, 145 ER 1022.
[125] *Griffith* (n 74) 1 Cox Eq Cas 386, 29 ER 1214 (emphasis added).
[126] ibid 1 Cox Eq Cas 388, 29 ER 1215.
[127] ibid 1 Cox Eq Cas 389, 29 ER 1215.
[128] *Fox* (n 49) 2 Bro CC 420–21, 29 ER 234.
[129] J Hovenden, *A General Treatise on the Principles and Practice by Which Courts of Equity Are Guided as to the Prevention or Remedial Correction of Fraud* (London, S Sweet, 1825) 18. See too J Barton, 'The Enforcement of Hard Bargains' (1987) 103 *Law Quarterly Review* 118, 136.

point. Consequently, rather than being told what was covered by this type of fraud – something one could then begin to interpret – one is merely informed of one way in which it could be proven.

In the end, taking into account all of the contents of the main clause, it appears that the third species of fraud identified in *Chesterfield* was, in fact, the 'taking [of a] surreptitious advantage of the weakness or necessity [or ignorance] of another'.[130] As shall be explained, the question is therefore whether this sort of fraud was, in substance, any different to that which could be inferred from, amongst other things, the fact of a one-sided transaction. Furthermore, the best view seems to be that the legally operative event involved in both cases was essentially the same: the abuse of interpersonal power.

As stated in Part II, it is true that as a matter of mid-eighteenth-century equity, some aspects of the abuse of interpersonal power could be inferred from other evidence. Indeed, this is what was being contemplated in cases like *Griffith v Spratley*. Hardwicke LC was therefore entitled to contrast the rules of proof relating to the taking advantage of another's weakness, necessity, or ignorance with the rules of proof relating to deceit. Of course, if the abuse of interpersonal power underpinned more than one of the other species of fraud which the Lord Chancellor identified – which it appears it did – then the fact that a surreptitious taking of advantage could be proven, in part, by inference from other evidence was *not* a defining feature of it. As a result, his Lordship's observations on that matter should be understood as made in addition to, not in lieu of, a substantive description of the legally operative occurrence type three fraud involved.

(b) Alternative Analyses

Various attempts have been made to sub-categorise the mass of cases which fall to be considered under Hardwicke LC's third head of fraud. In doing so, each one suggests – contrary to this chapter's position – that they were not all underpinned by the same one principle.

Sheridan, for example, devised what was formally a three-part scheme. He viewed the authorities as concerning one of 'undue influence', 'breach of fiduciary duty', or the 'taking [of an] advantage of weakness [or] necessity'.[131] To his mind, his last category was characterised by the fact that, in the cases which fell within it, 'there [had been] no [pre-existing] relation between the parties apart from the transaction impeached'.[132] In contrast, the first and second groups both concerned actions which occurred between people who shared relationships predating events.[133] The specific distinction between 'undue influence' and 'breach of fiduciary duty' is harder to pin down, as Sheridan himself admitted. The former, he stated, was no more than a subtype of the latter, limited to certain factually distinct acts of 'abuse of confidence'.[134] The latter covered all those 'remaining kinds of breach of fiduciary duty which [were] termed fraudulent'.[135]

[130] *Chesterfield* (n 13) 2 Ves Sen 156, 28 ER 99.
[131] Sheridan (n 18) 71.
[132] ibid 71.
[133] ibid 87.
[134] ibid 87.
[135] ibid 107.

In substance, then, they were the same and so for present purposes can be evaluated together.

Ashburner's analysis is premised on a sharp distinction between cases of 'fraud'[136] on the one hand and cases of what he calls 'undue influence'[137] and 'conflict of interest and duty'[138] on the other. What is more, he ascribes different and independent juridical bases to each of these concepts. Thus, while he thought that Hardwicke LC's judgment in *Chesterfield* covered 'fraud', he did not think that it touched either cases of undue influence or conflict of interest. As it happens, within his treatment of 'fraud', Ashburner *did* correctly consider that 'the second and third heads under which Lord Hardwicke LC arranged cases [were] properly considered together'.[139] Yet his discussion of both of those two kinds of fraud only refers to cases in which the court's focus was on whether there was a one-sided transaction. In other words, no true cases of type three fraud are mentioned. Further, when they *are* finally considered, type three fraud authorities are all said to involve either undue influence or a conflict of interest (and so are ascribed some other legal basis).

It is this chapter's argument that, for two reasons, both of these attempted classifications should be rejected. The first is that, properly understood, the cases which they purport to explain do not, in fact, conform to them. The second is that the same cases also indicate that the judges took exactly the opposite approach. They actively eschewed the sub-categorisation of cases, instead preferring to focus on the underlying question of principle before them. Indeed, these authorities thereby also add weight to this chapter's own analysis of type three fraud cases. The only principle the courts seem to refer to is, in substance, the abuse of interpersonal power.

(c) Unsatisfactory Explanations

The first reason for thinking that taking advantage of another's weakness, necessity, or ignorance was no more than the abuse of interpersonal power is that attempts to substantively sub-categorise the cases which involved it have failed to produce a convincing account of the law. This is because the true principle upon which each was decided was that which proscribed the abuse of interpersonal power, and so no further coherent division of them is possible.

Recall Ashburner's analysis. He explained all those cases concerning type three fraud on the basis of something substantively different to that which he said underpinned those involving type two. To his mind, they each turned on either 'undue influence' or 'conflict of interest and duty'. The problem is that these definitions are inconsistent with the authorities. The concepts they rest upon were not ones recognised by the judges.

Consider, for example, *Norton v Relly*.[140] It is a classic type three fraud case involving the taking of a surreptitious advantage of another's weakness. However, Ashburner

[136] W Ashburner, *Principles of Equity* (London, Butterworth & Co, 1902) 396.
[137] ibid 411.
[138] ibid 421.
[139] ibid 404.
[140] *Norton v Relly* (1764) 2 Eden 286, 28 ER 908.

did not think it was what he called a 'fraud' authority at all. Instead, he regarded it as one involving 'undue influence' and said it was decided according to the principle that:

> If A obtains any benefit from B, … by exerting an influence over B, which … prevents B from exercising an independent judgment in the matter in question, B can set aside the [transaction].[141]

Unfortunately, not only is it indisputable that the plaintiff in *Norton* based her bill on fraud, but it is also clear that it was the fact of at least one genuine type of fraud on the part of the defendant which grounded the judge's decision in her favour. Ashburner's explanation is therefore neither necessary nor sufficient to account for its outcome.

The facts of the case were as follows. The plaintiff was a wealthy unmarried woman from Leeds. The defendant was an itinerant preacher. They largely communicated by way of letter. Over time, the defendant convinced the plaintiff to join his congregation, and, for some years thereafter, the plaintiff made several gifts in his favour. Chief amongst these was an annuity worth £50. Eventually, the plaintiff came to regret her actions and sought relief.

Northington LC decreed that the defendant 'execute a release … of [his] annuity, and deliver up the deed [which created] it'.[142] He stated unequivocally that it 'was obtained [in] circumstances of the greatest fraud [and] imposition … that could be'.[143] In addition, this was not just because the defendant had committed actual fraud – there *was* evidence of knowingly made misrepresentations – but because he was also guilty of committing what this chapter has labelled an abuse of interpersonal power. The Lord Chancellor's reasoning on this second point was as follows:

1) Before the parties met, the plaintiff was a great religious 'enthusiast', but, although 'she was far gone', she was 'not gone far enough for [the defendant's] purpose'.[144]
2) When the defendant wrote, as he did in one letter, that 'your former pastor has … excommunicated you; but let not these things discourage you, … put yourself in my congregation, wherein dwells the fulness of God',[145] this was the start of a deliberate attempt to establish a (factual) power over the plaintiff.
3) This process was 'advanced step by step, and [she] imbibed his doctrines till she became quite intoxicated … with his madness and enthusiasm'.[146]
4) The plaintiff then started making what were sometimes expressly solicited gifts in favour of the defendant. Indeed, at least once, the defendant wrote that they were accepted 'in the name of [the] Saviour'.[147]
5) The defendant was thus 'a subtle sectary, who [preyed] upon his deluded hearers, and [robbed] them under the mask of religion'.[148]

This is, in substance, an abuse of interpersonal power analysis. Before they met, the plaintiff, although to some degree already vulnerable, was not under the defendant's

[141] Ashburner (n 136) 411.
[142] *Norton v Relly* (n 144) 291.
[143] ibid 291.
[144] ibid 289.
[145] ibid 289.
[146] ibid 289.
[147] ibid 290.
[148] ibid 289.

control. The defendant then initiated a process of establishing a power over her, and when that process was complete, she was rendered vulnerable to him. Unusually, there was also *direct* evidence from the defendant's own letters that he exercised his power in his own favour at various times. There was therefore no need to infer the fact of a causal link between the one-sided transaction in issue and the defendant's use of his influence. He manifestly procured her entry into a string of one-sided transactions which she would otherwise not have engaged in by way of various of his letters.

A second case for which Ashburner cannot properly account is *Whitackre v Whitackre*.[149] The best view is that it involved type three fraud: an idiosyncratic instance of a defendant knowingly taking advantage of another's (legal) weakness and therefore the abuse of interpersonal power. However, Ashburner did not believe it involved 'fraud', constructive or otherwise, at all. Instead, he considered it to have turned on the application of a wholly different principle: 'The desire to prevent a person from burdening his [own] conscience by the acquisition of property to which in conscience he has no right.'[150]

The defendant was the plaintiffs' agent, tasked with selling their stock. He arranged to sell it to a third party, but then exercised his power of disposal in his own favour for £600 less. He later passed on the stock to the third party for the price he had originally agreed with them, thereby making himself a £600 profit. The plaintiffs brought a bill seeking an account, and King LC allowed it. He stated:

> No trustee, or any person acting [in a similar capacity such as an agent,] can ever be a purchaser in this Court, on account of the great inlet to fraud.[151]

What really mattered in this case was that, by virtue of being an agent, the defendant had a (legal) power over the plaintiffs to cause them to enter into contracts. In exercising that power in his own favour, and therefore by locking them into a contract for £600 less than he might have, the defendant caused them to enter a one-sided transaction. He was therefore guilty of a textbook abuse of interpersonal power.

Sheridan's view on this material is similarly limited. The key distinction on which it rests: that between cases involving the taking advantage of weakness or necessity and cases involving a so-called breach of fiduciary duty, also fails to reflect the reasoning employed in the cases and so cannot adequately account for their results. Put simply, it does not appear that the fact that there was a pre-existing relationship between the parties was relevant to the disposal of a genuine type three fraud case.

Consider, for example, *Bennet v Vade*,[152] which Sheridan cited as an example of 'taking advantage of mental weakness', and *Clarkson v Hanway*,[153] said to involve 'undue influence'. As a matter of law, it is hard to see a meaningful difference between them. In *Bennet*, there was no pre-existing relationship between the parties. However, the court was happy to cast the defendant's conduct as 'undue influence'.[154] Indeed,

[149] *Whitackre v Whitackre* (1725) Sel Cas Ch 13, 25 ER 195.
[150] Ashburner (n 136) 421.
[151] *Whitackre* (n 149) Sel Cas Ch 13, 25 ER 196.
[152] *Bennet v Vade* (1742) 2 Atk 324, 26 ER 597.
[153] *Clarkson v Hanway* (1723) 2 P Wms 203, 24 ER 700.
[154] *Bennet* (n 152) 2 Atk 327, 26 ER 599.

that act is entirely consistent with various other contemporary decisions,[155] such that one might think that, at the time, that term was used only to describe certain factually similar instances of constructive fraud. In substance, the case was decided solely on abuse of interpersonal power terms. Hardwicke LC held that the plaintiff entered the one-sided transaction in issue because of 'the power [the defendant] had over him'.[156]

Conversely, in *Clarkson*, although one of the defendants was the victim's brother, it is not clear that their pre-existing relationship had any particular impact on the judge's reasoning. In setting aside the transaction in issue, Jekyll MR focused on the fact that there was 'proof that [the victim] was a weak man and easily to be imposed upon'.[157] Furthermore, it was for this reason that he found not just against the victim's brother but also a second defendant whom the victim had never previously met. Although potentially relevant for factual classificatory purposes, then, the fact there was a pre-existing relationship between the victim and one of the defendants seems to have been irrelevant as a matter of law.

(d) The Judges' Own Views

The second reason for rejecting any attempt to sub-categorise type three fraud cases is that, along with failing to conform to any other analyses, many cases positively eschew those analyses. There are therefore authorities which provide both negative and positive reasons for rejecting views like Ashburner's and Sheridan's. Ultimately, it appears that the judges had little regard for anything beyond the underlying question of principle in each case. They routinely spurned the chance to engage in any form of substantive sub-categorisation. Indeed, it is in this light that one can make sense of Hardwicke LC's otherwise puzzling comment, in *Thornhill v Evans* that:

> Where there is an act of extortion, this court will decree a refunding without inquiring into the particular circumstances of imposition.[158]

Further, the relevant cases are in fact doubly instructive. They also directly support this chapter's analysis of type three fraud. This is because, in substance, the single principle the judges return to again and again is the abuse of interpersonal power.

Of course, none of this is to say that previous decisions were never cited to – or even occasionally analysed by – the courts. They were. However, even then, the judges usually resisted the temptation to go farther. A clear example of this comes from Hardwicke LC's judgment in *Barnardiston v Lingood*.[159] During the course of argument, several allegedly analogous cases were cited, but, although he referred to them, it seems that the Lord Chancellor did so only out of courtesy to counsel. In substance, his focus was on the question of principle, not precedent, and it seems plain that he was interested

[155] See, eg, *Morris v Burroughs* (1737) 1 Atk 399, 26 ER 253; *Cocking v Pratt* (1750) 1 Ves Sen 400, 27 ER 1105.
[156] *Bennet* (n 152) 2 Atk 327, 26 ER 599.
[157] *Clarkson* (n 157) 2 P Wms 204, 24 ER 701.
[158] *Thornhill v Evans* (1742) 2 Atk 330, 331; 26 ER 601, 601.
[159] *Barnardiston v Lingood* (1740) 2 Atk 133, 26 ER 484. See too *Walmesley v Booth* (1739) 2 Atk 25, 29; 26 ER 412, 414.

in whether the facts of the case before him disclosed an abuse of interpersonal power. Consider, for example, the following passage:

> Without doubt, there are all the material ingredients in this case, as well as in those which have been cited: … *Comes Arglasse [v] Muschamp*, … *Berney [v] Pitt* … and *Knot [v] Johnson and Graham*, … to set aside this agreement as a catching bargain, against a necessitous and improvident heir. The very advancing [of] money in such small sums as has been done in the present case, [shows] the [plaintiff] to be in the utmost distress. … *But what the Court is guided by in all these cases is the taking an undue advantage of an heir's being in distressed and necessitous circumstances; and this is the principal ground of these decrees.*[160]

As Croft has noted, the decisions the Lord Chancellor cited were 'neither essential to, nor used as authorities for, any proposition [which formed] part of [his] reasoning process; they were merely [used to provide] analogies'.[161]

Now there *are* a handful of cases which point the other way. In them, when considering a mass of authorities, the judges occasionally referred to certain similar types of decision by reference to the factual nature of the abuse of interpersonal power within them. Indeed, as was hinted at above while discussing *Bennet v Vade*, it seems that this is how the term 'undue influence' first came into being. Yet, notwithstanding this behaviour, it must be recognised that even then the judges did *not* engage in any substantive sub-classifications of the authorities. Even if they *could* be sorted into certain factual types, the type three fraud cases constituting each of those categories turned on the same one legally operative occurrence. In *Blunden v Hester*,[162] for example, Parker LC specifically rejected counsel's attempt to sub-categorise the proceedings as necessarily involving 'the awe [a child] was presumed to have of his parent'.[163] Instead, he insisted on applying what were, in substance, abuse of interpersonal power rules. 'I do not see the argument from the father's power over the child to be of any weight', his Lordship explained, 'for if it should ever appear that this power has been abused, a court of equity would certainly set aside the [transaction in issue].'[164]

This approach fits in well with the general nature of all the reasons given for rejecting bills brought on the basis of constructive fraud discussed so far. They were not formalistic – 'the facts of this case are not those of a typical undue influence case etc.' – but substantive. They were consistently focussed on the fact that, whatever the circumstances of the case, there was no abuse of interpersonal power by the defendant.[165]

(iv) Conclusions

In the end, it seems that both type two and type three fraud cases concerned the same one ground of intervention, and, in substance, that ground of intervention was what this chapter has been calling the abuse of interpersonal power. Indeed, there is simply

[160] *Barnardiston* (n 159) 2 Atk 135, 26 ER 484 (emphasis added).
[161] Croft (n 70) 145.
[162] *Blunden v Hester* (1720) 1 P Wms 634, 24 ER 548.
[163] ibid 1 P Wms 639, 24 ER 549.
[164] ibid 1 P Wms 639–640, 24 ER 550.
[165] See, eg, *Duke of Hamilton v Lord Mohun* (1710) 1 P Wms 118, 24 ER 319, which does not fit easily into any factual category, but which clearly involved an abuse of interpersonal power.

no other coherent way of accounting for either of them. It therefore makes sense to describe both those species of fraud, plus all type five fraud cases (except insofar as any may *also* have concerned deceit), as constituting the law of constructive fraud. As said above, while they would occasionally involve instances of either type one or type four fraud, even in the absence of deceit, type five fraud cases *always* entailed a context-specific act of *both* type two *and* type three fraud.

Cases of type two fraud *did* differ from those of type three fraud. In the latter, the courts focused more on whether the defendant had a power over the plaintiff, and less on whether there was a one-sided transaction. In the former, the emphasis of this inquiry was reversed. Nevertheless, properly understood, all the authorities seem to show that, in the absence of actual fraud, in order to obtain relief on the basis of fraud in its jurisdictional sense, a plaintiff had to establish a causal link between an exercise of a power on the part of the defendant and his own entry into a one-sided transaction. Moreover, this means that, omitting (once again) type five fraud cases which *also* involved actual fraud, the second diagram set out above can be reworked as follows:

Table 15.3

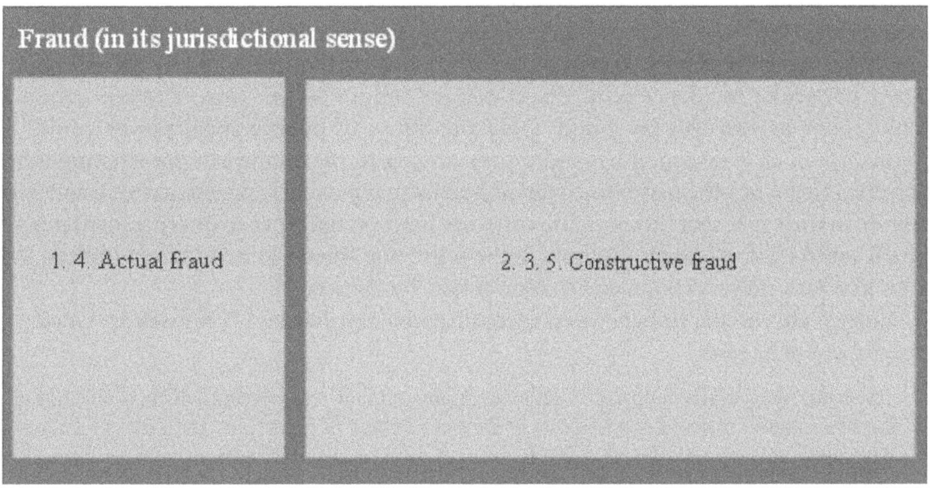

V. Lord Hardwicke's Letter

The most fundamental challenge to the type of analysis just advanced is probably the argument that, in the second half of the eighteenth century, the concept of 'constructive fraud' was not, in fact, fixed and determinable at all. Instead, it is suggested that the judges did not have a particularised understanding of that concept, nor did they wish to develop one. Indeed, if this were true, then no attempt to distil any principled basis for the court's intervention in cases which allegedly involved such conduct would be possible. However, there is good reason to doubt its veracity. All turns on the evidence which is usually cited in support of that proposition.

Consider, for example, Croft's work on this subject. Relying on a letter sent by Lord Hardwicke to Lord Kames in 1759, he has claimed that 'there were no rules laid down in relation to [any kind of] fraud for fear of assisting its perpetrators'.[166] In the letter, responding to the question of 'whether a court of equity ought to be governed by any general rules?',[167] and with a particular eye on the giving of 'relief against frauds',[168] the then-retired Lord Chancellor stated:

> No invariable rules can be established. Fraud is infinite, and were a court of equity … to lay down rules [saying] how far they would go … in extending their relief against it, or to define strictly the species … of it, the jurisdiction would be cramped, and perpetually eluded by new schemes which the fertility of man's invention would contrive.[169]

At first blush, much of this passage might seem to contradict this chapter's central thesis. After all, fraud – and, within it, constructive fraud – cannot simultaneously be both infinite and cover a limited number of grounds for judicial intervention. Nevertheless, properly understood, there is nothing in the text which should raise any genuine concerns. Lord Hardwicke's words are actually consistent with the claim, set out above, that the eighteenth-century courts of equity's jurisdiction over constructive fraud was limited to dealing with misconduct falling within the scope of the three requirements which have been identified.

Ultimately, if one accepts that constructive fraud covered *only* the abuse of interpersonal power, the letter upon which Croft puts so much weight can be read as referring simply to the *form* of such conduct. It should not be thought to go to the *substance* of any particular incidence of it. Fraud was *not* infinite in the sense that *any* conduct could count as constructive fraud. Only the abuse of interpersonal power could.[170] Nevertheless, as it extended beyond power arising in the context of pre-existing relationships (legal or otherwise) to cover ad hoc factual powers,[171] constructive fraud *was* infinite in the sense that there was no inherent limit on the types of interpersonal power which could exist. It was also infinite in the sense that there was no inherent limit to the ways in which powers could, as a matter of fact, be abused.[172]

Indeed, this seems to have been recognised by Hardwicke LC himself in *Lawley v Hooper* where he said:

> The court very wisely hath never laid down any general rule beyond which it will not go, *lest other means of avoiding the equity of the court should be found out*: Therefore they always determine upon the particular circumstances of each case; and wherever they have found the least tincture of fraud …, relief hath always been given.[173]

[166] Croft (n 70) 129.

[167] AF Tytler, *Memoirs of the Life and Writings of the Honourable Henry Home, Lord Kames*, 2nd edn (Edinburgh, T Cadell and W Stevens, 1814) vol 1, 338.

[168] ibid 341.

[169] ibid 341. For a judicial pronouncement to the same effect, albeit one made after the period under consideration, see Lord Wynford's judgement in *Blachford v Christian* (1829) 1 Kn 73, 81. However, for doubts as to its accuracy, see M Macnair, 'Sham: Early Uses and Related and Unrelated Doctrines' in E Simpson and M Stewart (eds), *Sham Transactions* (Oxford, Oxford University Press, 2013) 47–48.

[170] Indeed, recall the two categories of cases referred to in Part II, Section A, which show that, in the period under consideration, fraud in its jurisdictional sense was a firmly limited concept.

[171] Recall, eg, *Bennet* (n 156); *Clarkson* (n 157); *Griffith* (n 74).

[172] Indeed, this seems to be the point being made (with respect to late Victorian law) by Lord MacNaghten in *Reddaway v Banham* [1896] AC 199, 221.

[173] *Lawley v Hooper* (1745) 3 Atk 278, 279; 26 ER 962, 962 (emphasis added).

Likewise, as Fonblanque's treatise noted:

> Even in cases of fraud, *which from their nature must be almost infinitely various in their circumstances*, courts of equity constantly proceed upon some clear and established principle, sufficiently comprehensive to meet the circumstances of the particular case to which it is applied, and not upon a vague … and indefinite power.[174]

VI. Conclusion: The Decline and Fall of Constructive Fraud's Mid-Eighteenth Century Meaning

The unitary doctrine of constructive fraud described above lived on past the end of the eighteenth century. There are decisions right up to the 1830s which turn solely on the presence or absence of an abuse of interpersonal power.[175] However, beginning in the 1830s and over a period of approximately 50 years, the idea that all cases of fraud which did not involve actual fraud were regulated by the same one set of rules was almost entirely abandoned. What is more, several new, smaller, and substantively distinct doctrines arose to replace it. These included early versions of the law of fiduciaries and the law of undue influence.[176]

What happened was that, over time, the judges abandoned their old practice of refusing to turn various formal distinctions between constructive fraud cases into substantive ones. They therefore began to create the sort of legally operative subcategories which they had previously refused to create, and one consequence of this was that substantive differences between the rules thought to apply to each particular group of authorities began to emerge.[177]

As the switchover from constructive fraud to the various new and more discrete doctrines just referred to was not instantaneous, it is possible to find several examples of cases decided in old-fashioned abuse of interpersonal power terms, even though at the time they were heard alternative rules might have been thought to apply to them.[178] Yet these were the last of a dying breed, and it is hard to find any such authorities after the 1860s. Use of the term fraud to describe what was going on in cases which did not involve actual fraud but which did feature certain other legally operative occurrences which would previously have been classified as constructive fraud – not

[174] Fonblanque (n 53) 24 (emphasis added).

[175] See, eg, *Lady Ormond v Hutchinson* (1806) 13 Ves Jun 47, 33 ER 212; *Fawcett v Whitehouse* (1829) 1 Russ & M 132, 39 ER 51; *Hichens v Congreve* (1831) 4 Sim 420, 58 ER 157; *Dent v Bennett* (1835) 7 Sim 539, 58 ER 944.

[176] There was also a new law of duress and of unconscionable bargains: see, eg, *Parker v Clarke* (1861) 30 Beav 54, 54 ER 809; Sheridan (n 18) 132–144. In *Williams v Bayley* (1866) LR 1 HL 200, the former was assimilated into undue influence and so ceased to have any independent presence within English equity. A version of the latter still exists today, see J McGhee (ed), *Snell's Equity*, 34th edn (London, Sweet & Maxwell, 2019) 8-040–8-045.

[177] See, eg, *Wood v Rowcliffe* (1847) 2 Ph 382, 41 ER 990; *Barker v Harrison* (1846) 2 Coll 546, 63 ER 854; *Aberdeen Railway Co v Blaikie Brothers* [1843-60] All ER Rep 249, 149 RR 32 (all on fiduciaries); *Cooke v Lamotte* (1851) 15 Beav 234, 51 ER 527; *Smith v Kay* (1859) 7 HL Cas 750, 11 ER 299; *Re Holmes' Estate* (1861) 3 Giff 337, 66 ER 439 (all on undue influence).

[178] See, eg, *Clark v Malpas* (1862) 31 Beav 80, 54 ER 1067; *Baker v Monk* (1864) 33 Beav 419, 55 ER 430; *Summers v Griffiths* (1865) 35 Beav 27, 55 ER 804.

least what is nowadays called breach of fiduciary duty – *did* persist, albeit not in a particularly widespread way.[179] Furthermore, that habit was in no way designed to mask the true nature of the claims in relation to which the label fraud was then invoked. It was merely a convenient and historically pertinent synonym. In the end, then, it is perhaps unsurprising that the label constructive fraud has come to have the meaning it nowadays carries. The collapse of the eighteenth-century definition of the term constructive fraud and the coordinated rise of the law of fiduciaries and the law of undue influence and so on mean that they are genuinely its successors in law.

[179] See, eg, *Panama and South Pacific Telegraph Co v India Rubber, Gutta Percha, and Telegraph Works Co* (1874-75) LR 10 Ch App 515; *Bannister v Bannister* [1948] 2 All ER 133; *Pallant v Morgan* [1953] Ch 43.

16

Family Trustees and their Duties, c. 1740–1820

MICHAEL LOBBAN

I. Introduction

Eighteenth-century propertied families routinely made provision for their members through settlements and wills, which placed property in the hands of trustees. On the face of it, there were perhaps not many attractions to being a trustee: not only was it unremunerated, but it carried considerable risks for those who acted in breach of trust. It is therefore worth exploring how onerous the tasks of a trustee of family property were, and how active such trustees were expected to be. For Victorian Englishmen, it has been suggested, trusteeship was regarded as a moral duty, in the exercise of which trustees were 'expected to devote themselves wholeheartedly to the well-being and security of their beneficiaries'. In this era, family trustees looking after investments for middle-class widows and children had to devote much time to managing the trusts and were given a great degree of discretion in how they provided for their beneficiaries. The relationship between trustee and beneficiary at this time was (as its historian puts it) 'quasi-parental'.[1] In what follows, it will be suggested that in the Georgian era – when the paradigm family trust was an aristocratic landed one rather than a middle-class moneyed one – the burdens of family trusteeship were often rather lighter, and trustees had less room to exercise discretion.

As shall be seen, in many situations, while the trust was an essential vehicle to preserve, secure and transmit family property, the trustees themselves had few functions beyond being stakeholders. In many situations, it did not matter who the trustee was, provided that there was one, for control of the property itself remained in family hands. Besides such 'passive' functions, family trustees also had the more active role of raising and distributing money, particularly to pay off debts on a family estate or to provide jointures for widows

[1] C Stebbings, *The Private Trustee in Victorian England* (Cambridge, Cambridge University Press, 2002) 4, 8–9, 63. On the changes in family trusts between the eighteenth and nineteenth centuries, see MR Chesterman, 'Family Settlements on Trust: Landowners and the Rising Bourgeoisie' in GR Rubin and D Sugarman (eds), *Law, Economy and Society: Essays in the History of English Law, 1750-1914* (Abingdon, Professional Books, 1984) 124–67.

and portions for children. However, even in these areas, the room for trustees to exercise discretion was often quite limited. They were expected to ensure that the property in their hands remained intact and secure, and to make payments as directed under the settlement. The trust relationship was therefore more often a business relationship than a personal one, and there were high risks if a trustee went out of his way to help family members, in a way which jeopardised the fund for later generations.

Trustees were often lawyers or men of business. When Lady Mary O'Brien, daughter of the Earl of Inchiquin, married the son of the Earl of Shelburne, the articles of agreement provided for money to be raised to pay off her father's debts. The trustees of the settlement – who were also made trustees of a term of years to pay the debts – were the law agents of the respective parties.[2] In such cases, the intention was that these trustees, active in the financial affairs of the family, would perform the necessary tasks – of paying the debts – in a short time. Where there were fewer tasks to perform (as with trustees to preserve contingent remainders), it did not much matter who was trustee. As Lord Mansfield pointed out in 1785, Sir Edward Northey's clerk, Mr Green, 'was trustee of near half of the great estates in the kingdom; on his death it was not known who was his heir or representative'.[3] As this last comment shows, the trust might be executed not by the original trustees, but by the heirs or executors of the last surviving trustee.[4]

It often happened that the representative of the only surviving trustee – and consequently the only remaining trustee – was an infant or a lunatic. Since infants could not convey land, legislation was passed in 1708 to enable *cestuis que trust* to petition the court to direct a conveyance to be made of real property held by infant trustees or mortgagees.[5] Similar legislation was passed in 1731 to allow conveyances where the trustee had been found a lunatic.[6] The legislation did not solve all problems posed by the existence of such trustees, for until legislation was passed in 1825 to reform this,[7] the court would only act if the infant trustee had no duties to perform in executing the trust and had no beneficial interest of his own.[8] To fall within the legislation, the infant had to be a 'mere naked trustee'.[9] A trust coupled with a power of sale was therefore not

[2] *Shelburne v Inchiquin* (1784) 1 Bro CC 338, 28 ER 1166. See Stebbings (n 1) 22–24 on the choice of trustees (particularly noting the use of family friends and relations).

[3] *Doe d Bristow v Pegge* (1785) 1 TR 760n, 99 ER 1362n. Northey was Attorney-General in the reigns of William and Anne and he counted the Duke of Marlborough among his clients: S Handley, 'Northey, Sir Edward (1652-1723)' Oxford Dictionary of National Biography (Oxford University Press, 2004) doi.org/10.1093/ref:odnb/20330; AT Thomson, *Memoirs of Sarah Duchess of Marlborough and of the Court of Queen Anne* (London, H Colburn, 1839) vol 2, 339.

[4] In addition, as Lord Eldon explained, 'wherever a trust is created, and the execution of that trust fails, by the death of the trustee or by accident, this Court will execute the trust': *Brown v Higgs* (1801, 1803) 8 Ves Jun 561, 570; 32 ER 473, 476.

[5] 7 Ann, c 19.

[6] 4 Geo II, c 10. For this remedy to be available, the trustee's incapacity had to have been determined by a commission of lunacy, and not simply by the Master: *ex parte Gillam* (1795) 2 Ves Jun 587, 30 ER 790.

[7] 6 Geo IV, c 74, s 10. Both the original act and the consolidating one were held to apply only to express trusts, and not to constructive trusts: see *Dew v Clarke* (1828) 4 Russ 511, 514; 38 ER 898, 899.

[8] *Hawkins v Obeen* (1754) 2 Ves Sen 559, 28 ER 356.

[9] *Ex parte Swann* (1791) Dickens 749, 750; 21 ER 462, 462. According to Lord Eldon, he had to be 'a trustee without interest and without duties, for the simple purpose of parting with the estate': *Ex parte Tutin* (1811) 3 V & B 149, 150; 35 ER 435, 435 (referring to 4 Geo 2, c 10, which applied the same procedure in cases of lunatics). According to Sir Richard Arden MR, 'An infant trustee is never ordered to convey to another trustee upon trusts to be executed': *Ex parte Anderson* (1800) 5 Ves Jun 240, 243; 31 ER 566, 567.

regarded as falling within the Act.[10] In such cases, conveyances could not be completed until the trustee came of age. The trustee here had nothing substantial to do, but had to have the capacity to execute the formalities.

In what follows, we will explore some of the aspects of family trusteeship. As shall be seen, in many instances, trustees had no duties to perform at all, but were 'dry' trustees, only called upon to act (if ever) at the behest of the *cestui que trust*, and sometimes for formal purposes only. We shall then turn to different aspects of more active trusteeship, to explore how far the trustees were constrained in their powers, and to see how far their functions went beyond being mere stakeholders.

II. 'Dry' Trustees

In many family settlements, the trustees had no active duties to perform, but were 'mere naked trustees' (like the infants described above) or 'dry trustee[s], having no interest in the subject'.[11] A 'dry' trust was one where the legal estate was vested in the trustee, but the entire beneficial interest rested in another. According to James Hill, the duties of 'dry' trustees were straightforward:

> 1st, to permit the *cestui que trust* to have the beneficial enjoyment of the estate, by receiving the income and other profits arising from it. – 2nd, To execute such conveyances and dispositions as the *cestui que trust* may direct. – 3rd, To defend the title of his *cestui que trust* in any court of law or equity, or at any rate to suffer his name to be made use of for that purpose.[12]

'Dry' trustees could therefore be compelled to make conveyances of the legal estate, for instance to purchasers from the equitable tenant (when it was necessary for the trustee to join in making a title)[13] or to those who had acquired the right to the inheritance.[14]

In the 'driest' of trusts, where the trustees had no duties to perform, the trust might be regarded as executed by the Statute of Uses 1536, giving the *cestui que trust* a legal estate. This problem did not arise when settlements were made by deed, since conveyancers could easily evade the Statute by adding 'three words to a conveyance'.[15] Since common law courts did not recognise a use on a use, and only executed the first use, the Statute could be evaded by conveying land to the trustees

[10] *Ex parte Chasteney* (1821) Jacob 56, 37 ER 771. *Cf* R Preston, *An Essay in a Course of Lectures on Abstracts of Title* (London, W Clarke and Sons, 1811) vol 1, 320–21. See also *Riggs v Sykes* (1768) Dickens 400, 21 ER 325, where the Lord Chancellor decreed that the infant trustee should convey the land contracted to be sold when of age, and that in the meantime the purchaser could enjoy the property.

[11] Lord Eldon's phrase in *Anonymous v Handcock* (1810) 17 Ves 383, 384; 34 ER 148, 148.

[12] J Hill, *A Practical Treatise on the Law relating to Trustees* (London, V & R Stephens and G Norton, 1845) 308. This followed William Cruise's summary that 'pernancy of the profits, execution of estates, and defence of the land, are the three great properties of a trust': *A Digest of the Laws of England respecting Real Property*, 2nd edn (London, J Butterworth, 1818) vol 1, 524.

[13] eg, *Jones v Lewis* (1786) 1 Cox CC 199, 29 ER 1127.

[14] *Carteret v Carteret* (1723) 2 P Wms 132, 24 ER 670; *Willis v Hiscox* (1839) 4 Myl & Cr 197, 41 ER 78, where the plaintiff's mother (who had a life estate only) had suffered a recovery and resettled the estate (under which a remote interest was limited to the surviving trustee): here the trustee was compelled to convey to the son.

[15] *Hopkins v Hopkins* (1738) 1 Atk 581, 591; 26 ER 365, 372 (Lord Hardwicke).

'to use of' the same trustees, in trust for the beneficiary, whose interests would be protected in Chancery.[16] However, testators intending to leave property in trust did not always use such formulations. In the case of settlements under wills, the question was therefore raised whether the trust created by the will was executed by the Statute. Beneficiaries sometimes sought to establish that the trust had been executed, in order to allow them to dispose of the estate. This can be seen from *Broughton v Langley* in 1703, in which Chief Justice Holt held that a devise to trustees to permit George Ramsden, the testator's son, to receive the profits for his life, and then to stand seised to the use of the heirs of his body, was a trust executed by the statute.[17] This meant that the son had an estate tail (by the rule in *Shelley's case*) which he could bar. Whether the trust was in fact executed might be a difficult question, depending on the court's view of whether the trustees had any duties to perform.[18] In 1728, Lord King LC distinguished between cases where the trustees were to permit the *cestui que trust* to *receive* the rents (in which case the trust was executed) and those where they were to *pay over* the rents (in which case it was not).[19] The distinction could be a fine one, not least if a testator had used both formulations in the same will.[20]

Nor was the trust regarded as executed if the trustees could be seen to have had any kind of discretion. Courts were sometimes keen to find such discretion, even if it had never been exercised. For instance, in 1788, the King's Bench had to consider the 1732 will of Samuel Wilson, who had devised his land, first, to trustees to pay the rents of the estate for the subsistence and maintenance of his son John for life, and, then, to the heirs of John's body. John had aliened the land in his lifetime (after suffering a fine, assuming the trust to have been executed), and after his death, his son sought to recover it. Ashhurst J held the trust not executed, since he thought the testator had intended to give the trustees some discretion, by directing them to use the rents for his 'subsistence and maintenance'. Noting that John might have proved dissolute and extravagant, and squandered his money in gaming, Ashhurst J thought his father 'seems to have had some jealousy of his son's conduct, and to have wished that the trustees should have an eye to the application of the money'.[21] The case came to court 36 years after John had levied the fine, and two years after his own death: what was at issue here was not the conduct of the trustees – who do not seem to have played any active part in managing the estate – but John's property rights.

[16] See AWB Simpson, *A History of the Land Law*, 2nd edn (Oxford, Oxford University Press, 1986) 204–6. See also *Doe d Lloyd v Passingham* (1827) 6 B & C 305, 108 ER 465.

[17] *Broughton v Langley* (1703) 2 Salk 679, 91 ER 577; 1 Eq Ca Ab 383, 21 ER 1119.

[18] eg, *Shapland v Smith* (1780) 1 Bro CC 75, 28 ER 994.

[19] *Jones v Lord Say and Seal* (1728) 1 Eq Ca Ab 384, 21 ER 1119, more fully reported in 8 Vin Ab 262, pl 19. In this case, the trustees were to pay the surplus after paying annuities. It was also argued that this 'was a Trust for her separate Benefit, and for the Benefit of the Annuitants, and to construe it an Use executed would subject it to the Power and Controul of her Husband, contrary to the plain intent of the Testatrix' (8 Vin Ab 263).

[20] See *Doe d Leicester v Biggs* (1809) 2 Taunt 109, 127 ER 1017. If trustees were to 'receive and pay over' the profits or rents to another, it was settled that the trust was not executed by the statute: Eq Ca Ab 383n, 21 ER 1119, 2 *Comm* 336.

[21] *Silvester d Law v Wilson* (1788) 2 TR 444, 451; 100 ER 239, 243.

III. Trustees for Terms of Years

Family settlements often settled property on trustees for a term of years, to secure particular payments, such as an annuity or a jointure, or the payment of debts. The duty of these trustees was to make sure the money was paid, but it was usually left to the tenant to make the actual payments. In such cases, the estate subject to these charges generally remained in the possession of the tenant for life or in tail, with the trustees only expected to intervene if the payments were not made. The trustees' role here was again largely passive: they were in effect appointed to secure the interest of the annuitants, in case of default in payment. As Lord Eldon explained in 1820, though the trustee in such cases had the legal right to the estate, he had no right to make use of it until the tenant failed to make the payments due. Once this happened, however, the trustee was able to enter into possession, managing the estate and receiving the rents, to pay to the annuitant.[22] However, since annuitants were generally given their own remedies for late payment in the form of powers of distress and a right of entry after failure of payments, it was not essential for the trustees to intervene, and their attempt to do so might be resisted by the *cestuis que trust*.

Where terms of years were created for a particular purpose, the purpose for which the trust was created might be satisfied after a period of time, as where an annuity, jointure or portion had been paid. Equally, long terms of years might have been carved out of an estate to make provisions which turned out to be unnecessary: for instance, property might have been allocated to make provision for children who were never born. If there was no proviso in the original settlement for the term to cease,[23] it remained vested in the termor, as trustee for the owner of the inheritance. The outstanding term did not merge in the inheritance but would be attendant on the inheritance. In such cases, the trustee's duties were very limited: they were 'mainly to suffer his name to be used by the owner of the inheritance in any action at law respecting the title, and to assign or dispose of the term according to the requisitions of the same party'.[24] This was in effect a 'dry' trust: the trustee had no discretion over whether to assign but would be compelled to do so if and when required by the owner of the inheritance.[25]

There was some disagreement in the late eighteenth and early nineteenth centuries between common law courts and the Chancery over the question of whether an assignment of the trust term to the owner of the inheritance could be presumed. Some common law judges, aware that the surviving trustee of a long term of years (or his heir) might be hard to trace, feared that the existence of such terms might unduly fetter the owner of the inheritance in dealing with his property. Since the legal estate was

[22] *Jenkins v Milford* (1820) 1 J & W 629, 37 ER 508.

[23] It was prudent to include in marriage settlements 'provisoes for ceasing such term or terms of years, and such charge for portions and maintenance as aforesaid, when and so often as the same shall be raised and paid, or in case the same shall not become due or payable': G Horseman, *Precedents in Conveyancing* (London, H Lintot, 1744) vol 2, 195.

[24] Hill (n 12) 319.

[25] As Grant MR explained, 'When the purpose is answered, for which the legal estate was conveyed, it ought to be re-conveyed': *Hillary v Waller* (1806) 12 Ves 239, 252; 33 ER 92, 96. See also *Mole v Smith* (1822) Jacob 490, 498; 37 ER 935, 938.

outstanding in the trustees, he could not transfer it without their joining in any conveyance; nor could he assert his title in an action of ejectment against those who had gained wrongful possession. Faced with such a problem, in 1763 Lord Mansfield 'declared that he and many of the judges had resolved never to suffer a plaintiff in ejectment to be nonsuited by a term standing out in his own trustee, or a satisfied term set up by a mortgagor against a mortgagee, but direct the jury to presume it surrendered'.[26] Lord Kenyon was also prepared to allow juries to presume a surrender of the term by the trustee both in cases where there was an old satisfied term, and in cases where trustees had been directed to convey estates to *cestuis que trust* on reaching majority, but there was no proof that the conveyance had been made.[27]

In these cases, the King's Bench sought to protect the title of the owner of the inheritance from being undermined by the absence of formalities.[28] However, the presumption that the term had been assigned was more controversial when disputes arose between those who had purchased from the owner of the inheritance or lent on the security of his property. Such was the case in *Doe d. Putland v Hilder* in 1819, which concerned an estate purchased by John Newman in 1779. The estate was subject to a (satisfied) mortgage term of 1,000 years, which was assigned on the sale to a trustee, William Denman, in trust to attend the inheritance.[29] After John's death, the estate descended to his nephew Richard Newman, who had executed a marriage settlement in 1814 (giving himself a life estate, with remainder in strict settlement), and then conveyed his interest to his mother in 1816 as security for a debt. On neither of these occasions had the attendant term been assigned. Richard had previously incurred other debts, secured by a warrant of attorney, and in 1818 the plaintiff brought a writ of elegit to satisfy his debt from Richard's landed estates. This raised the question of which of Richard's creditors had the better claim to be satisfied on land in relation to which there was still an outstanding term of years. To resolve this matter, after the plaintiff's action commenced, Richard prevailed on John Denman, the next of kin of the now-deceased trustee William, who had died intestate in 1810, to take out letters of administration for his kinsman, and to assign the term to a new trustee, who would hold the term on behalf of those claiming under his mother.

The matter came before the King's Bench (in an action of ejectment), which had to decide which creditor had the better claim. If it could be presumed that the term, originally assigned to a trustee in 1779, had been assigned to Richard at some point thereafter, then the plaintiff would be able to recover; but if the term had remained outstanding until it was assigned to John Denman, then he could not. Following its earlier approach, the King's Bench held that the term must be presumed to have been assigned. Abbott CJ held that 'where acts are done or omitted by the owner of the inheritance … which ought not reasonably to be done or omitted, if the term existed in the hands of a trustee', then an assignment could be presumed.[30] Since the Chief Justice

[26] *Lade v Holford* (1763) in F Buller, *An Introduction to the Law Relative to Trials at Nisi Prius*, 5th edn (London, A Strahan and W Woodfall, 1790) 110. See also *Doe d Bristow v Pegge* (1785) 1 TR 760n, 99 ER 1362n.

[27] *England d Syburn v Slade* (1792) 4 TR 682, 100 ER 1243.

[28] As Kenyon explained, it was done 'in order to prevent a just title from being defeated by a matter of form': *Doe d Bowerman v Sybourn* (1796) 7 TR 2, 3; 101 ER 823, 824.

[29] *Doe d Putland v Hilder* (1819) 2 B & Ald 782, 106 ER 551.

[30] *Doe d Putland v Hilder* (1819) 2 B & Ald 782, 791–2; 106 ER 551, 554.

assumed that careful and cautious professional advisers would always make an assignment of such terms when marriage settlements were drawn up, he felt a jury might be asked to presume an assignment had taken place, thereby upholding the plaintiff's claim. This was, however, a controversial view to take. Counsel for the defendant in that case, Sir Edward Sugden, wrote that

> It is *not* the practice upon a marriage settlement to reassign attendant terms to new trustees; and no prudent practitioner declares the trust of attendant terms by the settlement, lest the parties upon an ejectment should be defeated by the production of their own conveyance, upon the face of which it would appear that the legal estate was outstanding.[31]

As Sugden pointed out, there was a good reason to keep the term outstanding in the hands of trustees: it was precisely to protect estates from encumbrances that such terms were kept on foot.[32] He explained that unless the *cestui que trust* concurred in the surrender of the term, it would be a breach of trust for the trustee to do so. Sudgen was also critical of Mansfield's fears about the practical problem presented by missing trustees: 'Is the whole system of trusts to be subverted because sometimes an obscure trustee dies without relations?'[33]

Sugden was not the only one to be sceptical. In 1806, Eldon commented that the King's Bench's approach to satisfied terms threatened the security of titles to property.[34] In his view, the purchaser or mortgagee who took care to secure the assignment of the term should be able to protect himself against an earlier one who had not. For a purchaser of property, there was much security to be had in having an outstanding term vested in a trustee for him: for if an ejectment was brought against him by a claimant under an adverse title arising subsequent to the creation of the term, he could not recover in such action during the continuance of the prior legal estate vested in the trustees.[35] The law as laid down in *Doe v Hilder* did not go down well: according to Sugden, it was 'repeatedly debated' before Masters in Chancery, when sellers argued that terms of years should be presumed to have been surrendered; 'but the general and prevailing opinion has been that that doctrine cannot be maintained; and the Masters have acted upon that principle'.[36] As the response of the Chancery lawyers to the initiative of the King's Bench showed, outstanding long terms of years in trustees served a

[31] EB Sugden, *A Practical Treatise of the Law of Vendors and Purchasers of Estates*, 6th edn (London, Joseph Butterworth, 1822) 394.

[32] As Lord Hardwicke had explained, such terms could be used 'as a guard and protection to an equitable owner of the inheritance against mesne conveyances, which would carry the fee at common law': *Willoughby v Willoughby* (1787) 1 TR 763, 767; 99 ER 1366, 1368.

[33] Sugden (n 31) 403.

[34] *Evans v Bicknell* (1801) 6 Ves Jun 174, 185; 31 ER 998, 1003. See also *Mole v Smith* (1822) Jacob 490, 496; 37 ER 935, 938 where he observed that '[i]f, upon grounds that are not extremely conclusive, it is now to be held, that terms are surrendered because they are satisfied, there will be an end of all that the Court has been doing upon this subject for a long time'.

[35] Hill (n 12) 318. As Fonblanque explained, 'though the trust or benefit of the term is annexed to the inheritance, the legal interest of the term remains distinct and separate from it at law; and the whole benefit and advantage to be made of the term arises from this separation, by affording the means of protecting *bona fide* purchasers of real estates, and also of enabling courts of equity to keep real estates in the right channel': J Fonblanque (ed), *A Treatise of Equity*, 2nd edn (London, W Clarke and Son, 1799) vol 2, 105–06.

[36] Sugden (n 31). See also *Doe d Blacknell v Plowman* (1831) 2 B & Ad 573, 577–78; 109 ER 1255, 1257. See also the discussion in JH Mathews, *A Treatise on the Doctrine of Presumption and Presumptive Evidence as Affecting the Title to Real and Personal Property* (London, J Butterworth and Son, 1827) 226–59.

function in protecting the title of the owner of the inheritance and purchasers or mortgagees from him. This debate over outstanding terms ended with the defence of the role of 'dry' trustees, who in this instance were effectively stakeholders, whose only role was to assign the estate as and when called on to do so, or to have it directed by the court. In such cases, it was not the *trustees* who were important, but the *trust*, which existed to perform a particular function of providing security for the estate.

IV. Trustees to Preserve Contingent Remainders

Another set of trustees whose existence was vital for family settlements, but who normally had no active duties to perform, were trustees to preserve contingent remainders. The invention of this class of trustees was the crucial step in the development of the strict settlement. Their function was to ensure that the tenant in possession under a family settlement could not dispose of the estate, and thereby prevent it from passing to the next generation, for instance, by a tortious feoffment or by a forfeiture. If the life estate of the tenant terminated before his death – destroying the freehold estate which supported the contingent entail – the estate would pass to the trustees, who would hold it until his death, when the next generation would enter.[37] For the most part, the role of these trustees was entirely passive: they existed as a kind of insurance to secure the transmission of the patrimony. However, on some occasions, they had a more active function. If the tenant's estate was forfeited, they would have to gather in the rents and profits of the estate and hold them for the remainderman to take.[38]

In an age when forfeiture was rare, trustees to preserve contingent remainders did not generally have to worry about running the estate. However, they did have to concur in certain cases when families sought to resettle estates, for instance, on the marriage of an eldest son. In such cases, their formal acquiescence was necessary for the resettlement to occur, since they were stakeholders in the family estates. However, their trusts were not entirely 'dry', since they were not simply trustees for those seeking to resettle the estate, but also for others who might be entitled in remainder on the happening of certain contingencies. They, therefore, might have to make a choice of whether to join in a resettlement or not.

In the common case where the estate was settled on a father for life, with a remainder to trustees to preserve contingent remainders and then a remainder to the eldest son in tail, the father and son could join in resettling the estate when the son came of age, and his estate vested: for at this point, the trustees were redundant. However, if the trustees joined in a resettlement before the first tenant in tail was of age, they were liable for a breach of trust by destroying the very remainders they existed to preserve.[39] For as Lord Chancellor King put it in 1732, where trustees 'appointed to preserve an estate in a family […] instead of preserving it, do a wilful act […] in order to destroy it', this was 'a

[37] L Bonfield, *Marriage Settlements, 1601–1740: The Adoption of the Strict Settlement* (Cambridge, Cambridge University Press, 1983) 55–6.

[38] Simpson (n 16) 230.

[39] *Pye v Gorges* (1710) 1 P Wms 128, 24 ER 323; *Biscoe v Perkins* (1813) 1 V & B 485, 491; 35 ER 188, 191. Every purchaser with notice was also liable.

plain breach of trust'.[40] Matters were more complicated where the concurrence of these trustees was needed in a resettlement of family estates in certain other situations where the eldest son had reached majority. Such was the case where an estate was settled in the trustees for the life of the father in trust for him, with remainder over to his eldest son. This form was used if a family sought to insure against the possible undue influence of a father, who might induce his son when of age to join him in barring the entail in order to secure his own interests, rather than those of the family.[41] Equally, if the estate were limited to the father for a term of years, rather than for life, the trustees would have to join in any resettlement, since the first legal estate of freehold was vested in them. They would also have to join where trusts were created under a will. In such cases, it was natural enough for families to seek to make resettlements, and the question was raised whether it was appropriate for trustees to join in destroying the contingent remainders it was their function to preserve.

If the eldest son was of age, the court would direct trustees to join in the conveyance in cases where the father had an estate for years or the estate was held by trustees, if they wanted to resettle the estate to allow a marriage settlement to be drawn up for the son.[42] Although the trustees were intended to preserve all contingent remainders, the court looked to the purposes of the original settlement, and those who could be seen as purchasers within it, and was not concerned to protect the interests of more distant potential claimants.[43] In 1719, Lord Chancellor Parker held that trustees would be directed to join if it was for the benefit of the family.[44] However, the court was not prepared to direct the trustee to join in a conveyance if there were younger sons who refused to consent.[45] Nor was it prepared to direct the trustees to join where the conveyance was not intended 'in some measure to answer the uses originally intended by the settlement', but simply to sell the estate.[46] The court was especially suspicious of requests to direct trustees to join in order to allow a resettlement requested by a father and son in order to pay the father's debts. As Lord Hardwicke observed in 1743, 'this was the very case which was intended to be prevented by the trust'.[47] Nor would the court direct the trustee to join in the sale of property where the tenant for life had no children, if there was any possibility – however remote – that he would have them in the future.[48]

According to Charles Fearne, 'the safest way for trustees' was 'not to act, except in the clearest cases, without the direction of the court'.[49] However, it had long been

[40] *Mansell v Mansell* (1732) 2 P Wms 678, 680; 24 ER 913, 914.

[41] T Lewin, *A Practical Treatise on the Law of Trusts and Trustees* (London, A Maxwell, 1837) 357.

[42] See *Frewin v Charlton* (1712) 1 Eq Ca Ab 386, 21 ER 1121 (where a provision was directed to be made for daughter, who was thought to have been intended to be included in the first settlement).

[43] See *Tipping v Piggot* (1713) 1 Eq Ca Ab 385, 21 ER 1120.

[44] *Winnington v Foley* (1719) 1 P Wms 536, 538; 24 ER 505, 506.

[45] *Townsend v Lawton* (1726) 2 P Wms 379, 24 ER 775. However, in *Moody v Walters* (1809) 16 Ves 293, 304; 33 ER 992, 1000, Lord Eldon suggested that equity only protected the interest of the eldest son, and not the second and other sons.

[46] *Symance v Tattam* (1737) 1 Atk 613, 26 ER 385; *cf Townsend v Lawton* (1726) 2 P Wms 379, 24 ER 775.

[47] *Woodhouse v Hoskins* (1743) 3 Atk 22, 24–5; 26 ER 816, 818.

[48] *Brown v Carter* (1801) 5 Ves Jun 862, 31 ER 898.

[49] C Fearne, *An Essay on the Learning of Contingent Remainders and Executory Devises*, 4th edn (London, Whieldon and Butterworth, 1791) vol 1, 493. The court's direction was also of course necessary where the only surviving trustee was an infant: eg, *Winnington v Foley* (1719) 1 P Wms 536, 24 ER 505.

clear that although judges would only compel trustees to join in conveyances in rare cases, they would not necessarily regard the trustees as acting in breach of trust if they joined in a conveyance where the court would not direct them to do so. In *Barnard v Large*, Sir Thomas Sewell MR observed that trustees to preserve contingent remainders, whose function was to preserve the estate from the father's power to destroy it and to guard against any improper influence he might have over his son, had a discretion. If they used it improperly, they would be punished by the court; if they refused to exercise it on 'a reasonable occasion', they would be compelled by the court to exercise it.[50] It was evident that there was also a space in between where the trustee had a discretion to join in a conveyance which the court would neither compel them to do nor regard as a breach of trust. It was this discretion which led Lord Hardwicke to refer to them as 'honorary trustees'.[51] According to Lewin, this phrase referred to the fact that once an eldest son had come of age, the question of whether the trustees should join in a resettlement 'becomes *matter of discretion:* they are said to be honorary trustees, that is, bound in *honour* only to decide on the most proper and prudential course'.[52]

As Lord Eldon pointed out in 1809, if trustees had to come to court every time they were asked to join in a conveyance, then the court itself would become in effect the trustee to preserve all contingent remainders in the country, 'and no one can say what is to be done, until a decree has been obtained'. Eldon realised that no one would be prepared to act as such a trustee under such circumstances: 'The principle therefore cannot be, that the absence of that sanction makes the act a breach of trust.'[53] Four years later, he explained,

> If they are honorary trustees to support contingent remainders for the benefit of the family, the interests of mankind require courts of justice to treat them as such; and, unless violation of the trust appears, not to take away all their discretion; and say, they are not to join, though their opinion is, that the interests of the family require it, without coming to a court of equity.[54]

For that reason, courts were not prepared to regard the exercise of their discretion, unguided by the court, as a breach of trust, for instance when asked to do so by purchasers who wished to resist specific performance on the ground that the vendor's title derived from a resettlement made by trustees who had failed to preserve the contingent remainders of possible claimants.[55] Nonetheless, while such trustees had a discretion, it was wise for them to be cautious, since they could be held liable for breaches of trust:[56] if the estate was sold to a purchaser without notice, so that it could not be undone, the trustees would have to purchase equivalent property for the estate.

[50] *Barnard* v *Large* (1781) 1 Bro CC 534, 536; 28 ER 1283, 1284.

[51] This phrase was used by Lord Hardwicke in *Woodhouse v Hoskins* (1743) 3 Atk 22, 24; 26 ER 816, 817. It was repeated by Sir Thomas Sewell MR in *Barnard v Large* (1780) Ambler 774, 776; 27 ER 496, 497, and by Lord Eldon in *Biscoe v Perkins* (1813) 1 V & B 485, 492; 35 ER 188, 188. See also Fearne (n 49) 492.

[52] Lewin (n 41) 361.

[53] *Moody v Walters* (1809) 16 Ves Jun 283, 311; 33 ER 992, 1003.

[54] *Biscoe v Perkins* (1813) 1 V & B 485, 492; 35 ER 188, 191.

[55] *Moody v Walters* (1809) 16 Ves Jun 283, 33 ER 992.

[56] *Garth v Cotton* (1750, 1753) 1 Ves Sen 546, 556; 27 ER 1196, 1199.

V. Trustees Managing Money

In many family settlements, the prime function of trustees was to receive and distribute money generated by landed estates. It was standard practice in marriage settlements to define the powers given to the trustees in relation to the management of the funds they were given. For instance, when money was settled on a marriage from the portion brought by the wife, trustees might be directed to use the money to buy real estate to be settled to the use of the husband for life, then to his wife for her life, then to the use of the children. The settlement would direct what was to be given to children and when (and whether maintenance was to be paid), and it might give the parents a power of appointment, to decide which child would get what. It might also include a provision for the eventual sale of the estate and the distribution of the proceeds (for instance, if the marriage only produced daughters who needed portions). The trustees were given firm directions on what to pay and when. In the meantime, the father of the family – whose tenure was habitually without impeachment of waste – would be in possession of the estate, in effect managing it.

Trustees might also be given more active powers of management. Where families were heavily in debt, it was common to give trustees power to discharge debts out of the rents and profits of the estate or by raising funds by mortgage or sale. In such cases, the life tenant's enjoyment of the income of the estate would be postponed (or at least reduced) until trustees had been able to reduce the debt. In such cases, the duties of the trustees might be burdensome, for they might have to deal with a large variety of creditors whose claims needed careful scrutiny before they were paid. However, whether it was a matter of paying debts or paying money to family members, the range of discretion they had in raising these funds – whether by mortgage or sale or only out of rents and profits – depended on the wording of the settlement or will.[57]

Normally, settlements would confer specific powers to demise or lease premises for long terms, if needed for the good management of the estate.[58] Sometimes such a power could also be inferred. As Eldon explained,

> Upon a devise to A. in fee in trust for his infant son, to be conveyed to him at the age of 21, and without imposing terms upon the trustee as to the rent, the length, or terms, of the lease, this Court would say, the trustee was to do what was reasonable; and [...] in the fair management of the estate.[59]

However, there was some debate about how far such inferences could be made. A power to grant leases was recognised in 1830 in *Naylor v Arnitt*, where lands were devised to trustees to pay annuities out of the rents and profits and, subject thereto, to pay the rents to William Naylor and his wife and children. A few weeks after the

[57] See, eg, *Ridout v Earl of Plymouth*, *Lingard v Earl of Derby* (1783) 1 Bro CC 311. *Cf* J Habakkuk, *Marriage, Debt, and the Estates System: English Landownership, 1650-1950* (Oxford, Oxford University Press) 322.

[58] Such powers of leasing might be needed where the beneficiaries of a trust were infants, since the court would not let beyond the period of minority. In *Sutton v Jones* (1809) 15 Ves Jun 584, 33 ER 875, the trustees were empowered to lease, 'if for the purpose of pulling down, and erecting new buildings, for a term not exceeding 99 years; if for repairing or considerably improving, for a term not exceeding 63 years; if for other reasonable purposes, not exceeding 21 years'.

[59] *Attorney-General v Owen* (1805) 10 Ves Jun 555, 560; 32 ER 960, 962.

death of the testator, they granted a ten-year lease of the land, which the family objected to. In the family's view, the trustees had no discretionary authority in the management of the estate but only had a power to let the lands from year to year and pay the proceeds. In this case, Leach VC held that they did have the power to grant such a lease.[60] On the face of it, this seemed to acknowledge that trustees must have the power to deal with an estate in the ordinary course of prudent management. Seventeen years later, however, Lord Langdale criticised the decision, 'for if the trustees, unauthorized by the will, have the power of leasing for ten years, I see no reason why they should not have power to lease for sixty'.[61]

Where trustees had active duties to perform, they ran a risk if they left it to beneficiaries to manage the estate, as trustees of the estate of Sir Benjamin Tebbs discovered. He left property to pay his widow an annuity, and to accumulate the surplus to be distributed among a number of beneficiaries after her death. The property consisted of a number of old houses, which required active management. However, Tebbs's executors had left the management of the estate to the testator's son-in-law, who was himself a beneficiary. The rents had fallen into arrears, and the trustees had not sought to replace the tenants or recover the rent at law. They had also retained sums in their bank account, in case it was needed to settle some of the testator's other affairs. Plumer VC was unsympathetic to the argument that they should not be liable. 'If persons accept the trust of executors, they must perform it,' he ruled, 'they must use due diligence; and not suffer infants [the other beneficiaries] to be injured by their negligence.'[62] They were held liable for the arrears they should have got in, and for interest on the sums left in the bank which should have been invested, since they had not proved it was needed for other purposes.

There were also risks for those trustees who failed to raise or invest the money which they were tasked with holding, even where they sought to be indulgent to the family. When the widow Ann Caffrey married Peter Prest, she settled her property – which consisted of her interest in her late husband's business, a public house in St Giles – on trustees, who were to raise £800 on the security of the property for the use of Ann and her children. They were also empowered to allow her husband to retain the premises and run the business, provided that he paid £100 per annum until the £800 was paid off (whereupon the business would be transferred to him). Prest paid the sums due for two and a half years, but then stopped making payments. He was eventually bankrupted and obtained his discharge. The trustees had in fact asked Prest to make the necessary payments but were frequently urged by Ann not to take steps against him, since she and her children were entirely maintained from income generated by the business, which had hit hard times. It was clear that the trustees had no corrupt motives and had acted for the benefit of the family. Sir William Grant MR was not sympathetic: given that the asset – a lease of the public house – was one which was diminishing in value – and given that they could have foreseen a conflict with Prest's creditors, the trustees should have taken steps to protect the interest of the children. Although in this case, the trustees had acted in good faith, Grant felt that to hold them not to be responsible 'would be an

[60] *Naylor v Arnitt* (1830) 1 R & M 501, 39 ER 193.
[61] *Wood v Patteson* (1846-7) 10 Beav 541, 544; 50 ER 690, 691.
[62] *Tebbs v Carpenter* (1816) 1 Madd 290, 298; 56 ER 107, 110.

encouragement to bad motives, and it may be impossible to detect undue motives'.[63] Their failure to act was regarded as negligence for which they were liable.

Trustees tasked with holding and investing funds had to invest them prudently, for the benefit of all the beneficiaries. Furthermore, each trustee had to ensure that no other trustee was allowed to invest the assets in a risky way, whatever the family pressures might be. This can be seen from the fortune of Isaac Donnithorne's granddaughter. In 1780, Isaac assigned a bond debt of nearly £8,000 to three trustees to pay the dividends to his daughter Joanna and her husband John Whitmore and to their children (with shares at their discretion), and after the parents' death to pay the money to any surviving child. The capital sum was at first invested in a mortgage, but in 1790 the mortgage was paid off. The money was then received (with the consent of the other two trustees) by the trustee Nicholas Donnithorne, who was himself the testator's son. Instead of investing it in government bonds, he invested it in more lucrative East India Company bills, which were payable at the end of two years. These attracted a higher interest rate than government securities, which was used to pay the Whitmores a higher income than they would otherwise get. When the bills were paid off, Nicholas proposed to Joanna Whitmore that the money should be invested in a mortgage on lands held by himself and his son Isaac in Cornwall. Joanna agreed to this, wanting it done as soon as possible. The money was to be secured in the meantime by a joint bond from Nicholas and Isaac. Although the other two trustees wanted the money to be invested in government bonds, they took the joint bond after Joanna had expressed her wishes. The mortgage was in fact never executed, and Nicholas died insolvent in 1796. Over 20 years later, Joanna's surviving daughter and her husband sought to recover against the two trustees (or rather their representatives), for breach of trust. In this case, Eldon held the trustees liable for permitting Nicholas to deal with the assets without investing them in government stock.[64] The trustees were expected to handle the money as cautious businessmen, and not deal with it in a discretionary way for the benefit of the immediate beneficiaries.

Clear rules were also developed about what kinds of investments trustees could make. In general, the view prevailed that trustees had to invest assets in 'proper' but productive investments. The prudent approach was seen in Lord Hardwicke's observations in 1746 that it was safe to invest in Bank of England annuities – since the income was guaranteed by the government and the capital would be redeemed – but not Bank stock, since that 'depends upon the management of the governors and directors, and are subject to losses'.[65] Lord Keeper Henley seemed to take a more relaxed approach when considering the case of executors who had lent £1,000 (with the consent of beneficiaries) to one of the executors, a large merchant at Bristol, on the security of his bond. Interest was paid on this loan for some time, but the merchant later died insolvent. 'No man can require, or with reason expect a trustee to manage his property with the same care and discretion that he would his own', Henley opined, adding that it would only be a breach of trust if the trustees had 'been guilty of a gross negligence'.[66] Later judges

[63] *Caffrey v Darby* (1801) 6 Ves Jun 488, 496; 31 ER 1159, 1162.
[64] *Walker v Symons* (1818) 3 Swans 1, 36 ER 751. Loveday Walker was also allowed to rescind an agreement made with Isaac which allowed him to settle with his father's creditors.
[65] *Trafford v Boehm* (1746) 3 Atk 440, 444; 26 ER 1054, 1056.
[66] *Harden v Parsons* (1758) 1 Eden 145, 149; 28 ER 639, 641.

took a different view of the trustee's duties, holding that they had to take care of trust property with the same care as they would their own.[67] It also came to be settled that trustees could not lend on personal securities, unless expressly empowered to do so.[68] Even when they were so empowered, trustees needed to be cautious, as the trustees for John Ollivant's daughter Betty found. Given a power to lend on personal security, they lent her husband £500 on their marriage on the security of his own bond to accommodate him. However, the court held their power did not extend to accommodation and so they were held liable for the sum after his bankruptcy.[69]

Just as trustees were required not to lend on the basis of personal securities, so they were required to call in money which was due to the estate on bonds. In *Powell v Evans* in 1801, executors were held liable for not calling in a bond from a debtor who later became bankrupt. The testator had left a £300 bond from Charles Price, which was among the assets which were to go to the plaintiff, should she attain the age of twenty-one. The executors – who had been unwilling to act as such – had been told by the testator that they would only have to receive the interest due on the securities. For three years, Price had paid the sums due, but he then failed. On his failure, the executor, Evans, asked the plaintiff's husband whether he should sign the bankrupt's certificate (which would exonerate him from the debt), and was told to do what he thought proper. On the advice of his lawyer son, he signed. Arden MR was not unsympathetic to the position of executors who had onerous and difficult trusts to deal with. He did not want to deter them from taking on the role and thought them 'entitled to great indulgence unless neglect is fully proved'.[70] In this case, however, he felt there was clear negligence, both in failing to convert the security and in signing the certificate.

Trustees were also forbidden from making use of the money for their own purposes, even when they paid the anticipated income to beneficiaries. William Reddington was made a trustee of a 99-year term of years under the will of John Pocock, to receive the rents and profits of Pocock's estates, pay an annuity to his widow, pay money at his discretion for the maintenance and education of his children, and then accumulate the surplus to be paid to them at majority. Pocock also left the residue of his personal estate to be invested for the same purposes. Reddington mixed the trust money with his own and lent some of it both to his business partner and to his brother-in-law, though he continued to pay the interest. As his lawyer Sir Samuel Romilly explained, '[t]his was a very troublesome trust' and the trustee had educated the children with great care from their father's death. However, Arden MR held it as very improper for him to have lent the money to his friends on their personal security: 'No man is justified in putting the property of which he is trustee in jeopardy.'[71] He went on,

[67] *Jones v Lewis* (1751) 2 Ves Sen 240, 241; 28 ER 155, 155. See also Lord Eldon's comment, that 'the Court does not expect them to take more care of the property entrusted to them than they would do of their own': *Massey v Banner* (1820) 1 J & W 241, 247.

[68] *Adye v Feuilleteau* (1783) 1 Cox CC 24, 29 ER 1045, where Lord Commissioner Hotham noted (at 1 Cox CC 25–6) that 'The court will always discourage lending trust money on private security, though larger interest may be gained. It becomes a species of gambling.' See also *Holmes v Dring* (1788) 2 Cox CC 1, 30 ER 1.

[69] *Langston v Ollivant* (1807) G Cooper 33, 35 ER 467.

[70] *Powell v Evans* (1801) 5 Ves Jun 839, 843; 31 ER 886, 888.

[71] *Pocock v Reddington* (1801) 5 Ves Jun 794, 799; 31 ER 862, 865.

> The rule upon this subject is, that when an executor or trustee, instead of executing the trust, as he ought, by laying out the property either in well secured real estates or upon Government securities, takes upon him to dispose of it in another manner, the *cestuis que trust* may call to him for an account either way: having an option to make him replace it, or, if it is for their benefit to affirm his conduct, and take what he has sold it for, they may take that, and charge him with 5 per cent interest.[72]

Just as trustees were to gather all the assets of an estate and invest them prudently, they were to handle the property with equal regard to all beneficiaries, present and future. This question was addressed by Lord Eldon in 1802 in *Howe v Earl of Dartmouth*, when he held that a tenant for life should not be allowed to obtain a higher rate of return by investing in a risky security which might endanger the interest of the remainderman.[73] In such cases, the life tenant (or his executors) would be called on to repay the surplus paid beyond the normal return on the three per cent Consolidated Bank Annuities; and trustees who had overpaid would be liable to make this good. The risks this might impose on trustees can be seen from *Dimes v Scott* in 1828: here, trustees were directed to invest the residue of a testator's personal estate in government stock or real securities, to hold in trust for his wife Mary, and after her death for Elizabeth Wintersgill. The assets in question consisted of an investment in an East India Company fund, which was irredeemable for over ten years from the beginning of 1800, and which gave a ten per cent return. The trustees sold the asset once it became redeemable and invested the proceeds in the three per cent government stock but, in the meantime, paid Mary the ten per cent earned. This was a breach of trust, and the trustees were held accountable for what they had paid her in excess of the three per cent return she should have obtained if the assets had been sold as directed.[74]

The point that the tenant for life could not be advantaged was also seen in *Bostock v Blakeney*. The case concerned a trust set up under the will of Field-Marshal Sir Robert Rich. He left over £45,000 invested in the public funds, which he directed to be used to purchase lands to go to his son for life, with remainders to his other sons and grandchildren. On his death, his eldest son Robert – who was also one of the trustees – prevailed on his fellow trustees not only to buy Waverley Abbey near Farnham at nearly £20,000, but also to spend money on making improvements to the estates. In the end, Robert spent almost £25,000 in enlarging and rebuilding the house and improving the grounds. He died in 1785, leaving a daughter, Mary, as his heir, and the next in remainder. He had fallen out with her some time before and had left her none of his own real or personal estate. However, not only did Mary succeed to the family estates, but she was also able to reclaim the money which had been spent on improvements. As Lord Thurlow explained, 'a tenant for life […] could not lay out a sum of money on the estate, and charge it on the reversion, although the estate itself would be benefited'.[75] By now, the trustees were all dead, but this was a way for Mary to reclaim the inheritance which her father sought to deny her.

[72] *Pocock v Reddington* (1801) 5 Ves Jun 794, 799–800; 31 ER 862, 865.

[73] *Howe v Earl of Dartmouth; Howe v Countess of Aylesbury* (1802) 7 Ves Jun 137, 32 ER 56. See further Stebbings (n 1) 68–74.

[74] *Dimes v Scott* (1828) 4 Russell 195, 38 ER 778.

[75] *Bostock v Blakeney* (1789) 2 Bro CC 653, 657; 29 ER 362, 364.

As these cases show, the degree of discretion enjoyed by trustees in managing family money was very limited. Their powers were normally closely defined by the settlement, and the way they were to be exercised was further regulated by the court's rules. Rather than being active managers, seeking to maximise returns from the assets, their task was to invest them in the safest assets, and make payments as directed by the settlement or will.

VI. Trustees of Separate Property

When marriage or family settlements were made, it was very common to settle property in trustees for the separate use of a married woman. Such provisions might be intended to give a wife a separate income which could not be controlled by her husband or to secure a separate stream of income for the family in case of her husband's insolvency. They might equally be intended to ensure that the capital fund which generated the income for the wife in her life would descend to members of her own family (including her children), rather than being diverted (for instance) to the children of her husband's second marriage. Given the law relating to married women's property, she could not hold the money herself, but it had to be vested in trustees. This raises the question of how much control the wife had over the property, and how much she was at the mercy of her trustees. A number of historians have suggested that the fact that property was put in the hands of trustees underscored the married woman's lack of capacity and imported a degree of (often masculine) control over her.[76]

How much control a married woman had over her separate property depended on the wording of the settlement. Late eighteenth-century settlors sought to protect a married woman from being 'kicked or kissed' out of their property by including a phrase attributed to Lord Thurlow that the wife should receive income 'from time to time' and 'not by way of anticipation'.[77] The 'restraint on anticipation' meant that a wife had no power to charge her separate property, for instance by way of mortgage: it ensured that she would always be sure of a future income, regardless of any present desire she (or her husband) might have in liquidating her assets. Where the trust included a restraint on anticipation, the role of the trustees was (as it was in other cases where they held funds) to hold the assets in safe investments, and to pay the income over in the way stipulated in the settlement. However, it is worth noting that the restraint on anticipation was itself developed as a way of restraining her from exercising the power she had over her own separate property in the absence of such a clause. For by the late eighteenth century, it was recognised that without such a clause, a married woman had the power of a *feme sole* over her separate property.

The married woman's power over her separate property was recognised by Lord Hardwicke in *Grigby v Cox*, where a wife who was entitled to rents and profits from an estate for her separate use sold part of her interest to the plaintiff, with the concurrence

[76] eg, SM Okin, 'Patriarchy and Married Women's Property in England: Questions on Some Current Views' (1983–4) 17 *Eighteenth-Century Studies* 125.

[77] See note 1 to *Chassaing v Parsonage* (1799) 5 Ves Jun 15, 31 ER 448, on the genealogy of the concept.

of her husband, but without consulting the trustees who held the property. She did so under a settlement which gave her a power of appointment which did not require their concurrence. Hardwicke stated, 'the rule of the court is, that where any thing is settled to the wife's separate use, she is considered as a feme sole, may appoint in what manner she pleases'.[78] In so holding, he rejected her argument that she should have been protected by her trustees. Taking the same view in 1778 in *Hulme v Tenant*, Thurlow LC held that a bond executed by a married woman to secure a loan to her husband bound her separate estate, so that her trustees had to use her income to satisfy her general engagements.[79] In *Pybus v Smith*, which came before the same judge twelve years later, Anna Maria Vernon had given her indebted husband's creditors a security charged on her separate property, and had appointed the income of her separate property to be paid by her trustees to her husband. On his bankruptcy, his creditors sought to be paid from her separate property. Upholding their claim, Thurlow also rejected the argument that Mrs Vernon should have been protected by her trustees. The trustees, he noted, 'are mere stakeholders': '[s]o far forth as the instrument creating her separate estate makes her proprietor, so far she is a feme sole: and if she has pledged her estate according to her power, the trustees must hold it to the uses she appoints'.[80] Once it was established that the wife 'knew what she was about', it allowed her to alienate her separate property.

The notion that the wife had full control over her separate property and was not to be protected by her trustees troubled Thurlow's successor as Lord Chancellor, Lord Loughborough. He clearly felt that trustees had a duty to protect the wife. As he put it in *Whistler v Newman*, '[s]he has trustees to guard her against those acts she might be induced to do by the influence of her husband.'[81] He thought that if the rule laid down in the earlier cases were to be followed to its full extent, a married woman with property in the hands of trustees would be less protected than a woman who had the full legal right to her real estate, which could not be taken from her unless she joined with her husband in levying a fine, during which procedure she would be separately examined by the court to confirm her consent. Loughborough's desire to protect a married woman was seen again in *Mores v Huish*,[82] where the couple – who had married as infants – granted an annuity secured on property which was settled for her separate use for her life, and then to her husband and children. The trustee, who was aware that the husband was a spendthrift, and that if he got hold of her money she and her children would end up on the parish, warned the lender off, but the loan went ahead. When the lender sought to recover payments due on his annuity, Loughborough approved of the trustees' refusal to pay: 'I must applaud the trustees, instead of condemning them, for not doing that, which, if they had done, would have involved them in a breach of trust.'[83]

[78] *Grigby v Cox* (1750) 1 Ves Sen 517, 27 ER 1178. See also *Allen v Papworth* (1748) 1 Ves Sen 163, 27 ER 958; Ves Sen Supp 88, 28 ER 465.

[79] *Hulme v Tenant* (1778) 1 Bro CC 16, 19–20; 28 ER 958, 960 (Lord Thurlow). However, he held that her creditors could not come directly to the separate (real) estate, as by requiring her to execute a power.

[80] *Pybus v Smith* (1790) 1 Ves Jun 189, 193; 30 ER 294, 296.

[81] *Whistler v Newman* (1798) 4 Ves Jun 129, 134; 31 ER 67, 70.

[82] *Mores v Huish* (1800) 5 Ves Jun 692, 31 ER 808.

[83] *Mores v Huish* (1800) 5 Ves 692, 694, 31 ER 808, 810. He also noted that the wife here did not have a power of appointment over the fund, which distinguished the case from *Pybus v Smith* (1790) 1 Ves Jun 189, 30 ER 294; 3 Bro CC 340, 29 ER 570.

Lord Eldon was another who felt the wife needed more protection. In 1804, he expressed the view that *Whistler v Newman* and *Mores v Huish* had qualified Thurlow's doctrine, and that it 'deserve[d] a very full review, whenever that point shall come distinctly before the Court'.[84] However, in the same year, in *Wagstaff v Smith*, Grant MR reiterated the previous approach in allowing a married woman to use her separate property to secure an annuity with her husband, even though she had no power of appointment. As he saw it, since she had 'an absolute, complete life-interest in the dividends to her separate use', she had a right to dispose of it as she saw fit.[85] He reiterated his views relating to a married woman's power in *Sturgis v Corp*, where a married woman and her husband sought specific performance of a contract to sell her reversionary interest in property settled to her separate use. In this case, he rejected the defendant's argument that the wife had to be privately examined by the court before she could consent to transfer her property: for Grant, no such protection was needed, as she had plenary powers.[86] Even Eldon had to concede the point, admitting (with some regret) that the authorities in equity were firm that if the wife had power under the terms of the instrument giving her separate property to deal with it, she had the powers of a *feme sole*.[87] As these cases showed, where there was no restraint on anticipation, trustees of married women's separate property were mere stakeholders, in effect 'dry' trustees who had to deal with the property as she wished.

VII. Trustees with Discretionary Powers

In the cases discussed so far, trustees had relatively little discretion. However, they might sometimes be given broad discretionary powers. This occurred, for instance, where they were empowered to give property to the 'most deserving' of a testator's relations. In such cases, the Chancery recognised the discretionary power given, but saw it as a personal one confined to the original trustees.[88] For instance, in his 1792 will, Sir Charles Booth left the residue of his estate to two trustees – and their executors, administrators and assigns – 'to dispose of the same for the use and benefit of such relations and kindred as they in their discretion should think proper'. Both trustees died before the trust was executed, and the surviving trustee named two executors to hold the property for the trusts of Booth's will. This raised the question of whether these men were to execute the trust – by investigating who was most deserving and allocating the funds there – or whether the real and personal property was to go to the testator's heir at law and next of kin, respectively.[89] In argument, Sir Samuel Romilly pointed to the inconvenience of conferring discretion on such representatives, noting that it might not only be difficult to find who were the heirs, executors or administrators of deceased trustees, but they might turn out to be infants, married women, or a range 'of different descriptions, whose conclusions might disagree'.[90] In his judgment,

[84] *Jones v Harris* (1804) 9 Ves Jun 487, 497; 32 ER 691, 695.
[85] *Wagstaff v Smith* (1804) 9 Ves Jun 520, 523; 32 ER 704, 705.
[86] *Sturgis v Corp* (1806) 13 Ves Jun 190, 33 ER 266.
[87] *Sperling v Rochfort* (1803) 8 Ves Jun 164, 177; 32 ER 316, 321.
[88] See also *Doyley v Attorney-General* (1735) 4 Vin Ab 485; 2 Eq Ca Ab 194, 22 ER 167.
[89] Matters were complicated by the fact that the will included wording which suggested that the representatives of the trustees might be given discretionary powers.
[90] *Cole v Wade* (1807) 16 Ves Jun 27, 33; 33 ER 894, 896.

Sir William Grant held that there was a trust in favour of the testator's relatives, which was coupled with a power of selection in the trustees: in his view, 'wherever a power is of a kind, that indicates a personal confidence, it must *prima facie* be understood to be confined to the individual, to whom it is given; and will not except by express words pass to others, to whom by legal transmission the same character may happen to belong'.[91] Since the court could not make the selection, the trust was to be executed by the court by giving the assets to the testator's next of kin, following the Statute of Distributions. As this case showed, where the trustees had not exercised their discretion in apportioning shares, the court would not do so, but would divide the funds equally between all of those among whom the trustees might have made a choice.[92]

However, not all powers which seemed discretionary had to be exercised personally by the original trustees. It was common to include a provision in settlements that property would be given to a young woman, on condition that she married with the consent of trustees.[93] The power to withhold or give consent might have been regarded as a discretionary one to be exercised by trustees who were familiar with the family, and who could judge whether the young man in question was a suitable match for the young lady. Yet settlements commonly conferred the power to consent to trustees and executors, or their survivors, heirs and executors. It was hard to argue that a father could have reposed much personal confidence in representatives of a surviving trustee, who might be unknown to him, and so there might have been room to argue that this discretion had to be a personal one in the originally named trustees. But this was not the case. Answering such an argument, Lord Eldon simply said 'if the testator has made that consent necessary, I have no authority to say it is not necessary'.[94]

In such cases, the court was generally less concerned with the personal judgment of the trustee on the suitability of the match than with the business side of ensuring that the bride obtained a suitable settlement. The case before Eldon concerned the provision made by Charles Elwes for his niece-by-marriage, which was conditional on the approval of three trustees, who were his cousins and unrelated to the beneficiary. When two of them objected to her proposed match, it was not because they disapproved of the groom, but because they were not satisfied with the proposed marriage settlement.[95] Similarly, when Elizabeth Callender's trustees refused their consent for her marriage, having approved of the young man and his family, it was because of his refusal to proceed with the settlement, after his father's death.[96] Such trustees were concerned not with matters of the heart, but with matters of business. This did not require the exercise of personal discretion. This can be seen from *Goldsmid v Goldsmid* in 1815, where the testator left money for his daughters if they married with the consent of his executors,

[91] *Cole v Wade* (1807) 16 Ves Jun 27, 44; 33 ER 894, 900. *Cf Doyley* v *Attorney-General* (1735) 4 Vin Ab 485; 2 Eq Ca Ab 194, 22 ER 167.

[92] *Longmore v Broom* (1802) 7 Ves Jun 124 129; 32 ER 51, 52. The court would only act if it considered the discretionary power to be coupled to a trust: if trustees failed to exercise a merely discretionary power, then the intended beneficiaries would have no claim, for there was no trust for the court to execute.

[93] See further RA Probert, 'Control over Marriage in England and Wales, 1753-1823: The Clandestine Marriages Act of 1753 in Context' (2009) 27 *Law and History Review* 413.

[94] *Clarke v Parker* (1812) 19 Ves Jun 1, 15; 34 ER 419, 424.

[95] A revised offer satisfied the trustees, but they continued to withhold their consent until they had been paid the costs of drawing up the settlement. *Clarke v Parker* (1812) 19 Ves Jun 1, 34 ER 419.

[96] *Dashwood v Lord Bulkeley* (1804) 10 Ves Jun 230, 32 ER 832.

who were his brothers. One of his daughters wished to marry and had the consent of her mother, but only one trustee survived, and he refused to act, not having been consulted on any other family matters. In this case, Eldon referred it to the Master to inquire whether this was a suitable and proper marriage and, if so, to receive proposals for a settlement or provision for the daughter.[97] In such matters, the court was as well placed as the trustees to see to the business.

Trustees were also often empowered to pay money for the education and maintenance of the children before their portions were paid, generally not exceeding the interest which would be earned on the portion when paid. Where they were given a discretion to make payments, the court would not interfere with their decision to make payments, provided that they did not act in a fraudulent or mischievous way.[98] Where the trustees refused to make payments, a bill could be filed in Chancery to direct them to be made.[99] However, the Chancery was very reluctant to order such payments when the child's father was still alive, for it took the view that provisions for maintenance in family settlements were to provide for children whose father had died before the time for the payment of their portions had come. They were not intended to give the father an additional income from which to pay for their children.[100] As Lord Hardwicke saw it, the law of nature obliged fathers to maintain their children, and the court would not direct the payment to be made 'unless the child from the mean circumstances of the parent is in danger of perishing for want'.[101] Trustees were reluctant to use funds for the maintenance of children who had other means of support, particularly where they were also directed to accumulate the income and settle it on the surviving children at majority. It was generally prudent for such trustees to seek the Court's guidance by bringing a bill, particularly where there was uncertainty about the exact interest of the child, or the powers of the trustees to make the payments.[102]

Trustees were also well advised to seek the court's guidance in cases where the right to portions given to children had vested, but the time for payment had not yet arrived. Settlements commonly provided that a portion was to be 'payable' at twenty-one or marriage but that it was only to be 'paid' after the death of the parents. In such cases, the child's right vested at majority or marriage, but the payment was postponed for the convenience of the estate. The children might, however, have need of the money before the time of the parents' death, and the question therefore arose whether trustees could sell or mortgage the reversionary estate. The early eighteenth-century view was summarised by Cowper LC in 1711:

> though a term is limited in remainder to commence after the death of the father, yet if the trust is to raise a portion payable at the age of eighteen or day of marriage, without question

[97] *Goldsmid v Goldsmid* (1815) 19 Ves Jun 368, 34 ER 554.

[98] *Collins v Vining* (1837) CP Cooper 472, 47 ER 472; *cf French v Davidson* (1818) 3 Madd 396, 56 ER 550; *Livesey v Beckett* (1830) Tamlyn 460, 48 ER 183.

[99] *Corbet v Tottenham* (1808) 1 Ball & Beat 59, 60.

[100] A Hofri-Winogradow, 'Parents, Children and Property in Late 18th-Century Chancery' (2012) 32 *Oxford Journal of Legal Studies* 741. See also *Jackson v Jackson* (1737) 1 Atk 513, 515; 26 ER 324, 325.

[101] *Butler v Butler* (1743) 3 Atk 58, 60; 26 ER 836, 837. The rule was relaxed in *Mundy v Earl Howe* (1793) 4 Bro CC 223, 29 ER 863, where a widower was permitted to use money settled by his wife for her separate use and the maintenance of her children from the marriage, since he already had six children from an earlier marriage who absorbed much of his income.

[102] See *Fairman v Green* (1804) 10 Ves Jun 45, 32 ER 760.

> the daughter shall not wait the death of her father; but at the age of eighteen or marriage may compel a sale of the term.[103]

This was not a view which was popular with parents – who often wished to maintain a degree of control over children – and so conveyancers drafted settlements which specified that portions were not to be paid until after the father's death. Lord Hardwicke was also inclined 'to lay hold of very small grounds, that speak of the intent of the parties, to hinder the raising of portions in the life of the father and mother'.[104] Some judges felt that Cowper's position encouraged improvident marriages by rebellious daughters; others felt that the court should recognise the financial needs of young adult women. When Eldon came to consider the question, he took the view that the court should 'hold an equal mind' on this question and thought that everything turned on the wording of the instrument. If it were certain that the daughter's right had vested, then money could be raised on it; but if there were any contingencies outstanding, then it could not. Trustees, therefore, had to be sure of the exact meaning of the instrument before acting, and in such cases, they were wise to be cautious.

VIII. Conclusion

Trustees played a central role in the holding and transmission of family property and family income. The very structure of the strict settlement required the existence of trustees to ensure the transmission of the family estate across generations. Trusts were also essential to secure the payment of debts and encumbrances on estates, as well as to provide for jointures and portions, and separate property for married women. In many respects trusts were more important to eighteenth- and early nineteenth-century families than particular trustees, for trustees were not generally expected to be particularly active, or exercise important discretion. Instead, they were often largely stakeholders, whose presence allowed the trust to exist and perform its function, but who did not need to take particular action. The trust could fulfil its function even if the trustee was an infant grandchild of the last surviving original trustee. Many family trusts were to a greater or lesser extent 'dry' trusts.

At the same time, many trustees did have active functions to perform, mainly in gathering and distributing money – or at least in checking and supervising whether money was gathered and distributed as directed under the settlement or will. Even here, however, they generally only had limited room to exercise discretion, and were expected to act as the court of Chancery itself would in managing an estate. While they were expected to ensure that assets remained productive – and consequently properly invested – their management of the assets was to follow the kind of prudence and caution which avoided any risk and ensured the preservation of the estate.

[103] *Corbett v Maidwell* (1711) 1 Salk 159, 91 ER 147.
[104] *Stanley v Stanley* (1737) 1 Atk 455, 26 ER 289.

17

Public Trusts, 1750–1850

CHARLES MITCHELL*

I. Introduction

In chapter sixteen, Michael Lobban discusses certain private trusts for beneficiaries that were common in the eighteenth and early nineteenth centuries, namely donative trusts for members of the settlor's family. At that time, there were also private trusts created by commercial parties for beneficiaries following a bargaining process, including trusts used in combination with contracts to create deed of settlement companies.[1] There were, in addition, public trusts, meaning trusts of property that was held not for the benefit of any person or group of persons as private individuals, but for public purposes, the accomplishment of which would benefit the community at large.

This chapter considers public trusts during roughly the same period as the one surveyed by Lobban, running on slightly to include discussion of the Municipal Corporations Act 1835,[2] but excluding discussion of the Charitable Trusts Act 1853,[3] which introduced a new regulatory regime for charitable trusts by creating a new body of Charity Commissioners.[4] Some attention is also paid to earlier periods, a knowledge of which helps to understand eighteenth- and nineteenth-century ideas about public trusts. The chapter examines town trusts (in Part II), statutory trusts for building and maintaining roads, bridges, docks, and harbours (in Part III), charitable trusts (in Part IV), and trusts of 'public money' owned by borough corporations (in Part V). These were not mutually exclusive categories of trust, and in practice they often overlapped, but it is helpful for expository purposes to divide the discussion in this way. Each type

* For their comments on drafts I thank David Foster, Jessica Hudson and Andreas Televantos.

[1] R Harris, *Industrialising English Law: Entrepreneurship and Business Organization, 1720–1844* (Cambridge, Cambridge University Press, 2000) 152–65; WR Cornish et al, *Law and Society in England 1750-1950*, 2nd edn (Oxford, Hart Publishing, 2019) 240–252; A Televantos, *Capitalism Before Corporations: The Morality of Business Associations and the Roots of Commercial Equity and Law* (Oxford, Oxford University Press, 2021) 35–52.

[2] 5 & 6 Will IV, c 76.

[3] 16 & 17 Vict, c 137.

[4] D Owen, *English Philanthropy 1660–1960* (Cambridge, MA, Harvard University Press, 1964) 182–208 and 247–308; SR Mealing, 'The British Charity Commission and the Cy-Près Doctrine, 1853–94: A Study in the Decline of Reforming Zeal' (1973) 6 *Histoire Sociale / Social History* 5; M Chesterman, *Charities, Trusts and Social Welfare* (London, Weidenfeld & Nicolson, 1979) 62–75; C Mitchell, 'Charitable Endowment and Social Change: Cy-Près Orders and Schemes, 1837–1901' (2020) 41 *Journal of Legal History* 29.

of trust was described by contemporary courts as a 'public trust',[5] but they did not pay much attention to what this term signified, nor did they discuss whether 'public trusts' were substantially different from 'private trusts' and, if so, what the consequences of that might be for the idea that trusts and trusts law comprised an integrated system of concepts and rules. These matters are considered further in Part VI.

It is useful to make some preliminary observations about borough corporations, since these make frequent appearances in the discussion. In the medieval and early modern periods, various towns obtained royal charters of borough incorporation. These created entities with legal personality that, for many purposes, was separate from the legal personalities of the town officials and town inhabitants.[6] At common law, borough corporations had the legal capacity to own property and powers to create regulatory bye-laws, breach of which could result in the levying of fines. It was obscure whether they also had common law powers to raise taxes, but this seems to have been untested because in practice the corporations (like towns without an incorporating charter) acquired statutory powers to levy rates when they wanted them in the 1700s and 1800s to fund town improvements.[7] Many corporations also borrowed money for this purpose, and before 1840, '80 per cent of local authority investment went on streets, bridges, docks, and harbours, largely to promote trade'.[8] Fines, rates and borrowing were relatively minor income sources for most corporations between 1750 and 1850, however; a larger proportion typically came from rents on property and receipts from charitable trusts for the provision of town amenities or for the general benefit of town inhabitants.[9]

By modern standards, central government in our period played only a small role in the formation of domestic social policy and provision of social welfare benefits. Much more work was done at the level of local government in both the towns and the country by self-actuating propertied elites who acted out of a sense of social and religious

[5] eg, *Boulton v Crowther* (1824) 2 B & C 703, 706; 107 ER 544, 546 (statutory turnpike trust); *Wilkinson v Malin* (1832) 2 Cr & J 636, 655–56; 149 ER 268, 275–76 (charitable trust); *AG v Cullum* (1836) 1 Keen 104, 104; 48 ER 246, 246 (town trust); *AG v Aspinall* (1837) 2 My & Cr 613, 630; 40 ER 773, 790 (trust of property owned by borough corporation).

[6] Recognised by the late 1490s: Sir J Baker, *Oxford History of the Laws of England, vol VI: 1483-1558* (Oxford, Oxford University Press, 2009) 626–27. It was not a given that liabilities incurred by a chartered corporation were separate from the legal liabilities of the corporation officials: *Charitable Corporation v Sutton* (1742) 2 Atk 400, 26 ER 642.

[7] S Anderson, 'Local Government' in WR Cornish et al, *Oxford History of the Laws of England, vol XI: 1820–1914 English Legal System* (Oxford, Oxford University Press, 2010) 427–28, noting that general acts also gave towns with exclusive quarter sessions the power to levy rates to pay for gaols, some bridges and various Poor Law purposes.

[8] I Webster, 'Making the Municipal Capital Market in Nineteenth-century England' (2022) 75 *Economic History Review* 56, 60. Sanitary improvements to alleviate public health problems became a concern only in the mid-1800s, reflected in the enactment of the Public Health Act 1848 (11 & 12 Vict, c 63) and the Public Health Act 1858 (21 & 22 Vict, c 97).

[9] This is described in many urban histories, eg, P Searby, 'Weavers and Freemen in Coventry, 1820-1861: Social and Political Traditionalism in an Early Victorian Town' (Warwick University PhD thesis, 1972; go.warwick.ac.uk/wrap/3472; last accessed 1 June 2023); G Bush, *Bristol and its Municipal Government 1820-1851* (Bristol, Bristol Record Society, 1976); AM Sparkes, 'The Municipal Corporation of Gloucester: Its Composition, Structure and Functions during the Early Nineteenth Century' (Gloucester University MA thesis, 2005; eprints.glos.ac.uk/2051/; last accessed 1 June 2023). See also K Grady, 'The Records of the Charity Commissions: A Source for Urban History' (1982) 9 *Urban History* 31, 32: in the early 1830s the combined incomes of the municipal charities of the main West Riding towns were: Sheffield £6,000; Leeds £4,800; Wakefield £3,000; Halifax £1,500; Doncaster £900; Ripon £600; Pontefract £500. With the exception of Doncaster, the corporations had much smaller incomes from property which belonged to them outright, eg, Leeds £200; Ripon £150.

obligation.[10] However, these elites also acted in self-interested ways and by 1750 there were many complaints that borough corporations were controlled by unelected, self-perpetuating oligarchies, Anglican in religion and Tory in politics, who used the corporation property as they chose, sometimes for the public good, sometimes for party political purposes, civic feasts, and perquisites escalating to a simple taking of the property for themselves.[11]

Pressure for reform mounted and eventually led to the Municipal Corporations Act 1835, although the immediate impetus behind the statute was political: it was a partisan Whig measure intended to break Tory control of the borough corporations, reduce their influence on parliamentary elections and redistribute their patronage.[12] The legislation preserved the legal status of the corporations as artificial persons but changed their political status by introducing town councils which were elected by the ratepayers and required to hold public meetings and have their accounts audited on an annual basis. As discussed in Parts IV and V, one result was the election of new town councillors, and the appointment of new trustees of municipal charities, many of whom then brought proceedings to recover property which had been misapplied under the old regimes.

II. Town Trusts

Although some towns obtained incorporating charters in medieval and early modern times, others did not, and in many of these, town elites used another device to secure the income needed to fund the construction and repair of town buildings, walls, streets, etc, and to care for the town poor – activities they wished to pursue out of social and religious duty, civic pride, economic self-interest, and the desire to obtain political power and independence from feudal lords. They bought land from the Crown and other territorial magnates and conveyed it to feoffees to uses, placing them under an obligation to apply the rent for the benefit of the town's inhabitants in specified ways. Some arrangements of this kind were made before the Reformation; more were made afterwards as land came onto the market following the dissolution of the religious houses and as the burden of social responsibilities on civic communities increased. They survived Henrician attacks on feoffments to uses[13] and later took the form of trusts, either because they were 'executed' by the Statute of

[10] See, eg, J Innes, 'Parliament and the Shaping of Eighteenth-Century English Social Policy' (1990) 40 *Transactions of the Royal Historical Society (5th series)* 63; P Langford, *Public Life and the Propertied Englishman, 1689–1798* (Oxford, Clarendon Press, 1991); D Eastwood, *Governing Rural England: Tradition and Transformation in Local Government 1780–1840* (Oxford, Clarendon Press, 1994).

[11] R Sweet, 'Corrupt and Corporate Bodies: Attitudes to Corruption in Eighteenth-Century and Early Nineteenth-Century Towns' in JR Moore and J Smith (eds), *Corruption in Urban Politics and Society, Britain 1780-1950* (Aldershot, Ashgate, 2007). At 45, Sweet notes Robert Tittler's contention that these problems and criticisms began in the 1600s: R Tittler, *The Reformation and the Towns in England: Politics and Political Culture c 1540-1640* (Oxford, Clarendon Press, 1998) 195–207.

[12] GBAM Finlayson, 'The Municipal Corporation Committee and Report, 1833–35' (1963) 36 *Bulletin of the Institute of Historical Research* 36; GBAM Finlayson, 'The Politics of Municipal Reform, 1835' (1966) 81 *English Historical Review* 673; J Phillips, *The Great Reform Bill in the Boroughs: English Electoral Behaviour 1818–1841* (Oxford, Clarendon Press, 1992) 42–44; P Salmon, *Electoral Reform at Work: Local Politics and National Parties, 1832–1841* (London, Boydell Press for the Royal Historical Society, 2002) 211.

[13] *AG v Porter* (1592) 1 Co Rep 22b, 24b; 76 ER 50, 54–55: 'For almost all the lands belonging to the towns or boroughs not incorporate are conveyed to several inhabitants of the parish and their heirs upon trust and

Uses 1536[14] or because they were drafted differently in later times. Their creation followed a common pattern, described by Richard Tittler:

> First, a group of townsmen secured sufficient funds to purchase from the Crown the desired properties. The Crown then granted the land to two or three of the townsmen who had been delegated by their fellows to receive it. These receivers then conveyed the same lands by formal deed to a larger group of named townsmen, usually a dozen or more, who then became the trustees or feoffees of that property. The deed in question conveyed to the feoffees not only the lands themselves, but also the powers of governance over them and control of rental income from them. In addition, such deeds also provided for the perpetuation of the feoffees, usually by co-option of replacements in their own numbers. In effect, deeds of trust granted both lands and governance and often served as governing instruments for the whole community. In some cases these endured, without incorporation or further enhancement, right up to the modern era.[15]

Some trusts were also created in towns where a charter had previously been obtained, and others in towns where a charter was obtained subsequently. In either case, the town trust then 'became a semi-autonomous but limited element of existing local government'.[16] Complicating the picture further, it often happened that later donors would gift more property to the trustees of town trusts. For example,[17] the Sheffield Town Burgesses' Trust began its life in 1297 when Thomas Furnival demised lands and tenements to free tenants in the town; additional property was added to the endowment for an assortment of public and charitable uses by later donors; by a 1681 decree of the Commissioners of Charitable Uses, all of these lands were then vested in trustees, their heirs and assignees, on trust for the repair of Lady's Bridge, the cleansing and repair of Barker's Pool for the use of the town inhabitants, the repair of causeways and highways in the locality, and other charitable and public uses in the town.[18]

Town trusts were trusts for the public purposes of the relevant town and were not trusts for the benefit of any of the town's inhabitants as private individuals.[19] To ensure continuity and share responsibilities, there were usually more trustees than would have

confidence to employ the profits to such good uses as defraying the tax of the town, repairing the highways, repairing the church, maintaining the poor of the parish, or supporting other charges of the parish, and no such uses (although they are common almost in every town) were ever made void by [the Mortmain Act 1532 (23 Hen VIII, c 10)].'

[14] 27 Hen VIII, c 10. Whether or not the statute applied to a feoffment to uses in this context would have depended on whether the uses were charitable. Charitable uses were active uses and not executed by the statute because this applied only to 'separated uses' (where a feoffee had seisin and a beneficiary had the use). Under an active use, seisin and use were conjoined: the feoffees had both seisin and the use in order to carry out their duties. Discussion in NG Jones, 'Uses, Trusts and a Path to Privity' [1997] *Cambridge Law Journal* 175, 179–82.

[15] Tittler (n 11) 82–3.

[16] ibid 85.

[17] Tittler discusses several other examples in Bridlington, Hungerford, Bury St Edmunds, Peterborough and Rotherham: ibid 84–7. See also D Pockley, 'The Origins and Early History of the Melton Mowbray Town Estate' (Leicester University PhD thesis, 1964; figshare.le.ac.uk/articles/thesis/The_origins_and_early_history_of_the_Melton_Mowbray_town_estate_A_study_in_the_government_of_an_unincorporated_town_/10178966/1; last accessed 1 June 2023); and *cf* MK McIntosh, *Poor Relief and Community in Hadleigh, Suffolk, 1547-1600* (Hatfield, University of Hertfordshire Press, 2013) 136–37.

[18] JD Leader (ed), *The Records of the Burgery of Sheffield, Commonly Called the Town Trust* (London, Elliot Stock, 1897).

[19] As recognised in the Municipal Corporations Act 1835, s 2, where a distinction was drawn between trusts 'for the particular benefit of the citizens, freemen, and burgesses of [cities, towns and boroughs]' – ie, for their benefit as private individuals – and trusts for 'public purposes'.

been appointed for a private trust, and for practical reasons the trustees were allowed to act by a majority (unlike private trustees who had to act unanimously).[20] Many town trusts predated the Statute of Charitable Uses 1601, legislation which created the Commissioners of Charitable Uses and gave them jurisdiction over trusts with the 'charitable' purposes described in the Preamble.[21] Many of these corresponded to the purposes of a typical town trust, including 'the relief of aged, impotent and poor people … schools of learning … the repair of bridges, ports, havens, causeways, churches, sea banks and highways … the relief, stock, or maintenance for houses of correction', and so on. The purposes of some town trusts were all charitable, and so they were 'charitable trusts',[22] but this was not always the case, and other town trusts were for charitable 'or other public' purposes – language used, for example, in *AG v Cullum* to describe the purposes of a town trust in Bury St Edmunds.[23]

Although the trustees of many town trusts were subject to the Commissioners' jurisdiction, the 1601 statute exempted them from the Commissioners' jurisdiction in cases where they had been created for the benefit of people living in incorporated towns, and were subject to the visitorial oversight of 'governors'. Proceedings could also be brought against the trustees of town trusts with charitable purposes by using the mechanisms for suing charitable trustees that are described in Part IV.

III. Statutory Trusts for Public Purposes

The purposes of many public trusts created by statute were similar to those of town trusts, and they were created for similar reasons by communally-minded propertied elites. Between 1689 and 1800, around 14,000 statutes were enacted, of which some 75 per cent – 10,000 statutes – were 'private' or 'local' Acts,[24] meaning that they were focused on particular regions and interests.[25] The dominance of private Acts continued into the nineteenth century, though the proportions changed: between 1800 and 1884, private Acts outnumbered public Acts by about 18,500 to 9,500.[26] Many private Acts

[20] *Wilkinson v Malin* (1832) 2 Cr & J 636, 654–6; 149 ER 268, 275–76.

[21] See further text following n 93.

[22] The legal form taken by such early town trusts as still survive, eg, (Barnstaple) Bridge Trust (Charity No 1184834); Bideford Bridge Trust (Charity No 204536); Bury St Edmunds Town Trust (Charity No 279477); Melton Mowbray Town Estate (Charity No 222142); Rochester Bridge Trust (Charity No 207100); Sheffield Town Trust (Charity No 223760).

[23] *AG v Cullum* (1836) 1 Keen 104, 104; 48 ER 246, 246.

[24] J Hoppit, 'Patterns of Parliamentary Legislation, 1660–1800' (1996) 39 *Historical Journal* 109; J Hoppit, *Britain's Political Economies: Parliament and Economic Life, 1660–1800* (Cambridge, Cambridge University Press, 2017) ch 2. In the 1700s and first half of the 1800s, most legislation of this kind was enacted as the result of local initiatives and it was notoriously expensive. In the 1830s the average cost of an unopposed town improvement bill was £1,627; opposed bills cost more and might fail: J Prest, *Liberty and Locality: Parliament, Permissive Legislation, and Ratepayers' Democracies in the Nineteenth Century* (Oxford, Clarendon Press, 1990) 5. The wording of one statute was often transplanted from another, but to reduce the overall expense of the process, Parliament began in the early 1800s to enact 'permissive' general legislation, setting out model clauses which the promoters of a private bill could adopt, or not, as they chose. An example is the Lighting and Watching Act 1833 (3 & 4 Will IV, c 90).

[25] 'Public' or 'general' acts, and 'private' or 'local' acts, were categories of legislation whose meaning shifted over time: S Lambert, *Bills and Acts: Legislative Procedure in Eighteenth Century England* (Cambridge, Cambridge University Press, 1971).

[26] F Clifford, *A History of Private Bill Legislation* (London, Butterworths, 1885) vol 1, vii.

were measures obtained by landowners to serve their own interests, most obviously the thousands of enclosure acts passed in the later 1700s (though it was argued that these were in the public interest because they increased agricultural productivity). Others were enacted for more self-evidently 'public' purposes, including[27]

> the paving, lighting or watching of streets, construction and regulation of market places, rebuilding of churches, improvement of roads, bridges and harbours, establishment of theatres, county halls and prisons, of small debt courts, workhouses and boards of poor law guardians.[28]

Some legislation empowered a borough corporation to levy rates to fund amenities such as water supplies, street paving and street lighting.[29] A still more common route was to obtain a private Act which appointed improvement commissioners who were given similar tax-raising powers for similar purposes.[30] None of this legislation expressly brought trusts into being, and the tax revenue was treated as property to which the corporation (or commissioners) were absolutely entitled – though as we shall see in Part V, an equitable rule emerged in the early 1800s that all property owned by borough corporations (or statutory commissioners) was held on trust for the public purpose of benefiting the community.

Other private Acts did expressly create trusts, for example, statutes which created trusts for the purposes of public infrastructure projects, such as the building and repair of bridges,[31] docks and harbours,[32] and turnpike roads. The following discussion will focus on turnpike trusts,[33] but bridge trusts, dock trusts and harbour trusts all worked in a similar way.

Historically, responsibility for maintaining the roads had been allocated to the parishes, and statute labour had been supplied by landowners (exercising powers to

[27] In addition, some legislation was enacted to create disaster funds, eg, the Blandford Forum (Rebuilding after Fire) Act 1732 (5 Geo II, c 16), which appointed 'managers' of a 'publick Trust' to rebuild Blandford after a fire; they owed accounting duties as 'undertakers' of the scheme prescribed by an earlier statute (3 & 4 Ann, c 14), as discussed in *ex parte Angle* (1740) Barn Ch 423, 27 ER 705; reported as *ex parte Angel* (1741) 2 Atk 163, 26 ER 502.

[28] J Innes, 'The Local Acts of a National Parliament: Parliament's Role in Sanctioning Local Action in Eighteenth Century Britain' (1998) 17 *Parliamentary History* 23, 24. See too Langford (n 10) 155–66; and *cf* S Handley, 'Local Legislative Initiatives for Economic and Social Development in Lancashire, 1689-1731' (1990) 9 *Parliamentary History* 14.

[29] eg, Gloucester Water Supply Act 1740 (14 Geo II, c 11); Norwich Water Act 1790 (30 Geo III, c 21).

[30] eg, Birmingham Street Improvement Act 1769 (9 Geo III, c 83); Mansfield Improvement Act 1823 (4 Geo IV, c 92) (discussed in C Smith, 'Urban Improvement in the Nottinghamshire Market Town, 1770-1840' (2000) 25 *Midland History* 98). One hundred and sixty Improvement Commissions were created between 1725 and 1799: EL Jones and ME Falkus, 'Urban Improvement and the English Economy in the Seventeenth and Eighteenth Centuries' in P Borsay (ed), *The Eighteenth Century Town: A Reader in English Urban History, 1688-1820* (London, Routledge, 1990) 139, Table 1. For a detailed account of town improvement acts, see FH Spencer, *Municipal Origins: An Account of English Private Bill Legislation Relating to Local Government, 1740-1835* (London, Constable & Co, 1911) 174–236.

[31] eg, Walton-Shepperton Bridge (Building and Tolls) Act 1747 (20 Geo II, c 22); Taunton Bridges Act 1809 (49 Geo III, c 84); Clifton Suspension Bridge Act 1830 (11 Geo IV, c 69) (regarding which see DR Portman, 'A Business History of the Clifton Suspension Bridge' (2002) 18 *Construction History* 3).

[32] eg, Scarborough Harbour Act 1731 (5 Geo II, c 11); Liverpool Dock Act 1737 (11 Geo II, c 32); Carnarvon Harbour Act 1793 (33 Geo III, c 123); Kingston-upon-Hull Docks Act 1802 (42 Geo III, c 91).

[33] Drawing on W Albert, *The Turnpike Road System in England, 1663-1840* (Cambridge, Cambridge University Press, 1972) chs 1, 2 and 4; E Pawson, *Transport and Economy: The Turnpike Roads of Eighteenth Century Britain* (London, Academic Press, 1977) chs 4 and 7.

make their tenants do the work), although by 1750 their obligation to supply statutory labour had generally been commuted into a duty to pay money.[34] Parish responsibility to maintain the highways remained the default position into the nineteenth century,[35] but long before then, many parishes had let the roads deteriorate rather than increase the parish rates to cover the costs of upgrading them and repairing the damage caused by the carriages and heavy carts of long-distance travellers and traders. A solution was found in the use of a toll system. In the late 1600s, turnpike acts were enacted to empower justices of the peace to maintain stretches of turnpike road, erect gates and collect tolls from users to pay for repair and improvement. In the early 1700s, these 'justice trusts' were replaced by 'turnpike trusts', also statutory creations, which conferred the same powers on independent bodies of trustees.

The legislation initially provided for appeals against the trustees' actions to be made to the justices, who could appoint inspectors to report back on abuses, but provisions of this kind disappeared from turnpike acts after 1750, freeing the trustees from immediate supervision and leaving them with 'extensive and virtually unchecked administrative and financial powers'.[36] They were accountable to Parliament, but in practice were paid little attention until widespread financial problems led to a series of select committees in the early 1800s and the introduction of a requirement in 1822,[37] that an audited account be sent annually to the Clerk of the Peace for the county in which the major part of the road was situated. The method used for presenting these accounts was modified in 1833,[38] after which a copy of the annual statement had to be sent to the Home Office for general publication. These measures increased the transparency of turnpike trustees' dealings, although in William Albert's words,

> Parliament seems to have been more concerned with protecting the creditors of the turnpikes than with effectively supervising the manner in which the trustees carried out their duties.[39]

Turnpike acts usually stipulated a twenty-one year perpetuity period for the trust, envisaging that the road would then be handed back to the parish authorities in good repair. This corresponded to the period (of twenty-one years after the death of a relevant life in being) that applied to common law trusts other than charitable trusts (to which no perpetuity rule applied). Frequently, though, acts were renewed by further legislation, and additional legislation was also passed in many cases to authorise extensions to the highway, variations in the route, increases in the tolls, etc.[40] Turnpike trustees sometimes

[34] Rates of commutation were standardised by the Highways Act 1773 (13 Geo III, c 78).

[35] The system for maintaining non-turnpike roads was overhauled by the General Highways Act 1835 (5 & 6 Will IV, c 50) which confirmed the parish as the responsible authority but dropped the requirement that inhabitants should maintain them and provided that this should be done by hired labour. The Highways Act 1862 (25 & 26 Vict, c 21) empowered the Home Office to force parishes into highway districts governed by Highways Boards consisting of locally elected members and JPs.

[36] Albert (n 33) 59. At 23, Albert suggests that the requirement for supervision by the justices was abandoned because they could not cope with the work in addition to their other duties.

[37] Turnpike Roads Act 1822 (3 Geo IV, c 126).

[38] Turnpike Trusts Returns Act 1833 (3 & 4 Will IV, c 80).

[39] Albert (n 33) 59.

[40] eg, the Bath Turnpike Trust was the subject of legislation in 1707 (6 Ann, c 42), 1721 (7 Geo I, c 19), 1739 (12 Geo II, c 20), 1757 (30 Geo II, c 67), 1759 (32 Geo II, c 51), 1761 (1 Geo III, c 31), 1793 (73 Geo III, c 144) and 1829 (10 Geo IV c 110); discussion in BJ Buchanan, 'The Evolution of the English Turnpike Trusts: Lessons from a Case Study' (1986) 39 *Economic History Review* 223.

owned the land over which the road passed,[41] and the toll houses,[42] but they did not always do so; nor did they own the right to pass along the highway, which belonged to the Crown. However, the legislation gave trustees the right to collect tolls, which they held on trust for the purpose of repairing the road, or more often, as Arden MR said in *Buckeridge v Ingham*, 'for borrowing money to be employed in repairing the road'.[43]

This was because trustees typically needed to raise money for repairs at the outset, and so in addition to their toll-charging powers, they were empowered to borrow money against the security of toll revenue[44] (the right to collect which was often leased on a fixed-term basis[45]) and sometimes the toll houses.[46] The legislation typically exempted the trustees from liability to repay the sums borrowed out of their personal funds: provided they had acted within their statutory borrowing powers,[47] they were liable only to pay creditors out of money which had been received as toll revenue.[48] The same rule also generally applied to trustee liability under contracts for repairs.[49] According to Lord Eldon in *Higgins v Livingstone*, however,

> when persons act under a parliamentary trust, and state themselves as so acting, they are not to be held personally liable. But this also, I think, rests on strong principle, that as the trustees must know whether there are funds to answer the purpose, they, when they contract with others who do not know, act as if representing that they had a fund applicable to the object, and are then personally bound to provide funds to pay the contractors.[50]

Between 1755 and 1845, most of the capital finance for turnpike road improvements came from individual lenders, most of whom lent sums of less than £100, ie, they were often small owners of capital seeking a steady income from the interest.[51] Larger lenders included borough corporations[52] and owners of agricultural estates. They calculated that apart from the interest earned on their loans, they would also benefit in other ways, either from the economic effects of enhancing the town's transport links or from increased land values and increased rental income as better roads made it easier to

[41] As in, eg, *R v Trustees of Great Dover Street Road* (1836) 5 Ad & E 692, 111 ER 1327.

[42] As in, eg, *Doe v Penfold* (1842) 3 QB 757, 114 ER 698.

[43] *Buckeridge v Ingham* (1795) 2 Ves Jun 652, 659; 30 ER 824, 829.

[44] RH Coote, *A Treatise on the Law of Mortgage* (London, J Butterworth & Son and J Cooke, 1821 and 1823) book 2, ch 12: 'Of Mortgages of Tolls'.

[45] As in, eg, *Paul v Meek* (1828) 2 Y & J 116, 148 ER 855; *Pearse v Morris* (1834) 2 Ad & E 85, 111 ER 32. General discussion in Pawson (n 33) 211–14.

[46] According to Lord Eldon in *Doe v Booth* (1800) 2 Bos & Pul 219, 223; 126 ER 1245, 1248, there was 'a great difference between a demise of tolls and of toll-houses' because 'the former gives only a personal interest, in respect of which an action for money had and received may be maintained', while 'the latter gives an interest in the land'. Neither would prove to be adequate security when toll income generally decreased in the 1830s: F Phillips, *Analysis of the Defective State of Turnpike Roads as Securities* (Manchester, Longman, 1834).

[47] For a case where this did not happen and the trustees were therefore personally liable to pay out of their own pockets, see *Parrott v Eyre* (1838) 10 Bing 283, 131 ER 913.

[48] *Pardoe v Price* (1844) 13 M & W 267, 284–85; 153 ER 110, 118.

[49] And to the personal liability of the trustees' clerk where the statute permitted the trustees to sue and be sued in the clerk's name: *Wormwell v Hailstone* (1830) 6 Bing 668, 130 ER 1438.

[50] *Higgins v Livingstone* (1816) 4 Dow 341, 355–56; 3 ER 1186, 1191.

[51] I Webster, 'The Public Works Loan Board 1817-76 and the Financing of Public Infrastructure' (Sheffield Hallam University PhD thesis, 2015; shura.shu.ac.uk/9939/7/10701157.pdf; last accessed 1 June 2023) 66–8.

[52] eg, in the early 1800s, Leeds corporation had £500 invested in the Leeds and Wakefield turnpike trust: BJ Barber, 'Leeds Corporation, 1835-1905: A History of its Environmental, Social, and Administrative Services' (Leeds University PhD thesis, 1975; theses.whiterose.ac.uk/26088/; last accessed 1 June 2023) 31.

travel and transport produce into markets.[53] More than one thousand turnpike acts were passed between 1760 and 1800, and the peak years for investment into the turnpike system were the mid-1820s.[54] However, many turnpike trusts were 'insolvent' for long periods because the toll income did not cover the trustees' debts, and this problem worsened as a result of competition from the railways. In 1834, turnpike trusts owed lenders nearly £1 million of unpaid interest on loans of around £8 million.[55] It came to be perceived that the turnpike system was unsustainable and that trusts needed to be wound down. At first, statutes were enacted to renew trusts if they were still in debt, but to abolish those which had achieved solvency;[56] insolvent trusts were then allowed to lapse as well, with the result that thousands of lenders lost £5.4 million between 1850 and 1880, more than one-third of the total amounts to which they were entitled.[57]

The trustees of a turnpike trust were often numerous: several hundred trustees were sometimes appointed, chosen for their wealth and social respectability to encourage lenders but without any expectation that they would participate in the trust affairs. These were managed by smaller groups of trustees – usually fewer than a dozen – who were unpaid but who directed a group of salaried officials – a clerk, treasurer and surveyor – who undertook the day-to-day business and whose salaries were paid out of the trust income. By modern standards, their accounting practices were crude: they had 'little idea of the costs of overheads, of capital, and of depreciation', there was 'no attempt by turnpike trusts to distinguish between new work and maintenance, and there was therefore no attempt to separate capital and current costs'.[58] Turnpike trustees were regularly criticised for these and other slack administrative practices and for their lack of accountability.[59] Turnpike roads were also unpopular with the inhabitants of localities through which they passed, who resented paying a toll to use roads which they had previously used for free,[60] and with the ratepayers who had to pay tolls although they also had to pay rates to fund the composition payments which were still payable by the parish authorities to the trustees.[61]

Turnpike trusts were not meant to be private profit-making ventures like canal and railway companies: the right to levy tolls was conferred on trustees on the basis that

[53] According to Dan Bogart land values and rental yields rose by 20 per cent as a result of road improvements delivered by turnpike trusts: D Bogart, 'Turnpike Trusts and Property Income: New Evidence on the Effects of Transport Improvement and Legislation in Eighteenth Century England' (2009) 62 *Economic History Review* 128.

[54] Webster (2015) (n 51) 68.

[55] *Returns from Turnpike Trusts* (PP 1836, XLVII).

[56] Starting with the Turnpike Acts Continuance Act 1834 (4 and 5 Will IV, c 10).

[57] Webster (2015) (n 51) 85.

[58] JE Ginarlis, 'Road and Waterway Investment in Britain, 1750-1850' (Sheffield University PhD thesis, 1970; etheses.whiterose.ac.uk/10379/; last accessed 1 June 2023) 28–9; and see 28–37 for detailed discussion of turnpike trust accounts.

[59] Albert (n 33) 61–4; Pawson (n 33) 178–80.

[60] Sometimes leading to rioting and destruction of toll gates, etc: D Lemmings, *Law and Government in England during the Long Eighteenth Century: From Consent to Command* paperback edn (Basingstoke, Palgrave Macmillan, 2015) 150–55; A Randall, *Riotous Assemblies: Popular Protest in Hanoverian England* (Oxford, Oxford University Press, 2006) 159–166 and sources cited in 161, fn 38.

[61] Parishes remained liable to provide statutory labour or to make composition payments in lieu of labour on turnpiked roads, though in practice trustees only demanded composition payments from wealthy parishes: Ginarlis (n 58) 51, noting a 'total lack of system in the relations between parishes and turnpikes'. If a turnpike trust became insolvent, the cost of maintaining the road fell back on the parish: *R v Inhabitants of Netherthong* (1818) 2 B & Ald 179, 106 ER 332; *R v Inhabitants of Preston* (1848) 12 QB 816, 116 ER 1076.

they would not keep the revenue for themselves and would apply it for the public good. This was why trustees were exempted from liability for the poor rate by the Turnpike Roads Act 1822, s 51.[62] In practice, though, it was common for trustees to invest their own capital,[63] producing a conflict between their personal interest in making a profit out of the road and the public interest in its improvement; there were also some trustees who obtained business as road contractors or lawyers through their trusteeships,[64] a practice criminalised by section 65 of the 1822 Act.[65] However, few civil proceedings were brought against trustees or their servants for theft or mismanagement,[66] the costs of proceedings often being prohibitive.[67]

IV. Charitable Trusts

As noted in Part II, the Statute of Charitable Uses 1601 created a body of Commissioners charged with overseeing trusts for the purposes listed in the Preamble. These purposes were described as 'charitable', but this was not a fully-fledged legal term of art at the time, and indeed the 1601 Act would itself subsequently play a significant role in turning 'charity' into a legal concept with a particular meaning that was separate from its everyday meaning.[68] Furthermore, the list in the Preamble was not intended to be exhaustive: many trusts for purposes which would also have been thought of as 'charitable' for legal purposes were not included because they were already overseen by a supervising authority, and so there was no need to subject them to the additional jurisdiction of the Commissioners. Most prominently, the list does not include the religious purposes of the Church of England, trusts for which were subject to the visitorial jurisdiction of Church officials.

As explained by Gareth Jones, it was therefore accepted in the seventeenth century that purposes other than those named in the Preamble could be legally charitable, and such efforts as were made by the courts to define these fastened on the idea of charity

[62] 3 Geo IV, c 126, considered in *R v Trustees of Great Dover Street Road* (1836) 5 Ad & E 692, 700; 111 ER 1327, 1330. *Cf Manley v St Helen's Canal and Railway Co* (1858) 2 H & N 840, 852; 157 ER 346, 353: 'turnpike trustees … are empowered to collect tolls, not for the benefit of themselves, but of the public; they are public officers discharging public duties for the benefit of the public.'

[63] Though the amounts lent by trustees and other investors varied, and in some cases, trustee lending was a relatively small part of the whole: Buchanan (n 40) 231–32.

[64] Albert (n 33) 98–100; Langford (n 10) 250, 253–54, 258–59, 261. But Pawson (n 33) 195 considers that although jobbery was probably widespread, 'the grounds for assuming that this led to high prices and mismanagement are from convincing'.

[65] 3 Geo IV, c 126; considered in *Towsey v White* (1826) 5 B & C 125, 108 ER 46.

[66] But *cf Earl of Lonsdale v Church* (1790) 3 Bro CC 41, 29 ER 396: receiver of harbour dues appointed by trustees of statutory trust for building and maintenance of Whitehaven harbour had to account for receipts and pay interest on the amounts if he applied funds to his own use without the trustees' permission.

[67] As in, eg, *Tredwyll v Byrch* (1835) 1 Y & C Ex 476, 160 ER 194 (proceedings struck out because insolvent plaintiff failed to give security for costs).

[68] According to Baker (n 6) 717, 'charity' had acquired no certain legal meaning in 1547. Fifty years on the same was true, although prior to the Reformation the ecclesiastical courts had already taken jurisdiction over the administration of testamentary estates, justified this on the basis that it was the Church's business to secure the enforcement of charitable bequests, and developed a set of legal rules to determine whether particular bequests were charitable: RH Helmholz, *Oxford History of the Laws of England, vol 1: The Canon Law and Ecclesiastical Jurisdiction from 597 to the 1640s* (Oxford, Oxford University Press, 2004) 417–19.

'as a *public use*', meaning that a charitable purpose was one from which a substantial portion of the public would derive a benefit.[69] This idea continued into the eighteenth century, when Lord Hardwicke stressed the 'extensiveness' of a charitable purpose,[70] and Lord Camden observed that a charitable gift was

> a gift to the general public use, which extends to the poor as well as the rich … many instances in the [1601 Act] carrying this idea, as for building bridges, &c. The supplying of water is necessary as well as convenient for the poor and the rich.[71]

Other eighteenth-century precedents about the definition of charitable purposes are confused and paradoxical, however, owing to the Mortmain and Charitable Uses Act 1736.[72] This was enacted out of anti-clerical sentiment and the fear that heirs would be cut out by testamentary gifts of land to ecclesiastical charities.[73] The statute invalidated testamentary devises of land to charity and vested the property in the testator's heir-at-law or next-of-kin. To invalidate as many devises as possible, the courts expanded the legal definition of charity beyond the list of purposes in the 1601 Preamble, with the result that testamentary gifts of land for newly recognised charitable purposes were void.[74] To achieve the same objective, the courts also took the opposite approach when considering testamentary trusts of money or chattels to which the 1736 Act did not apply: where these were for new purposes, they were excluded from the definition of legally charitable purposes and invalidated for breach of the perpetuity rules or the absence of anyone with standing to enforce the trust. Exemplifying the latter approach was *Morice v Bishop of Durham* where Grant MR and Lord Eldon held that legally charitable purposes were only those listed in the Preamble or within its 'spirit and intendment', and that with the exception of charitable trusts, the law did not generally permit trusts for purposes because there was no one at whose behest an order for execution of the trust could be made.[75]

In Jones's words, the effect of restricting the legal definition of charity in *Morice* was to drive 'a wedge between the charitable and public trust'. In other words, trusts for purposes which would benefit the community at large were no longer automatically held to be legally charitable. Instead, the 'spirit' of the Preamble was turned into a 'Delphic oracle' of charity,[76] with the result complained of by Sir Samuel Romilly in *Mayor and*

[69] GH Jones, *History of the Law of Charity 1532–1827* (Cambridge, Cambridge University Press, 1969) 120–22.

[70] *AG v Pearce* (1740) 2 Atk 87, 88; 26 ER 454, 454.

[71] *Jones v Williams* (1767) Amb 651, 652; 27 ER 422, 422. For discussion, see J Garton, '*Jones v Williams* (1767)': The First Definition of Charity in R Fry and J Picton (eds), *Landmark Cases in Charity Law* (Oxford, Hart Publishing, forthcoming).

[72] 9 Geo II, c 36; discussed in Jones (n 69) chs 6, 7 and 9.

[73] *AG v Day* (1748) 1 Ves Sen 219, 223; 27 ER 992, 995 (Lord Hardwicke LC): 'The particular views of the legislature were two: first to prevent the locking up of land and real property from being aliened;… second, to prevent persons in their last moments from being imposed on to give their real estate from their families … for by that means, in times of popery, the clergy got almost half the real property of the kingdom into their hands, and indeed I wonder they did not get the rest: as people thought they thereby purchased heaven.'

[74] As in, eg, *Townley v Bedwell* (1801) 6 Ves Jun 194, 31 ER 1008; *Trustees of the British Museum v White* (1826) 2 Sim & St 594, 57 ER 473.

[75] *Morice v Bishop of Durham* (1804) 9 Ves Jun 399, 32 ER 656 (Grant MR); (1805) 10 Ves Jun 522, 32 ER 947 (Lord Eldon); discussed in J Getzler, '*Morice v Bishop of Durham* (1805)' in C Mitchell and P Mitchell (eds), *Landmark Cases in Equity* (Oxford, Hart Publishing, 2012).

[76] Jones (n 69) 132 and 133.

Commonalty of Colchester v Lowten, that 'The Distinction between charitable and public Trusts is so nice and refined, that it can scarcely be followed.'[77] Whether a trust's purposes were charitable or non-charitable remained obscure for the rest of the nineteenth century (and into modern times), not least because there were different practical reasons why it could matter whether or not a trust was charitable. The cy-près doctrine applied primarily to charitable trusts; different perpetuity rules applied to charitable and non-charitable trusts; some fiscal exemptions were granted to charitable trusts but not to others;[78] and the Chancery originally took jurisdiction over trustees of charitable trusts but not over public trusts for other purposes, although as we shall see in Part V it was later extended to take in the latter type of trust as well.

Following the Reformation, charitable trusts were mainly endowed by donors actuated by religious and philanthropic motives to support the institutions and activities of the Church of England (but not 'superstitious' Roman Catholic religious observances and practices,[79] or indeed those of other religions), to establish dole funds or disaster funds, to endow almshouses, hospitals, and schools, to build and maintain public structures and amenities, etc. They did this either in their wills or, from the eighteenth century onwards, via public charitable subscriptions. Charitable trusts were also created in some other situations – for example, where they formed part of an enclosure award made under an enclosure act. Where common land had been used for parochial poor relief, or held on charitable trust for the relief of poverty,[80] enclosure awards often allotted part of the land to trustees to hold it on trust for the benefit of the 'labouring poor' in the neighbourhood. Such people might then be allowed to make direct use of the land, or it might be let and the income distributed as doles or used to defray the costs of poor relief and/or finance the construction and upkeep of parish and municipal buildings and infrastructure.[81]

Problems of interpretation could be caused by the wording of enclosure awards, which left it unclear whether land allotted for the use of the poor should be held on a stand-alone charitable trust or was meant to form part of a borough corporation's funds for application to its general purposes.[82] Uncertainty could also be created by gifts to the inhabitants of a town to build and maintain streets, walls, bridges, etc, without any clear direction that the property should be held on a charitable trust. An example is *AG v Corporation of Shrewsbury*,[83] where Romilly MR concluded that the Crown's gift of tolls to a corporation had been a

[77] *Mayor and Commonalty of Colchester v Lowten* (1813) 1 V & B 226, 240; 39 ER 89, 94.

[78] On income tax, see MJ Gousmett, 'The Charitable Purposes Exemption from Income Tax: Pitt to *Pemsel* 1798-1891' (University of Canterbury PhD thesis, 2009; ir.canterbury.ac.nz/bitstream/handle/10092/3448/thesis_fulltext.pdf?sequence=2&isAllowed=y; last accessed 1 June 2023). In earlier times, there were also charitable exemptions from the poor rate, house duty and window tax; their applicability to particular trusts was not infrequently litigated.

[79] *Cf* Chantries Acts 1545 (37 Hen VIII, c 4) and 1547 (1 Edw VI, c 14); discussed in Jones (n 69) ch 2.

[80] S Birtles, 'Common Land, Poor Relief and Enclosure: The Use of Manorial Resources in Fulfilling Parish Obligations 1601–1834' (1999) 165 *Past & Present* 74.

[81] As under an award made in Kendal in 1757 discussed in I Whyte, '"Wild, Barren and Frightful" – Parliamentary Enclosure in an Upland County: Westmorland 1767–1890' (2003) 14 *Rural History* 1, 25. An example from a later period is provided by an award made under the Nottingham Enclosure Act 1845 (8 & 9 Vict, c 7) that allotted 120 acres of land to the Nottingham Corporation in trust for the people of Nottingham for public baths and walks, cricket and football grounds.

[82] Sometimes after a very long period, as in *Densham v Charity Commission* [2018] UKUT 0402 (TCC), [2019] WTLR 473, which concerned an award made under the Inclosure Act 1845 (8 & 9 Vict, c 118) s 73.

[83] *AG v Corporation of Shrewsbury* (1843) 6 Beav 220, 230–31, 49 ER 810, 814.

> gift for a public and general purpose … for the benefit of the town in aid of a general charge or burden to which the burgesses and inhabitants of the town were liable … which under the equity of the statute of Elizabeth, ought to be considered as a gift to charitable uses.

Donors often appointed borough corporations or their officials (mayors, aldermen, etc) as the trustees of their charitable settlements. There were practical reasons for this: corporations never died, and their officials could easily be replaced; they held positions of authority in the community and were often already engaged in carrying out similar purposes.[84] However, two long-term effects were evident by the late 1700s: first, the income derived by many corporations from municipal charities was much larger than their other income;[85] and, second, all of the corporations' income was frequently mixed together and spent in ways that did not comply with the trust terms.[86] This was a breach of trust even when it was done in good faith, when the money was spent on some public purpose and when town officials took no personal benefit from the expenditure[87] – and when introducing the bill which became the Municipal Corporations Act 1835, the Whig government asserted that such practices were not always done in good faith. The solution they proposed was to empower the newly elected town councillors to appoint new sets of trustees of municipal charities, but the Tories objected that this would simply perpetuate political control of the charities' funds. The Tories therefore successfully introduced an amendment which led to sections 71–73 of the 1835 Act, which deprived town councils of any right to appoint trustees and gave a power of appointment to the Lord Chancellor (who delegated it to the Chancery Masters).[88] One result was that new charity trustees were appointed who brought proceedings against corporations to establish ownership rights in trust property which had previously been treated as belonging to the corporation outright[89] and proceedings for recovery against the recipients of misapplied trust funds.[90]

Charitable trusts were trusts for purposes, and so there were no beneficiaries to whom the trustees had to account for their handling of trust property. Some settlors

[84] *Cf Evan v Corporation of Avon* (1860) 29 Beav 144, 149; 54 ER 581, 584 (Romilly MR): 'a person might leave money to a corporation, in trust for the benefit of the inhabitants of a particular place or for paving or lighting the town. That would be a public trust for the benefit of all the inhabitants.'

[85] See n 9.

[86] RA McKinley (ed), *The Victoria History of the County of Leicester, vol 4: The City of Leicester* (London, Institute of Historical Research, 1958) 410: 'Most of the endowed charities established in Leicester between the Reformation and the Municipal Corporations Act of 1835 were vested in the corporation as trustee. The lands bought with the money left by the founders of charities were always regarded as corporation property and the money for the payment of the charities came out of the general funds of the corporation.' Similarly, see A Crossley and CR Elrington (eds), *The Victoria History of the County of Oxford, vol 4: The City of Oxford* (London, Institute of Historical Research, 1979) 462.

[87] eg, *AG v Mayor of Newbury* (1834) 3 My & K 647, 651–52; 40 ER 246, 248 (Lord Brougham); though a more lenient approach was taken in cases where trustees acted by mistake and in good faith: *AG v Mayor, Bailiffs, and Commonalty of the City of Exeter* (1826) 2 Russ 45, 54; 38 ER 252, 256 (Lord Eldon); and *AG v Bailiffs and Burgesses of East Retford* (1833) 2 My & K 35, 37; 39 ER 857, 858–59 (Leach MR). Anderson, 'Local Government' (n 7) 431–32 observes that at least some cases of this kind can plausibly be characterised as 'reasonable municipal management in changing times'.

[88] Anderson, 'Local Government' (n 7) 432–33.

[89] See, eg, Sparkes (n 9) 97–8, describing Chancery litigation between the trustees of the Crypt school in Gloucester and the Gloucester corporation which ran from 1844 to 1857 and finally ended in victory for the charity trustees.

[90] Trustees of Bristol charities brought proceedings to recover amounts assessed at £344,000, 'a sum almost equivalent to the entire municipal estate'; these were settled in 1841: Bush (n 9) 155–56; see also M Gorsky, *Patterns of Philanthropy: Charity and Society in Nineteenth-Century Bristol* (Woodbridge, Boydell Press for Royal Historical Society, 1999) 68–77.

of charitable trusts (and founders of charitable corporations) gave themselves (and/or their heirs or others) powers as 'visitors' to supervise the administration of the charitable funds and to take action against the trustees in the event of irregularities.[91] Where such visitors had been appointed, Chancery generally had no jurisdiction to hear complaints about trustee maladministration,[92] but otherwise it had a long-standing jurisdiction over charitable trustees.

The history of this has been set out by Gareth Jones,[93] whose account will be briefly summarised. By the mid-1500s, anyone alleging mismanagement of a charity could file a bill of complaint in Chancery, but few proceedings were brought because defendants could use delaying motions to drag matters out, and the sums at stake were often too small for litigation to be worthwhile. Many abuses therefore went uncorrected, and the Statute of Charitable Uses 1601 was designed to address this by appointing commissioners who would investigate misconduct brought to their attention by juries; after hearing witness testimony and other evidence, the commissioners could issue a decree. This system was initially a success but petered out after the Civil War.

During the 1600s, it was also established that the Attorney-General could bring misconduct into Chancery by filing an information using the bill and answer procedure, and that individuals could file an information in his name, acting as 'relators'.[94] This became the main process by which proceedings were brought against charity trustees in the 1700s, but the Attorney-General could not be made to pay the costs of an unsuccessful information,[95] and in practice he would act only on the relation of individuals who bore the risk of paying the costs. Few were willing to do this, although from time to time some appeared.[96]

An effort was made to address the costs problem by the Charities Procedure Act 1812 ('Sir Samuel Romilly's Act').[97] This empowered interested parties to file a petition with the Chancellor seeking a summary inquiry of an alleged charitable abuse and thereby avoid having to file a relator action. However, the legislation was restrictively

[91] OD Tudor, *The Law of Charitable Trusts*, 2nd edn (London, Butterworths, 1862) ch 4.

[92] As noted in, eg, *AG v Governors of Harrow School* (1754) 2 Ves Sen 551, 552; 28 ER 351, 352. Chancery judges were unimpressed by arguments that founders or settlors who did not appoint a visitor must have intended to exempt charitable trustees from any supervision at all. See, eg, *Eden v Foster* (1725) 2 P Wms 325, 326–27; 24 ER 750, 750 (Lord King): 'it would be of the most pernicious consequence imaginable, that any person intrusted with the receipts of rents and profits, and especially for a charity, though they misemploy never so much these rents and profits, should yet be unaccountable for their receipts; this would be such a privilege as might of itself be a temptation to a breach of trust'.

[93] Jones (n 69) 16–56 and 160–164.

[94] There was no requirement that a person acting as relator should have a private interest in the due administration of the charity: *AG v Bucknall* (1741) 2 Atk 328, 328; 26 ER 600, 600; followed in *AG v Vivian* (1826) 1 Russ 226, 236; 38 ER 88, 92.

[95] *Bailiffs, Burgesses and Commonalty of the Town or Borough of Ludlow v Greenhouse* (1827) 1 Bligh NS 17, 48; 4 ER 780, 791.

[96] eg, *AG v Mayor, Bailiffs and Commonalty of the City of Coventry* (1702) Colles 280, 1 ER 286; *Haberdashers Company v AG* (1702) 2 Bro PC 370, 1 ER 1003; *AG v Lady Hart* (1703) Prec Ch 225, 24 ER 109; *AG v Lord Gower* (1740) 9 Mod 224, 88 ER 412; *AG v Mayor, Aldermen and Burgesses of Stamford* (1747) 2 Swans 591, 36 ER 741; *AG v Griffith* (1807) 13 Ves Jun 565, 33 ER 406; *AG v Heelis* (1824) 2 Sim & St 67, 7 ER 270.

[97] 52 Geo III, c 101; considered in *ex parte Rees* (1814) 3 V & B 10, 12; 35 ER 382, 383 (Lord Eldon): 'in Cases, where there is a Charity Trust Estate, and the Question is only, whether the Revenues are properly distributed as between the Trustees and the Objects of the Charity, this Mode by Petition may be very convenient'.

interpreted by the courts, and its effect was muted.[98] A larger step was then taken by the appointment of the Brougham commissioners to inquire into abuses, initially by the trustees of educational trusts, then by the trustees of charitable trusts more generally. From 1818 to 1837 they investigated more than 29,000 charitable trusts and exposed many instances of bad practice in their published reports.[99] They referred some 400 cases to the Attorney-General for criminal prosecution,[100] and their reports were also a trigger for civil litigation by interested parties.[101]

Orders which the courts might make in cases of threatened or actual misapplication of property held on charitable trusts included: injunctions against the trustees;[102] orders that an account of trust income be taken and the trustees pay in missing funds;[103] orders that trustees compensate for loss caused by their negligence;[104] orders that trustees account for unauthorised profits;[105] orders to rescind contracts entered in breach of trust, eg, leases of trust land;[106] orders that defaulting trustees be replaced by new trustees;[107] orders that third parties return misdirected funds;[108] and orders that third parties account for profits.[109]

V. Trusts of 'Public Money' Owned by Borough Corporations

Partly as a result of the changes made to borough corporations by the 1835 Act, but partly also as an extension of principles which had begun to develop prior to 1835

[98] eg, 'a petition … which pray[ed] an account of the assets of a deceased trustee' was not within the terms of the statute: *ex parte Skinner* (1818) 1 Wils Ch 14, 15; 37 ER 7, 7 (Lord Eldon); nor was a petition for a declaration that third parties who had received charity land held it on constructive trust because such parties could themselves relevantly have committed a 'breach of trust' only after receiving the land: *ex parte Brown* (1815) Coop Rep 295, 35 ER 563.

[99] B Hargrove, 'The Reform of the Law and the Administration of Charities in the Nineteenth Century' (University of London PhD thesis, 1963) 17–280; RS Tompson, *The Charity Commission and the Age of Reform* (London, Routledge & Kegan Paul, 1979).

[100] Owen (n 4) 193.

[101] See the comments by counsel in *AG v Cullum* (1836) 1 Keen 104, 108–09; 48 ER 246, 248.

[102] *AG v Shrewsbury Corporation* (1843) 6 Beav 220; *cf AG v Governors of the Foundling Hospital* (1793) 2 Ves Jun 42, 30 ER 514.

[103] *AG v Mayor, Bailiffs and Burgesses of the Borough of Berwick upon Tweed* (1829) Taml 239, 248; 48 ER 95, 99–100. See too M Baker and M Collins, 'The Governance of Charitable Trusts in the Nineteenth Century: The West Riding of Yorkshire' (2002) 27 *Social History* 162, 178.

[104] *AG v Dixie* (1805) 13 Ves Jun 519, 533–34, 33 ER 388, 394. Trustees were not judged against a demanding standard of care.

[105] *AG v Mayor, Bailiffs and Commonalty of the City of Coventry* (1702) Colles 280, 1 ER 286; *AG v Dixie* (1805) 13 Ves Jun 519, 534; 33 ER 388, 394.

[106] *AG v Griffith* (1807) 13 Ves Jun 565, 5 ER 1005; and *cf AG v Plymouth Corporation* (1845) 9 Beav 67, 77–8; 50 ER 268, 272. But lapse of time and acquiescence could be bars: *AG for Ireland v Hungerford* (1834) 8 Bligh NS 437, 462–63; 5 ER 1005, 1012.

[107] *Mayor, Bailiffs and Commonality of the City of Coventry v AG* (1720) 7 Bro CC 235, 3 ER 153.

[108] *AG v Kell* (1840) 2 Beav 575, 48 ER 1305 (sale proceeds of charity land wrongfully paid by trustees to town improvement commissioners who were ordered to reconstitute trust fund by twenty annual payments taken out of rates). See too Baker and Collins (n 103) 168–69.

[109] *AG v Mayor, Aldermen and Burgesses of Stamford* (1747) 2 Swans 591, 592; 36 ER 741, 741 (but only where circumstances of collusion with trustees were 'very strong').

and were themselves founded on older authorities that subjected charitable trustees to Chancery oversight, the courts began to hold that corporation funds (and funds held by statutory improvement commissioners) were held on public trusts that were also subject to the supervisory jurisdiction of Chancery. The significance of this diminished in the second half of the 1800s when central government took responsibility for monitoring local government finances and public administrative systems were created to effect this.[110] However, such public trusts were clearly recognised in cases decided in the first half of the 1800s, as described in studies by John Barratt and Stuart Anderson.[111]

The cases can be divided into three groups. In the first, the courts affirmed that borough corporations could do what they liked with 'their' property and denied that they owed a duty to use it for public purposes. Examples are Lord Eldon's judgments in *AG v Carmarthen Corporation*[112] and *Mayor and Commonalty of Colchester v Lowten*, where he said that there never was 'a case, in which this court attached the doctrine of trust, as applied under the words "corporate purposes" to the alienation of a civil … corporation'.[113] For this reason, he denied that there was a Chancery jurisdiction over corporations and their officials in cases where they were alleged to have mishandled corporation property.

In the second group, the courts held that where improvement commissioners occupied the position of charity trustees, they should be subject to Chancery supervision for that reason. Leach V-C took this view in *AG v Heelis*,[114] referring back to *AG v Brown*,[115] where Lord Eldon had held that a Chancery jurisdiction existed but had left it unclear whether he was invoking the existing jurisdiction over charity trustees or recognising a new jurisdiction over the owners of 'public money' on the basis that they were trustees of it.

The latter position was then taken in the third group of cases, starting with *AG v Dublin Corporation*, where Lord Eldon said that his judgment in *AG v Brown*[116] had been misread, and where Lord Redesdale said that the court had a jurisdiction 'to see that right is done to … subjects who are incompetent to act for themselves, as in the case of charities *and other cases*'.[117] Where, as in the *Dublin* case, the only means of remedying the misuse of water rates was via parliamentary scrutiny of a statutory account, it was appropriate for Chancery to award a civil remedy. 'It is expedient,' said Lord Redesdale, 'that there should be a remedy, and highly important that persons in the receipt of public money should know, that they are liable to account, in a Court of Equity, as well for the misapplication of, as for withholding, the funds.'[118]

[110] Although the doctrine resurfaced in modern cases, eg, *Bromley LBC v GLC* [1983] 1 AC 768; *Porter v Magill* [2002] 2 AC 357, 463–4, citing *AG v Belfast Corporation* (1855) 4 IR Ch 119, 160–61.

[111] J Barratt, 'Public Trusts' (2006) 69 *Modern Law Review* 514, 514–25; Anderson, 'Local Government' (n 7) 433–37.

[112] *AG v Carmarthen Corporation* (1805) G Coop 30, 35 ER 466.

[113] *Mayor and Commonalty of Colchester v Lowten* (1813) 1 V & B 226, 244–45; 35 ER 89, 96.

[114] *AG v Heelis* (1824) 2 Sim & St 67, 76–8; 7 ER 270, 274.

[115] *AG v Brown* (1818) 1 Swans 265, 36 ER 384.

[116] *AG v Brown* (1827) 1 Bligh NS 312, 334; 4 ER 888, 897.

[117] ibid 1 Bligh NS 348, 4 ER 902 (emphasis added).

[118] ibid 1 Bligh NS 341, 4 ER 899, adding that where 'a public accountant clearly within the Act, who, having embezzled or misemployed the public monies, had rendered accounts which were imperfect or fabricated … the Attorney-General, upon discovery of the fact or the fraud, [could] proceed by information to recover the

Other cases post-dated the 1835 Act and attached particular significance to section 92. This stated that any surplus of borough funds, after all debts and expenses had been discharged, should be 'applied for the public benefit of the inhabitants and improvements of the borough'. In *AG v Aspinall*, for example, Lord Cottenham held that the effect of the section was that 'in the hands of the new council the capital was unalienable, and the whole income was subject to certain public trusts'.[119] Likewise, in *AG v Wilson* Shadwell V-C said that as a result of the section, 'there is a sort of public trust affixed upon that which, before the Act was passed, was mere corporate property, capable of alienation according to the uncontrolled will and pleasure of the body corporate'.[120] Lord Campbell said the same in *Parr v AG*, holding that the Act

> creates a trust for corporation purposes; first, for certain specified purposes, and then, when those are answered, for other general purposes, for the benefit of the town. Then this being trust property, there is nothing in the Act of Parliament to take away the jurisdiction, which the Court of Chancery would otherwise have over it, or to take away the right which the subject would otherwise have to relief in a court of equity, in case of any misapplication of trust property.[121]

It followed that new councils could recover funds alienated by corporation officials after the passing of the 1835 Act and before the local elections that followed – as in Leeds, for example, where incoming councillors were dismayed to discover on taking up office that their predecessors had deliberately paid out all the corporation's money to prevent them from having the use of it.[122] It also followed that in future, corporations could be enjoined from misapplying any part of the borough fund, whether this was ultimately sourced in the rates or rental income or borrowing,[123] and in cases where misapplications of the fund had already happened, an account could be ordered against corporation officials, and the property could be recovered from the recipients.[124]

It was also consistent with the courts' repeated statements that the public trust attached to *all* of a corporation's property, that although ratepayers were usually the relators in any proceedings (because in practice they were the only town inhabitants who could afford the costs of litigation), they had no equitable proprietary interest in the money which they had paid as rates. For these were not trusts for beneficiaries: they were trusts for public purposes, the accomplishment of which would benefit the whole community.

monies so fraudulently withheld or misappropriated', that 'the Court of Exchequer, upon such information, has jurisdiction to order such person to account and pay the money', and that a 'similar remedy is applicable, as I conceive, to any other person having the trust and management of public money'.

[119] *AG v Aspinall* (1837) 2 My & Cr 613, 630; 40 ER 773, 790.

[120] *AG v Wilson* (1837) 9 Sim 30, 48–9; 59 ER 267, 275.

[121] *Parr v AG* (1842) 8 Cl & Fin 409, 431–32; 8 ER 159, 168. See too the comments by Lord Lyndhurst at 8 Cl & Fin 431, 8 ER 168, and by Lord Cottenham at 8 Cl & Fin 433, 8 ER 168.

[122] D Fraser, 'Politics in Leeds, 1830-1852' (Leeds University PhD thesis, 1969; etheses.whiterose.ac.uk/2648/; last accessed 1 June 2023) 187–190. See also Jessel MR's comments about cases of this kind in *AG v Wandsworth District Board of Works* (1877) 6 Ch D 539, 542–43.

[123] *Cf AG v Mayor, Bailiffs, and Burgesses of Liverpool* (1835) 1 My & Cr 171, 202–03; 40 ER 342, 353.

[124] As in, eg, *AG v Dublin Corporation* (1827) 1 Bligh NS 312, 4 ER 888; *AG v Shrewsbury Corporation* (1843) 6 Beav 220, 49 ER 810; *AG v Belfast Corporation* (1862) 4 IR Ch 119. See too *AG v Compton* (1842) 1 Y & CC 417, 426–27; 62 ER 951, 955; *AG v Lichfield Corporation* (1848) 11 Beav 120, 131; 50 ER 762, 767.

VI. The Nature of Public Trusts

The point was made in Part I that the term 'public trust' was used by courts between 1750 and 1850 to describe all four of the categories of trust discussed here, but that they did not discuss conceptual questions about what this term meant, how 'public trusts' resembled or differed from 'private trusts', and whether or not these were sufficiently similar to say that both counted as 'trusts'. Judges of the eighteenth and nineteenth centuries, like their modern counterparts,[125] had little interest in classificatory questions of this kind, particularly when the answers made no difference to the outcome of disputes. Nevertheless, some inferences can be drawn about the views of contemporary lawyers and judges from some of the things which they did (and did not) say about public trusts.

First, we can distinguish the public trusts discussed in this chapter, which were clearly understood to be trusts of property settled on trustees for public purposes, from the principle established in a distinct line of eighteenth- and nineteenth-century cases, mostly at common law, that public officials who occupied positions of 'public trust and confidence'[126] owed duties to exercise their powers in accordance with the public's 'interest' in their doing so fairly, diligently and in good faith.[127] In practice, there were overlaps between these two ideas, because public officials might control property which they were obliged as trustees to apply for public purposes and, at the same time, by reason of their office, owe a duty to exercise their powers in good faith because the public trusted them to do so. Conceptually speaking, however, these two ideas of 'public trust' were distinct.[128]

Second, there was at least one contemporary lawyer who did attempt to define 'public trusts': Thomas Lewin, who wrote in the second edition of his treatise on trust law (published in 1842) that public trusts 'are constituted for the benefit either of the public at large or of some considerable portion of it answering a particular description'.[129] This glossed over the point that a public trust was a trust for public *purposes*, which did not fit with Lewin's view that 'trusts' were legal devices that conferred equitable proprietary interests on beneficiaries.[130] However, he also wrote that the class of 'public trusts' included 'all trusts for *charitable* purposes' before adding that '*public trusts* and *charitable trusts* may be considered as synonymous expressions'.[131] So even for Lewin, it was clear that 'public trusts' were not trusts for beneficiaries but trusts for purposes, and yet

[125] See, eg, Lord Millett, 'The Law of Restitution: Taking Stock' (1999) 14 *Amicus Curiae* 4, 4: 'I have to say that judges are profoundly uninterested in this kind of dispute. They take the pragmatic view that classification is important only as an aid to analysis and where correct classification is capable of affecting the outcome of [litigation].' (journals.sas.ac.uk/amicus/article/view/1503; last accessed 1 June 2023).

[126] *R v Bembridge* (1783) 22 State Tr 1, 155–6.

[127] Discussion in P Finn, 'The Forgotten "Trust": The People and the State' in M Cope (ed), *Equity: Issues and Trends* (Sydney, Federation Press, 1995).

[128] Overlaps between them can be seen in M Knights, *Trust and Distrust: Corruption in Office in Britain and its Empire, 1600-1850* (Oxford, Oxford University Press, 2021) ch 5. See also S Anderson, 'Central Executive: The Legal Structure of State Institutions' in WR Cornish et al, *Oxford History of the Laws of England, vol XI: 1820–1914 English Legal System* (Oxford, Oxford University Press, 2010) 367–68.

[129] T Lewin, *A Practical Treatise of the Law of Trusts and Trustees*, 2nd edn (London, A Maxwell & Son, 1842) 25. The nature of 'public trusts' was not considered in the first edition.

[130] S Anderson, 'Trusts and Trustees' in WR Cornish et al, *Oxford History of the Laws of England, vol XII: 1820–1914 Private Law* (Oxford, Oxford University Press, 2010) 240–41.

[131] Lewin (n 129) 25 (italics in original).

he still regarded them as a category of 'trust', and this was consistent with the way that the courts thought about them in the many cases discussed in this chapter.

The modern scholar Ron Harris has cast doubt on this, writing that a turnpike trust was 'not an extension of the trust in its equitable sense, but rather something quite different that can be termed a statutory trust',[132] reasoning that 'the equitable trust … is a personal relationship between beneficiaries and trustees, requiring no statutory sanction', but in a turnpike trust there 'were no beneficiaries other than the general public, and the latter had no legal standing regarding the trust'.[133] However, while Thomas Lewin might have agreed that 'trusts' *generally* created equitable proprietary interests for beneficiaries, he cannot have thought this was true of *all* trusts, since he recognised trusts for charitable purposes as 'trusts'. Nor is there any sign in the cases that the courts believed that statutory trusts (or any of the other public trusts discussed here) were not 'trusts' because they failed to conform with an idea of 'trusts' which required there to be beneficiaries with equitable proprietary rights. This should not surprise us, since the same could also be said of other trusts at the time, including trusts for unborn beneficiaries, trusts for married women with a restraint on anticipation, and debtor-initiated trusts for the payment of creditors (which the courts held did not vest proprietary interests in the creditors). In all of these cases, too, the purpose for which the trust was created was taken to be the guiding principle for the court when it came to issues of administration and enforcement. In none did the courts evince any particular concern to identify an individual with a vested beneficial interest in the subject matter of the trust – reflecting a general understanding of trusts that was less focussed on the question of whether there existed someone with equitable proprietary rights than on the question of whether the trustees were bound to administer the trust property in accordance with the terms of the settlement.[134]

Another modern scholar, Martin Loughlin, has written of trusts of 'public money' owned by borough corporations that they were trusts only in a 'metaphorical' sense, and that this language was 'essentially a Chancery device enabling the courts to assert jurisdiction' over the trustees.[135] That does not accord with the decisions considered in Part V, where the judges were explicit that the borough fund was property held on a trust for public purposes. Loughlin is correct, though, to say that the reasoning in this line of cases was initially focussed on questions of jurisdiction. And so far as that aspect of the cases is concerned, a third general point can be made about public trusts and the way in which they came to be understood in the later 1800s.

As noted in Part V, when the Chancery judges first held that they had a jurisdiction to oversee the uses made of property owned by borough corporations and improvement commissioners, they justified this by drawing an analogy with the long-standing supervisory jurisdiction exercised by Chancery over charitable uses. After the 1835 Act, they held that the legislation supplied another reason to draw the same conclusion, but traces of their earlier thinking appeared in *AG v Aspinall*, where Lord Cottenham described

[132] Harris (n 1) 88.

[133] ibid 88, fn 3.

[134] General discussion in D Foster, 'Historical Conceptions of the Express Trust, c 1600-1900' in S Degeling et al (eds), *Philosophical Foundations of the Law of Express Trusts* (Oxford, Oxford University Press, 2023).

[135] M Loughlin, *Legality and Locality: The Role of Law in Central-Local Government Relations* (Oxford, Clarendon Press, 1996) 208.

public trusts of funds held by public bodies as being for 'public, or in other words, charitable purposes'.[136] This dictum was the source of Lewin's statement, quoted above, that '*public trusts* and *charitable trusts* may be considered as synonymous expressions'. However, it would not have been accepted by earlier generations of lawyers, nor indeed by many of Lewin's contemporaries. Their conception of 'trusts for public purposes' included trusts for charitable purposes, but it also included trusts for non-charitable public purposes, which might have been created by settlements executed by property owners or by legislation. Nevertheless, it became judicial orthodoxy in the later 1800s and early 1900s.[137]

At the same time, the idea that there could be valid trusts for 'public' but non-charitable purposes took a battering in a series of decisions invalidating testamentary gifts of property to be applied for 'public purposes' which did not specify that these purposes should be charitable. Different explanations were given: that the word 'public', unlike the word 'charitable', was not a legal term of art and so the trust failed for uncertainty;[138] that a power of testamentary disposition could not be delegated and so executors could not validly be directed to apply funds to a 'public' purpose of their own choosing (although they could be directed to apply funds to a 'charitable' purpose of their choosing);[139] and that a trust is valid only if it is enforceable by a person with a right to beneficial enjoyment of the trust property (an exception being made for charitable trusts).[140] These cases contain much assertion and not much justification, and it was an under-examined question why technical legal advantages should be afforded to trusts for legally charitable purposes but withheld from trusts for purposes which were not legally charitable but which were assumed nevertheless to be publicly beneficial.[141]

Arriving at our fourth and final point, the idea that charitable trusts are the only legally valid public trusts also fails to account for trusts for public purposes created by legislation. These have always been legally valid – given their mode of creation, they could hardly be otherwise – but they are not charitable trusts. Judges of the eighteenth and early nineteenth centuries did not find this problematic because their world view included trusts for public but non-charitable purposes – and in this they had history on their side because, as noted in Part II, many feoffments to uses and trusts for the purposes of towns predated the recognition of such purposes as legally charitable. For modern courts, however, statutory trusts for purposes which are public but

[136] *AG v Aspinall* (1837) 2 My & Cr 613, 618; 40 ER 773, 776.

[137] eg, *Dolan v Macdermot* (1867) LR 5 Eq 60, 62–3 (Romilly MR): 'in a legal sense' public purposes 'are all charities'; *Goodman v Mayor and Free Burgesses of the Borough of Saltash* (1883) 7 App Cas 633, 650 (Lord Cairns): 'a charitable, that is to say a public, trust or interest'; *AG v De Winton* [1906] 2 Ch 106, 115 (Farwell J): 'property held for public purposes is held upon charitable trusts'.

[138] eg, *Blair v Duncan* [1902] AC 37, 42.

[139] eg, *Houston v Burns* [1918] AC 337, 342–44.

[140] eg, *Bowman v Secular Society* [1917] AC 406, 441.

[141] The further question whether non-charitable purpose trusts could have been valid within a perpetuity period 'seems not to have been explicitly addressed' in the cases during this period: Anderson, 'Trusts and Trustees' (n 130) 241, adding that on 'the rare occasions something like one appeared before a judge they seem to have escaped particular notice in the welter of more complex issues'. Later cases in which the point was considered, and the 21-year period was held to apply to trusts for non-charitable purposes, are discussed in JHC Morris and W Barton Leach, *The Rule against Perpetuities*, 2nd edn (London, Stevens & Sons, 1962) 321–27.

non-charitable present a conundrum, to resolve which they have determined that a trust of this kind is not a 'trust in the usual private law sense' but a 'statutory construct'.[142] The idea here seems to be not just that such statutory trusts differ from private trusts for beneficiaries, but that they are so different that they do not count as 'trusts' at all.[143] This is not how eighteenth- and early nineteenth-century judges thought about them. Nor is it what FW Maitland believed, writing in the early 1900s of the many statutory trusts created prior to 1835, 'now in this place, and now in that, now for this purpose, and now for that'. In his view, the corporate form could have been used to achieve the same ends, but it was not because the corruption of the borough corporations had brought the form into disrepute. So the form of the trust was used instead, and '[such] by this time had been the development of private trusts and charitable trusts, that English law had many principles ready to meet these "trusts of a public nature"'.[144]

[142] *R (Day) v Shropshire Council* [2020] EWCA Civ 1751, [2021] QB 1127 [21]; affirmed [2023] UKSC 8, [2023] AC 955 [50]–[52]. *Cf* Department of Transport, *Trust Port Study Key Findings and Recommendations* (Department of Transport, 2016) para 1.3, describing modern-day trust ports as 'independent statutory bodies without shareholders'.

[143] But *cf Re Lehman Bros International (Europe) (in administration)* [2010] EWCA Civ 917, [2011] Bus LR 277 [64]–[68]: where there is a gap in a statutory provision for the imposition of a 'trust', or the legislation is ambiguously worded, so that the rules governing the inception and/or operation of the 'trust' are not fully articulated or are unclear, the rules of general trust law will apply by default, to 'supplement', although not to 'supplant, or predefine the meaning of, the provisions expressly laid down' in the statute. See also *Rittson-Thomas v Oxfordshire CC* [2021] UKSC 13, [2022] AC 129 [29] and [39], following *Fraser v Canterbury Diocesan Board of Finance (No 2)* [2005] UKHL 65, [2006] 1 AC 377 [45].

[144] FW Maitland, 'Trust and Corporation' in HAL Fisher (ed) *The Collected Papers of Frederic William Maitland* (Cambridge, Cambridge University Press, 1911) vol 3, 399.

18

Equity and Legal Change, 1760–1875

STEPHEN WADDAMS

I. Introduction

In considering the scope and meaning of equity in English law in the (approximately) 100-year period before the Judicature Acts, it is not sufficient to look only at decisions of the Chancery Court. As John Mitford (later Lord Redesdale) wrote in 1780:

> The existence of courts of equity in England distinct from the courts of ordinary jurisdiction, has suggested an idea that the ordinary courts, and especially the courts of common law, have not in their administration of justice any recourse to such principles of decision as are merely rules of equity. But in fact those principles have been as constantly applied by the ordinary courts as by the courts of equity, except where they have clashed with established rules of the common law, and where the forms observed in the proceedings of the ordinary courts have not admitted of their application. And from time to time the courts of common law have also been induced to admit, as grounds of their decision, rules established in the courts of equity, which they had before rejected as clashing with established rules of the common law; and for some purposes they have noticed principles of decisions established in the courts of equity, which the forms of proceeding in the courts of common law have not permitted them directly to enforce.[1]

Equity is viewed in this chapter in the context of legal change, and is taken to include judicial modification by any court, for reasons of individual fairness, of a legal rule or legal position as previously understood. Principles of equity (in this broad sense of the word) can be seen to be operating during the period preceding the Judicature Acts, not only in the Chancery Court, but also in the courts of common law and in the Admiralty Court.

II. The Action for Money Had and Received

Although the origins of the modern law relating to unjust enrichment did not lie in the Chancery Court, there are close affinities between equity and the avoidance of

[1] J Mitford, *Treatise on Pleadings in Suits in the Court of Chancery by English Bill* (London, W Owen, 1780) 112 (note q). See also Wilmot CJCP's dicta in *Collins v Blantern* (1767) 2 Wils 347, 350; 95 ER 850, 852.

unjust enrichment. Lord Mansfield said, of the common law action for money had and received:

> This kind of equitable action, to recover back money, which ought not in justice to be kept, is very beneficial, and therefore much encouraged. It lies only for money which, *ex aequo et bono*, the defendant ought to refund .... [I]t lies for money paid by mistake; or upon a consideration which happens to fail; or for money got through imposition, (express or implied;) or extortion; or oppression; or an undue advantage taken of the plaintiff's situation, contrary to laws made for the protection of persons under those circumstances. In one word, the gist of this kind of action is, that the defendant, upon the circumstances of the case, is obliged by the ties of natural justice and equity to refund the money.[2]

In 1766 he said that it was 'a liberal action, founded upon large principles of equity, where the defendant cannot conscientiously hold the money';[3] and in another case he said that it was 'a liberal action in the nature of a bill in equity'.[4] Buller J also said, in 1788, that

> Of late years this Court has very properly extended the action for money had and received; it is founded on principles of justice, and I do not wish to restrain it in any respect. But it must be remembered that it was extended on the principle of its being considered like a bill in equity. And therefore in order to recover money in this form of action, the party must shew that he has equity and conscience on his side and that he could recover it in a court of equity.[5]

Equitable concepts can be seen here to have influenced the common law a century before the Judicature Acts. Probably Lord Mansfield was influenced by Roman and civil law concepts, including Scottish law.[6] The uses of the phrase 'bill in equity' and the reference to 'a court of equity' suggest that Mansfield and Buller also had in mind the English Court of Chancery, where 'bill' was the name of the originating process.[7] Lord Mansfield also said, of the action of indebitatus assumpsit, that 'the law allows a fiction for the sake of expediting the remedy'.[8]

III. Mistake and Unjust Enrichment

In *Kelly v Solari*[9] an insurer had paid out on a life insurance policy, mistakenly overlooking the fact that the policy had lapsed. In an action to recover the payment, Lord Abinger CB directed the jury that if the insurer had at one time known that

[2] *Moses* v *Macferlan* (1760) 2 Burr 1005, 1012; 97 ER 676, 681.
[3] *Sadler v Evans* (1766) 4 Burr 1984, 1986; 98 ER 34, 35.
[4] *Clarke v Shee* (1774) 1 Cowp 197, 199; 98 ER 1041, 1042.
[5] *Straton v Rastall* (1788) 2 TR 366, 370; 100 ER 197, 199. Further instances are given in B Kremer, 'The Action for Money Had and Received' (2001) 17 *Journal of Contract Law* 93, 102–03.
[6] D Ibbetson, 'Unjust Enrichment and Lord Mansfield' in H Dondorp et al (eds), *De Rebus Divinis et Humanis: Essays in Honour of Jan Hallebeek* (Göttingen, Vanderhoeck & Ruprecht, 2019) 193, 199–201; W Swain, *The Law of Contract, 1670-1870* (Cambridge, Cambridge University Press, 2015) 116–117.
[7] 'Bill' was also the term used on the equity side of the Exchequer Court: WH Bryson, *The Equity Side of the Exchequer* (Cambridge, Cambridge University Press, 1975) 93.
[8] *Holman v Johnson* (1775) 1 Cowp 341, 344; 98 ER 1120, 1121.
[9] (1841) 9 M & W 54; 152 ER 24.

the policy had lapsed, it could not later recover the payment by saying that it had forgotten the relevant facts. A verdict was given for the defendant, but with leave for the plaintiff to move to enter a verdict in favour of the insurer. On the application to the Exchequer Court a new trial was ordered. Lord Abinger expressly retracted his former view:

> I am now prepared to say that I laid down the rule too broadly at the trial, as to the effect of their [the directors'] having had means of knowledge. … I certainly laid down the rule too widely to the jury, when I told them that if the directors once knew the facts they must be taken still to know them, and could not recover by saying that they had since forgotten them. I think the knowledge of the facts which disentitles the party from recovering, must mean a knowledge existing in the mind at the time of payment.[10]

The other judges of the Exchequer Court agreed, emphasising the equitable perspective. Parke B said that 'it is against conscience to retain it [the money]'.[11] Rolfe B said that 'it cannot be otherwise than unconscientious to retain it'.[12] A new trial was ordered (rather than a verdict for the plaintiff) because a jury might find that the directors had not in fact forgotten that the policy had lapsed, and that they might have decided to pay out even knowing the true facts.

This case was perceived at the time to have changed the law, as is indicated by Lord Abinger's avowed change of opinion, and by a statement the next year in the Court of Common Pleas that

> the case of *Kelly v Solari* has certainly modified an impression which previously existed in the profession, that a party, in order to recover back money paid under a mistake of facts, should also show that he had no means of knowing them.[13]

Kelly v Solari, still cited as a leading case on unjust enrichment and mistake, shows that, despite a retrenchment from *Moses v Macferlan*,[14] a dynamic approach to equity in some common law courts was still being taken 81 years later. Twenty years later again, the case, though distinguished on the facts, was cited with approval, it having been, in the words of the Chief Justice of the Court of Common Pleas, 'against all equity and good conscience' that Solari should have been permitted to retain the money.[15]

IV. Dependent Covenants

In *Goodisson v Nunn*[16] Lord Kenyon addressed the then very controversial question of when contractual covenants were to be considered independent of each other. Older

[10] ibid 9 M & W 57–8, 152 ER 26.
[11] ibid 9 M & W 58, 152 ER 26.
[12] ibid 9 M & W 59, 152 ER 26.
[13] *Bell v Gardiner* (1842) 4 Man & G 11, 24; 134 ER 5, 10 (Coltman J).
[14] Swain (n 6) 139.
[15] *Chambers v Miller* (1862) 3 CB (NS) 125, 133–34; 143 ER 50, 53 (Erle CJ).
[16] *Goodisson v Nunn* (1792) 4 TR 761, 100 ER 1288.

cases[17] had laid down the rule that covenants were (unless the contrary was expressly stated) presumed to be independent, so that a party might be required to perform even though the other party had failed to render the counter-performance. Lord Kenyon, relying on more recent cases, said:

> The old cases ... have been accurately stated, but the determinations in them outrage common sense ... I am glad to find that the old cases have been over-ruled, and that we are now warranted by precedent as well as by principle to say this action cannot be maintained.[18]

Although Lord Kenyon said that the old cases *had been* overruled, his own decision played an important part in establishing the new legal position.[19] The underlying reason for his opinion that the old cases 'outrage common sense' was that requiring performance by a party who had failed to receive the promised counter-performance might lead, and had led, to absurd and unjust consequences, particularly where the claimant was insolvent.[20] The defendant would be compelled to perform in full (for example, to pay the price of land without receiving the promised conveyance in exchange) and would be left without any real prospect of obtaining either the counter-performance, or compensation for its failure. These are equitable considerations.

V. Lord Eldon

In the nineteenth century equity became more rigid in its attitudes.[21] The tendency of many nineteenth-century judges was to emphasise that equity, like the common law, adhered to precedents, and to understate the extent to which equity had exercised wide powers of modifying the common law. Lord Eldon said, in a case involving an injunction to prevent publication of private letters,

> The doctrines of this Court ought to be as well settled and made as uniform almost as those of the common law, laying down fixed principles, but taking care that they are to be applied according to the circumstances of each case. I cannot agree that the doctrines of this Court are to be changed with every succeeding judge. Nothing would inflict on me greater pain, in quitting this place, than the recollection that I had done anything to justify the reproach that the equity of this Court varies like the Chancellor's foot.[22]

This passage certainly indicates a tendency to favour predictability and certainty, but the word 'almost' and the reference to 'the circumstances of each case' show that Lord Eldon was not intending to abandon entirely the distinctive flexibility of equity. Recent research has shown that Eldon recognised the power of equity to control unfair contracts:

> [The Courts of Equity] ... will sometimes interpose where the conditions are manifestly and oppressively unequal, though no fraudulent act appears, for where the terms of a contract are

[17] Cases cited by counsel were *Carton v Dixon* (1640) Rol Abr 415; *Pordage v Cole* (1669) 1 Wms Saund 319, 85 ER 449; and *Blackwell v Nash* (1722) 1 Str 535, 93 ER 684.
[18] *Goodisson* (n 16) 4 TR 764–65, 100 ER 1290.
[19] S Waddams, *Principle and Policy in Contact Law* (Cambridge, Cambridge University Press, 2011) 1–7.
[20] Lord Kenyon made express reference to insolvency: *Goodisson* (n 16) 4 TR 765, 100 ER 1290.
[21] See Swain (n 6) ch 5.
[22] *Gee v Pritchard* (1818) 2 Swan 402, 414; 36 ER 670, 674.

> in a great degree disproportionate and that disproportion is made the subject of complaint, it is plain that if there were not fraud, there was error, that something was done which was not intended and the concurrent intention of the parties is necessary to the validity of a contract.[23]

In 1801 Lord Eldon said that

> Lord Chief Justice de Grey[24] said he never liked Equity so well as when it was like Law. The day before, I heard Lord Mansfield say that he never liked Law so well as when it was like Equity; remarkable sayings of those two great men, which made a strong impression on my memory.[25]

In considering the meaning of Lord Eldon's opinion in *Gee v Pritchard* that 'the doctrines of this Court ought to be as well settled and made as uniform almost as those of the common law', we should bear in mind that Lord Eldon was referring to what he perceived to be the common law of his own time, which itself incorporated elements of equity and flexibility, and that he would not necessarily have subscribed to the far more rigid attitudes that affected the common law a century later.[26]

VI. Action on the Case in Novel Circumstances

In *Grainger v Hill*[27] the defendant had taken advantage of the plaintiff's illness to threaten arrest for debt unless the plaintiff handed over a ship's register. The plaintiff, who was ill in bed at the time, yielded to the threat (held to amount, technically, to an actual arrest), handed over the register, and suffered loss through not being able to make use of the ship. The Court of Common Pleas, recognising that this was a novel claim, held that an action on the case could be maintained. Tindall CJ said,

> If the course pursued by the defendant is such that there is no precedent of a similar transaction, the plaintiff's remedy is by action on the case, applicable to such new and special circumstances … his complaint being that the process of the law has been abused.[28]

Park J said, distinguishing prior cases, that 'this is a case primae impressionis … and if an action on the case is the remedy applicable to a new species of injury, declaration and proof must be according to the particular circumstances'. It is clear that the court was influenced, in consciously making new law, by the inequity of denying a remedy in a case perceived by the judges as one of duress and extortion.[29] Blackstone had said,

[23] See M Johnson and J Oldham, 'Law versus Equity – as Reflected in Lord Eldon's Manuscripts' (2018) 58 *American Journal of Legal History* 208, 223, quoting from an unpublished manuscript, 'Of the Distribution of Justice in Courts of Equity with respect to Contracts.'

[24] Chief Justice of the Common Pleas, 1771–80.

[25] *Dursley v Fitzhardinge* (1801) 6 Ves Jun 251, 260; 31 ER 1036, 1041. See too WS Holdsworth, 'Blackstone's Treatment of Equity' (1929) 43 *Harvard Law Review* 1, 7–8.

[26] *London Street Tramways Co Ltd v London County Council* [1898] AC 375, *Sinclair v Brougham* [1914] AC 398, *Dunlop Pneumatic Tyre Co v Selfridge & Co Ltd* [1915] 1 AC 84; *Baylis v Bishop of London* [1913] 1 Ch 127.

[27] *Grainger v Hill* (1834) 4 Bing NC 212, 132 ER 769.

[28] ibid 4 Bing NC 221, 132 ER 773.

[29] ibid 4 Bing NC 219 and 220, 132 ER 772–73 (Tindall CJ, 'duress'); 4 Bing NC 223, 132 ER 774 (Vaughan J, 'extort'); 4 Bing NC 224, 132 ER 774 (Bosanquet J, 'duress').

referring to the action for money had and received, that it was 'the ground of an action on the case almost as universally remedial as a bill in equity'.[30]

VII. Inducing Breach of Contract

Another instance of a new action,[31] where the common law can be seen to have followed equity, is in the creation of the tort of inducing breach of contract. In 1852 there was a fierce rivalry between two London opera houses, Her Majesty's Theatre in the Haymarket, managed by Benjamin Lumley, and the Covent Garden Opera House, managed by Frederick Gye. Johanna Wagner, a highly renowned singer, having initially agreed to sing at Lumley's theatre, subsequently proposed to sing at Covent Garden. An interlocutory injunction to prevent her appearance at Covent Garden was upheld by the Lord Chancellor (Lord St Leonards).[32] The substantial and most difficult issue was perceived to be whether the court, not having power (as was conceded) actually to order Wagner to sing for Lumley, might nevertheless issue an injunction to restrain her from singing for Gye. This was a debatable point on which the authorities were divided:

> Now this case has been very elaborately argued upon the authorities. I bow to the authorities and I mean to execute the authorities. I am assuming no power of my own; I am giving no authoritative decision of my own; but I mean to follow the current of authority; and as there is no doubt a difference of opinion between the learned judges who have preceded me, I mean calmly and patiently to consider in what the difference consists, and to arrive at the best conclusion I can, but meaning to follow the better authority as I find it.[33]

It was argued for the defence that such an order would be an attempt to do indirectly what the court could not do directly. Lord St Leonards struggled with this point at considerable length, concluding that the court did have jurisdiction to issue the injunction, despite recognising the force of the argument that specific enforcement should not be decreed indirectly.[34] This would have been an unanswerable argument in the case of ordinary services, but a crucial aspect of the case was that Johanna Wagner's services were not ordinary.

Lord St Leonards evidently considered that the real dispute was between the two opera houses, and that a money remedy against Johanna Wagner personally would be wholly inadequate to protect Lumley's legitimate interest. Lord St Leonards said that

[30] TP Gallanis (ed) *The Oxford Edition of Blackstone's Commentaries on the Laws of England* (Oxford, Oxford University Press, 2016) [1769] vol 3, 432. See too Holdsworth (n 25) 12; and *Waterer v Freeman* (1618) Hob 266, 267; 80 ER 412, 413: 'Fairfax … saith well, that if men be good pleaders, there should not be cause of so many suits in Chancery.'

[31] 'New in its instance, but not new in the reason and principle of it': *Lumley v Gye* (1853) 2 El & Bl 216, 229; 118 ER 749, 754 (Crompton J).

[32] *Lumley v Wagner* (1852) 1 De GM & G 604, 42 ER 687; 21 LJ Ch 898; 16 Jur 871; 19 LT 264. For a fuller account see S Waddams, 'Johanna Wagner and the Rival Opera Houses' (2001) 117 *Law Quarterly Review* 431.

[33] *Lumley* (n 32) 19 LT 265.

[34] Although Lord St Leonards thought that the 'natural effect' of the order would be to induce performance of the original contract, and that it would be 'a fortunate thing for justice' if it did so, Johanna Wagner was not, as it turned out, induced to perform her contract with Lumley: she returned to Germany without performing anywhere in England in 1852. See Waddams (n 32).

'men are not suffered by the law of this country to depart from their contracts at their pleasure, and to leave the party with whom they have broken their contract to the mere chance of what a jury may give in point of damages', a probable reference to a then recent and notorious case (*Bunn v Lind*) in which a jury had awarded £2,500 as damages against another famous singer (Jenny Lind).[35]

Putting these points together, it is clear that Lord St Leonards formed a hostile view of Johanna Wagner's and Gye's actions and motives. He perceived the real dispute as being between the rival opera houses, and the existing state of the law as wholly inadequate to protect Lumley's interests: if Wagner sang for Gye, irreparable damage would have been done; an award of damages against Wagner by a common law court at some future date would almost certainly be too little and too late; even if a jury were prepared to award adequate damages (which he evidently thought very doubtful), Wagner might be unable to pay, or might very probably be beyond the jurisdiction of the English courts. In short, as one of Lumley's counsel had put it, 'to suppose that Lumley could be properly compensated by damages through an action at law was farcical'. An injunction against Wagner was therefore the only practicable way of protecting Lumley's legitimate interest against Gye, who had agreed to indemnify Wagner against all costs and damages, and who conducted, and was perceived to conduct, the defence. The same solicitor and counsel represented both, and Gye was in constant consultation with them. Gye was named as a defendant, and the injunction was issued against him personally, as well as against Wagner, although, as the common law then stood, Gye had committed no legal wrong.

The decision in *Lumley v Wagner* might be said to amount, in practical effect, to a decision that Gye (on the facts stated in the affidavits) was to be treated as a wrongdoer. It remained for the common law court to recognise this as a matter of law, something which was done the next year in *Lumley v Gye*, a case arising out of the same dispute. Lumley brought an action against Gye, claiming damages of £30,000. The declaration stated that Gye, knowing of the contract with Lumley, had 'wrongfully and maliciously enticed and procured' Johanna Wagner to break her contract. This was a novel claim in relation to professional services, and Gye demurred. This procedure (demurrer) enabled the Court of Queen's Bench to determine, before any evidence was heard, whether, assuming the facts alleged in the declaration to be proved, Lumley would be entitled to succeed.

It was vigorously argued on Gye's behalf that in order to succeed, 'the plaintiff must have a property in the thing taken away' and that 'the breach of contract is a wrong between the plaintiff and Johanna Wagner alone, and against her he may maintain an action on the contract, but not of tort'. It will be seen from this that the categorisation of the case was perceived to be crucial, and that property concepts as well as contract and tort concepts were in issue.

The Court of Queen's Bench, by a majority of three to one, decided the issue on the demurrer in Lumley's favour.[36] As in the Chancery Court, the majority emphasised the inadequacy of a contractual action against Wagner, and again it is likely that they had in mind the facts of *Bunn v Lind* (Erle J, one of the judges, had tried that case) and that they

[35] Reported in *The Times*, 23 Feb 1848, 7f.
[36] *Lumley v Gye* (1853) 2 El & Bl 216, 118 ER 749.

took account of the fact that Johanna Wagner was likely to be outside the jurisdiction of the English courts, and to lack the means of paying large damages. Crompton J said, of the contractual action, that

> The servant or contractor may be utterly unable to pay anything like the amount of the damage sustained entirely from the wrongful act of the defendant: and it would seem unjust, and contrary to the general principles of law, if such wrongdoer were not responsible for the damage caused by his wrongful and malicious act.[37]

The phrase 'unjust and contrary to the general principles of the law' indicates an equitable perspective.

Coleridge J, in a very vigorous dissent, argued that a rule that anyone who advised another to break a contract was guilty of a tort was far too wide, and that it amounted to the creation of a new legal rule:

> None of this reasoning [about liability for encouraging torts] applies to the case of a breach of contract: if it does I should be glad to know how any treatise on the law of contract could be complete without a chapter on this head, or how it happens that we have no decisions upon it. Certainly no subject could be more fruitful or important; important contracts are more commonly broken with than without persuaders or procurers, and these often responsible persons when the principals may not be so.[38]

This decision indicates the influence on the development of the common law of the Chancery decision in the previous year. It contains an element of backward reasoning, and the transmutation of an equitable into a legal wrong: if the Chancery decision enjoining Wagner and Gye was correct (and it was widely supported by public as well as by legal opinion), then Gye must have been guilty of some kind of wrongdoing. Equitable considerations were in play in both courts: success in the London opera scene at the time depended on securing the exclusive services of a star performer, and the production of an opera required very substantial reliance, preparation, and expense that could not be safely undertaken unless the commitment of the star performer could be relied on.

VIII. Restrictive Covenants

Another case involving a similar transmutation from equity to law was *Tulk v Moxhay*,[39] where the purchaser of land gave a covenant to maintain a garden square in London for the benefit of local residents. A subsequent purchaser, with notice of the covenant, proposed to disregard it. An injunction was given against the subsequent purchaser. Considerations of avoidance of unjust enrichment, and its relation to equity, were influential. Lord Cottenham said

> Of course the price would be affected by the covenant, and nothing could be more inequitable that that the original purchaser should be able to sell the property the next day for a greater

[37] ibid 2 El & Bl 230–31, 118 ER 755.
[38] ibid 2 El & Bl 250, 118 ER 761–62.
[39] *Tulk v Moxhay* (1848) 2 Ph 774, 41 ER 1143.

> price, in consideration of the assignee being allowed to escape from the liability which he himself had undertaken.[40]

The link with the concept of property is also apparent. The covenantee's interest may be described, and, since the decision in *Tulk v Moxhay*, has commonly been described, as a property right. The authors of a leading treatise on property law commented on *Tulk v Moxhay* 'thus was invented a new interest in land', describing it also as 'a new kind of property right created by equity'.[41] In this sense, as in *Lumley v Gye*, it may be said that the law followed equity. There are several other instances in which injunctions were issued to restrain conduct not previously recognised as wrongful, thus laying the groundwork for a later recognition, by courts and commentators, of new torts and new forms of property.[42]

IX. Implied Warranty of Authority

In 1858, in the case of *Collen v Wright*,[43] the Court of Exchequer Chamber created a rule that an agent who acted beyond his authority was liable to a third party who relied on the agent's claim to have authority, even if the agent honestly believed that in fact he did have the authority he claimed. This was new law, as pointed out by the dissenting judge (Cockburn CJ):

> It appears to me that there is not sufficient authority to warrant this position, and that, even assuming for the purpose of the argument that such a rule might be desirable, in establishing it we shall be creating a new law instead of expounding that which already exists. I believe I am justified in saying that this doctrine is altogether a novel one.[44]

The new rule, though depending formally on the finding of an implied contract, had the practical effect, remarkable against the common law background of the time, of creating a strict liability for an honest misstatement that caused purely economic loss.[45] The reasons of the majority, expressed by Willes J, depended on considerations of fairness to the party relying on the agent's claim to have authority:

> The fact that the professed agent honestly thinks that he has authority affects the moral character of his act; but his moral innocence, so far as the person whom he has induced to contract

[40] ibid 2 Ph 778, 41 ER 1144.

[41] R Megarry and H Wade, *The Law of Real Property*, 2nd edn (London, Sweet & Maxwell, 1959) 726 and 135.

[42] Such instances in this period include misuse of confidential information: *Prince Albert v Strange* (1849) 2 De G & Sm 652, 64 ER 293; see S Waddams, *Dimensions of Private Law* (Cambridge, Cambridge University Press, 2003) 76. Also innocent passing off: *Millington v Fox* (1838) 3 My & Cr 338, 40 ER 956; see H Carty, *An Analysis of the Economic Torts* (Oxford, Oxford University Press, 2010) 228; C Wadlow, *The Law of Passing-off: Unfair Competition by Misrepresentation*, 4th edn (London, Sweet & Maxwell, 2011) para 1-043.

[43] *Collen v Wright* (1858) 8 El & Bl 647, 120 ER 241.

[44] ibid 8 El & Bl 657, 120 ER 245.

[45] Forty-five years later, Pollock called the decision a 'brilliant and innovative fiction': Sir Frederick Pollock, *The Expansion of the Common Law* (London, Stevens, 1904) 136. As observed in M Lobban, 'Legal Fictions before the Age of Reform' in M Del Mar and W Twining (eds), *Legal Fictions in Theory and Practice* (Cham, Springer, 2015) 199, 218, while Cockburn CJ objected to the 'fiction of an implied contract hitherto unknown to our law' (8 El & Bl 663, 120 ER 247), the majority in *Collen v Wright* did not use the word 'fiction', and probably did not think of the reasoning as fictitious. They said (8 El & Bl 658, 120 ER 245) that 'the fact of entering into the transaction with the professed agent, as such, is good consideration for the promise', pointing out that the plaintiff incurred a potential detriment by exposure to the possibility of liability in case of ratification by the supposed principal.

> is concerned, in no way aids such person or alleviates the inconvenience and damage which he sustains.[46]

These may, in a broad sense, be described as equitable considerations.

X. The Postal Acceptance Rule

The rule that a contractual acceptance is effective on mailing is not usually considered from the point of view of equity. It has commonly been supposed that the choice of rule is arbitrary, and that certainty is the only consideration. But a case in the Chancery Appeal Court in 1872 shows that equitable considerations were prominent. Earlier cases[47] had held that a contractual acceptance was effective on mailing, but they had failed to give convincing reasons for the rule, which appeared to contradict the principle that contract formation required a meeting of the minds of the parties. In *Harris's Case*,[48] Mellish LJ elaborated the equitable reasons for favouring the rule:

> Now throughout the argument I have been forcibly struck with the extraordinary and very mischievous consequences which would follow if it were held that an offer might be revoked at any time until the letter accepting it had been actually received. No mercantile man who has received a letter making him an offer, and has accepted the offer, could safely act on that acceptance after he has put it into the post until he knew that it had been received. Every day, I presume, there must be a large number of mercantile letters received which require to be acted upon immediately. A person, for instance, sends an order to a merchant in London offering to pay a certain price for so many goods. The merchant writes an answer accepting the offer, and goes that instant into the market and purchases the goods in order to enable him to fulfil the contract. But according to the argument presented to us, if the person who has sent the offer finds that the market is falling, and that it will be a bad bargain for him, he may at any time, before he has received the answer, revoke his offer. The consequences might be very serious to the merchant, and might be much more serious when the parties are in distant countries. Suppose that a dealer in Liverpool writes to a dealer in New York and offers to buy so many quarters of corn or so many bales of cotton at a certain price, and the dealer in New York, finding that he can make a favourable bargain, writes an answer accepting the offer. Then, according to the argument that has been presented to us to-day, during the whole time that the letter accepting the offer is on the Atlantic, the dealer who is to receive it in Liverpool, if he finds that the market has fallen, may send a message by telegraph and revoke his offer.
>
> Nor is there any difference between an offer to receive shares and an offer to buy or sell goods. And yet, if the argument is sound, then for nearly ten days the buyer might wait and speculate whether the shares were rising or falling, and if he found they were falling he might revoke his offer. Those consequences are very extraordinary, and I always understood the law to be the other way until [a recent case] which has caused some doubt on the subject.[49]

These reasons explain, from an equitable point of view, why considerations of justice require protection of the reliance of a merchant who, in Mellish LJ's telling phrase, must, on

[46] *Collen* (n 43) 8 El & Bl 657, 120 ER 245.
[47] *Adams v Lindsell* (1818) 1 B & Ald 681, 106 ER 250, *Dunlop v Higgins* (1848) 1 HLC 381; 9 ER 805.
[48] *In re Imperial Land Co of Marseilles (Harris's Case)* (1872) LR 7 Ch App 587.
[49] ibid 594.

accepting a contract in a volatile market, go 'that instant into the market' in order to protect his position, and why, as company law then stood, it would be inequitable and unfair to creditors in a liquidation to permit a prospective shareholder to speculate by offering to subscribe for shares, and then revoking the offer while the message of acceptance was in transit, if the price of the shares on the market was falling. *Harris' Case* was expressly relied on in later cases decided shortly after the Judicature Acts that consolidated the postal acceptance rule in English law.[50] Recognition of the equitable reasons for the rule is desirable, not only from a historical perspective, but also because it is relevant to an assessment of the merits of the rule in an age of instantaneous communications.

XI. Reliance on Statements and Assurances

It was not until 1789 that the common law recognised the action of deceit for the deliberate making of a false statement causing loss. In *Pasley v Freeman*[51] the majority of the Court of King's Bench recognised such an action, relying on very general and equitable considerations, and clearly making new law, with one judge dissenting for this reason and Ashurst J saying that, though new in instance, the action was not new in principle.[52] The court was evidently strongly influenced by the injustice to the plaintiff of denying a remedy for loss deliberately caused by the defendant's knowingly false statement. Lord Kenyon said that 'all laws stand on the best and broadest basis which go to enforce moral and social duties',[53] adding that 'it is admitted that the defendant's conduct was highly immoral and detrimental to society and I am of opinion that the action is maintainable'.[54] DM Kerly, writing in 1890, said of *Pasley v Freeman* that it 'became the starting point of a series of decision which practically assimilated the doctrines of common law, in regard to fraud, with those of equity'.[55]

Loss may be caused by reliance on statements that are not fraudulent, in the common law sense of the word, that is, statements that are believed at the time to be true, but which turn out later to be false. Loss may also be caused by reliance on assurances that fall short of binding contracts. The common law courts in the nineteenth century gave no relief in such cases, but some cases in equity did so.

One line of cases came to be known as cases on 'making good' a representation. The leading case in this line was *Hammersley v De Biel* in 1845, where the following proposition was approved by the House of Lords:

> A representation made by one party for the purpose of influencing the conduct of the other party, and acted on by him, will in general be sufficient to entitle him to the assistance of the Court for the purpose of realizing such representation.[56]

[50] *Byrne & Co v Leon van Tienhoven* (1880) 5 CPD 344: *Household Insurance Co v Grant* (1879) 4 Ex D 216, overruling a case of 1871.

[51] *Pasley v Freeman* (1789) 3 TR 51, 100 ER 450.

[52] This could be said of any legal innovation, if the 'principle' is articulated in sufficiently general terms.

[53] *Pasley* (n 50) 3 TR 63, 100 ER 456.

[54] ibid 3 TR 65, 100 ER 457.

[55] DM Kerly, *An Historical Sketch of the Equitable Jurisdiction of the Court of Chancery*, (Cambridge, Cambridge University Press, 1890) 181.

[56] *Hammersley v De Biel* (1845) 12 Cl & F 45, 61n; 8 ER 1312, 1320n (Lord Cottenham, and headnote).

Lord Lyndhurst said:

> But the principle of law, at least of equity, is this, that if a party holds out inducements to another to celebrate a marriage, and holds them out deliberately and plainly, and the other party consents and celebrates the marriage in consequence of them, if he had good reason to expect that it is intended that he should have the benefit of the proposal which was so held out, a Court of Equity will take care that he is not disappointed, and will give effect to the proposal.[57]

The concept of 'making good' representations was applied in some other equity cases before the Judicature Acts,[58] but was later forcefully rejected.[59] The difficulty was that the concept of 'making good' a representation claimed too much from an equitable perspective. Equitable considerations may sometimes weigh in favour of protecting reliance, even where there is no fraud and no binding contract, but 'making good' the representation implies enforcement to the full extent of the plaintiff's expectation, which might produce extravagant results going far beyond what was necessary to prevent injustice, and not defensible in the absence of a contract. If the equitable concept had been more modestly framed, as doing only what was necessary in the particular circumstances to protect the plaintiff from injustice, the concept might perhaps have survived the Judicature Acts.

Another line of cases which did survive the Judicature Acts were those that came subsequently to be known as cases of estoppel. An example is *Dillwyn v Llewelyn*,[60] where the owner of land promised in a signed writing (but without consideration) to give the land to his son 'for the purpose of furnishing himself with a dwelling house'. The son made very extensive improvements at a cost far exceeding the value of the unimproved land.[61] The Court of Chancery held that the son was entitled to be declared the owner of the land. Lord Westbury LC said:

> A voluntary agreement will not be completed or assisted by a court of equity …. But the subsequent acts of the donor may give the donee that right or ground of claim which he did not acquire from the original gift. … So if A puts B in possession of a piece of land, and tells him, I give it to you, that you may build a house on it; and B, on the strength of that promise, with the knowledge of A, expends a large sum of money in building a house accordingly, I cannot doubt that the donee acquires a right from the subsequent transaction to call on the donor to perform that contract and to complete the imperfect donation which was made.[62]

As previously mentioned, cases of this sort came later to be known as cases of estoppel. The word 'estoppel', however, is not an ideal choice, and was not used by Lord

[57] ibid 12 Cl & F 78, 8 ER 1327.

[58] *Thomson v Simpson* (1870) LR 9 Eq 506, reversed on other grounds Ch App; *Coles v Pilkngton* (1874) 19 Eq 178; *Skidmore v Bradford* (1869) LR 8 Eq 134.

[59] The concept was said to be 'imaginary' in F Pollock, *Principles of Contract*, 3rd edn (London. Stevens and Sons, 1881) 687 and in the fifth edition (London, Stevens and Sons, 1889) 506, to be 'exploded'. The doctrine was described, and forcefully rejected, by G Spencer Bower, *The Law of Actionable Misrepresentation* (London, Butterworth, 1911) 191–94.

[60] *Dillwyn v Llewelyn* (1862) 4 De G F & J 517, 45 ER 1285; 6 LT 878; 31 LJ Ch 658.

[61] The LJ Ch report gives the unimproved value of the land as £1,500, and the cost of the improvements as £20,000.

[62] *Dillwyn* (n 60) 4 De G F & J 521, 45 ER 1286.

Westbury.[63] The court gave full enforcement of the promise in *Dillwyn v Llewelyn*, but later cases have held that the appropriate remedy will vary with the circumstances and that in some cases it is appropriate to protect only the claimant's reliance and not the expectation. The possibility of the more limited remedy, where appropriate, is in keeping with the underlying equitable reason for relief (to protect the claimant from injustice, not to enforce a contract that was never made) and has probably assisted in preserving this line of cases after the Judicature Acts.[64]

XII. Contractual Mistake

Equity recognised a power to set aside contracts for fundamental mistake in assumptions. In *Bingham v Bingham*,[65] an eighteenth-century case approved by the House of Lords in 1867,[66] where there was a mistake as to the title to land, the court said,

> though no fraud appeared, and the defendant apprehended he had a right, yet there was a plain mistake, such as the court was warranted to relieve against, and not to suffer the defendant to run away with the money in consideration of the sale of an estate, to which he had no right.[67]

The phrase 'run away with the money' plainly indicates an unjust enrichment perspective. The equitable power to give relief was recognised by Story,[68] Leake[69] and Benjamin,[70] was applied in several other nineteenth-century cases,[71] and was affirmed by the House of Lords in *Cooper v Phibbs* (1867),[72] where Lord Westbury said,

> at the time of the agreement … the parties dealt with one another under a mutual mistake as to their respective rights. … In such a state of things there can be no doubt of the rule of a court of equity with regard to the dealing with that agreement. … [If] the parties contract under a mutual mistake and misapprehension as to their relative and respective rights, the

[63] Neither was the word 'estoppel' used in *Hughes v Metropolitan Railway Co* (1876) 1 CPD 120 (CA), affirmed (1877) 2 App Cas 439 (HL).

[64] In *Hughes* (n 63) Mellish LJ said in the Court of Appeal at 135, in words approved by Lord Blackburn in the House of Lords at 452, that 'a Court of Equity, though they relieve against the forfeiture, will still compel the lessee to put the house into substantial repair, and will give the landlord all that he is really entitled to, only preventing him from enforcing a forfeiture that would be inequitable'.

[65] *Bingham v Bingham* (1748) 1 Ves Sen 126, 27 ER 934. Several other eighteenth- and nineteenth-century equity cases are listed in GE Palmer, *Mistake and Unjust Enrichment* (Columbus, OH, Ohio State University Press, 1962) 100, fn 14. The cases considered here are, in Palmer's phrase, cases of mistake in assumptions, ie, mistakes that relate to the reasons for entering into the transaction, rather than mistakes relating to what terms were agreed: ibid 6, 13.

[66] *Cooper v Phibbs* (1867) LR 2 HL 149.

[67] *Bingham* (n 65) 1 Ves Sen 126–27, 27 ER 934 (Fortescue MR).

[68] J Story, *Commentaries on Equity Jurisprudence: As Administered in England and America* (Boston, Hilliard, Gray, 1836) vol 1, s 140; maintained in subsequent editions: see, eg, 13th edn by MM Bigelow (Boston, Little, Brown & Co, 1886) vol 1, s 140.

[69] SM Leake, *The Elements of the Law of Contracts* (London, Stevens & Sons, 1867) 178.

[70] JP Benjamin, *A Treatise on the Law of Sale of Personal Property* (London, H Sweet, 1868) 303.

[71] *Hitchcock v Giddings* (1817) 4 Pri 135, 146 ER 418; *Hore v Belcher* (1842) 12 Simons 465; *Cochrane v Willis* (1865) LR 1 Ch 58; *Earl Beauchamp v Winn* (1873) LR 6 HL 223.

[72] *Cooper v Phibbs* (1867) LR 2 HL 149.

> result is, that that agreement is liable to be set aside as having proceeded upon a common mistake.[73]

The writer of the headnote also read the decision as affirming a wide general power: 'the agreement having been made in mutual mistake, the Plaintiff, though there was no fraud, was entitled to have it set aside'.[74] Relief was given, as Catharine MacMillan has said, 'for reasons related to conscience and not consent':[75] in some circumstances it was unconscientious to insist on enforcement of an agreement made by the other party under a mistake.

Though this aspect of equity came to be restricted in the twentieth[76] and twenty-first[77] centuries, Lindley LJ thought that it was still good law in 1895. Looking back on the cases, he said:

> I am aware that *Bingham v Bingham* has been occasionally criticised, and in some of the earlier editions of Lord St Leonards' book on Vendors and Purchasers he seemed to think that there was something wrong about it. In his last edition, however, he changed his opinion; and *Bingham v Bingham* was carefully examined in the House of Lords in *Cooper v Phibbs* and was distinctly affirmed. … It appears to me to be in perfect accordance with well-settled principles of law, both of this country and of all civilised countries, as far as I know.[78]

XIII. Subrogation

There are many statements to the effect that subrogation is a broad equitable remedy, not confined to particular categories, and available wherever justice and equity require it.[79] In *Jenner v Morris* (1861), Turner LJ said, quoting from Lord Redesdale's *Treatise on Pleading*:

> Cases frequently occur in which the principles by which the ordinary courts are guided in their administration of justice give a right, but from accident, fraud, or defect in their mode of proceeding, those courts can afford no remedy, or cannot give the most complete remedy, and sometimes the effect of a remedy attempted to be given by a court of ordinary jurisdiction is defeated by fraud or accident. In such cases courts of equity will interpose to give those remedies which the ordinary courts would give if their powers were equal to the purpose, or their mode of administering justice could reach the evil; and also to enforce remedies attempted to be given by those courts when their effect is so defeated.' It is therefore an ancient head of the jurisdiction of this court to interpose in cases in which the principle of law gives a right but the forms of law do not give a remedy.[80]

[73] ibid 170.
[74] ibid 150.
[75] C MacMillan, *Mistakes in Contract Law* (Oxford, Hart Publishing, 2010) 38. See also 53, 68, and 136. And see M Lobban, 'Contract' in W Cornish et al, *The Oxford History of the Laws of England, vol XII: Private Law, 1820-1914* (Oxford, Oxford University Press, 2010) 441–42.
[76] *Bell v Lever Bros* [1932] AC 161 (HL).
[77] *Great Peace Shipping Co v Tsavliris Salvage (International) Ltd* [2003] QB 679 (CA).
[78] *Huddersfield Banking Co Ltd v Lister & Son Ltd* [1895] 2 Ch 273, 281 (CA).
[79] *Orakpo v Manson Investments Ltd* [1978] AC 95, 110 (Lord Salmon) and 112 (Lord Edmund-Davies); *Boscawen v Bajwa* [1996] 1 WLR 328 (CA) 335 (Millett LJ); G Jones, *Goff and Jones, The Law of Restitution*, 6th edn (London, Sweet & Maxwell, 2002) 3-011 and 3-018.
[80] *Jenner v Morris* (1861) 3 De G F & J 45, 55; 45 ER 795, 799, quoting from J Mitford (Lord Redesdale), *A Treatise on the Pleadings in Suits in the Court of Chancery by English Bill*, 4th edn by G Jeremy (London,

This was said in the context of payments to a deserted wife for the purchase of necessaries: the payer was permitted to be subrogated to the rights of the tradespeople who had supplied the necessaries, and who had been paid from the money advanced to the wife but who, if they had been unpaid, would have had an action against the husband at common law. The words are very apt also in many other contexts, where it can often be said that 'the principles of law give a right but the forms of law do not give a remedy'. For example, where a contractual obligation is owed to one person, but the primary interest in performance of the contract is in another person, the latter might, where justice requires it, be subrogated to the contractual rights of the former. These are typically cases where the interests of the two potential claimants are closely aligned, and where the defendant would be unjustly enriched at the expense of the two potential claimants jointly if there were no liability to either.[81]

XIV. Good Faith in Partnership Agreements

In *Blisset v Daniel*,[82] articles of partnership included a power of a two-thirds majority to expel any partner. Following the plaintiff's objection to the appointment by one of the other partners of his own son as co-manager, the plaintiff was summarily expelled. It was held by Wood VC (later Lord Hatherley) that the power, though apparently unfettered, must be exercised in good faith. He spoke in strong terms:

> I must confess I never remember to have witnessed in this Court, among persons of the high station which these gentlemen … have occupied in the mercantile world, a course of proceeding so extremely unsatisfactory and harsh, and so wanting, not only in regard to any consideration, but, what I think is of much more importance in this case, any fair dealing towards the party who has been expelled from this partnership. I have said before that I have held with the defendants that they were competent to give a notice to dissolve without assigning any reason; that they were competent to exercise that power without holding any meeting with their co-partners; but then the power must be exercised *bona fide*. Good faith is unquestionably of the essence of all contracts. [Counsel for the defendants] has said that I could not introduce any new words into this contract. The Court does not do so, but the Court presupposes in every contract, and if there can be a difference, more especially in every contract of partnership, a basis of good faith, upon which all the stipulations contained in the deed must rest. This power would never be allowed to be exercised by this Court in a manner against what I may call the truth and honour of these articles, borrowing an expression which has been applied to another description of contract. It is quite clear that this power was never intended to be exercised by any two-thirds of the partners merely and solely for their own exclusive benefit.[83]

J & WT Clarke, 1827) 112, and 5th edn by JW Smith (London, V & R Stevens and GS Norton, 1847) 134. Lord Campbell LC, at 51–2, characterised the legal problem in *Jenner v Morris* as lack of privity, but this was not a reason for withholding the remedy of subrogation; on the contrary it was the very reason why an equitable remedy was necessary. He also explained the result on the basis of imputed assignment: 'it may possibly be that equity considers that the tradespeople have for valuable consideration assigned to the party who advanced the money the legal debt that would be due to them from the husband on furnishing the necessaries, and that, although a chose in action cannot be assigned at law, a court of Equity recognizes the right of the assignee'.

[81] See S Waddams, 'Breaches of Contract and Claims by Third Parties' in JW Neyers et al (eds), *Emerging Issues in Tort Law* (Oxford, Hart Publishing, 2007) 191.

[82] *Blisset v Daniel* (1853) 10 Hare 493, 68 ER 1022.

[83] ibid 10 Hare 522, 68 ER 1034.

This wide concept of good faith, depending on the court's understanding of the underlying basis ('truth and honour')[84] of the contract, rather than on the construction of particular words or implication of terms, has potentially far-reaching implications, not only for partnership agreements, but for all contracts.[85]

XV. Wayleave

Where use had been made by a trespasser of underground passages without causing damage to the value of the claimant's land, there was doubt as to whether a court, either of law or of equity, could make any money award. In 1871 Lord Hatherley held that a court of equity could do so:

> I at first felt some doubt as to compensation for wayleave; but on further consideration I think that on principle it ought to be given, whether the cases have as yet gone that length or not. Here is a man doing a surreptitious act, which cannot be discovered except through the medium of a bill. Under the old practice there would have been a bill for discovery of the thing, and then an action for damages in respect of it would have been brought; but this Court has now the power to grant compensation in respect of a continuously accruing damage de die in diem, arising from a continuous trespass underground, which can only be stopped by injunction restraining any further conveyance of coal through the Respondents' property. These damages cannot be better assessed than by an inquiry what is fit and proper to be paid for wayleave for the coals carried through the property.[86]

Lord Hatherley was conscious of making an innovation ('whether the cases have as yet gone that length or not'), and the concept that he introduced, of a money award based on a hypothetical bargain to pay a fair price for permission, has played an important part in later debates on the difficult issue of gain-based awards for wrongs.[87]

XVI. Maritime Salvage

It was stated in various contexts that the Admiralty Court was a court of equity, and this concept had important implications in respect of enforceability of contracts. Maritime salvage contracts were enforced by the court only if fair and reasonable and if made with full knowledge of relevant facts. The Admiralty Court took a more flexible approach than the common law to questions of mistake and unfairness, and a much more fluid approach to the relation between the principle of contractual

[84] See *Woodcock v Duke of Dorset* (1789) 3 Bro CC 569, 571; 29 ER 704, 705 (Lord Thurlow LC): 'Though the words are strong and difficult to manage the intention of the settlement is the truth and honor of the case'; *Buhner v Jay* (1830) 4 Sim 48, 54; 58 ER 19, 22 (Shadwell V-C): 'I decide not on the literal construction of the words but on the truth and honour of the settlement.'

[85] P Sales (Lord Sales), 'Use of Powers for Proper Purposes in Private Law' (2020) 136 *Law Quarterly Review* 384, 394.

[86] *Phillips v Homfray* (1871) LR 6 Ch App 770, 780–81.

[87] See *One Step (Support) Ltd v Morris-Garner* [2018] UKSC 20, [2019] AC 649.

enforceability and its exceptions. Admiralty, never having had a separate system of equity, partly because of its civilian origins, thus achieved a more harmonious relation between the concepts of strict law and equity than did the common law system, where, even after the Judicature Acts, the fusion/fission debate remained unresolved.

It was frequently asserted that the Admiralty Court was a court of equity, as well as a court of law.[88] One characteristic, shared with the Chancery Court, in contrast to the courts of common law, was the ability of sailors to join together in a single action against the ship to recover unpaid wages:

> The suit of the seamen in the court of Admiralty is frequently spoken of as an excepted case, and an indulgence granted to them on account of the convenience and advantage of proceeding in a Court in which all may join in one suit, and payment may be made out of the value of the ship.[89]

A common law judge commented,

> And there is great reason why they should have this remedy, because in the Admiralty the body of the ship is liable, and the seamen may join in action.[90]

Another common law court commented that

> one of the privileges of suing for wages in the Court of Admiralty is, that two or more mariners may join in a suit in that Court, and not be put to the inconvenience of bringing separate actions, which they must do, if they sue in a Court of common law.[91]

It did not follow, however, that the Admiralty Court followed the Chancery Court in all respects. Lord Langdale said in *The Saracen*

> It is true that in the decisions of cases, properly within the jurisdiction of the Court of Admiralty, equitable considerations ought to have their weight; but it does not thence follow that the Court of Admiralty has jurisdiction to do all that Courts of Equity may do.[92]

In *The Don Francisco*,[93] Dr Lushington said

> It was said by Lord Stowell … and I could not appeal to higher authority, that the Court of Admiralty was a court of equity as well as of law; but to what extent it is a court of equity is nowhere defined.[94]

Lushington went on to refuse to allow an equitable set-off in the particular case because he thought the inconvenience to the plaintiff of permitting the set-off would be greater

[88] *The Juliana* (1822) 2 Dods 504, 521; 165 ER 1560, 1566–67; *The Minerva* (1825) 1 Hag Adm 347, 357; 166 ER 123, 127; *The Prince Frederick* (1832) 2 Hag Adm 394, 396; 166 ER 287, 288; *The Trident* (1839) 1 W Rob 29, 35; 166 ER 484, 486; *The Heart of Oak* (1870) 21 LT (NS) 727; *Atlantic Mutual Insurance Co v Huth* (1880) 44 LT (NS) 67, 71; FL Wiswall, *The Development of Admiralty Jurisdiction and Practice since 1800: an English Study with American Comparisons* (Cambridge, Cambridge University Press, 1970) 71–2.

[89] C Abbott, *A Treatise of the Law relating to Merchant Ships and Seamen*, 9th edn by W Shee (London, Shaw & Sons, 1854) 536.

[90] *Wells v Osman* (1704) 2 Ld Raym 1045, 1045; 92 ER 193, 194 (Powell J).

[91] *Mills v Gregory* (1754) Sayer 127, 127; 96 ER 826, 826.

[92] *Bernard v Hyne (The Saracen)* (1847) 6 Moo PC 56, 74; 13 ER 604, 611.

[93] *The Don Francisco* (1861) Lush 468, 167 ER 210.

[94] ibid Lush 472, 167 ER 213.

than the inconvenience to the defendant of refusing it. In *The Harriett* he said, on a question concerning sureties,

> If a Court of Equity would relieve, and a Court of Law could not, I consider that it would be my duty to afford that relief under the circumstances of the present case. The jurisdiction which I exercise is an equitable as well as a legal jurisdiction, and I must relieve the parties in this suit, if they are entitled to be relieved in law or in equity.[95]

The law of maritime salvage was regarded by the Admiralty Court as a 'mixed question of private right and public policy'.[96] Dr Lushington, judge of the High Court of Admiralty from 1838 to 1867, said that the court seeks not only 'to do that which is just and right for [the salvors'] interests', but also for 'the interests of the public, which is to encourage them, and give that amount of salvage reward which is due to them'.[97] The reward is given 'not merely to remunerate the effort made to save the ship, cargo, and lives of the persons on board, but also to encourage others to make similar attempts'.[98] In another case he said:

> Say what you will, so long as human motives operate on conduct, unless you give a reward you must take away all incitement to service. It is all very well to talk of the abstract question of fulfilling duty and obeying commands; and I have no doubt that, so long as men can execute the duty and perform the commands entrusted to them, they will do so; but in cases of doubt and difficulty, and where great and extraordinary exertions have to be made, reward according to human exertions is the only great stimulus to their performance.[99]

Salvage was also regarded as governed by equitable principles, being called 'a loss for which an equitable compensation may reasonably be demanded',[100] 'a general principle of natural equity',[101] and 'founded on the equity of remunerating private and individual services'.[102]

Not infrequently, contracts were made affecting the amount of salvage, but Lushington had little hesitation in setting them aside if he considered them to be contrary to public policy, or unfair as between the parties. In one case he said that 'it has been the practice of this Court not to allow agreements barring salvage, in order that the spirit of enterprise should not be interfered with'.[103]

On questions relating to mistake, Lushington was more willing than the common law courts, and perhaps more willing than the courts of equity, to set aside agreements:

> An agreement to bind two parties must be made with a full knowledge of all the facts necessary to be known by both parties; and if any fact which, if known, could have any operation on

[95] *The Harriett* (1841) 1 W Rob 182, 192; 166 ER 541, 545.

[96] *The Albion* (1861) Lush 282, 284; 167 ER 121, 122. Dr Lushington attributed the saying to the American judge, Mr Justice Story, with reference probably to *The Henry Ewbank* 1 Sumn 400, 11 F Cas 1166, 1170 (CA Mass, 1833): 'mixed question of public policy and private right'.

[97] *The Magdalen* (1861) 31 LJPMA 22, 24.

[98] *The William Hannington* (1845) 9 Jur 631, 632. Similar statements appear in *The Albion* (n 96); *The Ocean* (1843) 2 W Rob 91, 166 ER 689; and *The Swan* (1839) 1 W Rob 68, 166 ER 499.

[99] *The Rosalie* (1853) 1 Sp 188, 189; 164 ER 109, 110.

[100] *The Vine* (1825) 2 Hag Adm 1, 2; 166 ER 145, 145.

[101] *The Calypso* (1828) 2 Hag Adm 209, 218; 166 ER 221, 224.

[102] ibid.

[103] *The Pensacola* (1864) Br & Lush 306, 310; 167 ER 376, 379.

> the agreement about to be entered into is kept back, or not disclosed to either of the contracting parties, that would vitiate the agreement itself. It is not necessary, in order to vitiate an agreement, that there should be moral fraud; it is not necessary, in order to make it not binding, that one of the parties should keep back any fact or circumstance of importance, if there should be misapprehension, accidentally or by carelessness; we all know that there may be what, in the eye of the law, is termed equitable fraud.[104]

On the question of unexpected events occurring after the contract, a topic which may be regarded as an aspect of mistake,[105] Lushington showed himself willing to give relief. In allowing compensation additional to that agreed in a towage contract that had proved unexpectedly burdensome, he said:

> I think I should be laying down a very dangerous doctrine if I were to hold that, where a person agrees to perform the simple duty of towing from the Nore [the North Foreland in the Thames estuary] to London, if from stress of weather, from an accident happening to the ship, or other circumstances of a like nature, it should so happen that other and different services have to be discharged, the original agreement is binding on the parties. … Am I to consider £16, the original amount agreed upon, as sufficient under these circumstances? I am of a contrary opinion. I think £16 might be a fair reward for a purely towage service; but I think that another service grew up on it, over which the master of the tug had no control, and that he is entitled to be paid for that also.[106]

Lushington did not wholly disregard the force of contracts, and in some cases he enforced contracts that he recognised as onerous.[107] He said, in another case of a towage contract, that 'when an engagement is made – a contract – for a specific time, that contract must be adhered to, and is not to be broken hastily', but the force of this consideration was not conclusive. He added immediately:

> unless it be shown that circumstances have occurred which could not have been within the contemplation of the parties, and that such is the state of circumstances, that to insist upon the contract and hold it binding would be contrary to all principles of justice and equity …. If the tugs were merely ordinarily delayed in performing the service they must not have additional remuneration; but if the delay was unexpected, and beyond all contemplation, they must have something additional.[108]

Unlike the common law in the nineteenth-century frustration cases, Lushington perceived the question as one of justice, and not mere interpretation, and he did not hesitate to modify the contract, rather than abrogating it entirely, where justice required that result. In case of unexpected danger in carrying out a towage contract, the obligation to render services continued, but at (higher) salvage rates, rather than at the rate agreed to in the contract.[109]

[104] *The Kingalock* (1854) 1 Sp 263, 265; 164 ER 153, 154.

[105] See S Waddams, *Sanctity of Contracts in a Secular Age: Equity, Fairness and Enrichment* (Cambridge, Cambridge University Press, 2019) 140–42.

[106] *The William Brandt Jr* (1842) 2 Not Cas Supp lxvii, lxviii.

[107] *The Jonge Andries* (1857) Swab 226, 166 ER 1108, affirmed by the Privy Council, (1857) 11 Moo PC 313, 14 ER 714; *The True Blue* (1843) 2 W Rob 176, 166 ER 721.

[108] *The White Star* (1866) LR 1 Ad & E 68, 70–71.

[109] *The William Brandt Jr* (n 106); *The Saratoga* (1861) Lush 318, 167 ER 140; *The Hebe* (1844) 2 W Rob 246, 166 ER 747 (pilotage); *The Black Sea* (1855) Pritch Dig 337.

In stating that contracts should be enforced, Lushington frequently added the words 'if just and equitable', or 'if fair and equitable' or words to the same effect.[110] In considering the question of unfairness in salvage contracts, the danger of extortion by the salvors springs first to mind. Lushington, in one such case, described the salvors' demand as 'exorbitant, and such as no Court of Justice would be justified in carrying into effect'.[111] This feature of admiralty law survived the Judicature Acts, but only in relation to maritime matters. In *The Port Caledonia and the Anna* a tugmaster refused to rescue a ship that was drifting towards another, and thought likely to collide with it, unless the ship's master agreed to pay £1,000 for the service. The ship's master agreed, and the service was rendered, but the court refused to enforce the agreement. Considerations of fairness and avoidance of extravagant enrichment were prominent. Bucknill J said:

> I have to ask myself whether the bargain that was made was so inequitable, so unjust, and so unreasonable that the Court cannot allow it to stand .... This was an inequitable, extortionate, and unreasonable agreement ...[112]

This approach avoids many of the difficulties associated with the common law concept of duress. The agreement was set aside, but the court made a salvage award of £200, showing that the court's object was not to deprive the tugmaster of reasonable payment for the service, but to prevent the enforcement of an agreement that the court thought to be highly unreasonable. There was no need for the ship's master to prove that his action was involuntary, or that his will was overborne, or that the action of the tugmaster was illegal.

In *The Theodore*, mentioned above, Dr Lushington said that 'the Court would be just as ready, in favour of salvors, to set aside an agreement, if satisfied that it was wholly inequitable',[113] and he had more cases of the latter kind. In one case a mariner, John Armstrong, having performed a very valuable service in saving life and in unloading silver bullion from a vessel that had run onto rocks and might have been about to break up, had agreed to accept a small reward (11 shillings), signing a receipt 'in full of all further demands'. The court set aside the agreement and awarded him £50 – more than 90 times as much as had been agreed. Lushington, having quoted Lord Stowell to the effect that 'ignorant persons of this description were not competent judges', added:

> Now, I have always a certain suspicion of these papers. I do not mean to say that this receipt was not honestly obtained, but the inclination of the Court is to look at the circumstances of the case, and not allow a paper to operate as a bar. And upon that principle I shall continue to act.[114]

It is evident that the principle was one of avoiding unfairness and disproportionate enrichment – Armstrong had sold his claim for a small fraction of its value – and that it

[110] *The Arthur* (1862) 6 LT 556; *The Crus V* (1862) Lush 583, 167 ER 266; *The Helen & George* (1858) Swab 368, 166 ER 1170; *The Enchantress* (1860) Lush 93, 167 ER 49; *The Resultatet* (1853) 17 Jur 353; *The Firefly* (1857) Swab 240, 166 ER 1116; *The British Empire* (1842) 6 Jur 608; *The Henry* (1851) 16 LT (OS) 553; 15 Jur 183.

[111] *The Theodore* (1858) Swab 351, 352; 166 ER 1163, 1164.

[112] *The Port Caledonia and the Anna* [1903] P 184, 189–90.

[113] *The Theodore* (n 111).

[114] *Silver Bullion* (1854) 2 Sp 70, 75; 164 ER 312, 315. See also *The Enchantress* (n 110) and *The Phantom* (1866) LR 1 Ad & E 58.

did not depend on any finding of wrongdoing on the part of the advantaged party ('I do not mean to say that this receipt was not honestly obtained').

Lushington was very hostile to agreements whereby mariners gave up potential future salvage claims. Here considerations of public policy were relevant, as well as considerations of fairness between the parties. In one case Lushington held such an agreement to be 'highly prejudicial to the public interests' on the ground that it would 'take away … the motives to all enterprise and energy', adding, 'Until, therefore, I am compelled by superior authority, I never will consider articles of this nature, made previous to the performance of the salvage service, binding and conclusive upon my judgment.'[115] In other cases he described such agreements as 'against equity and public feeling',[116] 'contrary to all justice',[117] and 'inequitable'.[118]

These salvage decisions show that the Court of Admiralty, before the Judicature Acts, was administering a system that combined law and equity with each other, and with considerations of public policy. At this date the common law courts and the Court of Chancery were still operating separately, as they continued to do until 1875. The practice of the Court of Admiralty in salvage cases offers an illustration, from within English law, of how a single court may simultaneously administer both law and equity. The court, lacking an institutional division between law and equity, in part because of its civilian tradition,[119] accepted and incorporated the concept of equity as something like a reserve power, or safety valve, in order to avoid unfair results and disproportionate enrichments. Contracts were usually enforced, but contractual obligation in salvage cases was not elevated to the level of 'sanctity'.[120]

XVII. Conclusion

Legal history, Sir John Baker has said, is the study of legal change,[121] and legal change has very commonly occurred in response to a perception that an older law, if not modified, would operate inequitably. Equity, in the period preceding the Judicature Acts, was not all to be found in one place. The common law courts often invoked equitable considerations, either of their own motion, or in response to decisions of the Chancery Court. Separately from both the common law and from Chancery, the Admiralty Court also administered equity. A considerable measure of what might be described as 'diffusion', rather than fusion, may thus be discerned in aspects of English law in the period between

[115] *The Louisa* (1843) 2 W Rob 22, 23–24; 166 ER 664, 664. See also *The Pensacola* (n 103).
[116] *The Columbine* (1843) 2 W Rob 186; 166 ER 724.
[117] ibid.
[118] *The Enchantress* (n 110) Lush 96, 167 ER 50.
[119] HJ Bourguignon, *Sir William Scott, Lord Stowell: Judge of the High Court of Admiralty, 1798-1828* (Cambridge, Cambridge University Press, 1987) 12–28, 68, 94–96.
[120] Lushington did say, in *The Vibilia* (1838) 1 W Rob 1, 4; 166 ER 474, 475: 'All legal agreements, all contracts sanctioned by the law, are sacred; that is they are to be enforced by every court of law and equity.' But the question at issue there was not whether the contract was unfair, but whether it had the effect of creating a lien on the ship as a bottomry bond.
[121] JH Baker, 'Why the History of English Law Has Not been Finished' [2000] *Cambridge Law Journal* 62, 63, reprinted in id, *Collected Papers on English Legal History* (Cambridge, Cambridge University Press, 2013) 1544, 1544–45.

Lord Mansfield's decision in *Moses v Macferlan*, and the abolition of the Chancery Court. The nineteenth century has sometimes been thought of as a time of judicial rigidity,[122] and it is true that there was a retreat from Lord Mansfield's expansive view in *Moses v* Macferlan,[123] but, as we have seen, equity, in the broad sense of the word, remained active during this period.[124] Recognition of this activity has important implications for the perception of the powers of the modern court: the equity inherited by the new court in 1875 from several sources was not a collection of fossilised antiquities, but a dynamic and active aspect of the legal system. Its subsequent neglect was neither attributable to the earlier period, nor authorised by the Judicature Acts.

[122] CK Allen, *Law in the Making*, 6th edn (Oxford, Clarendon Press, 1958) 402, spoke of a '*rigor aequitatis* as austere as the *rigor juris*', and Lord Simon, in *Steadman v Steadman* [1976] AC 536, 560, spoke of a 'hardening of Equity's arteries'.

[123] Swain (n 6) 126.

[124] See Pollock (n 45) and R Stevens, *Law and Politics: The House of Lords as a Judicial Body, 1800-1976* (Chapel Hill, NC, University of North Carolina Press, 1978) 135 ('The "new" House that appeared in 1877 was, if anything, heir to an expanding rather than a contracting view of judicial legislation – at least in those areas traditionally left by Parliament to the judges').

19

Equity, Legal Coding, and the Foundations of Banking: *Foley v Hill* (1838–48)

JOSHUA GETZLER*

I. A Seminal Decision, a Hotbed of Theories

In the leading House of Lords decision of *Foley v Hill* in 1848, it was ruled that if a banker had failed to account for a customer's bank balance, including a failure to acknowledge or pay over the agreed interest, for a period longer than six years, then the extant limitation statute[1] was effective to bar the customer's claim to an account of the balance, and hence the value of both deposited principal and notionally accrued interest could not be claimed.[2] As part of their reasoning, the Lords affirmed Lord Lyndhurst C's view[3] that a customer depositing money in a bank account has only a conventional debt claim against the banker, and cannot normally demand an account in equity to measure a fluctuating balance, and so cannot use an equitable procedure to maintain the banker's duties. Some five separate courts heard the cause across a ten-year span of litigation, and of these, only the first instance judge, Knight Bruce V-C thought that a Chancery court had power to enforce return of the bank money by finding a continuous equitable duty of account binding the banker that was effective to circumvent the limitation period.[4] According to the appellate courts, the claim embodied in a positive bank balance was a simple debt subject to normal limitation rules, even though the debt has no terminus or maturity date. It was true that the banker's debt to the customer was accompanied or

* Thanks are owed to Mitchell Cleaver, Nuncio D'Angelo, David Fox, Jeremiah Lau, Hin Liu, Lionel Smith, Stephen Smith, Robert Stevens, Peter Watts, and seminar participants at the Banking and Financial Services Law Association, UCL Laws, and UNSW Law & Justice, for contributing important points and queries.

[1] Limitation Act 1624 (21 James I, c 16) s 3.

[2] *Foley v Hill* (1848) 2 HLC 28, 9 ER 1002.

[3] *Foley v Hill* (1844) 1 Phillips 399, 41 ER 683 (Ch, LC). Curiously, Lord Lyndhurst sat in both this, the intermediate appeal, and then the further Lords appeal, where he gave his speech last despite his precedence as former chancellor, gratefully agreeing that his earlier decree should be affirmed. *Cf FHR European Ventures LLP v Cedar Capital Partners LLC* [2014] UKSC 45, [2015] 1 AC 250 where Lord Neuberger overruled his own judgment in *Sinclair Investments Ltd v Versailles Trade Finance Ltd* [2011] EWCA Civ 347, [2012] Ch 453.

[4] (1843) 13 Law J Rep (NS) 182 (Ch, V-C). The exclusion of trustee liabilities and running merchant accounts from the conventional operation of the statutory limitation periods for obligations is explained in M Macnair, 'Length of Time and Related Equitable Bars 1660-1760' in H Dondorp et al (eds), *Limitation and Prescription: A Comparative Legal History* (Berlin, Duncker & Humblot, 2019) 337, 343–51.

augmented by implied and express contractual terms typically according the customer a right to payment on notice or demand, plus some level of reporting of the balance. In addition it was normal to offer a facility for drawing payment orders on the bank for the benefit of third-party payees, such as personal or negotiable cheques, giving the payee an autonomous claim to payment from the bank/drawee at the order of the depositor/drawer and payable upon acceptance; and there might further be an overdraft facility annexed to the deposit account.[5] After extensive grappling with the distinction between bailments of money as specie, debts of sums certain, and accountability for control of assets, the judges came to insist on the banker-depositor relation as a simple fluctuating debt relationship, with superadded, limited, and malleable customary and contractual rights. The augmentations do not transform the basic banking relationship into any type of bailment or trusteeship over the money value accorded to the bank via the deposit; nor should the banker be regarded as an accountable agent or fiduciary of the customer (unless he or she takes on a role as adviser or manager). It was crucial to the relationship that the bank should have full title to the money and power to direct its use value, so that the bank could personally lend it out under contract to other customers, or invest in the bank's own name in external security instruments in order to earn the bank income.

By excluding troublesome and hampering doctrines of property, agency, trust, and fiduciary law from the pure contractual streams of banking law, *Foley v Hill* was received as a welcome clarification and simplification of the law, providing a foundation for modern fractional reserve banking as a means of credit expansion and financial intermediation in the mid-Victorian economy.[6] Indeed, the decision is universally celebrated in modern banking texts as the *locus classicus* of modern banking law, as *Saloman v A Saloman Ltd*[7] sits within the development of company law, or *Donoghue v Stevenson*[8] within tort. But not all commentators have been so sanguine about the consequences of the decision. Economists of a libertarian bent, notably from the Austrian school beginning with Ludwig von Mises, have seen this stream of case law as undermining the historical banking institution of *depositum irregulare*, whereby a 100 per cent level of circulating security for any placed deposit must be warehoused within a fungible mass by a deposit-accepting bank, giving the depositor a complete commercial and legal security, and confining the bank to cashier and payment services rather than lucrative and risky intermediations and maturity transformations, operations deemed more appropriate for other financial institutions.[9] Critics have also doubted the legal logic of

[5] The autonomous payment obligation represented by a cheque or bill of exchange representing a cancellation of debt to the drawer balanced by bank payment to a payee is explained in *London Joint Stock Bank v Macmillan* [1918] AC 777 (HL) and *Libyan Arab Foreign Bank v Bankers Trust Co* [1989] QB 728. For history and analysis see B Geva, "Bank Money': The Rise, Fall and Metamorphosis of the Transferable Deposit' in D Fox and W Ernst (eds), *Money in the Western Legal Tradition – Middle Ages to Bretton Woods* (Oxford, Oxford University Press, 2016) 358–86; R Cranston et al, *Principles of Banking Law*, 3rd edn (Oxford, Oxford University Press, 2018) 335–55; E McKendrick, *Goode and McKendrick on Commercial Law*, 6th edn (Penguin, Harmondsworth, 2021) chs 17–21.

[6] For an insightful contemporary note, see Anon, 'Bankers' Current or Deposit Accounts, and the Statute of Limitations' (1853) 13 *The Bankers' Magazine; Journal of the Money Market, and Railway Digest* 275, 275–81. For a representative modern celebration of the case, see Cranston, *Banking Law* (n 5) 190–92.

[7] *Saloman v A Saloman Ltd* [1897] AC 22 (HL).

[8] *Donoghue v Stevenson* [1932] AC 562 (HL).

[9] HE Batson (trans), L von Mises, *The Theory of Money and Credit* [Vienna, 1912] (1st English edition, London, Jonathan Cape, 1934; 2nd English edn, New Haven, NJ, Yale University Press, 1953); MN Rothbard,

the decision: how can a banker be said to own client money outright, yet be expected to repay a like value on demand, unless the law imposes some set of obligations on the banker to ensure that such ready money is available, thus undermining the simple debt premise?

Two general observations may be registered about the case. First, the judges in *Foley* thought they were deciding a narrow range of legal questions concerning legal defences and were not trying to transform or codify banking practice. Later courts and commentators have read into the decision the larger legal policies they would have liked to exist. Secondly, much legal to-and-fro followed the decision, as uncertainty remained about the nature of the basic bank deposit, reflecting perhaps a deeper fragility and instability within the growing banking sector of Victorian Britain.[10] There remains to this day an ineluctable tension between a banker's power over deposit values and the risks this imposes over customers' savings. A host of legal, regulatory, and social devices have had to be invented over time to deal with this uncertainty, from reputational control and personal liability of bank directors and investors, to inter-bank lending pacts, government deposit insurance, ring-fencing of savings and commercial banking, macro-prudential banking regulation requiring capital buffers, and ultimately the threat or promise of government nationalisation.[11] The apparently simple debt answer given in *Foley v Hill* to the question of bank liability only threw up a more complex set of legal and financial puzzles that continue to exercise courts and regulators to this day. Hence, it is well worth understanding more deeply the historical genesis and content of the decision, and not rest content with the received and compressed view of the case presented in modern literatures.

The case also presents an opportunity to test Katharina Pistor's hypothesis of the legal coding of capital, taking her enquiry into the terrain of nineteenth-century equity. Pistor, in her 2019 instant classic *The Code of Capital*, argued that the law constructs capital with a 'code' of shifting ascriptions of rights, powers, duties and liabilities between various parties to legal relationships. In her vision, legal history joins to political economy, charting how the law enhances or undermines the claims of original owners, assignees, trustees and beneficiaries, directors, shareholders, secured and unsecured bondholders, employees, fiscal authorities, public and private reinsurers, heirs, tort victims … in fact, every type of party seeking benefit from economic relations or recourse against assets. By uncovering the coding of capital, we may discover how elite lawyers, who typically serve powerful corporate and financial interests, can re-engineer assets and transform how risks and profits attach to those assets to favour clients' interests, often

The Mystery of Banking (Richardson & Snyder, Dutton, New York, NY, 1983); MA Stroup (trans), JH de Soto, *Money, Bank Credit, and Economic Cycles* [Madrid, 1998] (1st English edn, Auburn, AL, Ludwig von Mises Institute, 2006).

[10] JD Turner, *Banking in Crisis: The Rise and Fall of British Banking Stability, 1800 to the Present* (Cambridge, Cambridge University Press, 2014).

[11] For analysis and synthesis see CW Calomiris and CM Kahn, 'The Role of Demandable Debt in Structuring Optimal Banking Arrangements' (1991) 81 *American Economic Review* 497; D Focarelli and AF Pozzolo, 'Banking Industry' in SN Durlauf and LE Blume (eds), *The New Palgrave Dictionary of Economics*, 2nd edn (London, Macmillan, 2008) online version link.springer.com/referencework/10.1057/978-1-349-95121-5 (last accessed 21 February 2023); PE Strahan, 'Bank Structure and Lending: What We Do and Do Not Know' in AV Thakor and AWA Boot (eds), *Handbook of Financial Intermediation and Banking* (Oxford, Elsevier, 2008) 108–31; P Krugman and R Wells, *Economics*, 6th edn (Basingstoke, Macmillan, 2021) chs 25 and 29.

at the expense of wider social efficiency, equity and macro-stability.[12] Pistor prescriptively argues for a stronger public order disciplining the experimentation of cautelary lawyers and restraining their relentless pursuit of monopolist income and market-shaping power on a tilted legal playing field. Her theory can neatly be applied to *Foley v Hill*, as a decision privileging banker profits and reducing their liabilities, whilst cutting away the protections of commercial, industrial, and family savers. Pistor's analysis can be seen as a descendant of the radical muckraking and realist movements in Gilded Age, Progressive, and Depression America. Indeed in 1914 a famous Boston lawyer soon to join the United States Supreme Court made just such arguments, assailing the power of monopolist bankers who diverted wealth from the working population, using complex trust and corporate structures to attain their goals.[13]

So, we have three framing models available for our leading case: a salutary clarification of existing and successful banking practice making the future possible; an incoherent decision opening the door to unbridled credit creation and financial instability; or a gift to the banking interest by lawyers caught within a financialising ideology and lending the authority of the courts to an intra-capitalist class war.

Let us turn now to the historical legal record to see if any of these theories have traction. A theory of historical law can only be as good as its grasp of the laws being described.

II. The Bank Balance as Debt not Deposit: *Carr v Carr* (1811)

There was a good deal of litigation over the legal nature of money instruments and payment mechanisms in early modern law; lawyers might struggle to distinguish bullion, fiat, and fiduciary currency from bills, notes and money orders; and liquid sums might be awarded alternatively or concurrently as finite promises of value, as damages awards protecting expectation and reliance, or as covenanted sums or debts encompassing interest awards in addition to the face value or principal owed.[14] Lord Mansfield offered the definitive treatment of the legal nature of money and currency in *Miller v Race* in 1757,[15] perhaps influenced by the theories of his intellectual companion and compatriot Adam Smith. In this case a stolen banknote had been delivered on to an innocent third party for consideration, who sued when the bank refused to honour the note. This raised the deeper question of the legal nature of a banknote and the relation of title to the paper and money value as embodied in coin or specie. Lord Mansfield

[12] K Pistor, *The Code of Capital: How the Law Creates Wealth and Inequality* (Princeton, NJ, Princeton University Press, 2019).

[13] LD Brandeis, *Other People's Money – And How the Bankers Use It* (New York, NY, Frederick A Stokes Co, 1914).

[14] See, eg, *Hawley v Cutts* (1677) 2 Freeman 24, 22 ER 1034 (LC). Further on the legal history of money: C Desan, *Making Money: Coin, Currency, and the Coming of Capitalism* (Oxford, Oxford University Press, 2014); R Kreitner, 'Legal History of Money' (2012) 8 *Annual Review of Law and Social Science* 415; Fox and Ernst (eds), *Money in the Western Legal Tradition* (n 5).

[15] *Miller v Race* (1757) 2 Kenyon 189, 96 ER 1151 (KB).

explained that banknotes were paper money and that title passed on delivery. To reach this point, he had to dig deeper and explain money itself:

> Money, properly speaking, is whatever common consent has fixed upon as a sign denoting a certain value; and though, commonly, of gold, or silver, yet, sometimes, of mixed metals: and leather stamped has been used; so may paper; seeing, whatever the material is, common consent may make it money, to all intents, and purposes; and that banknotes are so received, and not considered as documents of a debt, or securities for money only, appears from many determinations. 1. A man devised all his securities for money: it was held, bank notes did not pass. 2. "All my ready money, or cash:" it was held, they did pass. …
>
> The use of current specie is, that, where it passes from one to another for good consideration, and without collusion, it can never be traced, or demanded, by any former possessor: which has given rise to a quaint expression (which, however, is not warranted by the fact), that money has no ear mark, and therefore cannot be followed. Now this is not true; for money, when it can be distinguished (as some particular pieces may, or in a purse), may be followed, as far as a bank-note may.[16]

In this case the note had not been segregated when placed with the bank but had been presented in the ordinary course for exchange into some other money form. The plaintiff could insist on the value of his paper money, and recover by assumpsit for money had and received a sum equivalent to the note value, or alternatively a remedy in trover, from the defendant bank who had received the note. This was not a deposit, but an exchange of one form of money for another.

Lord Mansfield's reserved judgment on the legal nature of money made an enormous impact on the commercial world. Legal analysis of the nature of a money deposit at a bank was not to arrive for fifty years and more, and then by a sidewind involving parsing of the language of an obscurely formulated legacy. In the 1811 case of *Carr v Carr*,[17] a testator bequeathed to the plaintiff 'whatever debts might be due to him (the Testator) *from the Plaintiff or others*, at the time of his death'. This clause seems to have been intended as a forgiveness of a debt owed by the plaintiff to the testator effected through the drawing of a bill of exchange by the plaintiff in the testator's favour, which had been lodged with his bank but which had not yet become payable. The testator, in addition, was owed debts by other parties; and further had a cash balance due to him on his banker's account. The residue of his personal estate was granted to the defendant. There was no question that the third-party debts should go to the plaintiff. The question before the court, with the distinguished Chancery judge Sir William Grant MR sitting, was 'Whether this bill of exchange, and the said cash balance, or either of them, passed to the Plaintiff by the above bequest.' If a money claim in the hands of the testator's bank could be described as ready money at the testator's demand and disposal, then the defendant could lay claim to that money value as 'residue' rather than 'debt'.

Sir Samuel Romilly[18] for the plaintiff contended that the bill and the balance were both choses in action, that could only be recovered by action, and therefore must be considered as debts. Anthony Hart KC[19] for the defendant, submitted that the bill of

[16] ibid 2 Kenyon 199, 96 ER 1154.
[17] *Rolls*, 30 November 1811, reported (1816) 1 Mer 529, 541; 35 ER 767, 771 (note 2 to *Sleech's Case*).
[18] A distinguished counsel, politician and law reformer, Solicitor-General 1806–07.
[19] Briefly Vice-Chancellor (1827), then Irish Lord Chancellor (1827–30).

exchange 'was delivered to the bankers by the Testator as money', and through their control was 'as if in his own possession'. Moreover,

> the cash balance … could not be considered as a debt in the contemplation of the Testator; that, though strictly speaking, a debt, yet it was, in the common opinion of mankind, considered as money deposited with the banker; that, in construction of Wills, words ought not to be taken according to their strict legal meaning, but according to the intention of the Testator; and that, in this case, the Testator could not have conceived it to be a debt.

Romilly rejoined that a deposit claim against a bank was clearly nothing but a debt, as 'it might be proved under a commission of bankrupt; or a commission might be taken out upon it; it would not pass under a bequest of all the Testator's ready money, and therefore must clearly pass as a debt'.

Grant MR found for the plaintiff on all counts. It was clear that the bill of exchange, like the third-party claims, passed as debt being a chose in action. It did not matter that the plaintiff himself had armed the bank with the power to draw the funds as a debt claim for the testator; its legal characterisation as debt was always maintained. The bank balance, however, gave the judge more pause:

> He had entertained some doubt on the other point; but thought that the money which had been paid into the banker's ought also to pass as a debt. This was not a despositum [sic]. A sealed bag of money might, indeed, be a despositum; but money paid in, generally, to a banker could not be so considered. He observed, that money had no ear-mark; that, when money is paid into a banker's, he always opens a debtor and creditor account with the payor. The banker employs the money himself, and is liable merely to answer the drafts of his customer to that amount. This would clearly support a commission of bankrupt; it would not pass by the description of ready money; and, therefore, it must be considered as a debt, and must pass by that description.

The plaintiff was declared due the debt due on the bill with interest once payable, and the balance of cash at the banker's, with interest from the testator's death, as well as the third-party debts. Interestingly, Grant MR simply assumed that the debt owed to a customer by a banker must yield interest at all times when the value had fallen into the bank's own joint estate, as it was then presumably available to the bank for its own use.

Finally, Grant MR's observation that a bank balance is debt, not deposit, as a banker 'is liable merely to answer the drafts of his customer to that amount', gave no trace of a concept of *depositum irregulare*, being the loan of a fungible where a 100 per cent floating reserve is kept in place to restore a like value to the customer on demand.[20] The judge thus seems to have assumed that the custom and expectation of fractional

[20] For the historical background, see L Waelkens, *'Amne Adverso'. Roman Legal Heritage in European Legal Culture* (Leuven, Leuven University Press, 2015) 401–04; de Soto, *Money* (n 9) 1–36. A summary of common-law irregular deposit was offered in *South Australian Insurance Company v Randell* (1869) LR 3 PC 101, relating to wheat merged in a fungible common stock with a right to revest title in replacement stock; and a modern instantiation is found in *Mercer* v *Craven Grain Storage Ltd* (17 March 1994, HL, unreported), discussed in LD Smith, 'Bailment with Authority to Mix – And Substitute' (1995) 111 *Law Quarterly Review* 10. *Re Goldcorp Exchange Ltd* [1995] 1 AC 74 (PC) rehearsed the same set of issues in the guise of a failed attempt to enforce a claim to residual value of fungibles by means of an equitable charge enhancing the priority of a debt claim. The history of the older common-law debt actions enforcing claims to a 'sum certain' embodied in currency, fungible goods, and even specific chattels, is narrated in AWB Simpson, *A History of the Common Law of Contract: The Rise of the Action of Assumpsit* (Oxford, Clarendon Press, 1975, reprinted 1987) 53–196.

reserve banking was in play, and that all the parties expected it. Thus, it could not be said that money at the bank could be classified as specie or 'ready money', even if it could normally be assumed to be freely available on demand. There was behind this a stream of authority classifying a demand triggering an immediate obligation to pay a debt, loan or sum certain as merely the perfection of a debt already in existence and sounding *in personam* from the time the note or covenant constituting the debt had been inscribed.[21]

III. Balances Held by Bank Partners are Joint and Several Debts: The *Devaynes Case* (1816)

The debt obligations of bankers were soon elaborated by Sir William Grant MR and Lord Eldon C, dealing with problems raised by the insolvency of a partnership bank. The banking firm of Devaynes, Dawes, & Co failed in 1810, giving rise to a complex series of litigation.[22] Devaynes was a founding partner of the bank but died in 1809, and his son and heir took over his estate, including initial rights to partnership profits. However, the son did not join the partnership, and he took out the inherited partnership capital some nine months later, requesting then that his deceased father's name be removed from the trading name of the continuing banking business where it had been used without overt authority. Customers continued to trade with the renamed and reorganised firm, but the bank failed within a few months, and its surviving partners became insolvent and liable to the creditors of the bank. Certain creditors also sued the son, Devaynes, for bank debts amassed by the partnership at the time of his father's death, claiming that they should have satisfaction against the deceased estate for the partner's share of firm debt run up whilst the father was a member of the firm, taking priority once any personal debts outside the business had been paid under the so-called 'jingle rule'. In an initial hearing in 1811, Lord Eldon upheld the basic principle that a partner, even having left the firm, remained liable for partnership debts contracted whilst still a partner, unless that debt had been released by the creditors and adopted by the remaining partners.[23] The case was then remitted for accounting by a master in

[21] *Rumball v Ball* (1712) 10 Mod 39, 88 ER 616 (QB): 'a debt [is] plainly precedent to the demand'; *Norton v Ellam* (1837) 2 M & W 461, 150 ER 839 (Ex), where Baron Parke said: 'It is quite clear that a promissory note, payable on demand, is a present debt, and is payable without any demand, and the statute begins to run from the date of it'. The common-law rules for pleading of debt and the role of demand are explored in *Young v Queensland Trustees Ltd* (1956) 99 CLR 560, 562–70 and *Ogilvie v Adams* [1981] VR 1041, 1049 ff (Fullagar J). Judges were pragmatic as to when conventional interest burdens would lie against a debt payable on demand without maturity, raising difficult points as to whether interest was a primary or remedial obligation: see *Pinock v Willett* (1734) Barnes 228, 94 ER 889 (KB); *Blaney v Hendricks* (1771) 2 Black W 761, 96 ER 445 (CP); *Calton v Bragg* (1812) 10 East 223, 104 ER 828 (KB). The matter of demandable debt is further discussed in Sections V. & VI., below.

[22] *Devaynes v Noble* (1816) 1 Mer 529, 35 ER 767 – some three main cases reported plus various ancillary cases. See A Televantos, *Capitalism Before Corporations: The Morality of Business Associations and the Roots of Commercial Equity and Law* (Oxford, Oxford University Press, 2020) 151–62, focussing on partnership insolvency aspects. I am indebted to Televantos' analysis.

[23] *Ex parte Kendall* (1811) 1 Rose 71; 17 Ves Jun 514, 34 ER 199. The principle was consistently replied in later cases of bank insolvency, and was also used to enforce calls on unpaid capital: see *Wallworth v Holt, in re The Imperial Bank of England* (1841) 4 My & Cr 619, 41 ER 238 (LC).

Chancery, and various creditor claims were proved. Devaynes junior, the son, appealed the master's findings.

In *Sleech's Case* in 1816,[24] counsel for Devaynes junior (again Hart KC) argued that since Sleech, as a particular creditor, had been paid a dividend from the failed bank by the surviving partners and had then settled and composed her claims against those partners, she was shut off from suing the deceased partner's estate for debts contracted during his lifetime as a partner. The overall argument was that Sleech had in effect settled her claims against the bank as a group or entity, accepting impliedly that the dealings with the live partners had shifted her legal claims to them and them alone. Moreover, her composition had in any case embraced the departed partner's liability. Counsel for Devaynes junior further tried to argue that the continuation of Devaynes senior's name in the partnership and the leaving of his capital in the firm should not be taken as any representation that the creditor claims against the surviving partners could be attached to the deceased estate. Moreover, by failing to sue the deceased estate at the time of the death and partnership dissolution and reformation, Sleech had foresworn the Devaynes debt, and could not now revive it due to the operation of the laches defence.

Perhaps the most interesting argument adduced by Hart KC was that Devaynes senior did not in law owe a debt as a banker, but was rather a bailee of a deposit, such that a delay in retrieving a deposit from a surviving partner presented a strong case of laches:

> The case of bankers is stronger than that of ordinary traders, because the money in their hands is rather a deposit than a debt, and may therefore be instantly demanded and taken up; and this is the reason why nobody ever hears of an action against a banker to pay a balance, unless in the case of disputed items. If a man deposits a collection of pictures in the hands of a partnership, and one of the partners dies, and nine months afterwards a fire happens, by which the pictures are consumed; can he come into a Court of Conscience, and say to the Executors of the deceased, you must make good the loss sustained by the surviving bailees? The trust reposed in a banker arises out of personal confidence …

If the banker leaves the partnership, trust in the maintenance of the deposit must be reposed in the remaining bailees who run the bank. This was a radical alternative hypothesis going beyond the initial arguments that Sleech's debts had been composed or abandoned.

In response, John Bell, counsel for Sleech (and regarded by Lord Eldon as the best Chancery barrister then in practice), opposed the initial idea that a customer must be taken to have acquiesced in the acquittance of a deceased partner's estate for debt, if she continues to deal with the surviving partners and does not remove her balance forthwith, settling all claims as the partnership bank is reconstituted. Sir William Grant MR agreed with Bell, and did not accept the defence arguments that Sleech had foresworn Devaynes' debt when she failed to sue his estate on his death, nor that she had composed the debt implicitly by dealing with the other partners and settling their parts of the extant debt. He applied Lord Eldon's earlier ruling that individual partnership liabilities survived departures from or dissolution of a partnership, and each individual partner's liability stood independently of the position of the others. The bank was not to be taken

[24] Reported in *Devaynes v Noble* (1816) 1 Mer 529, 539; 35 ER 767, 771.

as an entity holding debt only against present membership, even if traders customarily treated it as such; quotidian mercantile practice did not change basic principles of property and obligation.[25] To accept the defence case that customers must sue for their deposits instantly on the death of a bank partner or face a laches defence for surrendering their claim would only encourage depositors to make a run on the bank and recover their money every time a bank partnership changed its membership and so was legally reconstituted. This would be intolerable, and so it was preferable simply to maintain the usual rule that departing bank partners remained fixed with extant debt liabilities in the normal way of partnerships. Grant MR explicitly rejected the defence claim that the custom of bankers meant that the personal debt relationship should be shifted on a dissolution of the remaining partners of a reformed bank that carried on the same business; counsel could not simply appeal to some vague *lex mercatoria* to shift the normal principles of the law.

Sir William Grant also took time to discern and reject the alternative bailment/deposit hypothesis advanced by Hart KC in Devaynes' defence:

> But it is supposed that there is a considerable difference between the case of bankers and that of any other partnership; and that it is impossible for the creditors of a banking-shop to permit their money to remain in the hands of the surviving partners for such a space of time as eight months – (indeed, the argument went to eight days, or even to a shorter period), – without recognizing those surviving partners to be the depositaries of the balance due, and therefore exclusively responsible to make what is called the deposit forth-coming. There is a fallacy in likening the dealings of a banker to the case of a deposit, to which, in legal effect, they have no sort of resemblance. Money paid in to a banker's becomes immediately a part of his general assets; and he is merely a debtor for the amount. Therefore, when a man lodges money with a partnership of bankers, he is as much concerned to look to the solvency of each particular partner, as if he was lending the money to any other partnership. The money, in each case, equally ceases to be his the moment he has parted with it, and he has only to trust, for the return of it, to the solvency of the persons into whose hands it passes: but he has, in each case alike, the credit, and the responsibility of all the partners in the firm. Then, when one partner dies, what is to be inferred from the mere circumstance of allowing the debt upon the banking account to remain uncalled for in the hands of the surviving partners, beyond what would be inferred from not immediately calling in any debt due by the surviving partners, in any other trade, where money had been advanced or lent to that partnership? The security is permitted to stand just as it did, the party doing nothing to alter it. There is no *novatio debiti* – no new contract – no relinquishment of the old security, whatever it may, either in law or equity, be defined to be.[26]

Sir William Grant went on to decide another creditor claim involving problems of ordering the timing of receipts and payments in a running set of joint bank accounts in *Clayton's Case.*[27] Clayton had contracted a debt against the bank whilst Devaynes was

[25] ibid 1 Mer 563–71, 35 ER 778–81. For a later case showing how an explicit release by creditors of a retiring partner could work, see *Attwood v Banks* (1839) 2 Beav 192, 48 ER 1153 (MR). Agreements could work in the reverse direction, guaranteeing a retiring partner a share of future debt accruals or profits in the residual partnership: *Lees v Laforest* (1851) 14 Beav 250, 51 ER 283 (MR).

[26] ibid 1 Mer 568–69, 35 ER 780.

[27] ibid 1 Mer 572, 35 ER 781; and see also a much later airing of the same issue before Lord Brougham C, reported (1831) 2 Russ & M 495, 39 ER 482 (LC).

alive, and then a further debt after he died. The surviving partners had paid a sum equal to the prior debt. The question arose whether Clayton could count this payment against the later debt, and so revive the earlier debt against Devaynes' estate. Grant MR stated the 'first in first out rule' to deny the creditor a power to determine which debts had been paid out of a consideration from the debtor; the court would simply take the first return of deposited money as retiring the first liability. This celebrated part of the decision is not as strongly relevant to our enquiry into the particular nature of bank deposit and debt, but it does further affirm the obligational or debt nature of bank deposit.

IV. 'Money in Hand', 'Ready Money', and the Will Cases

Sir William Grant MR was esteemed as one of the great lawyers of his time, and his decisions in *Carr v Carr* and *Sleech's Case* stood within the precedents and had a power of legal logic behind them. But the heterodox concept of the bank balance as an asset in the nature of a demandable deposit, rather than a simple debt, did not vanish as a result of his judgment, and re-emerged in a scattering of will cases. In *Vaisey v Reynolds* (1828),[28] a testator made a will giving 'to my wife all … all and every my book debts, *monies in hand*, stock in trade [etc]'. He next gave to the named executors 'all and every my monies out at interest on mortgage, notes of hand, or any other security whatsoever, together with all my monies vested in the public funds'. The issue was whether a bank balance fell into the money-in-hand class, ie, immediately available, or money in the form of a chose in action that had to be realised via a prestation, security, or sale. The banker had no overt duty to pay interest, and balances were payable on demand, but the banker customarily paid three per cent on balances left for more than nine months. Sir John Leach MR found as follows:

> The testator has referred to two descriptions of monies – monies in hand – and monies out at interest on mortgage, notes of hand, and other securities whatsoever. The balance in the banker's hands, though it carried interest, was not out at interest on security; and it was in the same order and disposition of the testator, as if it had been deposited in his own drawer. It must be inferred that the testator meant to pass it by one of the two descriptions which he has used. In no sense was it money on security; and, in a reasonable sense, it was money in hand, and passed, therefore, to the wife.[29]

A decade later in *Taylor* v *Taylor*,[30] Lord Langdale MR summed up this stream of authority as follows:

> It is true that in strict legal language, what is called money deposited at a banker's is nothing more than a debt, and cannot be called ready money, but in the ordinary language of mankind money at a banker's is called ready money, and we must construe a will according to the ordinary language of mankind.

[28] *Vaisey v Reynolds* (1828) 5 Russ 12, 38 ER 931 (MR).

[29] ibid 2 Russ 14–16, 38 ER 932.

[30] *Taylor* v *Taylor* (1837) 1 Jur 401. For a full exploration of the early nineteenth-century authorities, see HD McLeod, *The Theory and Practice of Banking*, 3rd edn (London, Longmans, 1875–76) vol 2, 279–333, 495–500.

The courts soon noticed that the quality of demandability or readiness of payment for the bank depositor matched the quality of negotiability of debt to third-party payees via issuance of bills and cheques. In *Marzetti v Williams* (1830),[31] the duty of a banker to honour cheques drawn for third parties was held in a strong Court of King's Bench[32] to be an express or implied contract quite independent of the nature of the balance as a debt. The court would imply an actionable contractual duty into the usual banking relationship because this was the strong expectation of the parties. In light of these vested expectations, it would be disruptive and harmful to a customer's credit and reputation for a cheque unreasonably to be dishonoured where a positive balance was in place or nearly in place, and a banker who had refused a reasonable and expected payment order should pay at least nominal damages to maintain expectations. By so building into a bank balance an expectation of instant payment to the depositor or his or her payee, the courts recognised a legal quality of control or 'order and disposition' over bank deposits which they compared to possession.

The *Marzetti* control and disposition doctrine of the King's Bench went beyond the Chancery cases where the judges were straining to characterise bank balances as ready assets in order to enhance inheritance expectations. Indeed, doubts over the pure debt model may have grown as the credit economy expanded in mid-Victorian England, and parties wished to manipulate their payment expectations in order to generate further credit. The judges remained ambivalent, however; shortly after *Marzetti*, in the 1833 King's Bench decision of *Sims v Bond*, Denman CJ and a full court insisted that an undisclosed provider of a loan paid into a bank account could not claim the account value on the analogy of an undisclosed principal enforcing a contract via an agent. 'Sums which are paid to the credit of a customer with a banker, though usually called deposits, are, in truth, loans by the customer to the banker.' Only the direct provider of the value could claim the account at law, reasserting an obligational, personal concept of bank accounts as personal debts, not as assets of wider exigibility.[33] Perhaps it was expedient to keep the doctrinal choices open, sometimes favouring the debt end of the spectrum, sometimes the asset end.[34]

In *Parker v Marchant*, the asset/debt dichotomy was tested in another testamentary case, coming before Vice-Chancellor Knight Bruce in 1842,[35] and appealed the next year before Lord Lyndhurst C.[36] Knight Bruce V-C prefaced his judgment by setting out an interpretative methodology for wills, taking general constructions of expressions in the first place, but allowing special meanings, as used in a locale or community or by particular individuals, to displace general meanings, with wide use of extrinsic evidence to establish those additional interpretative norms.[37] This liberal approach might have

[31] *Marzetti v Williams* (1830) 1 Barn & Ad 415, 109 ER 842 (KB).

[32] Tenterden CJ, Parke, Taunton, and Patteson JJ.

[33] *Sims v Bond* (1833) 5 Barn & Ad 389, 392–93; 110 ER 834, 835 (KB). Concomitantly the agent of an undisclosed principal could render the principal's property liable to general banker's lien: *Brandao v Barnett* (1846) 12 Cl & Fin 787, 8 ER 1622 (HL). Remedies for wrongful payment of principal's monies into a mixed bank account and the passing of title to money generally were thoroughly explored much later in *Pennell v Deffell* (1853) 4 De G M & G 72, 43 ER 551 (Ch – LJJ) and *Re Hallett's Estate* (1880) 13 Ch D 696 (CA per Jessel MR).

[34] *Cf Governor of the Bank of England v Booth* (1837) 2 Keen 466, 48 ER 655 per Langdale MR, on the porous lines between bank deposits, bills, and notes.

[35] *Parker v Marchant* (1842) 1 Y & Col 290, 62 ER 893 (V-C).

[36] (1843) 1 Phillips 356, 41 ER 667 (LC).

[37] *Parker* (V-C) (n 35) 1 Y & Col 299–304, 62 ER 897–900.

left some doubt whether testamentary causes are safe arenas of law-making for general commerce.[38]

In *Parker* the testator by his will made a series of bequests as follows: (1) 'in the first place, all of my debts are to be paid'; then (2) £60,000 worth of consols to his wife; (3) the remaining £10,000 of consols to A.; (4) £500 to B.; (5) £100 to C; (6) 'to D. and E. all the rest and residue of my ready money, securities for money, and monies in the funds, upon trust to invest, &c., and to pay the dividends to my wife for life, and after her decease to divide the capital amongst F., G., H. and I'; (7) all real estate to the same trustees upon certain trusts; (8) a gift of the residuary personal estate to the testator's wife in terms: 'And I do further give and bequeath to my said wife all my jewels, plate, linen, china, carriages, wines and other goods, chattels and effects whatsoever, as her own goods and chattels for ever; and I do hereby constitute and appoint her, my said wife, sole executrix of this my will.'[39]

The court held that in the normal way general debts should be paid out of the personal estate first, and only turn to the realty in case of shortfall. This was uncontroversial and of no moment since the personal estate was very large. The pertinent question was whether the final bequest of personalty to the wife, which in its latitude was held to be a gift of the entire residuum, encompassed two sizeable bank balances amounting to over £21,000 held to the account of the testator at banks in Bath and London. There was only some £116 in ready cash left amongst the possessions of the testator. If the bank balances were characterised as 'ready money', they would be grouped with the 'securities for money, and monies in the funds', and those sums would pass into the specific trust of personalty to be distributed as income for life to the wife with a gift-over of capital to named legatees; the result would be to deny the greater sum of bank capital to the wife as residuary. If the more usual meaning of 'ready money' as physically available cash was rather deployed, the bank money as capital would not touch the trust but go directly to the wife. So, everything depended on the characterisation of the nature of the bank balances.

Knight Bruce V-C began by observing that the will was ambulatory, and would apply to all wealth fitting the named categories at time of death, not at time of testation – a canon of interpretation established in the prior century but still occasionally challenged.[40] Hence the term 'ready money' applied to such money as was held at death. The judge held that the £116 cash '[c]learly is ready money'. He continued:

> It is, I think, on the other hand, equally clear that the debts due to the testator at his death from his agents and other persons, however safe, and with whatsoever facility obtainable, were not included under that description, with the exception only of the two [bank] sums … [at] the

[38] Compare in modern law the tensions over the application of proprietary estoppel and constructive trust doctrines in commercial cases (eg, *Yeoman's Row Management Ltd v Cobbe* [2008] UKHL 55, [2008] 1 WLR 1752) and cases concerning family inheritance (eg, *Thorner v Major* [2009] UKHL 18, [2009] 1 WLR 776; *Guest v Guest* [2022] UKSC 27, [2022] 3 WLR 911).

[39] *Cf Jones v Curry* (1818) 1 Wils Ch 25, 37 ER 11 (MR).

[40] Counsel cited a stream of authority for the ambulatory principle including *All Souls' College v Coddrington* (1720) 1 P Wms 597, 24 ER 533, but clearly the judge thought that the point of timing the extent of the estate fund had to be resolved on a case-by-case analysis. See further B Häcker, '*All Souls College v Codrington* (1720): Money, Books and the Interpretation of Wills – A Testamentary Drama in Three Acts' in B Sloan (ed), *Landmark Cases in Succession Law* (Oxford, Hart Publishing, 2019).

> testator's bankers at Bath [and] London. The argument has proceeded on the basis that these two sums were ordinary bankers' balances on banking accounts of the usual description, kept in the usual manner, that neither of them bore interest, and that in the customary mode it was competent to the testator at any moment to have drawn cheques payable to the bearer on demand for the whole. … The main dispute on this part of the case has been whether these two sums are to be considered as "ready money". According to the decision in *Carr* v. *Carr* (1 Mer. 541, n.), they would have passed, or might have passed, under a bequest of debts due to the testator. That, I think, is not conclusive against their capacity of passing under a bequest of ready money.[41]

Knight Bruce V-C then laid out a careful set of reasons to depart from the bank-balance-as-debt orthodoxy propounded earlier with such authority by Grant MR:

> Undoubtedly, an ordinary balance in a banker's hands is in a sense a debt due from him – certainly, he may be sued for it as for a debt. But it may be equally true that in a sense it is ready money; and, if that description may in general be justly held applicable to it, possible difficulties, not existing here, which may exist in other cases, as of a bequest in the same will of the debts due to the testator to one person, and of his ready money to another, without an explanatory context, or of interest being allowed by the banker, or of a contract that unless upon a certain notice the balance should not be reduced below an agreed amount, or of acceptances by the banker for the customer, not at maturity at the latter's death, or of drafts upon the banker, drawn by the customer, but not at maturity, not presented, or not paid, ought not to prevent the Court from giving full effect, according to a fair interpretation of the will, to the language which the testator has used. The term "debt," however technically correct, is not colloquially or familiarly applied to a balance at a banking-house. No man talks of his banker in that character being indebted to him. Men, speaking of such a subject, say they have so much at their bankers, or so much in their bankers' hands, a mode of expression indicating virtual possession rather than that right to which the law applies the term chose in action. Again, a man having not enough in his purse or in his house to pay a tradesman's bill for which he is asked, but having a large balance at his bankers, says that he has not so much about him, or that he has not so much in the house; he does not say that he has not so much ready money. Agreeing that this term is applicable to money in the purse, or the house, I cannot agree that it is confined to money so placed. Money paid into a banking-house in the ordinary mode is so paid for the purpose of being not safe merely, but ready as well as safe – available upon the instant for any exigency or object which may arise; according to a definition of the word "bank" in a book of high character[42] – "a place where money is laid up to be called for occasionally." It is true that the deposit is one which the banker is not bound to return in specie; that is, he satisfies the engagement if he has always ready for his customer a sum equal to the amount deposited. That, however, I think too thin and narrow a distinction to render the banker more in substance than a depositary, though technically, a debtor as well as a depositary. I consider, therefore, these two balances as ready money – a conclusion at which, as it differs, though not necessarily from the decision, yet, from an opinion expressed in *Carr* v. *Carr* by one of our greatest Judges, I have arrived, not without feelings of embarrassment and distrust. But it is my unavoidable duty to express and act upon my own opinion in the present case, however slightly I may and must estimate it in comparison with

[41] *Parker* (V-C) (n 35) 1 Y & Col 306, 62 ER 901.

[42] The judge is coyly referring to Samuel Johnson's *Dictionary of the English Language*, 9th edn (London, Longman, 1805) sv 'Bank', 4.

> that of a man such as Sir William Grant. I have the relief, certainly, of considering that the view which I take seems to be in accordance with the impression of two eminent Judges – I mean Sir John Leach and the present Master of the Rolls [Lord Langdale];[43] and that the Plaintiff has the right of bringing my judgment under the review of the Lord Chancellor.[44]

For all the politesse offered to Grant MR, this amounted to a major weakening of the bank debt principle enunciated in *Carr*. In Knight Bruce V-C's view, a bank balance, to be paid on demand to the depositor or his assignee without question, was a type of quasi-possession of the money, perhaps bailed as a shifting fungible mass to the bank, with a floating claim to severance from the mass always left in the depositor. The expectations of the parties placing a high level of control in the depositor fed back into the law to create a kind of modified *depositum irregulare*. In the result, the Vice Chancellor found against the widow, with the large bank balances described as 'ready money' to be taken into the trust for legacies. She was therefore to receive the income as a life beneficiary but not the capital as residuary.

On the appeal,[45] Lord Lyndhurst C first observed that the testator had used his own private language to denote various classes of 'ready money' encompassing both cash and convertible stock, to be rendered as initial pecuniary legacies. The testator then goes on to say: 'All the rest and residue of my ready money I dispose of' via the trust clause. The words of this grant to trust did not distinguish the large bank balances, nor the small sum of £116 cash left in the testator's house at death. It seemed unlikely that the elaborate trust settlement raising legacies and income for a range of beneficiaries had been predicated solely on the small cash amount left over. More likely the clause showed a testamentary intention to put all the remaining bank wealth, described here as 'ready money', to that beneficial end. The court should respect the testator's particular and non-legal use of language, as an objective understanding of his intentions that could be collected from the overall structure of the settlement.[46] Lyndhurst C concluded that such quotidian usage could feed back to change the legal concepts themselves:

> The question therefore is, whether the terms he [the testator] has used are sufficient for that purpose. Now, in construing a will of personal property, the terms that are used in the will are to be construed according to the ordinary acceptation of language in the transactions of mankind; and nobody can doubt that, in the ordinary use of language, money at a banker's would be considered as ready money. Everybody speaks of the sum which he has at his banker's as money: "my money at my banker's" is a usual mode of expression. And if it is money at the banker's, it is emphatically ready money, because it is placed there for the purpose of being ready when occasion requires: it is received upon the understanding that it shall be so ready. If a man goes to his banker, the money is counted out to him on the table. If he sends

[43] These supportive authorities are not identified in the judgment; he clearly means *Vaisey v Reynolds* and *Taylor v Taylor*, discussed above.

[44] *Parker* (V-C) (n 35) 1 Y & Col 306–08, 62 ER 901.

[45] *Parker* (LC) (n 36).

[46] This subjectivist canon of interpretation later hardened into the so-called 'arm-chair' rule stated by James LJ in *Boyes v Cook* (1880) 14 Ch D 53, 56: 'You may place yourself, so to speak, in his [the testator's] arm-chair, and consider the circumstances by which he was surrounded when he made his will to assist you in arriving at his intention'; see also *Loring v Woodland Trust* [2015] 1 WLR 3238, [2014] EWCA Civ 1314 [21] (Lewison LJ).

> an order for the money, it is counted out to his servant, or the person in whose favour that order is made. I consider, therefore, that it is strictly ready money according to the ordinary acceptation of those terms among mankind.[47]

This decision established the testamentary rule that bequests of bank debt using language of money would be effective.[48] This led to a new bout of litigation outside testamentary causes, testing if the banker's duty to have customer money payable on demand had now become the core of a revamped depositor's right.

V. Are Bankers Accountable for Deposits? *Foley v Hill* (1838–48)

Foley v Hill concerned a bank partnership with roots in the early industrial revolution. The Stourbridge Old Bank, as it came to be known, was founded in 1762, and served as a provincial or country bank providing payment and financial services to the local glass and iron trade in this quintessential Midlands industrial town. It survived as a banking partnership until its takeover by the Birmingham & Midland Banking Company in 1851. This was the first of many acquisitions of smaller provincial and country partnership banks by a new-model joint stock bank that grew to become the Midland Bank, one of the four largest national banks until its takeover by HSBC in 1992. The original Stourbridge Old Bank issued not only notes and cheques but also banknotes, which served as good tender in the locale, providing much-needed payment systems where there was a dearth of issue of note and coin with general tender in the late eighteenth century.[49] Local banking up to the mid-nineteenth century tended to rely on personal relationships and the local reputations of the partner-directors, and shareholders were counted as partners with full and unlimited liability for losses. The staking of personal reputations and fortunes was held to be the essential counterbalance for the great power that bankers wielded over client fortunes. That personalised system was shaken first by the crisis following the fall of Overend, Gurney, & Co, in 1866, followed by the still greater City of Glasgow Bank crash of 1878.[50] After this long decade of financial rupture, the banking trade began to amalgamate into large joint stock companies with limited liability, trading with customers at arm's length and deploying actuarial calculation of risks. At any rate, the defendant bank in the case in hand was known as 'Messrs. Hill & Co.', comprising a co-partnership of three bankers named Hill, Bates and Robbins. Hill, in fact, left the firm in 1834, but the remaining partners continued to trade under his name. So, in fact, the instant case had no real connection to the name of Hill; it was in reality a case against the firm of Bates & Robbins, with Robbins as the active partner signing the receipts.[51]

[47] *Parker* (LC) (n 36) 1 Phillips 360, 41 ER 669.
[48] See, eg, *Manning v Purcell* (1854) 2 Sm & Giff 284, 65 ER 402 (V-C); (1855) 7 De G M & G 55, 44 ER 21 (Ch – LJJ).
[49] LS Pressnell, 'Public Monies and the Development of English Banking' (1953) 5 *Economic History Review (NS)* 378; LS Pressnell, *Country Banking in the Industrial Revolution* (Oxford, Clarendon Press, 1956).
[50] Turner, *Banking in Crisis* (n 10) 79–88.
[51] See the narration of fact in *Foley v Hill* (1843) 13 Law J Rep (NS) 182 (Ch, V-C).

Foley, the plaintiff, belonged to a well-established Stourbridge family who had pioneered metallurgy and iron smelting in the earliest phases of the industrial revolution. Richard Foley had founded the family fortunes, opening ironworks in Staffordshire between 1624 and the Civil War, including multiple furnaces, forges, and mills, fired by charcoal and using the most advanced water power technologies for the milling process. Richard and his son Thomas developed the family business to a national position rivalling the London works, and supplied ordnance to the King's armies in the 1640s, though they were also sympathetic to the Parliament. The family moved its seat to Stourbridge in 1631 and then to Stoke Edith in Herefordshire in 1670. The family business grew apace, with generations of Foleys joining the management of the family partnership, and owning hundreds of iron works by 1700. Sons of the fourth and fifth generations were educated at Cambridge and Inner Temple, and entered politics, finance and law; a daughter married Robert Harley, Earl of Oxford and later Prime Minister in a Tory administration. The Foleys now became gentrified and ennobled, and by the early 1700s the speaker of the House of Commons and five MPs were Foley cousins. The iron works that had been the foundation of the Foley fortune passed to other hands from the 1710s, and from the sixth generation onwards the Foleys concentrated on managing their financial and banking interests and three large landed estates.[52] This was a classic case of a rising family moving from trade and industry to finance, politics and landed society.

Edward Thomas Foley, the plaintiff in the instant case, was born in 1791 and educated at Brasenose College, Oxford, rising to become a member of Parliament on the Tory side for Ludgershall (1826–32) and Herefordshire (1832–41). Foley attended the Commons throughout the tumultuous administrations of Wellington, Grey and Peel, and he is recorded in many votes, generally in lockstep with his party; but no parliamentary speeches are recorded. He died without heir in March 1846, leaving his estate freely to his wife, and presumably with his executors maintaining his suit in the House of Lords, which concluded some two years after his death. There is a certain irony in the fact that this well-connected magnate could not protect his liquid wealth from the neglect and depredation of his local bankers and, in a twist worthy of *Bleak House*, died before the resolution of a decade's worth of fruitless Chancery litigation.

The initial suit of *Foley v Hill* was filed in January 1838 in the Court of Chancery, with the bill narrating that the plaintiff had deposited the initial sum of £6,117, 10s with the defendants as his local bankers in April 1829.[53] This was a large sum of equivalent purchasing power of around £0.75 million in today's pounds. Foley received an account receipt for that sum, and the bankers agreed to pay the conventional three per cent interest. It seems that Foley deposited the funds simply to pool their value, and there was little account activity. Foley could prove that he had drawn two cheques for £1,700 and £2,000 prior to July 1830. He also claimed that fresh profits had been paid semi-annually into his sole account up to August 1834, being his share of income from a local colliery. The colliery account was in fact held at the Hill & Co Bank by Foley as joint holder with his colliery partner Scott, and the bankers denied that the colliery, whether directly or through agents, had ever paid money over to the sole Foley account.

[52] Family history from MB Rowlands, 'Foley family (per c. 1620–1716)' Oxford Dictionary of National Biography (Oxford University Press, 2004), doi.org/10.1093/ref:odnb/47491 (last accessed 22 September 2022).
[53] *Foley v Hill* (1838) 3 Mylne & Craig 475, 40 ER 1010 (Ch) per Lord Cottenham C.

Foley further claimed four cheques were drawn for payment to third parties in each year from 1831 to 1834. Foley claimed that interest had accrued and 'was duly entered or credited to the Plaintiff in the said account'; but all the defendants acknowledged was that interest was calculated at six-month stops up to the end of 1831 and the sums recorded in a ledger, but were never actually credited to the account. By 1837 Foley sought to close the account, and narrated that he had asked the defendant bankers 'to render a statement of their receipts and payments on his account, and of the interest accruing on the balance'; but

> they [the bankers] refused, under the pretence that no entries had been made to or on account of the Plaintiff's account within six years then last past, and that no written acknowledgment of the existence of any such account, and no written promise to pay the balance thereof, had been signed by the Defendants, or any member of their firm, since the accountable receipt of April 1829, and that the claim was barred by the Statute of Limitations.[54]

Foley could not say how much value was left in the bank account beyond estimating it was a large balance; he sought an account first, to find out the level of the account after the purported payments of interest, profits, disbursements and so on, and then have the balance paid over. Alongside the substantive accounting process, Foley also sought procedural discovery of bank documents showing acknowledgement of more recent account activity and so permitting a traversal of the limitation defence.

The defendants initially mounted a surprising double limitation defence, arguing not only that the remedy of account was time-barred, but also that the plaintiff's seeking of evidence by interrogatories and discovery, in order to dispel the operation of the limitation period by showing proof of account activity, was itself a time-barred action. In other words, no proof of the live nature of the account within the past six years could be made out, because the evidence had not been properly assembled within the past six months. The Rolls court[55] in a preliminary hearing rejected this secondary defence, as did Lord Cottenham C at second instance. Lord Cottenham cited the equity eminences Lord Redesdale and Lord Eldon as authorities for the proposition that the defendant could not presume the success of a legal bar in order to exclude facts and procedures that would test for the existence of that bar:

> I have always understood that where a bill contained an allegation which would meet the legal bar, the Defendant could not plead the legal bar without negativing that allegation. That applies to all cases of this kind – to pleas of the Statute of Limitations, pleas of fraud, and so forth.[56]

The defence counsel for this unmeritorious procedural defence at the first appeal was none other than Solicitor-General Robert Rolfe, later to become Lord Chancellor Cranworth. One can only assume that the large sum of money at stake warranted the hiring of an impressive Chancery silk to try out an *outré* argument. But as we shall see in the appeals that followed, in the end the limitation strategy succeeded, and Hill & Co resisted paying back any balance.

[54] ibid 3 Mylne & Craig 476, 40 ER 1010.
[55] Decision of Sir Lancelot Shadwell MR, noted in (1838) 3 Mylne & Craig 475, 40 ER 1010; a verbatim printed report cannot be located.
[56] (1838) 3 Mylne & Craig 475, 481, 40 ER 1010, 1012.

Knight Bruce V-C took the first substantive hearing of the account claim some five years later, in 1843.[57] He found a continuous duty on the part of the bankers to account for both principal and interest that took the duty outside the ambit of the limitation statute. This was a variation on the liability-generating maxim 'equity sees as done that which out to be done', expressed in the language of account:

> It appears to me, that the mode in which the persons whose duty it was to keep the account – that the mode in which they actually kept it is perfectly immaterial, because they are to be charged according to their duty. And suppose that bankers do receive sums of money from their customers, and do not make any entry of the receipts, are we to be told that they are not responsible, or that they may take the benefit of the Statute of Limitations, because they do not do their duty? If a customer proves that money was received by his bankers' at any time after the last item in the bankers' account, that is enough to charge the bankers; and when I find there is a statement that it was agreed in the language of the answer, that Hill & Co. should allow interest at the rate of 3l. per cent. per annum, it is the same thing, in my mind, as if there had been the interest at 3l. per cent. from time to time paid by them on the balance to the credit of the customer. The fact that they have not chosen to enter the items, never could be beneficial to them, and they are therefore by virtue of this agreement liable down to this time for that interest, at the rate of 3l. per cent. per annum on the balances, which they agreed should be allowed; and therefore it must be considered as a specific account; and my opinion is, that the bankers are responsible. There must be an account taken.[58]

Lord Lyndhurst C heard an initial appeal against the Vice-Chancellor's account order the next year, in 1844.[59] By this stage all that had been added to the evidence by Foley's earlier discovery efforts were two post-1831 letters between the banking partners acknowledging the existence of Foley's sole account, but no direct communication or receipt showing transactions on an operating account. Lord Lyndhurst held that this private letter evidence, though adverse to defendants, was not legally an acknowledgement of any debt and was not probative of the live, performed state of the bank account in the years between 1831 and 1837, when the time of limitation had run.

Lord Lyndhurst focussed on whether the application of the six-year limitation applied to debts by the 1623 statute should apply to a money claim where an account in equity was sought to calculate a running balance over the course of a relationship. If the account was an equitable auxiliary action, did this procedural device displace the operation of the statute? An alternative enquiry was to postulate that the reason why an accounting remedy was applicable to a bank balance in the first place was because the banker-customer relationship was inherently based on accountability, that is, it was in substance a trusteeship or fiduciary relation. The two strands of justification were mutually entwined: if a complex loan and credit relationship entangles the parties so far that equity must order an account to unscramble their affairs, then a fiduciary element comes into the legally founded relationship, just as the Chancery court comes to regulate the continuous relations of contractually bound partners.[60]

[57] *Foley v Hill* (1843) 13 Law J Rep (NS) 182 (Ch, V-C).
[58] ibid 183.
[59] *Foley v Hill* (1844) 1 Phillips 399, 41 ER 683 (Ch, LC).
[60] The affinity assumed here between accountability and fiduciary duty is notably challenged by JE Penner, 'Distinguishing Fiduciary, Trust, and Accounting Relationships' (2014) 8 *Journal of Equity* 202; a lot of filigree

Lord Lyndhurst first cited the key passages in *Carr*, *Sims*, and *Devaynes* to deny the fiduciary element in a banker-customer relation (the substantive fiduciary duty question), and then posed the question of whether equitable accounting applied to the bank balance made any difference:

> It is quite clear that a banker is not to be considered a trustee for his customer in the legal sense of the term. Money advanced by a customer to a banker is a loan, and constitutes a debt. … Here there was a loan by Foley to the Defendants, to be repaid with interest at 3 per cent.: that was the simple transaction between them, and if this were a case at law, a plea of the statute would be a sufficient answer, unless there were some special circumstances to take the case out of the statute; and the only question, therefore, is whether that defence is to have the same effect in a Court of Equity.[61]

Lyndhurst noted that the high authority Lord Redesdale had affirmed that the limitation statute ought to apply directly to equitable causes where possible. He then set out how it might be possible to defeat the operation of limitation in the instant case, based on some equity in the statute interacting with a duty of account:

> It is further said, however, that it was the duty of the Defendants, as bankers, or by reason of the mode in which they usually conducted their business, to have entered the interest half-yearly in their books, on the balance remaining due; that if such entries had been regularly made, the case would have been taken out of the statute; and that, having neglected to do this, they ought not to be allowed to profit from their neglect by setting up the Statute of Limitations as a defence founded on their own omission. But no such question is raised by the bill: no such equity is insisted upon or suggested. The bill is confined entirely to the statement of subsequent transactions for the purpose of taking the case out of the statute.

Foley had not alleged a fraudulent concealment of interest to bring him within the equity court's remedial power to suspend the statute; and for him to claim that the omission to record and pay over alleged interest on a time-barred principal debt should remove the time bar would potentially undermine the policy of limitation in a wide swathe of debt cases. Foley should have gathered his evidence of breach more vigorously and earlier; he only had weak evidence of recent acknowledgement of the bank account in subsequent transactions, and so it was his own ineptitude that had subjected him to the barring of his debt. The judge concluded: 'I think, therefore, the Statute of Limitations is a sufficient defence, as the record is at present constituted.'[62] He added that the state of the alleged account, with just three proven payment transactions, the initial deposit and two withdrawals, was so simple as to best be decided in a court of common law using money had and received counts: there was no room for a special order of equitable accounting. As Lyndhurst put it: 'A party has no right to come here upon a simple transaction of this kind, when justice may be administered in a more simple way and at less expense in a Court of law.'[63] Foley's bill was accordingly dismissed with costs. But too much was at stake to let the matter rest, and a third appeal was taken to the House of Lords.

historical work remains to be done exploring the linkages between such categories, see, eg, J Watson, *The Duty to Account: Development and Principles* (Annandale, Federation Press, 2016); M Cleaver and A Televantos, ch 20 in this volume.

[61] *Foley* (Ch, LC) (n 59) 1 Phillips 404, 41 ER 685.

[62] ibid 1 Phillips 407, 41 ER 686.

[63] ibid.

The House of Lords judicial committee took the final appeal of *Foley v Hill* four years later, in 1848,[64] and perhaps the time gap plus a shortage of legal personnel made it seem acceptable for Lord Lyndhurst himself to join the ad hoc panel. This was still some years before eminent judges such as Baron Parke were appointed to serve as appellate judges in the Lords so as to produce a stable and professionalised final court distinct from the legislature. As it happened, the Court of Exchequer (including Baron Parke) had examined a like issue the year before the Lords hearing of *Foley v Hill*. The existence of this judgment from a strong common-law court may have influenced the Lords appeal. In *Pott, Assignees of Ryle v Clegg*,[65] the assignees of a bankrupt claimed that the bankrupt's written admissions that he might claim an old and untouched sum in a bank account did not take the time-barred enforcement of the banker's duty out of the statute of limitations. The Attorney-General, representing the bankers, cited Lyndhurst C's judgment in *Foley v Hill*, arguing that a failure by the banker to acknowledge an account or pay over any sum or add any expected interest for six years sufficed to invoke the limitation statute and time-bar the creditor-customer's claim to the account. An articulate criticism of this position was then offered by the defence counsel, Chilton:

> If the argument on the other side be well founded, it follows that a banker, who neglects to balance the account of his customer for six years, may keep for his own use the money deposited with him by the customer, who may have been abroad the whole time, and may have had no occasion to draw a cheque. Surely that would be contrary to the policy of the law … But the true relation between the parties is this, that the banker holds the money under a special contract to honour the cheques of the customer; who on his part cannot, so long as the banker is solvent, support an action for it without a previous demand of it in writing. This view of the case appears to be supported by the decision in *Marzetti* v. *Williams*. In Pothier on Contracts, by Evans, vol. 2, p. 126, it is said – "Where a man deposits money in the hands of another, to be kept for his use, the possession of the custodee ought to be deemed the possession of the owner, until an application and refusal, or other denial of the right; for until then there is nothing adverse; and I conceive that, upon principle, no action should be allowed in these cases, without a previous demand; consequently that no limitation should be computed further back than such demand."[66]

The court was not convinced and held that the limitation period ran from the time of the making of the bank debt, and could have been interrupted at any time by a demand for principal or interest; but the accrual of interest over time, and the inchoate duty to pay that sum only affected the quantum of the existing debt and did not refresh it with fresh obligation. Pollock CB, giving the judgment of the court, fell in with the decision but expressed himself uneasy, and thought it possible that money could be bestowed on a bank under a contract of deposit, hinting that such a claim could stop the limitation clock:

> I must, certainly with considerable doubt and diffidence, confess the hesitation of my own opinion, whether there is not a special contract between the banker and his customer as to the money deposited, which distinguishes it from the ordinary case of a loan for money. It seems to me that is a question for the jury, who ought to decide what is the liability of the banker, and

[64] *Foley* (HL) (n 2).
[65] *Pott, Assignees of Ryle v Clegg* (1847) 16 M & W 321, 153 ER 1212 (Ex).
[66] ibid 16 M & W 325–26, 153 ER 1213–14.

> whether the money deposited with him is money lent or not. I could not concur in the judgment of the rest of the Court without expressing this doubt, in which, however, they do not partake, as they are of opinion that money in the hands of a banker is merely money lent, with the superadded obligation that it is to be paid when called for by the draft of the customer.[67]

A few months later, Stuart, arguing for Foley in the Lords, seized on Pollock CB's remarks and invited the Lords to adopt this line of reasoning. He argued that a banker's debt obligation had 'various superadded obligations' that transformed the banker into an accountable party in equity. He had to repay money deposited, honour depositors' cheques, and by special contract (commonly applied), pay interest on positive balances. Moreover, a banker had to keep clear and intelligible accounts, calculate interest from time to time, enter that interest in the account, and preserve evidence of all transactions of value (deposits, withdrawals, payments, offsets, charges) affecting the balance of the account.

> These duties and transactions constitute a relation more complex than that of mere debtor and creditor, and an account of them is a fit subject for a bill in equity, not only by reason of the admitted concurrent jurisdiction of Courts of Equity with Courts of law in matters of account, but also because the account here sought is of moneys received by the respondents, the receipt of which is within their own knowledge, and the entries and record of which they were bound to keep.[68]

Counsel denied the theory that equity would not order an account in case of a small number of simple transactions when the law could provide a balance of claims and counter-claims; the right to account in equity could be concurrent with common law claims, as was the longstanding practice with stewards, agents, and factors; and the same should apply to the banker-customer relation. Moreover, the facts strongly suggested fraud by the bankers even if the bill had not spelt this out, in the sense that they seem to have refrained from making any entries or formally accounting to the customer for the considerable sums he had banked with them, precisely in order to run down the clock on limitations and make it possible for them to take the money value. They had admitted transactions in the adjacent joint colliery account, and these could be taken as acknowledgement of their overall banker's duty to Foley in the sole account as well.[69] It was not a case of barring a debt, but controlling a relationship. Ample authority, notably from Lord Redesdale and Lord Eldon, was given showing that an equity court would order an account and stave off defences when it saw a need to regulate a continuous relationship.[70]

The Lords would have none of it, and did not even hear counsel for the defence before finding for Hill & Co. Lord Cottenham, the present Lord Chancellor, commenced. He denied that the tangled state of the account presented any procedural reason for equity to be involved; only in cases too complex for a common-law jury trial was there a call

[67] ibid 16 M & W 37–28, 153 ER 1214–15.

[68] *Foley* (HL) (n 2) 2 HLC 31, 9 ER 1003–04 *in arguendo*.

[69] A further point might have been added that multiple accounts in the name of a single customer could be merged or set off against each other by the bank, suggesting that the law treated the group of accounts as a composite single account, on the analogy of an 'account stated'; see *Laycock v Pickles* (1863) 4 B & S 497, 122 ER 546 (KB) per Blackburn J; SJ Stoljar, 'What is Account Stated?' (1964) 2 *Sydney Law Review* 373.

[70] *Foley* (HL) (n 2) 2 HLC 32–33, 9 ER 1004.

to move a case over to the concurrent equitable jurisdiction to administer the case.[71] The only other reason to enforce an account would be 'upon the supposed fiduciary character existing between the banker and his customer'. The analogies suggested all failed: a factor and agent might act as a trustee or '*quasi* a trustee' in the sense of being accountable for the proceeds of sales or contracts, but neither actor owned the goods of the owner-principal. The Chancellor explained:

> Money, when paid into a bank, ceases altogether to be the money of the principal; it is then the money of the banker, who is bound to return an equivalent by paying a similar sum to that deposited with him when he is asked for it. The money paid into the banker's, is money known by the principal to be placed there for the purpose of being under the control of the banker; it is then the banker's money; he is known to deal with it as his own; he makes what profit of it he can, which profit he retains to himself, paying back only the principal, according to the custom of bankers in some places, or the principal and a small rate of interest, according to the custom of bankers in other places. The money placed in the custody of a banker is, to all intents and purposes, the money of the banker, to do with it as he pleases; he is guilty of no breach of trust in employing it; he is not answerable to the principal if he puts it into jeopardy, if he engages in a hazardous speculation; he is not bound to keep it or deal with it as the property of his principal, but he is of course answerable for the amount, because he has contracted, having received that money, to repay to the principal, when demanded, a sum equivalent to that paid into his hands.[72]

Lord Cottenham cited *Parker v Marchant* for the debt theory, which was strange considering that this case had established that a passing of 'money in hand' or 'ready money' in a will encompassed a bank account payable on demand. The judge dealt with this objection with a classic floodgates argument: if any demandable debt could be said to be accountable as resting on a continuously accountable duty, then equity would have to involve itself with every type of debt where forbearance could be ended and payment demanded. Lord Cottenham also disposed of the argument that the failure to pay over the agreed interest renewed the breach of the banker's contract: there was no breach unless the banker had resisted an overt demand to account and accrue the interest, which had not happened. He concluded that the equity court did not even have jurisdiction to adjudge the case using account techniques, and so he did not have to decide the limitation point.

The other lords agreed, with Lord Brougham adding some verbose remarks about the function of banking. A banker commonly received money from customers on condition of paying it to the order of the customer on demand, but all the while the banker who receives the money

> has the use of it as his own, and in the using of which his trade consists, and but for which no banker could exist, especially a banker who pays interest. But even a banker who does not pay interest could not possibly carry on his trade if he were to hold the money, and to pay it back, as a mere depositary of the principal. But he receives it, to the knowledge of his customer, for

[71] Citing *O'Connor v Spaight* (1804) 1 Sch & Lef 305 (Ir Ch) per Lord Redesdale C (ie, John Mitford, the acknowledged expert on equitable pleading). But this case was on landlord and tenant accounting for rent and allowances, and it may not have been correct to take the judgment, now nearly a half century old in a pre-fusionary system, as legislating for all cases.

[72] *Foley* (HL) (n 2) 2 HLC 36–37, 9 ER 1005–06.

> the express purpose of using it as his own, which, if he were a trustee he could not do without a breach of trust.[73]

In particular cases a banker might serve as agent or intermediary, or bailee or depositary of specific financial instruments, but these fiduciary acts were distinct from the core function of keeping customer balances and reinvesting the money stock, and here equity had no role.

VI. What Follows?

The Lords' speeches in *Foley v Hill* offered a simple, perhaps shallow, answer to an interlocking puzzle that had disturbed the judges since the beginning of the nineteenth century – what were the duties of a banker to a depositing customer, where money to repay the debt was to be ready on demand, yet the value was free to be used and dispelled by the banker? Did the solution lie in fiduciary regulation of the relationship, or were the consequences of such legal characterisation too disruptive to be contemplated? *Foley* did not, could not, settle the issues forever. Let us take some of the issues in turn.

The core practical finding in *Foley* was that a banker's neglect to pay or report principal and interest could be shielded from action by the limitation defence, keeping out troublesome equities of due continuous performance. The rule was restated and perhaps confused in the important 1921 case of *Joachimson v Swiss Bank Corporation.*[74] In that case the plaintiff, a German national, sought to disburse the assets of a partnership that had dissolved on the death of a partner of his firm on 1 August 1914. These assets included a deposit in an account at the defendant bank; and after the outbreak of war, the plaintiff, as an enemy alien, had been barred from seeking to recover any assets, relying on a fresh cause of action accruing after the time of hostilities. However, a cause of action accruing before 14 August could have been pursued, on the return of peace. Plaintiff argued from *Foley v Hill* that since limitation ran against claims to recover a bank deposit from the moment the debt was incepted on payment in by the depositor, the law must assume there was a cause of action for debt in place at that same instant of deposit for other legal purposes, such as the timing of a claim before or after the outbreak of war. The Court of Appeal affirmed that authority of *Foley*, namely that a bank deposit was a simple debt with superadded banker's duties. But the plaintiff's claims still failed, on the basis that the obligation of a bank to pay out from an open-ended bank deposit was only triggered by a depositor's demand for payment (which could include a writ of action); before that demand the claim did not solidify as a cause of action, but was only the basis for a cause of action. In the instant case, since there had been no demand before 14 August, the bank was able to treat any demand by nationals of an enemy state after that date as barred by the outbreak of hostilities. This appeared to set up the depositor's cause of action as a version of Schrödinger's Cat – simultaneously existing from the inception of deposit for some purposes (initiating the running of a time limitation) but not for others (dating the claim against the outbreak of hostilities).

[73] *Foley* (HL) (n 2) 2 HLC 43–44, 9 ER 1008.
[74] *Joachimson v Swiss Bank Corporation* [1921] 3 KB 110.

The implication of the 1921 case was that *Foley v Hill* may have been wrongly decided, at least on the limitation point, because of the peculiar nature of a bank deposit; it was unlike a simple debt where there was an implied term that a borrower would make efforts to locate the lender and repay by the due date without waiting for a demand.

The need for an explicit demand by a depositor was affirmed by Lord Sumption in the Hong Kong Final Court of Appeal in the case of *PT Asuransi Tugu v Citibank NA*,[75] where it was argued that the fraudulent emptying and closure of a company account with negligent cooperation by the bank did not excite a debt cause of action initiating the running of a limitation period. This was because the bank's breach of the banking contract by unauthorised closure would only give rise to a valid demand if the customer noticed and affirmed the breach, perhaps by suing for damages. In the absence of such an acceptance of the wrong and turn to secondary remedy, the bank had a continuous primary duty to reconstitute the bank account that it had wrongfully closed; and the alternative cause of action for the recovery of the debt still owed only arose when a demand for the missing funds was made much later by the successors of the company management.[76] This decision, by preserving a duty of reconstitution immune to limitation, would seem to further distance the law from the conclusions of *Foley* that bank accounts were simple debts incepted from deposit.

The paradoxical conclusions set up by the *Joachimson* doctrine were only laid to rest in English law with the passing of section 6 of the Limitation Act 1980. Here Parliament finally rid the law of the defence of limitation initiated from the date of inception of a loan without term:

> (1) … this Act shall not bar the right of action on a contract of loan to which this section applies.
>
> (2) This section applies to any contract of loan which—
>
> (a) does not provide for repayment of the debt on or before a fixed or determinable date; and
>
> (b) does not effectively (whether or not it purports to do so) make the obligation to repay the debt conditional on a demand for repayment made by or on behalf of the creditor or on any other matter …

A deeper unresolved question left by the cases is whether an open-ended obligation to hold a credit and use its value at will can even count as an existing legal duty, if split off from an ancillary or posterior duty to repay on subsequent demand. If I lend a friend £10 to pay for his pizza on a night out when he forgot to bring his wallet, and I make the transfer with no repayment schedule mentioned, then in a sense I have made a gift with an expectation of a counter gift in some future part of our shared life (if at all). The absence of term suggests no intention, and no possibility, of imposing coercive legal relations. The failure to repay on demand or reminder might be damaging to the friendship, but that is to characterise the duty as relational and continuous, rather than focussed on the imperfect debt.

[75] *PT Asuransi Tugu v Citibank NA* [2023] HKCFA 3, noted J Lau, 'Limitation in Bank Fraud Claims: Effect of Account Closure' (2023) 82 *Cambridge Law Journal* 224.

[76] [2023] HKCFA 3, [23]–[28].

The *Foley v Hill* dogma about excluding a concurrent equitable accounting function when common law damages or restitution could work a solution also turned out to be less than easy to apply. A host of cases were fought over this point where parties sought an account to police their relationships, including determining the flow of money, goods, and opportunities in and out of their shared affairs.[77] In English fiduciary and tort law the past ten or so years have seen renewed controversy over this very issue.[78] In the United States of America we have a reverse problem, where parties asserting a right to jury trial must overcome a bar based on the need to have a juryless court exploring complex issues through an account mechanism grounded in equity.[79]

There are also implications beyond the law, returning to the political economy mood of our opening pages. The fact that City commentators of the time warmly welcomed the courts' legal innovations is particularly striking. Henry Dunning McLeod, in his brilliantly argued and widely read *Theory and Practice of Banking*,[80] thoroughly reviewed the course of the banking, credit and currency laws of the mid-nineteenth century across hundreds of tightly written pages, including the legal run-up to *Foley v Hill*. In his discussion of ready or demandable money, he bestowed special praise on the English courts for liberating the law from crude deposit theories of banking. He offered these reflections on how bank debt could be liberated to do good:

> Nothing can be more unfortunate or misleading than the expression which is so frequently used that banking is only the "Economy of Capital," and that the business of a banker is to borrow money from one set of persons and to lend it to another set. Bankers no doubt do collect sums from a vast number of persons, but the peculiar essence of their business is, not to lend that money to other persons, but on the basis of this bullion to create a vast superstructure of Credit; to multiply their promises to pay many times: these Credits being payable on demand and performing all the functions of an equal amount of cash. Thus banking is not an Economy of Capital, but an increase of Capital; the business of banking is not to lend money, but to create Credit: and by means of the Clearing House these Credits are now transferred from one bank to another, just as easily as a Credit is transferred from one account to another in the same bank by means of a cheque. And all these Credits are in the ordinary language and practice of commerce exactly equal to so much cash or Currency.[81]

This is a very confident political economy of law; it is also the Austrian school's nightmare, an invitation to recurring credit bubbles and crashes, and increasingly straitened political interventions to rescue the flailing financial markets. The idea that was rejected in *Foley v Hill* was a model of the banking relationship whereby bankers should be seen as accountable stewards of deposits backed by adequate capital. By characterising the banker-customer relationship as pure debt, largely untouched by wider duties, private

[77] See, eg, *Corporation of Carlisle v Wilson* (1807) 13 Ves Jun 276, 33 ER 297 (Ch); *The Taff Vale Railway Co v Nixon* (1847) I HLC 111, 9 ER 695; *Nixon v The Taff Vale Railway Co* (1849) 7 Hare 136, 68 ER 55 (Ch); *Padwick v Hurst* (1854) 18 Beav 575, 52 ER 225 (Ch).

[78] Compare *AIB Group (UK) Plc* v *Mark Redler & Co* [2014] UKSC 58, [2015] AC 1503 and *Main v Giambrone & Law* [2017] EWCA Civ 1193, [2018] PNLR 2.

[79] P Devlin, 'Equity Due Process and the Seventh Amendment: A Commentary on the Zenith Case' (1983) 81 *Michigan Law Review* 1571.

[80] HD McLeod, *Theory and Practice of Banking*, 1st edn (London, Longmans, 1855–56; 3rd edn, London, Longmans, 1875–76).

[81] ibid vol 2, 304.

law effectively abandoned any dynamic role in controlling the solvency of banks by arming customers with tools to monitor capital and hold banking directors or partners to account.[82] In effect the only real legal recourse left to depositors was to claim priority over the partnership or equity investors of the bank if capital proved inadequate and the institution was wound up.[83] Even that discipline was abated in the wave of bank amalgamations and the adoption of limited liability regimes, accelerating in the wake of the crises of 1866–67 and 1878–79.[84] Instead of private law disciplines to enforce capital adequacy, novel political measures aimed at maintaining banking stability had to be invented over the next fifty years, including government deposit insurance and guarantees of capital adequacy balanced by monitoring and supervision.[85] But public underwriting to minimise the risk of bank failure fomented fresh moral hazard, as banks evaded supervision in the knowledge that the state would likely provide a backstop if risk-taking went wrong. The country was left with banks that were too large to fail, and too powerful and independent to regulate effectively, even when it became plain that the interests of the controllers were divorced from those of their customers.

We learn from this story that small shifts in private law doctrine can contribute to large effects in the public, political-economic spheres. We need to ask sharper questions about the constant coding and re-coding of capital effected in our courts and legislatures, and the longer-term consequences when legal controls are relaxed at the bidding of financial actors. The legacy of *Foley v Hill* leaves us with some intriguing counterfactuals. Could more rigorous private law controls have reshaped credit production and better aligned the interests of British industry and commerce with the financial sector in the later nineteenth century? Could heightened duties of care and accountability for bankers sounding in private law have curbed the irrational exuberance and dangerous credit bubbles of more recent times?[86] The judges in *Foley* dimly perceived that their pure debt theory would free up the banking sector to create credit without restriction. They could not foresee where it would end.

[82] I am grateful to David Fox for discussion of these points.

[83] *Cf Sinclair v Brougham* [1914] AC 398 (HL), where depositors were granted an equity to claim their payments in priority to shareholders in a situation where the financial institution eliciting their deposits lacked legal power to do so; an equity was granted because a common-law debt recovery was held to excluded by the lack of deposit-taking capacity, and it would have been wrong to have left the monies in the errant company's proprietary capital for distribution to shareholders. It would be a stretch to create a fiduciary control of deposits where bankers misbehave in other ways with deposited capital. See further SJ Stoljar, 'Re-Examining *Sinclair v Brougham*' (1959) 22 *Modern Law Review* 21. The remedial response evolved in *Sinclair* to bail out the depositors was always controversial and ultimately overruled in *Westdeutsche Landesbank Girozentrale v Islington LBC* [1996] AC 669.

[84] See text accompanying nn 49–51, above.

[85] W Bagehot, *Lombard Street: A Description of the Money Market* (London, Henry S King, 1873) is the seminal work grounding the mission of the Bank of England as the lender of last resort with responsibility to neutralise banking crises.

[86] See N Morris and D Vines (eds), *Capital Failure: Rebuilding Trust in Financial Services* (Oxford, Oxford University Press, 2014).

20

Accounting and Breach of Trust in the Nineteenth Century

MJ CLEAVER AND ANDREAS TELEVANTOS*

I. Introduction

This chapter examines suits against trustees in the nineteenth century and their relation to court-supervised accounting.[1] The topic has been recognised as an important one but has received little attention from historians. Most historical work on accounting is rooted in descriptions of medieval procedures outside of the trusts law context,[2] and legal histories of trusteeship in the nineteenth century, such as those by Chantal Stebbings[3] and Stuart Anderson,[4] do not consider accounting. Even legal historical work on Chancery procedure and its reform in the nineteenth century has neglected accounting.[5]

In contrast, modern scholarship concerning equitable compensation for breach of trust is often premised on assertions about nineteenth-century law.[6] Jurists have distinguished between two types of claim.[7] The first, sometimes called a 'substitutive'

* We are grateful for very helpful comments from Matthew Conaglen, Joshua Getzler, Jessica Hudson, Michael Lobban, Charles Mitchell, Aruna Nair, Timothy Pilkington, and Luke Rostill.

[1] This chapter does not consider profit stripping. For recent work, see M Conaglen, 'Identifying the Profits for which a Fiduciary Must Account' [2020] *Cambridge Law Journal* 38.

[2] See, eg, JA Watson, *The Duty to Account* (Sydney, Federation Press, 2016); A Licht, 'Lord Eldon Redux: Information Asymmetry, the Roots of Accountability, and the Structure of Fiduciary Loyalty' (2017) 37 *Oxford Journal of Legal Studies* 770; JS Getzler, '"As If" Accountability and Counterfactual Trust' (2011) 91 *Boston University Law Review* 973.

[3] C Stebbings, *The Private Trustee in Victorian England* (Cambridge, Cambridge University Press, 2001).

[4] S Anderson, 'Trusts and Trustees' in WR Cornish et al, *The Oxford History of the Laws of England, Volume XII, 1820–1914: Private Law* (Oxford, Oxford University Press, 2010).

[5] P Polden, 'The Court of Chancery, 1820–1875' in WR Cornish et al, *The Oxford History of the Laws of England, Volume XI 1820–1914: English Legal System* (Oxford, Oxford University Press, 2010).

[6] See, eg, S Elliott, *Compensation Claims against Trustees* (Oxford University DPhil thesis, 2002); J Edelman, 'Money Awards of the Cost of Performance' (2010) 4 *Journal of Equity* 122; C Mitchell, 'Stewardship of Property and Liability to Account' [2014] *Conv* 215; L Ho 'An Account of Accounts' (2016) *Singapore Academy of Law Journal* 849; J Edelman, 'An English Misturning with Equitable Compensation' in S Degeling and J Varuhas (eds), *Equitable Compensation and Disgorgement of Profits* (Oxford, Hart Publishing, 2017).

[7] Elliott (n 6) 10–14, 50–59; S Elliott and C Mitchell, 'Remedies for Dishonest Assistance' (2004) 67 *Modern Law Review* 14, 23–25; J McGhee and S Elliott (eds), *Snell's Equity* 34th edn (London, Sweet & Maxwell, 2019)

or 'falsification' claim, involves a beneficiary enforcing a trustee's primary 'custodial stewardship duty'[8] to 'maintain the fund or disburse it in an authorised manner'.[9] This claim does not turn upon wrongdoing but is rather about 'enforcing performance of an obligation':[10] the beneficiary is entitled to have the trustee produce the trust property, or 'substitutively perform this duty by payment of a money sum'.[11] When quantifying trustee liability, 'causation, foreseeability and remoteness do not readily enter the matter'[12] because 'the amount due is not compensation for loss but payment of the sum necessary to make good a deficit in the trust account'.[13] Thus the burden is on the trustee 'where authority for a disbursement' is in issue:[14] a trustee unable to identify a ground of discharge will owe an equitable debt to pay 'the objective value of the property'.[15]

The second, sometimes called a 'reparative' or 'surcharging' claim, involves the beneficiary enforcing a secondary duty 'to make good the damage caused by a breach of trust'.[16] Although both the former and the latter types of claim were historically conceived as suits for the recovery of an 'equitable debt',[17] Lord Millett espoused the view in more recent times that the latter type of claim resembles a modern common law action for negligence and considered that there was 'no reason in principle why the common law rules of causation, remoteness of damage, and measure of damages should not be applied by analogy'[18] – although his views on this point are controversial.[19]

The distinction between substitutive and reparative claims has often been associated with historical accounting procedures by modern scholars: substitutive claims are said to reflect the 'common' accounting procedure, and reparative claims the 'wilful default' accounting procedure.[20] As a matter of modern law, the distinction between the two types of claim has been made controversial by the decisions in *Target Holdings Ltd v Redferns (a firm)* (1996)[21] and *AIB Group (UK) plc v Mark Redler & Co (a firm)* (2015)[22] that causation is always relevant to quantifying trustee liability.[23] Although modern debates often invoke 'orthodox' or 'traditional' accounting principles, it is only relatively

[30-011]–[30-018]. The nomenclature is not uniformly accepted: L Tucker et al, *Lewin on Trusts*, 20th edn (London, Sweet & Maxwell, 2020) ch 41; D Heydon, M Leeming and P Turner, *Meagher, Gummow & Lehane's Equity: Doctrines and Remedies*, 5th edn (Chatswood, LexisNexis Butterworths, 2015) [23-610]–[23-615].

[8] *AIB Group (UK) plc v Mark Redler* [2015] UKSC 58; [2015] AC 1503 [51].

[9] J Edelman and S Elliott, 'Money Remedies against Trustees' (2004) 18 *Trusts Law International* 116, 131.

[10] *Libertarian Investments Ltd v Hall* [2014] 16 HKCFAR 681 [167].

[11] J Hudson, B McFarlane and C Mitchell, *Hayton, McFarlane and Mitchell on Equity and Trusts*, 15th edn (London, Sweet and Maxwell, 2022) [13-010].

[12] *Re Dawson (deceased)* (1966) 2 NSWR 211; 84 WN (Pt) (NSW) 399, 404.

[13] P Millett, '*AIB v Redler*' (2018) 32 *Trust Law International* 44, 48.

[14] *Chong v Channell* [2009] NSWSC 765 [7].

[15] *Libertarian* (n 10) [168].

[16] P Matthews et al, *Underhill and Hayton: Law of Trusts and Trustees*, 20th edn (London, Sweet & Maxwell, 2022) [91.11].

[17] *Ex parte Adamson* (1878) 8 Ch D 807, 819.

[18] *Bristol and West Building Society v Mothew* [1988] Ch 1, 16–17.

[19] *AIB* (n 8) [118]–[119], [123]; *Youyang Pty Limited v Minter Ellison* (2003) 212 CLR 484, [39]; *Stevens v Hotel Portfolio II* [2025] UKSC 28, [2025] 3 WLR 293 at [44].

[20] See R Chambers, 'Liability' in P Birks and A Pretto (eds) *Breach of Trust* (Oxford, Hart Publishing, 2002). See too *Agricultural Land Management Ltd v Jackson (No 2)* (2014) 48 WAR 1 [349], [437].

[21] *Target Holdings Ltd v Redferns* [1996] AC 421.

[22] *AIB* (n 8).

[23] The distinction has been recognised in later Court of Appeal cases: *Interactive Technology Corp Ltd v Ferster* [2018] EWCA Civ 1594, [2021] WTLR 561 [16]–[18]; *Auden Mackenzie (Pharma Division) Ltd v Patel* [2019] EWCA Civ 2291, [2020] WTLR 1133 [31]–[32]; *Mitchell v Al Jaber* [2023] EWCA 423, [2024] BCC 934 at [62]–[66].

recently that scholars have begun to test the historical assumptions on which the 'substitutive/reparative compensation' model is based: for example, by examining accounting principles in greater detail, and by reference to particular historical periods.[24] Further, assertions in legal scholarship about substitutive claims and the irrelevance of the 'moral quality'[25] of trustee conduct sit uneasily with historical scholarship emphasising the centrality of fault to the Victorian treatment of transgressions by trustees.[26]

This chapter argues that nineteenth-century accounting procedures did not straightforwardly enshrine a distinction between substitutive and reparative compensation claims against trustees. Although a distinction was recognised between suits in respect of 'ultra vires dispositions of trust property' and those in respect of 'failures in the management of the trust',[27] the extent to which it shaped contemporary thinking about the measure of trustee liability[28] has been exaggerated by modern scholars. Although the logic of charge and discharge accounting made liability stringent, a trustee who made an unauthorised disposition was not automatically liable for the full value of the asset disposed of without authority. Courts had regard to the purpose of the particular trust and, via discrete mechanisms, could reduce or extinguish trustee liability. Further, in awarding relief against trustees, courts acted upon a general notion of replicating due performance. This applied both to 'substitutive claims' in respect of unauthorised dispositions and 'reparative claims' in respect of 'negligent'[29] management of trust property. This concept involved enforcing the trustee's primary duties to 'carry out the [settlor's] directions' and 'place the trust property in a state of security'.[30] In other words, courts were concerned that trustees dealt with trust assets in the authorised manner according to the terms, the settlor's intention in creating the trust, and Chancery's own policies concerning proper trust administration. The due performance concept was particularly useful early in the century, when trustees had few discretions, and so determining what proper performance of the trust would have involved was not difficult. However, 'due performance' became a less useful concept as trustees were given more discretions, and so determining what due performance would have involved became harder. This, combined with the ultimate decline of the accounting procedures, prompted some lawyers to see some kinds of breach of trusts claim as analogous to common law actions for damages.

In the following discussion, Part II examines the court-supervised accounting procedures in their heyday, the period 1790–1852. Part III then considers the gradually emerging principles of trustee liability in light of those procedures until the Judicature Act reforms of 1873–1875. Part IV returns to procedure, discussing the major reforms

[24] M Conaglen, 'Equitable Compensation for Breach of Trust: Off *Target*' (2016) 40 *Melbourne University Law Review* 126; M Conaglen, 'Judicature and Accounts' in B McFarlane and S Elliot (eds), *Equity Today: 150 Years after the Judicature Reforms* (Oxford, Hart Publishing, 2023).

[25] P Birks, 'Equity in the Modern Law an Exercise in Taxonomy' (1996) 26 *University of Western Australia Law Review* 1, 47.

[26] Stebbings (n 3); Anderson (n 4); J Getzler, 'Duty of Care' in P Birks and A Pretto (eds), *Breach of Trust* (Oxford, Hart Publishing, 2002) 41; J Getzler, 'Laying the Axe to the Root of the Tree'? Shielding a Co-trustee from Liability' in P Davies and others (eds), *Defences in Equity* (Oxford, Hart Publishing, 2018).

[27] Birks (n 25) 46.

[28] On our usage of 'liability', see section II.A below.

[29] The term 'negligence' and 'negligent' here is not used in this chapter as a reference to the common law tort of negligence, but instead in the sense that contemporaries used it in assessing trustee conduct, see, eg, text to (n 140) and text to (n 156) below.

[30] EHT Snell, *The Principles of Equity*, 1st edn (London, Stevens and Haynes, 1868) 123–24.

that enabled beneficiaries to obtain money decrees in a more summary fashion and without a full accounting, thereby reducing the central place of court-supervised accounting in suits against trustees.

II. Accounting Procedures and Trustee Liability: 1790–1852

At the beginning of the nineteenth century, proceedings alleging a breach of trust and seeking money relief often, though not invariably, involved an administration suit to which all beneficiaries and trustees were usually joined.[31] A preliminary step in such proceedings, often decreed as a matter of course, was a court-supervised accounting. This part explains the nature of accountability, the mechanics of charge and discharge accounting, and why these had the practical effect of making trustee liability stringent.

A. The Centrality of Accounting Procedures and 'Automatic' Liability

To account is 'to tell the story of one's management or stewardship of resources'.[32] As accounting parties, trustees were obligated to maintain accurate records of the assets under their care. These written statements (or 'accounts') had to record all receipts (the 'debit' or incoming side of the account) and all disposals (the 'credit' or outgoing side). The trustee charged himself with an asset by including it on the debit side and could later discharge himself of that asset by including an entry on the credit side. The latter had to be supported by appropriate documentary proof called a 'voucher'.[33] It was the 'first duty' of a trustee to be 'constantly ready with his accounts'[34] and to be 'at all times willing to inform the Court' concerning its administration.[35] No breach of trust was required to enforce these duties and obtain a court-supervised accounting: the 'mere relation' of trustee and beneficiary sufficed.[36]

Trust accounts – whether accepted as settled for the purpose of proceedings or taken under judicial direction – provided an indispensable factual foundation for curial relief, but they did not necessarily determine the form or indeed the measure of that relief. This is because to be *accountable* for trust assets was distinct from being *answerable* for those assets.[37] Accountability was concerned with an anterior question, the factual

[31] Elliott (n 6) ch IV.

[32] J Getzler, 'Magna Carta Clauses 4 and 5 and the Origins of Accountability' in C MacMillan and C Smith (eds), *Challenges to Authority and the Recognition of Rights* (Cambridge, Cambridge University Press, 2018) 140.

[33] That is, 'any acquittance or receipt, discharging a person, or being evidence of a payment': TW Williams, *A Compendious and Comprehensive Law Dictionary* (London, Gale & Fenner, 1816) *sv* 'Voucher'.

[34] *Pearse v Green* (1819) 1 Jac & W 135; 37 ER 327, 329.

[35] *Freeman v Fairlie* (1817) 3 Mer 29, 42; 36 ER 12, 17.

[36] G Jeremy, *A Treatise on the Equity Jurisdiction of the High Court of Chancery* (London, J & WT Clarke, 1828) 523.

[37] See, eg, I Cory, *A Practical Treatise on Accounts* (London, Pickering, 1839) 228–29, 256, 264.

state of the trust fund. Answerability involved what we might today call liability,[38] and involved a judicial determination. If a trustee were charged with an asset, and he could not show that asset remained in his hands for the benefit of the trust, a court could order that he buy a substitute asset on behalf of the trust with his own money – or else appropriate and segregate a sum of his own money for the benefit of the trust.

The liability of a trustee was undoubtedly straightforward in many cases, the measure of a trustee's liability being the state of account determined by a master. We can see this from the mechanics of 'charge and discharge accounting',[39] discussed further below. If a master properly charged the trustee with an item for which there was no accompanying discharge, then the balance was struck against the trustee and in favour of the trust estate. After confirming the master's report, a court might simply decree payment of that balance. In this way, the procedures for ascertaining the factual state of the trust fund, and the substantive principles governing trustee liability were closely intertwined. Accounting before a master was not simply a neutral fact-gathering exercise. The practical effect of charging a trustee with a particular item could render the trustee personally liable for the value of that item. Even so, accountability did not *necessarily* generate any duty to pay. For instance, charges might be disallowed, or discharges might be allowed, either in whole or in part; the balance might be in favour of the accounting party; beneficiaries might be entitled to make particular elections; or some other factor might bar a prayer for a particular decree.

B. The Mechanics of Court-Supervised Accounting

The fact-finding nature of court-supervised accounting is one reason why accounting was a common preliminary step in breach of trust litigation. What is today described as the quantum or measure of 'equitable compensation' often expressed the monetary equivalent of items in the debit (or incoming) side of trust accounts. The trustee would be decreed to pay the 'equitable debt'[40] revealed by curial investigation and would thereby be 'compelled to make restitution'.[41] The trustee would owe a debt because he had to pay a liquidated sum (namely, the balance owing after charges and discharges were taken into account), and this was payable out of the bankrupt[42] or deceased (personal) estate of a trustee.[43] This 'debt' was 'equitable' because it could not be sued upon in a common law court.[44]

For present purposes, there were two principal forms of court-supervised accounting: common accounting and accounting on the basis of wilful default, the principal difference being the items for which a trustee was chargeable.

[38] We are not using the term 'liability' in a Hohfeldian sense.
[39] Licht (n 2) 775.
[40] *Ex parte Blencowe* (1866) LR 1 Ch App 393.
[41] *The Solicitors' Journal & Reporter*, Vol 1 (6 June 1857) 513.
[42] *Re Warne* (1816) 2 Rose 413.
[43] *Vernon v Vawdry* (1740) 2 Atk 119, 27 ER 474.
[44] *Pardoe v Price* (1847) 16 M & W 451, 458–59; 153 ER 1266, 1269. One exception existed if the accounts were closed and the trustee admitted to an unconditional obligation to pay: *Case v Roberts* (1817) Holt 500, 171 ER 317; *Edwards v Lowndes* (1852) 1 El & Bl 81, 89–91; 118 ER 367, 370–71.

(i) Common Accounting: Actual Receipts

The 'common' or 'usual' decree directed a master[45] to take an account of all that the trustee had received, but no more than this.[46] This involved the accounts being 'passed' – that is, assembled and proved ('vouched') item-by-item – by a master in Chancery, assisted by his clerks. Proceedings generally took the following course.

First, the debit (or incoming) side of the account was prepared. Written interrogatories could be put to the trustee; if necessary, the trustee could be examined on oath; and orders for the delivery up of documentary material could be obtained. With this evidence – the trustee having already sworn in his answer that he had provided 'the best account' and 'fullest information' he could[47] – the beneficiary prepared a 'charge': 'a written statement of the items with which the beneficiary claimed to be entitled, upon proof, to charge the defendant'.[48] The beneficiary's charge and proofs were confined to 'actual or constructive receipt[s]'.[49] These were considered by the master, and the trustee would either accept or object to each item. The master ruled upon any objections, *pro tanto* charging the trustee.

Secondly, the credit (or outgoing) side of the account was prepared. The trustee submitted a discharge: 'a statement of payments and disbursements made by him, and other matters, by which he claimed to discharge himself from the debt attempted to be made out against him by the charge'.[50] The master would go through the discharge. The 'strict practice' of the masters – even if there were 'no real dispute between the parties as to many of the items' – was that *every* item above 40 shillings had to be proved by 'independent evidence'.[51] One beneficiary's acceptance was not decisive: absent a voucher, or in exceptional cases a supporting affidavit, each item would be disallowed. The evidential burden was firmly upon the trustee as the accounting party.

There were several well-recognised grounds of discharge.[52] The first was due performance: here, the trustee produced a voucher as proof of due application. Thus, trustees might produce a receipt evidencing payment to a named beneficiary or, if trustees had retired, proof of delivery to new trustees.[53] Secondly, the usual practice was to empower

[45] Masters assisted the judicial officers of the Chancery: see generally, WH Bennet, *A Short Dissertation on the Nature of the Various Proceedings in the Masters' Office in the Court of Chancery* (London, H Butterworth, 1831).

[46] *Blue v Marshall* (1753) 3 P Wms 381, 24 ER 1110; *Hodson v Ball* (1841) 11 Sim 456, 461–62; 59 ER 949, 951.

[47] *White v Williams* (1803) 8 Ves Jun 193, 194–95; 32 ER 327, 328.

[48] ER Daniell, *A Treatise on the Practice of the High Court of Chancery* (London, WT Clarke, 1838) vol 2, 877–78 (describing pre-1828 procedure).

[49] *Terrell v Mathews* (1841) 1 Mac & G 436; 41 ER 1333; *Re Fryer* (1857) 3 Kay & J 317; 69 ER 1129. As Conaglen observes, this could be used to strip unauthorised profits: the beneficiary could charge the trustee with assets actually received but, in breach of fiduciary duty, not recorded in the trust accounts: Conaglen (n 1).

[50] Daniell (n 48) 877.

[51] Chancery Commission, *First Report of Her Majesty's Commissioners Appointed to Inquire into the Process, Practice, and System of Pleading in the Court of Chancery* (London, Clowes & Sons, 1852) 35, 48, 92–93, 101, 179.

[52] These grounds were common to all forms of accounting.

[53] Trustees might retire under an express power, but otherwise the circumstances in which they could do so changed throughout the century see Stebbings (n 3) 45–57 for an overview. For precedents for deeds for the replacement of trustees see, eg, G Crabb, *A Complete Series of Precedents in Conveyancing*, 3rd edn (London, H Butterworth, 1845) 277–79; F Prideaux, *Forms and Precedents in Conveyancing*, 6th edn (London, Stevens & Sons, 1870) 462–74.

masters to make 'just allowances':[54] trustees were allowed discharges for expenses properly incurred in administering the trust.[55] Thirdly, theft: discharges were allowed if the trust asset had been stolen by a third party[56] or an agent of the trustee.[57] Trustees were permitted to tender an affidavit outlining the circumstances. Fourthly, restoration: discharges were allowed based on documentary proof of '[re]payment or something equivalent to it', to the extent these 'reproduce[d] the trust fund'.[58]

In the final stage, the master prepared a report. Having ascertained the state of the trust fund and assets still retained by the trustee, the master reviewed the verified charge and discharge, deducted any credits (ie, items of discharge) from the debits (ie, items of charge), and stated any balance due from the trustee to the trust estate. The case then returned to court.

(ii) Wilful Default Accounting: Charging Beyond Actual Receipts

If a beneficiary wished to charge a trustee beyond actual receipts, a decree for wilful default accounting was required. This directed an accounting not only of what the trustee received – exactly like a common accounting – but also 'what he might, without his wilful neglect or default, have received, although he has not received it'.[59] It was therefore not confined to 'reparative claims'; it simply involved investigating the state of the trust fund and, like a common accounting, could be followed by a decree to pay 'substitutive compensation'.[60]

To obtain a wilful default accounting, 'Lord Eldon's general rule'[61] was that the beneficiary had to aver a 'special case'[62] of wilful default or neglect and satisfy the court at the hearing that there had been at least one instance thereof.[63] Although 'wilful default' was not 'precisely defined',[64] it connoted voluntary acts or omissions infringing a judicial standard of prudence or reasonableness.[65] Thus, it included failures to: (i) enforce covenants given by, or debts due from, a third party; (ii) sell or realise investments; (iii) segregate trust from personal assets; (iv) supervise co-trustees, agents, or a banker; or (v) exercise due care and skill in the selection and management of investments. Proof of any of these could entitle a beneficiary to charge beyond actual receipts.

[54] *Howell v Howell* (1837) 2 My & C 478, 486; 40 ER 722, 725.
[55] See Conaglen (n 1) 42–44.
[56] *Morley v Morley* (1678) 2 Chan Cas 2; 22 ER 817.
[57] *Knight v Lord Plimouth* (1747) 3 Atk 380, 26 ER 1076; reported *sub nom Knight v Earl of Plymouth* (1747) Dick 127, 21 ER 214. The discharge for the original receipt would be disallowed if the theft had in fact resulted from a breach of duty: eg, a failure to exercise due care and skill: *Jones v Lewis* (1750) 2 Ves Sen 240, 28 ER 155; *Ex parte Belchier* (1754) Amb 218, 27 ER 144.
[58] *Bacon v Clarke* (1837) 3 My & Cr 294, 300–01; 40 ER 938, 941; *Lander v Weston* (1855) 3 Drew 389, 61 ER 951.
[59] *Partington v Reynolds* (1858) 4 Drew 253, 256; 62 ER 98, 99.
[60] *Cf Agricultural Land* (n 20) [349], [437].
[61] *Sleight v Lawson* (1857) 3 Kay & J 292, 294; 69 ER 1119, 1120 (in argument).
[62] *Lord Kensington v Bouverie* (1855) 7 De G M & G 134, 156; 44 ER 53, 61–62.
[63] *Coope v Carter* (1852) 2 De GM & G 292, 297–99; 42 ER 884, 887; *Jones v Morall* (1852) 2 Sims NS 241, 249–51; 61 ER 333, 336–37; *Partington* (n 59) 4 Drew 253–62, 62 ER 98–101.
[64] G Spence, *The Equitable Jurisdiction of the Court of Chancery* (London, V and R Stevens and GS Norton, 1849) vol 2, 923–924; *cf Re Owens* (1882) 47 LT 61, 64.
[65] JE Stannard, 'Wilful Default' [1979] *Conv* 345, 346, 349.

(iii) Stated Accounts: Liberty to Surcharge and Falsify

Chancery would not always take accounts from scratch, and perhaps the simplest way for a trustee to avoid a court-supervised accounting was by entering a 'plea of stated account'.[66] The trustee would plead that he had already accounted to the beneficiaries – that the account was 'closed', 'stated', or 'settled', rather than 'open'. Upon the matter coming up for hearing, the court ruled upon the plea. There were four basic possibilities. First, the plea might succeed, barring so much of the suit as sought an accounting.[67] Secondly, the plea might fail, and the court would decree a common accounting (or rule on any prayer for a wilful default accounting). Thirdly, if the beneficiary established a prima facie case of 'fraud or imposition', as distinct from mere error, the court could treat apparently settled accounts as open: the accounts would be taken *de novo*.[68] Fourthly, if a beneficiary identified an error in apparently settled accounts, the beneficiary could be given liberty to challenge particular items. This was called 'liberty to surcharge or falsify' settled accounts. A beneficiary could obtain this decree without proving every asserted error; a single, precisely identified[69] error might be enough.[70] If liberty were granted, a master would rule upon each of the beneficiary's challenges. If the beneficiary averred that the trustee had failed to include items on the debit (or incoming) side, this was called a 'surcharge'. A surcharge could relate to assets a trustee had received, or might have received, but for a wilful default. In modern terms, a surcharge could lay the foundation for an account of profits, or for substitutive or reparative compensation. If, instead, the beneficiary averred that the trustee had improperly included an item on the credit (or outgoing) side – for instance, by recording an unauthorised disposition or investment as if it had been authorised – this was a 'falsification'.[71] In either case, the evidential burden was upon the beneficiary. If the beneficiary's challenges succeeded, the court could grant relief on that basis: for example, it could decree payment of the revised balance, plus interest.[72]

(iv) Reform to Court-supervised Accounting: 1828–1852

In 1828, at the very peak of the backlog in Chancery, a limited range of reforms were made to Chancery procedure.[73] Although accounts were sometimes taken in the old way,[74] the revised practice was as follows.

First, trustees – whether under a common accounting or a wilful default accounting – were now required to supply a full statement of the debit and credit sides of the account in the first instance.[75] Trustees would supply an affidavit with four schedules.[76]

[66] Daniell (n 48) 186–89.
[67] *Dawson v Dawson* (1737) 1 Atk 1, 26 ER 1; *Taylor v Hayling* (1788) 1 Cox Eq Cas 435, 29 ER 1237.
[68] *Vernon* (n 43).
[69] *Kinsman v Barker* (1808) 14 Ves Jun 579, 33 ER 643; *Parkinson v Hanbury* (1867) LR 2 HL 1, 8–9, 12–13, 19–20.
[70] Daniell (n 48) 190.
[71] On the terms, see *Pitt v Cholmondeley* (1754) 2 Ves Sen 565, 565–66; 28 ER 360, 360; Cory (n 37) 260–261.
[72] *Brownell v Brownell* (1786) 2 Bro CC 62, 29 ER 35.
[73] Polden (n 5) 652–55.
[74] Cory (n 37) 262.
[75] S Miller, *The Orders of the High Court of Chancery* (London, Butterworth, 1841) 295.
[76] Cory (n 37) 256–57, 332–40 (illustrative schedules).

This affidavit replaced the lengthier process of written interrogatories and examination. By the first schedule, the trustee recited that which was to be held upon trust. The second schedule contained the credit side of the account; that is, the trustee's actual receipts – the assets for which he admitted he was chargeable. The third schedule contained the debit side; that is, the claimed discharge for each asset.[77] The fourth schedule listed the documentary proof relevant to each item of discharge.[78]

Secondly, the same process of charge and discharge then followed. The beneficiary prepared a charge, and the master examined it item-by-item.[79] Items agreeing with the trustee's affidavit would be allowed as a matter of course.[80] Otherwise, the master ruled on any objections by the trustee. The trustee then prepared a discharge, making clear on what basis the trustee sought to be relieved from each item in the charge.[81] As before, other than in a wilful default accounting, charges were confined to actual receipts. Likewise, in supporting his discharge, the trustee was required to prove 'not only the fact of the payment', supported by vouchers, but also to show 'the *propriety*' of such payment.[82]

Although these procedures could have the practical effect of making trustee liability stringent, liability was not automatic. Parties aggrieved by a master's report could dispute its findings by 'taking exception' to all or part of it: for example, by challenging a decision to allow or disallow a particular item in a charge or discharge, in whole or in part. Exceptions were ruled upon in open court – bringing debate to the attention of law reporters and requiring courts to state their reasons for measuring trustee liability in a particular way. Having allowed or disallowed any challenges to the master's report, the court would confirm it and determine the appropriate form of relief. How, then, did accounting principles shape trustee liability?

III. Emerging Principles for Quantifying Trustee Liability: 1790–1875

In this part we argue that, when quantifying a trustee's pecuniary liability, nineteenth-century courts acted upon a general notion of replicating due performance. As we show below, this idea of due performance could in some cases result in extensive trustee liability, but in others it allowed trustees to escape liability for diminution of the trust estate. This approach applied to 'substitutive claims' arising from unauthorised dispositions as well as 'reparative claims' for negligent management. Indeed, we suggest that contemporaries did not see the distinction as central. First, we discuss the concept of replicating due performance, and examine how trustees who made unauthorised dispositions could be discharged. Secondly, we argue that whether a suit involved an

[77] ibid 258.

[78] ibid 259.

[79] ibid 262–263.

[80] Indeed, charges often duplicated material already before the master, Chancery Commission, *First Report* (n 51) 167, 179.

[81] JS Smith, *A Treatise on the Practice of the Court of Chancery*, 2nd edn (London, R Saunders and W Benning, 1837) vol 2, 117.

[82] Cory (n 37) 263 (emphasis in original).

unauthorised disposition or other kinds of mismanagement, contemporary courts were concerned with 'due performance or its monetary equivalent'.[83]

We use the term 'due performance' because it neatly captures what courts thought they were doing. Curial relief was designed to give effect to how a prudent trustee would have acted. In determining this, courts did not only consider the express terms of the trust, but also had regard to its own policies about good trustee conduct. Courts would also draw inferences about the settlor's intention in creating the trust. The idea, therefore, is perhaps wider than some modern conceptions of a trustee's duty of due administration, which focus on the limits placed by the trust's terms on the free use of the rights and powers held on trust.[84]

A. Aim of the Remedy: Replicating Due Performance

Chancery's jurisdiction to order trustees to make money payments was rooted in the 'duty of the Court to enforce the execution of trusts'.[85] The centrality of replicating due performance is well-illustrated by James Hill's *A Practical Treatise on the Law Relating to Trustees* (1845).[86] Hill divides his chapter on the powers and duties of trustees according to different types of trust. Each section opens with an explanation of the function served by each and a discussion of the trustee's powers and duties given that function – the remedial consequences in each case flowing from that function.[87]

The importance of this approach to unauthorised disposition cases is clear.[88] Importantly, however, the fact that trustees were *accountable* for everything received did not mean that trustees were automatically *answerable* for the full monetary equivalent of assets disposed of without authority. Even if assets were disposed of without authority, trustee liability still turned on the terms and function of the trust. A good example of this is *Bacon v Clark* (1837).[89]

A settlor wanted to raise £10,000 for a marriage settlement in England by selling an estate in India. To do this, the settlor conveyed the Indian estate to a trustee. The trustee was under a duty to sell the estate and to take £10,000 from the proceeds and send this to England. The trustee sold the estate for 145,000 sicca rupees, separated 80,000 sicca rupees (then equivalent to £10,000), yet, in breach of trust, remitted the 80,000 sicca rupees to a partnership in India (in which he was a partner). The partners lent this sum to the East India Company and only years later, after the settlor and trustee had died, took steps to remit the separated proceeds by purchasing a bill of exchange for £7,979 – a sum equal to 80,000 sicca rupees at then-prevailing exchange rates. This

[83] L Ho and R Nolan, 'The Performance Interest in the Law of Trusts' (2020) 136 *Law Quarterly Review* 402, 412–13. See too W Strachan, 'Compensation for Breach of Trust' (1918) 34 *Law Quarterly Review* 168, 170; Ho (n 6) 849, 854–57, 882.

[84] eg, see, *Hayton, McFarlane and Mitchell* (n 11) at [3-143].

[85] *Adair v Shaw* (1803) 1 Sch & Lef 242, 262.

[86] J Hill, *A Practical Treatise on the Law Relating to Trustees* (London, V and R Stevens and GS Norton, 1845).

[87] ibid 307–517.

[88] See, eg, *French v Hobson* (1803) 9 Ves Jun 103, 106–07; 32 ER 540, 541–42.

[89] *Bacon* (n 58).

remittance failed because all the obligors on the bill became insolvent. The beneficiaries sued the trustee's personal representatives and succeeded.

Lord Cottenham LC emphasised that the trustee was accountable for the *full proceeds* of the estate: the effect of the trust deed was that 'the whole proceeds' remained 'liable to the payment of £10,000' unless 'payment or a sufficient excuse for non-payment [could] be shown'.[90] Importantly, neither separating the 80,000 sicca rupees (for the purpose of the unauthorised partnership loan), nor the remittance of £7,979 (ie, the unsuccessful attempt to make payment to the beneficiaries), were allowable discharges. Nevertheless, Lord Cottenham only decreed payment of £10,000 – not the full proceeds of sale of the estate. The fact that the trustee was accountable for 145,000 sicca rupees did not make the trustee automatically liable for that amount. There was no suggestion that the beneficiaries could recover *more* than the terms of the trust would have given them, nor indeed that the remedy was *limited* by the fact that the value of the originally separated amount had fallen by the date of judgment.[91] The result was reached not by causal analysis, but by charging the trustee by reference to the trust's purpose: raising £10,000.

B. Relieving Trustees Following Unauthorised Dispositions

It is well recognised that nineteenth-century trustees who exceeded their powers – for example, by selling without authority,[92] or by acquiring an 'improper' (ie, unauthorised) investment[93] – were in a precarious position. As we have seen, trustees were chargeable with what they received, and masters, noted for their strict approach to discharges,[94] generally disallowed disbursements 'not expressly authorized by the trust instrument, or sanctioned by necessary construction'.[95] Thus a trustee who admitted having sold out investments, but who was unable to explain what had happened to the sale proceeds, might be declared answerable even in advance of a court-supervised accounting.[96] Nonetheless, nineteenth-century courts went beyond the narrow question of whether trustees had acted within the strict terms of their powers. Even if recognised grounds of discharge – for example, administrative outlays or theft – were unavailable, trustees who acted beyond their powers could be relieved. We consider two categories of case: invalid exercises of powers and court-sanctioned departures from the terms of the trust. Courts had the tools to relieve trustees in such cases, but used these tools sparingly to preserve the integrity of the trust institution. The cautious judicial policy is one reason why, later in the century, it fell to Parliament to confer a general power to relieve honest and reasonable trustees.[97]

[90] ibid 298–99; 940.
[91] *cf Re Dawson* (n 12).
[92] *Adams v Clifton* (1826) 1 Russ 297, 38 ER 115.
[93] *Knott v Cottee* (1852) 16 Beav 77, 51 ER 705.
[94] Chancery Commission, *First Report* (n 51) 43, 48, 179.
[95] Hill (n 86) 597.
[96] *Meyer v Montriou* (1841) 4 Beav 343, 49 ER 372; (1842) 5 Beav 146, 49 ER 532; (1846) 9 Beav 521, 50 ER 445.
[97] Stebbings (n 3) 188–92.

(i) Invalid Exercise of a Power

The first class of cases concerned trustees who had the power to make particular investments, or to advance money to a particular beneficiary, but acted beyond the terms of their power. Trustees in such cases could *in principle* escape liability for trust assets disposed of under an imperfectly executed power. Courts had jurisdiction to aid the defective execution of powers[98] in certain cases,[99] for instance, 'saving' a purported exercise of a power even if stipulated formalities were not followed.[100] However, this doctrine had limits. Courts would not intervene if doing so would defeat 'the intentions of the author of the power' or deprive relevant persons of protections served by the formalities.[101]

These principles are relevant because cases involving defectively executed powers to sell or to lend might give the impression that contemporaries regarded trustee liability for unauthorised dispositions as 'strict' or 'automatic'. These cases are better understood in terms of judicial sensitivity to the function played by certain kinds of trust. In the nineteenth century it was regarded as important that property settled on trust for a married woman be protected from her husband. The concern was that a husband might exercise undue influence and procure a disposition for his own purposes. Typically, a wife's father would settle property for her separate use, thereby providing for her and any children even if, for instance, the husband became bankrupt.[102] One way of safeguarding the wife's fortune was through a trust, not otherwise recognised by the law,[103] whereby the wife was treated as acquiring an interest in the trust property but had no powers of alienation over it.[104] Trustees for a married woman – whether or not the trust also restrained the wife's power of alienation – were sometimes also given power to advance money to the husband (whether by way of loan or gift), subject to obtaining the wife's prior consent in a particular form. If trustees, without obtaining this consent, purported to exercise this power, courts would refuse to perfect it, on the basis that the formalities were 'matters of substance and not of form'.[105]

The classic illustration is *Cocker v Quayle*,[106] cited today for a more general proposition that causation was irrelevant in cases of unauthorised dispositions.[107]

[98] Whether dispositive or administrative: *Harvey v Harvey* (1739) Barn Ch 103; 37 ER 572; 9 Mod 253; 88 ER 433.

[99] See FT White and OD Tudor, *A Selection of Leading Cases in Equity*, 2nd edn (London, W Maxwell, 1858) vol 1, 185–90; E Sugden, *A Practical Treatise on the Law of Powers*, 8th edn (London, H Sweet, 1861) chs X and XI. Excessive execution of powers could also be perfected: see, eg, *Harvey* (n 98).

[100] See, eg, *Tollett v Tollett* (1728) 2 P Wms 489, 24 ER 828; *Cockerell v Cholmeley* (1830) Tam 435, 48 ER 173; 1 Russ & Myl 318, 39 ER 161 (MR), affirmed in *Cockerell v Cholmleley* (1832) I Clark & Fin 60, 6 ER 839; VI Bligh NS 120, 6 ER 543 (HL).

[101] White and Tudor (n 99) 194; *Thackwell v Gardiner* (1851) 5 De Gex & Smale 58, 65; 64 ER 1017, 1020.

[102] See WH Hart 'The Origins of Restraints on Anticipation' (1932) 40 *Law Quarterly Review* 221, E Spring, *Law, Land and Family* (Chapel Hill, NC, University of North Carolina Press, 1993) 115–16.

[103] *Brandon v Robinson* (1811) 18 Ves Jun 429, 34 ER 379. See Anderson (n 4) 246–49.

[104] See, eg, *Sockett v Wray* (1794) 4 Brown CC 483.

[105] *Hopkins v Myall* (1830) 2 Russ & My 86, 39 ER 327. See also *Bateman v Davis* (1818) 3 Madd 98, 56 ER 446; *Kellaway v Johnson* (1842) 5 Beav 319, 49 ER 601; *Thackwell* (n 101).

[106] *Cocker v Quayle* (1830) 1 Russ & My 535, 39 ER 206.

[107] See, eg, *Underhill* (n 16) [91-01], [91-15].

Trustees for a married woman had the power to lend to the husband if they obtained the wife's written consent and the husband's bond. The trustees obtained neither, and the money was lost in the husband's bankruptcy. The trustees were made answerable for the full value of the sum given to the husband, despite later obtaining the wife's consent in the proper form,[108] and despite the fact the trust estate would have sustained the same loss had this been done in the first place. Although the case is consistent with the default stringency of charge and discharge accounting, it does not follow that contemporaries were ignoring the moral aspects of trustee conduct. The limits on the trustee's power were 'prescribed in order to protect [the wife] against the influence of her husband'.[109] Discharging trustees in such cases would strip those restrictions of their purpose – it would frustrate the settlor's purpose in setting up such a trust.

(ii) Court-sanctioned Dispositions where Trustees Had No Powers

A second category of case involved courts allowing discharges for payments for which trustees lacked any power. Early examples concern executors[110] and trustees[111] making bona fide distributions to infant legatees out of income or capital for maintenance. These cases illustrate contemporary willingness to relieve trustees from the stringency of charge and discharge accounting, though once again there were limits to this jurisdiction, and it would only be exercised in certain categories of case. Although there was uncertainty about the precise ambit of judicial power to sanction departure from trust terms,[112] courts had power to relieve prudent trustees ex post for unauthorised disposals that they would have sanctioned ex ante. In other words, dispositions of a kind not authorised by the trust's terms could nevertheless be seen by the court as involving due performance of the trust.[113]

In *Nelson v Duncombe* (1846),[114] for example, a trustee used trust money to pay for the beneficiary's removal from prison to an asylum, his upkeep in that asylum, and for a commission of lunacy to be sued out against him. The commission, however, returned a verdict that the beneficiary was not a lunatic. The trustee later sought a declaration that he was entitled to 'allowances' (discharges) in a court-supervised accounting based on implied contract, while the beneficiary denied that the court had jurisdiction to do this. Lord Langdale MR ruled for the trustee. Although he acknowledged that the 'shocking' prospect that trustees in such cases had no power to act did not 'determine the question of jurisdiction', he was evidently influenced by a concern that trustees could intervene in extreme cases of necessity – as here, where a beneficiary was 'without friends,

[108] *cf Stevens v Robertson* (1867) 37 LJ Ch 499.

[109] *Cocker* (n 106) 1 Russ & My 538, 39 ER 207.

[110] See, eg, *Franklin v Green* (1690) 2 Vern 137, 23 ER 696; *Andrews v Partington* (1790) 2 Cox 223; 30 ER 103; *Davies v Austen* (1790) 3 Bro CC 178, 29 ER 475; 1 Ves Jun 247, 30 ER 325; *Lee v Brown* (1798) 4 Ves Jun 362, 369; 31 ER 184, 188.

[111] See, eg, *Bruin v Knott* (1845) 1 Phillips 572, 41 ER 750; *Prince v Hine* (1859) 26 Beav 634, 53 ER 1043.

[112] See, eg, *Blacklow v Laws* (1842) 2 Hare 40, 46–47; 67 ER 17, 19–20; *Harrison v Randall* (1852) 9 Hare 397, 407; 68 ER 562, 567; *cf Johnstone v Baber* (1845) 8 Beav 233, 235; 50 ER 91, 92.

[113] *Cf* J Hudson, 'Equity's Gloss on Authority' in McFarlane and Elliot (n 24).

[114] *Nelson v Duncombe* (1846) 9 Beav 211; 50 ER 323.

relations, or anybody but the trustee to take care of him'.[115] Emphasising the power to require beneficiaries seeking an account 'to do equity and justice', he laid down a general principle:

> if a trustee is sued for an account in this Court, and it shall appear that he has properly expended sums of money for the protection and safety or for the maintenance and support of his *cestui que trust*, at a time when the *cestui que trust* was himself incapable of taking care of himself, this Court will allow him credit for such sums of money.[116]

Lord Langdale then directed further inquiries, evidently willing to give discharges for trust money paid without power if 'properly expended' according to a judicial standard of reasonableness. A similar approach is evident in infant maintenance cases such as *Brown v Smith* (1878),[117] where Stuart VC in 1853 authorised trustees to pay £140 to a widow for the education and maintenance of her daughter. Their power to pay expired when the widow subsequently remarried, yet the payments continued. The daughter-beneficiary later sought an account, arguing that a proper allowance would have been £80 and that the surviving trustee and mother should repay the difference. Sir George Jessel MR refused to grant the prayer of the bill: notwithstanding that the payments were made without authority, the court could sanction them ex post, and, taking 'the whole circumstances together', £140 was a 'fair allowance'.[118] He justified his decision by reference to what would benefit orphaned infants – it was desirable that they should be looked after by relatives or willing friends; these persons might refuse to take orphans in return only for the bare cost of care; and this beneficiary had received a good education and been dressed and presented to society as a lady. The Court of Appeal upheld his decision, saying that even if money had been spent to keep up her stepfather's house, the daughter had clearly benefited from such expenditure. The trustee and the mother were accordingly discharged of the full value taken from the trust estate without authority – the trustees had acted prudently.

By the end of the nineteenth century, lawyers were rationalising these and analogous cases into a general principle: equity might relieve trustees in cases of 'practical necessity' neither foreseen nor expressly forbidden by a trust's express terms,[119] provided that relief would not transform the character of the trust.[120] Assessing the historical ambit of this jurisdiction is difficult, as applications were usually heard privately in chambers.[121] For present purposes, the point is that the 'moral quality' of trustee conduct for an 'ultra vires disbursement' did not 'only become material' when trustees invoked statutory jurisdiction 'to be excused on the ground of having acted honestly and reasonably'.[122] Nineteenth-century courts had the power to relieve trustees, even if judicial policy placed a heavy burden on the trustee seeking such relief.

[115] ibid 9 Beav 218, 50 ER 326.
[116] ibid 9 Beav 232, 50 ER 332.
[117] *Brown v Smith* (1878) 10 Ch D 377.
[118] ibid 382.
[119] *Re Tollemache* [1903] 1 Ch 457, 462.
[120] See, eg, *Re Crawshay* (1888) WN 246; 60 LT 357, 359; *Re New* [1901] 2 Ch 534.
[121] For later views on its scope see *Chapman v Chapman* [1954] AC 429.
[122] Birks (n 25) 47. See too Judicial Trustees Act 1896 (59 & 60 Vict c 35) s 3.

C. Proper Investments

It has been suggested that 'substitutive claims' were fundamentally distinct from 'reparative claims' arising from negligent management: the latter were 'equity's equivalents to a damages claim at law',[123] and 'it is possible to forget altogether about the formal relationship of the breach to the trustee's accountability'.[124] That is not true of the nineteenth century. In both contexts, monetary relief was designed to replicate the effect of due performance upon the trust estate. In most eighteenth- and early nineteenth-century trusts this was straightforward, in that trust drafting at that time tended to give trustees few discretions, and so what due performance involved was unambiguous.[125] For instance, trustees who failed to accumulate income were to be 'charged precisely in the same manner as if [they] had performed'.[126] Conversely, if a trustee failed to enforce debts or sell assets as directed, courts were anxious to *limit* liability to the sum that would have been recovered by a prudent trustee.[127] Further, whether a trustee engaged in an 'active' breach (for example, by selecting an improper investment) or merely failed to act (as by failing to sell at the proper time), the trustee's liability crystallised as 'part of the duty which the trustee [...] had undertaken to perform'.[128] The focus was the trust estate, not the loss suffered by any particular beneficiary, and trustees were treated as having prudently performed and charged themselves in the trust accounts at the relevant time.

This focus on 'deemed performance'[129] is clearly illustrated in the Chancery's approach to investments, perhaps one of the most controversial areas of trustee liability in the nineteenth century and one in which remedial principles were more explicitly discussed than in other areas. The default rule was that trustees had to make 'proper' investments – those which Chancery itself would choose. Trust money must neither 'lie unproductive', nor 'be exposed to hazard', a tension resolved by a default policy that 'prudent' trustees should invest in government consolidated annuities ('consols'), yielding a three per cent return.[130] Difficulties arose as investment opportunities opened up in the nineteenth century which trustees and beneficiaries might wish to take advantage of. While settlors[131] or Parliament at times increased the range of proper investments, the change was a slow one.[132] Trustees often found themselves trapped between beneficiaries keen to maximise investment return and legal rules premised on eighteenth-century

[123] Elliott (n 6) 178–79.
[124] Birks (n 25) 47.
[125] Stebbings (n 3) ch 5; A Televantos, *Capitalism Before Corporations* (Oxford, Oxford University Press, 2020) 33–5.
[126] *Raphael v Boehm* (1807) 13 Ves Jun 407, 411; 33 ER 347, 348; affirmed *Raphael v Boehm* (1807) 13 Ves Jun 590, 591–92; 33 ER 415, 416. See also *Dornford v Dornford* (1806) 12 Ves Jun 127; 33 ER 49.
[127] The burden of proof, however, was upon the trustee: see, eg, *Blue* (n 46); *Maitland v Bateman* (1844) 13 LJ Rep NS (Ch) 273, 275; *Fenwick v Greenwell* (1847) 10 Beav 412, 50 ER 640; *Wiles v Gresham* (1854) 5 De GM & G 770, 43 ER 1069; *Clack v Holland* (1854) 19 Beav 262, 269–71; 52 ER 350, 353–54; *Lord Gainsborough v The Watcombe Terra Cotta Clay Company* (1885) 54 LJ Ch 991, 997.
[128] *Devaynes v Robinson* (1857) 24 Beav 86, 96; 53 ER 289, 293; 5 WR 509, 510.
[129] Ho (n 6) 855.
[130] See generally, Stebbings (n 3) 68–78, 131–51; *Howe v Earl of Dartmouth* (1802) 7 Ves Jun 137, 32 ER 56; *Norbury v Norbury* (1819) 4 Madd 191, 192; 56 ER 677, 678; *Robinson v Robinson* (1851) 1 De G M & G 247, 255–56; 42 ER 547, 550.
[131] *Brown v Gellatly* (1867) LR 2 Ch App 751, 758; *Re Brown* (1885) 29 Ch D 889.
[132] See Stebbings (n 3) 136–45.

investment practices.[133] As Maitland put it: 'Long ago the Court of Chancery came to an opinion as to what the prudent investor does'[134] yet allowed the conception to ossify and '(so to speak) screwed up the standard of reasonableness to what many men would regard as an unreasonable height.'[135]

In this way, fault-based reasoning was a feature of all investment cases, regardless of whether the alleged breach involved unauthorised investments, or authorised but negligently selected investments. That is not to say that contemporaries did not recognise a distinction between trustees who acted beyond their powers, and those who negligently exercised their powers – the distinction between ultra vires and intra vires (but negligent) conduct.[136] That distinction was discussed[137] and mattered, for instance, as regards burden of proof. A trustee who had a voucher evidencing a disposal within the letter of the trust's terms might obtain a discharge as a matter of course – being answerable for any diminution in the trust estate would require proof of wilful default or neglect.[138] In contrast, trustees lacking a voucher and investing without power to do so had to justify their conduct.

Even so, the distinction is less significant than modern literature would suggest. More significant in contemporary reasoning was a morally laden distinction between 'proper' (or 'prudent' or 'provident') and 'improper' (or 'imprudent' or 'improvident') conduct. Courts emphasised their own policies about proper trust administration. Thus in *Ryder v Bickerton* (1743),[139] a trustee had power to invest 'at interest' upon the 'best security', yet lent upon a promissory note with no interest, and so the investment was a 'direct contradiction of the words of the trust'. However, Lord Hardwicke LC grounded the trustee's liability in 'gross negligence', not the unauthorised disposition.[140] Throughout our period, what could have been characterised as unauthorised dispositions were debated in terms of irregularity, impropriety, imprudence, or culpable neglect.[141] Indeed, judges were often averse to characterising investments as 'authorised' even if within the literal terms of powers[142] – evidently to encourage what they saw as prudent management.[143]

[133] ibid 65–69.

[134] AH Chaytor and WJ Whittaker (eds), FW Maitland, *Equity: A Course of Lectures* (Cambridge, Cambridge University Press, 1936) 95, 99.

[135] ibid 104.

[136] P Birks and A Pretto, 'Preface' in P Birks and A Pretto (eds), *Breach of Trust* (Oxford, Hart Publishing, 2002) viii–ix.

[137] See, eg, GF Hampson, *A Short Treatise Endeavouring to Point Out the Means by which Those who Accept the Situation of Trustees May Perform Their Duties Without Incurring Responsibility* (London, A Maxwell, 1825) 31–32.

[138] *Knight* (n 57) Dickens 126, 21 ER 216; *Buxton v Buxton* (1835) 1 My & C 80; 40 ER 307; *Re Chapman* [1896] 2 Ch 763, 776.

[139] *Ryder v Bickerton* (1743) 3 Swans 90, 36 ER 782. A brief manuscript report of the same case is printed as note 1 in *Harden v Parsons* (1758) 1 Eden 145, 28 ER 641.

[140] ibid.

[141] See, eg, *Harden* (n 139) 1 Eden 145, 148–50; 28 ER 641, 641; *Caffrey v Darby* (1801) 6 Ves Jun 488, 495–96; 31 ER 1159, 1162; *Clough v Bond* (1838) 3 My & C 490, 496–97; 40 ER 1016, 1018.

[142] *Wilkes v Steward* (1801) G Coop 6, 35 ER 457; *Langston v Oliphant* (1807) G Coop 33, 35 ER 467; *Dickonson v Player* (1838) Coop Pr Cas 178, 179–80; 47 ER 455, 456; *Simson's Trust* (1860) 1 John & H 89, 70 ER 674; *Harris v Harris* (1861) 29 Beav 107, 54 ER 567. Note that the cases do not involve allegations that the trustees acted for improper purposes, so as to engage what we today regard as the fraud on the power doctrine.

[143] See, eg, *Holmes v Dring* (1788) 2 Cox 1, 30 ER 1; *Mant v Leith* (1852) 15 Beav 524, 527–28; 51 ER 641, 642–643. See also Anderson (n 4) 280–81.

(i) Replicating Due Performance in 'Improper' Investment Cases

Given judicial concerns about trustee prudence, it makes sense that there was no categorical distinction between how contemporaries approached unauthorised investments and the negligent selection of otherwise authorised investments. Take cases where trustees improperly sold consols, consolidated government annuities which generated a three per cent return and were the default proper investment for trusts of personalty. The circumstances could vary. Sometimes trustees did have a power to sell consols with a view to reinvestment, but sales were made without complying with preconditions for exercising the power. In other cases, trustees complied with those conditions, but then selected investments of a type not authorised by the power or made investment decisions negligently. In each case, courts took the same general approach. In a court-supervised accounting, beneficiaries could usually elect between charging the trustee with: (i) the original receipt (the consols); or (ii) the subsequent receipt (for example, the sale proceeds of the consols; or an asset acquired with such proceeds, with any income derived therefrom).[144] The court's decree carried this state of account into execution. In the former case, the trustee might be ordered to acquire equivalent investments and pay amounts referable to the dividends that would have accrued – or pay the monetary equivalent, plus interest. In the latter case, the trustee might be ordered to pay the monetary equivalent of the substituted asset and interest. In either case, the measure of liability was the sum required to replicate due performance.

Importantly, a similar position obtained if the trustee had failed to acquire consols. Unless displaced by an express term, trustees were under a duty to convert trust personalty and invest in consols. In accounting terms, beneficiaries could charge trustees with: (i) the original receipt (the sum to be invested); or (ii) that which might have been received but for the trustee's default (the amount of consols the trustee was duty-bound to purchase at the appropriate time, plus dividends that would have accrued). The beneficiary having elected, the decree put the trust estate into a position conforming to court-drawn accounts: for example, if the latter election were made, the trustee could be directed to buy so many consols as he would have been able to buy at the relevant time;[145] or to pay an amount enabling this to occur (even if the stock had subsequently risen in value).[146] In such cases, the trustee's lack of discretion meant that it was straightforward to determine what due performance would have involved.

More difficult were cases where the trustee's duty to invest was coupled with discretion to elect between consols and another permitted investment. If a trustee made an unauthorised investment, how was a court to measure liability to reconstitute the trust estate? By reference to the sum to be invested or one of the permitted investments?

[144] See, eg, *Harrison v Harrison* (1740) 2 Atk 121, 26 ER 476; reported *sub nom Harrison v Pryse* (1740) in Barn Ch 324, 325–26; 27 ER 664, 664–65; *Bostock v Blakeney* (1789) 2 Bro CC 653, 656; 29 ER 362, 364; *Ex parte Shakeshaft* (1791) 3 Brown CC 197, 29 ER 487; *Pocock v Reddington* (1801) 5 Ves 794, 799–800; 31 ER 862, 865–66; *Long v Stewart* (1801) reported in note 1 to *Pocock* ibid; *Docker v Somes* (1834) 2 My & K 655, 39 ER 1095; *Fletcher v Green* (1864) 33 Beav 426; 55 ER 433; *cf O'Brien v O'Brien* (1828) 1 Molloy 533. It was for the beneficiary, not the trustee, to elect: *Pinkett v Wright* (1844) 2 Hare 120, 127–28; 67 ER 50, 53.

[145] *Byrchall v Bradford* (1822) 6 Madd 235, 56 ER 1081; *Brown v Gellatly* (n 131).

[146] *Byrchall* (n 145) 6 Madd 240, 56 ER 1082–83; *Pride v Fooks* (1840) 2 Beav 430, 48 ER 1248; *Starkey v Dyson* (1875) 24 WR 7.

After a series of conflicting decisions,[147] in *Robinson v Robinson* (1851)[148] it was settled that the beneficiary could only charge the trustee with the original receipt – the beneficiary could not charge the trustee *as if* the trustee had exercised his discretion in a particular way and received a particular asset and derived certain income. After acknowledging the importance of putting an injured party 'in the same situation in which he would have stood if the wrong had not been done', Lord Cranworth LC emphasised that the beneficiary could compel due administration of the trust *according to its terms*: 'the measure of [the trustee's] responsibility' was what the beneficiary 'must have been entitled to do', and the beneficiary never had any right 'to compel' the trustee to perform in a particular way.[149] Allowing the beneficiary to charge the trustee beyond the actual receipts – notwithstanding the negligent management – would not replicate due performance: it would give the beneficiaries 'an option which certainly did not belong to them by the terms of the trust'. The trustee being at liberty to invest in either of two lawful investments, liability was measured by that which 'is *least*, not that which is most beneficial' to the trust estate.[150] The case shows how the growth in trustee discretions strained the utility of 'due performance', forcing judges to make decisions about how trustee liability should be measured where the trust could be performed in more than one way. The answer to that question in *Robinson* was perhaps influenced by mid-century concerns that trustee liability was growing too burdensome as more and more came to be demanded of trustees.[151] Nevertheless, Lord Cranworth framed the issue of the trustee's liability explicitly within the then orthodox idea that trustee liability turned on what due performance of the trust demanded. That idea remained fundamental to judicial treatment of both charges for unauthorised dispositions ('substitutive claims') and negligent failures to invest ('reparative claims').

That there was no sharp remedial distinction between unauthorised and negligent investments is illustrated by *Phillipson v Gatty* (1848).[152] Trustees had powers to vary investments and to invest in real property. With a view to reinvestment, they sold consols and lent the sale proceeds out on a mortgage of real property. Although the trustees argued that the original sale was 'lawful' (ie, within the scope of their powers), the court considered that the mortgage was imprudently selected, treating the entire dealing as 'one transaction'.[153] In accounting terms, the trustees remained chargeable for their original receipt: although acting within the letter of their power, imprudent conduct barred the trustees from claiming any discharge. Similar reasoning appears in *Norris v Wright* (1851),[154] where trustees had to reconstitute the trust fund in respect of

[147] Compare *Marsh v Hunter* (1822) 6 Madd 295, 56 ER 1103; *Shepherd v Mouls* (1845) 4 Hare 500, 67 ER 746; *Rees v Williams* (1847) 1 De Gex & Sm 314, 63 ER 1083 (trustee only liable for the sum to be invested) with *Hockley v Bantock* (1826) 1 Russ 141, 38 ER 55; *Watts v Girdlestone* (1843) 6 Beav 188, 49 ER 797; *Ames v Parkinson* (1844) 7 Beav 379, 49 ER 1111; *Ouseley v Anstruther* (1847) 10 Beav 453, 50 ER 656 (trustee liable for what the present value of consols would be, had they been purchased).

[148] *Robinson v Robinson* (1851) 1 De G M & G 247, 42 ER 547.

[149] ibid 1 De G M & G 258–60, 42 ER 550–51.

[150] ibid 1 De G M & G 258, 42 ER 551 (emphasis added).

[151] Stebbings (n 3), ch 6.

[152] *Phillipson v Gatty* (1848) 7 Hare 516, 68 ER 213.

[153] ibid 7 Hare 528, 68 ER 219.

[154] *Norris v Wright* (1851) 14 Beav 291, 303–05; 51 ER 298, 303–04.

both unauthorised and negligent investments. The point was made most clearly in the later case of *Re Massingberd's Settlement* (1890).[155] Counsel argued that:

> [T]here is a broad distinction … between [1.] investments which are proper so far as relates to the mere instrument creating the trust[,] investments which satisfy those terms, but which may be affected by negligence in the mode of carrying them out, and [2.] investments which are entirely outside the terms of the trust; … [and] with regard to the latter class … the measure of relief given was or might be greater than with regard to the first.[156]

Fry LJ rejected the argument for two reasons. First, it was irrelevant on the facts: the investments were outside the terms of the trust. Secondly, and crucially, he denied that there was a remedial difference between the two categories.[157] *Phillipson v Gatty* illustrated that this was not a 'proper distinction' because there the trustee had acted negligently within the terms of his powers, but was ordered to 'reinstate the original fund to its original amount'.[158] Relief replicated due performance – the trustees were charged as if they had retained the fund.

IV. Towards a Discrete Claim for Equitable Compensation

This final part of the chapter examines the procedural reforms which made it easier to litigate discrete breaches of trust without a court-supervised accounting and the effect the reduced focus on accountability had upon legal thinking about suits against trustees and the replication of due performance.

A. Summary Procedures and Narrowing Dispute to Contested Items: 1841–1875

From 1841, beneficiaries who had a joint and several demand against co-trustees were permitted to proceed against a sole trustee. Courts allowed these suits if there was a 'definite breach' or 'ascertained' liability, if the sum was liquidated, and if the matter could be 'separately dealt with' without co-trustees.[159] Such suits were not permitted, however, if a general administration of the trust estate was sought or required.[160] In 1852, more wide-ranging reforms were enacted.

First, a simple summons for general administration could be brought, and decrees for the payment of money obtained, in cases where there was 'no substantial dispute

[155] *Re Massingberd's Settlement* (1890) 63 LT 296.

[156] ibid 298.

[157] Fry LJ acknowledged the procedural distinction discussed above at text from (n 136) to (n 139), in that the burden was on the trustees to show that any given investment was authorised: ibid 299.

[158] *Massingberd* (n 155) 298.

[159] See, eg, *Perry v Knott* (1842) 5 Beav 293, 49 ER 590; *Kellaway* (n 105); *Biggs v Penn* (1845) 4 Hare 469, 471–72; 67 ER 733, 734; *Shipton v Rawlins* (1846) 4 Hare 619, 622–24; 67 ER 795, 796–97; 2 Holt Eq 109, 112–19; 71 ER 813, 814–16. *Cf Meagher, Gummow & Lehane* (n 7) para [23-030].

[160] *Coppard v Allen* (1864) 2 De G J & Sm 173, 179–82; 46 ER 341, 343–44.

as to the facts'.[161] Full pleading remained the proper course for more complex cases. Secondly, objections for want of proper parties were reformed, enabling decrees for administration and the judicial execution of trusts to be obtained in a more summary fashion and, if appropriate, without joinder of all those beneficially interested.[162]

Thirdly, courts could now determine questions *without* decreeing administration and judicial execution of a trust, or requiring a common accounting – this remained a discretionary decision, however, to be refused if the application was 'fraudulent', 'collusive', or avoiding administration was otherwise thought inappropriate.[163] Fourthly, the office of master was abolished, and any accounting was thereafter to take place under judicial supervision with the assistance of clerks.[164]

Finally, and most importantly, the traditional procedures for charge and discharge were abolished. Instead, trustees were to verify their accounts by affidavit, and beneficiaries could put specific items in issue through a concise statement with brief particulars.[165] Although the reformers considered the possibility of treating all trustee accounts as presumptively settled,[166] courts were instead given a narrower power to make 'special directions' about the taking and vouching of accounts when appropriate:[167] for example, courts could direct that a trustee's books of account be taken as prima facie evidence, subject to liberty to surcharge and falsify.[168] It seems likely that these reforms encouraged the wider application of the terms 'falsify' and 'surcharge' to *all* accounts:[169] from 1852, asserting that items ought to be omitted from, or included in, trust accounts was analogous to falsifying or surcharging a specific item in a settled account. However, the analogy was superficial – the distinctions remained between common and wilful default accounting and between open and closed accounts.

B. Dispensing with Accounting: 1875–1901

The Judicature reforms assigned the execution of trusts to the Chancery division.[170] Although full pleading remained the norm for breach of trust cases or when seeking a wilful default accounting, these reforms continued the trend towards summary procedures. Thus beneficiaries could issue a specially endorsed summons for recovering a 'debt' or 'liquidated demand' arising 'on a trust' and obtain summary judgment;[171]

[161] Chancery Commission, *First Report* (n 51) 11–14.
[162] Court of Chancery Procedure Act 1852 (15 & 16 Vict c 86) ss 42–45.
[163] ibid s 51.
[164] Polden (n 5) 678–82.
[165] *General Orders and Rules of the High Court of Chancery* (London, Stevens, 1852) 8–10; L Field and EC Dunn, *Daniell's Chancery Practice*, 5th edn (London, Stevens and Sons, 1871) vol 2, 1122–27.
[166] Chancery Commission, *First Report* (n 51) 48, 100–01.
[167] Court of Chancery Procedure Act 1852 (15 & 16 Vict c 86) s 54.
[168] See, eg, *Banks v Cartwright* (1857) 15 WR 417.
[169] These terms were usually confined to settled accounts, discussed in Section II.B.(iii) above. See too PG Turner, 'Want of Causation as Defence to Liability for Misapplication of Trust Assets' in P Davies et al (eds), *Defences in Equity* (Oxford, Hart Publishing, 2018) 160. For illustrative modern usage, see *Ultraframe (UK) Ltd v Fielding* [2005] EWHC 1638 (Ch) [1513].
[170] Supreme Court of Judicature Act 1873 (36 & 37 Vict c 66) s 34(3).
[171] RSC Order III, r 6; JM Lely and WDI Foulkes, *The Judicature Acts of 1873 and 1875*, 2nd edn (London, H Sweet, 1877) 126–27.

or seek a common accounting, which was to be ordered forthwith, unless there was 'some preliminary question to be tried'.[172] Courts also took a liberal view of the rule that they had power 'at any time' to direct 'any necessary inquiries or accounts',[173] thereby altering the earlier practice[174] and partially relaxing the distinction between common and wilful default accounting.[175]

Although these changes brought the procedure closer to its modern form, the decisive step did not occur until the revised Judicature Rules of 1883.[176] As Conaglen observes, one can discern in the 1883 rules and related case law an increased judicial focus on the issue necessary to rectify a breach of trust and a willingness to do so without a full administration.[177] These revised rules clarified, and extended, previous reforms. First, the situations in which a beneficiary could commence by summons, dispensing with full pleadings, were enlarged: for example, when seeking orders for furnishing and vouching accounts, or directing the trustees to do or not do something in their capacity as trustees.[178] Otherwise, the proper course was to adopt or adapt prescribed forms.[179] Secondly, courts were given a discretionary power to refuse prayers for 'the administration of any trust' – and hence a common accounting – if the dispute could be 'properly determined' without it.[180] This reversed the default position that a common accounting was obtainable as 'a mere matter of course'[181] or as 'a matter of right'.[182] Thirdly, courts could direct that the vouching of trust accounts occur at the office of the trustee's solicitor, 'or at any other convenient place' – only 'contested or surcharged' items were now adjudicated in judge's chambers.[183]

By these steps, court-supervised accounting lost its central place in legal debate about the measure of trustee liability. Principles governing 'compensation for the loss the trust estate had sustained'[184] were now unhooked from the procedures on which they were premised: breach of trust could be litigated without explicit reference to charge and discharge accounting concepts. Thus in *Speight v Gaunt* (1883)[185] it was uncontroversial that loss to a trust estate occasioned by wilful default could be remedied without court-supervised accounting; in *Re Brogden* (1888)[186] the quantum of liability for wilful default was determined on the papers, both sides assuring the court that preliminary inquiries were unnecessary; and in *Re Salmon* (1889)[187] the beneficiaries simply sought

[172] RSC Order III, r 8; XV, r 1.
[173] RSC Order XXXIII.
[174] See text above at text from (n 61) to (n 63).
[175] Conaglen (n 24) 132.
[176] FP Tomlinson, *The Judicature Acts and Rules of the Supreme Court, 1883* (London, Clowes, 1883) 302–06.
[177] Conaglen (n 24) 135.
[178] RSC Order LV, r 3. Breaches of trust could in principle be remedied this way (as in, eg, *Re Stuart* (1896) 74 LT 546; *Re Newland* [1904] WN 181), though it was usually inappropriate in hostile proceedings (*Dowse v Gorton* [1891] AC 190, 202–03).
[179] Tomlinson (n 176) 179, 421 (Appendix C, Numbers 2, 4, 9 and 10).
[180] RSC Order LV, r 10.
[181] *Re Wilson* (1885) 28 Ch D 457, 460–61.
[182] *Campbell v Gillespie* [1900] 1 Ch 225, 228–229. See also *Re Blake* (1885) 29 ChD 913, 916, 919–20; *Re Gyhon* (1885) 29 Ch D 834, 838.
[183] RSC Order LV, r 4A: *Re Lockwood* (1892) 8 TLR 293, 294; *Re Fish* [1893] 2 Ch 413, 426–28.
[184] Lewin (n 53) 630–634.
[185] *Speight v Gaunt* (1883) 22 Ch D 727, 736, 739; *cf Speight v Gaunt* (1883) 9 App Cas 1.
[186] *Re Brogden* (1888) 38 Ch D 546, 558–60, 567–68, 572–73.
[187] *Re Salmon* (1889) 42 Ch D 351, 353.

a declaration that an investment was a breach of trust and that the fund be replaced, or the trustee otherwise make good the loss.

These reforms seem to have prompted some judges to state accounting principles,[188] and reaffirm the 'equitable debt' characterisation'[189] more clearly than earlier in the century, when the procedural framework meant that these points could simply be assumed. The continued influence of historical accounting procedures upon substantive principle is neatly illustrated by Ashburner at the close of the Victorian era: in his view, the measure of trustee liability is derived from two principles – trustees who 'improperly' dispose of trust assets are chargeable *as if* they have retained the asset; and trustees guilty of neglect are treated *as if* they have obtained the asset at the proper time.[190]

At the same time, it seems likely that the new direct practice influenced contemporary thinking in another direction. Lawyers began to draw analogies between the 'sui generis'[191] equitable wrongdoing of a negligent trustee and a tortious claim for damages. Other factors perhaps encouraged this development too. On the one hand, the Trustee Act 1888 introduced for the first time statutory limitation periods for 'any action or other proceeding' in respect of negligent breach of trust, but none where the 'claim' was 'founded upon any fraud' to which the trustee was privy, or was brought 'to recover trust property'.[192] On the other hand, the increasing range of discretions given to trustees puts further strain on 'due performance' as a concept for quantifying trustee liability. Take a case where a trustee had negligently mismanaged trust property. How was the court to measure liability by reference to a 'due performance' idea, if a reasonable trustee could have performed in several different ways? As Getzler has shown, late nineteenth-century courts came to examine the prior question of breach of duty by reference to a reasonableness standard.[193] In turn, 'reparative claims' for breach of trust could more easily be analogised to tortious claims for damages. Thus, in *Re Massingberd's Settlement* (1890),[194] counsel (albeit unsuccessfully) argued that trustees were not bound to reconstitute the trust estate, because trustees negligently exercising their powers only bear 'ordinary responsibility for actual loss'; and in *Webb v Jonas* (1888)[195] and *Re Salmon* (1889),[196] we see a sharper distinction being drawn between unauthorised investments and negligently exercised investment powers. Similarly, in *Re Bowden* (1890), a limitation dispute, counsel argued that suits against trustees for negligent mismanagement were 'equitable action[s] on the case for negligence'.[197] The persistence of accounting ideas is illustrated by opposing counsel's reply: the claim was 'entirely different from an

[188] See, eg, *Head v Gould* [1898] 2 Ch 250, 266–27; *Re Stevens* [1898] 1 Ch 162, 169–70; *Re Wrightson* [1908] 1 Ch 789, 798–99.

[189] See, eg, *Adamson* (n 17) 819; *Webb v Stenton* (1883) 11 QBD 518, 526–27, 531; *Sharp v Jackson* [1899] AC 419, 426.

[190] W Ashburner, *Principles of Equity* (London, Butterworth & Co, 1902) 196–97.

[191] A Underhill, *A Practical and Concise Manual of the Law Relating to Private Trusts and Trustees*, 4th edn (London, Butterworth & Co, 1894) 585.

[192] 51 & 52 Vict. c 59, s 8.

[193] Getzler, 'Duty of Care' (n 26) 62–69. See in particular, *Speight* (n 185).

[194] *Massingberd* (n 155) 297.

[195] *Webb v Jonas* (1888) 58 LT 882.

[196] *Salmon* (n 187) 368–69.

[197] *Re Bowden* (1890) 45 Ch D 444, 448 (arguendo).

action to compel a trustee to replace a fund' – it was an action 'to pay money into a fund as against which the applicant has a claim'.[198]

V. Conclusions

The challenges of doctrinal legal history are well-known: the conceptual framework within which adjudication took place is often difficult to discern, known only to a small legal community;[199] and it is all too easy to read modern legal ideas into historical material.[200] Both issues are especially acute when studying the pre-history of 'equitable compensation' for breach of trust and its relation to court-supervised accounting. After all, 'difficult legal and equitable questions' were constantly arising in court-supervised accounting;[201] masters did not always act uniformly in resolving such difficulties;[202] and even when exceptions were taken to a master's report, judicial statements 'did not necessarily clarify the principles'.[203] Even so, it is possible to reconstruct the procedural framework assumed by the earlier case law – one which changed much more than existing literature suggests. Moreover, we have seen that accounting procedures did not recognise 'substitutive claims' for unauthorised dispositions and 'reparative claims' for negligent management as equivalent to distinct causes of action with different elements and measures of relief. This is not to deny the stringency of the default position produced by the accounting relationship, well-recognised by contemporaries.[204] It is rather to emphasise that the purpose and terms of a trust always mattered in determining trustee liability, which was always designed to replicate due performance.

This historical analysis has implications for lawyers today too. Although the extent to which trustees should be able to limit their liability by raising questions of causation is an open one,[205] the general approach taken by modern courts is less unorthodox than usually supposed. Modern authorities emphasise that a beneficiary is entitled to due performance of the trust according to its terms, and that the scope of a trustee's duties, as well as the purpose and function of the trust, should always inform the measure of liability.[206] This suggests that *Target Holdings* and *AIB* need not be treated as a clean slate for a new law of equitable compensation. In both cases, the trustees had duties to make dispositions following particular steps, and it perhaps makes sense that relief was given by reference to a counterfactual where the trustees had taken those steps. The trustees, after all, had few discretions and so it was clear what due performance

[198] ibid. See too *Howe v Earl Winterton* [1896] 2 Ch 626, 642–43.

[199] Sir J Baker, *The Law's Two Bodies* (Oxford, Oxford University Press, 2001).

[200] F Maitland, *Why the History of English Law is Not Written: An Inaugural Lecture* (Cambridge, Cambridge University Press, 1888) 13–15.

[201] Chancery Commission, *First Report* (n 51) 77.

[202] See, eg, Polden (n 5) 676.

[203] Conaglen (n 1) 40.

[204] See, eg, *Fyler v Fyler* (1841) 3 Beav 550, 563–64; 49 ER 216, 222.

[205] See, eg, *Auden McKenzie* (n 23) [57]–[64].

[206] *Target Holdings* (n 21) 434, 436; *Youyang Pty Limited v Minter Ellison* (n 19), [36], [40], [49]; *AIB* (n 8), [70]–[71], [108], [136]–[137].

would have involved. That does not mean that principles formulated to deal with trusts drafted in the nineteenth century necessarily hold the key to solving modern problems – especially in light of recent trends towards widely drafted discretionary powers.[207] Nonetheless, it is easier to appreciate the reasons behind legal rules by taking a long view of their development. In the case of trustee liability, this is not possible without understanding the procedures through which such liability was determined.

[207] See L Smith, 'Massively Discretionary Trusts' (2017) 70 *Current Legal Problems* 17; Getzler, 'Duty of Care' (n 26).

21

Equity after Fusion: The View from Legal Treatises

CATHARINE MACMILLAN

I. Introduction

What happened to equity after the fusion of law and equity in nineteenth-century England? Discussion of this question frequently concentrates on whether the fusion which occurred was substantive or procedural.[1] The general consensus is that it was largely procedural, although, as Joshua Getzler has observed, the best view is that the two systems have been converging ever since.[2] Confusion attends this convergence, however. In some areas equity has a strong and certain presence. Trust law is one example. In other areas uncertainty attends the role of equity in relation to the common law. Contract law is an example of that. Writing extra-judicially, Lord Burrows has noted the puzzling distinction between law and equity in private law.[3] The puzzlement and uncertainty are greatest in those areas of law where the Court of Chancery's equitable jurisdiction was concurrent with the common law jurisdiction of the courts of common law. It is argued in this chapter that an important factor underlying these puzzling distinctions and uncertainties is the way in which legal treatises and their use in legal education, from fusion onwards, synthesised and analysed the interface between the common law and equity in areas of concurrent jurisdiction. The way in which knowledge about the changes brought about by the Judicature Acts 1873–1875[4] was formed and transmitted amongst law students and lawyers provides a novel explanation for modern uncertainties about fusion. It is argued here that treatises concerned with both common law and equity, and with a readership of both students and lawyers, approached

[1] See, eg, JCP Goldberg et al (eds), *Equity and Law: Fusion and Fission* (Cambridge, Cambridge University Press, 2019); P Sparkes, '*Walsh v Lonsdale*: The Non-Fusion Fallacy' (1988) 8 *Oxford Journal Legal Studies* 350; B Fitzgerald, '*Walsh v Lonsdale*: Eighties Style?' (1990) 6 *Queensland University of Technology Law Journal* 119; PM Perell, 'A Legal History of the Fusion of Law and Equity in the Supreme Court of Ontario' (1988) 9 *Advocates Quarterly* 472.

[2] J Getzler, 'Patterns of Fusion' in P Birks (ed), *The Classification of Obligations* (Oxford, Clarendon Press, 1997).

[3] A Burrows, 'We Do This at Common Law but That in Equity' (2002) 22 *Oxford Journal of Legal Studies* 1.

[4] 36 & 37 Vict, c 66; 38 & 39 Vict, c 77.

fusion in a way which tended to ignore, marginalise or re-characterise the role of equity in contract law. The result has been to leave modern lawyers with a sense that they have somehow missed something: in Lord Burrows's words,

> I began to think that the explanation for all this was in a crucial lecture or tutorial in the contract course that I had missed or that it was buried in the pages in the text that I had somehow overlooked.[5]

It is also a result which fulfils some (but not all) of the fears of the pre-fusion Equity Bar that equity would lose its distinct character following the enactment of the Judicature Act 1873.

This chapter examines the enactment of the Judicature Act 1873 and the attendant concerns of contemporaries. It then explores two interrelated topics, legal education and legal treatises. While these subjects have received some consideration in legal historical scholarship, this chapter explores several new areas: the writing of equity treatises; the activities of law coaches and crammers in the role of legal education; and the production by law coaches of manuals or 'low' treatises in equity and contract. The chapter then reaches new conclusions as to why modern lawyers are left with the sense that, somehow, something is missing or overlooked in the study of equity in contract law.

II. The Judicature Act 1873: Fusion and its Critics

One of the most significant legal reforms of the nineteenth century was the amalgamation of the administration of common law and equity in a single court by the Judicature Acts 1873–75. The legislation followed decades of debate as to how to create a convergence of law and equity to alleviate problems of cost and delay,[6] and several earlier statutes which had unsuccessfully attempted some procedural convergences between courts of common law and equity.[7] Different visions of fusion existed in the nineteenth century.[8] In 1867 a royal commission was established to examine the situation. Chaired by Lord Cairns, the Judicature Commission had a distinguished membership and a novel remit, the focus of which was on the administration of justice and how the procedures surrounding the dispensation of justice 'may be advantageously made so as to provide for the more speedy, economical, and satisfactory dispatch of the judicial business now transacted' by the courts.[9] After years of deliberation the Judicature Commission's recommendation was the consolidation of the superior courts of law and

[5] Burrows (n 3) 2.

[6] M Lobban, 'Preparing for Fusion: Reforming the Nineteenth Century Court of Chancery [Parts 1 and 2]' (2004) 22 *Law and History Review* 389 and 565; P Polden, 'The Judicature Acts' and 'The Court of Chancery' in WR Cornish et al *The Oxford History of the Laws of England, vol XI: 1820-1914 English Legal System* (Oxford, Oxford University Press, 2010).

[7] Chancery Amendment Act 1858 (21 & 22 Vict, c 27); Common Law Procedure Act 1852 (15 & 16 Vict, c 76); Common Law Procedure Act 1854 (17 & 18 Vict, c 125); Common Law Procedure Act 1860 (23 & 24 Vict, c 126).

[8] M Lobban, 'What Did the Makers of the Judicature Acts Understand by 'Fusion'?' in Goldberg et al (n 1).

[9] PP 1868–9 [4130] 4.

equity, together with the courts of Probate, Divorce and Admiralty, for such a 'consolidation would at once put an end to all conflicts of jurisdiction'.[10] While this was a procedural consolidation, the Commissioners acknowledged that the ancient division between the courts of common law and equity had

> led to the establishment of two systems of Judicature, organized in different ways, and administering justice on different and sometimes opposite principles, using different methods of procedure, and applying different remedies.[11]

No attempt was made to accomplish a substantive fusion of the jurisprudence of these two systems or to consider how this might come about by reason of an administrative fusion. This appears odd, given that the substance of English law, both common law and equity, had largely developed under the influence of procedures. However, contemporaries generally viewed such a substantive fusion as best arising from the codification of English law, and the prospect of codification was lost when the Digest of Law Commission of 1866, chaired by Lord Westbury, and with an overlapping membership with the Judicature Commission, abandoned attempts even to digest English law because the expense was prohibitive.

Lord Selborne's Judicature Bill of February 1873[12] sought to implement the procedural convergence recommended by the Judicature Commission. Bringing together 'many divided Courts and divided jurisdictions' in one Supreme Court of Justice in which judges exercised an undivided jurisdiction would 'unite within itself all the jurisdictions of all the separate Courts of Law and Equity'.[13] Lord Selborne, a member of the Digest of Law Commission, was well aware of the challenges of a substantive fusion of law and equity and desired to bring forward a Bill that would pass. He resisted calls to abolish the distinction between law and equity because to do so would be to abolish trusts, and thus the distinction between legal and equitable estates.[14] Instead, he proposed to resolve those ('not very numerous')[15] discrepancies between law and equity by allocating certain cases to a particular division and with the general proviso that where there was any conflict between the two, equity would prevail. The legislature would effect an administrative fusion, leaving to judges the determination of how such fusion would occur as a matter of substantive law. Although it was not framed in these terms, the effect of the Bill would be to assign that which formed the exclusive jurisdiction of equity to the Chancery Division and to assign much of the concurrent jurisdiction to the other divisions.[16] The Judicature Bill had the support of three eminent Equity judges in the House of Lords, namely Lord Selborne, Lord Cairns and Lord Hatherley, and along with cross-party political support, this persuaded many who might otherwise

[10] ibid 9.

[11] ibid 5.

[12] Supreme Court of Judicature Bill (1873) HL Bill 158.

[13] Hansard, 3d series, vol 214 cols 336–7 (13 February 1873).

[14] ibid col 339. Lord Hatherley, on the second reading, reaffirmed the view that 'the distinction between law and equity could not be at once abolished by any measure [for] … [t]here must be a distinction between legal and beneficial ownerships, and this Bill did not seek to wipe away those distinctions': Hansard, 3d series, vol 214 col 1717 (11 March 1873).

[15] ibid.

[16] Discussed in greater detail below at 466–71.

have doubted the Bill.[17] Lord Westbury, a proponent of a substantive fusion,[18] was too ill to attend the debates, and the absence of one 'whose attacks [upon the Judicature Bill] were most to be feared'[19] was a further reason for its successful enactment.

The Judicature Bill was, though, subject to an extraordinary criticism by almost all of the Equity bar. In two letters, one signed by nearly all the Queen's Counsel at the Equity Bar and the other signed by nearly all the remaining members of the outer Equity Bar,[20] these barristers expressed their concern that equity jurisprudence would be damaged if it were no longer devised and maintained by the Court of Chancery. They said that equity 'has hitherto been administered by Judges trained in its doctrines and imbued with its traditions'.[21] The establishment of the proposed divisions within the Supreme Court of Judicature was one in which three-quarters of the judges would be common law judges, and, in the Court of Appeal, none were to be equity judges. Equity would thus be applied by common law judges, men untrained in equity. The result, the Equity barristers feared, would 'endanger the very existence of Equity jurisprudence'.[22]

The Equity barristers' concerns that equity would be diminished in this proposed fusion were also presented in newspapers and periodicals. The greatest of these criticisms came from the equity barrister GW Hemming,[23] writing anonymously in *The Saturday Review*. Hemming argued that equity and law differed in substance, and accordingly, as equitable principles were more consonant with rational justice than those of the common law, the common law ought to be adapted to the standard of equity. The Bill proposed a reform, the effect of which would be that 'the principles of Equity will perish in an uncongenial atmosphere'.[24] This would follow from the abolition of the Court of Chancery and its writ of injunction over common law proceedings. In the new system of judicature, the numerical superiority of the common law judges would keep the equity judges in a helpless minority with no choice but to submit to the law as it would be administered.[25]

The Spectator advanced further concerns that the proposed fusion was 'a measure under which, if Equity is not to be at once extinguished it will "dwindle, peak, and pine," till its once beneficent power has ceased to be remembered'.[26] While an 'inner' equitable system, most noticeable in trusts or the married woman's separate estate, was a substantial part of the law, equity also consisted of 'a peculiarly subtle and complicated mass of "principles", [and] a still more involved and intricate accumulation of

[17] Anon, 'Law Reform. The Judicature Bill' (1873–1874) 8 *American Law Review* 175; Anon, 'The Judicature Bill' (1873) *Law Journal* 270; Anon, 'The Debate on the Judicature Bill' (1873) 55 *Law Times* 116, 117.

[18] FR Burns, 'Lord Westbury, Law Reform and Fusion' (2008) 29 *Journal of Legal History* 1, 30–36.

[19] Anon, 'The Ordeal of the Judicature Bill' *The Economist* 3 May 1874, 524.

[20] The letters were published: 'The Judicature Bill' *The Times* 28 April 1873, 8; 'The Judicature Bill' *The Times* 1 May 1873, 12.

[21] *The Times* 1 May 1873.

[22] *The Times* 28 April 1873.

[23] He later published these articles in GW Hemming, *Thoughts on the Fusion of Law and Equity suggested by the Lord Chancellor's Bill* (London, Macmillan, 1873).

[24] Anon (GW Hemming), 'The Lord Chancellor's Bill' *The Saturday Review* 22 February 1873, 232.

[25] Anon (GW Hemming), 'The Chancellor's Bill' *The Saturday Review* 1 March 1873, 267. See also 'The Chancellor's Defence of His Bill' *The Saturday Review* 15 March 1873, 332 and 'The Judicature Bill' *The Saturday Review* 5 April 1873, 436.

[26] Anon, 'The Revolt of the Equity Bar' *The Spectator* 3 May 1873, 565.

precedents'.[27] The continued existence of this particular jurisprudence was endangered because common law judges, 'trained in another school', one reliant upon the Court of Chancery to overturn the rigidities of this other school, could not safely be presumed to administer justice in the way that it was currently administered. The problem was particularly acute where the equitable principle arose by way of a defence in a common law claim before a court composed exclusively of common law lawyers.[28] The critics' proposed solution was to increase the number of equity judges at both first instance and appellate level. It was also suggested by many critics that an equity judge should always sit with common law judges.[29] A 'parsimonious spirit'[30] which animated the cabinet meant that neither proposal was implemented.

The criticisms of these equity barristers were not universally accepted. A paper on 'The Re-organisation of our Judicial System' at the Law Amendment Society found discussants largely in support of the Bill.[31] The view in *The Law Journal* was that the judgments of Equity judges in the Court of Appeal would be sufficient to 'control and educate common law lawyers'.[32] Arthur Wilson, writing anonymously[33] in the *Solicitor's Journal*, thought Hemming's claims exaggerated[34] and that the effect of the reforms would be very slight.[35] Wilson agreed that the majority of judges would be common law judges, but of necessity, as most judicial business was common law. While common law judges would have to learn equity, this was something they were capable of doing. Equity was 'not an aroma, nor a mystic tradition ... but a body of positive law' which every man of sufficient intellectual capacity was capable of understanding and applying.[36] It was also observed that since the mid-century common law courts had taken a broader and less technical view of the law 'to do ... substantial justice between the parties without violating settled principles of Law'.[37] Common to these viewpoints was the belief that if the Judicature Bill did not pass, the reform agreed by all to be needed would be most unlikely to occur. Reform was necessary to deal with the most pressing of problems, namely the increase of litigation that required adjudication.[38]

In the end, the Judicature Bill was passed with little substantive amendment made to address the criticisms that equity would suffer. The accommodation of equity and common law was achieved in three critical sections of the Judicature Act 1873. By section 24 the High Court of Justice and the Court of Appeal were able to administer law and equity concurrently in every civil matter or cause commenced in the High Court. Section 25 provided rules for the adjudication of certain points and concluded

[27] ibid 565–66.

[28] GW Hemming, 'Equity, Law and Justice', Letter to the Editor, *The Times* 15 May 1873, 12.

[29] 'A Q.C.', 'To The Editor of The Times' *The Times* 1 May 1873, 12; Anon, *The Times* 2 May 1873, 10; 'Revolt of the Equity Bar' (n 26).

[30] 'Revolt of the Equity Bar' (n 26) 566.

[31] Anon, 'Societies and Institutions: Law Amendment Society The Judicial System' (1872–1873) 17 *Solicitors' Journal* 388–89 (15 March 1873).

[32] Anon, 'The Judicature Bill' (1873) 8 *Law Journal* 193 (5 April 1873).

[33] His articles were later published: A Wilson, *Equity and the Judicature Bill* (London, King & Co, 1873).

[34] Anon (A Wilson), (1872–1873) 17 *Solicitors' Journal* 475 (19 April 1873).

[35] Anon (A Wilson), 'The Projected Law Reform' (1873) 17 *Solicitors' Journal* 361 (8 March 1873).

[36] Anon (A Wilson), 'Fusion' (1873) 17 *Solicitors' Journal* 513 (3 May 1873).

[37] W Forsyth, 'Law, Equity and Justice', Letter to the Editor, *The Times* 12 May 1873, 13.

[38] Anon, (1873) 55 *Law Times* 116, 117 (14 June 1873).

in subsection (11) with the stipulation that in all matters not specifically provided for in the Act and where there existed 'any conflict or variance' between the rules of equity and those of common law, the rules of equity prevailed.[39] Finally, section 34 established which causes and matters were to be assigned to particular divisions of the High Court. The Chancery Division was to hear all matters given to the exclusive jurisdiction of the Court of Chancery under any Act of Parliament.[40] To this was added specific causes and matters pertaining to what had been the core, and exclusive, jurisdiction of the Court of Chancery.[41] As observed in *The Times*, the result was, at least initially, 'business shall be so distributed as to run in the old grooves so far as possible'.[42]

In the case of contract law, though, a separation had been inadvertently made. In those cases where a contract came within the enumerated divisions of section 34, or where the cause sought an equitable remedy (specific performance, rectification or cancellation of deeds and written instruments), the matter would be heard by the Chancery Division; in this sense the business ran in the old groove. However, in the case of contracts outside these enumerated instances, many such cases would now be heard in a common law division of the High Court and not in Chancery. An important consequence was that such cases would be separated out from a distinctly equitable environment where cases were decided with reference to encompassing considerations such as conscience,[43] which, because it related to the particular parties, was necessarily discretionary. Henceforth cases heard in common law divisions would be decided by judges who might not appreciate the finer equitable jurisprudence and who were attempting to adjudicate on the basis of a less discretionary, more rules-based approach.

A century and a half after the passage of the Act, it is clear that English law retains a distinct body of equity jurisprudence, of which the law of trusts is the most obvious manifestation. And yet, it is apparent that in contract law the Judicature Acts worked a substantive change in the progress of those areas where the jurisdiction of equity had been concurrent with that of common law.[44] As Stephen Waddams has demonstrated, subsequent developments in contract law indicate that there was some substance to the concerns of the Equity bar.[45] Common law courts, which had been confident in their ability to lay down rules in rather absolute terms and accustomed to the amelioration of

[39] Judicature Act 1873, s 25(11). As Maitland later observed, since the relationship between law and equity was not one of conflict, this was a subsection with a very limited operation: FW Maitland, *Equity: A Course of Lectures* (Cambridge, Cambridge University Press, 1936, reprinted 1969) 152–153.

[40] ibid s 34(2).

[41] ibid s 34(3). These were: the administration of estates; the dissolution of partnerships or the taking of partnership or other accounts; the redemption or foreclosure of mortgages; the raising of portions or other charges on land; the sale and distribution of the proceeds of property subject to any lien or charge; the execution of trusts; the rectification, or setting aside, or cancellation of deeds or other written instruments; the specific performance of contracts between vendors and purchasers of real estates; the partition or sale of real estates; and the wardship of infants and the care of infants' estates.

[42] Anon, 'The Lord Chancellor's "Supreme Court of Judicature Bill"' *The Times* 27 February 1873, 9.

[43] M Macnair, 'Equity and Conscience' (2007) 27 *Oxford Journal of Legal Studies* 659 has argued that the meaning attributable to 'conscience' lay in the private knowledge of the parties, that this had moral overtones, and that it formed a theoretical basis for Chancery intervention.

[44] C MacMillan, 'The Lasting Impact of the Judicature Acts 1873-75 upon Contract Law' in TT Arvind and J Steele (eds), *Contract Law and the Legislature* (Oxford, Hart Publishing, 2020).

[45] S Waddams, 'Equity in English Contract Law: The Impact of the Judicature Acts (1873-75)' (2012) 33 *Journal of Legal History* 185.

their decisions in cases of severe injustice by Chancery, now operated alone. Important elements of equity doctrine disappeared as they were inconsistent with common law rules. Patrick Polden has demonstrated the challenges that arose from a combination of equity and common law judges, which required those trained in the common law to undertake justice in another form.[46] This worked to produce a new form of contract law which had 'a distinctly individualistic tone where parties contracted at their own risk' and which tolerated few excuses for non-performance.[47]

This chapter explores a new reason behind this changed role of equity within contract after the Judicature Act. Students learned law differently after the Judicature Act, and jurists wrote about equity and contract in different ways. There was, in short, a change in the perception of equity within contract law, as a result of which the traditional equitable concerns of Chancery in contract adjudication lost their importance in the areas of concurrent jurisdiction in contract law. In 1873 critics were concerned that common law judges, untrained in equity, would somehow fail to do equity. They were concerned about 'how to secure the administration of justice while we are educating a race of judges under the new system'.[48] What they did not consider was that the very substance of the law would change in areas such as contract law because they envisioned a static rather than a dynamic body of equity. In addition, they did not anticipate how perceptions of equity could be altered through changes in legal education and legal writing.[49]

III. Legal Education: Universities, Crammers and Coaches

In the years after fusion, the numbers of legal practitioners in both branches of the legal profession increased, and legal education changed. The Bar, during Victoria's reign, experienced a complete change in its professional ideas.[50] The close of the nineteenth century saw a profoundly different landscape of legal education from that which existed at its beginning. In 1846 the Select Committee on Legal Education found '[n]o Legal Education worthy of the name of a public nature at this moment' in England or Ireland;[51] this altered entirely within seventy-five years. An increasingly professional and systematic form of legal education replaced an earlier form based on practical learning acquired in a barrister's chambers or a solicitor's office.[52] Legal

[46] P Polden, 'Mingling the Waters' [2002] *Cambridge Law Journal* 575.

[47] W Cornish et al, *Law and Society in England 1750-1950*, 2nd edn (Oxford, Hart Publishing, 2019) 216.

[48] AE Miller, 'General Correspondence: Fusion' (1872–73) 17 *Solicitors' Journal* 556 (17 May 1873).

[49] This is not to say that these participants were unaware of the importance of legal education to the profession. See, eg, the observations of Lord Selborne to the Legal Education Association: Anon, 'Lord Selborne on Legal Education' *The Times* 9 July 1874, 7.

[50] R Cocks, *Foundations of the Modern Bar* (London, Sweet & Maxwell, 1983) 5.

[51] Report from the Select Committee on Legal Education (1846) PP [686] lvi.

[52] The processes of this transformation are described in B Abel-Smith and R Stevens, *Lawyers and the Courts* (London, Heinemann, 1967) chs 3, 7 and 13. See also WW Pue, 'Professional Legal Education at Queen's College, Birmingham, in the 1850s' in WW Pue, *Lawyer's Empire: Legal Professions and Cultural Authority 1780-1950* (Vancouver, University of British Columbia Press, 2016); MH Hoeflich, 'The Americanization of British Legal Education in the Nineteenth Century' (1987) 8 *Journal of Legal History* 244. For earlier nineteenth-century teaching practices and calls for reform see CW Brooks and M Lobban, 'Apprenticeship or Academy? The Idea of a Law University, 1830-1860' in JA Bush and A Wijffels (eds), *Learning the Law: Teaching and the Transmission of Law in England 1150-1900* (London, Hambledon Press, 1999).

education shifted to one based upon lectures, tutorials and set reading;[53] ultimately, examinations were also integral to such modes of institutional learning. Institutional legal education occurred at two levels: the universities and private crammers or law coaches who taught to the professional examinations. While law was taught only in Oxford, Cambridge and London before fusion, by 1909 HD Hazeltine could speak of the existence of English law schools,[54] and in 1908 the Society of the Public Teachers of Law was formed.[55] David Sugarman has considered how university law teaching and the creation of treatises by academics to facilitate this teaching had an enduring impact on the way in which modern common law lawyers think about law.[56] Contract and equity were subjects of study for both universities and the professional bodies. The teaching of each was facilitated by the creation of subject-specific treatises which sought to make the law understandable to the novice by rationalising and systematising it, usually through an architecture of inter-locking principles. The academic teaching of law thus improved the quantity and quality of legal treatises.[57]

While this process has been examined in relation to universities, it has not been scrutinised in relation to private crammers or law coaches, of whom little study has been made.[58] While the full scale of their activities cannot be gauged, it is apparent that as a group they taught law to more students than the universities and the professional bodies.[59] The Judicature Act 1873 followed upon the 1872 introduction of a written examination for the Bar, bringing entrance requirements closer to those which already existed for solicitors. This was not entirely accidental, as the administration of justice was linked to legal education and professional standards. What was accidental was the way in which most students came to be prepared for their professional examinations.

As potential entrants to the professions increased, there was a rapid growth in a new legal education 'industry'.[60] This industry centred around professional crammers or law coaches and took a large variety of forms, from private sessions or classes in

[53] P Polden, 'The Education of Lawyers' in *OHLE vol XI* (n 6) 1175–1201; AH Manchester, *Modern Legal History* (London, Butterworths, 1980) 54–66.

[54] HD Hazeltine, 'Present State of Legal Education in England' (1910) 26 *Law Quarterly Review* 17. Hazeltine included not only those law schools to be found at universities (Oxford, Cambridge, London, Manchester, Liverpool, Sheffield and Leeds) but also those of the professional societies at the Inns of Court and the Law Society. To this latter group he also included the provincial law schools concerned with the instruction of articled clerks.

[55] AD Bowers, 'The Founding of the Society' (1959) 5 *Journal of the Society of Public Teachers of Law (NS)* 1. The President of this new Society linked the academic teaching of law to its practice: WS Holdsworth, 'The Vocation of a Public Teacher of Law' [1925] *Journal of the Society of Public Teachers of Law* 1, 11.

[56] D Sugarman, 'Legal Theory, the Common Law Mind and the Making of the Textbook Tradition' in W Twining (ed), *Legal Theory and Common Law* (Oxford, Basil Blackwell, 1986).

[57] Holdsworth (n 55) 10–11. Anson's *Principles of the English Law of Contract* was written around the particular requirements of the Oxford Law School: FH Lawson, *The Oxford Law School 1850-1965* (Oxford, Clarendon Press, 1968) 41. On the influence of American treatise writers, particularly Joseph Story, see Hoeflich (n 52) and GB Baker, 'Story'd Paradigms for the Nineteenth-Century Display of Anglo-American Legal Doctrine' in A Fernandez and MD Dubber (eds), *Law Books in Action* (Oxford, Hart Publishing, 2012).

[58] There is some consideration of crammers in Abel-Smith and Stevens (n 52) ch 4; P Leighton, 'The LLB as a Liberal Degree? A Re-assessment from an Historical Perspective' (2015) 22 *International Journal of the Legal Profession* 87, 93–97; RH Kersley, *Gibson's 1876-1962 A Chapter in Legal Education* (London, Law Notes Lending Library, 1973). I am indebted to David Sugarman for the last two references.

[59] Patrick Polden, in *OHLE vol XI* (n 6) 1195–1201, details the low attendance rates at both the Council of Legal Education and Law Society lectures.

[60] Leighton (n 58).

London to correspondence courses by post, from a detailed series of formal teaching over a course of several months to last-minute revision sessions. While many crammers operated individually, often for short periods of time, two organisations grew large enough to generate a considerable amount of legal literature over several decades. Both were formed by solicitors who were also in active legal practice. John Indermaur began his teaching on Chancery Lane in 1873 and was joined by a partner, Charles Thwaites, in 1888. Five doors down Chancery Lane, Albert Gibson began in 1876, and Arthur Weldon joined him in 1881. The teaching efforts of both entities were more deserving of the title law coach than crammer, a term they justifiably resisted.[61] Both sets of coaches ran sophisticated teaching operations: in addition to the classes they gave, they established lending libraries for students, produced periodical literature aimed at their students,[62] and wrote and published legal literature that was designed to assist students in the preparation of both Bar Council and Law Society examinations. Some students read this literature while undertaking university studies in other subjects;[63] there are also indications that it was read by students at the law schools in Oxford and Cambridge while undertaking their university studies.[64]

There has been no consideration of this literature or its impact upon legal knowledge or the development of English law. This is surprising because by the Second World War, Gibson and Weldon had effectively become a general law school for both branches of the profession,[65] and their candidates' examination results were enormously successful.[66] Indermaur and Thwaites, who ceased operation during the First World War, not only coached large numbers of students but were also prolific writers. The literature ranged from examination aids, in which suggested answers to questions were given along with study revision and preparation tips,[67] to reasonably detailed manuals devoted to the substantive consideration of a legal subject. These works crossed the Atlantic and were found in American and Canadian collections, giving an indication of the desire for these manuals.

The reception of such 'low' treatises was varied and also changed over time. The legal profession largely viewed them as helpful to students.[68] University professors, keen to establish their own faculties, were at best disdainful and at worst hostile towards

[61] Kersley (n 58) 2.

[62] Gibson and Weldon, and then the College of Law, published *Law Notes* from 1885 to 1994; Indermaur, and then Thwaites, published the *Law Students' Journal* from 1879 to 1917.

[63] See, eg, the autobiography of Patrick Yu Shuk-siu, *A Seventh Child and the Law* (Hong Kong, Hong Kong University Press, 1998) 100–108.

[64] See, eg, the many advertisements in the *Oxford and Cambridge Undergraduate's Journal* and note A Gibson, 'A Law University: To Be or Not To Be?' (1887) 6 *Law Notes* 16, 20. 'Where well-paid professors with fixed salaries are gathered together, there, too, will be found the 'coach,' and with more work than there would be for him without the University and its teachers.'

[65] Abel-Smith and Stevens (n 52) 183.

[66] 337 out of 394 candidates who attained First Class Honours in the Law Society examination between 1900 and 1939 were Gibson and Weldon students: Kersley (n 58) 3. Gibson and Weldon themselves published the many prizes won by their students: see, eg, A Gibson et al, *Gibson & Weldon's Aids to Equity*, 8th edn (London, Law Notes Publishing Office, 1908) i–iv.

[67] See, eg, A Gibson, *Aids to the Final; being A Complete Guide to Self-Preparation for the Final (Pass and Honors) Examinations of the Law Society*, 3rd edn (London, Reeves & Turner, 1885).

[68] See, eg, Anon, 'Law Library' (1873) 55 *Law Times* 163: 'it must prove of great assistance to beginners' (writing of Indermaur's *Leading Conveyancing and Equity Cases*).

them. One reviewer, probably Fredrick Pollock, wrote that the student who relied on one such manual 'will never be a sound lawyer, and we are sorry for him and his future clients';[69] of another he wrote 'this is one of a class of books – examination manuals – on which we think it right to look with suspicion';[70] of yet another, 'Messrs. Indermaur and Thwaites … present their customers with a bewildering succession of gross elementary blunders.'[71] At times the criticisms were deliberately cutting: reviewing the *Guide to Specific Performance*, the reviewer, likely Pollock again, described it as 'slovenly and inaccurate' and stated that 'it is with much regret that we point out so many serious errors in books likely to be used extensively by students'.[72] The view of the *Law Quarterly Review* was that there was no point in writing such books because there was no reason to compete with established authors such as Snell and Smith.[73] Successive editions of low treatises indicated otherwise. For present purposes, however, what is important is how both high and low treatises presented equity after fusion to law students and to lawyers.

IV. Legal Treatises

A change in legal education, combined with a new employment of novel forms of treatise writing, worked to change the perceptions of lawyers in relation to equity in contract. Students learning law in an institution studied a particular presentation of equity in contract rather than witnessing contract cases in Chancery. And lawyers in practice, and judges in giving judgments, both looked back to their earlier legal education and actively referred to the treatises which had supported this education. Treatises assumed a greater importance by the last quarter of the nineteenth century. Treatise writers planned to set the foundations of knowledge which students were expected to carry into their professional careers: 'the result [of understanding the treatise] was satisfactory and abiding'[74] and 'the law student of one year is the practitioner of the next'.[75] Treatises were often intended, in the words of the Scottish jurist George Joseph Bell, 'for the sudden occasions of practice'.[76] While the influence of jurists upon judges is complex and difficult to establish,[77] treatises have had a powerful impact upon the development

[69] Anon, '[Review of] *The Student's Conveyancing*: being specially intended for the use of Candidates at the Final and Honors Examinations of the Law Society. By Albert Gibson and Robert McLean. (London: Reeves and Turner. 1885. La. 8vo. Lx and 552pp.' (1885) 1 *Law Quarterly Review* 511, 512.

[70] Anon, '[Review of] *The Student's Guide to Trusts and Partnership*. By John Indermaur. (London: George Barber, 1885)'. 8 vo. 14pp. (1886) 2 *Law Quarterly Review* 106.

[71] Anon, '[Review of] *A Guide to the Criminal Law at the Bar Final and for Students generally*. by Charles Thwaites (London: George Barber, 1885). *The Student's Guide to the Principles and Practice of the Common Law* by John Indermaur (London: George Barber 1886)' (1886) 2 *Law Quarterly Review* 258.

[72] Anon, '[Review of] *The Student's Guide to Specific Performance and Mortgages* by John Indermaur and Charles Thwaites (London: George Barber, 1886)' (1886) 2 *Law Quarterly Review* 402, 403.

[73] Anon, '[Review of] A *Manual of the Principles of Equity*, by John Indermaur (London: Law Student's Journal Office, 1886)' (1887) 3 *Law Quarterly Review* 246.

[74] A Brown, *The Principles of Equity*, 10th edn (London, Stevens & Haynes, 1892) vii.

[75] HG Rivington and AC Fountaine, *The Principles of Equity*, 17th edn (London, Stevens & Haynes, 1915) v.

[76] KCG Reid, 'From Text-Book to Book of Authority: The Principles of George Joseph Bell' (2011) 15 *Edinburgh Law Review* 6, 12.

[77] N Duxbury, *Jurists and Judges: An Essay on Influence* (Oxford, Hart Publishing, 2001) 5–22.

of English contract law.[78] There is also a close relationship between the operation of the law and sources available to the lawyers who operate it.[79]

The late nineteenth century saw a changed approach to the writing of legal treatises. Writers sought to adopt a scientific approach, what Pollock termed a 'well devised order' and an easily accessible form of introduction for the student to elementary jurisprudence.[80] These treatises differed from earlier compilations of precedents or abridgements of cases. Treatises vary in form, but generally their authors attempt to take a legal subject and to provide a methodological exposition of the principles of the law.[81] Often the treatise works to 'crystallise' the understanding of a certain subject;[82] and this makes the treatment of equity in contract post-fusion significant. Importantly, the treatise purports 'to deal only with a single branch of the law that is conceived of as possessing some quality of unity'.[83] This desire for unity was challenged by the Judicature Acts on the problem of how to deal with both the equitable and common law aspects of contract law. Treatises had previously been written either on the common law of contract or on equity: this division largely continued after 1873. As we shall see, the effect was to separate the concurrent jurisdiction of contract away from treatises on equity and to separate equity from contract treatises.

A. Equity Treatises

The initial flurry of treatises specifically on the Judicature Acts 1873–75, whether written for practitioners[84] or students facing examinations,[85] were concerned with the new practice and procedures of the Acts. Despite the concerns that the Acts would in somehow diminish equity, this was not a point considered in these treatises. Nor was there any great analysis of any sort presented in these treatises: 'there was no room, or very little, for originality in a work on the subject which should be useful to the body of practising lawyers'.[86]

How, though, did works on equity consider fusion, particularly in relation to contract? Did they anticipate any conflict between the common law and equity? Did they posit how contract issues would best be resolved in this new fused administration? The extent to which writers of equity avoided these questions is rather remarkable. Once a treatise has

[78] AWB Simpson, 'Innovation in Nineteenth Century Contract Law' (1975) 91 *Law Quarterly Report* 247. See also S Waddams, 'The Authority of Treatises in English Law (1800-1936)' in M Godfrey (ed), *Law and Authority in British Legal History 1200-1900* (Cambridge, Cambridge University Press, 2016).

[79] D Ibbetson, 'Legal Printing and Legal Doctrine' (2000) 35 *Irish Jurist (NS)* 345, 345.

[80] F Pollock, 'Oxford Law Studies' (1886) 2 *Law Quarterly Report* 453, 455–56.

[81] The definition is from A Fernandez and MD Dubber, 'Introduction: Putting the Legal Treatise in Its Place' in *Law Books in Action* (n 56) 2.

[82] MJ Horwitz, 'Part III – Treatise Literature' (1976) 69 *Law Librarian's Journal* 46.

[83] AWB Simpson, 'The Rise and Fall of the Legal Treatise: Legal Principles and the Forms of Legal Literature' (1981) 48 *University of Chicago Law Review* 632, 633.

[84] A Wilson, *The Supreme Court of Judicature Acts, 1873 and 1875* (London, Stevens and Sons, 1875); A Rogers, *The Law and Practice of the Supreme Court of Judicature* (London, Butterworths, 1875); WD Griffith, *The Supreme Court of Judicature Acts 1873 and 1875* (London, Stevens and Haynes, 1875).

[85] J Indermaur, *The Students Guide to the Supreme Court of Judicature Acts 1873 & 1875* (London, Stevens and Haynes, 1875).

[86] Griffith (n 84) v.

been written, it is then unlikely to be substantially altered. This general point is supported by this particular study of post-fusion equitable treatises. To modern eyes, works on equity prior to fusion took a curious series of forms: few sought an orderly and scientific presentation of their topic, and none made any concessions to the novice. Some were concerned with Chancery practice, such as Jarman's *Practice of the Court of Chancery*[87] and Daniell's *Practice of the High Court of Chancery*,[88] and contained the minutia of a myriad of Chancery rules and procedures. Another form was a collection of cases, such as White and Tudor's *Leading Cases in Equity*,[89] containing leading cases, organised thematically, to which the compilers appended notes observing the principles laid down or acted upon in these cases. Neither format lent itself to any sort of predictive analysis of fusion.

A better format for such analysis lay in the construction of a treatise organising the substance of equity jurisprudence around principles.[90] This format had already been adopted in America in 1836 when the prolific treatise writer, Joseph Story, published *Commentaries on Equity Jurisprudence*[91] as a necessary obligation of his role at Harvard. Story wrote the first scientific treatise of equity, applicable in America and England. He sought to collect the general principles of equity from the case law and, in so doing, to 'define the various sources and limits of Equity Jurisdiction'.[92] A further object was to set out the leading doctrines (and the underlying reasons for the doctrines) which guided and governed courts of equity in exercising their jurisdiction, particularly where these doctrines were unique to equity or applied in a manner unknown in common law courts. To synthesise and analyse his treatment of equity, Story adopted[93] a three-fold division: first, the concurrent jurisdiction of courts of equity with common law; second, the exclusive jurisdiction of courts of equity; and third, the auxiliary or assistant jurisdiction. Although Story sought to give clarity to his subject with this division, Mike Macnair has observed that in dividing the jurisdiction up in this manner, Story and those who followed him, such as Snell, 'made their accounts less conceptually coherent' than if an historical approach had been taken to classifying equity jurisdiction.[94]

This approach to equity, though, was greatly reflected in the division of jurisdiction made by the Judicature Act 1873. Story 'was a master of exhaustive description and of consequentialist reasoning … a gifted technician with a knack for seeing the architectonic structure of legal systems'.[95] Story's abstraction of legal rules, designed to promote

[87] H Jarman, *The Practice of the High Court of Chancery*, 3rd edn (London, W Maxwell, 1864).

[88] L Field and E Clennell Dunn (eds), ER Daniell, *The Practice of the High Court of Chancery*, 5th edn (London, Stevens and Sons, 1871).

[89] FT White and OD Tudor, *A Selection of Leading Cases in Equity*, 4th edn (London, W Maxwell and Sons, 1872).

[90] Waddams's observation that the concept of principles in contract law was an elusive one is equally applicable to equity: S Waddams, 'Nineteenth-Century Treatises on English Contract Law' in *Law Books in Action* (n 57).

[91] J Story, *Commentaries on Equity Jurisprudence, as Administered in England and America* (Boston, MA, Hilliard, Gray & Co, 1836).

[92] ibid v.

[93] The same approach was taken in J Fonblanque, *A Treatise of Equity* (Dublin, J Byrne et al, 1793) and G Jeremy, *A Treatise on the Equity Jurisdiction of the High Court of Chancery* (London, J and WT Clarke, 1828).

[94] Macnair, 'Equity and Conscience' (n 43) 666.

[95] Baker, 'Story'd Paradigms' (n 57) 84. Baker also notes Story's tendency to verbosity, his adoption of popular jurisprudential buzzwords without an apparently complete sense of their meaning and only a limited reflection of the scientific epistemology in law or the theory of juristic knowledge.

uniformity of interstate or international practice, led to an instrumentalisation in law by him of scientific method, terminology and purposes.[96] His organisation, his appeal to reason, his use of English cases and the lack of a similar English work made his treatise hugely influential in England and formed the basis for English treatises.[97]

Edmund Snell's *Principles of Equity* became the greatest equity treatise of them all; it survives into the twenty-first century in a current edition. Its endurance, surprising given that Snell wrote only the first edition, indicates the overwhelming need of practitioners and students alike for a treatise on equity.[98] Like so many treatise authors, Snell's work grew from his lecture and study notes. Snell, born in India and a graduate of Madras University, was admitted to the Middle Temple in 1865 and attended the lectures of WL Birkbeck, the Inns of Court reader on equity. Snell adopted the organisation and analysis of *Story's Commentaries upon Equity* in his attempt to produce a treatise exploring equity jurisprudence on the basis of the principles he discerned from the cases. Snell began with a history of equity and equitable maxims and then followed Story's three-fold division of the jurisdictions of equity. Within the concurrent jurisdiction, where the law did not give adequate relief or gave relief only by a circuity of action but equity could give complete justice, he placed cases of accident, mistake, fraud and specific performance. After the publication of *Principles of Equity* in 1868, Snell returned to India, where he died of tuberculosis. The second (1872) and third (1874) editions of his work were written by his friend, John Griffith, before Griffith's own untimely death.

After this unpromising start of short-lived authors, further editions of the treatise were written by Archibald Brown for the next three decades. Under Brown, Snell's *Equity* became 'the student's favourite text-book',[99] recommended as a good work to prepare candidates for their law examinations.[100] Brown, a Scot and the son of a Selkirk factory manager, had an impressive academic background. Another member of Middle Temple, a recent graduate of both Oxford (MA, BCL) and Edinburgh (MA), a fellow attendee of Birkbeck's Inns of Court equity lectures, Brown had earlier translated and epitomised Savigny's treatise on obligations in Roman law.[101] He combined a practice at the Chancery Bar with the production of various legal treatises, of which *Principles of Equity* was the most significant. He characterised his purpose in 1875 as suggesting how fusion would operate and endeavoured to demonstrate in successive editions how it had operated.[102]

One might have thought Brown would adopt a more critical and scholarly approach to the issue of fusion, given his bold statement that the Judicature Acts meant that 'law and equity have in substance and effect been fused into one system'.[103] However, his

[96] ibid.

[97] See, especially, JW Smith, *A Manual of Equity Jurisprudence as Administered in England* (London, V and R Stevens and GS Norton, 1845) and EHT Snell, *The Principles of Equity, Intended for the Use of Students and the Profession* (London, Stevens and Haynes, 1868).

[98] R Griffith and R Castle, 'Who Was Snell?' (1991) 135 *Solicitors' Journal* 1041. I am indebted to Joanna McCunn for this reference.

[99] Anon, 'New Editions' (1898) 104 *Law Times* 603 (30 April 1898).

[100] Anon, 'Examinations at the Incorporated Law Society' (1893) 95 *Law Times* (15 July 1893) 245, 259.

[101] A Brown, *An Epitome and Analysis of Savigny's Treatise on Obligations in Roman Law* (London, Stevens & Haynes, 1872).

[102] A Brown (ed), EHT Snell, *The Principles of Equity*, 16th edn (London, Stevens & Haynes, 1912) v.

[103] A Brown (ed), EHT Snell, *The Principles of Equity*, 4th edn (London, Stevens & Haynes, 1878) 12.

retention of Snell's threefold division of equity jurisdiction meant that he did not, in truth, envision a substantive fusion. While every jurisdiction was, he explained, concurrent, reasons of convenience caused much of the former exclusive jurisdiction to be assigned to the Chancery Division.[104] His treatment of the former concurrent jurisdiction was unchanged, and while he recognised that the categorisation of an auxiliary jurisdiction was now completely meaningless, he nevertheless retained the threefold division because it illustrated the historical growth of equity[105] and for reasons of 'practical utility'.[106] His treatment of the Judicature Acts was confined to practical points in particular instances. He emphasised that equity would prevail in any conflict with law. Under his editorship, the treatise therefore affirmed the view expressed at the enactment of the Judicature Act 1873 that no substantive change had occurred while powerfully reinforcing this view.

Far more significant changes occurred in the next edition of *Snell* in 1915.[107] For the first time, *Snell* was written not by barristers but by a pair of solicitors, Henry Gibson Rivington and Arthur Clifford Fountaine. Moreover, they were not practising solicitors but partners in the law coaching business of Gibson and Weldon.[108] This meant that the same authors who wrote low treatises now also wrote high treatises. Changes in structure and approach were made. Removed was the threefold distinction of equity jurisdiction ('rendered obsolete by the Judicature Acts'[109]) and any consideration of auxiliary jurisdiction, although the order of topics remained the same. A new preliminary chapter concerned with the Judicature Acts was added: the Acts, it was explained, were necessary to fuse the administration of law and equity – 'a fusion of administration rather than of principles'[110] – and to remove any possibility of conflict between these systems. Section 25 of the 1873 Act, they emphasised, provided that in any conflict between the two, the rules of equity prevailed over the common law: *Walsh* v *Lonsdale* and *Job* v *Job* were studied as applications of the section.[111] Section 34 meant that matters formerly considered by the Court of Chancery were assigned to the Chancery Division, 'so that in practice equitable matters are usually dealt with in a separate Court'. The treatment of subjects within the former concurrent jurisdiction, small in comparison to that devoted to trusts, gave no hint of any form of fusion or amalgamation. For example, the mistake chapter (a subject 'of much difficulty') made no distinction between mistake at common law and mistake in equity despite the introduction of cases decided at common law. And while the discussion was brief, relief for mistake appeared to be explained as an absence of agreement between parties rather than Brown's vague explanation that mistakes fit for equity involved 'questions of construction, questions of conduct, &c., &c.'.[112] As we shall see, this

[104] ibid 14.
[105] ibid.
[106] ibid 15.
[107] HG Rivington and AC Fountaine (eds), EHT Snell, *The Principles of Equity*, 17th edn (London, Stevens and Haynes, 1915).
[108] Kersley (n 57) 15–23.
[109] Snell's *Equity* 17th edn (n 107) 11.
[110] ibid 11.
[111] ibid 9–10.
[112] Snell's *Equity* 16th edn (n 102) 396.

was a treatment much closer to that of contract treatises than to that of traditional equitable treatises.

Rivington undertook the next five editions, the final two on his own after Fountaine's premature and tragic death in a climbing accident. While he had many legislative changes to incorporate, most notably the fundamental changes brought by the 1925 property legislation, his treatment of topics surrounding fusion was unchanged since his first edition. A careful reader of the treatise would discern the influence of *Pollock on Contracts*, but there was no attempt to analyse equity in relation to common law in matters concerned with contract. Nor was the possibility considered that the substance of the law as it had existed prior to the Judicature Acts might have changed.

Subtle changes were wrought to the treatment of fusion and its effect upon the former concurrent jurisdiction of equity in contract with the authorship of Robert Megarry, which began in 1947. Megarry, now largely remembered as a Chancery judge, had been a teacher at Gibson and Weldon for a short period and continued to teach law until the 1960s.[113] His teaching titles (he also wrote *A Manual of the Law of Real Property*) were written with clarity and a certain levity. In *Principles of Equity* he hoped to 'relieve the prevailing gloom which so often seems to attend the subject'.[114] Megarry entirely reworked the structure of the book. While he opined that 'the substance of *Snell* is relatively little changed: this edition is less a case of putting new wine into old bottles than of making a new bottle for old wine',[115] his changes meant that the treatise was now resolutely focussed upon trusts and land. He severed the remaining vestiges of Snell's threefold distinctions of equity jurisprudence by removing the order and enumeration of the chapters and replacing them with new chapters. Equity was defined as that portion of natural justice suitable for judicial enforcement, historically provided by the Court of Chancery: 'the whole distinction between equity and law is not so much a matter of substance or principle as of form and history'.[116] The Judicature Act 1873 worked a fusion of administration, rather than of principles, which solved the mischief of parties being 'driven backwards and forwards' between courts of law and equity in a system where no 'Court had full power to grant relief in all cases'.[117] While it was important to distinguish between equitable and legal rights and remedies,[118] the Judicature Act placed 'most' of the equitable matters dealt with by the Court of Chancery in the Chancery Division.[119] Each High Court division was, though, vested with all jurisdiction. He emphasised the intention of the legislature that equity would prevail in cases of conflict by reason of section 25 and illustrated the judicial fulfilment of this intention in various areas.[120]

[113] P Gibson, 'Megarry, Sir Robert Edgar (1910–2006)' Oxford Dictionary of National Biography (Oxford University Press, 2004) doi.org/10.1093/ref:odnb/97469; Kersley (n 58).
[114] R Megarry, *Snell's Principles of Equity*, 23rd edn (London, Sweet & Maxwell, 1947).
[115] ibid vi.
[116] ibid 2.
[117] ibid 5.
[118] ibid 8.
[119] ibid 6.
[120] ibid 7. Four examples were given: *Walsh* v *Lonsdale* (1882) 21 Ch D 9 (equitable leases); *Berry* v *Berry* [1929] 2 KB 316 (variation of deed); *Job* v *Job* (1877) 6 Ch D 562 (executor's liability for assets); and *Lowe* v *Dixon* (1885) 16 QBD 455 (contribution claims between sureties). Such a short list indicates that in many cases a potential conflict was not considered.

Megarry made no reference to the fact that this administrative fusion resulted in a situation where common law divisions considered matters that had previously lain within the concurrent jurisdiction of equity without the all-encompassing considerations of equity. Indeed, the reverse is true of his treatment of this issue, since he ignored the substantive results of administrative fusion, a curious omission in a text which tried to stimulate further intellectual questions. Megarry also served 'notice' that some topics would be removed altogether in his next edition. These topics included mistake, a subject he identified as more properly belonging in a contract treatise. In what became the final chapter concerned with mistake in *Snell's Equity*,[121] the impact of contract treatises upon the topic is obvious. Removed from the Court of Chancery, mistake had become a subject 'of much difficulty' in which it 'is not easy to deduce a consistent body of doctrine from the decisions', which often contained other elements such as fraud and misrepresentation.[122] Megarry presented a confused accumulation of authorities on mistake without offering an underlying rationale for relief nor making any attempt to find one. The remedies of specific performance and rectification were granted where mistake worked a hardship, but contracts were avoided for mistake because the necessary element of true consent between the parties was not present. Consensus was a rationale borrowed from the contract treatises. Megarry also omitted to mention any distinction between mistake at law and in equity whilst simultaneously providing detailed consideration of older equity cases, such as *Cooper* v *Phibbs*. It was probably with relief that Megarry removed mistake from his next edition.

While the changes made in successive editions of *Snell's Equity* were gradual, it had become a title largely concerned with trusts. The structure of the Judicature Act 1873 – which worked well to preserve the traditional exclusive jurisdiction of the old Court of Chancery by placing it within the new Chancery Division – allowed treatise writers to write about fusion, and the subjects which had been within the concurrent jurisdiction, in a way which marginalised and overlooked the equitable principles, discretionary approach and concerns of conscience within the Court of Chancery. Fusion, it was repeatedly asserted, was administrative only. No attempt was ever made to consider the substantive changes wrought by fusion in areas such as mistake or undue influence. Increasingly, as we shall see, these were topics left to contract treatises. That equity would prevail over a conflicting principle of law was constantly stated without consideration of how such a conflict might arise. This was coupled with the endless, albeit confusing and unquestioning, reiteration that the difference between law and equity lay in history, not in principle.

Other equity treatises followed the same approach to fusion. Josiah Smith's *Manual of Equity Jurisprudence*,[123] also based *on Story's Commentaries*, was three decades old when fusion occurred. Smith dismissed the Judicature Acts as relating

[121] In the next edition, the chapter on mistake was removed and rectification was added to a new composite chapter on equitable remedies: R Megarry and PV Baker, *Snell's Principles of Equity*, 24th edn (London, Sweet & Maxwell, 1954).

[122] Snell's *Equity* 23rd edn (n 114) 441.

[123] JW Smith, *A Manual of Equity Jurisprudence, for Practitioners and Students*, 13th edn (London, Stevens and Sons, 1880).

almost entirely to practice and procedure, and not to jurisprudence, the subject of his treatise. The Acts 'do not make any general fusion of Law and Equity'. Indeed, the effect of the Judicature Acts was to 'leave the Chancery Division and other Divisions to themselves as heretofore'.[124] In his *Principles of Equity*, Thomas Roberts added a new chapter on the Judicature Acts but confined himself to quoting statutory sections with the added observation that equity prevailed in the event of any conflict.[125] Freeman Haynes went a bit further. He was the equity lecturer for the Incorporated Law Society whose verbose and rambling treatise on equity goes some way to explaining why so many students engaged the services of crammers and law coaches. He acknowledged the concerns that the effect of the Judicature Act 1873 might be 'to arrest the fair natural development of Equity Rules and Doctrines' but also stated that this apprehension had not as yet been realised and that any such danger would lessen every year.[126] In all other respects, his approach to fusion was that it was administrative only.

What of the treatises begun after 1875? The enactment of the Judicature Acts prompted WE Grigsby, sometime Vinerian Scholar and onetime Professor of Law at the Imperial University of Japan, to produce an English version of *Story's Commentaries*. The promise of this work was disappointed with Grigsby's focus upon the procedural aspects of the Acts, with his observation that the Acts 'relate in a very slight degree, if at all, to the principles of equity jurisprudence which are the subject of the present treatise'.[127] Ashburner's *Principles of Equity*[128] provided a more detailed and thoughtful consideration of the procedural role of the concurrent jurisdiction of equity in contract law, but did so in the complete absence of any consideration of how this might affect the substantive development of the law. He identified as the Acts' main object the ability for litigants to obtain the same remedy regardless of whether their claim or defence was legal or equitable. And it was in this context that he created the famous metaphor of two streams of jurisdiction flowing in the same channel without mingling their waters.[129] Following a scathing review in the *Law Quarterly Review*,[130] probably by Frederick Pollock, Ashburner never wrote another edition of his treatise (he also quit England and gave up law for many years). Something of a different approach can be found, however, in the writing of Harold Hanbury. In 1929 he delivered a paper at the Society of Public Teachers of Law meeting, in which he was critical both of the treatment of equity within contract treatises and also the absence of equity in the teaching of law. Concerned with

[124] SE Williams(ed), JW Smith, *A Manual of Equity Jurisprudence*, 15th edn (London, Stevens and Sons, 1900) 11.

[125] TA Roberts, *The Principles of Equity, as administered in the Supreme Court of Judicature*, 3rd edn (London, Butterworths, 1877).

[126] FO Haynes, *Outlines of Equity*, 5th edn (London, W Maxwell & Son, 1880) 14, fn (b).

[127] AE Randall (ed), Hon Mr Justice Story, *Commentaries on Equity Jurisprudence*, 3rd English edn (London, Sweet and Maxwell, 1920) 31.

[128] W Ashburner, *Principles of Equity* (London, Butterworth & Co, 1902).

[129] ibid 23. The repeated use of this metaphor is ironic because the treatise appears, otherwise, to have had little impact. It did not appear in a second, and last, edition until 1933, then under the authorship of Denis Browne.

[130] Anon, review of 'Principles of Equity. By W. Ashburner' (1903) 19 *Law Quarterly Review* 230. The review opened with the sentence '[t]his book contains the most extraordinary statement that it has ever been our fate to read' and concluded that the book 'contain[s] too many pitfalls to be a safe road for the student': at 234, 236.

the study of equity post-fusion, he strongly advocated that equity should be taught early in a programme of legal education:

> Students must early learn that in the field of contract law and equity have both played big parts, that the whole subject is a medley of legal and equitable rules and ideas, and it is on the solution of the ambiguities to which this dualities of origin has given rise … that the mastery of the law of contract depends.[131]

Hanbury had probably been influenced in this view by his own teacher, William Holdsworth.[132] In the first edition of *Modern Equity* in 1935, Hanbury sought to implement this ambition. While the 'lion's share' of his treatise was about trusts, he was also concerned to consider the relationship of law and equity post-fusion in a separate chapter. With regard to the Judicature Act 1873, he wrote that

> few great statutes have accomplished at once so much and so little; so much in that it replaced the old separate Courts of law and equity … and so little in that it dd not fuse the substantive rules of equity with the substantive rules of law.[133]

Hanbury viewed the influence of equity upon contract as profound, particularly with regard to mistake, misrepresentation and undue influence.[134] His treatise, though, primarily inspected the relationship of equity with contract law in relation to the equitable remedies of specific performance, injunctions and rectification.

The narrow approach to equity post-fusion was even more apparent in the much briefer guides, epitomes and outlines of equity, the 'low' treatises used by law students. These low treatises sometimes shared the same publishers as the high and it is clear that publishers often worked cooperatively with the editors and authors of low treatises. Six of the most important were written as direct guides or complements to Snell's *Principles of Equity*: Rivington's *Epitome of Snell's Equity*,[135] Blyth's *An Analysis of Snell's Principles of Equity*,[136] Indermaur's *Manual of the Principles of Equity*, and Gibson and Weldon's *Aids to Equity*. They all adopted the same approach to equity post-fusion as *Snell's Equity*, a narrowness exacerbated by the simplicity of their discussion. This is not surprising: Gibson and Weldon's *Aids to Equity* came to be written by Rivington when he also wrote *Principles of Equity* itself.[137]

While it is unfair to expect a study guide or outline to attempt an analysis of deeper questions of legal development, particularly given the comparative simplicity and limit of the questions set to the students by their examiners, the fact remains that these low treatises undoubtedly served as the sole source of legal information for many students,

[131] HG Hanbury, 'The Place of Equity in a Curriculum of Jurisprudence' (1930) 1930 *Journal of the Society of Public Teachers of Law* 28, 31.

[132] WS Holdsworth, 'Equity' in AL Goodhart and HG Hanbury (eds), WS Holdsworth, *Essays in Law and History* (Oxford, Clarendon Press, 1946).

[133] HG Hanbury, *Modern Equity, being the Principles of Equity* (London, Stevens and Sons, 1935) v.

[134] ibid 17.

[135] Rivington wrote the work as a companion to, rather than a replacement for, *Snell's Principles of Equity*; the title carried on after his death: P Jenkin (ed), *Rivington's Epitome of Snell's Equity, Twenty-Fourth Edition*, 4th edn (London, Sweet & Maxwell, 1954).

[136] EE Blyth, *An Analysis of the Twelfth Edition of Snell's Principles of Equity, with Notes Thereon* (London, Stevens and Haynes, 1898).

[137] A Gibson, A Weldon and H Gibson Rivington, *Gibson & Weldon's Aids to Equity: Intended as a Guide to that difficult but essential Work Snell's Principles of Equity* (London, The "Law Notes" Publishing Offices, 1908).

with the result that this was the basis of their knowledge and informed their understanding of equity post fusion. In essence, this boiled down to the propositions that equity was distinct from common law and that equity was that portion of natural justice usually administered in the Chancery Division to which the Judicature Acts, passed to better administer the law, had assigned most of Chancery's exclusive jurisdiction.[138] The difficult questions regarding the effect of the legislation on matters of concurrent jurisdiction were unmentioned and unapparent.

The great rival to Gibson and Weldon in the law coaching business, John Indermaur, produced a series of short study guides to equity,[139] longer manuals of equity[140] and epitomes of leading equity cases.[141] Here the student found that, to the extent that the Judicature Acts were mentioned, it was to state that they brought about an administrative fusion, that all divisions of the Supreme Court administered both systems of law and that in the event of a conflict, the rules of equity prevailed. Most of the work was concentrated on trusts and mortgages. Indermaur's *Student's Guide to the Supreme Court of Judicature Acts* simply explained that there was a nominal fusion of the Courts of Common Law and Courts of Equity to prevent the anomaly of two distinct courts with different jurisdictions.[142] Blyth's *Analysis of Snell's Principles of Equity* neatly summed up the situation by observing that while the fusion was procedural, section 34 assigned matters of exclusive jurisdiction to the Chancery Division with the effect that the exclusive jurisdiction was practically retained. So far as the concurrent jurisdiction was concerned, it was simply stated that '*legal* rights are enforced'.[143]

B. Contract Treatises

It was the writers of contract treatises who integrated equity with law in their consideration of contract law. The enactment of the Judicature Acts occurred as a revolution was underway in the writing of contract treatises. The archaic approach of Chitty's *Law of Contracts*, arranged around forms of contracts and procedural details, was giving way to a new scientific form of orderly compositions based on principles and structured around a will theory of contract. In developing this new approach to contract treatises, the authors were quick to realise the utility of equitable cases in contract law after the Judicature Acts, and they incorporated equitable cases within their treatises. The result was not always a happy one.

[138] ibid 2–3.

[139] J Indermaur, *The Student's Guide to the Principles of Equity* (London, G Barber, 1894); a second edition was written five years later with his partner, Charles Thwaites. The work set questions for students sitting the Bar Final based on Indermaur's *Manual of Equity*.

[140] J Indermaur, *A Manual of the Principles of Equity: A Concise Explanatory Treatise Intended for the Use of Students & the Profession*, 5th edn (London, G Barber, 1902).

[141] J Indermaur, *An Epitome of Leading Conveyancing and Equity Cases*, 8th edn (London, Stevens and Haynes, 1897). The work was intended as a guide to *Tudor's Leading Cases on Conveyancing* and *White and Tudor's Leading Cases in Equity*.

[142] J Indermaur, *The Student's Guide to the Supreme Court of Judicature Acts 1873 & 1875* (London, Stevens & Haynes, 1875) 9–10, 32.

[143] EE Blyth, *An Analysis of the Twelfth Edition of Snell's Principles of Equity with Notes Thereon* (London, Stevens and Haynes, 1898) 4 (original italics).

Stephen Martin Leake produced the first modern contract treatise in 1867.[144] Martin Leake sought to discern from cases the 'elementary rules and principles of the law of contracts',[145] and he then synthesised and analysed English law with the assistance of civilian jurisprudence.[146] The treatise was largely concerned with the common law but in a substantially revised second edition of 1878.[147] Martin Leake incorporated equitable aspects of contract law. To his section on duress he added a further section on undue influence, and he considered the jurisdiction of the court of equity to set aside agreements which had been induced by undue influence or pressure. He also moved from a consideration of 'Damages' for a breach of contract to a more comprehensive consideration of 'Remedies for Breach of Contract', where he wrote of the equitable relief provided by specific performance and injunctions.

Frederick Pollock's treatise, tellingly entitled *Principles of Contract at Law and in Equity*,[148] made the first real attempt to present a unified analysis of contract law post-fusion. Pollock began from the premise that the principles of English contract law had been concurrently developed in courts of law and equity and that this had 'led unavoidably to a … lamentable division of exposition in text-books'.[149] Writers on contract confined themselves to common law cases, leaving the equitable cases to works on equity, which rarely developed contract cases fully. The result was that the 'permanent elements and the broader principles of law on which the rules were in truth founded, were in danger of falling out of sight'.[150] Pollock was right in this diagnosis, but the manner in which he sought to cure the problem was an unfortunate one. In general terms, he was to employ equitable cases, particularly those which were involved with the vitiation or non-enforcement of contracts, to support his broader will theories of contract, which he derived from the work of the German jurist, Frederich von Savigny, and the French jurist, Robert Joseph Pothier.[151] Possibly because of his early experiences in the chambers of a conveyancer, Pollock tended to find equity 'peculiar': the technical language of equity jurists left much to be desired, for there were too many words and phrases imbued with a mysterious value which did not correspond to any definite ideas.[152] Probably because of this view, and because he did envision a substantive fusion of law and equity, Pollock was to employ equitable cases in which courts of equity had avoided a contract for reasons related to conscience and found that these cases supported Pollock's proposition that these were factors which disrupted the consent necessary to form a contract. One example is his treatment of the equitable mistake case, *Cooper* v *Phibbs*.[153] In successive editions Pollock began to obscure even the equitable origins of these cases.[154] Mistake was not an isolated example of this sort of treatment, for

[144] S Martin Leake, *The Elements of the Law of Contracts* (London, Stevens and Sons, 1867).

[145] ibid v.

[146] C MacMillan, 'Stephen Martin Leake (1826-1893)' in J Goudkamp and D Nolan (eds), *Scholars of Contract Law* (Oxford, Hart Publishing, 2022) 115–119.

[147] S Martin Leake, *An Elementary Digest of the Law of Contracts* (London, Stevens & Sons, 1878).

[148] F Pollock, *Principles of Contract at Law and in Equity* (London, Stevens and Sons, 1876).

[149] ibid v.

[150] ibid.

[151] See C MacMillan, *Mistakes in Contract Law* (Oxford, Hart Publishing 2010) 148–50.

[152] F Pollock, 'The Science of Case Law' in AL Goodhart (ed), F Pollock, *Jurisprudence and Legal Essays* (London, Macmillan & Co, 1961) 184.

[153] *Cooper* v *Phibbs* (1867) LR 2 HL 149, discussed in Pollock, *Principles of Contract* (n 148) 400–01.

[154] MacMillan, *Mistakes* (n 151) 167.

one finds Pollock doubting the wisdom of equitable cases in relation to representations,[155] and he added undue influence to the considerations of duress. While Pollock is now largely forgotten,[156] he had an outsized influence upon the development of contract law. This influence was reinforced by the vociferousness of his criticisms of scholarship and cases that did not fit with his own view.

While Pollock did not write for beginners, Sir William Anson did: AV Dicey wrote that no writer 'ever published a work more useful for the man just beginning his legal studies than Anson's *Principles of the English Law of Contract*'.[157] The treatise was written for students who studied contract law at Oxford, a subject begun in 1877. Like Pollock, Anson was a will theorist, influenced by both Pothier and von Savigny, and defined contract as an agreement enforceable in law made between two or more persons by which rights are acquired.[158] Having established what was required to reach a binding contract, Anson then turned to a chapter entitled 'The Reality of Consent'.[159] Here he considered circumstances which might remove the consent of both or either contracting party because there was no real expression of consent. Most of these circumstances were ones which fell within the concurrent jurisdiction of equity: mistake, misrepresentation, fraud, and undue influence. The significance of this inclusion is that these topics were moved from treatises on equity to those of contract. As we have seen, with the passing of time the equity treatise writers came to view this as the correct location for discussion of these circumstances.

There were fewer low treatises of contract law than of equity, possibly because Anson wrote with such clarity that the need for outlines was removed. The indefatigable Indermaur undertook *Principles of the Common Law*[160] which outlined contract and tort, primarily to prepare students for the Law Society examinations. The title began before Pollock's treatise had been published and adopted the then-prevailing practice of examining types of contracts rather than principles of contracts; it also considered contract at common law and not in equity. Indermaur was of the view that while the Judicature Acts worked 'to a certain extent' to fuse law and equity, equitable rules prevailed in any clash, and, in any event, the allocation of jurisdictions between the High Court divisions meant that the division of law and equity largely continued.[161] Indermaur retained this view throughout the period of his authorship,[162] but when the work was revived in 1922 by AM Wilshere,[163] he undertook a substantial revision of the title. While particular types of contract were still considered, the topic of contract

[155] Pollock, *Principles of Contract* (n 146) 478–480. By the fifth edition, the consideration of equity was diminished in relation to misrepresentations: F Pollock, *Principles of Contract*, 5th edn (London, Stevens and Sons, 1889) 542–576.

[156] N Duxbury, *Frederick Pollock and the English Juristic Tradition* (Oxford, Oxford University Press, 2004); S Hedley, 'Frederick Pollock and the Teaching of English Law' in Bush and Wijffels (n 52).

[157] HH Henson (ed), *A Memoir of the Right Honourable Sir William Anson* (Oxford, Clarendon Press, 1920) 93.

[158] Sir WR Anson, *Principles of the English Law of Contract* (Oxford, Clarendon Press, 1879) 8.

[159] ibid 115.

[160] J Indermaur, *Principles of the Common Law: An Elementary Work intended for the use of Students and the Profession* (London, Stevens and Haynes, 1876).

[161] ibid 3.

[162] J Indermaur and C Thwaites, *Principles of the Common Law*, 12th edn (London, Stevens and Haynes, 1914).

[163] AM Wilshere, *The Principles of the Law of Contracts and Torts* (London, Sweet & Maxwell, 1922).

was prefaced with an exposition of contract principles. This exposition was derived from the treatment of the subject by Pollock and Anson. Contract was a product of will, and in a new section on the 'Reality of Consent', vitiating elements were considered. While the Judicature Acts were mentioned, and it was stated that equity prevailed in a fused administration of justice, the consideration of vitiating elements was a distinctly common law one.

A few examples make the point. In outlining equitable fraud, the unconscionability upon which the court gave relief in *Aylesford* v *Morris* was greatly diminished with the direction that such a situation would now be considered under the Moneylenders Act 1900.[164] In considering mistake, Wilshere stated that in certain circumstances at common law, mistake prevented the formation of a contract. While he acknowledged that in a limited number of circumstances equity would provide relief in cases of a mistake (in cases of mistakes as to private law, or in the rectification of contracts, or in the refusal of specific performance), no basis was given for why equity so intervened.[165] The influence of the high treatises upon the low meant that the latter followed the former with the incorporation of equity into contract law in ways that tended to overlook the uniqueness and original flexibility of the Court of Chancery in determining these cases.

V. Conclusions

A number of conclusions can be drawn about the nature of equity after fusion. Lord Selborne introduced a major change in a deliberately conservative manner. This was a virtue insofar as it facilitated the passing of the statute, but it has created problems for the development of equity in areas of what had been the concurrent jurisdiction of equity. These were marginalised and ignored in the debates surrounding the Judicature Bill, as was the question of what sort of substantive fusion would occur outside those matters heard exclusively in the Chancery Division, and these issues remained unexamined in legal treatises. This mattered because these treatises were the principal form of legal literature of the day and also became the principal mechanism by which law students were educated. The development of large numbers of low treatises used extensively in teaching, the end of which was to attain examination success, further reinforced this state of affairs.

The examination of both high and low treatises in this chapter demonstrates how classifications create conceptual understanding. This arises not only in the classification within a particular treatise but also in how treatises on seemingly different subjects, in this case equity and contract, work to develop not only a particular genre but also the ambit and reach of that genre. In the consideration of equity post-fusion, treatises on equity ignored or marginalised the extent to which equity had in any way changed. At the same time, they reinforced the increasingly meaningless message that equity was 'that body of jurisprudence administered by the old Court of Chancery'. Changes to the substance of equity in areas where its jurisdiction was concurrent to the common

[164] ibid 86–89.
[165] ibid 89–95.

law were ignored by equity writers. Contract writers, who had previously approached the subject from a largely common law perspective, were much quicker to incorporate considerations of equity into their treatises. This is likely to have come about due to the development of a more dynamic tradition of treatise writing in contract law than in equity. This is probably because there was no great equity treatise produced in the nineteenth century by an author who was also closely associated with the new teaching of law in university faculties. The result of this treatise writing in both areas, though, was to both marginalise the role of equity in contract and re-cast equitable cases as essentially similar to common law cases. These treatises, as we have seen, were remarkably unchanged. This static treatment was accompanied by a high degree of similarity between treatises within a particular subject. These treatises worked, from the commencement of legal studies through to legal practice, to reinforce the essential message that nothing had really changed in the substance of equity. This created a certain rigidity of understanding around the subject, and the end result was that many of the concerns of the Equity bar in 1873 were realised.

What is curious about this process is less the inherent conservatism presented in treatise writing and education and more that treatise writers were largely reluctant to recognise that the body of law upon which they wrote was formed by precedents, themselves decided in accordance with particular procedures, and that as the procedures changed, so, too would the substance of the law. Instead, the statements made about the Judicature Bill 1873 when it was introduced and debated in Parliament, namely that fusion was administrative only, were maintained in treatises and legal education. While much of both the common law and equity did follow along the same grooves, in certain areas it did not. In these areas a certain puzzlement attended efforts of trying to reconcile legal and equitable doctrines in contract law. The result has been that the rigours of the common law in the modern law of contract have often not been ameliorated by equity. That this occurred is, in no small part, a result of the way in which legal treatises were written.

www.ingramcontent.com/pod-product-compliance
Ingram Content Group UK Ltd.
Pitfield, Milton Keynes, MK11 3LW, UK
UKHW020226290926
15470UKWH00001B/399

9 781509 955121